Reader's Digest

Our Magnificent Wildlife

How To Enjoy and Preserve It

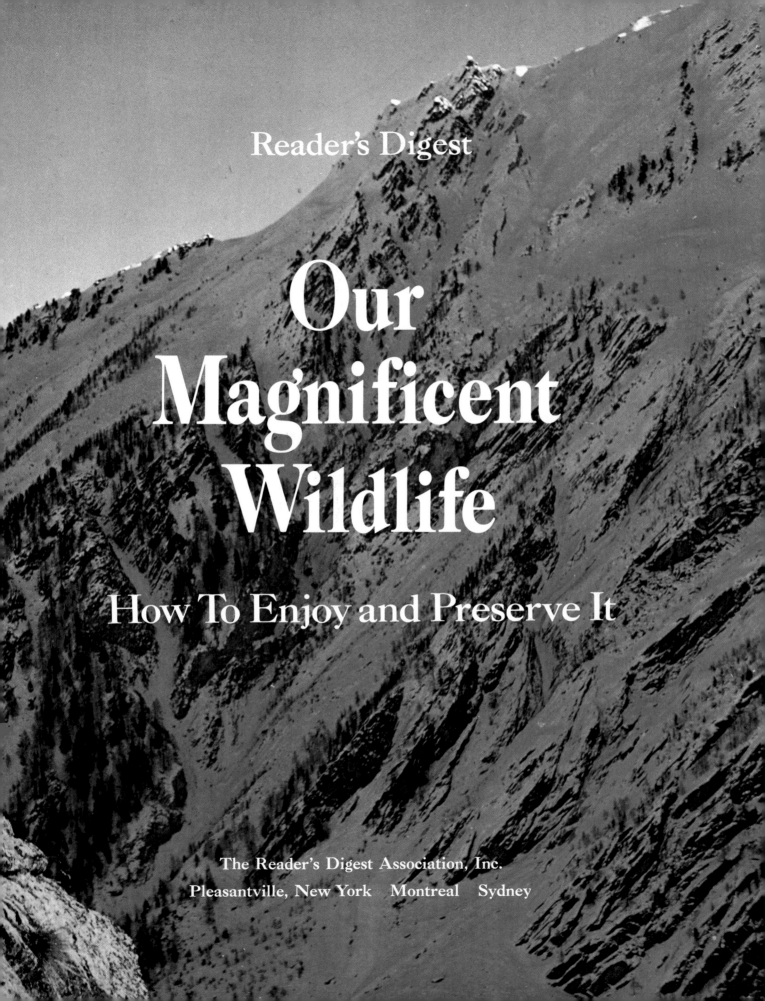

Reader's Digest

Our Magnificent Wildlife

How To Enjoy and Preserve It

The Reader's Digest Association, Inc.
Pleasantville, New York   Montreal   Sydney

Consultants

Durward L. Allen, *Purdue University*

William G. Conway, *New York Zoological Society*

Raymond F. Dasmann, *International Union for Conservation of Nature and Natural Resources*

Norman Myers, *Consultant in Conservation Ecology*

CONTENTS

Wild Worlds   104

The Web of Life   154

An Endangered Heritage

Is there hope for the splendid wild animals and
the last great wilderness areas of our planet?
The answer is a resounding yes! Awareness
of nature—and of human responsibility for our
wildlife heritage—has finally become widespread.
More and more people are concerned about
the fate of the eagle, the tiger, the polar bear.
And there is a growing recognition that every plant,
every animal—from the fragile butterfly to
the mighty whale—has a place in nature's plan.

A Bengal tiger in algae-covered water demonstrates that tigers are not afraid of water; indeed, tigers swim very well. A recent tiger census listed 1,827 tigers in India—a dangerously low figure.

The Magnificent Tiger

Leland Stowe

The tiger lives in a closing trap. Still shot for its skin, this great cat is also menaced by loss of prey and living space.

Crouching at the edge of a clearing in an Indian jungle, Ranjit Singh, a veteran tiger hunter, raised his rifle as beaters drove his quarry nearer. Suddenly a beautiful male tiger burst out of the high grass, loping straight across the open corridor only 30 yards away.

In the morning sunlight its striped reddish coat gleamed so splendidly, and its muscular body rippled with such liquid grace, that Singh gazed spellbound. In a moment the animal vanished. "I wanted to kill that tiger," recalls the hunter, now an expert wildlife photographer, "but it was simply too beautiful to kill. And I will never shoot another." That promise was a fitting tribute to one of the most fascinating and graceful of all animals.

Though tigers are large animals, they are seldom seen. On exposed terrain the tiger's camouflaged body can enable it to vanish before observers' eyes. Sometimes a mere 10-inch tuft of grass can serve as "cover."

A tiger can glide silently through the driest thicket, its huge, cushioned paws traversing brittle twigs and leaves without causing a single crackle. Hunter Sher Jung once sat in a jungle copse, his senses alerted for the slightest sound or movement. Suddenly he glanced sideways and saw—only 20 to 25 feet away—a massive tiger languidly licking its forepaws. Jung had heard nothing at all.

A tiger possesses phenomenal hearing and sight, which compensate for a mediocre sense of smell. Sher Jung reports that a tiger's ears register more than the seven octaves normal for humans. As for its vision, nighttime hunters know that a tiger will see even the slightest movement.

Tigers sleep or catnap by day; it is not till evening that they start hunting. An hour or two before dusk they start their rounds, roving up to 10 or 15 miles nightly. An adult tiger devours 40 to 70 pounds at a single meal, yet may top that off with several additional snacks the same night. But it may not eat again for several days.

Man-eating tigers?

The popular conception of the tiger as savagely aggressive applies only to the man-eating individuals. Although few in number, India's man-eaters took a toll of more than 1,000 persons annually until well into this century. Most man-eaters had been disabled—usually by being wounded by a hunter—and were unable to catch their normal prey.

The average tiger tends to give man as wide a berth as possible, even in face-to-face confrontations. A forest ranger was cycling round a bend on a woodland track one day when he nearly collided with a tigress. Twice she reared up, snarling and growling, but the ranger remembered the standard instructions for such encounters: "Never panic; stare the beast down." He did just that, and the tigress grumbled off.

Tigers are generally solitary creatures except during the brief mating season. Two or more suitors may fight for the female in bloody battles. The female takes no part in the fray. The winner drives off his competitors, and mating ensues. Shortly thereafter the male and female part company. About 16 weeks after conceiving, the tigress bears her cubs (each weighing 2½ to 3 pounds). The usual litter size is two to four, though litters of five or six sometimes occur. Fewer than half of the cubs ever reach maturity. Predators (chiefly hyenas, wild dogs, and crocodiles) and disease are the major causes of this high mortality rate.

Frolicsome as kittens, cubs tumble, grapple, and pounce at shadows, including their own. They display affection for their mothers, readily shifting from play to caresses. American zoologist George Schaller watched one take its mother's head between its forepaws and smother her face with fervent licks.

In the first 4 weeks the cubs quadruple in size; in another few weeks, still unweaned, they begin to eat

Scantily striped, powerfully built, and heavily furred, Siberian tigers are the world's largest cats. This zoo-born cub and its mother belong to a captive population that is fortunately growing; only about 300 Siberian tigers survive in the wild.

The Tiger and Its Prey

During the day a tiger is likely to be inactive, but its nighttime search for food may cover 10 to 20 miles. In India's Kanha National Park, where zoologist George B. Schaller studied the Bengal tiger, tigers eat gaur (wild cattle) and several kinds of deer: Chital, barasingha, and sambar. Because of increasing encroachment on the forest for grazing lands, natural prey has become scarce, and the great cats supplement their diet with domestic animals. An adult tiger needs an average of 15 pounds of food a day.

Stalking

Attacking

Dragging kill to a secluded place

Hiding kill

What a Tiger Kills in a Year

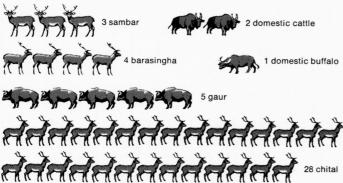

3 sambar

2 domestic cattle

4 barasingha

1 domestic buffalo

5 gaur

28 chital

A tiger's prey is mainly hoofed animals of various sizes. An adult tiger requires about 7,600 pounds of prey a year, which it takes in some 43 kills.

How a Tiger Hunts and Feeds

Between dusk and dawn a tiger is on the prowl. It does not run down its prey or pursue a fleeing animal. Instead, it usually stalks its prey to within 30 to 80 feet. Avoiding any horns or antlers, the tiger aims for the animal's side or rear, topples the prey, and seizes its throat; some species, such as barasingha, are killed by a bite on the neck. The tiger often drags its kill to a secluded place, preferably near water. It may feed for an hour or so and then bury the rest of the kill. Later it will return and eat all but the largest of the bones.

---

chewed meat disgorged by the mother. Trailing her on hunting forays, they imitate her every move. Then, when the cubs are about 6 months old, the mother initiates them in the skills of the hunt. At first they learn to stalk and kill small creatures. Gradually they progress to assaults on deer, buffalo calves, and larger game, until at the age of 2 they have become fully independent of their mother.

Today tigers are close to extinction. Tigers are endangered because the land they need has been taken for farming and logging. They have no place to go. Sanctuaries in India, Nepal, and other countries protect tigers and their prey and habitat. But much more land needs to be set aside, for tigers are wanderers, and each individual animal needs at least 10 square miles of living space.

A demand for tiger skins and heads also jeopardizes the tiger. In most of the animal's range, tiger hunting is illegal, but poachers threaten the continued existence of the great cat.

In the 18th century William Blake praised this magnificent creature in a stirring poem: "Tyger, tyger, burning bright/ In the forests of the night. . . ." The tiger's light may not go out completely. But the future is precarious indeed, for the species is at the mercy of its mortal enemy—man.

The Tiger's Narrowing Range

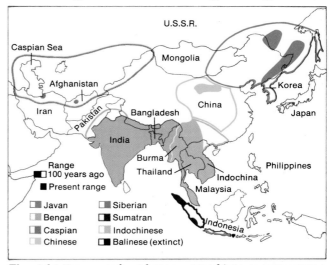

U.S.S.R.

Caspian Sea

Mongolia

Afghanistan

Korea

Iran

China

Japan

Pakistan

Bangladesh

India

Burma

Philippines

Range
■ 100 years ago
■ Present range

Thailand

Indochina

Malaysia

Javan   Siberian
Bengal   Sumatran
Caspian   Indochinese
Chinese   Balinese (extinct)

Indonesia

The eight tiger races have been squeezed into an ever-narrowing range as an expanding human population turns forests into farms. Hunting is another cause of the tigers' decline, though they are now legally protected over most of their range. To save the Bengal tiger, whose population is only about one-tenth of what it was in 1900, the World Wildlife Fund is raising money to buy land for tiger sanctuaries.

Chimney Pets of Europe

Bernhard Grzimek

The beloved white storks of Europe have adjusted amazingly well to the presence of man. But drained marshes and lingering pesticides spell trouble.

Storks are like me: When winter approaches, I set off for Africa; so do they. The storks, however, take longer to get there. A white stork has been known to cover 400 miles in 2 days, but in general these striking birds make a fairly leisurely journey southward. If they leave Germany in August, they do not reach Africa until sometime in November.

Averse to moving their wings, storks fly by gliding and need thermal upcurrents to maintain altitude. Since there are practically no thermals over large expanses of water, storks usually do not fly over the Mediterranean but concentrate at the shortest possible crossing points for the over-water journey. The West European population travels in a southwesterly direction via Spain and Gibraltar, then across the Sahara and thence to South Africa; the East European storks migrate southeast through the Balkans, over the Bosporus, and through Turkey to East Africa.

Naturalists have tried to discover why some storks fly southeast and others southwest. Working in East Prussia at a time when storks were still very prolific

White storks and small towns seem made for each other. In this town in southern Turkey nearly every house has its own nest in April. Most storks return year after year to the same area and many to the same nest, adding to it each season.

When Storks Court

Courtship ceremonies are all-important in the life of white storks. Males and females look alike but behave differently. The male's performance at the nest site signals his sex to other storks and attracts a mate, which must make the correct female response.

A male entices a female by grasping at sticks and preening his wings.

When mated birds meet, they raise their bills and clap them noisily.

The greeting ceremony includes wing fluttering on the part of both birds.

there, a German ornithologist sent fledgling storks west to the Rhineland for rearing. In August the native Rhineland storks set off southwestward for Spain, but the young East Prussian storks, which were not released until long after all the adults had migrated, turned southeastward, as was proper for their breed. Their instinct to fly southeastward was evidently inherited and not learned from their parents or other adult storks.

One day I received a letter from a game warden at Serengeti National Park in East Africa, saying that a dead stork with an aluminum ring around its ankle had been found there. The ring was marked MOSKWA 6069. (Whenever a ring like this is found, it should be sent to the nearest ornithological station, which will transmit the information to the ornithologists who ringed the bird—in this case almost certainly from the city of Moscow.)

Storks have discovered Russia

This particular find is evidence that some of the storks wintering in East Africa had hatched in Russia. Fifty or a hundred years ago this would have been impossible: There were then no storks in the Moscow region. They have only recently settled in that area, while they are growing ever scarcer in other parts of Europe. At the turn of the century Switzerland had 150 breeding pairs of storks; today there is not one.

The decline of the stork population has caused disquiet in Alsace in eastern France. In 1947 there were still 177 breeding pairs in Alsace, by 1958 only 135. This situation prompted an industrialist to found the Society for the Preservation of Storks of Alsace. The members built 25 artificial nests and even bought fields and made small ponds, into which schoolchildren put tadpoles. The following April the storks came back as usual from Africa. They inspected the friendly welcome prepared for them, but the majority flew on northward. Nevertheless, three extra pairs stayed in the locality. This example, widely mentioned in the newspapers, prompted many people to take measures to encourage their storks.

A stork's instinct to return to its birthplace is extremely powerful. Even though many young storks stay in Africa for their first summer—they are not sexually mature until the age of 4—8 percent of them eventually settle down to breed in their home village, 41 percent settle within a radius of 6 miles, and another 21 percent at distances between 6 and 15 miles from the spot where they were hatched. Storks, it appears, are attached not only to their home district but also to their nest. Of 60 storks, 37 were found a year later at the same nest, 11 after 5 years, and 1 even after 7 years.

As parents, storks are exceptionally faithful. A male stork in Germany flew into high-tension wires and was electrocuted. His mate continued to incubate the eggs alone for 3 days, during which she left the nest only once for a short time to look for food. Her persistence was remarkable because usually male and female storks,

like many other birds, take turns in sitting on the eggs. This female stork reared her brood alone, presumably because the male was killed just a few days before the eggs were due to hatch. In another case, when the female stork was shot, the father reared the young. Storks such as these, brought up by one parent, are slow to develop and are usually a few weeks later than other storks in being ready to fly.

When feeding their young, adult storks have to forage for food in considerable quantity and variety. A stork that was following a plow was reported to have caught 44 mice in an hour. Another stork's meal consisted of 76 large beetles, 674 small ground beetles, 730 sawfly larvae, and 1,315 grasshoppers. In fact the Zulu name for the stork translates as "locust eater," which aptly describes its eating habits.

It was long thought that adult storks had to show their young how to fly. You have only to rear some orphaned young storks to convince yourself that this is not so. In addition, young storks are quite willing to take food—finely chopped meat and fish—from a feeding bowl. They are used to having their parents deposit food in the nest before them, whereas many other young birds are fed by having the food put directly into their beaks or throats. For this reason it is possible to feed young parentless storks in the nest by passing their food up to them in a basket on a long pole.

In Münster, Germany, a pair of storks that had lived in the zoo for 8 years with clipped wings reared two

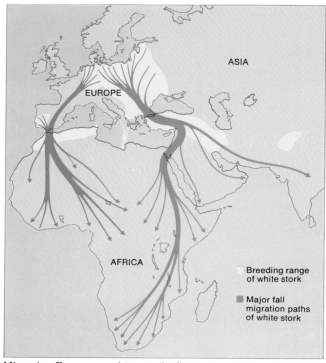

Migrating European white storks *flying to and from their winter homes in Africa avoid crossing the widest part of the Mediterranean Sea. Western storks cross at Gibraltar and fly over the Sahara; eastern birds wing their way over Turkey.*

North America's Only Stork

Its magnificent wings spanning a full 5 feet, the wood stork sails in a wide circle over its breeding colony.

Late in the afternoon wood storks fly in to their roosts at Corkscrew Swamp Sanctuary. Though wood storks formerly nested in much of the southeastern United States, at present no U.S. breeding sites are known outside Florida, and the Corkscrew Swamp Sanctuary is the largest in that state. These heavy-billed, black-necked birds (known locally as ironheads or flintheads) have suffered greatly from lumbering, swamp drainage, and droughts. At the beginning of the nesting season the pairs put on an elaborate ceremony of bill clapping and wing flapping. The nests are untidy stick platforms, usually built in bald cypresses. Both parents incubate the eggs and feed the young with small fish, up to 50 pounds per nestling. In summer, when food is scarce and the young are able to fly, the storks wander into other states—occasionally as far as Maine and Montana. After a bad nesting season they scatter farther.

Hardly moving, a wood stork may stand for hours on a limb near its nest in a bald cypress tree.

Breeding colonies of wood storks are scattered over Florida in swamps surrounded by marshy feeding sites.

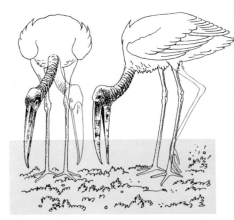

As a wood stork moves slowly through the water, groping side-to-side motions of its bill locate small fish.

young, while the keepers reared a third young stork artificially. Between the 31st and 48th days of a young stork's life its great black wing pinions grow three-eighths of an inch a day; at 2½ months it is capable of flight. At this age the young storks of the Münster Zoo began flying over the town.

Unfortunately the young stork that had been artificially reared insisted on regarding human beings as its friends. Even when it was far from Münster with its two companion storks, it would joyfully greet any man, woman, or child who approached. It would squat down, flap its wings, and make hissing and meowing noises. Children and unthinking adults poked the bird with sticks, threw stones at it, and made its life a misery. When the Münster storks finally flew away, they were first spotted at the Dutch frontier; a fortnight later one of them was shot near Marseilles.

A Czechoslovakian circus once bought 50 young storks in Romania and allowed these birds, which could not yet fly, to walk around freely in the fenced-in area around the circus caravans. They were well fed, but when the time came to cage them as the circus was moving on, they all flew away. The circus people had forgotten that the birds had in the meantime grown big enough to fly. At the next stand, several hundred miles away in Czechoslovakia, suddenly there were the storks again, perching on the guy ropes of the big tent.

Bill clapping begins early

People who bring up a young stork from the egg are often puzzled by the hatchling's odd behavior: As soon as it crawls out of the egg, it lays its head on its back and makes snapping movements with its bill. This is not some kind of cramp, as is often thought, but a preliminary stage in the stork's characteristic bill clapping. The little bird is trying to clap its bill, but the clapping is inaudible because the bill is still soft. A slight noise can be heard after 6 weeks. One expert in raising storks has said: "One has the feeling that storks would rattle their bills while they were still inside the egg, if only there were room." Young storks clap their beaks whenever they are fed, at least in their early days.

When an adult stork claps its bill, it simply means the bird is excited. Whether the emotion is anger or love or something else can be determined only by what the stork does next. Sometimes a newly arrived stork is so shocked at the condition of its nest that it forgets even to clatter its bill. In one German village a farmer noticed that a stork, just back from Africa, had leaped up into the air as if horrified by something; without even a single clap it settled on a neighboring roof and kept looking back at the enormous pile of its nest. Finally the farmer got a ladder and climbed up to the nest—and a mallard flew into his face. In the stork's nest were 10 blue-green duck eggs. As soon as the squatters had been evicted, the stork, visibly relieved and noisily clapping its bill, reoccupied its old home.

What is happening to these attractive and popular birds, the European white storks? From the end of the last century until 1928 their numbers steadily de-

Different Storks, Different Foods

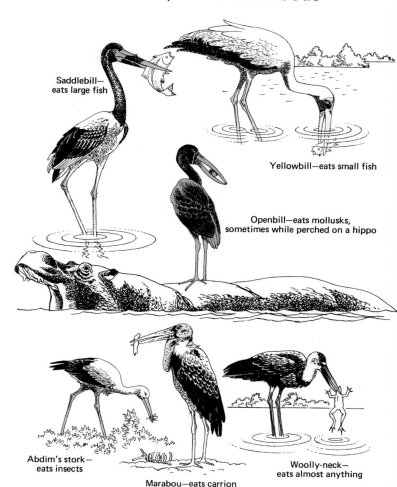

Sharing the same habitat, six species of storks live side by side in East Africa. There is little competition among the species, for each has its own food preference. The European white stork also winters in the same region; though its varied menu is similar to that of the woolly-neck's, it usually avoids conflict by staying away from its potential competitor.

creased. Then they rose steeply until 1937, but since then they have been on the decline.

Are western European storks dying out because swamps and ponds are being drained? Are too many areas growing steadily drier because great cities are pumping ground water into their water systems? Are too many western European storks shot during their migrations? Or has the chemical destruction of locusts in Africa depleted the food supply?

But the fact that storks are declining in some parts of Europe does not necessarily mean that they are disappearing. Great numbers of storks are now breeding in North Africa, and they are moving into new territories in eastern Europe. If they are made welcome, perhaps the sight of a great white bird alighting on a rooftop to a noisy clatter of bills will remain a welcome sight for centuries to come.

A group of mountain gorillas —bigger, hairier, and rarer than their lowland cousins—takes a midday rest in a central African forest. As one female relaxes comfortably, another grooms her, carefully picking off parasites and flaky bits of skin. During this rest most gorillas simply lie or sit where they are, but a few build rudely constructed nests, which are indistinguishable in a short time from the surrounding vegetation. The rest period is longer on warm, sunny days than when the weather is cool and cloudy. It is broken up as first one animal and then another rises and begins to feed.

The Gorilla, Greatest of Apes

Allen Rankin

**Behind the gorilla's fearful roars
and chest beating is a peaceful plant eater.
But a gentle nature will not save
this huge animal if men destroy its forests.**

He's the hulking monster of horror tales and nightmares, a beetle-browed killer that's supposed to get his kicks from making off with luscious young women or rending jungle explorers limb from limb. Such is the lurid legend of the gorilla, but this mystique is a far cry from reality. In their native habitat, the rain forests of equatorial Africa, gorillas are among the gentlest and most peaceable of animals.

Dian Fossey, an American zoologist, lived for 3 years among wild gorillas in central Africa. She reported that in 2,000 hours of direct observation they showed less than 5 minutes of aggressive behavior.

Her observations confirmed the findings of George Schaller, of the New York Zoological Society, who in 1959 undertook the first thorough scientific study of these mystery-shrouded animals. An adult male gorilla, 6 feet tall and weighing between 400 and 500 pounds, is many times as powerful as the strongest man. But gorillas use their menacing display of power not to seek trouble but to avoid it. When Schaller approached a troop, it frequently retreated in orderly fashion, with only its leader standing fast. Facing Schaller, the leader—always a male—ripped up and hurled masses of underbrush, slapped his chest till it resounded like a bongo drum, and gave a cavernous show of teeth and horrific roars. Occasionally he would charge, always stopping just short of the mark.

"It's all a masterful bluffing act," concluded Schaller. "The big fellows seem to be torn between their duty to defend their troops and their desire to flee from danger. So, to blow off tension and frighten their enemies, they pound their chests and throw things around. It doesn't mean much."

Gorillas live a peaceful existence. They eat only plants. No animal preys on them. And they don't fight among themselves. Several groups frequently share the same territory, meet on friendly terms, and even exchange members.

Their government is a benign dictatorship. The leader of a troop does sometimes assert his right to the choicest food, the most receptive female, or the driest spot when it's raining. But in general he's tolerant; intelligence and a knack for getting along seem to count as much as brawn in determining which adult

A Day in the Life of a Gorilla

Mountain gorillas are slow risers, usually stirring in their nests for about an hour after sunrise. During their leisurely 2-hour morning meal the gorillas sit down, eat the plants within reach, get up, walk a few steps, grab more food, and sit again. Another meal, accompanied by more movement, follows the midday rest. Before night—or earlier on rainy afternoons—the gorillas build their individual nests and settle down for the night.

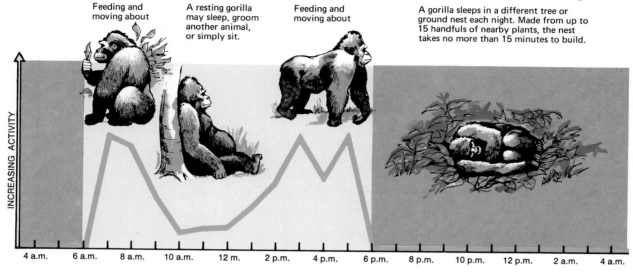

Feeding and moving about

A resting gorilla may sleep, groom another animal, or simply sit.

Feeding and moving about

A gorilla sleeps in a different tree or ground nest each night. Made from up to 15 handfuls of nearby plants, the nest takes no more than 15 minutes to build.

INCREASING ACTIVITY

4 a.m. · 6 a.m. · 8 a.m. · 10 a.m. · 12 m. · 2 p.m. · 4 p.m. · 6 p.m. · 8 p.m. · 10 p.m. · 12 p.m. · 2 a.m. · 4 a.m.

male gorilla becomes and remains chief of the troop.

The gorillas' world is far from all bliss, however. They're plagued with the same diseases as people are, especially the common cold and other respiratory ailments. Their average lifespan in the wild is probably only about 25 years.

By far their greatest enemy, however, is man. The expanding human population, with its proliferating farms and roads, is encroaching on the habitat of these great apes. All three types of gorillas are now threatened with extinction—lowland gorillas, restricted to the Zaire River Basin, and the two races of mountain gorillas, living in the mountains of central Africa. The three types belong to the same species, but mountain gorillas have thicker and finer coats and are much rarer than the lowlanders.

Gorillas born in zoos

Wildlife sanctuaries such as the vast Virunga National Park in Zaire (formerly the Democratic Republic of the Congo) offer the best hope of saving the great apes. But zoos are playing an increasingly important role in perpetuating the species. In 1956 at the zoo in Columbus, Ohio, two gorillas, Baron and Christina, finally did what no caged gorillas had ever done: they produced an offspring. In the years since there have been numerous other gorilla births in zoos.

At model zoos gorillas (usually the lowland type) live in spacious indoor-outdoor complexes closely resembling their natural habitat. The gorillas are treated like stars, and rightly so. For, like other top stars at zoos, they render a vital service to the cause of conservation. William Conway, director of the New York Zoological Society, explains: "By fascinating city people, zoo animals do more than anything else to interest these people in the fate of wildlife and awaken them to the urgent need of saving at least a token number of our wild creatures before it is too late—for them and for us."

Chimpanzee (up to 150 lb.)

Gorilla (up to 500 lb.)

Gibbon (up to 15 lb.)

Orangutan (up to 200 lbs.)

Dominated in size by the gorillas, the apes—tailless primates with arms much longer than their legs and with more intelligence than monkeys—inhabit tropical Asia and Africa.

Monarch of the North

Fred Bruemmer

**The polar bear is king of the arctic
ice pack and the bleak tundra world.
Only man's weapons can threaten
the supremacy of this crafty seal hunter.**

A polar bear mother and her half-grown offspring amble across the

At first the footprints we were following seemed to show an aimless amble, but then a purposeful patrol pattern emerged. The polar bear had wandered from one hillock on the ice to another, approaching from leeward and paying particular attention to huge snow-drifts. It was seeking lairs excavated by ringed-seal mothers as nurseries for their pups. Until the pups molt, at the age of 3 to 4 weeks, they are easy prey; they cannot swim and therefore cannot use the sea as a refuge from polar bears.

At the fourth hillock the trail indicated success. After scooping great chunks of compacted snow from a drift, the bear reared up on its hind legs, then drove down with all its force to break through the ice-coated roof of the lair. Two limp, furry flippers in the snow were all that remained of the pup.

A single seal pup, weighing perhaps 15 pounds, is not much of a meal for a large polar bear, which can devour 150 pounds of blubber at a sitting. With its peculiar broad-legged, shuffling gait, our bear wandered on, its great furry paws leaving tracks 12 inches across. Abruptly it turned and dug up something. A few feathers told of a dead bird that had lain beneath the surface. The polar bear is both hunter and scavenger.

The bear climbed the next rise, evidently spotted a seal from it, and slid down the other side, front paws outstretched to break the descent.

End of a hunt

Now its tracks revealed a long, deliberate stalk. First, the bear moved toward a ridge and advanced behind it, obviously careful to keep downwind and out of sight of a seal snoozing beside its hole on a level stretch of ice. Then, from the point of the sheltering ridge closest to the seal, the bear emerged between two ice blocks; keeping flat on the ground, it pulled itself forward with its front paws and pushed cautiously with its hind feet.

A seal is a fitful sleeper. It dozes, raises its head, and looks around for about 30 seconds; when satisfied that all is well, it slumps down to sleep for another minute. A polar bear stalks a seal in a series of stops and starts. The instant the seal goes to sleep, the bear inches forward. At the seal's slightest move, the bear freezes into

a motionless and indistinct yellowish hump. Only its big shiny nose stands out, coal-black in the surrounding whiteness.

Ten yards from the seal, our bear hunched up and with a tremendous burst of speed rushed upon the sleeping prey, grabbing it with teeth and claws. It stripped the carcass of blubber and ate some of the intestines; the rest was food for the arctic foxes that followed the bear in hope of leftovers. Replete, the bear shuffled back to the ridge, where it fell asleep on a sheltered ice block.

The polar bear's realm is vast—more than 5 million square miles of northern land, sea, and ice. The bear has been seen within 150 miles of the North Pole. A heavy fur coat and a thick layer of body fat insulate the animal against the cold; a streamlined shape and nonskid soles give it speed and maneuverability.

Polar bears avoid the worst days by escaping into dens. Males generally live in dens for only short periods of time, but a female may hole up for as long as half the year in a snowdrift on the leeward side of a hill. The air in the den is usually some 40 degrees warmer than the outside air.

In late November or December a pregnant female gives birth, usually to one cub if it is her first, and to twins thereafter. Newborn cubs weigh only 1 to 2 pounds. They lie not on the chilly floor but in their mother's thick fur.

In March or April the mother bear digs a passage out of the dark den, and the cubs, now chubby and

...ce near Point Barrow, Alaska. Cubs usually stay with their mothers for 2 years, while they learn to swim and hunt seals.

The Yearly Cycle of the Polar Bear

Climate, pregnancy, and the supply of seals determine a polar bear's schedule. Pregnant bears always den; others do so in very cold winters. If seals are scarce bears seek food on land.

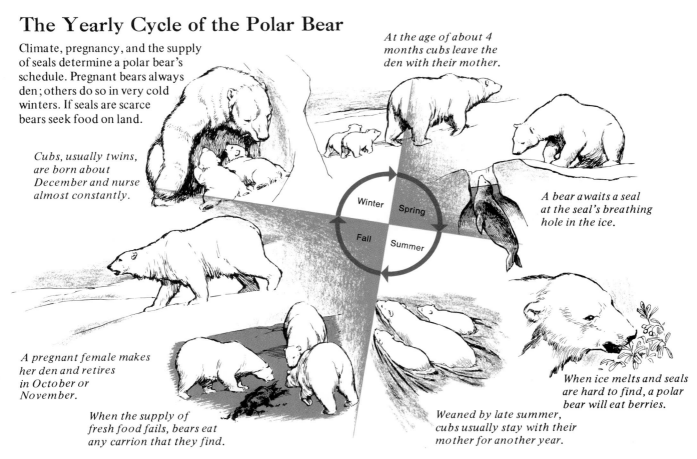

Cubs, usually twins, are born about December and nurse almost constantly.

At the age of about 4 months cubs leave the den with their mother.

A bear awaits a seal at the seal's breathing hole in the ice.

A pregnant female makes her den and retires in October or November.

When the supply of fresh food fails, bears eat any carrion that they find.

Weaned by late summer, cubs usually stay with their mother for another year.

When ice melts and seals are hard to find, a polar bear will eat berries.

Winter · Spring · Fall · Summer

heavily furred, have a first look at the sparkling world of ice and snow. For the next 2 years they will stay close to their mother, who looks after them with great solicitude mingled with disciplinary sternness. From her they learn the art of the stealthy stalk and the location of hunting grounds.

Spring is the season of plenty for polar bears, and by this time many are grimly in need of food. The fat reserves of nursing females are used up during the long sleeping period. Other bears have prowled the frozen bays and fiords, searching for the breathing holes that seals cut through the ice for air vents. There the bears scoop out the seals when they come up to breathe. But each seal has many vents, and a bear may wait for days in vain.

When the ice breaks up and moves with the currents, most bears remain on the floating pack, traveling from floe to floe in search of seals. But once this pack ice begins to disintegrate, polar bears move to the nearest coast. Although they are good swimmers, seals are better swimmers and can escape their pursuers in water. So, until new ice begins to form in the autumn, the bears stay on land and change from a pre-dominantly meat diet to one that is mainly vegetarian. They eat grass, sedge, sorrel, seaweed, and berries. In lemming years, when the populations of these rodents peak, polar bears eat lemmings. Occasionally the bears raid colonies of eider ducks and snow geese, eating the eggs and catching a few brooding birds. A hunter on the shore of Hudson Bay watched a polar bear stalk one of his goose decoys with great patience and skill. At 10 yards it pounced, but when it got only a mouthful of papier mache, the frustrated bear flattened every decoy in sight.

In summer, when seals are scarce, some polar bears go into a temporary sleep. They dig pits as deep as 5 feet and sleep in them for days or even weeks, expending a minimum of energy.

Despite their impressive size (an adult male usually weighs 700 to 1,000 pounds), polar bears are not normally aggressive. They are, however, extremely curious. They will go far out of their way to examine anything unusual. Where the bears are not hunted, they show the same mixture of curiosity and indifference to man that amazed and often frightened the early European explorers and traders.

Where Polar Bears Are Born

The polar bear's range circles the Arctic, though the most important denning sites are in Canada and Greenland and on Norwegian and Soviet islands. Because the seals on which the bears live follow migration patterns, many denning sites are used regularly. But in years when seal hunting is poor, the bears may wander far inland looking for other food.

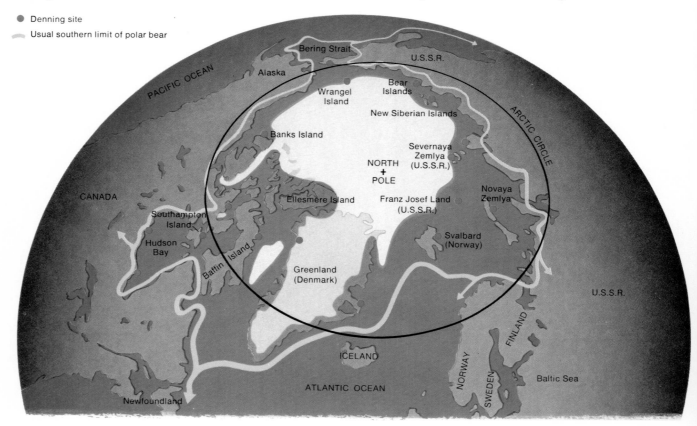

● Denning site

〜 Usual southern limit of polar bear

In the sea a walrus or killer whale may attack a polar bear, but the bears have no natural enemies on land. Only man captures or kills them there. Long ago the Romans brought polar bears back to their cities, where they pitted them against seals in aquatic battles staged in flooded arenas.

New dangers for polar bears

But it was not until the era of arctic exploration and exploitation that Europeans, and later Americans, encountered and killed polar bears in large numbers. Whaling had a lot to do with the fate of polar bears. Whalers brought bowhead whales and walruses to shore by the tens of thousands and stripped them of blubber. Polar bears congregated near the carcasses, led to this feast by their acute sense of smell. As the whale population declined, whalers supplemented their income by shooting polar bears. In recent decades the yearly average of polar bears killed has been about 1,000. The total number left in the world is now estimated at about 20,000.

Recently some measures have been taken to preserve the remaining polar bears. They have been completely protected in the Soviet Union since 1955; only a few cubs can be captured for zoos. In all other northern countries they receive at least partial protection: neither cubs nor females with cubs may be shot.

But polar bears are a slow-reproducing species. Thanks to the prolonged period of maternal care, most cubs grow to maturity, but a female has only one or two cubs every 3 years. So the polar bear population may continue to decline unless additional protective measures are established and enforced.

The polar bear, one of the largest carnivores in the world, has been known to European man for nearly 2,000 years; yet its seasonal movements or possible annual migrations remain a mystery. Does it really travel from country to country, even from continent to continent, with the drift of the polar ice, as some scientists claim? Or does each polar bear belong to a purely regional group that moves only within a limited area? Today no one really knows the answers. Scattered over the vastness of the arctic seas and their sparsely inhabited shores, the polar bear pursues its lonely patrol across the endless ice and snow, still far from the ken of its worst enemy and only friend, man.

Polar Bear Nurseries

Digging into a drift of new snow, a pregnant polar bear hollows out a 6-foot entry with an oval den at the end. Body heat will enlarge the chamber and keep an air vent open. Later the bear may add an alcove or a second room. Hudson Bay bears sometimes dig in soil, then add an upper room as snow accumulates. The female sleeps part of the time she is in the den; but she must be alert in early winter, when her cubs, usually twins, are born. The cubs, born naked and about the size of guinea pigs, are kept warm in their mother's furry embrace until they have grown their own soft fur. They nurse almost constantly and grow rapidly on their mother's rich milk.

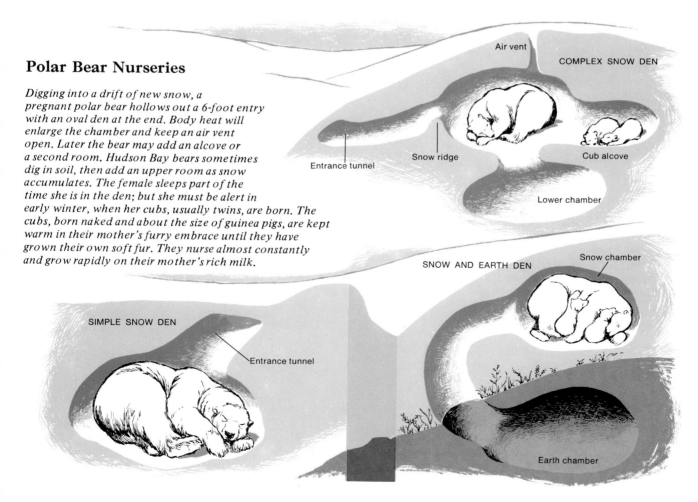

Air vent

COMPLEX SNOW DEN

Entrance tunnel

Snow ridge

Cub alcove

Lower chamber

SNOW AND EARTH DEN

Snow chamber

SIMPLE SNOW DEN

Entrance tunnel

Earth chamber

Butterflies in Jeopardy

Jo Brewer

Few of us would set out to harm butterflies, but these delightful insects are among the unintentional victims of pesticides and habitat destruction.

What is your idea of the quintessence of beauty in a butterfly? Probably to many people's minds would come, in answer to this question, the image of an iridescent blue morpho, often sold as an art object. Observers have striven in vain to explain the impact of morphos, which have been compared to stars, flowers, flames; the sun is reflected so brilliantly from the wings, 7 or 8 inches across, that the insects can be seen from low-flying airplanes. Time was, but is no more, when the tropical American morphos appeared in swarms, dominating the landscape.

In 1848 the British naturalists Henry Bates and Alfred Russel Wallace found about 700 species of butterflies within an hour's walk of Pará, Brazil. Modern writers love to recall and describe the clouds of butterflies they saw as children beside flower-bordered dirt roads. But far fewer are seen today, for butterflies have suffered a dramatic decline in numbers.

The earliest threat to butterflies in modern times was probably the collecting mania that struck the Western World with the awakening of scientific interest. Fos-tered by greed and vanity, the interest in collecting increased. The populations of some of the loveliest tropical butterflies were decimated by collectors' nets, some insects ending up in museums or in cases in private homes, others appearing in jewelry, on box lids, on trays, in pictures, wherever an exquisite bit of color and workmanship could be admired. Prisoners deported from France to a penal colony in South America picked up extra funds by capturing morphos for the European market. Even as recently as 1967 a private collector paid $2,500 for a birdwing butterfly.

In spite of the temptations implicit in such sums of money, the great majority of butterflies now faces far more serious threats than collecting for either scientific or commercial purposes. One is the increasing use of insecticides, which are seldom aimed specifically at butterflies in the vicinity. A few years ago about 600 species of butterflies inhabited the meadows and marshes of Sikkim, a small Indian protectorate in the Himalayas. Unfortunately malaria-carrying mosquitoes also lived there, and the area was massively sprayed with DDT. Along with the mosquitoes most of the butterflies perished.

Orchards and butterflies

Many commercial orchards have been so saturated with insecticides that they have become barren of both butterflies and insect-eating birds. The giant swallowtail butterfly, whose caterpillars feed on leaves in the citrus groves of Florida, is not a target of the spraying. But it will eventually disappear from groves that are regularly sprayed, and the groves will be poorer, not richer. The blemish-free fruit that we buy has been paid for in part with the lives of viceroys, red-spotted purples, and striped hairstreaks.

The tiger swallowtail, which ranges from the Hudson Bay region in Canada to Florida, spends its time flying

---

The Splendor of a Morpho Butterfly Wing

If you look through a morpho butterfly's wing at a strong light, you will see only brown because the pigment in the scales on both sides is brown. The fiery blue that makes the male's wings commercially valuable is produced by structure, not by pigment, and therefore it will never fade. The tiny scales on the upper side of the wing are ridged with minute layers that, together with the air spaces between them, bend (refract) and reflect light beams, destroying all the colors except blue. Some morphos have additional glassy scales on top of the others. These reflect even more light and give the wings a paler, more opalescent quality.

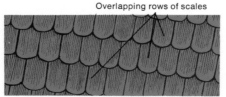

The color-producing scales of a morpho wing are laid in rows overlapping each other like shingles on a roof.

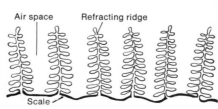

An electron microscope shows in cross section the light-refracting ridges that project up from a morpho wing scale.

There are about 50 species of morpho butterflies, all South American, the males of most of them blue. Their wingspans range from 3 to 8 inches; shown here is a 5½-inch insect.

England's most striking butterfly, the British swallowtail, lives in just one marshy region in the eastern part of the country. Swallowtails bred in captivity are released into a protected reserve there, where the caterpillars feed on parsley.

in and out of woods, stopping to visit flowers in a meadow, disappearing into the woods a few minutes later. The trees afford this lovely yellow and black insect a perfect camouflage as sunlight streams through the leaves onto its wings.

After mating, the female swallowtail lays her eggs on the new growth of trees, especially birches. She requires not just one birch but many, for she lays her eggs one at a time and on different trees. The eggs develop into caterpillars that feed on birch leaves. At the end of summer, those caterpillars that have not become butterflies crawl or drop to the ground and develop into pupae in sheltered spots, where they remain hidden until spring. The tiger swallowtail needs meadows, woods with birch trees, and sufficient debris for hiding places, free of insecticides and herbicides.

Butterflies as a group, of course, are not considered pests and are simply innocent casualties in man's war against unwanted plant growth and destructive insects. In a great many cases the caterpillars of butterflies feed on and probably help control weeds such as thistles, nettles, knotweed, chickweed, sneezeweed, and milkweed. Many desirable wildflowers and other plants actually *need* butterflies; as pollinators, butterflies are second only to bees.

The gravest and most widespread danger to butterflies all over the globe is not pesticides; it is the disturbance or destruction of habitats. Draining and excavating bogs in Canada and the United States are endangering the bog copper butterfly; draining the marshes is endangering Britain's largest butterfly, a swallowtail living only on the Norfolk Broads in eastern England. The building boom in Florida has nearly eliminated Schaus' swallowtail, which occurs nowhere else in the world.

Near San Francisco once lived the xerces blue butter-

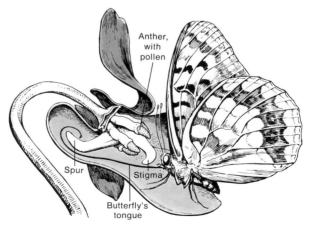

As a butterfly sips nectar from a sweet violet, pollen from the anthers sticks to its body. The pollen will be left on the stigma of another flower, and seed formation may result.

23

A Butterfly Grows Up

A butterfly goes through four stages in its life: Egg, caterpillar, pupa, adult. After mating, the female butterfly lays her eggs on or near the plant where the caterpillars will feed. A caterpillar eats voraciously, and as long as it eats it grows, shedding its skin a number of times. Eventually it stops both eating and growing, attaches itself to a support, and scuffs off its final caterpillar skin, revealing the pupal case underneath. Inside the case the pupa's organs change to those of the adult butterfly, which in time splits the case and emerges.

1　*A California checkerspot lays eggs on the underside of a sticky monkey-flower leaf, the caterpillars' food plant.*

2　*A silk tent keeps young caterpillars safe from strong winds and rain.*

3　*A pupa has sloughed off the caterpillar's old spiny skin.*

4　*About 10 days later the pupa's translucent skin begins to split.*

5　*The wings of the newly emerged butterfly steadily expand as blood is pumped into the intricate network of veins.*

6　*An adult checkerspot assumes a typical butterfly pose as it rests on a twig while the wings take shape.*

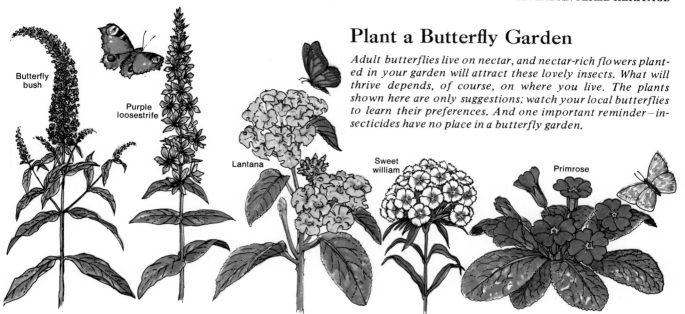

Plant a Butterfly Garden

Adult butterflies live on nectar, and nectar-rich flowers planted in your garden will attract these lovely insects. What will thrive depends, of course, on where you live. The plants shown here are only suggestions; watch your local butterflies to learn their preferences. And one important reminder—insecticides have no place in a butterfly garden.

Butterfly bush

Purple loosestrife

Lantana

Sweet william

Primrose

fly, which fed on a trefoil growing on sand dunes. But the trefoil could not tolerate disturbance of its soil, and when people began to move in in numbers both plant and butterfly disappeared.

Two British butterflies, the large tortoiseshell and the white-letter hairstreak, are dependent on elm trees for food for their caterpillars. The Dutch elm disease, which has killed well over a million elm trees in southern England, has had its effect on these butterflies too.

Sometimes the cause of the decline of a species is much more complicated. No one knows why the numbers of meadow browns and chalkhill blues have decreased so markedly in certain areas of the chalk hills of southern England. But one explanation traces the decline to an epidemic of myxomatosis (a viral disease) that killed a great many rabbits in England in 1953. The rabbits had been the chief natural grazers on the chalk hills. As they vanished, longer grasses and shrubs invaded the hills. Then small mammals—voles and shrews—moved into the area. And since shrews are known to feed on the young of butterflies, shrews may have caused the decline in the butterfly population.

The new awareness

Fortunately the world became aware a few years ago of the very real possibility of silent springs and summers without the flash of butterfly wings. And fortunately the new awareness came in time to save several species of butterflies. In the northwestern United States a private conservation organization, the Nature Conservancy, bought 14 acres of land, enough to preserve the silver-bordered fritillary in that area. Near Sydney, Australia, a 35-acre park for butterflies has been established. Morphos used commercially are now bred commercially, like mink, and so is Australia's largest butterfly, the Cairns birdwing.

Many governments have taken steps to give butterflies the protection of the law. In Pacific Grove, California, where huge numbers of migratory monarch

butterflies spend the winter, there are strict laws against disturbing them. Papua and New Guinea forbid export of seven species of birdwing butterflies, including the world's largest butterfly, with a wingspan as great as 10 inches. Other nations throughout the world, including Japan, Mexico, Ecuador, and Switzerland, are also protecting their rare butterflies.

The story of the large copper in England shows the increasing concern people are giving to butterflies. Both overcollecting and marsh drainage had contributed to the extinction of the British large copper by the middle of the 19th century. Then in 1915 schoolboys in the Netherlands discovered some close relatives of the extinct butterfly. After careful preparation of wetlands, including the establishment of food plants, eggs and larvae were brought from the Netherlands and bred in captivity. Some butterflies were set free in 1927, and the introduction was so successful that 4 years later 100 living pupae were returned to the Netherlands for the reserve that country had set up. Conservationists have kept a careful watch on the Dutch large copper colony in Britain; though drastically affected by a flood in 1969, the colony is thriving once again.

Every nature lover can do something to help preserve butterflies. Letting a corner of a garden go wild or growing plants on which butterflies will feed is a good start. Even developing a caterpillar tolerance helps. A woman in the United States once frantically sprayed a willow "because it is simply alive with worms, and they are completely destroying it!" The "worms" were full-grown caterpillars; they had by no means completely destroyed the tree, and would have done no further damage. Out of ignorance, this well-meaning householder had eliminated mourning-cloak butterflies that would have added life, color, and beauty to the entire neighborhood 2 weeks later. If she had looked at the "worms" through sympathetic eyes, she might even have found the frosty, scarlet-studded caterpillars rather striking, if not handsome.

The Sociable, Curious Prairie Dog

Mary Cable

Prairie dogs once covered the North American plains with their tremendous "dog towns." Now they are outlaws, poisoned in their burrows, safe only in refuges.

An unusual tourist attraction at Alcalde, New Mexico, has been luring motorists from their journeys. Roadside signs point to PRAIRIE DOG TOWN. From a distance the town looks as devoid of interest as the rest of the barren range that borders the highway. But inside the entrance gate a large signboard informs the visitor of the habits and merits of the prairie dog, and beyond—stretching over 30 acres—are dirt roads that lead the visitor through a genuine prairie dog town.

It's not exactly the Serengeti Plains of Africa, but it represents an effort on the part of the U.S. Department of the Interior to protect a rapidly diminishing species. Prairie dogs have for years been systematically poisoned and otherwise destroyed by ranchers, often with the assistance of the U.S. Fish and Wildlife Service. This poisoning is still going on despite the hue and cry raised by conservationists, and refuges such as this could eventually save the species.

Ranchers dislike prairie dogs because their burrows sometimes cause horses and cattle to stumble and break their legs, and because they eat grass that would otherwise be available as forage for stock. The first charge is undeniably true; the second, debatable. Prairie dogs do eat grass and a lot of range weeds, but they also aerate the soil. The land where prairie dogs live makes fertile pasture. If they are driven out, the soil may become harder, and after a few years the grass less abundant. In the days when bison roamed the land, prairie dogs did their ecological bit to counteract the packing down of grassland by millions of hooves.

Some of the vanished natural marvels of the North American continent are easy to imagine—skies darkened by the flight of migrating birds, for instance, or vast herds of bison. We have seen simulations in the movies; besides, the game of East Africa is still abundant enough to suggest what the American West used to be like. But the phenomenon recorded in 1901 of a prairie dog town covering more than 25,000 square miles and inhabited by up to 400 million prairie dogs is mind boggling. There is nothing like it anywhere in the world today.

Early chroniclers of the western plains spoke of these towns with wonder. Meriwether Lewis, of the Lewis and Clark expedition, wrote that a prairie dog town, seen from a distance, reminded him of a "beautiful bowling-green in fine order." Its grass was nibbled short and was therefore of a uniformly lighter green than the surrounding sea of prairie grass. There were always sure to be rattlers and other snakes in the towns, sunning themselves and apparently ignoring the prairie dog life around them. And, as the American historian Francis Parkman noted in *The Oregon Trail*, there were also "demure little gray owls [burrowing owls] with a large white ring around each eye . . . perched side by side with the rightful inhabitants."

Affable antics charmed the pioneers

The little rodents made their homes not only on the prairie but in semidesert as well. "Frequently the hard and dry plain was thickly covered, for miles together," wrote Parkman, "with the little mounds which they make at the mouth of their burrows, and small squeaking voices yelped at us as we passed along. . . . Some of the bolder dogs . . . would sit yelping at us on the top of their mounds, jerking their tails emphatically with every shrill cry they uttered. As the danger drew nearer they would wheel about, toss their heels into the air and dive in a twinkling into their burrows. Towards sunset, and especially if rain was threatening, the whole community made their appearance above ground. We saw them gathered in large knots around the bur-

How Prairie Dogs Communicate

All-clear signal

Warning signal

A bark and an erect tail indicate the approach of a coyote or another potential danger. In the all-clear, expressing well-being, the tail is held downward.

Identification kiss

With heads side by side and teeth showing, prairie dogs from the same part of town meet and greet one another. The identification kiss may last more than 10 seconds.

Grooming

Nibbling and touching make up grooming, a frequent activity among prairie dogs.

Black-tailed prairie dogs are social animals that use both sounds and gestures to communicate. A warning bark tells of possible danger. The all-clear signal announces that the danger is past; it also claims territory. Prairie dogs that know each other kiss upon meeting. Grooming, which often follows kissing, is an expression of sociability among friends.

A black-tailed prairie dog family pauses warily beside its burrow entrance. The young emerge from the burrow about 6 weeks after birth and then gradually explore the neighborhood, learning their way around and the rules of prairie dog social behavior.

row of some favorite citizen. There they would all sit erect, their tails spread out on the ground, and their paws hanging down before their white breasts, chattering and squeaking with the utmost vivacity."

To western adventurers the harmless and engaging prairie dog was a pleasant contrast to the perils of the unknown wilderness. The little animal is equally appealing to modern urbanites, perhaps because some of its behavior reminds them of their own. Monkeys are similarly fascinating, but they have the drawback of looking like unflattering caricatures of people. A prairie dog, on the other hand, is "cute"—a Walt Disney natural. It looks like a large, short-tailed squirrel and is, of course, not a dog at all but a rodent and a member of the ground-squirrel family. As one early explorer put it: "Its yelp, which resembles that of the little toy dog, seems its only canine attribute." It weighs 2 to 3 pounds and has a squirrel's habit of sitting erect on its haunches and holding food in its front paws.

White-tailed prairie dogs live in grassy prairies and uplands; black-tailed ones prefer plains and semidesert. There are several subspecies of each. Before the West became settled, there were literally billions of the black-tailed variety. Yet the creatures produce but one litter a year of two to eight pups, which are regarded as a tempting meal by badgers, coyotes, bobcats, ferrets, large snakes, and birds of prey.

A prairie dog burrow is among the special wonders of nature. From its main entrance a tunnel may descend steeply for 6 or 7 feet, then turn slightly upward and continue for a distance of as much as 80 feet. About 3

Prairie Dog Country

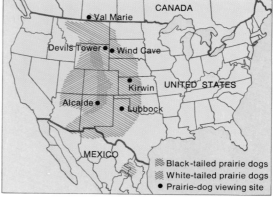

Black-tailed prairie dogs, more numerous than their white-tailed relatives, live in North American grasslands from southern Canada to northern Mexico. Though greatly reduced in number by poisoning campaigns, they flourish in national parks and wildlife refuges; some States and municipalities have also set aside land for prairie dog parks where people can watch these appealing creatures. White-tailed prairie dogs live as high as 10,000 feet in the Rocky Mountains. Unlike their gregarious lowland cousins, they are usually loners, not town dwellers; high-altitude prairie dogs spend most of the winter in their burrows beneath the snow.

feet below the entrance there is usually a "guard chamber," where an embattled resident may listen and judge what dangers lie overhead. Other rooms and side corridors lead from the main tunnel, and at the far end of it there is often a cozy nursery lined with soft grasses. The upward turning of the tunnel causes an air pocket and enables the inhabitants to survive drownings.

With such a comfortable and ingeniously designed bastion, it is not surprising that the prairie dog is greatly concerned with property maintenance. It nibbles away all vegetation that grows within several feet of the burrow entrance, making it almost impossible for enemies to approach unobserved. Using its nose, the prairie dog tamps the earth around the hole into a mound that keeps out water and serves as a lookout post. And the rodent is constantly bringing up debris from inside the burrow and pushing it away or incorporating it into the mound, leaving a neat and tidy dooryard of bare earth.

Like the beaver, the prairie dog has a strong sense of territory. One burrow or several neighboring burrows are the home of a "coterie," consisting of one or two males, several females, and their descendants. When one prairie dog meets another in the feeding areas that surround the burrows, they exchange a kind of kiss—a touching of mouths and teeth—that is believed to be a means of identifying fellow members of a coterie. Friends may pause to groom one another and have even been observed sitting side by side on their haunches, with forepaws carelessly thrown over one another's shoulders. Strangers, on the other hand, are chased back to their own territory, although those in dire need of shelter, as when pursued by a coyote or a hawk, may get sanctuary in an unfamiliar part of the town. At sunset on a fine summer day all members of a coterie assemble in the open, apparently just to enjoy togetherness for a while.

Prairie dogs, like people, are sensitive to weather changes. When the weather is very hot or very cold or rainy, they pass much of their time indoors, where the temperature may vary but the atmosphere remains humid in winter and summer alike. Abandoned burrows are attractive to other creatures—snakes and burrowing owls, as well as ferrets, mice, and various insects—and become a sort of ecological melting pot. The black-footed ferret was once Public Enemy No. 1 to the prairie dog, but now, as a result of the wholesale use of poison in dog towns, this ferret has become an almost extinct species.

After feeding voraciously during the early autumn, prairie dogs return underground for the winter months. On bright days the black-tailed variety comes out to feed and enjoy the warmth, but the white-tails seem to remain dormant, if not exactly hibernating. The unpleasant weather of February and March passes unnoticed: it is mating season. The young are born 30 days after the mating.

Permissive parents

Prairie dogs are permissive and affectionate parents. As soon as the young ones are ambulatory, they are allowed out of the burrow and are to be observed playing tag, wrestling, and cavorting. At first they are friendly to all. According to one writer on prairie dogs, David F. Costello, they "sometimes go around kissing every prairie dog they see." Adult members of other coteries are tolerant of such behavior, but as the young grow up, they are taught to be more discriminating.

Many Animals Share in the Benefits of a Burrow

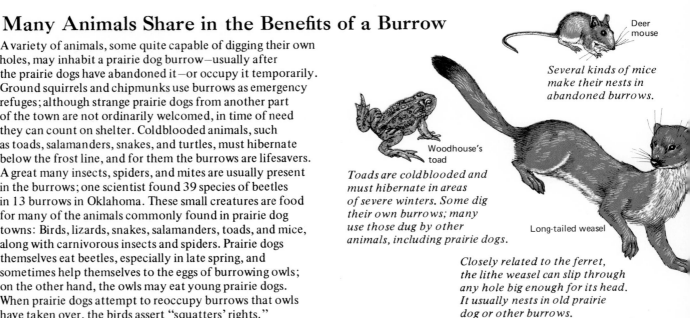

A variety of animals, some quite capable of digging their own holes, may inhabit a prairie dog burrow—usually after the prairie dogs have abandoned it—or occupy it temporarily. Ground squirrels and chipmunks use burrows as emergency refuges; although strange prairie dogs from another part of the town are not ordinarily welcomed, in time of need they can count on shelter. Coldblooded animals, such as toads, salamanders, snakes, and turtles, must hibernate below the frost line, and for them the burrows are lifesavers. A great many insects, spiders, and mites are usually present in the burrows; one scientist found 39 species of beetles in 13 burrows in Oklahoma. These small creatures are food for many of the animals commonly found in prairie dog towns: Birds, lizards, snakes, salamanders, toads, and mice, along with carnivorous insects and spiders. Prairie dogs themselves eat beetles, especially in late spring, and sometimes help themselves to the eggs of burrowing owls; on the other hand, the owls may eat young prairie dogs. When prairie dogs attempt to reoccupy burrows that owls have taken over, the birds assert "squatters' rights."

Deer mouse

Several kinds of mice make their nests in abandoned burrows.

Woodhouse's toad

Toads are coldblooded and must hibernate in areas of severe winters. Some dig their own burrows; many use those dug by other animals, including prairie dogs.

Long-tailed weasel

Closely related to the ferret, the lithe weasel can slip through any hole big enough for its head. It usually nests in old prairie dog or other burrows.

They learn to know their own territory and, since they are not remarkably fast on their feet, to stay near the entrances of their underground burrows.

The chief weakness of prairie dogs is intense curiosity. They are continually looking about with eyes that have wide-angle vision, like a rabbit's, and contain orange pigment that protects them from the glaring sun. Their hearing is acute, and it is almost impossible to sneak up on them; but they may linger too long in the open just to see what's going on. However, they have a warning system that is understood by the whole town: a high, fast bark, which means "Everyone into the burrows and don't stop to ask questions!"

Unlike rats, prairie dogs have developed neither wariness nor immunity to poisoned bait, and it has proved their terrible undoing. It is possible that before long they will no longer be found on private lands.

The Alcalde prairie dog town is still only a hamlet, with perhaps a hundred inhabitants, and is not expected to become much larger. Other towns may be observed in U.S. national lands in the Dakotas and Wyoming. A 7-acre town in Lubbock, Texas, is said by the local Chamber of Commerce to attract more than a million tourists yearly. In western Canada the Saskatchewan Natural History Society has leased 160 acres near Val Marie, where there is a prairie dog town in its natural setting of cactuses and primroses, pronghorn antelope, and burrowing owls.

Given the prairie dogs' amiability and lively sense of curiosity, they seem not to mind the role of tourist attraction. And although never again will there be those astonishing "bowling green" prairie dog towns of the old West, these appealing rodents may yet survive the depredations of man because they amuse him.

The Architecture of a Burrow

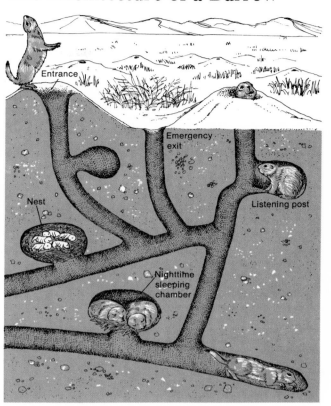

Entrance

Emergency exit

Nest

Listening post

Nighttime sleeping chamber

No two prairie dog burrows are exactly alike, nor does any burrow stay the same for a long time. Like human householders, prairie dogs make alterations as they live in the burrows, plugging and unplugging entrances and digging new tunnels and rooms or enlarging or closing off old ones.

Burrowing owls

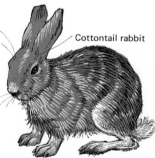

Cottontail rabbit

Burrowing owls occupy old prairie dog homes after enlarging and cleaning them.

Abandoned burrows provide cottontails with shelter and nest sites.

Prairie rattlesnake

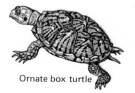

Ornate box turtle

Rattlesnakes find refuge in a burrow during the heat of the midday sun.

Ornate, or western, box turtles often hibernate in prairie dog burrows.

Black-footed ferrets peer from the entrance of a prairie dog burrow. Ferrets prey on prairie dogs, which have now become so scarce that the black-footed ferret is believed to be the rarest mammal in North America.

Peril Point for Sea Turtles

Archie Carr

A hundred eggs in every nest once meant survival for the green turtle. But now that turtle oil and soup are in such demand, this number may not be enough.

Sea turtles are among the most confirmedly aquatic of all reptiles. In body form, musculature, and behavior, they are marvelously equipped for successful life in the water. But they have retained one old reptilian feature that ties them to the land. That is the shelled egg that has to be lodged on shore.

At breeding time female sea turtles leave the safety of the sea, where they have grown to a size that makes them almost immune to predators, and lumber ashore. There they are exposed to the hazards of the land. A sea turtle on shore is defenseless. She weighs on the average nearly 300 pounds but seems almost wholly unable to use her bulk and strength in active self-defense.

One variety of sea turtle—the Atlantic green—was important in the colonization of the Americas. It was abundant and edible, populating tropical coasts throughout the Caribbean. The British and Spanish fleets counted on turtle meat to feed their forces while cruising in New World waters. A green turtle was as big as a heifer, easy to catch, and easy to keep alive for many weeks on its back in a space no greater than the turtle itself.

It is impossible to say how widely the green turtle nested in primitive times. Today the Atlantic green has only two major Caribbean nesting beaches left, at Tortuguero in Costa Rica (where it is now protected) and on the tiny island of Isla Aves.

The ruthless exploitation that has brought the green turtle to the edge of extinction has beset all sea turtles: green turtles, loggerheads, ridleys, hawksbills, and leatherbacks. These peaceful creatures have been persecuted from the Indian Ocean to Ascension Island in the middle of the South Atlantic.

First step in the rescue

To save sea turtles and if possible reestablish them where they once flourished, it is necessary to know more about their life history. There are only two times in the life of a sea turtle when a zoologist can count on making contact with it: When it hatches, and when the female goes ashore to nest. The rest of its life is lived away off somewhere out of sight and has to be reconstructed from fragmentary observations. Scientists put an identification tag on an adult turtle so that they can recognize it from one year to the next. (So far, no way has been devised to mark a 3-ounce hatchling so that it can be identified when it reaches 300 pounds some years hence.)

Like all other sea turtles, the green turtle lays more than once during her season at the breeding beach. Most of the females probably lay from three to five times, at intervals of about 12 days. One of the few things known about these intervals between trips to the breeding beach is that a lot of strenuous romance goes on out in the surf. This became obvious during the first season of the tagging program at Tortuguero, when many turtles came back with their tags gone. The tags had apparently been ripped off violently, with the wires either broken or pulled right through the quarter inch of solid shell.

A tempestuous engagement

The loss of tags was the work of the rutting males. Sea turtles in love are appallingly industrious. It is not easy to observe their conduct because observations come only in snatches, from airplanes or from shore when the turtles rise on wave crests. The male turtle holds himself in the mating position on top of the smooth, curved, wet shell of the wave-tossed female by employing a three-point grappling rig. This consists of his long, thick, curved, horn-tipped tail and a heavy, hooked claw on each front flipper. Turtles are air-breathing animals; so both sexes naturally try to stay at the surface during the violent mating engagement. This adds to the acrobatic problems of the male. Besides all that, the female generally stays coy and resistant for what seems an unnecessarily long while. Other males gather, and all strive together over the female in a vast frothy melee.

The nesting rites begin at night. The female stands in the surf, blinks and peers, turns her nose down and presses it into the wave-washed bottom, then looks up

---

From Eggs to Hatchlings

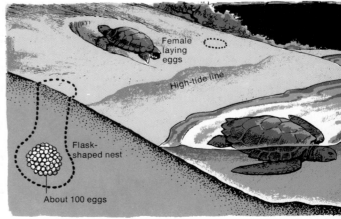

In the dark of night a female green turtle lumbers up the beach, digs a nest in the sand, and lays about 100 eggs.

In nature, golf-ball-size turtle eggs hatch among dozens of other eggs buried in the sand. Here, a single egg was brought to the surface to show how a green turtle hatchling works itself free of its leathery shell with help from a horny "egg tooth."

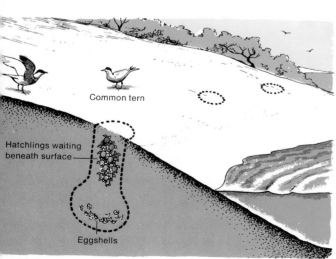

After 60 days the eggs hatch. The young wait near the surface, perhaps for the sand to reach the right temperature.

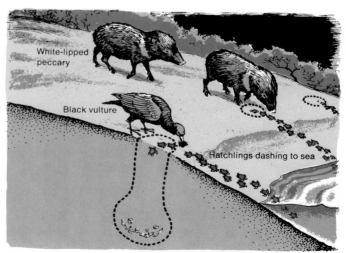

The dash to the sea is the most perilous time in the turtles' lives. Even in the darkness predators take many hatchlings.

and all around. She is clearly making a decision. What her criteria are, nobody knows. The turtle is skittish when she first touches shore; anything but steady quiet will scare her back into the sea.

The female turtle is awkward of gait, myopic of vision, and single track of mind. Once she has gone up into the dry windblown sand and begun to lay, she will go stubbornly through the hour-long ceremony of nest digging and egg laying oblivious to any amount of hullabaloo. She can be watched by gangs of people waving flashlights or set upon by packs of dogs.

This inconvenient, hazardous nesting venture on land complicates life for both the female turtle and her young, and it is surely influential in determining how many eggs must be laid to ensure survival. Each time, the female lays roughly 100 eggs. They are big, round, and white, and they seem a great many when seen all together. One marvel is how great the number is compared with the eggs of lizards, snakes, and other land animals; but another is how small the number is compared with those of wholly aquatic animals, such as mackerel or lobsters.

A great deal of biology is packed into that figure. The turtles have hit on a formula for outwitting predators, or at least for surviving in spite of them. The formula is simply 100 turtle eggs. Any fewer, and the predators prevail and the species wanes. Any more, and the eggs are too heavy to be carried or too energy consuming to produce.

Predators are the most obvious factor that determines the magic number. The whole world seems against the hatchlings during their trip from the nest to the surf and for an unknown amount of time after they enter the sea. Animals that feed on turtle eggs and young range in size from ants and crabs to bears and Bengal tigers. Some of them live along the beach itself, some in the coastal scrub. Some come from far back in the interior, showing up for the turtle season. At Tortuguero the most important nonhuman predators are dogs and vultures. The egg eaters are a menace while the eggs are being laid and for a day or two afterward. This is followed by a peaceful period of about 60 days when no animal seems able to locate turtle eggs.

There is no parental care and no guarding by any adult turtle. When the masses of baby turtles first hatch in their deep sandy nest, they respond to being crowded, jostled, and trod upon by flailing about. The hatchlings on top of the heap scrape sand off the "roof" and push it down. Those on the bottom pack the sand into the "floor." This flailing movement takes the baby turtles steadily up to the surface.

The test of teamwork

An experiment demonstrated the utility of this involuntary teamwork. Single eggs were buried, and the burial places were watched. Out of 22 eggs that hatched, only 6 hatchlings reached the surface. All these were too weak to continue across the sand to the shoreline nearby.

Baby sea turtles come out of the sand as a small eruption. They are really a kind of little team, a simpleminded, cooperative brotherhood in which each member is better off because its siblings are there. They have all contributed to the job of getting the troop out of the predicament of being buried in sand. Then they go on working mindlessly together to lower the penalties of being succulent on a hostile shore.

When the little turtles come out, usually after midnight, they waste no time about it. By the thousands they flail across the beach, hurried, paddle-footed little creatures the size of a silver dollar. On the beach each depends on its own senses to take it across the sand in the right direction, toward the sea. Even here, however, the hatchling that is one of a hatful of nestmates

Who's Who Among Sea Turtles

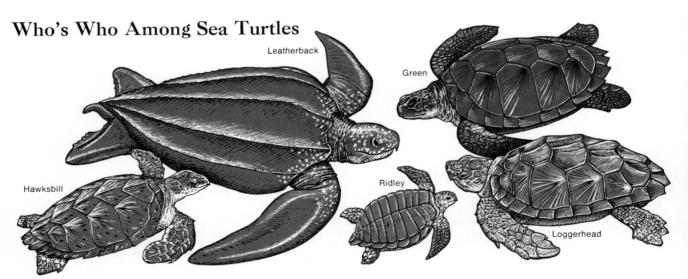

There are five major kinds of sea turtles, reptiles that come ashore only to lay eggs. The largest is the leatherback, whose tough shell measures up to 6 feet in length; smallest is the ridley, at 2 feet. The most endangered are the Atlantic ridley, one of two ridley species, and the hawksbill; the ridley is commercially valuable because of its eggs and hide, the hawksbill for its tortoise shell. The leatherback turtles, which lack the usual hard shell of turtles, are the least endangered.

seems to have an advantage over one that comes out as a single individual.

In tests with young hawksbills, hatchlings that were allowed to crawl singly across the beach stopped oftener than siblings released in groups; they also seemed to lie still longer during stops. Thus single turtles are on the beach longer and are likelier to be caught by a ghost crab or to dry up. When a nestful of hatchlings comes out all at once, there are fewer and shorter hesitations simply because the turtles keep bumping into one another. If a sprinkling of hatchlings has stalled for a time, and a nestmate comes charging up from behind and touches one of them, the action spreads.

There is also some evidence that big groups of hatchlings go more directly toward the sea than turtles traveling separately. The main body of the group is nearly always well oriented. When a single hatchling strays across the stream of traffic, it usually corrects its course to conform to that of the group.

So long as the dangers of this time on land remained natural ones—jaguars and pumas for the adult turtles; gulls, vultures, coatis, and the like for the eggs and young—the populations held their own. But when modern man gave rein to his greed, the sea turtles began to dwindle in number. Only international cooperation can save them now. The Caribbean Conservation Corporation has made efforts to transplant colonies to other beaches where conditions seem favorable. We do not yet know if these efforts will succeed.

In Mexico a New Chance for the Atlantic Ridley

Like the green turtle and other sea turtles, the Atlantic ridley comes ashore to lay its eggs. But unlike all the others, it does this by day rather than by night. This small turtle also nests in denser concentrations than any other reptile; its entire world population uses a few miles of sand near Rancho Nuevo on Mexico's east coast. On the other hand, the Pacific ridley, the second species of ridley, comes ashore at night and uses more space; a mile of beach holds dozens or hundreds of Pacific ridley nests rather than tens of thousands.

The Atlantic ridley's habit of nesting in huge concentrations in the daytime has made it extremely vulnerable to hunters and egg collectors. The number of nesting Atlantic ridleys declined from 40,000 in the late 1940's to 5,000 some 20 years later. It is now probably the most endangered species of sea turtle.

But just because the Atlantic ridley nests in such a limited area, it is also the easiest sea turtle to protect. Each year since 1967, from the time of egg laying to the time of hatching 2 months later, the nesting beach is guarded against human and animal predators. Only a few people, who will themselves eat the eggs, are permitted to collect them; no turtles may be killed either on the beach or in the water.

In addition to this protection, some Atlantic ridleys are caught just after hatching, raised in tanks for 3 months, and then released on the beach where they hatched. Scientists hope that this special handling will give the young turtles a headstart in life and a better chance against their countless natural predators in the sea.

A Mexican marine guards a ridley as she lays her eggs. Human egg hunters, dogs, and birds would gladly take fresh eggs.

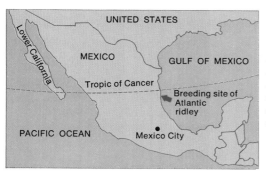

Each year Atlantic ridleys nest somewhere within a 90-mile stretch of Mexico's eastern coast.

These young ridleys, raised in a tank, will later be released into the sea.

The powerful hind legs of a kangaroo may carry it more than 25 feet in a single leap, though if it is not in a hurry, 8 or 10 feet is more usual. If pressed, a kangaroo can reach 30 to 40 miles an hour; females, fleeter than males, are sometimes called fliers.

The Incredible Kangaroos

Roger Tory Peterson

World champion hopper, the red kangaroo belongs to Australia's vast plains. Its friends are trying to convince sheep and cattle ranchers that there is room for all.

We were pacing a red kangaroo, a male of the sort that an Australian would call an "old man." But no oldster this; as our Land Rover careened over the arid plains of inland Australia, its speedometer showed 26 miles an hour. I started shooting with my 16-mm camera gun. The big red was performing beautifully, his pistonlike legs hurling his 150 pounds in 20-foot leaps, his diminutive forepaws tucked inward, his long tail maintaining the balance.

Then he veered closer to our line of travel until he was much too near for me to continue filming. Retiring the camera gun across my knees, I watched at arm's length, then leaned out and patted the animal on the back as he raced beside us. Graham Pizzey, my Australian host, commented: "You are probably the only American who has ever patted a kangaroo on the back in full flight."

Kangaroos and over half of Australian mammals are marsupials, animals that rear their young in pouches. Zoologists recognize about 50 species in the kangaroo family, ranging from the three or four man-sized species properly called kangaroos to numerous smaller wallabies, pademelons, and other forms.

Although marsupials are born in much the same way as other mammals, their infancy is unique. At birth the forelimbs of a kangaroo are more developed than the hindlimbs, allowing the infant, scarcely three-quarters of an inch long, to drag its way to the pouch. It is a climb of only 6 inches, but a phenomenal effort for a creature weighing about $\frac{1}{35}$ ounce. Finding one of four teats, the blind, groping infant fastens itself and remains firmly attached for nearly 7 months. During the next month or so the joey (as young kangaroos are called) spends more and more time outside the pouch, then leaves the pouch permanently but continues nursing for another few months.

The fossil record reveals that kangaroolike animals have lived in Australia for at least 30 million years. Man has been on the continent fewer than 30,000 years; yet he has had considerable impact on the kangaroo population, probably beginning when immigrants from New Guinea brought in the dingo. This reddish dog was imported as a hunting companion and then ran wild, preying on the smaller kangaroos.

But the arrival of European man as a colonizer some 200 years ago has posed the greatest threat to kangaroo survival. Three species have become extinct because of the introduction of the European red fox, land clearance, and other factors; several others exist today only marginally.

"You may be surprised," Pizzey said to me, "to know that a great many people who live in Australia's big cities have never seen a kangaroo in the wild."

Encounter with kangaroos

To see red kangaroos, one must drive to a ranch where the owner tolerates the 'roos. "I know such a ranch," said Pizzey. "If it's pictures of reds you're after, it's the most accessible place I know. We've had a succession of drought years, and the kangaroos have suffered almost as much as the sheep. In some areas they have been nearly eliminated by ranchers who blame all their troubles on the kangaroo. But this ranch is different."

We set out early the next morning, reaching the ranch just before noon. It was hot; so I reclined in the shadow of the bush and relaxed. How long I dozed I don't know, but a thumping sound suddenly intruded into my consciousness. I raised my head and, half turning, saw a big kangaroo scarcely 50 feet away, looking me over. I tried to swing the camera around; but before I could, the kangaroo was off. Next time I would be ready. I didn't have to wait long.

There has been a lot of controversy about kangaroo conservation. Of the small species of kangaroos, some are near extinction and others are already extinct. The large kangaroos—the "Big Red," the gray, and the wallaroo—seem to be doing better, and sheep farmers sometimes consider them pests. The recent near-elimination of the dingo (because it kills sheep) may have helped the large kangaroos. In addition, sheep eat the coarser plants, allowing the more succulent grasses preferred by some large kangaroos to proliferate.

No one knows how many kangaroos—large or small —there are. But conservationists fear that a continuation of the kill rate of the 1960's—more than 1,500,000 each year—could threaten the large kangaroo species. Since 1973 the Australian Government has prohibited the export of kangaroo meat (used in pet foods) and skins, although domestic manufacturers may still use the meat and fur. Some of my Australian friends are indignant that the kangaroo, which adorns Australia's coat of arms, should be sacrificed to sustain pets. As one expressed it: "As a national conservation symbol, as a unique animal, and as a protein source for man, it is too important for such a frivolous use."

A Kangaroo's First 50 Days

Blind and naked, a red kangaroo at birth weighs only about 1/35 of an ounce. Crawling hand over hand with its forelimbs, completely unaided, it takes about 3 minutes to climb from the opening of the birth canal to the opening of the pouch.

Inside the pouch the kangaroo clamps onto one of four teats, where it remains for more than 6 months.

At 50 days, although it still has no fur and its eyes are only bumps, the infant, called a joey, has well-developed hind legs and a tail.

This family of gray kangaroos includes, besides the parents, a nearly grown joey and a younger one still in its mother's pouch. *Gray kangaroos live in open forests; red kangaroos, their larger relatives, are animals of somewhat more arid country.*

Rare Marsupials of Australia

Marsupials, mammals that usually carry their young in pouches, are a trademark of Australia. At first sight the variety of marsupials in Australia seems to be almost endless; in reality, however, this variety is limited and diminishing. The arrival of people 30,000 years ago, accompanied by the dingo (a kind of dog), meant extermination for some species.

European settlement in the last 200 years has had a much more profound effect. Europeans introduced rabbits and deer (which compete with the vegetarian marsupials) and foxes (which prey upon them). In addition, the Europeans took huge tracts of land for tree farms, mining, and sheep and cattle grazing. Now many marsupials are in trouble.

Alert and strong, the tiger cat lives in eastern Australia and Tasmania. Slightly larger than a domestic cat, this marsupial pursues its prey on the ground or through the treetops. Hunting by night, it catches mammals, birds, and insects.

Closely related to the large kangaroos and wallabies, the small potoroo survives in isolated colonies on the Australian mainland but is commoner in Tasmania. It feeds at night on plants, digging holes in the ground to get at their roots.

An inveterate and efficient digger, the hairy-nosed wombat burrows in hard, arid soil in southern Australia. It is losing ground because sheep farmers see its holes, which may be 2 feet across, as a threat to livestock.

The numbat, also called the banded anteater, lives almost entirely on termites. No longer in eastern Australia, it still lives in the forests in the southwestern part of the continent.

The yellow-footed rock wallaby, 2 feet tall and one of the handsomest marsupials, was once killed in large numbers for its pelt. Rock wallabies scale cliffs and climb rocks with superb agility and can leap sizable chasms. Because their habitat is relatively inaccessible to grazing animals, rock wallabies have generally fared better than the other small members of the kangaroo family.

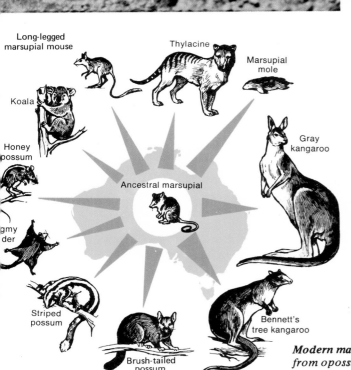

Long-legged marsupial mouse

Thylacine

Marsupial mole

Koala

Honey possum

Ancestral marsupial

Gray kangaroo

gmy der

Striped possum

Brush-tailed possum

Bennett's tree kangaroo

The spotted cuscus inhabits a strip of rain forest in northern Queensland, where it pursues its slow way through the trees, searching for leaves and fruits and trying to avoid the python, its chief predator.

Modern marsupials, *scientists believe, have evolved from opossumlike creatures that lived about the same time as the last of the dinosaurs. They have adopted almost every lifestyle possible for land animals.*

At an aerie in Florida's Everglades, a female bald eagle and her 21-day-old eaglet await the arrival of the male with a fish. Both parents feed the young, and meals arrive two to eight times a day—more frequently as the young appetites grow.

The Bald Eagle:
Symbol and Victim

George Ott

Time was when a soaring bald eagle was a familiar sight in North American skies. Today over most of the continent bald eagles are rare birds indeed.

Lord of the skies, the eagle has stirred the mind of man for ages. More than 5,000 years ago the Sumerian city of Lagash adopted the bird as its divinity. Later, imperial Rome's conquering legions bore standards topped by sculptured eagles. Napoleon, too, favored the eagle as a symbol of empire.

Although for millennia eagles represented imperial power, one species—the bald eagle—now symbolizes freedom and democracy. Because it is native only to North America, and because of its great strength and grandeur in flight, the Continental Congress in 1782 chose the bald eagle to be the national bird of the new United States.

Today the U.S. national emblem is seldom found aloft in its native skies. For almost two decades the number of bald eagles has shown a steady decline as advancing civilization, illegal shooting, and poisons pouring into lakes and rivers have taken their toll. Should this tragic trend continue, the harsh, creaking cry of the bald eagle may be heard no more.

Before the arrival of white men the bald eagle ranged through most of North America, from what is now Alaska and northern Quebec to Mexico and Florida. Today, although it may pass through in migration, the bald eagle no longer breeds within much of this vast territory. Scattered pairs remain in eastern Canada and Maine, around the western Great Lakes and the upper Mississippi, in the mountain States and the Northwest. Only British Columbia, Alaska, and Florida have bald eagles in appreciable numbers.

The bald eagle was named the national bird almost two centuries ago, but it was not until 1940 that the U.S. Congress passed the Bald Eagle Protection Act, which (though it banned the molesting or killing of the birds in the then 48 States) contained loopholes and lacked enforcement provisions. Even this limited eagle protection was not extended to Alaska, the bald eagle's last stronghold. There the birds have been subjected to more than four decades of persecution, mainly by bounty hunters and fishermen who begrudge them their take of small fur-bearing mammals and salmon. Since 1912, when Alaska passed its first bounty law, more than 100,000 bald eagles have been killed there. Not until the 1960's did Alaska finally adopt the national protection act and repeal the bounty law.

Molesting or killing a bald eagle today is a Federal offense punishable by a sizable fine or imprisonment or both. But enforcement is still feeble or lacking, and bald eagles are becoming increasingly rare. In several western States illegal shooting from planes and electrocution by power lines have threatened the bald eagle as well as the commoner golden eagle. Lumbering operations and burgeoning real estate and industrial developments have invaded the birds' retreats, disturbing and destroying nests.

In the last decade bald eagles have suffered from an even deadlier peril, which was first noted on Florida's west coast, a favorite nesting area of southern bald eagles. There, starting about 1950, the reproductive rate of bald eagles began to drop. Suspicions arose that pesticides were the cause.

Field research and feeding experiments point to accumulating residues of chlorinated hydrocarbons, of which DDT is one, as a major factor in the decline in the bald eagle's reproduction. These residues upset the female's calcium metabolism, causing her to lay eggs with thin, easily broken shells or even no shells at all. Though most uses of DDT have been banned in the United States and Canada, DDT already in the soil will remain in the environment.

What kind of creature is North America's most celebrated bird, which has been so harried? With its great size, beauty, and magnificent wingspread, the

Fully feathered but not yet flying, young eagles wait in vain for food. After several weeks of frequent feeding, the parents may starve and torment the young into hungry flight by showing them the fish and then eating it themselves.

The Eagle and Its Food Chain

The bald eagle is in trouble because of loss of habitat and also because of what it eats. It feeds mainly on water birds and large fish, which eat small fish, which eat minute forms of aquatic life. The small organisms at the bottom of this food chain absorb long-lasting pesticides (notably DDT) from the water, where eroded soil, dry leaves, and dead insects have carried them. The poison becomes more and more concentrated at each link, and the birds of prey at the top of the chain get a heavy dose. In eagles DDT can cause male sterility or defects in eggs, such as easily broken shells or no shells at all. Although this pesticide is still used in fighting malaria, many countries, including those controlling the bald eagle's destiny, have banned or reduced its use.

Living principally on fish and fish-eating birds, the bald eagle is at the top of its food chain and inexorably gets a heavy DDT dose.

Bald eagle

Tiny aquatic plants and animals absorb DDT from the water.

The grebe, a fish-eating diver, accumulates DDT from its food.

Grebe

Catfish

Fish that eat other fish concentrate pesticides from their prey.

DDT

Algae

Zooplankton

Yellow perch

Minnows

Great Birds of Prey

Although from the human point of view birds of prey seem to be the villains in the drama of nature, they play vital roles as predators and clean-up squads. Without eagles, hawks, and owls, the rabbits, mice, and rats would destroy grain fields; without vultures, decaying material would remain on the ground. Shooting, the use of long-lasting pesticides, and the loss of habitat through man's intrusions have caused a disastrous decline in the numbers of birds of prey; more than 50 species are now endangered worldwide.

With its 9-foot wingspan, the California condor is among the largest North American birds. Fewer than 60 of these supervultures survive.

Europe's rarest bird, the majestic Spanish imperial eagle, is barely holding its own in a few protected areas of Spain.

The lammergeier is a cliff-dwelling vulture of Europe, Asia, and East Africa. It drops bones from a height to get at the marrow.

Only about 100 Everglades kites are now left in the swamps of Florida.

The Galápagos hawk now lives only on the relatively remote islands of the archipelago.

The Philippine monkey-eating eagle suffers from loss of rain forests.

Pesticide poisoning has nearly wiped out the peregrine falcons from their former range in Europe and North America.

In a battle of wings and talons, bald eagles compete for a piece of carrion, though they prefer live prey. They catch fish, birds, and small mammals for themselves; or they may rob ospreys and vultures in spectacular midair confrontations.

soaring eagle demonstrates power, majesty, and freedom. From wingtip to wingtip it spans 6 to 8 feet; its overall length is 30 to 37 inches.

This eagle is not really bald, of course. Snowy white head feathers, like those of the tail, are marks of maturity that do not become prominent until the bird is 3 to 5 years old. An adult bald eagle, with its shining white head and tail and its yellow beak, legs, and feet, cannot easily be mistaken for any other bird.

During courtship the male bald eagle puts on a fantastic display of aerial acrobatics. He may roll over onto his back and glide briefly, or in this unusual position he may beat his wings a few times. Sometimes a pair of courting eagles will lock talons, fold their wings, and plummet earthward.

After mating, the birds build a nest of sticks and branches high in a tree or on a cliff. Because the bald eagle's diet is principally fish, the nest is usually built close to the ocean, a lake, or a river. Bald eagles generally return to the same nest each year, gradually enlarging it as they mend damage incurred during their absence. In time their home becomes enormous. One nest measured more than 8 feet across and 12 feet deep; it was estimated to weigh 2 tons.

Model parents

Bald eagles breed at 3 or 4 years of age, and the annual clutch of eggs usually numbers just two. These eagles are model parents, feeding their young faithfully for the 3 to 4 months they are in the nest and often for some time after they learn to fly. Because of this prolonged period of parental care, young eagles are reasonably well equipped for survival when they leave the nest.

Like other birds of prey, female bald eagles are larger than males. Strangely, young bald eagles, before leaving the nest, are considerably larger than either parent. Loss of weight due to the strenuous exercise of learning to fly may bring them down to size.

There are two races of bald eagles, the northern and the southern. The larger northern birds range over the vast zone extending from the Arctic south to the northern United States. They usually winter and nest near the southern limits of that area. The southern bald eagles, listed as an endangered subspecies, once ranged over the entire United States and the northern half of Mexico. Now they winter and nest largely along the coasts and rivers of the southern States, although some migrate well into Canada during the warm months. Probably as few as 600 southern bald eagles now survive.

Although it may be a matter of too little and too late for the southern bird, there are some encouraging signs. In U.S. national wildlife refuges a square mile has been measured around each nesting tree, and timber cutting within this area is prohibited. Weakened trees are reinforced to prevent loss of the nest.

Private conservation associations, too, are moving to aid the bald eagle. Nesting success or failure is recorded, and eggs that fail to hatch are sent to laboratories to be tested for pesticide content. The Florida Audubon Society has persuaded owners of land where bald eagles nest to post more than 2 million acres as cooperative sanctuaries. The Continental Bald Eagle Project, sponsored by the National Audubon Society and supported by the World Wildlife Fund, is actively engaged in bald eagle research and census taking, and so is the Canadian Wildlife Service.

Despite these belated efforts to save this magnificent bird, much remains to be done. In particular, better protective measures and stronger penalties for infringement are urgently needed.

Great Goats of the Gran Paradiso

Verna Mays

A century ago Europe had only some 60 alpine ibexes, all in Italy. Today 50 times as many live in that area alone, and ibexes have spread to other parts of Europe.

Men have seen in the ibex everything from a tasty stew to an arena performer to a cure for gout. The Romans of the Empire watched pairs of sturdy bucks clash horns in the arenas. Unfortunately, the easiest way to capture an ibex was to kill a mother and take the young.

In the Middle Ages ibexes, admired and misunderstood because they dwelt in remote regions of rock and wind, earned a reputation for magic. Ibex blood was supposed to remove calluses. Hard balls composed of hair, resin, pebbles, and other indigestibles, taken from ibex stomachs, were pronounced a cure for various illnesses.

Hunted to provide medicine and food, the alpine ibex quickly declined in numbers. Laws enacted to protect them only seemed to make the animals more desirable. Ibexes disappeared from the Central Alps. Medieval and Renaissance records show the history of the animal in Switzerland: last ibex killed in Glarus, 1558; last ibex seen in the Gotthard region, 1583; Grisons, 1650; Waldstatten region, 1661. By 1700 Switzerland had no living ibexes. The species miraculously survived in France until about 1800.

By 1816 only a few dozen alpine ibexes remained, all in the Italian Alps. In 1856 the Italian mountain area known as the Gran Paradiso was proclaimed a royal hunting preserve, and a substantial and well-armed group of wardens was maintained to protect the ibexes from all but a very limited amount of hunting.

During the 19th century there were other efforts to save the alpine ibex. Well-meaning conservationists captured living ibexes and placed them in zoos and game parks, where they were expected to thrive and reproduce. But usually they did not live long enough to reproduce. Sometimes ibexes and chamois (a kind of mountain goat) were confined in the same enclosure. The two species often fight when penned in a small space; and since the chamois attacks straight and low, and the ibex stands on its hind legs, the ibex invariably lost the battle.

The Swiss were determined to return the ibex to their slopes; they even established the Peter and Paul Game Park for future ibexes. Unfortunately, the Italians had all the purebreds, and they were reluctant to part with them. In 1906 the Swiss smuggled a few animals into Peter and Paul. The Italians then relented and began to sell stock. Since that time ibexes have been successfully reintroduced to other mountainous regions of Switzerland and to the Alps of Austria and France as well. A German attempt to reestablish the ibex in that country failed; all but 10 ibexes contracted "rubbers," a contagious disease, from resident chamois and died. The 10 survivors escaped to Austria.

A spectacular recovery

Although their numbers dropped drastically during World War II, today there are more than 6,500 alpine ibexes in Italy, Switzerland, Austria, and France. All are descendants of the few dozen that lived in the Italian Alps in the early part of the 19th century. In addition, more than 8,000 Spanish ibexes—another species—live in the mountains of Spain. Smaller numbers of other species inhabit mountainous regions from Europe eastward as far as China and Siberia, and southward in Africa to the Sudan and Ethiopia.

Why have these Olympians of goatdom been prized,

Where To See Ibexes in Europe

A quest for the alpine ibex will lead you, of course, to the Alps. But not to just any spot in the Alps. This animal—once endangered, now recovering—is secure only in parks where it is protected from hunting. The largest colony is in Italy's Gran Paradiso National Park. During the summer the ibexes usually remain above the 10,000-foot elevation; in winter they move to the lower slopes, where they find more food and where the wind is less fierce. Another European species, the Spanish ibex, inhabits the Pyrenees; other kinds of ibexes live in Asia and Africa.

Alpine ibex

Spanish ibex

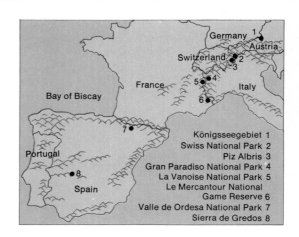

Königsseegebiet 1
Swiss National Park 2
Piz Albris 3
Gran Paradiso National Park 4
La Vanoise National Park 5
Le Mercantour National
Game Reserve 6
Valle de Ordesa National Park 7
Sierra de Gredos 8

hunted, cherished, fought over, almost exterminated, and finally saved? The alpine ibex is, after all, nothing but a goat. But even one sight of the male's tremendous ribbed horns sweeping from the forehead backward over the shoulders, then tapering to fine points, is enough to establish beyond a doubt that this is no ordinary goat. A full-grown male ibex weighs as much as 200 pounds; nearly a tenth of its weight is in its magnificent horns.

A rocky road

The alpine ibex is at home only high in the mountains and rarely descends to an elevation below 6,500 feet. Alpine ibexes are born in late spring or early summer and are surefooted almost from the time they are born; within a few hours after birth they are able to follow their mothers in search of shrubs, grasses, and other plants. Except during the late fall breeding season, the sexes live separately. The mature males, which climb higher up the slopes, form herds of as many as 50; the groups of females (which have shorter, straighter horns), yearlings, and kids consist of as few as 6 animals.

Poaching is the principal threat to the ibex today. Most of the animal's natural enemies—wolves, lynx, bears, and golden eagles—have vanished from the mountain slopes occupied by ibexes. The largest population of alpine ibexes—more than 3,000 animals—is in the Gran Paradiso, now an Italian national park. Especially in the morning and evening, visitors willing to do a little climbing there can observe these rugged mountain goats at a surprisingly close distance.

Playfully sparring, young male ibexes stay near their mothers on an alpine slope. Magnificent horns on adult males curve backward as much as 5 feet and may weigh 20 pounds; the horns on these female and young goats are shorter and lighter.

Is There Room for the Horned and Antlered?

It is one of nature's paradoxes that the animals with the most conspicuous weapons are all vegetarians. No hoofed creature uses its horns or antlers to kill prey; they are used to threaten and, less often, to fight. But, except in defense against predators, the opponents are members of the same species, usually male, and the contest is generally over possession of space or of females. Why are so many of these creatures endangered? Man's hunting for food or sport has taken a toll. In addition, throughout the world man has occupied the habitats of many species, using the land for agriculture, cutting forests for lumber. Other hoofed animals have been eliminated because they competed with livestock for grazing.

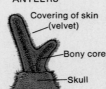

ANTLERS
Covering of skin (velvet)
Bony core
Skull

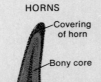

HORNS
Covering of horn
Bony core

While growing, an antler is covered by living "velvet"; a horn is always covered by a fingernail-like substance.

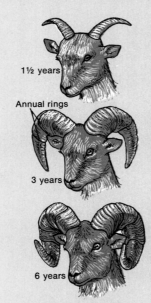

1 year

4 years

6 years (12 points)

RED DEER

1½ years

Annual rings

3 years

6 years

BIGHORN SHEEP

Antlers grow anew each year, though older deer have more points. Horns are permanent; annual rings tell age. Horns usually occur on both sexes, antlers on males.

Extinct Antlered Animals

Bush-antlered deer
The bush-antlered deer was an ice age European form.

Schomburgk's deer
The last of these deer was killed in Thailand in 1932.

Irish elk
The antlers of the giant deer spanned 12 feet.

Extinct Horned Animals

Syndyoceras
About 20 million years ago the Syndyoceras, a four-horned deerlike animal, lived on the Nebraskan plains of North America. It stood about 3½ feet tall at the shoulders.

Aurochs
The last European aurochs, which died in 1627, lived in dense forest, perhaps driven there by man.

Blaubok
This South African antelope was exterminated at the end of the 19th century.

Threatened Antlered Animals

Peruvian guemal

These Andean deer live at elevations of 10,000 feet to 15,000 feet, forming small herds. They are threatened by overhunting.

Barasingha

Small numbers of the overhunted barasingha, or swamp deer, survive in India and Nepal.

Manipur brow-antlered deer

This deer lives in only one reserve in India, though a related race is found in Thailand.

Fea's muntjac

The muntjac, also called the barking deer because of its alarm call, is protected by law in Thailand and Burma but is killed illegally.

Persian fallow deer

Twice given up as extinct, this deer is losing out to domestic goats. Zoos are trying to establish breeding groups.

Key deer

Once numbering only 50, the smallest North American deer has been protected for several decades. The population is now about 600, but road accidents kill deer even in protected areas.

Threatened Horned Animals

Mountain anoa

Habitat destruction and hunting have nearly exterminated these small buffaloes of Indonesia. The lowland anoa is also endangered.

Slender-horned gazelle

This gazelle inhabits the Sahara Desert from Algeria to Libya and south to Chad. Hunting has severely reduced its numbers.

Kabul markhor

Domestic goats have taken over most of the range of this wild goat of Afghanistan.

Wild yak

The few remaining wild yaks, much larger than their domestic relatives, live in remote Asian mountains.

Arabian oryx

Zoos are breeding the oryx in order to restore the vanishing wild herds of Arabia.

Western giant eland

The largest antelope lives in West Africa.

45

In Search of the Right Whale

Roger Payne

Who has seen the mighty whale in love or at play? One man's quest led to southern Argentina, where groups of rare right whales sported just offshore.

One early fall afternoon, from a high cliff on the shores of Argentina, my wife and I observed a display that few people see. It was late in the day, and the sky was turning pink and red as we scanned the sea. Suddenly, as our eyes strained in the fading light, a massive black column surged out of the water, then toppled back in a welter of spray, making a sound like the boom of distant artillery. We had caught a glimpse of a creature seldom seen in modern times: a right whale, one of the rarest and largest mammals on earth.

The sight of this huge whale crashing into the sea was once common on the shores of all continents, but to see it we had to travel to the remote and sparsely inhabited region of southern Argentina. A small colony of these playful and unaggressive creatures, hunted for six centuries to a state of near extinction, survives in this isolated corner of the world.

Even before the heyday of whaling, the right whale was worth a fortune. It earned its name because it was the "right" whale to kill—slow enough to catch, fat enough to float after the kill, and with a treasure in whalebone between its jaws. The right whale's habits also made it an attractive target. Right whales approach the shore so closely that they are sometimes within reach of a harpoon hurled from the beach, a kill that requires very little courage or equipment.

Right whaling flourished during the 12th and 13th centuries in the Bay of Biscay, off Spain and France.

Right whales were given their name because they were the right kind to hunt —rich in blubber and whalebone and slow enough to catch easily. Recently a small herd of right whales was discovered off the coast of Argentina. For the first time scientists have been able to study them in the winter breeding season. The two whales (left) are probably courting. The whale breaching (above) is apparently simply playing.

When the Pilgrims arrived in the New World in 1620, they saw whales, probably right whales, in Massachusetts Bay. The crew of the *Mayflower* thought that Massachusetts Bay might be an even better site for whaling than the "Greenland fishery," which had at that time the densest concentration of the right whales known anywhere.

Toward the end of the 19th century the right whale carnage dwindled, along with the demise of sperm whaling, but whaling was to undergo yet another boom. In 1901 scientists developed a chemical technique for removing the unpleasant taste of whale oil, which made it possible to use the oil in food products. The few remaining right whale concentrations were sought out as the industry began its final and greatest expansion, the one that almost wiped out blue and humpback whales.

In the 1930's the principal whaling nations finally agreed on the protection of right whales, but they made no provision for international observers. By this time right whales were no longer of commercial interest; their remnants were too scattered.

The Most Endangered Whales

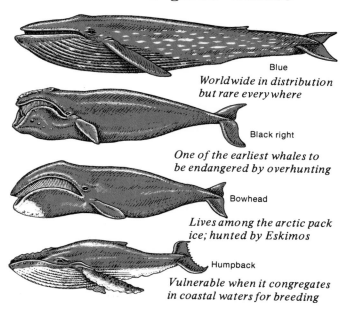

Blue
Worldwide in distribution but rare everywhere

Black right
One of the earliest whales to be endangered by overhunting

Bowhead
Lives among the arctic pack ice; hunted by Eskimos

Humpback
Vulnerable when it congregates in coastal waters for breeding

An inquisitive right whale, its barnacle-encrusted head mostly submerged, cruises toward a small boat. The paired slits of its blowhole are immediately to the left of the diver's wristwatch; the lower lip nearly reaches the top of the head.

In 1970 the New York Zoological Society sponsored an exploratory expedition to Argentina, and in due time I experienced the realization of a lifelong dream. For 6 days we stayed in the area, going out in a tiny skiff to make recordings of the whales' sounds.

The next year we returned to the area on a 3-month expedition sponsored by the New York Zoological Society and the National Geographic Society. In late winter we set up camp where we could live in sight of right whales even when cooking or eating. On calm nights when the whales came near shore, the sounds of their breathing often woke us.

Whale courtship

In the two areas in which we made most of our observations different herd structures seemed to predominate. Toward the end of our stay one herd was almost entirely composed of females and calves, while the second had few calves but many mating whales. One area seemed to be a nursery, the other a courting and mating ground.

Mating in right whales appears to be promiscuous. Once we saw two males mate with the same female within a short time; one of these males mated with a second female only a few minutes later.

During mating the female remains on an even keel, with the male under water, belly up, beneath her. She can avoid mating simply by rolling upside down at the surface. But she must right herself periodically in order to breathe. When she does so, the males drifting by her side (as many as six, but usually two or three) dive rapidly beneath her with much pushing and shov-

ing. There is considerable competition among the males for a single female. But when a male is not competing with others while mating, much apparently tender stroking between male and female takes place.

The sense of touch seems to be important to these whales. A female often dallies with her calf for long periods, lying on her back with the calf draped across her chest. Occasionally she pats it or allows it to play on her tail. There it slides repeatedly off one fluke or tries to swim and wriggle over its mother's back when she is breathing quietly at the surface.

We also saw whale calves playing with kelp (a giant seaweed) after a bad storm had left long strands floating in the bay. A calf would make a shallow dive and come up with a strand draped over its head like a comical hat. The calf would then submerge and swim forward, allowing the seaweed to slide slowly down its back. Just as the kelp was about to slip off the tail, it would twist its tail around, grab the kelp with its flippers, and pat it vigorously between them. This form of play was repeated many times and was made all the more fascinating by the very slow rate at which it all occurred. Such is the pace of the lives of right whales. Often the whales simply drifted quietly near the surface for hours, moving only enough to take an occasional breath.

We shall be going back to Argentina soon, hoping that when we return no illegal whaling operations in the area will have encountered the right whales and turned them into dog food, margarine, or soap—things from which I, for one, have never gained the least inspiration.

The California Gray Whale Returns

California gray whales are making a comeback. They have been protected from whaling for more than 30 years, and the result has been an encouraging and dramatic rise in their population.

What imperiled these gray whales in the first place was not just their commercial value but their extreme vulnerability. Each year they migrate from summer feeding grounds in the Arctic, traveling more than 6,000 miles to breeding lagoons off Baja California in Mexico. As they approach their destination, they swim in the shallow waters close to shore.

In the 19th century this annual coastal parade attracted many whaling vessels. The shore-hugging whales were easy to find. And the gray whale's habit of clustering in just a few shallow lagoons to mate and give birth made harpooning a simple matter.

On their northward migration the whales travel much farther from shore and are seen much less often.

No one knows how large the original gray whale population actually was. Estimates range from a high of 50,000 to a conservative guess of 25,000 in 1840, when the whaling industry began its incredible slaughter. By the 1930's only about 100 of these animals could be found. Not until then did the whaling nations of the world agree to prohibit the killing of grays. This ban, dating from 1937, is still in effect.

The California gray whale has shown an astounding ability to come back. There are now about 11,000 of these gentle giants. Although a gray whale may live to an age of 50 or more, few of the gray whales alive today are more than 35 years old—a reminder of how recently the hunting stopped and the recovery began.

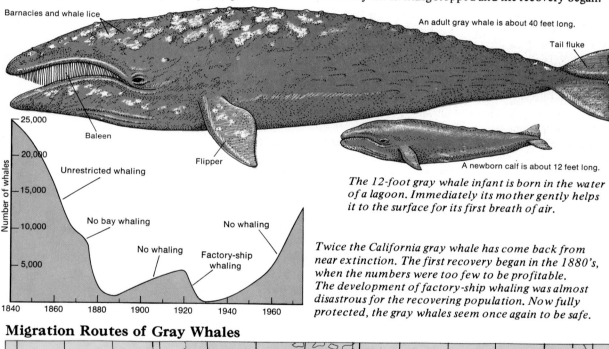

Barnacles and whale lice
An adult gray whale is about 40 feet long.
Tail fluke
Baleen
Flipper
A newborn calf is about 12 feet long.

The 12-foot gray whale infant is born in the water of a lagoon. Immediately its mother gently helps it to the surface for its first breath of air.

Number of whales — 25,000, 20,000, 15,000, 10,000, 5,000
Unrestricted whaling
No bay whaling
No whaling
No whaling
Factory-ship whaling
1840 1860 1880 1900 1920 1940 1960

Twice the California gray whale has come back from near extinction. The first recovery began in the 1880's, when the numbers were too few to be profitable. The development of factory-ship whaling was almost disastrous for the recovering population. Now fully protected, the gray whales seem once again to be safe.

Migration Routes of Gray Whales

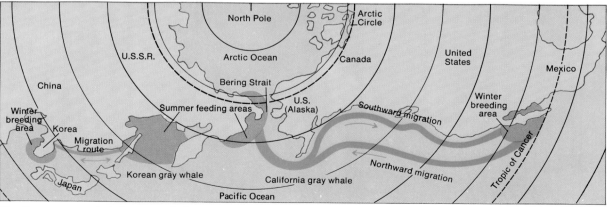

North Pole
Arctic Circle
U.S.S.R.
Arctic Ocean
Canada
United States
Mexico
China
Bering Strait
Winter breeding area
Korea
Summer feeding areas
U.S. (Alaska)
Southward migration
Winter breeding area
Migration route
Tropic of Cancer
Japan
Korean gray whale
California gray whale
Northward migration
Pacific Ocean

The Korean gray whale has a much shorter migration route than that of the California race, though both go north in summer and south in winter. Fossils of ice-age gray whales are found on the coasts of Europe.

Wildlife Living Free

A living wall of greater flamingos edges Kenya's Lake Elmenteita. When the chicks are independent (about 75 days after hatching), the adults may leave for nearby Lake Nakuru, a favorite feeding area and a national park.

Living space is the key to wildlife survival. The activities of an expanding human population have reduced the world's wilderness areas, making parks, reserves, and refuges increasingly significant as havens for wildlife. Wisely managed, these sanctuaries can provide land and protection for their animal inhabitants and rewarding experiences for their human visitors.

The Challenge of South Asia

George B. Schaller

Retreating before the human flood, Asia's wildlife can find refuge only in sanctuaries, now too small and too few.

On a boulder-strewn slope in the shadow of 25,230-foot Tirich Mir, highest peak in Pakistan's Hindu Kush, I looked into the pale, haunting eyes of a female snow leopard. She lay on the crest of a spur, her fur blending into the rocks so that she seemed almost a part of them. A rare, elusive inhabitant of isolated mountains, the snow leopard typifies not only the delights and problems of studying large mammals in South Asia but also the special plight of many South Asian animals.

I had come to Pakistan to make a survey of wildlife in the Chitral Gol Reserve. This reserve, comprising about 30 square miles of rugged mountains, has for many years belonged to the royal family of Chitral. Now its owners hope to convert it from a hunting reserve into a sanctuary where visitors will observe and enjoy the wildlife.

Pakistan, India, Bangladesh, Nepal, and Sri Lanka (Ceylon) possess a wildlife heritage few areas can equal. But in its impact the tiger so overshadows all other species that most people forget or are unaware that South Asia also has lions, leopards, and clouded leopards, as well as snow leopards. In addition, there are gaurs (wild oxen), elephants, one-horned rhinoceroses, four species of bears, and several kinds of deer. The high mountains harbor such unfamiliar animals as the Himalayan tahr, takin, bharal, urial, markhor, serow, goral, and Marco Polo sheep.

Few visitors travel to South Asia especially to view wildlife. But for the person willing to seek out remote places and perhaps even physically exert himself, the experience can be very rewarding.

Vanishing species

Many large mammals are now rare and others have disappeared. In the 16th century Akbar the Great is said to have kept 1,000 cheetahs for the chase; the last wild cheetah in India was shot in 1952. The Sumatran rhinoceros probably has disappeared, as has the Sikkim stag. Other species cling to a last vestige of their former range, some tenuously protected in small sanctuaries: About 175 Asiatic lions in the Gir Wild Life Sanctuary of Gujarat State; about 400 Indian wild asses, almost all in the Little Rann of Kutch; about 40 Javan rhinoceroses in an Indonesian reserve; about 600 Indian, or one-horned, rhinoceroses, most of them in Kaziranga and in a Nepalese sanctuary; about 100 Manipur brow-antlered deer in the swamps of Assam's Keibul Lanjao sanctuary. In Kanha National Park I found some 100

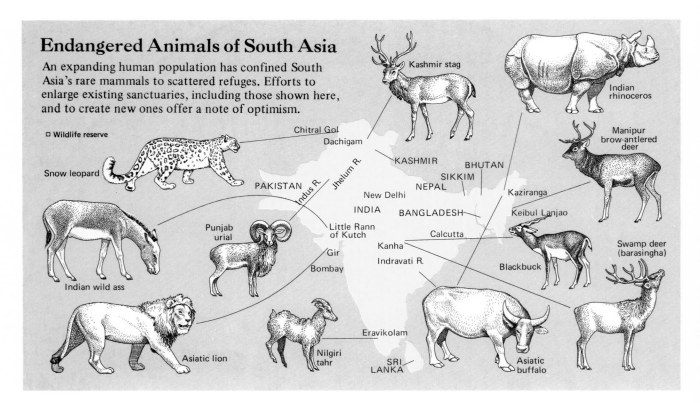

Endangered Animals of South Asia

An expanding human population has confined South Asia's rare mammals to scattered refuges. Efforts to enlarge existing sanctuaries, including those shown here, and to create new ones offer a note of optimism.

□ Wildlife reserve

Snow leopard

Indian wild ass

Punjab urial

Asiatic lion

Nilgiri tahr

Chitral Gol
Dachigam
KASHMIR
SIKKIM
BHUTAN
NEPAL
PAKISTAN
Indus R.
Jhelum R.
New Delhi
INDIA
BANGLADESH
Little Rann of Kutch
Gir
Bombay
Kanha
Indravati R.
Calcutta
Eravikolam
SRI LANKA

Kashmir stag

Indian rhinoceros

Manipur brow-antlered deer

Kaziranga
Keibul Lanjao

Blackbuck

Swamp deer (barasingha)

Asiatic buffalo

swamp deer, last remnants of this species' southern race; in 1938 some 3,000 were estimated there. The northern race numbers about 4,500.

In central India I helped the Bombay Natural History Society make a census of the Asiatic buffalo. Along the remote Indravati River we finally saw a herd; the animals were strikingly different in their tense vitality from their domestic counterparts. Perhaps no more than 200 buffaloes survive in that area and 2,000 elsewhere in India and in Nepal, a quarter of them in the Kaziranga sanctuary.

One day in October as I walked along the Dagwan River in Kashmir, with snow far down on the slopes of the Himalayan peaks around me, I heard a wild bugling —eee-oo-uuu—beginning harshly and ending on a deep, clear note, the mournful call of a dying species. It was a Kashmir stag. There were few hinds to answer his call. Twenty years ago perhaps 2,000 stags wintered in the Dachigam sanctuary, but now fewer than 200 make their last stand there.

In southern India the cloud-shrouded cliffs of the Nilgiri highlands are the home of the Nilgiri tahr, a unique goat whose closest relatives live in the Himalayas and Arabia. Possibly fewer than 1,500 Nilgiri tahrs still exist, a third of them in the private Eravikolam Reserve, but even the existence of this reserve is threatened by the Kerala State Government, which wants the land for agriculture.

In Pakistan I observed the Punjab urial, a sheep that once inhabited the low dry hills between the Indus and Jhelum Rivers. Today about 500 animals survive in a private sanctuary. The blackbuck, once the most abundant large mammal of the open woodlands and semi-deserts, with herds in the Punjab numbering up to 10,000 animals, has been so persistently shot that it is almost extinct in Pakistan, Nepal, and most of the Indian States.

Tigers need their own home

Predators have special problems. In 1967 about 55 tigers were legally shot by foreigners in India. Such hunting has now been stopped. But how many tigers are killed each year by villagers? Thirty-two tigers were found dead from poison in 1969 in one district of central India. The only hope for the tiger lies in large reserves and special restricted sanctuaries.

Several factors have contributed to the decline in Asian wildlife. Today less than 20 percent of India is still forested. In the past 3 centuries man's misuse of land has turned much of western India and Pakistan into desert. In areas that cannot be cultivated, forests have been cut for firewood. Livestock, particularly goats, have scoured the hills for centuries, eating every sapling, every blade of grass. India alone has more than 350 million head of goats, cattle, and buffaloes.

The overpowering impression of South Asia is people. More than 1,000 human beings per square mile are crowded into the Ganges Basin. The only hope for the survival of wildlife is in sanctuaries. But many existing sanctuaries contain villages, virtually all permit livestock grazing, some extract timber, and poaching is common. A comprehensive system of sanctuaries must be established in this generation, or the remaining lands will be swamped by the human tide.

A rare view of one of the world's rarest cats, this color photograph by George Schaller is the first ever taken of a snow leopard in the wild (Pakistan's Hindu Kush). Scientists estimate that only about 500 snow leopards survive today, including 100 in zoos.

From the broad back of an elephant tourists watch a rhinoceros cross a forest path in Nepal. Only a few hundred one-horned Indian rhinoceroses remain in India and Nepal; the rhino is losing its jungle habitat to domestic animals and agriculture.

Elephantback in Nepal

Erwin A. Bauer

At Tiger Tops, in a new national park, the safest way to view a one-horned rhino is as a passenger atop an elephant.

For several hundred yards the mahout had prodded our elephant through an almost impenetrable swamp, where grass grew 20 feet tall. Visibility was zero. When we finally emerged into a clearing, we could hear the excited shouts of other mahouts, for this was a big-game drive. Next we heard the angry snort of the animals being driven toward us.

An instant later a huge female one-horned rhino broke out of the swamp, followed closely by a small calf. The two stopped and stood facing us, the female on the verge of charging. Even though we were safely atop an elephant, it was a chilling confrontation. My first instinct as a wildlife photographer was to focus my camera on the pair and shoot. But our elephant had another idea: A mother rhino is nothing to trifle with.

An instant later the elephant fled, and the rhinos bolted back into the swamp.

The young mahout apologized for the animal's nervous behavior, explaining that at only 21 it was very young. "Don't worry," he said in accented English, "we soon see more rhinos." And before that morning had ended we flushed out three more and had a very close look at a large bull lumbering across a stream.

Watching rhinos is nothing special nowadays. Anyone who joins a photo safari to eastern or southern Africa is certain to see many of both the black and white varieties. White rhinos even roam freely in the new "safari parks." But the great Indian, or one-horned, rhino is one member of the family that is not easy to see. Probably fewer than 600 still survive—250 to 300 of them in the Kaziranga and Manas sanctuaries of Assam, in India. The rest occur in the Terai, a little-visited region of southern Nepal. A portion of the Terai is now Royal Chitwan National Park.

Less than 100 miles from the peaks of Everest and Annapurna, the Terai is a lowland jungle fringed by the swamp habitat of the rhino and laced by clear, cool streams. In 1965 the region was declared a wildlife sanctuary, and attempts were made to control the poaching of rhinos for their horns, which were thought to act as an aphrodisiac. At the same time, with an eye toward improving Nepal's balance of payments, a facility was built to attract tourists. Completed in 1968 and called Tiger Tops, it consists of twin lodges built on mahogany stilts at treetop level. Its rattan walls and thatched roofs blend into the environment. The showers are cold water, and Tiger Tops has no telephones, no radio, no television, not even electricity. A small concession to luxury is a circular dining room and bar, built beside a large fireplace, a pleasant place to wait for a tiger or leopard to show up at the baits placed nearby.

Watching rhinos

Just getting to Tiger Tops can be an adventure. It is first necessary to fly to Katmandu from New Delhi or Bangkok. From Katmandu it is a 40-minute hop by air to Meghauli "airport"—nothing more than a level cow pasture. Elephants carry travelers and luggage to Tiger Tops, 8 miles away.

All rhino viewing out of Tiger Tops is done on elephantback for two good reasons. It is the best way to approach rhinos, which are far less suspicious of the tuskers than of four-wheel-drive jeeps. And in some places it is the *only* way. Vehicles are impractical without extensive road building, and that would destroy the wilderness atmosphere.

The Indian one-horned rhino is even more grotesque and intimidating in appearance than its African cousins. The hide of this massive animal folds and seems to overlap on its neck, shoulders, and thighs; it is studded with masses of tubercles that resemble steel rivets. Except for the horn, the large face and head are piglike; the eyes are small and the upper lip is prehensile. But the low-slung armored body and short legs are deceptive—the rhino is more agile than it appears. One-horns are solitary, sedentary, and almost entirely grazers. The average weight of an adult is less than the African white rhino's and greater than that of the black rhino.

Even in the densest cover, rhinos are not too hard to find. They bathe or wallow daily in the same place as long as the water supply remains. Tramped-down trails lead to these wallows. Individual one-horns also defecate in the same place, each establishing its own latrine until large piles of dung accumulate.

In former centuries the one-horned rhino was abundant; it ranged from Kashmir in the west, along the Himalayan foothills, the Ganges and Brahmaputra headwaters, to the Burma border. On the edges of the Terai, teams of farmers once used gongs, firecrackers, and other noisemakers to drive rhinos from their fields. Today there is only the relic population in Nepal and India, and the rhinos of India's Kaziranga sanctuary are by no means secure. Domestic stock is still permitted to compete for available food, and the small staff cannot cope with the continuous poaching on the fringes. But compared with the fate of the disappearing Javan and Sumatran rhinos, the future of the great Indian species in its Nepalese and Indian sanctuaries is positively bright.

The Beleaguered Rhinos

Thick-skinned and powerful, rhinos once ranged over Asia, Africa, Europe, and North America. Climatic changes initially narrowed the rhinos' range; hunting, especially for their horns, has been a major factor in their decline more recently. Rhinos are now confined to small areas of Asia and Africa, and all five species are endangered.

White rhino

Black rhino

*The second-largest land animal, the white rhino is named for its wide (*wijd *in Dutch) upper lip, adapted for grazing; but this rhino is really gray. Its numbers are increasing in South Africa.*

The black rhino, most numerous of the rhinos, lives in East and South Africa. Like its Asian cousins it browses on trees and bushes.

Javan rhino

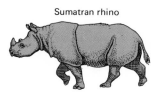
Sumatran rhino

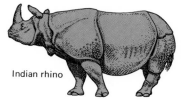
Indian rhino

There are fewer than 100 Javan rhinos, mainly in one Indonesian reserve.

The smallest rhino (4½ feet high) only numbers a few hundred.

Fewer than 600 of this rhino live in the tall grasses of India and Nepal.

Last Stand of Asia's Lions

Eliot Elisofon

Once protected as royal game, the lions of Gir faced a meager future until the tourists came to their assistance.

There were about 20 of us, including several young children. A father held his daughter high up on his shoulder so that she could see the seven lions stalking slowly up the dusty hill.

The lions passed us by, intent on a black goat. The goat was led by a uniformed tracker called a shikari, who also carried a shotgun. Wherever the goat went, the lions followed.

This was the lion show held nearly every day late in the afternoon in the famous Gir Wild Life Sanctuary in western India. Normally the lions stay hidden deep inside the dense scrub. Every morning shikaris look for fresh pugmarks; once they locate the lions, a decision is made where to hold the day's show. Luring lions past tourists may seem artificial, but it is the only way they can be seen. And the Gir Forest in the State of Gujarat is the only place in the world where one can still see the Asiatic lion in its natural habitat.

The Asiatic lion differs only slightly from the lion of Africa. It has larger tail tassels, elbow tufts, and belly fringes, and is longer in the head and a bit stockier. But peering through the thickets, one is likely to notice only that the Asiatic lion has less mane.

Originally Asiatic lions ranged from Greece to India, but by A.D.100 they had disappeared from Europe. They held their own in the remainder of their range until the use of firearms became widespread. By 1844 only a dozen or so were to be found in the Gir hills; thenceforth, they were protected as royal game.

In 1955 Prime Minister Nehru visited the Gir Forest and observed what may have been the first lion show. Impressed, he recommended that a tourist industry be built up around the lions. By 1965 the area had been reclassified from game reserve to wildlife sanctuary, and more than 5,000 tourists a year were watching much the same kind of lion show that I saw.

After their performance the lions did not get to eat the black goat, but neither were they turned away empty. When the tourists left and darkness fell, a water buffalo was tethered to a tree for the lions.

The Gir Forest is the largest wildlife sanctuary in India, spanning some 500 square miles of semiarid hills. Besides the cover of thorny scrub and acacia trees, it contains commercially exploited stands of teak. The only bright color is the orange-red flower of the flame-of-the-forest trees.

When I arrived, Gujarat was suffering from the

Lions Today and Yesterday

Many thousands of years ago two species of gigantic lions roamed Europe, one of them living as far north as Poland. Both are long gone, and so are the smaller lions that roamed Europe in ancient times. The Berber lion of northern Africa and the Cape lion of southern Africa are extinct, and the Asiatic lion is seriously endangered. Though its range is much reduced, the lion of central Africa still prowls its native plains.

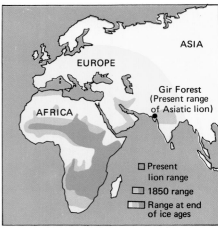

Most of its habitat and natural prey destroyed by man, the lion now occupies a fraction of its original range.

A 500 B.C. seal, now in the British Museum, depicts a lion hunt of King Darius I of Persia. In the upper center Darius appears as an eagle.

Under the watchful eyes of gamekeepers a pride of lions in India's Gir Wild Life Sanctuary eats a leisurely meal of buffalo, which is provided on a regular basis by the park authorities. This teak forest is the only home of the Asiatic lion.

worst drought in 10 years. There was little grass, an ominous situation for the already hard-pressed wild herbivores. The most common of these is the chital or spotted deer. Less common are the sambar or large Asiatic deer, the nilgai or blue bull, and the rare four-horned antelope. Other prey species available to the Gir lions, as well as to leopards, jungle cats, hyenas, and jackals, are wild boar and hares. During my visit I saw only a few of these prey species, but even so I got a sense of the dynamics of prey and predator as it must once have been in the Gir Forest. But no longer.

Competing with cattle

The Gir Forest is now grazed by thousands of domestic cattle, mostly water buffalo. They are raised for milk, which is made into ghee (a semifluid butter), the cash crop of the maldharis—colorful camel-riding people who have lived for many years in the Gir. Some 5,000 maldharis keep more than 20,000 cattle there.

Cattle in a wildlife sanctuary make wildlife managers extremely uncomfortable. The cattle compete with wild herbivores for available fodder, and they destroy the habitat. Predators may take to attacking the cattle; disgruntled villagers who lose cattle sometimes poison lions. A census showed a dramatic decline in Gir lions from an estimated 285 in 1963 to 177 in 1968. In that year scientists joined in an ecological survey of the Gir Forest, sponsored by the Smithsonian Institution and the World Wildlife Fund.

Their findings were grim: The Gir Wild Life Sanctuary exhibited overwhelming evidence of accelerating deterioration. Around its boundaries it was being hemmed in by cultivated lands, and cultivation had spilled over into the sanctuary itself.

The survey proved what most people already suspected—the lions lived almost entirely on cattle. The herders, carrying only sticks, have no means of preventing a lion from taking livestock; they sometimes keep a few cheaper cows or bullocks in the herd to satisfy the lions. (The Government of Gujarat compensates maldharis who lose cattle to lions.)

But the report confirmed that the lions clearly did not get to eat most of the cattle they killed. Well over half the kills were appropriated by harijans—untouchables, most of whom live outside the sanctuary and who chase the lions away so they can eat the meat and sell the hides. About the only thing going for the lions, it seemed, was the tourist business, since the lions were provided with food. Yet the lions I saw were in prime condition; there were many litters, and all appeared well fed.

Well fed or not, however, the Gir lions by no means face an assured future. It is not even known whether they are increasing or decreasing now. Indian officials have taken a number of steps to put the survey research into practice: The scavenging of lion kills has been outlawed. The cutting of teak will be discontinued. To keep cattle from entering the sanctuary, a low stone wall is being built around a large section of the forest. The maldharis and their cattle will be moved outside the sanctuary with land and compensation.

Such measures may save the forest itself, but what will they do to the predators now living mostly on domestic cattle? The vegetation will revive quickly, but it may take years for the wild herbivores to increase. There is one optimistic sign: Plans have been suggested for reintroducing the Asiatic lion elsewhere in its former range, thus increasing its chances of survival.

Sri Lanka's Wildlife Heritage

In wildlife conservation Sri Lanka has an enviable record: One of the first countries in Asia to pass protective wildlife legislation, it established hunting controls in 1908. Today Sri Lanka's major national parks—Ruhunu in the south and Wilpattu in the northwest—are models of management. Their visitors are always accompanied by guards, and their forests are fully protected from human interference. Not that the island, formerly called Ceylon, is untouched; as elsewhere in Asia, poaching is a problem, and agricultural developments destroy wild areas. But sea turtles and nearly all birds are protected; dugongs and elephants find refuge in the national parks; conservationists are working to include threatened habitats in the system of parks and reserves; and an active wildlife society has educated several generations of citizens to care about their remarkable heritage.

Sri Lanka's largest carnivore, *the leopard was once considered vermin to be shot on sight. Now that a license is required to hunt these secretive cats, they are becoming more common throughout the island's national parks.*

Alert in the dense jungle *of Wilpattu National Park, this crested hawk eagle is about 18 inches tall. A small, pale race of an eagle that ranges from India to Indonesia, the striking bird preys on lizards, small mammals, and domestic fowl.*

Two star tortoises encounter one another in Ruhunu National Park; the larger one is about 12 inches across. On Sri Lanka these reptiles live in dry lowland forests; their relatives in central and southern India prefer high, grassy jungles.

A Ceylonese gray langur – identified by its pointed head – perches in Wilpattu National Park, supported by the tough buttock pads possessed by all Old World monkeys. The gray langur is the Sri Lankan form of India's sacred monkey.

A 5-year-old elephant and its mother drink from a waterhole late in the afternoon in Ruhunu National Park. The mother is standing over a drowned infant, a victim of an encounter with a crocodile; she is still trying to protect the baby.

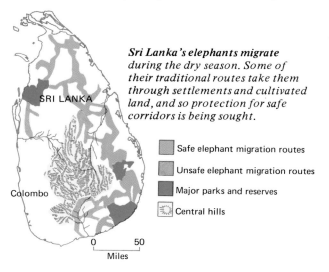

Sri Lanka's elephants migrate during the dry season. Some of their traditional routes take them through settlements and cultivated land, and so protection for safe corridors is being sought.

SRI LANKA

Colombo

Safe elephant migration routes

Unsafe elephant migration routes

Major parks and reserves

Central hills

0   50

Miles

Well equipped for desert life, addaxes get needed water from the plants they eat. But prolonged drought has devastated the Sahara's addax population, giving increased importance to the small (but breeding) herd at Hai-Bar South.

Bringing Biblical Animals Home

Martin Zucker

A dream of restoring Israel's vanished wildlife is becoming a reality at Hai-Bar South, thanks to a retired general.

The Bible called it a land with brooks of water. Here the ancient Israelites encamped during their 40-year journey from Egypt to Canaan. Now this same land is giving refuge to wildlife that roamed the area 33 centuries ago.

The refuge, Hai-Bar South, is the work of a group of conservation-minded Israelis concerned about the destruction of wildlife during millennia of neglect and armed struggle, and most recently through mechanized hunting by military patrols, oil surveyors, and tribesmen. Hai-Bar South will be used to restore species mentioned in the Bible to Israel.

Hai-Bar's 10,000 acres of savannalike, semiarid land, rich with acacia trees and grazing grasses, lie in the hot rift valley called the Arava, about 25 miles north of Elat on the Gulf of Elat. The reserve is just north of Timna, site of King Solomon's copper mines.

The driving force behind Hai-Bar South is General Avraham Yoffe, who retired from the Israeli Army some years ago to become the first director of the Israel Nature Reserves Authority. He is responsible for the development of habitat parks and bird sanctuaries and for the protection of coral reefs.

The Hai-Bar refuge is one of Yoffe's leading projects. He feels an urgency to save the historical wildlife of the region. "Many of these creatures are extinct in Israel and fast disappearing elsewhere," Yoffe points out. But the purchase of rare animals and the fencing off of thousands of acres have been a slow process because of a small budget. The Israeli Government has provided about half of the required funds. Additional contributions have been received from private sources and the World Wildlife Fund.

Yoffe hopes to build up small breeding herds of endangered species. These would form the nucleus of larger herds that would freely roam the area and the Negev Desert to the west.

The reserve started out with addaxes, scimitar-horned oryxes, onagers, Nubian ibexes, and dorcas gazelles. Yoffe added Ethiopian ostriches, similar to the Syrian ostriches that once roamed the Holy Land (last seen in the 1920's), and caracals, lynxlike cats.

No one knows for sure if the addax is the *dishon* mentioned in the Bible. At any rate, this unique animal, which ranges in decreasing numbers through the Sahara, has found a home in Hai-Bar South. A true denizen of the desert, the addax has adapted itself to some of the most extreme conditions on earth. It obtains moisture only from the vegetation; broad hooves assist it in traveling over sand. Wild addaxes were last seen in Palestine in 1863.

Related to the addax but less hardy is the scimitar-horned oryx; in the oryx both sexes have long horns that arch backward. Less than a century ago this species was well distributed on the fringes of the Sahara from Senegal to the Nile, but because of climatic changes and overuse of the ranges in recent years it is reportedly extinct in most of this area. The total population may be well below 10,000.

Smaller and rarer than the scimitar-horned oryx is the Arabian species. It once ranged west to the Sinai and east to Mesopotamia, but it is now confined to a small area of the Arabian Peninsula, where fewer than 200 are believed to survive in the wild. To save the Arabian oryx from extinction, "Operation Oryx" was staged in 1962. Three individuals were caught and transferred to the Phoenix (Arizona) Zoo; later additions and highly successful breeding have boosted their number. The sheik of Qatar also maintains a private zoo with about 50 Arabian oryxes; other zoo herds exist in the United States and in Saudi Arabia.

Yoffe wants to obtain a pair of Arabian oryxes from the United States and reintroduce them to the Holy Land—rock paintings of these oryxes have been found at ancient copper mines there. But they are expensive. King Saud of Saudi Arabia paid $25,000 for a pair some years ago.

Some species are recovering

One desert animal that has been badly mauled by motorized hunting is the graceful dorcas gazelle. Both Israelis and Arabs have been guilty. The species is now fully protected in Israel, and the population, formerly estimated at about 500, is increasing steadily. The Nubian ibex, like the dorcas gazelle, has also made a remarkable recovery since coming under protection in 1955. There are now more than 1,000 of these spectacularly horned wild goats in Israel, with several herds located in nature reserves, including Hai-Bar South. The Nubian ibex is a muscular animal with great crescent-shaped horns. So striking is this animal that its head is used as the insignia of the Israel Nature Reserves Authority.

Gone from the Holy Land is the Syrian wild ass,

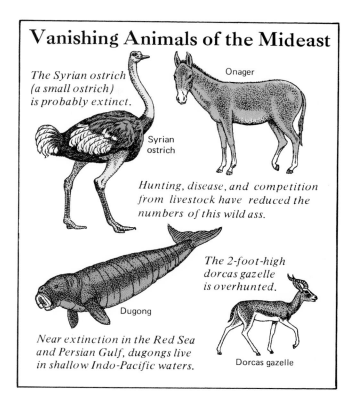

Vanishing Animals of the Mideast

The Syrian ostrich (a small ostrich) is probably extinct.

Syrian ostrich

Onager

Hunting, disease, and competition from livestock have reduced the numbers of this wild ass.

Dugong

The 2-foot-high dorcas gazelle is overhunted.

Dorcas gazelle

Near extinction in the Red Sea and Persian Gulf, dugongs live in shallow Indo-Pacific waters.

which once roamed widely over the Fertile Crescent. To replace the extinct Syrian race, Hai-Bar South acquired a number of extremely rare Somali wild asses from Ethiopia, which are now breeding in the reserve.

Hai-Bar South is still in process of completion. Yoffe hopes to obtain funds that will enable him to build observation towers and visitors' facilities. After these improvements are completed, he wants to create two other reserves: Hai-Bar North for the fallow deer and Syrian bear that once frequented the heights of the Holy Land; and Hai-Bar Carmel for the herds of roe deer and Palestinian gazelles that once frequented the slopes of Mount Carmel.

A slowly growing herd of scimitar-horned oryxes at Hai-Bar South includes six purchased by the Holy Land Conservation Fund, a U.S.-based organization that also provided three addaxes. The 5½-inch bronze oryx is a detail from a first-century-B.C. incense burner found in southern Arabia.

Europe's Wildlife Wonderlands

Lawrence Elliott

A variety of parks and reserves are saving rare animals and preserving scenic beauties—to the delight of ever-growing numbers of vacationers.

A few summers ago I spent an unforgettable vacation touring some of Europe's national parks and nature reserves. I soon found I had joined a growing four-season parade of campers, hikers, and Sunday drivers to these lovely last refuges of wildlife. Indeed, of all the surprising things I saw, none struck me more forcibly than the way nature's wonders were reflected on the faces of these visitors.

In France's La Vanoise National Park on the mountainous Italian border, I saw a couple from Marseilles watching their two young sons stand motionless in a field of alpine wildflowers, hypnotized by the antics of a family of marmots. "They have never seen anything like this," said the father. Then, gazing out over a spectacular range of 10,000-foot peaks, he added, "And neither have I."

His feelings typify those of thousands of Europeans who have discovered that a national park vacation can be educational, inspiring, and inexpensive. In the eight countries I visited, I saw them everywhere—traveling in automobiles, some hauling trailers full of camping gear, or on bicycles with only a simple pack. By day they were scattered across the landscape, studying animals through binoculars, photographing wildflowers, or just sitting by a stream in quiet contentment. And most wore an expression that seemed to ask, "How long has this been going on?"

Royal hunting ground to nature reserve

With a few exceptions, not long. Ironically, the first steps toward nature conservation were a result of the arbitrary fiats of kings. Nine centuries ago William the Conqueror decreed that a great stretch of woodland in southwest England be preserved as a royal hunting ground. Known as the New Forest, it is the oldest and one of the largest of British reserves.

But in most cases man remained at odds with nature well into this century—waterways had to be dammed,

---

A Magnificent Mountain Park in France

La Vanoise, France's first and largest national park, occupies a spectacular part of the Savoy Alps. The park's highest peak, Monte Casse, reaches more than 12,600 feet; outside the park nearby Mont Blanc and Gran Paradiso are both above 15,000 feet. The 200-square-mile park adjoins Italy's Gran Paradiso National Park for a short stretch along the border; more than 500 square miles of buffer zone, owned by neighboring communities, protect it on other sides. The area surrounding La Vanoise is famed as a ski and tourist resort, and the park itself narrowly escaped the developers. Now its continuous expanse of alpine valleys, forested slopes, jagged ridges, and snowcapped peaks shelters a variety of birds and mammals.

FRANCE

La Vanoise
National Park

Preserving spectacular scenery and wildlife, France's largest national park, La Vanoise, adjoins the Gran Paradiso Park in the Italian Alps. Rising 12,470 feet over this peaceful river valley, Mont Pourri is the third-highest peak in the park.

marshes drained, wildlife slaughtered for food or the protection of domestic animals. Finally, naturalists, desperate to save threatened refuges, began a series of last-ditch battles.

Most notable among their successes has been the preservation of Spain's Coto Doñana in the delta of the Guadalquivir River. In 1961 Coto Doñana's marshy thickets, home to nearly half the bird species of Europe as well as the endangered Spanish lynx, were about to be drained. Spanish naturalists appealed for help. The World Wildlife Fund coordinated a drive to save the area. Coto Doñana is now a national park.

Similarly, the World Wildlife Fund provides money to lease threatened Austrian marshlands around the Neusiedler See. This important ecological area contains colonies of great white and purple herons, European spoonbills, and white storks. A rare sight in the surrounding grasslands is the ostrichlike great bustard. One of the world's largest flying birds, it can weigh as much as 30 pounds.

The work goes on, but there are problems. One of the most serious is how to invite man, that inveterate disturber of the peace, into a relatively constricted setting where peace is essential if wildlife is to thrive. To this end, park planners have come up with some remarkably imaginative solutions. La Vanoise, for example, is laid out in two concentric circles. In the cen-

ter is a cluster of isolated areas in which all human activity, except that connected with scientific study, is forbidden. Around these is the park itself, where visitors are welcomed with the strict understanding that living things are inviolate. Finally, surrounding the park is a "peripheral zone" where all tourist needs are met: Hotels, campgrounds, parking facilities, restaurants, and shops.

Parks cross international borders

Even more significant is the development of wildlife sanctuaries astride international frontiers. Poland has pioneered this concept on two of its borders—in the south with Czechoslovakia, where the two High Tatra parks are set in the lush Carpathian Mountains, and in the northeast with the Soviet Union. The great Bialowieza Forest, which crosses the U.S.S.R. border, has, since World War II, been prized by both nations as Europe's last stand of virgin forest.

Poland's Bialowieza National Park is famous because it is home to a species saved from extinction. Decimated by the hungry soldiers of three armies in World War I, the great European bison herd of the Bialowieza Forest had dwindled by 1921 to a few specimens in zoos. By careful breeding a vigorous new herd was established and returned to the forest.

The trend toward adjoining parks has been con-

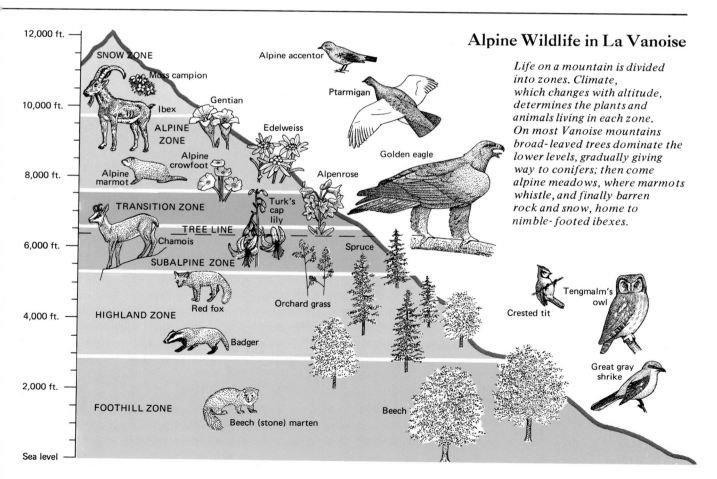

Alpine Wildlife in La Vanoise

Life on a mountain is divided into zones. Climate, which changes with altitude, determines the plants and animals living in each zone. On most Vanoise mountains broad-leaved trees dominate the lower levels, gradually giving way to conifers; then come alpine meadows, where marmots whistle, and finally barren rock and snow, home to nimble-footed ibexes.

In Sweden's Sarek National Park *a hiker (above) surveys the source of the Rapa River, which drains 30 glaciers. Located in the Swedish mountains just north of the Arctic Circle, the three adjoining national parks of Sarek, Padjelanta, and Stora Sjöfallet cover more than 2,000 square miles, the largest wild area in Europe. Wildlife abounds in the parks, including such mammals as bears, moose, and lynxes. Among the world's oldest the Swedish mountains (below) were formed 300 million years ago. Since then weathering and glaciers have worn down the mountains, smoothing their once jagged profiles.*

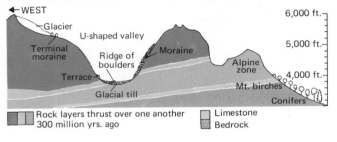

tinued in western Europe. In France, La Vanoise National Park shares a common frontier with Italy's Gran Paradiso to create a vast area of wild heights where the rare alpine ibex can find safety and a compatible environment. France's new Pyrénées Occidentales National Park, patterned after the "peripheral zone" plan of Vanoise, was created opposite Spain's Valle de Ordesa National Park; this large area protects the brown bear, chamois, wild boar, lynx, and imperial eagle.

Italy's Gran Paradiso National Park, the largest in western Europe, was created in 1922 to save the dwindling ibex herd. But it long suffered from indifferent management; many young ibexes were smuggled into Switzerland and sold. In 1945 Dr. Renzo Videsott, a biologist, was put in charge. He began hiring local poachers as wardens on the ground that no one knew the ibex better or was more interested in its survival. He had made a shrewd guess—hunting violations dropped off dramatically. The trails Videsott laid out in Gran Paradiso stop short of the heart of the park, where animals are beyond the reach of man.

The French have made their own imaginative provision for an ever-mounting flow of visitors. They have trained teams of monitor-guards—emphasis on "moni-

tor"—who are expert mountain men. Besides caring for trails, wildlife, and flora, they make visitors feel welcome and instruct them in the park's natural wonders. Camping facilities and mountain shelters are increasing slowly, for materials come by helicopter.

Another successful synthesis of natural resources and people has been devised by Dr. Robert Schloeth, director of the Swiss National Park. Here, up to 150,000 visitors come each year to observe the wildlife and flora along nearly 50 miles of spectacular alpine trails. At each of the 14 park entrances there are large maps, with trails plainly marked and rules and regulations depicted in cartoons to get around language barriers. "If you are to teach anything," says Schloeth, "the 'why' is vital. And keeping one's distance is important. The alternative is to bring people so close that the animals would get used to them and come begging for food. And that can hardly be termed wildlife!"

As in these alpine parks of France and Switzerland, other European national parks attract the young and hardy with mountain trails and shelters. Poland's High Tatra National Park, adjoining the Czechoslovakian park of similar name, is another mountain reserve with marked trails and huts for hikers. The three adjacent Swedish national parks of Sarek, Padjelanta, and Stora Sjöfallet, in Lapland close to the Norwegian border, make up Europe's largest wild area. Their 2,105 square miles contain rugged mountains, glaciers, lakes, and tundra. Sarek is only for the hiker with mountain-climbing experience who comes equipped with tent and provisions and knows how to cope with true wilderness. Nomadic Lapps and their reindeer herds excite the visitor's interest in Padjelanta.

Water birds on beaches

At the opposite extreme are the accessible dunes, beaches, and tidal flats of the Dutch Frisian Islands. Reserves on Texel and Terschelling are breeding areas for terns and gulls, avocets and godwits, eiders and shelducks, and important transit stops for migrating shorebirds. Nearby waters are wintering grounds for thousands of brants.

Of Europe's several wetlands reserves, one of the wildest is the Camargue in the Rhône delta west of Marseilles. Here black bulls and white horses thunder along the beaches and through the marshes. In spring pink flamingos color the shores of the salt lagoons. Although parts of the Camargue have been protected since 1928, the reserve owes much of its development to Luc Hoffmann, a Swiss biologist who, seeing the scientific possibilities in its lonely reaches after World War II, set up his own biological laboratory. Now the French Government has established a scientific station close by, and in 1971 the World Wildlife Fund contributed a million francs to consolidate and enlarge the Camargue Zoological and Botanical Reserve.

More and more vacationers, from overseas as well as the Continent, are discovering the rewards of visiting Europe's national parks. With patience and education, authorities are finding it is possible to reconcile the needs of people and of wildlife.

British Sanctuaries for Wildlife

One of the astronaut teams called Great Britain the greenest spot it saw from outer space. A great number of organizations—local and regional, governmental and private— are dedicated to seeing that it remains so. But the protection of wild areas is complicated. The national parks are in an ambiguous position. Sections of them are in the hands of Government agencies, but most of the land is privately owned. The parks are not inviolate: Military maneuvers, mining, lumbering, and agriculture are practiced in them. The nature reserves are safer havens for wildlife. Scotland has its own National Trust, but the Nature Conservancy, the Government agency most directly concerned with wildlife, covers all of Britain. The map shows only a selection of reserves (the Royal Society for the Protection of Birds alone runs about 50 of them), many animals are not shown, and most of them occur in more than one place.

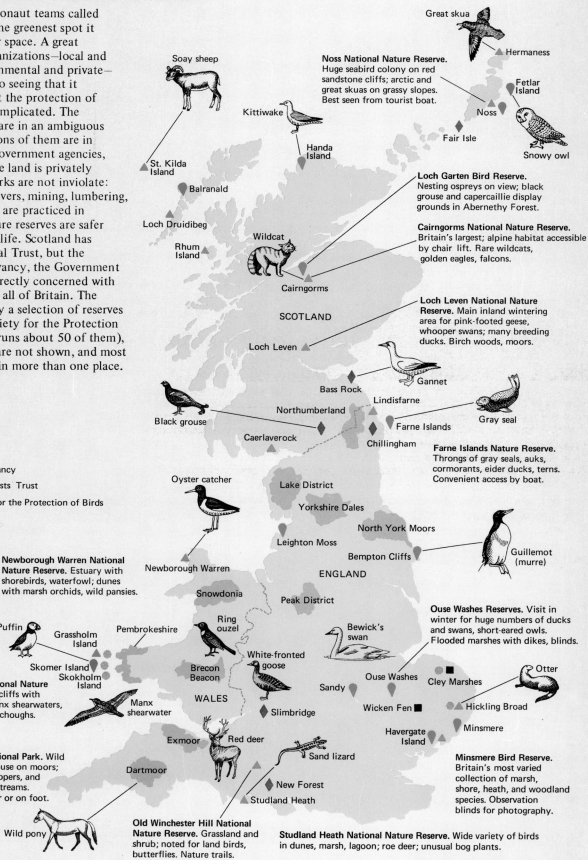

Great skua

Noss National Nature Reserve. Huge seabird colony on red sandstone cliffs; arctic and great skuas on grassy slopes. Best seen from tourist boat.

Hermaness

Fetlar Island

Noss

Fair Isle

Snowy owl

Soay sheep

Kittiwake

Handa Island

St. Kilda Island

Balranald

Loch Druidibeg

Rhum Island

Wildcat

Cairngorms

SCOTLAND

Loch Leven

Loch Garten Bird Reserve. Nesting ospreys on view; black grouse and capercaillie display grounds in Abernethy Forest.

Cairngorms National Nature Reserve. Britain's largest; alpine habitat accessible by chair lift. Rare wildcats, golden eagles, falcons.

Loch Leven National Nature Reserve. Main inland wintering area for pink-footed geese, whooper swans; many breeding ducks. Birch woods, moors.

Gannet

Bass Rock

Lindisfarne

Gray seal

Black grouse

Northumberland

Caerlaverock

Chillingham

Farne Islands

Farne Islands Nature Reserve. Throngs of gray seals, auks, cormorants, eider ducks, terns. Convenient access by boat.

Legend:
- National park
- National Trust
- Nature Conservancy
- County Naturalists' Trust
- Royal Society for the Protection of Birds
- Other reserve

Oyster catcher

Lake District

Yorkshire Dales

North York Moors

Leighton Moss

Bempton Cliffs

ENGLAND

Guillemot (murre)

Newborough Warren National Nature Reserve. Estuary with shorebirds, waterfowl; dunes with marsh orchids, wild pansies.

Newborough Warren

Snowdonia

Peak District

Ouse Washes Reserves. Visit in winter for huge numbers of ducks and swans, short-eared owls. Flooded marshes with dikes, blinds.

Puffin

Grassholm Island

Pembrokeshire

Ring ouzel

Bewick's swan

Otter

Skomer Island
Skokholm Island

White-fronted goose

Brecon Beacon

Ouse Washes

Cley Marshes

Skomer Island National Nature Reserve. Towering cliffs with nesting puffins, Manx shearwaters, fulmars, razorbills, choughs.

Manx shearwater

WALES

Sandy

Wicken Fen

Hickling Broad

Minsmere

Slimbridge

Exmoor

Red deer

Sand lizard

Havergate Island

Dartmoor National Park. Wild ponies and grouse on moors; ring ouzels, dippers, and wagtails near streams. Explore by car or on foot.

Dartmoor

New Forest

Studland Heath

Minsmere Bird Reserve. Britain's most varied collection of marsh, shore, heath, and woodland species. Observation blinds for photography.

Wild pony

Old Winchester Hill National Nature Reserve. Grassland and shrub; noted for land birds, butterflies. Nature trails.

Studland Heath National Nature Reserve. Wide variety of birds in dunes, marsh, lagoon; roe deer; unusual bog plants.

Spanish Haven for Wildlife

The sun-warmed marshes and dunes of a duke's hunting reserve are now a national park of worldwide renown.

A living encyclopedia of the wildlife of Europe, less than 2 hours by car from Seville—this is Spain's Coto Doñana. The wetlands and sand dunes between the Guadalquivir River and the Atlantic Ocean attract tremendous flocks of birds; they also provide a haven for animals that rarely breed elsewhere in Europe.

The word *coto* means a private hunting reserve; Doñana is a contraction of Dona Ana, the name of the original ducal owner's wife. But the bands of hunters who for centuries harassed the animals of Doñana have gone. The reserve has been a sanctuary since 1964, when lands used for recreation by the wealthy were acquired by Spain's Council of Scientific Research. The Spanish Government supplied 51 percent of the cost; the balance came from the World Wildlife Fund. Further gifts from the Fund and from a private donor have enlarged the reserve to 131 square miles; in 1969 it became a national park.

But Doñana, with its reedy marshes, muddy savannas, sand dunes, freshwater lagoons, and scrubby vegetation, with its cycle of intense summer drought and life-giving fall and winter floods, is surrounded by contaminating and uncontrolled progress.

The neighboring beaches of fine white sand are a powerful temptation to vacationers avid for sun and sea. Hotel owners and promoters of tourism have already taken possession of the narrow strip of land that separates the national park from the Atlantic. Doñana itself has less than 2 miles of access to the sea. The land at each side of this narrow corridor is owned by a construction firm that is erecting many high-rise hotels in the style of Miami Beach, putting up tourist apartments, and laying roads. The human sea of summer visitors has not yet reached its maximum, but when that happens, heavy traffic, noise, pollution, and trespassers will inevitably follow.

Already agricultural activities are threatening all that Doñana signifies. A plan to drain the marshes of the Guadalquivir is being activated, and nearby properties are being converted to rice fields. Insecticides, weed killers, and fertilizers could contaminate the reserve's air and water. And when weeds and insects are destroyed, the foods of many animals are destroyed.

In the midst of all this commercial activity on its outskirts, Coto Doñana remains an oasis of peace. A permit is necessary to enter the national park, and lodging there is limited. Only the 15th-century Palacio, which once housed visiting dukes and kings, puts up a few visitors. Don't be deceived by the high-sounding name of "Palacio." It is a large old house with clean bedrooms but without luxury of any kind.

The entrance permit is issued in Seville, at the Biological Station of Doñana. When applying, sufficiently

Blanketing the crown of a cork-oak tree, gregarious spoonbills rest in Spain's Coto Doñana. The great birds nest as far north as the Netherlands but winter in Africa. They find their fish, amphibian, and crustacean food in marshes and lakes.

What Lives Where in the Coto Doñana

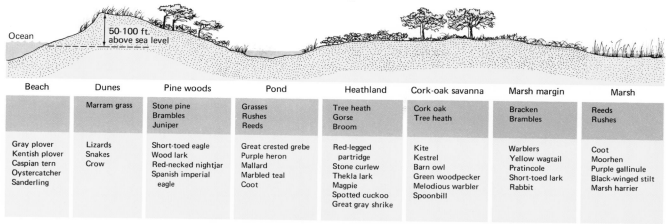

Beach	Dunes	Pine woods	Pond	Heathland	Cork-oak savanna	Marsh margin	Marsh
	Marram grass	Stone pine Brambles Juniper	Grasses Rushes Reeds	Tree heath Gorse Broom	Cork oak Tree heath	Bracken Brambles	Reeds Rushes

Gray plover
Kentish plover
Caspian tern
Oystercatcher
Sanderling
	Lizards
	Snakes
	Crow
		Short-toed eagle
		Wood lark
		Red-necked nightjar
		Spanish imperial
		  eagle
			Great crested grebe
			Purple heron
			Mallard
			Marbled teal
			Coot
				Red-legged
				  partridge
				Stone curlew
				Thekla lark
				Magpie
				Spotted cuckoo
				Great gray shrike
					Kite
					Kestrel
					Barn owl
					Green woodpecker
					Melodious warbler
					Spoonbill
						Warblers
						Yellow wagtail
						Pratincole
						Short-toed lark
						Rabbit
							Coot
							Moorhen
							Purple gallinule
							Black-winged stilt
							Marsh harrier

A profile of Coto Doñana habitats—from beach and dunes, to freshwater ponds, to the marshes of the Guadalquivir River—shows its alternating dry and wet areas. Each habitat has its characteristic vegetation and resident wildlife community. Huge flocks of ducks, geese, and shorebirds arrive during the migration seasons. Several factors combine to make Spain's Coto Doñana a wildlife haven: Diversity of habitat; a warm, damp climate; and a strategic location where the fauna of Europe and Africa overlap.

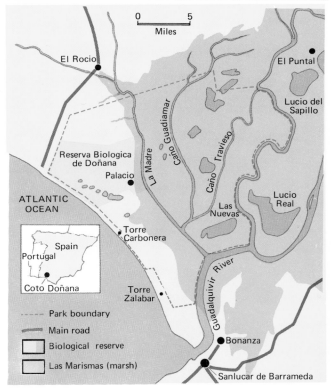

ahead of time, you should specify the day you plan to arrive and the length of your stay. Anyone proceeding directly to the reserve without a permit would be wasting his time.

Doñana's wardens orient visitors and supply vehicles (animal-drawn or mechanical) for exploring the reserve. These wardens, who know the animals, their habits, and their probable location at any moment, will show you where you can see the most exciting spectacles, according to the season. For the enthusiastic animal photographer, Doñana is a paradise. The reserve has blinds and portable huts.

Spying on eagles

Each spring, in the midst of thickets of cork oak and pine, high wooden towers are set up; there is even a collapsible metal tower, gift of the Royal Zoological Society of Antwerp. You need permission to climb these towers, but when that has been secured, you will find yourself face to face with the nest of one of the world's rarest birds of prey—the Spanish imperial eagle. Most photographers get sensational pictures of eagles posing on the nest, taking off, or feeding young.

Besides the imperial eagle, 135 other bird species, 9 species of amphibians, 19 reptile species, and 24 mammal species are resident the year round. About 130 species of migratory birds also nest in the reserve. In summer as many as 70 nests of eagles and hawks have been counted. In a single winter day, if you are lucky, you might see black and griffon vultures, lammergeiers, and golden, tawny, spotted, and imperial eagles.

Great nesting colonies of herons and egrets are scattered through the oak groves and the reedbeds. In

some years as many as 6,000 pairs of purple herons have nested in Doñana. Here, too, is one of the rare colonies of spoonbills in western Europe. A few white storks also nest in the area. Flamingos have not bred here in many years, but large flocks sometimes come to Doñana's shallow lagoons to feed.

The stars of the winter at Doñana are the geese. Nowhere else in Spain, and rarely in the rest of Europe, can 10,000 geese be seen at one time. Almost all are greylag geese, but with them are occasional white-fronted and barnacle geese. They start arriving in Doñana by the end of October, accompanied by great flights of ducks representing almost all the European species. These flocks can be closely observed from blinds near the lagoons.

Considered the most endangered bird in Europe, with a total population of about 100, the Spanish imperial eagle breeds at Coto Doñana. Both parents incubate the eggs, but only the female broods the chicks, while the male brings food.

Standing guard over its ground nest, a purple heron waits for its mate to return with food for their scrawny chicks. Doñana's reedbeds conceal many colonies of this species, which is widespread in southern Europe, Asia, and Africa.

Throughout the year hundreds of red and fallow deer and wild hogs run through the low brush. Viewed from a vehicle, they make an exciting spectacle. But the specialties of Doñana are the Spanish imperial eagle and the Spanish lynx. Doñana is a refuge for these animals, which are close to extinction.

Spanish imperial eagles prefer the plains and nest in low-growing trees, where they are extremely vulnerable to hunters. Probably only about 100 eagles of this sub-species survive in central and southern Spain, Morocco, and Algeria. The reserve's three pairs of imperial eagles nest in the tops of cork oaks. They may often be seen soaring majestically or scanning the horizon from the topmost branches. The adult is brownish black, with a distinctive white patch on the shoulders and an ashy head; younger birds are cinnamon brown.

How to find a lynx

If you see a group of magpies dashing about over a thicket and scolding loudly, you can be sure that it conceals a lynx, the largest European cat. Doñana has perhaps six pairs of lynxes and some 30 single animals. But although their rounded tracks can readily be found, it is truly difficult for a visitor to locate these elusive animals.

Two systems are recommended. The surer one is to climb at dusk into one of the cork oaks at the edge of the marshes. Stay there completely immobile—it doesn't matter if you are in full sight, for the lynx's legendary vision is concentrated on movement. If you are lucky, the lynx may come as close as a few yards from your tree without discovering you. The other system is to drive down the access road, also at dusk. Every day the lynxes cross this road. If you see one cross, drive close to it and stop as noiselessly as possible. Usually the cat will be seated in the brush at the roadside, looking out at the vehicle, without being frightened away by your presence.

Coto Doñana National Park has one suggestion for the visitor: To enjoy its rare sights, you must be as quiet and inconspicuous as possible. If you are part of a noisy group, or are wearing too brightly colored clothing, you will find yourself surrounded by vacant space. But if you walk silently, face to the wind, you will be able to spy on the intimate life of Doñana: A nestful of egrets clamoring for food, a wild hog nursing her young, or, greatest luck of all, a family of lynxes at play.

Only one thing is asked of you in exchange for these marvels: You must not hinder the work of Doñana's scientists. Basically, there are three types of scientific work going on in the reserve: A daily record of each species throughout the year; a detailed study of the biology of certain species; and bird banding so that migration patterns can be determined. (In a recent year Doñana's workers banded 14,000 birds belonging to 103 species.)

Doñana is not just a national park for the re-creation of man's spirit. It is a gigantic living laboratory where specialists and students from all over the world seek to penetrate the mysteries of ecology and animal behavior.

The Contracting World of the Spanish Lynx

With every sense alert a Spanish lynx feasts on a hare. The lynx may attack a deer but prefers smaller animals.

Once ranging throughout Spain and Portugal, the Spanish lynx has survived in a few isolated spots in southern Spain. Its natural habitat is the mountain forest, but deforestation and loss of prey have driven the Spanish lynx to less favorable regions. Its chief refuge today is the marshes and scrubby pine copses of Coto Doñana National Park, where its major prey is rabbits. Outside the park the lynx is sometimes hunted for its handsome, heavily spotted coat. It is accused of killing livestock and classified as "vermin" to be shot on sight. Now probably the largest predator living in Spain, the lynx has no enemy except man. But it is especially vulnerable because of its small numbers, scattered populations, and limited range.

Wherever lynxes occur in the world, they are the victims of human persecution. The northern lynx of Scandinavia and the U.S.S.R. and the closely related Canada lynx (found in Canada and the extreme northern United States) have thicker and paler fur than that of their southern cousin, and hunters consider them even more valuable. The smaller caracal lynx of Asia and Africa, with its long ear tufts, has fared better, though as human populations grow all wildcats will lose.

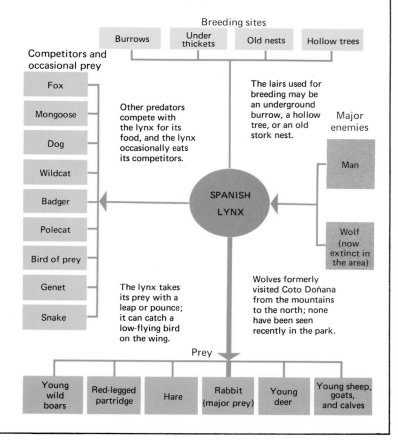

Frosted by an early snowfall, bare trees await winter beside Meach Lake in Gatineau Park. One of the loveliest of central Canada's parks, with a wealth of lakes, woods, streams, and hills, Gatineau has beavers, deer, black bears, and wolves.

Wild Nature in Ottawa's Backyard

Sheila C. Thomson

A wooded park on Ottawa's doorstep lures city dwellers with its promise of wilderness and peace. But urban pressures threaten its very survival.

Between the valleys of the Gatineau and the Ottawa Rivers, a rocky spur of the Canadian Shield extends southeastward to touch the city of Hull. It is this spur of the Shield that forms the backbone of Gatineau Park, an 88,000-acre tract of rocky woodland owned by the Canadian Government. During its 35-year history, it has been maintained as a "wilderness park," the gem of the nation's capital. People from many walks of life are drawn to the Gatineau hills in every season of the year. Families like to picnic by the shores of the park's streams and lakes. Naturalists search for the hidden bogs where wild orchids grow. Rock climbers scale the cliffs. Cross-country skiers explore the interior hills and valleys, free from the tyranny of designated routes and ready-made trails. And, spring after spring, hundreds of city dwellers return to the park to see the native wildflowers. The park has become Everyman's wilderness, its southernmost tip only a 20-minute drive from the Parliament Buildings in Ottawa.

The hills of Gatineau Park are the stumps of a very ancient mountain range, formed in a geological age further back in time than the earliest fossil records of life on earth. When the glaciers of the Pleistocene finally retreated from the region, a mere 10,000 years ago, they left the hills scraped, gouged, denuded of soil, and strewn with boulders. In poorly drained depressions, small sphagnum bogs were formed. Today these are the habitat of wild orchids, insect-eating plants, Labrador tea, bogbean, cotton grass, and all the strange community of bog plants that intrigue the botanist and delight the naturalist.

For 10,000 years life has been creeping back over the hills, clothing first the sheltered valleys and finally even the rocky hilltops with vegetation. Today only the most exposed hilltops are still bare of soil and plants. Even here the lichens are creeping across the bedrock, creating soil for the plants to follow.

As the hills became forested again, the wild creatures of the Shield began to move in, each settling into its preferred niche and adding to the diversity of living things in the region. In the wild deserted country that lies between Harrington Lake and the Eardley Escarpment, a few timber wolves have established their territory, while black bears roam throughout the entire park. Few animals have chosen the high, open scrub oak forest of the rocky escarpment, but to man this is exhilarating country, shared with white-tailed deer and raven, red squirrel and boreal chickadee. The escarpment also provides the student of ferns with exciting terrain for exploration. Several ferns considered rare or absent from the region have recently been discovered happily established there in small colonies.

In the interior of the park, the moist woods and the meltwater ponds of April provide habitat and mating territory for a host of vociferous or voiceless amphibians. When the April chorus of spring peepers and woodfrogs is heard in the hills, the salamanders crawl silently to the ponds to mate. There follows, in the dark, a throng of curious naturalists creeping stealthily around the ponds, flashlights in hand, hoping for a glimpse of mating newt or singing frog.

Winter wonderland

Another habitat is revealed by a winter ski through the hardwoods and along the streambeds joining frozen lakes and ponds. The characteristic tracks of otter, fisher, mink, and pine marten give unmistakable proof of their presence in the park, although only a stroke of luck will afford a glimpse of one of these graceful fur-bearers. The tiny tracks of white-footed mice, the broad troughs gouged in the snow by waddling porcupines, and the distant rhythmic hooting of the barred owl are further clues to the wildlife of the seemingly deserted winter woods.

The tangled evergreen swamps provide wintering territory for an interesting community of animals. To don snowshoes after a light snowfall and visit a cedar swamp on a mild winter day is to become suddenly aware of the great numbers of wild creatures that continue to move about in the park in winter—snowshoe hare and cottontail, weasel and muskrat and raccoon, deer and fox and grouse. Many a tale of hunter and hunted can be read from the tracks in the snow.

Beavers now occupy many of the park's lakes and streams. Extensive beaver floodings (habitat for osprey, heron, muskrat, mink, and snapping turtle) are a decided impediment to summer exploration, but in winter their frozen surfaces provide excellent and easy routes for travel. Beaver dams are the crossroads of the wild, where the trails of animals following the easiest routes through the forest converge.

Other animals have chosen habitat in different terrain. The open-water marshes, rich wooded valleys, spring-fed lakes, beaver meadows, rocky ravines, and sandy lakeshores all have their own distinctive communities of plants and animals. Diversity of habitat accounts in part for the great variety of species in so small an area as Gatineau Park.

The postglacial invasion of the hills by plants and animals has not proceeded at a steady pace. Some species formerly present seem to have disappeared, for example, the cougar and bald eagle. Others, such as the fisher and the pileated woodpecker, disappeared for a time, only to return again. The southern flying squirrel and the gray squirrel appear to be reaching the Gatineau in our own century for the first time, while loons may have been returning here to nest in ancestral breeding grounds century after century. The cutting of the white pine forest, now replaced by hardwoods, has no doubt encouraged the northward migration of a number of spring wildflowers such as bloodroot, Dutchman's-breeches, and white trillium. It seems safe to assume, too, that scarlet tanagers, rose-breasted grosbeaks, and many other songbirds have moved into the park in greater numbers in the last 100 years as habitat more to their liking became available.

Finally, man himself has invaded, retreated, and invaded again, causing a shift in the populations of other living things, but until recent years leaving only superficial scars on the landscape. The Indians who roamed the Gatineau hills left no footprints behind. When the Irish settlers arrived before the middle of the 19th century, they came to a Canadian wilderness. A magnificent white pine forest then covered the land. To all appearances the hills were still untouched by man. In fact, however, the trappers of the fur-trade days had left a negative legacy. Not one beaver remained in the hills. It now seems certain that no beavers were seen here during the entire period of settlement, although evidence of their former abundance was everywhere. (The return of the beaver to the park about 30 years ago coincided with a spectacu-

The Spotted Salamander's Year: From Land to Water and Back Again

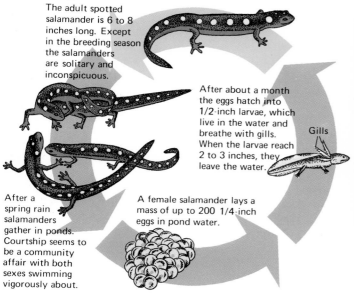

The adult spotted salamander is 6 to 8 inches long. Except in the breeding season the salamanders are solitary and inconspicuous.

After about a month the eggs hatch into 1/2-inch larvae, which live in the water and breathe with gills. When the larvae reach 2 to 3 inches, they leave the water.

Gills

A female salamander lays a mass of up to 200 1/4-inch eggs in pond water.

After a spring rain salamanders gather in ponds. Courtship seems to be a community affair with both sexes swimming vigorously about.

Spotted salamanders, amphibian residents of Gatineau Park and other North American woodlands, grow up in ponds, then move onto land. In spring they return to ponds to breed, then disperse to damp hiding places under stones and logs.

Far-flung Parks Protect Canada's Wildlife

High in Jasper National Park mountain goats pause on a steep slope. They prefer life at or above timberline, but in winter they escape deep snow by coming lower. In some areas they have been overhunted and are becoming scarce.

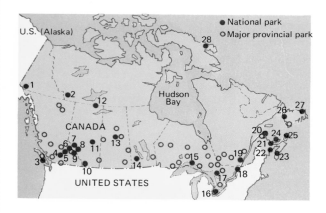

- ● National park
- ○ Major provincial park

CANADIAN NATIONAL PARKS

1 Kluane	15 Pukaskwa
2 Nahanni	16 Point Pelee
3 Pacific Rim	17 Georgian Bay Islands
4 Mount Revelstoke	18 St. Lawrence Islands
5 Glacier	19 La Mauricie
6 Yoho	20 Forillon
7 Jasper	21 Kouchibouguac
8 Banff	22 Fundy
9 Kootenay	23 Kejimkujik
10 Waterton Lakes	24 Prince Edward Island
11 Elk Island	25 Cape Breton Highlands
12 Wood Buffalo	26 Gros Morne
13 Prince Albert	27 Terra Nova
14 Riding Mountain	28 Baffin Island

Canada's 28 national parks and hundreds of provincial parks protect a remarkable fauna. Wood Buffalo, one of the world's most extensive parks, with 17,300 square miles, not only has the largest living herd of bison but also is the nesting area for the endangered whooping crane. Pacific Rim has a fine herd of sea lions. Other parks are key points on waterfowl migration routes. The eastern fox snake finds refuge in one provincial park; another was established for polar bears.

The parks encompass a variety of some of the most glorious scenery in the Western Hemisphere. Prince Edward Island is a 25-mile strip of quiet shore; the coast of Terra Nova is rugged and deeply indented. Such parks as Prince Albert, the St. Lawrence Islands, and Kejimkujik preserve typical local landscapes.

The park system is growing rapidly. When the system was formalized by the 1920 National Parks Act, there were 14 national parks; of those now in existence 8 date only from the 70's, including the 3 northernmost. Banff, established in 1887, is the oldest; it now adjoins three other parks (Jasper, Yoho, and Kootenay) for a total of more than 7,800 square miles of protected peaks, forests, glaciers, gorges, and wildlife—eagles, bighorn sheep, mountain goats, and grizzly bears.

But with all their splendor the parks do have problems arising from their history. Some of them allow permanent residents, some permit logging (albeit controlled), some are crossed by railways. Canadian conservationists are working hard to make the parks more truly natural areas.

lar continent-wide recovery of the beaver populations.)

By the middle of the 19th century, a sprinkling of tiny clearings was scattered through the hills. At the edge of each clearing nestled the log cabin of the settler. A wagon track winding through the bush provided the link with neighbors. At the peak of settlement days there were throughout the area of the park perhaps fewer than 100 families living "on the mountain," although many more small log homes were strung along the roads through the valleys and at the foot of the hills.

In the end, however, it was clear that the rocky terrain was unsuitable for farming. In places the soil was so shallow as to leave bedrock exposed. The resourceful settlers turned to the forest for their livelihood. The huge white pines were harvested from the hills and hauled or floated to the lumber mills. Meantime, the valleys of the Ottawa and the Gatineau were cleared and opened up for farming. By the turn of the century, most of the mountain families had moved down to an easier and more prosperous life in the farming communities of the valleys. Their mountain properties, kept as woodlots or for hunting camps, were finally sold to the Federal Government to form the nucleus of Gatineau Park.

Nature takes over again

In the decades that followed the exodus of the settlers, a forest of maple, beech, and yellow birch replaced the pines of presettlement days. The encroaching hardwood forest has advanced steadily, swallowing up the clearings and log cabins, until today there is little evidence that three generations of Canadians made their homes in these hills.

The years since the establishment of the park have brought a number of changes to the land. A few, wrought by dynamite and bulldozer, have come about swiftly and scarred deeply. It is worth noting that where serious damage to the landscape has occurred, it has usually resulted from man-made improvements designed specifically to attract crowds of human beings into mass-recreation situations. Nevertheless, with a few deplorable exceptions, Gatineau Park is still wild and beautiful and teeming with wilderness life.

But to some who use the park, the meaning of wilderness is not diversity of living things, but freedom. Freedom to roam through wild country has become a rare privilege for most Canadians. As urban populations continue to grow, wild lands are shrinking and becoming more and more remote from the everyday lives of Canadians. Yet the psychological need for this kind of freedom is greater than ever. It is needed to counteract the stifling effects on the spirit of an all-protective state and a technology that renders almost obsolete the need to exert oneself either physically or mentally. A journey of discovery through some of the wilder parts of Gatineau Park is an exhilarating way for the city man to test mental and physical resources that are in danger of shriveling from lack of use.

Although a Federal park, Gatineau Park is not part

A porcupine perches on its larder in Gatineau Park; it can eat almost any part of a tree but prefers the bark. Under attack a porcupine swings its tail, loosening barbed quills that lodge in the skin of the enemy and may work their way inside.

of Canada's national parks system. There is no legislation to indicate its status or restrict its use. From time to time, various schemes for exploiting the park have been put forward. Even the National Capital Commission, misreading the mood of the public, began in the late 1960's to draw up elaborate plans for large-scale development of the park. In the public furor that followed, citizens were startled to learn that their wilderness park had, in fact, no legal status whatsoever and therefore no legal protection.

The advocates of wilderness, of tourist attractions, of mass recreational developments, of prestige hotels, of superhighways, and of scenic locations for public buildings are all eager to influence Gatineau's development. It is true that there are superb alternative sites in the region for all but the first-mentioned choice, but the cheap (Government-owned) land of the park makes it of course the most sought-after site. The advocates of wilderness have a formidable obstacle, too, in the widely held notion that undeveloped land close to large urban populations is "too valuable" to be left in an undeveloped state.

But perhaps (and this is not impossible) man, in a glimmer of wisdom, will choose to cherish this relic of an earlier age and to build his modern world around the margin of this miniature wilderness.

A great egret comes in for a landing in the marshes of Bombay Hook, a U.S. wildlife refuge on Delaware's coastal plain. Snowy egrets, a Louisiana heron, and a great blue heron are other wading birds in this companionable fishing party.

Sanctuaries From Sea to Sea

Robert Murphy

From Hawaii to Maine, from the Aleutians to the Florida Keys, more than 300 U.S. refuges help preserve America's wildlife legacy.

I don't recall how many years ago it was that I first heard of a place called Bombay Hook. Bombay Hook, it appeared, was a U.S. national wildlife refuge. At certain seasons great congregations of migratory birds—Canada and snow geese, shorebirds, herons, ducks, and other marsh birds as well as songbirds—could be seen there, close at hand, unconcerned and living their natural lives. This sounded very interesting, so I went to Bombay Hook.

The refuge is not far from Dover, Delaware, on the coastal plain—farming country with patches of brushy woodland. I registered in the small building across the road from the headquarters and followed the gravel road. Soon I was driving along the top of a long dike that held the first freshwater impoundment at the refuge. The impoundment was to the left, and there were a great number of black ducks, mallards, pintails, and Canada geese on the water; to the right there were a ditch and the great tidal marsh, golden in the autumn sun, extending far eastward to Delaware Bay. Red-winged blackbirds flitted among the reeds; an egret waded offshore. A slowly beating marsh hawk and a pair of red-tailed hawks hunted the marsh. A bald eagle perched on a distant dead tree.

All of these creatures were aware of me, but not too aware; they went about their business with evident feeling of confidence, as if they knew they were in a sanctuary. All the while there were, scaling down through the air, an occasional bunch of geese conversing together in that mellow music that never fails to stir the blood. That wide sweep of golden marsh and blue water, infused with life and vitality, was the sort of place that I had often wished I could reach.

I went on to the next impoundment, stopping often, then through fields where grain was grown for the avian visitors, and finally into a wooded swamp. Several times as I moved about, deer watched me from the edge of their cover; great blue herons, egrets, or curlews gathered together here and there.

The geese come home

Toward dusk, just before I went home, I stood in a low tangle of trees and greenbrier near the first impoundment and watched (and listened to) company after company of geese go over me in the rosy sky, set their wings, and plane down toward one of the ponds for the night. Some that came in high suddenly broke ranks and sideslipped down like great falling leaves, and it was evident that they enjoyed this playful maneuver. The rise and fall of their voices and the welcoming voices of those already on the water accompanied me to the car and followed me toward the gate. It had been one of my most invigorating and satisfactory days in a long time.

I picked up a refuge leaflet when I left, and from it I learned something about Bombay Hook. The

How a National Wildlife Refuge Changes the Environment

Of the more than 300 national wildlife refuges scattered over the United States, those on the Atlantic Flyway, such as New Jersey's Brigantine (right), were planned as resting areas for thousands of migrating ducks and geese. A constant source of food was essential, and this was ensured by creating impoundments of fresh or brackish water where small fish, snails, frogs, and aquatic plants flourish.

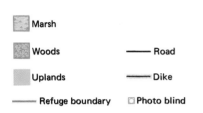

Marsh

Woods — Road

Uplands — Dike

— Refuge boundary □ Photo blind

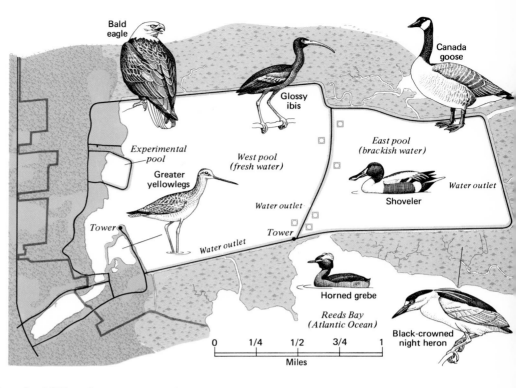

Bald eagle

Glossy ibis

Canada goose

Experimental pool

West pool (fresh water)

East pool (brackish water)

Greater yellowlegs

Water outlet

Shoveler

Water outlet

Tower

Water outlet

Tower

Water outlet

Horned grebe

Reeds Bay (Atlantic Ocean)

Black-crowned night heron

0   1/4   1/2   3/4   1
Miles

marsh had been bought from the Indians in 1679 and was known to the Dutch settlers as Boompies Hoock. Salt hay was cut from it, and muskrats were trapped in the tidal creek; the uplands were farmed.

The geese that I had watched were part of a total of 25,000 that now winter at Bombay Hook. At one time they hadn't been there in such astonishing numbers; in 1950 only about 350 wintered on the refuge. This increase, oddly enough, is due to the mechanical corn picker, which leaves a lot of corn in the fields. The geese, observing this, have changed their ancient

pattern of migration; rather than fly farther south, they stay where the corn is. The many geese, as well as the 30,000 ducks that stop on migration, require a lot of food, and more than 500 acres of upland are planted with corn, wheat, rye, clover, millet, sorghum, and soybeans for them.

A fair proportion of the refuge is composed of three marshy islands fronting Delaware Bay. There are more than 15,000 acres in Bombay Hook, of which about 10,000 are salty and brackish marsh and 1,200 are impoundments—freshwater pools where water levels

A flock of North America's largest geese floats on the water of Bombay Hook National Wildlife Refuge. Canada geese breed from Labrador to Alaska. The V-shaped wedges flying south in autumn are prime targets for hunters.

U.S. National Wildlife Refuges— Safe Stopovers for North America's Birds

Four great flyways channel millions of North American migratory birds between northern breeding grounds and warmer wintering areas. Spaced along the flyways are more than 300 U.S. national wildlife refuges. They were established mainly to protect geese and ducks, but many other migrants take advantage of the refuges' food, water, and shelter.

U.S. (Alaska)

Pacific Flyway
Central Flyway
Mississippi Flyway
Atlantic Flyway
• U.S. National Wildlife Refuge

CANADA

UNITED STATES

MEXICO

Merging and diverging, the four flyways cover the continent. Birds that travel the Pacific Flyway have the shortest way to go. Because of California's equable climate, millions of ducks from Alaska and Canada winter in the refuges in its interior valleys.

Refuges on the Central Flyway shelter mostly ducks and geese but are also used by white pelicans, trumpeter swans, and sandhill cranes. The Mississippi and Atlantic Flyways also carry a heavy traffic of ducks and geese; hawks and eagles, along with smaller birds, share these routes, too.

White pelicans take to the air in a North Dakota refuge. Poisoning from grain treated with pesticides and changing water levels in the few lakes where white pelicans still breed may put this magnificent bird on the endangered list.

are manipulated for the best growth of aquatic plants.

Bombay Hook has become increasingly important to waterfowl and shorebirds since its establishment in 1937, for the once vast area of marshland along the Atlantic Flyway—that ancient aerial path used by millions of birds migrating along the coast from their northern nesting grounds to winter in the South—has been steadily shrinking, making it harder and harder for the migrants to find places to stop on their way. More and more people and industries have moved into the area, draining it for building, mosquito control, and whatnot, and increasingly polluting it. The refuge, one of a series of stepping-stones on the East Coast, was established when it became evident to the United States Biological Survey (now the Bureau of Sport Fisheries and Wildlife of the Department of the Interior) that this trend would continue and accelerate.

In addition to migrating visitors, geese, black and wood ducks, mallards, gadwalls, and blue-winged teal nest at Bombay Hook. More than 300 bird species have been identified there. All of the mammals characteristic of the region live on the refuge, but they are not as easily seen as the birds.

After such a pleasant day at Bombay Hook, I fell into the habit of returning there. Getting to know one refuge made me want to know more of them. I made some inquiries and was given a good deal of information by the U.S. Government. I began to see the scope of the thing, and it appeared to me that the history of the refuges, which began in 1903 on a 3-acre island in

A handsome male pronghorn assumes a habitual pose in Oregon's Malheur National Wildlife Refuge. Millions of pronghorns once roamed the Plains; by the early 1900's they were almost extinct. Now they thrive in a number of reserves.

Florida's Indian River, where brown pelicans nested and were shot by plume hunters, was the history of conservation in the United States.

The National Wildlife Refuge system is divided into five regions, covering roughly the flyways over which waterfowl migrate: Region One, the Pacific Flyway; Two, the Central Flyway; Three and Four, the Mississippi Flyway and the southern part of the Atlantic Flyway; Five, the northern part of the Atlantic Flyway. Alaska and Hawaii have their own refuges. Not all of the more than 300 national wildlife refuges are managed for waterfowl; some are for large mammals and several are for certain endangered species.

Refuges around the country

The typical Atlantic Coast refuge is a waterfowl marsh—often with impoundments—such as Bombay Hook, Mattamuskeet in North Carolina, or Brigantine in New Jersey. Moosehorn in Maine, Cape Romain in South Carolina, and Okefenokee in Georgia are beautiful and unique. Florida has fine refuges with a great variety of wildlife, and many people have a great affection for North Carolina's Outer Banks, where the Pea Island refuge is located. Most of the Atlantic Coast refuges are fairly close to areas of high population and are easily reached. So are those in the Middle West. Some of the refuges farther west or in Alaska and Hawaii are more difficult to get to but well worth the effort required.

Sabine and Lacassine in Louisiana and Aransas in Texas are typical refuges of the Gulf Coast. Of the many refuges along the Mississippi River and the Central Flyway, including the prairie pothole country where a vast number of ducks and geese are hatched, I would select Agassiz and Tamarac in Minnesota. The West is well represented by Cabeza Prieta in the western Arizona desert, the Red Rock Lakes and the Bison Range in Montana, and Bear River in Utah. The Santa Ana Refuge on a bend of the Rio Grande in Texas is a living museum of a unique lowland forest that has disappeared elsewhere.

At one time the Bureau of Sport Fisheries and Wildlife was not enthusiastic about the idea of welcoming people to the refuges. They were sanctuaries where attempts were being made to bring back mammals or birds that were in trouble, and people would interfere with this difficult enterprise. In many cases the enterprise has been unusually successful—as, for instance, in the cases of the American bison, the pronghorn, and the trumpeter swan. These successes have been enough to change the Bureau's original thinking. No one wants to see the refuges invaded by the hordes who now crowd the national parks, but the Bureau is now giving a lot of thought to how best to share the refuge system with those who are genuinely interested in wildlife. A great many Americans, as well as overseas visitors, are unaware that there is a great U.S. refuge system to visit and explore. I hope that they will look into it and receive as much outdoor pleasure as it has given me.

Rare Animals in North American Sanctuaries

Man has preempted so much of the earth for his own use that most rare and endangered animals can find safety only in national parks or refuges set aside to preserve wildlife and natural habitats. In the United States farsighted people reserved large areas of federally owned land in time to save many threatened species. Canada, whose national parks protect bighorn sheep, wood bison, whooping cranes, and other animals, has established an

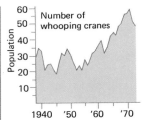

Rarest of North American birds, whooping cranes nest only in Canada's Wood Buffalo National Park. They migrate to and from their main wintering area, Aransas National Wildlife Refuge in Texas. The number of whooping cranes fluctuates, though it has increased in the last few decades. The flock reached its recent maximum (59) in 1971; the 1973 count was 48.

The world's largest herd of wood bison lives in Canada's Wood Bison National Park, straddling the Alberta-Northwest Territories li

8,200-square-mile sanctuary for the polar bear on Baffin Island, north of the Arctic Circle. But even the existence of parks and refuges does not guarantee a secure future for many species. Wolves or cougars, for example, cannot be confined to a reserve, and whooping cranes exist in such precariously small numbers that a natural disaster could wipe them out. Aware of the challenges, North Americans are cooperating to protect their common wildlife heritage.

The elusive Florida panther probably numbers fewer than 300. Sighted in Everglades National Park and other Florida refuges, it seems to be extending its range, possibly because of an increased population of its deer prey.

North America's largest bird of prey, the California condor, is also the rarest. It once lived from Oregon to Mexico. Today the entire population (50 to 60 birds) inhabits two Forest Service sanctuaries in southern California.

The rare bison subspecies is slowly building up its numbers.

Escaping the winter chill, this manatee swims in one of Florida's hot springs. The half-ton Florida manatees range the shores of Everglades National Park; smaller numbers live on several island refuges in the State.

How To Rescue a National Park

Jean George

Yellowstone started it all. Now this great U.S. national park and many others are struggling to save themselves from the hordes of their admirers.

The summer before the centennial of Yellowstone National Park, I visited the spot where, on September 20, 1870, the idea of a national park was born. There, at the confluence of the Firehole and Gibbon Rivers, the men of the Doane-Langford-Washburn expedition camped for the night. They were discussing parceling out the area's scenic wonders among themselves for profit when one of them—Cornelius Hedges, lawyer, journalist, and educator—reminded them that 6 years earlier President Lincoln had deeded Yosemite Valley to the people of California.

Hedges suggested that Yellowstone be claimed by the Federal Government so that it could belong to everyone in the nation. Upon their return home, the men worked diligently to have their idea presented to Congress. As a result of their efforts President Ulysses S. Grant, on March 1, 1872, signed the bill that made Yellowstone the world's first national park.

Today there are more than 40 national parks, seashores, and lakeshores in the United States, and about 1,400 national parks around the globe. The U.S. parks are administered under guidelines laid down in 1918 by Secretary of the Interior Franklin K. Lane, who decreed that they be "maintained in absolutely unimpaired form for the use of future generations as well as those of our own time."

As I pondered these words beside the Firehole River,

Popular Old Faithful, always surrounded by geyser watchers, spouts at intervals of approximately 1 hour. Yellowstone National Park's thermal areas contain more than 100 geysers and about 3,000 hot springs, the world's largest concentration.

a rifle shot rang out nearby. A boy explained to me: "Problem bear. If they're real troublemakers and keep coming back into the camps, they're shot."

Conflicting needs of people

The incident highlighted the question that many concerned people are asking at the beginning of the second century of national parks. The U.S. population has doubled since Lane's time, and our parks are suffering from civilization's severest problems—overcrowding, riots, vandalism, the advance of technology. With many millions of people visiting the parks each year, these irreplaceable sanctuaries are being damaged. Can they continue to be "maintained in unimpaired form"? Can man and beast still be "contained in the wild freshness of nature"?

Recently I visited several parks to see how they are holding up. I began with a grand tour of Yellowstone, that huge volcanic plateau 8,000 feet high and one-tenth the size of Scotland. Towering beyond Old Faithful were snowcapped mountains, and throughout the park I encountered waterfalls. I saw a mountain of black glass (obsidian), petrified forests, many of the more than 10,000 hot springs, and the famous Mammoth Terrace. I visited wildernesses of lodgepole pine, spruce, and Douglas fir and bright green meadows ablaze with wildflowers.

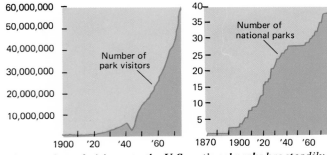

The number of visitors to the U.S. national parks has steadily increased, the impressive curve broken only by a dip during World War II. The war also briefly checked the rise in the number of national parks. The increase in park visitation is the result of growth in population and in leisure time.

Also in Yellowstone Park I found hotels, lodges, cabins, a trailer village, restaurants, stores, churches, gas stations, visitor centers, 14 campgrounds, and two marinas, all connected by 300 miles of road. And, of course, in man-created areas of congestion, there were people. I heard their car horns, motorcycles, voices, radios, tape decks, and the incessant click of their cameras. I saw their mobile homes with dishwashers, refrigerators, and showers, their bikes, canoes, and patio chairs, also their garbage, litter, bottles, and cans.

This is the big problem of the U.S. National Park Service today: people. We have overloved and over-used our parks; we have demanded conveniences at the expense of nature. The Park Service, by trying to please everyone—campers, trailer owners, lodge dwellers, motorboaters—has created vast areas of discontent. Hikers come upon an elegant hotel with country club facilities in the middle of Yosemite and write letters protesting the "misuse" of public property. Adults protest the appearance and conduct of the young, and the young protest right back.

Another Park Service headache is simple ignorance on the part of the traveling public. Until recent years most park visitors were outdoor people who knew how to handle themselves in the wilderness. Today more than 85 percent come from cities, and accident rates have soared. I saw a woman walking a forest trail in high heels. She twisted her ankle so badly she had to be stretchered out. In Yosemite two people slipped at the top of a waterfall and plunged to their deaths. The superintendent of California's Sequoia-Kings Canyon National Parks told me, "Almost every day I'm sending out rescue teams."

Saving the seedlings

Sequoia has a unique problem, and its superintendent regards solving it as a sacred mission. "These giant trees must reproduce for the future," he commented, "but people are trampling the seedlings to death. And even the grown trees are sometimes endangered. The General Sherman tree is the biggest and one of the oldest living things on earth. Yet people have chopped pieces out of it for souvenirs!" Fences and rangers now guard the giant trees and the soil beneath them where the seedlings lie.

Thus does one find park personnel rallying to crises on many fronts. The most popular hot springs in Yellowstone have been girded with railings or posted with warning signs, and park visitors can tune in on a special radio frequency to hear safety instructions con-

Avoiding Yellowstone's summer crowds, a lone snowshoer encounters elks near hot springs. In winter heat in the ground adjacent to the springs melts enough snow to let grazing animals reach grass. The animals also use the nearby natural salt licks.

Visitors to Rocky Mountain National Park avoid damage to tundra vegetation by keeping to a paved walk. Because mountain plants grow slowly, the alpine tundra may take decades to recover from any destruction of ground cover.

cerning hazardous areas, as well as talks on ecology. In the aftermath of the Yosemite riot several summers ago (a nightlong clash between counterculture young people and the police), the Park Service launched a two-pronged preventive campaign: It formed a mobile riot squad and put 224 rangers through 12 weeks of police training. And it inaugurated a number of educational programs for young people.

"The time of additional expansion of existing campgrounds and facilities in the established national parks must be behind us," says Harthon Bill, former deputy director of the National Park Service. "The day is coming when a visitor will have to make reservations for a campsite long in advance." Thus one evening when I arrived late at my selected campsite, a ranger told me it was full and then showed me several campgrounds outside the park border. That night I did what many of us will be doing in the future—I pitched my tent in a U.S. Forest campground, a far more spacious and undisturbed site than those in the park.

The National Wildlife Federation and the National Parks and Conservation Association, both private groups dedicated to ecological protection, are behind this trend. They are urging that new tourist facilities be placed outside the parks and that, as far as possible, existing facilities in need of major repair also be rebuilt beyond park borders. These steps would bring revenue to local communities while helping to conserve the parks. A permit system for rationing backcountry

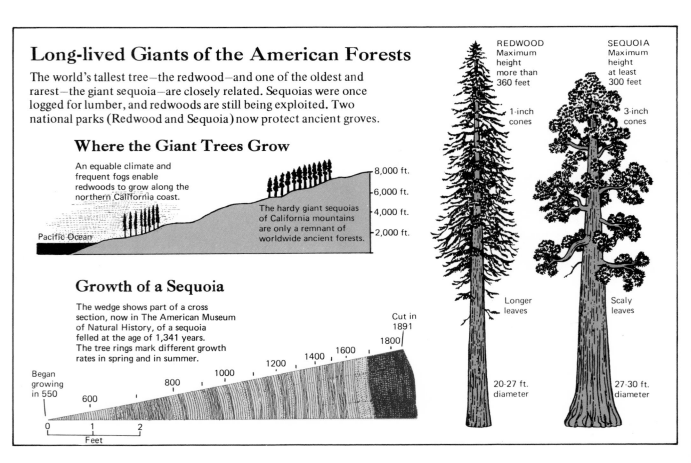

Long-lived Giants of the American Forests

The world's tallest tree—the redwood—and one of the oldest and rarest—the giant sequoia—are closely related. Sequoias were once logged for lumber, and redwoods are still being exploited. Two national parks (Redwood and Sequoia) now protect ancient groves.

Where the Giant Trees Grow

An equable climate and frequent fogs enable redwoods to grow along the northern California coast.

Pacific Ocean

The hardy giant sequoias of California mountains are only a remnant of worldwide ancient forests.

8,000 ft.
6,000 ft.
4,000 ft.
2,000 ft.

Growth of a Sequoia

The wedge shows part of a cross section, now in The American Museum of Natural History, of a sequoia felled at the age of 1,341 years. The tree rings mark different growth rates in spring and in summer.

Began growing in 550

600   800   1000   1200   1400   1600   1800   Cut in 1891

0   1   2
Feet

REDWOOD
Maximum height more than 360 feet

1-inch cones

Longer leaves

20-27 ft. diameter

SEQUOIA
Maximum height at least 300 feet

3-inch cones

Scaly leaves

27-30 ft. diameter

A Crowded Park Copes with Traffic

California's Yosemite National Park, with some of the most spectacular mountain scenery in the United States, has long had a traffic problem. Now, as private cars are phased out, free public buses and trackless trams serve the narrow Merced River Valley, where traffic is heaviest, and a sequoia grove. Service to the scenic attractions and places of accommodation is frequent and convenient; air pollution and noise have been reduced. And oldtimers say the park has never been lovelier.

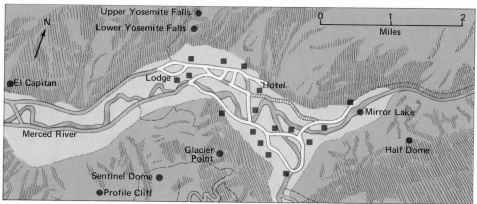

travel in certain of the most visited parks is another step in conserving the fragile wilderness environment.

It has been demonstrated, too, that another park problem—bumper-to-bumper traffic—can be effectively controlled. For years the 5-mile valley where the Yosemite waterfall spills like a ribbon of lace was choked by gas fumes. In 1970 the National Park Service decided to experiment with public transportation. When I arrived, I was asked to leave my car in the campground and use the free buses that carry visitors to the scenic wonders and spectacular trails.

Public transportation helps

Some major roads and parking areas have now been closed to cars, and other parking lots have been torn up and returned to grasses and flowers. A shuttle service of trackless minitrains supplements the free bus system. At a campfire one night, a ranger gave a hint of things still to come. "Perhaps in the near future," he said, "there will be no cars at all in this valley. You will leave your car outside, ride electric buses into the park, and then get out and walk." There was a moment of thoughtful silence, then spontaneous applause.

When I shouldered my pack and took a trail into Yosemite's high country, I came upon a huge pile of trash. Trees had been chopped down for campfires, wildflowers trampled by horses. Even health and sanitation become problems. While I was hiking a trail in the Tetons, a helicopter came clattering over a peak,

transporting a twirling privy into the backcountry!

Great Smoky Mountains National Park, athwart the Tennessee-North Carolina border, is the most visited of all the parks in the United States (more than 7 million people a year). I approached it with considerable apprehension. Up to 400,000 hikers tramp its 800 miles of paths each year. And yet I found Great Smoky to be serene and beautiful.

This is largely because of two factors: the lack of suitable sites for development within the park and the proximity of communities eager to establish facilities for park visitors—all to the advantage of the park's conservation. I drove 20 miles without coming to a hotel, lodge, or concession of any kind. The traffic was heavy, but many pullouts allow visitors to stop, walk trails, or look back across the rolling carpet of forest.

Still, this park has one problem in common with the great western parks—the more popular trails have eroded by overuse. But that summer 50 local high school students worked 6 weeks on these trails, and when I arrived they had the backcountry in good shape. I sought out the biologist in charge of the work.

"We just took those youngsters out there and showed them how to replant eroded areas," he said. "They learned quickly, because they've been picking up ecological information in school. And they *really care.*"

Suddenly it struck me: The biologist was right—it *is* the kids who care and who are doing something about preserving the wilderness.

Yellowstone National Park: Heart of a Wilderness

Magnificent Yellowstone, largest U.S. national park, lies at the heart of a vast Rocky Mountain region that is almost as big as Scotland—27,000 square miles of national forests and wilderness areas. A long-range master plan will take the pressure off the park itself by encouraging overnight stays outside the park. Many changes have already been made: Buildings have been torn down, roads rerouted. Tomorrow's park will be a place to leave your car, walk the trails, and enjoy its wonders in peace.

Yellowstone of the Future

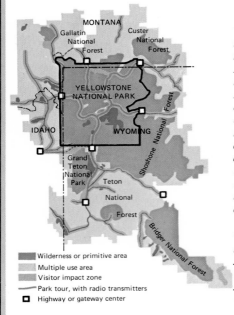

The master plan for the Yellowstone region includes Grand Teton National Park and five national forests. Multiple-use areas are open to grazing, tree cutting, hunting, and recreation. Wilderness and primitive areas are accessible only by trails. Heavily traveled areas near roads and tourist attractions make up the visitor impact zone. On highways into the park the plan calls for information centers with parking, food, lodging, and transportation available.

- ■ Wilderness or primitive area
- ■ Multiple use area
- ■ Visitor impact zone
- — Park tour, with radio transmitters
- □ Highway or gateway center

Wildlife in Yellowstone

Pronghorn
Elk
Summer ——
Winter ----

Bison
Grizzly bear
Summer ——
Winter ----
Year-round ——

Scientists have mapped the ranges of Yellowstone's large mammals. Pronghorn shift little from summer to winter; elks and bison range more widely. Grizzlies concentrate in the same areas all year.

Williamson's sapsucker
Western bluebird

Areas where fires are allowed to burn

Natural fires helped create the Yellowstone ecosystem. In two park areas fires are not put out but are allowed to burn. Woodpeckers nest in burned stubs of trees; bluebirds move in later.

The Yellowstone Food Web

Some food chains are simple—just the eater and the eaten. But Yellowstone has a complex web, involving life on land and in water and including bacteria, fungi, and other organisms of decay right up to the big predators and scavengers. Within the park each strand of the web is protected—there is no spraying or shooting. Nature regulates Yellowstone National Park.

Fire can be a beneficial force in the park ecosystem. Heat opens the cones of lodgepole pines; each wave of fire is followed by vigorous new growth. Burned-over aspens put out fresh shoots, relished by elk and moose.

A hot spring has its own food chain. Small brine flies feed on blue-green algae. The flies are food for larger insects, which are snapped up by birds. In winter the heated soil is like a hothouse—bison, elks, and moose feed in these green areas.

LAND PLANTS

PLANT-EATING ANIMALS
bears, bison, deer, pronghorns, bighorns, rodents, seed-eating birds

PREDATORS AND SCAVENGERS
bears, cougars, wolves, coyotes, ravens, eagles, insect-eating birds, insects

FIRE

NUTRIENTS   DECAY

moose, swans, crustaceans, mollusks, minnows, tadpoles

pelicans, eagles, gulls, ospreys, minks, otters, trout, insects

WATER PLANTS

PLANT-EATING ANIMALS

PREDATORS AND SCAVENGERS

The presence of people has caused problems for the Yellowstone ecosystem. Begging or marauding bears used to be a nuisance, if not a danger. But closing dumps, moving campsites from grizzly haunts, and banning handouts have forced bears back to the wild for food. In park waters alien fish once almost crowded out native cutthroat trout, and overfishing limited the food available for ospreys and pelicans. Now no alien fish may be introduced, there's a two-fish catch limit, and catch-and-release fishing is encouraged.

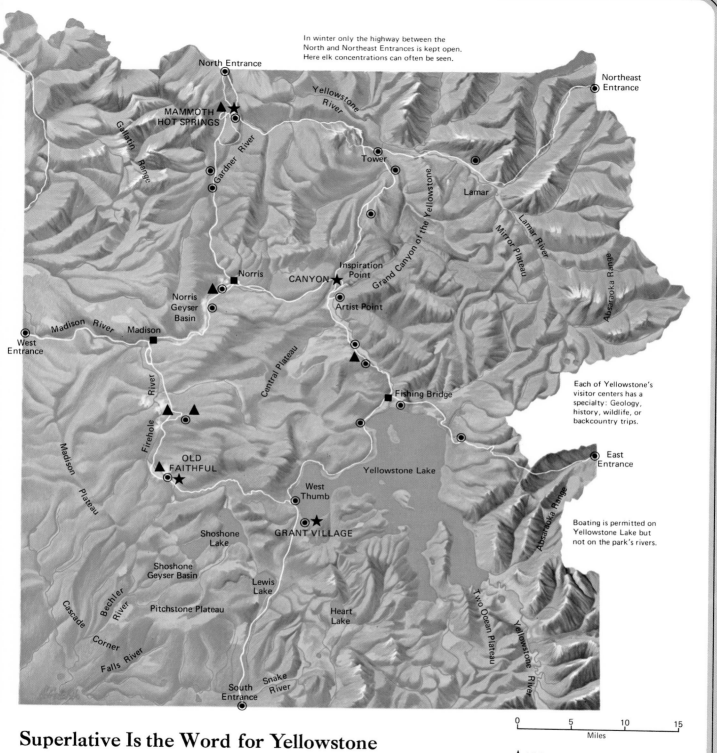

In winter only the highway between the North and Northeast Entrances is kept open. Here elk concentrations can often be seen.

North Entrance

Northeast Entrance

Yellowstone River

MAMMOTH HOT SPRINGS

Gardner River

Gallatin Range

Tower

Lamar

Lamar River

Mirror Plateau

Absaroka Range

Norris

Norris Geyser Basin

CANYON

Inspiration Point

Grand Canyon of the Yellowstone

Artist Point

Madison River

Madison

West Entrance

Firehole River

Central Plateau

Madison Plateau

Fishing Bridge

Each of Yellowstone's visitor centers has a specialty: Geology, history, wildlife, or backcountry trips.

OLD FAITHFUL

Yellowstone Lake

East Entrance

Absaroka Range

West Thumb

GRANT VILLAGE

Shoshone Lake

Boating is permitted on Yellowstone Lake but not on the park's rivers.

Shoshone Geyser Basin

Lewis Lake

Heart Lake

Bechler River

Cascade Corner

Falls River

Pitchstone Plateau

Two Ocean Plateau

Yellowstone River

South Entrance

Snake River

Superlative Is the Word for Yellowstone

The 3,400 square miles of Yellowstone National Park contain the largest—and best protected—concentration of gushing geysers, terraced hot springs, and bubbling mud volcanoes in the world. Seeping water, heated by underground lava flows, created this thermal wonderland; displays in the Old Faithful Visitor Center demonstrate how the volcanic plumbing system works. Scattered over the Yellowstone map are other natural wonders: Petrified trees standing as if still living (near Lamar and Tower); an obsidian cliff resembling black glass (near Norris); beautiful falls and cascades; and the Grand Canyon of the Yellowstone River. Numerous transmitters along park roads broadcast information—a 24-hour service to car radios.

0   5   10   15
Miles

★ Visitor center   ◉ Radio transmitter
▲ Interpretive trail   ■ Museum

CANADA

Yellowstone National Park

UNITED STATES

MEXICO

El Dorado on the Manú

Tony Morrison

Peru's new national park near the headwaters of the Amazon is protecting rare animals and habitat already threatened by advancing civilization.

Although a modern population map of South America shows many large cities and towns, it still seems easy to pinpoint thousands of square miles of virgin territory, apparently uninhabited and inaccessible.

This does not, however, mean a complete absence of human intrusion. Although the wildest parts of the continent are inhabited only by primitive Indians, the influence of civilized man has permeated to many of the tribes, with disastrous effects on their environment. In 1967 Ian Grimwood, a naturalist, visited Peru in search of an area suitable for a national park; along the entire jungle-covered eastern side of the Andes he found only one place in a nearly pristine condition.

Most areas have developed rapidly in the past decade, and new roads have been carved down the precipitous Andean slopes to open up the rich forest land below. Trading along the rivers of Amazonas has increased, and products ranging from valuable timber to rare wildlife are exported to the outside world. With reliable light aircraft, powerful outboard motors for canoes, and easy access by road to headwaters of the major Amazon tributaries, it is hardly surprising that in regions marked "uninhabited" a few years ago there are now pockets of colonization with forest clearings every few miles.

The relatively small area that Ian Grimwood found unspoiled was the Manú River, part of the Madre de Dios system flowing into the Amazon. The river rises in the Andes east of Cuzco, the ancient mountain capital of the Incas, its course descending the steep eastern slopes through dark cloud forest to the warm lowland jungle. A major factor contributing to the preservation of the Manú has been its inaccessibility. Only one road penetrates the northern part of the Madre de Dios watershed, and until recently this road terminated at a point known as Atalaya, about 130 rough miles from Cuzco.

The abundant wildlife in the region led the Peruvian Government to act quickly by declaring a Manú National Park in March 1968. Brazil and neighboring

Who's Who Among South American Cats

Chief predators of the South American rain forest are its cats, ranging in size from the 250-pound jaguar to the small margay, which may weigh as little as 13 pounds. Adaptable hunters, they feed on a wide variety of prey. The spotted coats of the jaguar, ocelot, and margay are an effective camouflage in the dappled light and shade of the deep forest; the plain-coated jaguarundi hunts in the forest openings.

Jaguar

Largest of the South American cats, the 7-foot jaguar is a good swimmer and does much of its hunting in the water, sometimes capturing crocodiles. Black jaguars (which have nearly invisible spots) are frequently seen.

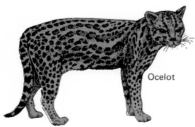
Ocelot

A skilled climber, the 4-foot, 35-pound ocelot does much of its hunting on the ground, preying on lizards, snakes, and small- to medium-sized mammals. It is threatened by the demand for its fur.

Jaguarundi

Despite its short legs the 4-foot, 20-pound jaguarundi runs down its prey – mostly groundbirds – rather than leaping at it from an ambush. Unlike most cats it eats fruit. Both gray and reddish jaguarundis exist.

Margay

Little is known of the habits of the 3-foot margay, a small cousin of the ocelot. Shy and solitary, the long-tailed, lightweight margay probably spends most of its time in the trees hunting birds.

countries of the Andes have plans for reserves in similar regions, but Peru was the first to enforce some protection.

Within the boundaries of the park there are more than 5,000 square miles of virgin land, whose varied terrain includes high Andean puna, or tableland, falling away steeply through deep canyons to the typically Amazonian lowlands. A variety of habitats are represented, and many species of Peruvian fauna are known to exist within the limits now protected by law.

Giant armadillos, giant rodents

The Manú River, the focus of the new park, is sluggish and brown; above each bank tall forest trees press together in an impenetrable wall. The fauna is exceedingly rich and varied. There are sloths, three species of anteaters, and armadillos, including the rare giant armadillo. Elsewhere, hunters have reduced the numbers of this armored mammal, which on average weighs more than 100 pounds and is highly prized for food. Among the rodents are agoutis roughly the size of a hare, pacas and pacaranas that are somewhat bigger, and the semiaquatic capybaras, the largest rodents in the world. Capybaras may be seen sunning themselves on sandy beaches or swimming in the river; elsewhere these animals have been overhunted.

The Manú area contains populations of the spectacled bear; inhabiting isolated areas of the Andes, it is South America's only bear. The giant otter, often nearly 7 feet long, has been seen in the river. It is danger-listed by the International Union for Conservation of Nature and Natural Resources and has reached extremely low numbers on account of its fine skin, which fetches a price equal to the pelt of a jaguar. Traders admit the giant otter, jaguar, and ocelot are becoming scarce, but each of these animals can still be found in the Manú.

Other animals in danger elsewhere include alligator-like caimans, notably the black caiman; these giant reptiles are common in the Alto Manú, with some specimens attaining more than 10 feet in length. In the same area the river turtles, on the danger list after the egg-collecting predations of colonists, have remained abundant. Now the only disturbance is from the careful work of the wardens, who are keeping notes on the nesting beaches within their territory.

Of the 1,500 species of birds listed for Peru, many occur in the park area, and the most spectacular can be seen easily from a canoe. There are the enormous jabiru stork, wood ibis, roseate spoonbill, limpkin, jaçana, and horned screamer, a curious swan-sized bird with a resounding call. Primitive hoatzins, whose young are born with claws on their wings, are always present on the borders of quiet lagoons. Between Tres Cruces and the Manú River is unexplored cloud forest, with a wealth of birdlife including brilliant cock-of-the-rocks and tail-twitching motmots. Steep canyons, where streams pour over boulders into deeply scoured potholes, are perfect homes for torrent ducks, birds found only in Andean streams.

Grasping wing claws, found on no other bird, help hoatzin chicks clamber along branches reptile fashion and hint at a close link with birds' reptilian ancestors. Adult hoatzins lack wing claws but use wings as "arms" for climbing. Weakly muscled, the 2-foot birds, which weigh less than a pound, can glide from a branch but can barely fly.

Clinging upside down to a branch is the normal posture of the two-toed sloth. The slow-moving, 2-foot-long animal spends most of its life in the trees, feeding on immense quantities of leaves. Almost helpless on the ground, it is a good swimmer.

Animals with Five Feet

South America's lowlands contain a greater variety of animals with prehensile tails—able to curl around a support and grasp it—than any other region of the world. Scientists speculate that species like those shown here have adapted to the frequent floods of the Amazon and other great river basins. An animal with a prehensile tail, functioning as a fifth foot, can climb more easily and escape a flood; a prehensile tail also prevents falling.

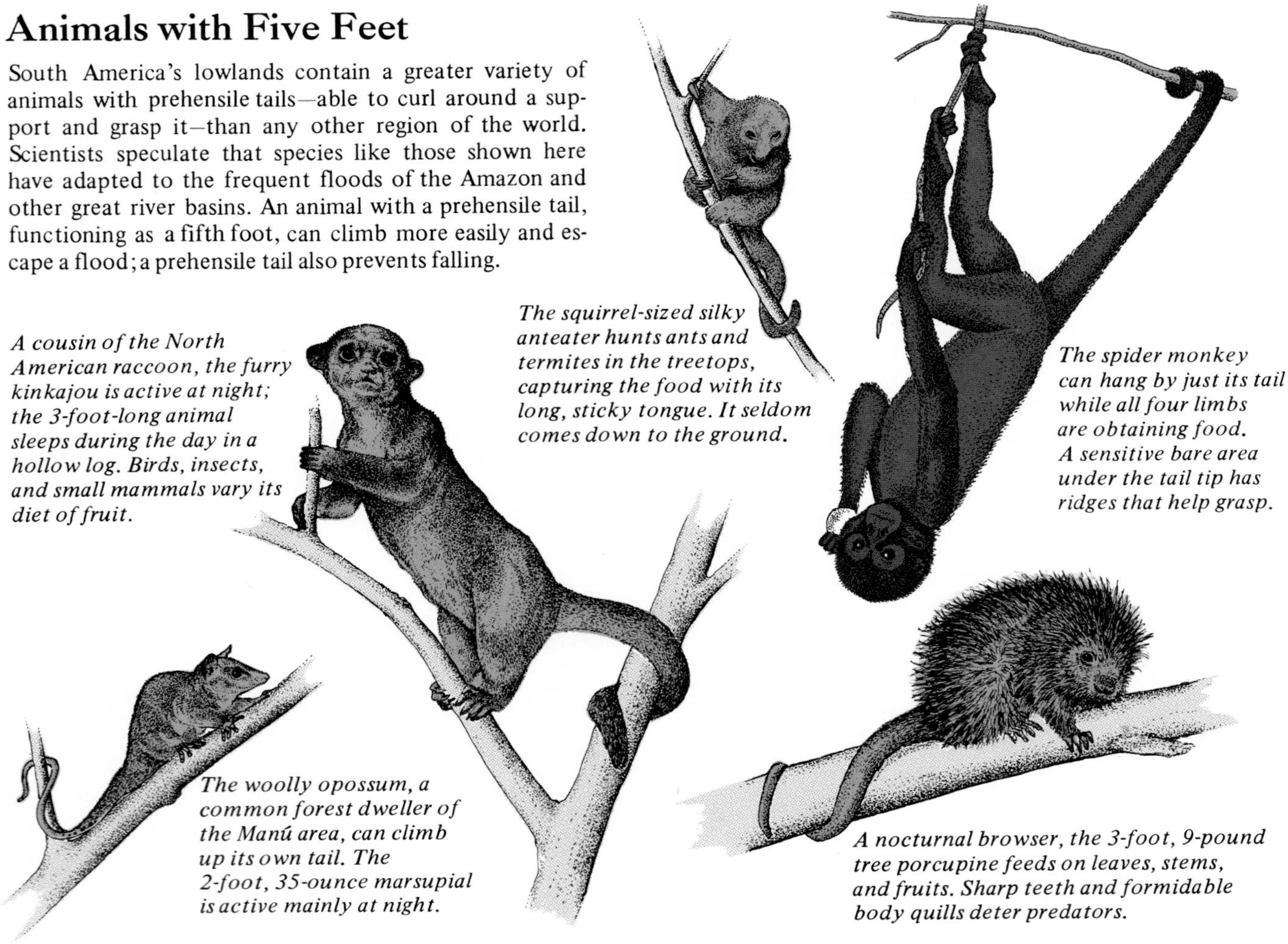

A cousin of the North American raccoon, the furry kinkajou is active at night; the 3-foot-long animal sleeps during the day in a hollow log. Birds, insects, and small mammals vary its diet of fruit.

The squirrel-sized silky anteater hunts ants and termites in the treetops, capturing the food with its long, sticky tongue. It seldom comes down to the ground.

The spider monkey can hang by just its tail while all four limbs are obtaining food. A sensitive bare area under the tail tip has ridges that help grasp.

The woolly opossum, a common forest dweller of the Manú area, can climb up its own tail. The 2-foot, 35-ounce marsupial is active mainly at night.

A nocturnal browser, the 3-foot, 9-pound tree porcupine feeds on leaves, stems, and fruits. Sharp teeth and formidable body quills deter predators.

Hunting animals for food is a problem that has affected many areas of South America now being opened up. Mining companies and lumber camps employ hunters to provide meat for their crews. The main species shot for this purpose are the larger rodents, the tapirs, and the monkeys. Red howler monkeys, which have disappeared from all areas close to settlement, are present in the Manú, a heartening sign that protection has arrived in advance of exploitation. And other monkeys are plentiful, particularly spider monkeys, squirrel monkeys, capuchins, sakis, and woolly monkeys, together with some species of marmosets.

The future of the park

Indians are a threat to the monkey species, particularly spider and woolly monkeys, which are said to be the best eating. At present the only group of Indians within the boundaries of the national park is a score of families belonging to the Machiguenga tribe. Amahuacas Indians move occasionally into the Machiguenga territory. The problem of the forest Indians is just one of the difficulties that will have to be solved if the Manú National Park is to be a success.

The park's immediate future is a guaranteed period of complete protection. A control post has been established at the confluence of the Panahua and Manú rivers to guard the main entry point used by waterborne hunters and woodcutters; other boundaries are in wild Indian country or densely forested terrain.

Park administration is financed by the Peruvian Government; in the initial stages it was helped by a grant from the World Wildlife Fund. Once protection was established in 1968, plans were prepared for the development of the park as a tourist attraction; a small airstrip has been planned at Tayakome. The administration has set up a field base not far from the Machiguenga village and has built an observation post at Cocha Cascho, 2 hours upriver from Panahua. These facilities are already being used by biologists and expeditions, but Manú is not yet ready to receive tourists.

It is as a biological reservoir, with many unique ecosystems enclosed in a relatively small area, that Manú National Park is important. Even if only a fraction of the park's fantastic variety of wildlife is seen by the rare visitor, it will remain for the benefit of future generations—a secret wildlife El Dorado that will attract naturalists as the *conquistadores* were lured to South America four centuries ago.

High in the Andes the Vicuña Is Making a Comeback

Shy highland dwellers, vicuñas live in small herds, consisting of an adult male, several females, and young under a year.

Centuries ago vast numbers of vicuñas grazed on the scanty grass on South America's Andes Mountains. Protected by Inca law, the fleet-footed animals were not killed but were rounded up in annual hunts, sheared, and then released. After the 16th-century Spanish Conquest vicuñas were hunted ruthlessly for their valuable fleece and meat. An estimated pre-Conquest vicuña population of 1 million declined to several thousand, most of them in Peru. Alarmed by the near disappearance of this graceful animal, the Peruvian Government established a 15,000 acre vicuña reserve at Pampa Galeras in 1966. By 1974 about 6,500 vicuñas lived there, and nearby reserves in other Andean countries brought the total to 15,000.

Herders and hunters reduced the vicuña's original range. Several herds now thrive on scattered reserves.

Natives of the high, arid Andean grasslands, these closely related animals share a common ancestor with the camels. Bred by man for generations, llamas and alpacas do not exist in the wild. Guanacos and vicuñas have never been domesticated.

Standing 4 feet at the shoulder, this all-purpose animal carries loads, yields meat, wool, hides.

Bred for its long, fine wool, it was the Incas' equivalent of sheep.

Slender, speedy, and alert, the guanaco is hunted for its meat.

The most delicate cameloid is only 2½ feet tall.

Llama   Alpaca   Guanaco   Vicuña

Scanning the shattered trunk of a baobab tree, a female elephant and her calf seek food and moisture. In their desperate quest the powerful animals have damaged and uprooted trees and devastated large areas in Tsavo and other African parks.

Tsavo: Too Many Elephants?

John Reader

What is a national park to do when the habitat is being destroyed by the animals it protects? This is the life-or-death problem facing Tsavo.

If you had visited Kenya's Tsavo National Park during the 1971 drought and had seen the carcasses of some of the thousands of elephants, or had watched the gaunt survivors looking, as one observer put it, "like bundles of bones with an old rug thrown over them," you might well have thought the African elephant was headed for extinction.

Elephants are so grand, they seem so self-sufficient. Once they roamed most of the continent, but since man began to live from the land of Africa, the elephants have been jostled along to make way for agriculture and habitation. They have been hunted with bow and arrow, with spear and rifle, for meat, for sport, and for their ivory.

Now there are probably about a million savanna elephants left, plus almost as many more of a different variety in the Zaire rain forests. In East Africa there are approximately 680,000. Most of these are in the national parks, which, though vast (about 30,000 square miles), represent a small fraction of the total area.

Tsavo National Park covers more than 8,000 square miles—about the size of Israel. No one knows just how many elephants were there when the park was established in 1948, but when the long rains failed at the end of 1971 there were far too many: 20,000. During this drought the seasonal water holes dried out entirely. An elephant needs to drink at least every second day, and many chose to stay near the few permanent water sources. As the elephants consumed all the edible vegetation in the vicinity of water, the distance between food and water stretched alarmingly, sometimes to 30 miles. All the elephants grew weak from lack of protein. Of the 13,500 elephants in the eastern section of the park, at least 6,500 died.

Tsavo was chosen as a national park, not so much because it was particularly suitable for a park, but because it was unsuitable for anything else: The tsetse fly made ranching impossible, and the low and erratic rainfall made agriculture difficult. Now Tsavo is one of the largest sanctuaries in the world and carries the highest populations of elephants and black rhinos in Africa.

Sliced by a railroad

The Mombasa-to-Nairobi road and railway slice the park into Tsavo West and Tsavo East. They cover 3,000 and 5,000 square miles respectively and are administered separately.

Drawing a line on a map does not make a national park, but, once that initial step is taken, man's influence becomes paramount. Tsavo was never entirely devoid of people. There were always nomads passing through, while along the Galana River were the Waliangula, hunters who killed elephants for their meat and ivory.

There is no fence around Tsavo, but the encircling human settlements and hunting blocks are, in most cases, just as effective. As these external pressures increased, more elephants found safety within the park—and they began to knock down trees.

In 1954 Tsavo East's warden, David Sheldrick, drew attention to the growing elephant population and the consequent destruction of the Commiphora woodland. In 1963 a zoologist conducted a survey of the park and concluded: "If the habitat is to be preserved in its present form . . . the numbers of elephants will have to be controlled." In 1966 the Ford Foundation financed a 3-year research project. The project director was Richard Laws.

Laws had worked on seals and whales in Antarctica, elephants and hippos in the Uganda national parks. He began his study by analyzing physiological data from 300 elephants shot at his request in Tsavo East; he found that instead of a single homogeneous population, the Tsavo complex, in fact, held 10 distinct elephant populations of which nine were in a state of decline.

The decline was most marked in those ranges that were most overused. Laws suggested that some populations should be allowed to continue their decline, to see what the ultimate effect on the animals and the

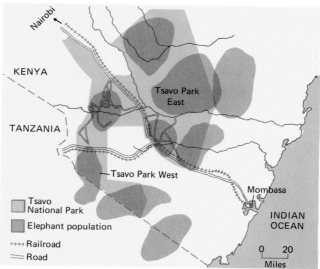

A recent elephant survey in Kenya's Tsavo National Park and its vicinity counted nine separate elephant populations. Two were outside the park's limits; all could enter or leave the park (which is divided in two parts by a road and a railroad) at will by crossing its unfenced boundaries.

Rwenzori: Too Many Hippos?

Hippos laze cheek-to-cheek at Rwenzori. On the shore a line of yellow-billed egrets forms a snowy backdrop.

In Uganda's Rwenzori National Park hippos wallow in two large lakes and the connecting channel. After dark they eat their daily 400 pounds of grass on the shore. As their numbers multiply, these forays denude the grassy areas. Hippo dung deposited in the water fertilizes the algae, which in turn feed large schools of Tilapia. Marabou storks eat their fish. The storks roost on a rare species of Euphorbia; their weight breaks limbs, and droppings burn the trees. Park officials are now controlling hippo numbers, and the grasslands are recovering. Hopefully the chain of destruction will eventually be broken.

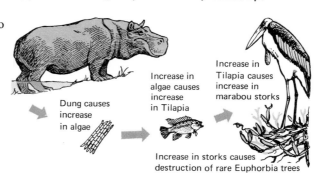

Dung causes increase in algae

Increase in algae causes increase in Tilapia

Increase in Tilapia causes increase in marabou storks

Increase in storks causes destruction of rare Euphorbia trees

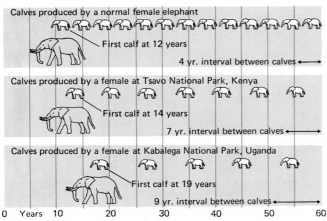

Elephants respond to crowding by producing fewer offspring. Some people argue that with time the elephant overpopulation problem will solve itself; others argue that this will not be soon enough and that man must intervene.

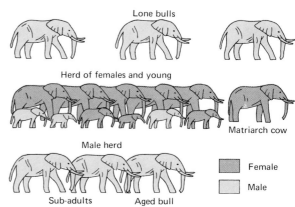

Elephants form two kinds of herds: Bachelor groups are made up of nonbreeding bulls; family groups, led by an old female, are made up of cows and calves. Breeding males sometimes live alone, sometimes in the family groups.

habitat would be. Others, he said, should be manipulated to establish what might be called halfway habitats, while yet others should be drastically reduced to keep the area as it was. Such a program would require more research, more samples, and more killing (or, more politely, cropping).

Critics looked hard at the Laws proposals and found that they could mean the slaughter of a further 2,700 elephants. Suppose Laws was wrong? The national park trustees overruled him, and Laws resigned.

Meanwhile the Tsavo elephant population continued to grow. Over the last 20 years the elephants have brought about profound changes in the habitat in Tsavo. Vast tracts that once were thick woodland are now sparse grass plain studded with the stumps of dead trees. Most of the larger trees that the elephants eat (Commiphora, baobab, acacia) are dying out and being replaced by grass and shrub. Thus the 1971 drought brought to a crisis a problem that everyone had seen coming for years. Having destroyed most of their food resources, the Tsavo elephants began dying by the thousands.

In the view of the national park trustees, this is merely a harsh demonstration of natural cause and effect, with the emphasis on "natural." The drought apparently took mainly the weaker elephants and small calves. An opposing school of thought holds that there is nothing more unnatural than a national park, and that Tsavo's optimum elephant population level must be established and the excess shot.

Those who advocate intervention maintain that the 1970's will very likely see the end of the myth of a vast African wilderness. East Africa's population is growing at an annual rate of 3.3 percent, a rate that will double the population in 20 years.

Pressures on land resources will increase, and ultimately, the hard fact will have to be faced that Africa cannot have both truly wild animals and human development. Critics point to the ambiguity of policies that allow the shooting of 4,000 to 5,000 elephants annually outside the parks in the defense of human interests—while refusing to control the numbers within the parks.

Ian Parker, who carried out elephant cropping for Laws in Uganda and Tsavo, says, "Tsavo is a political unit, not an ecological one. The elephants are not natural there; they have been forced in by surrounding human population. What you see now is the result of intense compression. It is in circumstances like this—drought, starvation, and the chance of disease—that the extinction of a species becomes a real possibility."

Natural controls or human controls?

The opposition to direct human intervention is personified in David Sheldrick, warden for more than 20 years of Tsavo East, where the effects of the drought have been most severely felt. It is his opinion that nature should be allowed to take its course.

"People tend to apply the standards of a temperate climate to Tsavo. But here we deal in extremes, and there are so many species involved. If you treat just one, you really don't know what you're doing to the rest. The only thing that can satisfactorily control large animals like elephants and rhinos is drought.

"When I first came to Tsavo, it was thick bush virtually all over. You were lucky to see an elephant disappearing into the bush.

"In 1954 I drew attention to the destruction of the Commiphora. It was a problem. Our future was uncertain; we got maybe one tourist a week. We knew nothing about elephants, and there weren't any scientists who wanted to get involved. Then came the 1960–61 drought. Everyone said the place was going to become a desert. Reduce the elephant population by one-third, they said. But no one knew how many there were. We began counting them. I was all for culling in those days. But you can't shoot elephants out of a herd without making the rest of them savage.

"The other possibility was to shoot whole herds. Then people said you can't just shoot the animals and leave them to rot, they must be utilized. But the recovery and marketing problems would be enormous.

The Orphans of Tsavo Find a Home

David Sheldrick, the warden of Kenya's Tsavo East, and his wife Daphne keep an open house and garden for lost and abandoned animals, ranging in size from 6-inch weaverbirds to elephants. They rear the orphans not as pets but as animals that will eventually be given a chance to return to the wild. Observations of the orphans during their stay at the Sheldricks have provided new information on such subjects as the animals' behavior, growth rates, preferred diets, and diseases.

A zebra nibbles the front horn of a young black rhino, which seems to be indifferent.

Daphne Sheldrick, accompanied by an assistant, walks with four of her orphans—two elephants, a rhinoceros, and a water buffalo.

A mischievous and rambunctious zebra conducts experiments on how far it can impose on an elephant's good nature.

"We decided to let things ride. I began to have doubts about culling. Looking around the park, I could see that nature was taking a hand. As the trees were knocked down, the park was being colonized by grasses and creepers. There was a buildup of plains game, and with the bush opening up, the park was becoming better for tourists. It was doubtful if Tsavo would have survived as a park with tourist potential if it had remained as it was; tourists wouldn't come to see the backside of an elephant that was disappearing into the bush.

"And now we have another drought. The surviving elephants are in terrible shape. They haven't the reserves to take another long dry period. More of them will die. But are we interested in maintaining such large numbers of elephants?"

To critics of David Sheldrick's view, the choice is simple: Introduce a program of planned killing or allow all the elephants to die. Against this contention the national parks trustees can pitch only their longer experience at Tsavo and a questioning doubt of the scientific evidence collected so far.

Time will tell who is right. Unavoidably the score will be the number of dead or living elephants.

Guardians of Africa's Wildlife Heritage

The wardens and rangers in Africa's national parks, like their counterparts everywhere, perform a variety of functions. In almost every park one urgent task is to protect their charges against poaching. Orphaned youngsters and sick or injured animals require special care. Ecology studies involve keeping records of such statistics as the numbers of animals in herds and directions and times of migrations. Conditions in the park or refuge may require the movement of certain animals from one area to another or even from one park to another, if a population has built up beyond the carrying capacity of the range. One of the most important long-term tasks of wardens and rangers is public education. Schoolchildren come to the parks in buses for specially guided tours, and so do groups of teachers. The paperwork that is part of any administrative job—keeping up with new ideas, preparing literature, answering correspondence—fills the rest of a warden's day.

In the combined orphanage, hospital, and retirement home in Kenya's Nairobi National Park a warden, assisted by a ranger, feeds a wildebeest calf. Sick and injured animals are treated here. One of the residents is a lion so old that rangers have to cut up its meat for it. Any sick or injured animals or orphans that can return to the wild are freed as soon as they can take care of themselves.

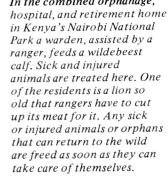

An antipoaching unit uses whatever transportation is most appropriate: Plane, jeep, bicycle, or camel. Men keep in touch with each other by radio. The work includes finding and arresting poachers, looking for snares, and rescuing trapped animals. A unit may be on patrol for days or weeks at a time; poachers with poisoned arrows or powerful guns make the work dangerous.

After a ride several zebras captured in an overgrazed area of a South African national park are released in a region with more food. Moving animals from one place to another in order to keep the park healthy is part of the warden's job.

Education is an important part of a warden's job. Kenyan schoolchildren touring the 44-square-mile Nairobi National Park learn how valuable wildlife is to their country—and how fascinating in itself.

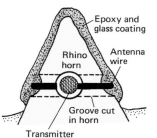

Epoxy and glass coating

Rhino horn

Antenna wire

Groove cut in horn

Transmitter

A tranquilized black rhinoceros in the Hluhluwe Game Reserve in South Africa receives a radio transmitter in a hole drilled in one of its horns; a groove cut around the horn will hold the antenna. The radio will enable rangers to keep track of the rhino's movements as part of a long-term study of this endangered mammal.

At Africa's oldest wildlife-management college on the slopes of Kilimanjaro in Tanzania, students from the whole continent learn about animals in the field, lecture hall, library, and laboratory.

A mixed herd of zebras and wildebeests grazes on the vast plains of Tanzania's Serengeti National Park. The two species oft

Living Laboratory of the Serengeti

Niko Tinbergen

The great spectacle of migrating herds and the predators that live on them— so thrilling to the tourist—is a research challenge to the ecologist.

The Serengeti, the naturalists' paradise in northwestern Tanzania, is known to thousands around the world who have never visited the park. It first captured the public's imagination when Bernhard Grzimek and his son Michael published their stimulating book *Serengeti Shall Not Die* and released their fine film with the same title. The great merit of the Grzimeks was that they foresaw that conservation of the rapidly dwindling African fauna would not be possible without intensive studies of its ecology—and, more important still, that they set out to give the research a start.

The government of the young State of Tanzania, keenly interested in preserving its national parks, retained the services of John S. Owen, national parks director, who with great tenacity of purpose built up a field research group. This was in 1966. Now the Serengeti Research Institute is one of the world's outstanding study centers of plains game ecology.

To see this part of Africa for the first time is to enter a new world, almost unreal in its beauty and its riches. A local plane takes you in an hour from Nairobi in Kenya into the heart of the Serengeti plains. Here the headquarters of the Serengeti National Park, the tourist lodges and campsites, together with the houses of personnel and scientists, form the settlement of Seronera. One low swoop over the airstrip drives off the antelopes, storks, or other animals that might endanger both themselves and the aircraft. Then you land in the middle of the vast plains and at once feel the wonderful, invigorating warmth of the equatorial sun, which in the dry atmosphere is not at all oppressive. The air is incredibly clear—the mountain wall of the Ngorongoro Crater, 80 miles away, is always visible.

Man and animals live peacefully together at Seronera. From the veranda of a comfortable bungalow one can observe the small groups of grazing antelopes; an occasional giraffe browses in a tree less than 30 yards away; lovebirds, splendidly colored starlings, barbets, and many other birds come to drink at the water trough near the house. In the distance you hear the barking of zebras. Even lions and hyenas are at home in Seronera, and you sometimes find their footprints under your window in the morning.

In the crystal-clear atmosphere after an afternoon rain one can see the animals miles away in astonishing detail. This is the time to see the predators at work— particularly the wild dogs, those efficient hunters that work in packs and run down the antelopes. Lions, leopards, and hyenas become more active at dusk; as it darkens, one imagines that one can feel the tension among the herbivores.

It is in this animal wonderland that the biologists of the Serengeti Research Institute are studying the ecology of the plains and of the animals living there. The research program has been carefully thought out and is based on the following reasoning: The upkeep of Tanzania's vast national parks puts a heavy burden on a young and by Western standards very poor coun-

ether but do not compete. Wildebeests eat tender grass shoots; zebras crop tall, tough grass that the wildebeests cannot bite off.

try that can ill afford to set aside for wildlife land needed for grazing or agriculture.

Fortunately the Tanzanian national parks, famous all over the world, are attracting an increasing number of tourists, and this tourist trade is one of the country's most important sources of income. The parks' interest for tourists will obviously depend on the maintenance of their rich and varied fauna. Since all animals depend ultimately on their habitats, it is the richness and variety of habitats that have to be maintained—for purely economic as well as for idealistic reasons.

We know it is wrong to assume that just leaving such areas undisturbed will ensure their continued existence. The Serengeti is hardly primeval; it has been shaped by the hand of man. The main factor by which man has influenced this and many other parts of Africa is undoubtedly fire. To put a stop to all grass fires might allow the open Serengeti plains to develop into a bush-covered habitat; on the other hand, too much burning would destroy first the undergrowth and then the trees of these parkland areas. Either course could lead to a reduction in the variety of habitats and so of animal life.

Why research is necessary

The answer, therefore, is management. But how to manage the habitats, and through them the animals? Sound management can be achieved only on the basis of wide and detailed knowledge of the animals' habitat requirements.

This is the reason why the Serengeti Research Institute was set up primarily for ecological research. The Institute's scientists concentrate on habitat research.

The plains offer a variety of habitats. This is at once clear when one begins to visit them in order to assess the numbers of animals found there. For census purposes, each member of the Institute's re-

A Big Park That Should Be Bigger

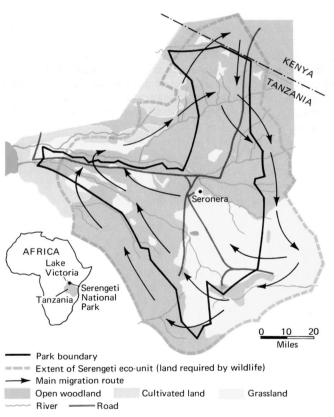

— Park boundary
--- Extent of Serengeti eco-unit (land required by wildlife)
→ Main migration route
  Open woodland   Cultivated land   Grassland
  River   Road

The immense mammalian herds of Tanzania's Serengeti National Park are perpetually on the move in search of food and water, one species following another in a regular succession. Although the park is huge—about 5,400 square miles—it does not form a complete ecological unit; some animals migrate outside its boundaries, creating problems for local farmers and for the migrating wildlife itself.

Leisurely lounging in the midday heat, a pride of lions ignores busloads of camera-clicking tourists in Tanzania's Serengeti National Park. In the park a pride consists of two to four adult males, several females, and their young.

search team has a Land Rover, and in addition shares a small spotter plane, contributed by the New York Zoological Society. The plane is used to collect systematic photographic data on numbers, age compositions, and movements of the large herbivores. Thus the scientists are able to study the animals' impressive seasonal migrations and their rhythm of reproduction. The antelopes and zebras spend the dry season in the bush area of the north and west, and pour out over the plains in their hundreds of thousands when, in December, the rains begin to fall and the plains turn green.

These migrations must be seen to be believed. There are now approximately 250,000 zebras, 900,000 wildebeests, 600,000 Thomson's gazelles, and more than 140,000 other antelopes in the Serengeti. Photographs give only a faint impression of the tremendous scale of this phenomenon—probably the largest of its kind in the world.

The herds do not scatter uniformly over the plains. They concentrate in certain areas to calve; they entirely avoid others. It is clear that here is a task for the grassland ecologist, who will have to look at the vegetation with, so to speak, the eyes of a herbivore (and a different set of eyes for each species, at that). The zoologist will have to discover what it is in the vegetation that makes the various herbivores take up the habitat they select. This is certainly not merely a matter of available food but of other, possibly equally vital factors, such as cover. Some species avoid cover so that they can keep a good lookout for predators, but others need it, paradoxically, for the purpose of hiding from predators. Thus while Thomson's gazelles, wildebeests, and zebras like the open plains and may well be less vulnerable there, others, such as waterbucks, reedbucks, and duikers, take shelter in places with denser vegetation.

The matter is further complicated by the seasonal changes in habitat selection. Even though zebras and wildebeests prefer the open plains, they have to spend the dry season in bush country, simply because the plains are then too arid; they also seem to have special preferences at mating time and especially for calving.

How many predators?

From a comparison of diets, hunting methods, and available numbers of prey animals, it becomes clear that predators such as lions, hyenas, and wild dogs have an easy time when they can hunt the herbivores' newborn young. This at once gives rise to the question: Why are these predators not much more numerous? Could not these teeming masses of game feed many more of them? Probably they can't. This seems to be due to various circumstances. For example, the wildebeests all calve at about the same time, so that the season of abundant, easy-to-catch calves is very short. Furthermore, most herbivores migrate, and some predators do not; as a result these predators live in plenty only when game passes through. In other words, there are lean seasons as well as fat seasons for the predators.

And there is another question: How do the predators select their prey? Do they, for instance, really take predominantly young and weak animals? We recently

A trio of giraffes lopes easily past a grove of the thorny savanna trees on which they browse. Obtaining moisture from their food, giraffes seldom need to drink. Their height—up to 18 feet—permits them to utilize food other herbivores cannot reach.

observed a mother cheetah with her two nearly full-grown young during a successful hunt. The mother walked leisurely at a distance of some 150 yards past several herds of Thomson's gazelles, as if just "window shopping." Suddenly a young Tommy jumped up about 50 yards ahead of the mother cheetah. A marvelously fast sprint brought her up with the desperate kid; its zigzag jumps were of no avail, and through the cloud of dust we saw the cheetah knock it down with one quick blow. She took it in her mouth and walked back to her young.

Upon meeting the cubs, the mother cheetah dropped the Tommy, and we saw to our surprise that it was alive; it jumped up and ran away! But the mother did not follow—she allowed the cubs to hunt it down. This they did enthusiastically but clumsily. They knocked the Tommy down twice, but they could not kill it. After some minutes the mother took over and killed it.

Apart from the interesting fact that the cheetah actually took a live prey to her young and gave it to them for hunting practice, the observation suggests that the cheetah selected an easy prey among hundreds of Tommies. Of course, in order to be able to say whether or not the weaker prey are taken more often than those in prime condition, one has to collect many of these observations, each made with great accuracy. This is just one example of the problems being studied at the Serengeti Research Institute. With the knowledge thus gained, the animals of the Serengeti can be fully understood and helped to survive.

Serengeti Around the Clock

This "clock" shows the daily schedule of the large mammals in Serengeti National Park. Midday is the period of least activity, the time when both predators and prey seek shelter from the heat; early and late day are full of activity. The Serengeti cycle is typical of East Africa's grasslands, though there are many variations from region to region.

NIGHT

FEEDING: buffalo, elephant, gazelle, rhino, wildebeest, hippo, zebra
DRINKING: buffalo, elephant, rhino
RESTING: cheetah, gazelle, wild dog, wildebeest, zebra
HUNTING: hyena, jackal, leopard, lion

EARLY DAY

FEEDING: buffalo, elephant, gazelle, giraffe, rhino, wildebeest, zebra
DRINKING: giraffe, wildebeest, zebra
RESTING: hippo
HUNTING: cheetah, hyena, jackal, wild dog, leopard, lion

LATE DAY

FEEDING: buffalo, elephant, gazelle, giraffe, rhino, wildebeest, zebra
DRINKING: buffalo
RESTING: rhino, hippo
HUNTING: cheetah, hyena, jackal, leopard, lion, wild dog

MIDDLE DAY

FEEDING: elephant, gazelle, giraffe, wildebeest
DRINKING: elephant, gazelle, rhino, wildebeest, zebra
RESTING: buffalo, cheetah, elephant, hyena, jackal, leopard, lion, rhino, wild dog, wildebeest, hippo, zebra
HUNTING: cheetah

Giant eucalyptus trees tower above the floor of the rain forest in eastern Australia's Lamington National Park. The massive roots of a strangler fig have nearly enveloped the trunk of the big tree at the left; eventually, the strangler fig will kill its host.

Australia's Rain Forest Wonders

Allen Keast

Relics of an ancient past, the unique plants and animals of Queensland's mountains and plateaus are protected for the future in parks of great beauty.

Back from the sea along the borders of New South Wales and Queensland is a magnificent mountain sector of lush jungles, tall eucalypt forests, and misty valleys. It is Lamington National Park, a reserve of 48,510 acres, created in 1915 mainly as the result of the campaigning of a young pioneer, Romeo Lahey, who was appalled at the rapid cutting of the best forests in the rugged McPherson Ranges.

Today, from guesthouses in the center of the park, tracks radiate out to high points with such fascinating names as Mount Bithongabel and Mount Hobwee, through dense forests and thick scrub, and along swift-running creeks and still pools. These are the haunts of rare jungle birds such as the Albert lyrebird, rufous scrubbird, and riflebird (a bird of paradise). Forest wallabies, koalas, and large fruit bats (flying foxes) are not uncommon. The McPhersons contain the last of Australia's large surviving tracts of temperate rain forest. The importance of Lamington National Park in the survival of the wildlife peculiar to this habitat is, accordingly, considerable.

Distinctive trees

The gnarled and ancient trees of the McPhersons, known as antarctic beeches, are said to be more than 1,000 years old. This is the northernmost stand in Australia. Other trees include the giant evergreen tristania, the rough-barked hoop pine, or araucaria, and the stinging tree, whose large leaves are covered with stiff, pain-inflicting hairs. Among the flowering species are the flame tree, which begins blooming in November, and the firewheel tree, whose deep crimson tubular flowers appear in January. Piccabeen palms with scarlet fruit, climbing lawyer palms, ferns of many kinds, and, in open places, tall grass trees or black boys (so-called because of their resemblance to grass-skirted aborigines) are some of the more striking forms of the lower forest levels.

In late spring flowering orchids adorn many of the trees. They include the delicate spider orchid, the orange-blossom orchid, the yellow-green olive orchid, the white and mauve sprays of the ravine orchid, and the spectacular golden king orchid.

The McPherson trails are famous for lookouts on high cliffs from which the entire northeastern corner of New South Wales can be seen spread out like a relief map: Spirelike Mount Warning, the meandering Tweed River, the Terranora Lakes sparkling in the sun, the coast extending away to the south as far as the eye can see. Dropping away from the cliffs at one's feet are gorges, precipices, and waterfalls. They echo and seem to amplify the notes of the birds from the forest canopy below—the loud whipcrack of the whipbird, the "walk-to-work" call of the brilliantly colored pitta, the "calung-calung" of the pied currawong, the bubbling notes of the wompoo pigeon, and the excited screeches of a flock of rainbow lorikeets.

The birds are among the main attractions of Lamington National Park, for they include many rain forest forms that are rare elsewhere. The brush turkey, a mound builder or megapode, is a common sight on guesthouse lawns. The male riflebird, resplendent in iridescent greens and purples, sends pieces of bark tumbling as he prods the cracks and fissures of trees with his long, down-curved bill. Several kinds of fruit pigeons and the tiny fig parrot feast high in the tall trees. The Albert lyrebird scratches up showers of fallen leaves in its search for insects. The somber blue satin bowerbird decorates its playground with bits of blue paper and other blue oddments retrieved from paths and lawns; the black and gold male of the regent bowerbird, a species that seldom builds a bower, flies across a jungle clearing.

Australia's tropical rain forest

North of Lamington and the McPhersons, in the northeastern corner of Queensland, is the greatest remaining belt of tropical rain forest in Australia. The Atherton Tableland and the Bellenden-Ker Plateau are the habitat of striking plant and animal forms with strong New Guinea affinities.

Large sections of these highlands have been set aside as reserves. Bellenden-Ker National Park includes the two highest peaks in Queensland. Two small national parks surround Lakes Barrine and Eacham, at 2,400 feet, near the top of the tableland. One comes upon them suddenly from the jungle—clear, deep bodies of water occupying old volcanic craters.

The visitor strolling along a road or track on the Atherton Tableland will note that a tropical rain forest differs from forests in other areas. The trees are tall, commonly between 150 and 180 feet high, and they grow so closely together that their foliage is continuous,

Architects of Australia's Rain Forest

The tailorbird stitches a covered, pouch-shaped nest of grass stems and living leaves, using spiderwebs as thread.

The paradise riflebird builds its shallow nest of vines and dead leaves, often decorated with a castoff snakeskin.

The scrub fowl builds a huge mound of leaves and earth in which it lays its eggs. Heat from the rotting vegetation incubates the eggs.

A sacred kingfisher hollows out a nest in an arboreal termite colony.

Constant opening and closing of its tail have given the rufous fantail its name. The 6-inch insect eater nests in the rain forest thickets of eastern Australia. Its wineglass-shaped nest is built of bark fibers bound with spider silk.

Australia's Parks: Scenic Diversity

Colorful desert rock formations, spectacular river gorges
that rival the Grand Canyon, wave-lashed seacoasts,
and cool highland forests and alpine meadows—
all are features of Australia's more than 200 major
national parks and other reserves. Each shelters its
own characteristic plant and animal communities.

*Around the colorful rock formations of Mount Olga-Ayers
Rock National Park, kangaroos, bandicoots, dingoes, and
wedge-tailed eagles survive in the desert of central
Australia. These rocks are sacred to the aborigines.*

*Rivers carved deep gorges in the ancient red rocks of Western
Australia's Hamersley Ranges National Park. Birds are the
major form of wildlife here. Flocks of budgerigars, winging
through the gorge, often form a green cloud against the rocks.*

*Eroded rock formations, called "sea stacks," mark the
shoreline of Port Campbell National Park in Australia's
Southeast. Muttonbirds, famed for their long migrations,
and fairy penguins nest on rugged offshore islets.*

*Snow drapes the flank of Cradle Mountain, towering above a
glacier-created lake. Eucalypts, antarctic beeches, and heath
thrive in Tasmania's Cradle Mountain/Lake St. Clair National
Park; Tasmanian devils and wallabies are wildlife highlights.*

providing a closed canopy. The interior is, accordingly,
in dense shade, and ground vegetation is scanty. Here
and there are fallen branches and trunks, moss-covered
and crumbling. Huge vines, some the thickness of a
man's thigh, hang like cables between the trees. Creepers cling in sinuous curves around the trunks. The
humidity is high, and the still air has an earthy smell.

In the rain forest, softwoods of Malaysian origin
predominate. Among the more curious trees is the
strangler fig. Scattered by flying foxes and birds, the
seeds lodge and germinate on a tree branch, producing
roots that grip the host tree. A wood tuber develops
and then drops a root to the ground. Other roots follow until finally the host is enmeshed in a stout cage of
fig roots. When the tree has been strangled, the
strangler fig inherits its position.

Climbers include several species of lawyer vine, or
scrambling palm, the most obstructive of all vegetation,
equipped with prickly stems and long, hooked tendrils.
Tree ferns are plentiful. Staghorn and elkhorn ferns

grow outward from huge bowl-like holdfasts attached to tree trunk or branch; the holdfasts gather debris and the ferns may be said to grow in a soil of their own making.

The early morning is the best time to see birds, for then they are feeding actively. One of the tamest is the tiny yellow-breasted sunbird, often seen flitting among the scarlet hibiscus flowers. This dainty bird bears a superficial resemblance to a hummingbird.

The flame trees and umbrella trees reveal a number of different honey eaters tumbling among the blossoms. Scrub wrens and log runners rake over the debris of the forest floor. Gray and rufous fantails flutter about the low shrubbery, taking insects on the wing. Yellow and gray-headed robins drop down from their tree-trunk perches to pick up insects on the ground. The pied flycatcher hops around the gnarled trunks and vines. Whistlers and shrike thrushes search the branches and leaves. Topknot pigeons feed in the treetops. Occasionally a party of large white cockatoos will come screeching over a ridge and make their leisurely way down the valley.

Two elusive rain forest birds are the golden and tooth-billed bowerbirds. The golden bowerbird's display structure, built against small saplings, is huge. The walls are 3½ feet or more high, spaced about 2 feet apart, and there is a lichen-strewn runway elevated 10 inches or more. The male, brilliant gold and brown in color and about the size of a thrush, glows like a fireball as he displays. The toothbill, a plain brown bird, has a serrated beak, a development apparently associated with its habit of sawing off large leaves for use in its "circus-ring" play area on the jungle floor.

Cuscuses, bandicoots, and others

Three large birds of exceptional interest frequent the rain forest: The jungle fowl, the brush turkey, and the cassowary. All three will sometimes be seen crossing the jungle tracks or roads. The first two are mound-nest builders, depending on the heat generated by rotting vegetation to hatch the eggs. The mounds after some years of use may be enormous—40 to 50 feet across and 7 to 8 feet high.

Cassowaries, giant flightless birds, stand about 5 feet high. Their plumage is black; the head and neck are bare and mostly blue, and a large red wattle hangs from the foreneck. The wings are rudimentary, the legs very powerful; the inner toe has a greatly enlarged nail, used in defense. Cassowaries are shy and difficult to see in the scrub. When alarmed they run through the undergrowth with amazing speed. They feed mainly on berries and palm seeds. The young birds are striped. The cassowary is one of the many Australian animals that originated in New Guinea.

The Queensland rain forests are the home of several kinds of kangaroos and wallabies, three species of ring-tailed possums, the striped possum, two kinds of cuscuses, the tiger cat, the long-nosed bandicoot, and fruit bats. Most unusual of the kangaroos are the musk kangaroo, a stumpy marsupial that is the most primi-tive member of its family, and the tree kangaroo.

Tree kangaroos probably originated in New Guinea. Despite their bulk, they are not easily seen in the dense rain forest canopy. Tree kangaroos have lengthened forelimbs, long, sharp claws, and "skidproof" foot pads. The tail, however, is not prehensile and functions merely as a balancer.

Cuscuses are woolly arboreal marsupials with protruding eyes and small ears. They are nocturnal feeders, but are occasionally seen by day, curled up high in a tree. Most cuscus species occur in New Guinea.

The striped possum also is of New Guinea origin. It has thick, woolly fur, white on the back with three blackish-brown lengthwise stripes. One of its fingers is long and thin and has a long nail, a device for extracting insects from cracks in the bark.

One of the great delights of walks along rain forest trails is the sight of many butterflies. The majority of the 250 Australian species inhabit these northern forests. Most brilliant is the metallic blue and black Ulysses, or imperial, swallowtail. The large Cairns birdwing male is strikingly marked in yellow-green and black. Both butterflies have New Guinea relatives.

The exchange of plants and animals between Australia and New Guinea, once linked by a land bridge, has obviously gone on intermittently over a vast period of time. The Cape York Peninsula, which includes the Atherton Tableland and the Bellenden-Ker Plateau, is the channel through which most recent exchanges have taken place. Thus to visit Lamington and the other parks of northern Queensland is to sample the wonders of Australia's neighbor island.

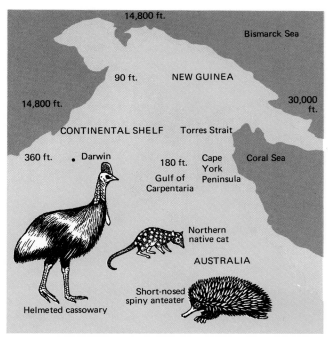

The helmeted cassowary, the northern native cat, and the spiny anteater were among the animals that moved freely between northern Australia and New Guinea over an ice age land bridge. Today they live on both sides of the shallow sea.

Wild Worlds

*Blowing antarctic snow partially conceals a colony of
Adélie penguins. In some of the worst weather in
the world—but in the least spoiled environment—Adélie
and emperor penguins live and raise their young.*

Desert, grassland, rain forest, polar tundra,
sea—each kind of habitat has its own complex
community of living things. Man and his
works have touched every spot in the world,
and no natural area is still completely wild.
But mingled with built-up and cultivated areas
are many fine wild places. Their preservation
for future generations should have priority.

The Vanishing Prairie

John Madson

The plows that broke North America's prairies almost brought about the demise of the wild grasslands. But scattered remnants worth saving can still be found.

The old-time American prairie was a grandmother's quilt of color and form shifting constantly as the wind breathed life into the grass. Novelist Willa Cather remembered Nebraska when "there was so much motion to it; the whole country seemed, somehow, to be running."

Why all that grass? Why, suddenly, in Indiana, did the land begin running out of trees?

Mostly, prairies are a matter of rainfall. Forests are in wet climate while grasslands are in drier country. The American plains and prairies lie in the rain shadow of the Rocky Mountains—a lofty barricade to the moisture-laden winds from the Pacific. Prevailing winds carry enough rain to grow grasses, but not forests.

But grasslands result not only from low rainfall but from evaporation caused by incessant exposure to wind, low relative humidity, and frequent high temperatures. The wind breaks twigs and leaves, and drives dust and sand against delicate tissues, abrading and tearing them. Wind shaking a plant increases its rate of transpiration —in a climate where a tree can't afford to lose too much water vapor.

Grasslands Around the World

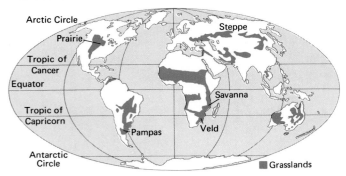

Covering about a quarter of the earth's total land surface, grasslands occupy much of the most productive land on the globe. The steppes of the U.S.S.R., the savannas of tropical Africa, the velds of southern Africa, the pampas of South America, and the prairies of North America are home to most of the world's hoofed animals and to vast numbers of birds.

Even at the eastern edge of the grasslands, where rainfall is sufficient to support trees, the dividing line is abrupt. Prairie is a closed community; tree seedlings can seldom live in prairie sod with its intense competition, crowding, and ground-level shading.

My feeling for tallgrass prairie is like that of a modern man who has fallen in love with the face in a faded tintype. Only the frame is still real; the rest is illusion and dream. So it is with the original prairie. Its beautiful face had faded before I was born, before I had a chance to touch and feel it, and all that I have known of the prairie is the setting and the mood—a broad sky of pure and intense light, with a sort of loftiness to the days, and the young prairie-born winds running past me from open horizons.

The tallest prairie grasses never reach their highest growth in the richest soils, but in lower, marshier land in the Eastern States. Where clay lies near the surface the big bluestem can grow to 12 feet. Cows can get lost in it and may be found by a mounted man only when he stands in the saddle.

The many kinds of grasses

The size of prairie grass is proportional to moisture. The dark green slough grass, called "ripgut" because of its saw-edged leaves, grows in dense stands on low flats. Indian grass is tall, coarse, and up to 8 feet high. Farther west, as rainfall diminishes, the well-drained uplands are home to the shorter midgrasses. Still farther west, with even less rainfall, midgrasses are replaced by the shortgrasses of the true plains, such as buffalo grass and blue grama.

The colors and texture of tallgrass prairies vary with the season and elevation. In early spring the pasque-flower, or prairie crocus, blossoms, not in sheltered woods but out in the big open where the wind cuts to the bone in late March. Then, one bright morning, the south-facing slopes look as if patches of spring sky had fallen on them, and you know that bird's-foot violets are in bloom.

Colors of the prairie

By early June daisies begin to appear, and larkspur and purple coneflower. There is a foot-high prairie lily with a red flower, and with this lily come clouds of prairie roses. Summer brings wild indigo, with its heavy, creamy blooms. White larkspur stands above many grasses; so do ox-eye daisies, sunflowers, goldenrod, and compass plants—the set of their oarlike leaves marking the prairie meridian. The autumn prairie flames with blazing star, tall purple spikes whose root bulbs were fed to Indian ponies to increase their speed and endurance.

But in color and form the grasses have the last word. By September they have lost their greens and have deepened into tones of gold and bronze. There are tawny stands of ripe Indian grass, patches of airy switch grass heavy with seed, and the wine-red fields of bluestem. As winter comes on the grasses bleach and fade, and the prairie world retrenches.

In a North Dakota wildlife refuge needle and thread, a midgrass, flourishes on the prairie beneath a June sky. In early summer, when groundbirds nest, grazers avoid this grass because of its sharp-pointed seeds but eat it the rest of the year.

North America's Prairies— Where They Grow and Why

Three types of prairie occur in North America—shortgrass, midgrass, and tallgrass. In the arid country just east of the Rocky Mountains is the shortgrass prairie, which slopes up to meet the foothills. To the east, where rainfall is more ample, are grass species that grow taller. Still farther to the east, in a region of still greater rainfall, is the tallgrass prairie. In past years these grasslands teemed with wildlife, including millions of bison, pronghorn antelopes, rodents, and birds. Now they are the most productive cattle and grain lands on earth, and the native vegetation and wildlife are largely gone. The map shows several places where original prairie remains on public lands in Canada and the United States.

Shortgrass prairie receives relatively little rainfall because prevailing westerly winds drop much of their moisture as they cross the Rocky Mountains. To the east the midgrass and tallgrass prairies receive more rainfall as moist air sweeps in from the north and south.

Rain or snow

Moist air   Dry air

Annual rainfall:
Rocky Mountains

10-20 in.
Short-grasses

20-30 in.
Mid-grasses

30-40 in.
Tall-grasses

The three types of prairie grasses— the shortgrasses, the midgrasses, and the tallgrasses—reflect the amount of moisture they receive. Toward the west native shortgrasses only grow up to 16 inches. To the east midgrasses may reach 4 feet; some tallgrasses tower 8 feet.

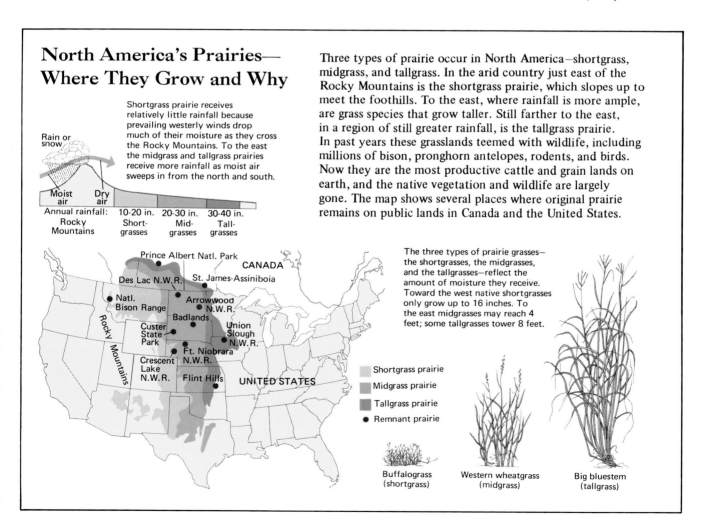

Prince Albert Natl. Park

CANADA

Des Lac N.W.R.

St. James-Assiniboia

Natl. Bison Range

Arrowwood N.W.R.

Badlands

Union Slough N.W.R.

Custer State Park

Ft. Niobrara N.W.R.

Crescent Lake N.W.R.

Flint Hills

UNITED STATES

Rocky Mountains

Shortgrass prairie
Midgrass prairie
Tallgrass prairie
Remnant prairie

Buffalograss (shortgrass)

Western wheatgrass (midgrass)

Big bluestem (tallgrass)

This tallgrass prairie once swarmed with wildlife. Out on the open ground were bison. There were bear, ruffed grouse, and turkeys in the forests, and deer and elk in and around the forest edges.

The openness of these prairies, and their frequent wetness, drew countless waterfowl: Ducks, geese, pelicans, sandhill cranes, whooping cranes, egrets, and whistling swans. Shorebirds came in vast spring clouds: In March and April golden plovers on their way from Argentina to the Arctic stopped on the prairie; the dark slopes were spangled with moving gold and silver as the great flocks of plovers fed.

Music for the settlers

Even without trees the prairie drew songbirds. There was our western meadowlark, singer laureate of the tallgrass prairie, almost identical with the eastern meadowlark but singing a longer and more tuneful song. Dickcissels and lark buntings sang from tall flower stalks; longspurs and bobolinks simply sang on the wing.

The first prairie pioneers settled in low-lying timber. Forests had building materials and fuel, clear streams, and abundant game. These settlers failed to see that these trees grew on the prairie's poorest soils and that forest soils were a thin veneer of fertility that was a delusion, for it would quickly erode without trees to stabilize it. But in spite of the prairie's strangeness, the pioneer farmers soon found that it was where the

Endangered Prairie Birds

Sandhill crane

Though protected by law, the greater sandhill crane is still hunted. Also the marshes where it nests are being drained.

Prairie falcon

Like other birds of prey, the prairie falcon suffers from disturbance of its nesting sites, from shooting, and from accumulated pesticides.

Attwater's prairie chicken

Only Texas still has any Attwater's prairie chickens. Reduction of habitat is their most serious problem.

action was. Farmers, using a walking plow with a three-horse team, could break the dense prairie sod with amazing efficiency.

During the early years of prairie settlement there were strange and primitive dangers. Tall prairie grasses, especially in dry autumns, became tinder of almost explosive quality. Prairies have always burned from fires set by lightning, and sometimes by man. The windless prairie fire would advance deliberately, marching across the grassland while tufts of bluestem vanished in puffs of flame. Coyotes and foxes exploited this, hunting before the flames to catch dispossessed mice and rabbits.

But if there was wind, there was a fire blizzard— one of the greatest horrors of prairie life. It came with walls of flame 30 feet high and a deep devouring roar, and the sun darkened and animals went mad. The glow of these great prairie fires could be seen for 40 miles, and showers of ash and flake would be carried that far ahead by the wind.

We spent our tallgrass prairie with a prodigal hand, and it probably had to be that way, for these are the richest farm soils in the world. But spending is one thing; bankruptcy is another. To destroy the last of the native prairie would be as criminally stupid as burning history books, for prairie is a chronicle of human courage, endurance, and victory, as well as a rich and complex natural system.

Original tallgrass prairie is the end point of 25 million years of evolution; it cannot be restored overnight, if indeed it can be restored at all. Imitation prairies have perhaps 30 plant species instead of the original 200 or more.

The Flint Hills prairie in Kansas has survived because beds of limestone lie so close to the surface that the land can't be plowed. It is heavily grazed, and has been for a hundred years, but it is still prairie, rolling in long waves from the Nebraska line down into the Osage Hills of Oklahoma. There is a proposal to create from it a Prairie National Park. It has all the elements —a splendid roll to the land, most of the original plants and animals, and enough physical dimension to look as prairie ought to look.

We need the big park. But we need prairie remnants, too, such as those surviving in fragments along old railroad rights-of-way and in neglected fence corners and farm lanes. Of the relic prairies that I know, none is as poignant as the tiny scrap that I found years ago in the center of an intensely farmed section of Iowa. It was a small, lost graveyard, all that remained of the little settlement of Bloomington, wiped out by diphtheria over a hundred years ago. About a dozen weathered stone markers leaned and lay in a patch of original bluestem. Among the graves were those of a young mother and her children, and when I found the place in late summer their graves were set about with a few tall magenta torches of blazing star, stateliest of all prairie flowers. It was part of an original time and place. That patch of tallgrass prairie was a more enduring memorial than the stones that stood there, and infinitely more appropriate.

The Bison: Symbol of the Prairie

For thousands of years the economy of North American Indians on the plains and prairies depended on the bison (buffalo): Bison meat was the principal source of protein; bison hides the principal material for clothing and shelter; bison dung, dried, the principal fuel; bison bones the principal tools. Whole villages searched for or followed bison herds; possessions were few and easily carried; and from century to century life remained much the same. The arrival of white settlers from the East changed everything. Bison were slaughtered to feed crews building railroads, to furnish hides for the leather industry, to make way for cattle and sheep— even, some hinted, to destroy the Indian way of life. In 1804 a sergeant with an expedition exploring the West described "verry large innumerable quantyties of buffalow." In 1885 Theodore Roosevelt, later President, met a rancher who in a 1,000-mile journey the previous year "was never out of sight of a dead buffalo, and never in sight of a live one." By 1900 the United States had only 20 wild bison, and poachers killed 16 of these. Fortunately, a few hundred had been preserved in zoos, and from them have come the herds now found in western national parks and wildlife refuges.

1500
1850
1870
1880
1906
O Large present-day herd

The bison's range was rapidly eroded, but its numbers are now increasing.

Driving a large number of bison over a cliff, especially in autumn, was one way Indians made sure of a meat supply for lean months ahead.

Indians began acquiring horses in the 17th century. The horses made them much more effective hunters and also made it possible for them to transport and to own more goods, thus raising their living standards.

This 1871 engraving shows a hazard of early travel on the Kansas Pacific Railway. A bison herd could hold up a train for hours; on the other hand, both passengers and crew appreciated the chance to break the trip with some shooting.

109

Hidden World of the Hedgerow

Ted Walker

For centuries British hedgerows have supported their own wildlife communities. Modern farming methods threaten both the hedges and their animal inhabitants.

I find it almost impossible to visualize an England devoid of hedgerows. Over the centuries they have created the essential Englishness of the English landscape—that patchwork effect of small and often irregularly shaped fields that provide such infinite variety to our countryside, whether hilly or flat.

Our forefathers transformed the landscape into a vast and subtly composed artifact of straight lines and curves dividing shape from shape, arable ground from pasture, color from color. Not, of course, that the planters of hedgerows had motives other than the strictly pragmatic ones of separating livestock from crops or establishing property boundaries. But what they created unwittingly was not only the characteristic face of the English pastoral scene but also a world in which some of our wild flora and fauna could survive and flourish.

It is unthinkable, then, that we should do away with all our ancient hedgerows. England would not be England without them. And yet this is precisely what we are doing at a rate that frightens and saddens me; for the stern practicality of the English farmer, to which we owe the existence of our huge network of hedges, is now turned toward destroying the creation of several centuries.

Modern husbandry doesn't need hedges. Not only are barbed wire, electric fences, and sheep netting

Animals of the Hedgerow

A hedgerow is at the same time a compact habitat and a wildlife pathway between woodlands. Some of Britain's hedgerows are many hundreds of years old; most date from the 18th century. There has been plenty of time for a stable community of wildlife to become established. Songbirds feed their young on weed seeds and insects; insects lay their eggs on tree leaves and weeds; small mammals burrow in the soil. Besides the permanent residents of the hedge, migrant birds visit the trees and bushes to harvest berries and seeds. Some crop-destroying insects live in hedgerows, but so do many insect eaters.

Whitethroat · Hawthorn · Blackbird · Hawthorn shield bug · Chinese character moth · Yellowhammer · Froghopper · Long-tailed tit · Orange-tip butterfly · Great green bush cricket · Hedge brown butterfly · Ladybird · Blackthorn · Hedge brown butterfly · Stinging nettle · Wren · Garden spider · Dog rose · Burnished brass moth · Garlic mustard · Hedgehog · Hedge sparrow · Grass snake · Common toad · Common shrew · Earthworm · Common wasp · Violet ground beetle · Wood mouse · Weasel

English hedgerows were originally planted to separate fields and pastures and to mark property lines, but they have actually accomplished much more: They serve as effective windbreaks and play an important part in soil and wildlife conservation.

quicker to erect and cheaper to maintain, they also have the extra advantage of being movable.

Five years ago it was estimated that there were upward of 600,000 miles of hedgerows in the whole of Britain. If the average width of a hedge is 2 yards, this mileage represents nearly a half million acres of habitats for birds, small mammals, insects, and flowers —an astonishingly large area, very much greater than all our national nature reserves put together. And the alarming fact is that we are grubbing up 2,000 miles of hedgerows every year.

Well, no doubt there will be infinitely worse problems for my children to face during their lifetime than the disappearance of hedgerows and the unique community they sustain. However, I would wish them to inherit from us more than just some artificially preserved remnant of the countryside. The not-so-distant prospect of England as a monotonous farmland relieved only by dead rivers and a thickening network of motorways appalls and saddens me. Also, I consider

it a huge responsibility that man should so heedlessly deprive the wild plants and animals of the living space he himself originally provided.

If now I write with nostalgia of a fast-vanishing scene, I hope that I do so without sentimentality. I see man as part of nature, a creature who can mold his environment according to his will. He has a duty toward his own kind, the future generations, and to the indigenous wildlife of his homeland. While I recognize the exigencies of modern farming methods and accept that land must be made available for housing and roads, I still believe that with thought and compassion we can achieve a satisfactory compromise of interests.

Man belongs to nature

One of the most disturbing aspects of this change on the farming scene is the very speed at which it is happening. When I was born, in the mid-1930's, the countryside still looked much as it looked before the Great War. True, farming was slowly becoming mechanized, but the days of free cropping (or movable fences), combine harvesters, battery houses for chickens, and the like were not yet dreamed of by the ordinary agricultural community.

I acquired most of my love and knowledge of nature from the endless mazes of hedgerows, as much a habitat for us gangs of marauding boys as they were for chaffinch, shrew, or honeysuckle. Deplorably I spent a good part of every springtime looking for birds' nests and robbing them. But we had an unwritten law, which

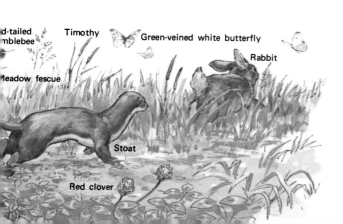

111

The Hedgerow Web of Life

The plants of the hedgerow—hawthorns, blackberries, stinging nettles, dog roses—support a surprisingly varied community with a complicated food web. Snails, caterpillars and other insects, and small rodents such as bank voles eat leaves; hedgehogs, voles, and insects eat berries; hedgehogs and voles eat insects; songbirds eat insects and berries; song thrushes and hedgehogs eat snails. Owls and hawks prey on rodents, songbirds, snails, and insects; foxes and weasels catch hedgehogs, rodents, and even insects. Actually most meat-eating animals sometimes eat grass and berries. Finally the lowly scavengers, such as earthworms, ground beetles, and bacteria, clean up the leftovers.

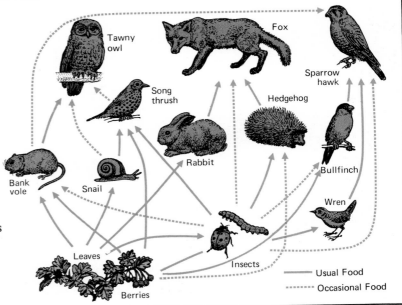

most of us, I think, obeyed, that you should never swipe more than one egg from any one nest.

All country people considered the hedgerows as a kind of unofficial extension of their gardens, to be harvested freely in due season. Autumn, of course, was the busy time. There were blackberries to be gathered, and hazelnuts to be picked and kept for Christmas; these were, and still are, the commonplace fruits of the hedgerow, and to this day we keep the annual rituals of blackberrying and nutting. There were elderberries for making dark, rich jelly or tart red wine, rose hips for a syrup to keep colds away, sloes from the blackthorn with which to make sloe gin, crab apples and wild pears, whose dry acidity was transformed by some alchemy into the most delicious conserve.

If we lose the countryside as we know it, of which the hedgerow is such a predominating feature, we are the first to lose. We could even affect the temperate nature of our climate, for the hedgerow network of England acts as a kind of gigantic and complex wind barrier against the blustery weather systems of the northeast Atlantic Ocean. But while we can be quick to adapt to a worsening situation, buying supermarket jam and deep-frozen Argentinean rabbits and turning to the national parks for our pleasure, the wild creatures to which we surely owe a living are losing not only their food but also a place to live.

As the plow turns up more and more grassland, certain species will be favored with the kind of open environment they prefer. The hares will prosper, as will the lapwings and skylarks and the semitame partridges. But the wild creatures that are inevitably bound to lose, because they need dense cover as a prerequisite of their way of life, are too numerous to mention. They are the birds and mammals (as well as the insects and flowers) that over the centuries have come to depend entirely on that linear extension of the woodland habitat, the hedgerow: blackbirds, fieldfares, redwings, robins, yellowhammers, whitethroats, hedge sparrows; and also, apart from the common rabbit, the voles and shrews, the badgers and foxes, the stoats and weasels. All of them, to a greater or lesser extent, have made the hedge bank their customary home. They cannot find alternative quarters in the roomier, open-plan fields created by the new farming methods; they require a more stable and permanently sheltered surrounding than is offered by the short period of crop growth, and they simply could not find the means to survive when the land reverts to winter bareness. There are no longer the rich pickings to be had from the stubble fields. There are fewer weeds and insects, and the chemicals

Young hedgehogs acquire their coats of tough spines by the time they are 3 weeks old. Their principal defense against predators is to roll into balls with spines erected. Hedgehogs build ground nests of leaves and grass, where they hide by day.

Originally a woodland nester, Britain's national bird, the robin, has invaded hedgerows and gardens. It searches for worms and insects on the ground. A year-round resident, it mates in winter, when both sexes defend territories.

Britain's smallest mouse, the harvest mouse, is only 2½ inches long and light enough to climb a wheat stalk. In winter it may dig a burrow beneath a hedgerow, but in spring and summer the female builds a grass nest aboveground for her young.

responsible for this are often deadly poison to wild creatures that ingest them.

Knowledge, together with public awareness and education, might yet save much of the English hedgerow and the life it supports. Ordinary people can, and do, alter the course of events such as this, once they are aroused. Some farmers have begun a benign policy of providing alternative habitats for wildlife, planting on those patches of ground that exist on all farms and cannot be used in the large-field system.

The Crown Estate Commissioners, who manage 155,000 acres of farmland in England, made an encouraging gesture when they began a system of payments to tenants for preserving trees—both those newly planted and those spared in trimmed hedgerows —and at the same time ordered that when hedges are removed in the interest of farm efficiency, twice the number of trees thus lost are to be planted elsewhere on the farm. What is now needed is strict Government legislation to limit the rate at which all other hedgerows are grubbed up and to require alternative and suitable cover to be planted as replacements.

Rural England will, in time, look different from the present patchwork effect, but it won't necessarily be displeasing, and it is a small price to pay for maintaining the priceless heritage of our wildlife. Nobody would suggest that farmers should subsidize the continuance of the English wild flora and fauna by keeping to the

agricultural methods of a past age. If they need to create larger, open fields, then we must all accept the fact that the face of the countryside is bound to change.

The British countryside must change

I believe that there is plenty of space still left in England where hedgerow habitats could be provided, in addition to the odd corners of farms where the large machines don't have room to maneuver efficiently. Municipal and suburban parks could provide more cover than they do, and so could the larger private gardens. Above all, I am certain that public authorities could do much with the considerable acreage of grounds that fall within their jurisdiction. Notably, the ever-increasing mileage of motorways should be bordered along their entire length by thick hedgerows as a matter of course. I have noticed that at least the rook and the kestrel have adapted well to living on the roadside pickings; the hedgehog has even lost its habit of rolling into a ball at the approach of danger, and instead runs for its life. Motorway hedgerows would be a boon to the driver, for they would soften the drab monotony of his journey.

Perhaps, then, there is reason for guarded optimism. There is room for us all, and none of us need be the loser, but it will take a sense of urgency, education, and goodwill—now, before we lose our chance.

In a maze of shifting loops and meanders a small tributary of the Amazon makes its way through the rain forest. A seemingly limitless expanse of green, the 2 million square miles of the Amazon Basin is the largest forest on earth.

Fabulous Forest of the Amazon

Lorus and Margery Milne

This forest harbors one of the greatest aggregations of wildlife on earth. Plants and animals occur in fantastic variety.

The first time we set foot on South America we stepped from the gangplank of a bauxite ore boat at a mining town in Surinam. Within hours we were afloat again in a dugout canoe powered by an outboard motor. Slowly we chugged upstream on the Cottica River far beyond any sign of civilization.

On both sides the dense rain forest came right to the river's edge, presenting a vertical wall of vegetation. Monkeys and macaws screamed at us from high trees. Over the water blue iridescent butterflies 5 inches across flitted erratically, rose above the forest canopy, and disappeared.

In much of South America the rivers are still the principal highway for human travel at ground level. And from a boat a traveler may get a false impression of the country through which he goes. Like the shrubs and trees landscaping a modern highway, the forest extends along the rivers. On the banks, with both light and moisture available, the undergrowth is likely to be dense. Even in drier regions the groundwater spreads out through the soil enough to support a narrow belt of trees, the gallery forest, perhaps only 10 to 50 yards wide.

From the northern coast the rain forest continues across much of Brazil for about 1,400 miles. Most of it has soggy soil, tall trees, and few people. Through it flow the tributaries of the largest river on earth, the mighty Amazon. This one broad basin occupies nearly a third of South America, collecting water from more than 2 million square miles. After the heaviest downpours, in January and February, the Amazon spreads out to a width of 50 to 60 miles, and by the time the melting snows from the mountains have been gathered, the river level has risen 30 to 40 feet above normal.

A tree on the flood plains of South America's great rivers needs a sturdy trunk to resist the current, as well as an extraordinary tolerance for having much of its trunk submerged for weeks or even months each year. Yet literally thousands of kinds of trees hold their place. To any visitor from the temperate zones walking over the muddy forest floor in dry season, the most astonishing feature is that on a given acre of ground there may be no two trees of the same species.

From these rain forests come trees important in commerce: the most desired among mahoganies; the Brazil-nut tree, which yields valuable timber as well as nuts; the silk-cotton tree, the source of kapok; and the cinchona tree, from the bark of which the Incas extracted bitter quinine to treat malaria.

During the wet season no one walks through the forests on the flood plains; instead, fish swim among the tree trunks. Some of these rain forest fish provide unusual hazards. Four kinds of piranhas attack wading animals and quickly strip them of flesh. An electric eel produces pulses as powerful as 600 volts to immobilize its prey or to defend itself against would-be predators.

Reptilian hunters

Crocodiles and caimans lurk at the surface of the rivers, with only their eyes and nostrils exposed as they wait for prey. A giant constrictor snake, the anaconda, drapes its heavy body, as much as 25 feet long, on sturdy tree limbs arching out over the water. Its victim may be a rain forest otter, 7 feet from tip of nose to tip of tail, searching for fish. Only the manatees, up to 400 pounds in weight, seem too big to be disturbed.

Most of the plants and animals in the rain forest live far above the floor. Every horizontal branch is loaded with orchids and other rootless perching plants. Some have enlarged storage organs for water and starch, which allow them to survive a dry season and then grow and bloom when the humidity increases.

Other brilliantly flowering air plants hold great quantities of rainwater in the whorled bases of their stiff leaves. Known as "tank epiphytes," they provide places for tiny aquatic animals high above the ground. Tadpoles of frogs and toads hatch from eggs deposited in these miniature ponds, and so do mosquitoes and other aquatic insects. On rainy days and nights, small crustaceans may climb the trees and make themselves

Tropical Rain Forests of the World

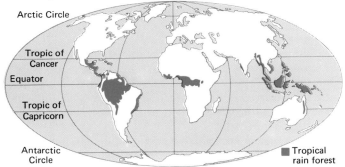

A diminishing resource as great trees fall to lumbering and agriculture, tropical rain forests still girdle the earth. From continent to continent plants and animals differ, but all require continuously high temperatures and humidity.

Layers of Life in a Tropical Rain Forest

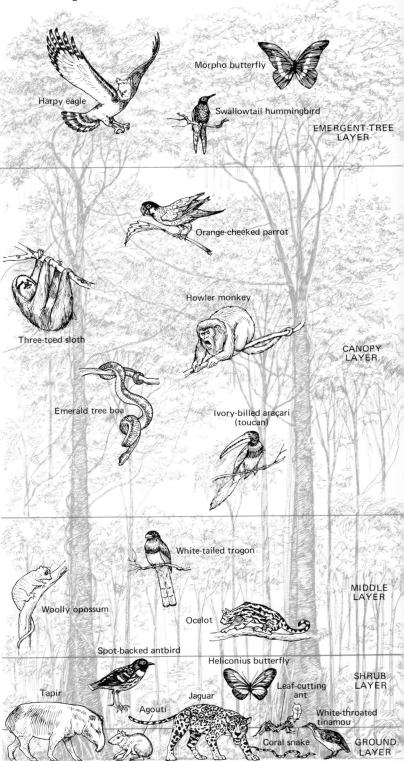

From sunlit tree crowns to the gloomy forest floor, each layer in a rain forest has its own distinct population of animals. Light, temperature, humidity, and the types of food available are some of the factors determining what lives where.

Born to the treetops, this young spider monkey (named for its spidery, immensely long limbs) rarely descends. A superb acrobat though its hands lack thumbs, it flies through the forest using its prehensile tail as a fifth arm.

Able to swallow a deer, the anaconda of the Amazon is South America's largest boa constrictor, sometimes reaching a length of 20 feet or more. It lies in ambush among aquatic vegetation and seizes hapless mammals or birds.

at home in the tank epiphytes; one species of crab has been found only in such tanks.

Vying with the flowers for space on the tree limbs are ferns, mosses, liverworts, and lichens. In combination the plants perching on a single branch may weigh a ton and hasten the day when the whole branch will break off and, with its load of life, crash to the ground. Probably fungi, wood-boring beetles, and termites will have weakened the structure. Sometimes a whole tree collapses, usually knocking down several smaller trees in its path.

A bare floor

In dry season these calamities in the rain forest benefit the peccaries, wild pigs that find an abundance of food among the broken branches. But soon the floor is clean again, just bare slippery mud. It is not only the dim light that discourages new growth. In the constantly high humidity and temperature, organic material decays rapidly, and the almost daily rains, even in dry season, wash everything away.

Vines growing on trees tie together the forest canopy; their roots may extend 150 feet to reach the ground. The animals of the high trees use the vines as travel routes. Only here do animals of so many kinds have prehensile tails, used like an extra hand. The various kinds of monkeys are all experts at hanging by their tails. Tree porcupines, kinkajous, tree anteaters, and most of the opossums are similarly equipped. The emerald boa constrictor, hanging by its prehensile tail, can catch birds in flight.

The sloth has virtually no tail, but its hooked claws support its upside-down body so well that even after it dies it may hang in place for days or weeks. The large, crested harpy eagle takes monkeys and sloths as its favorite prey. Rarely does the bird fly *over* the rain forest. Instead, it darts and dodges among the branches.

The rain forest has an incredible variety of birds, including dozens of species each of hummingbirds, flycatchers, and tanagers. The derby flycatcher or kiskadee catches fish as well as insects. The dully colored, 2-foot hoatzin is of special interest because the young have hooks on their wings like those of the oldest bird fossil known, *Archaeopteryx.* The hooks are used in climbing about the trees. Since the nests are always located on branches over water, the young throw themselves overboard if they are disturbed, swim to shore, and climb back up the tree.

The South American parrots called macaws are the noisiest birds in the world and as colorful as they are noisy. The bright bills of toucans may be as long as their bodies; the bills, much lighter in weight than they appear, reach for berries at the end of small tree branches.

The Amazonian rain forest has more kinds of bats than any other area its size in the world. A few hide in caves by day but more sleep in the trees, clustering on the trunks. The tent-building bat may use its sharp teeth to cut a leaf until the leaf folds over and provides a shelter. Most of the bats feed on fruit and nectar,

An adroit plucker of fruits and berries, the toucan manages its enormous bill with ease. Actually the bill is very light—the horny surface covers a network of bony threads. More than a dozen toucan species inhabit the Amazon rain forest.

incidentally pollinating the plants. But fishing bats, skimming the surface of streams, snatch fish without stopping, and vampire bats lap blood from other mammals or from birds whose skin they have slit with a painless bite.

Insects of the forest

A few kinds of ants nest underground. The leaf cutters bite off pieces of foliage, which they carry through tunnels to subterranean chambers as large as a bushel basket. Fungi grow on the compost thus prepared and furnish almost the sole food of the ants. Before a virgin female goes out on her mating flight she stuffs into her cheeks samples of fungus, which inoculate the compost in her new nest.

Day-flying moths and night-flying butterflies occur in the rain forest among others with more usual habits. Two moth species, each with a wingspan up to 12 inches, hold the record for size among modern insects. Click butterflies sound like crackling paper when they fly, but no one knows what produces the sound. The wings of glass-winged butterflies are transparent except for spots or lines of color, so that they look like petals blown in the wind.

Many lasting changes have already come to the New World tropics, and others are sure to come. Brazil's new highway-building program is posing the most serious threat the Amazonian rain forest has ever had to face. One naturalist compares even the narrowest road to a razor cut on the skin—a focus for infection. The people of Brazil need and must have economic development. But those who deplore the destruction that has impoverished so much of the rest of the world, where landslides follow strip mining and dust storms follow sod breaking, will devoutly hope that Brazil will be wiser in its development.

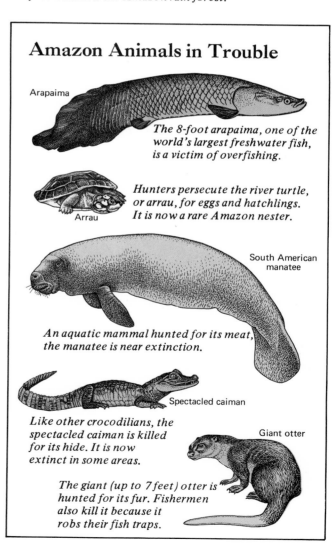

Amazon Animals in Trouble

Arapaima

The 8-foot arapaima, one of the world's largest freshwater fish, is a victim of overfishing.

Arrau

Hunters persecute the river turtle, or arrau, for eggs and hatchlings. It is now a rare Amazon nester.

South American manatee

An aquatic mammal hunted for its meat, the manatee is near extinction.

Spectacled caiman

Like other crocodilians, the spectacled caiman is killed for its hide. It is now extinct in some areas.

Giant otter

The giant (up to 7 feet) otter is hunted for its fur. Fishermen also kill it because it robs their fish traps.

Near the Xingu River, a brother and sister, members of an Indian family, play with a pet macaw. In this area Brazil has set up an enormous reserve for forest Indians; scattered tribes are encouraged to move there for protection.

Brazil's pioneer highway was planned to draw the Amazon's vast assets, including minerals, into the national economy.

A Land Besieged– The South American Rain Forest

The Amazon River and its many tributaries flow through the greatest rain forest in the world. Tropical rain forests are so lush, so rich in diversity of animals and plants, that they have always tempted land-hungry men. But once the forest's trees are removed, the heavy tropical rains wash the nutrients and humus out of the scanty topsoil; the subsoil

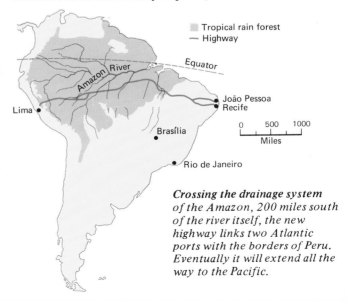

Crossing the drainage system of the Amazon, 200 miles south of the river itself, the new highway links two Atlantic ports with the borders of Peru. Eventually it will extend all the way to the Pacific.

118

Watched by his family, a Bolivian Indian from the highlands clears forest land in the Amazon Basin. Like many other emigrants, he hopes to eke out a living by "slash-and-burn" farming.

A natural forest is a nearly closed system: Most of the nutrients in it are recycled indefinitely. Planting for crops disturbs the soil and encourages erosion; harvesting forever removes some of the nutrients and impoverishes the system, which produces less and less.

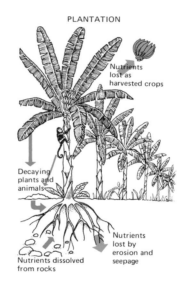

PLANTATION

Nutrients lost as harvested crops

Decaying plants and animals

Nutrients dissolved from rocks

Nutrients lost by erosion and seepage

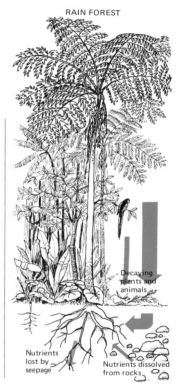

RAIN FOREST

Decaying plants and animals

Nutrients lost by seepage

Nutrients dissolved from rocks

quickly turns to rocklike clay, useless for agriculture because it cannot be plowed.

With the building of the 3,400-mile Trans-Amazon Highway and its feeder roads, this previously undeveloped rainforest region, which covers a quarter of South America, has been opened up to the exploiters. Small river villages have become booming frontier towns. Large lumbering outfits are cutting 3 million trees a year. Following the log cutters and bulldozers, "slash-and-burn" farmers move in to raise a few crops before the soil is depleted. The most remote areas are now invaded by hunters and wild-animal dealers in search of endangered species, despite Government attempts to protect them. The primitive jungle Indians are perhaps the most endangered of all.

One of South America's best known products, cattle graze from one end of the continent to the other. Cattlemen utilize the extensive grasslands for this purpose, but in addition vast areas of rain forest are being cut and turned into ranchland.

The Fragile Northland

William O. Pruitt, Jr.

Animals of the Arctic live in a precarious balance with the environment. If technology upsets this balance, some may not survive.

One late July afternoon I was returning to my field camp north of Beverly Lake in the Northwest Territories of Canada. I trudged wearily along a ridge, thinking of the mug of strong, scalding hot tea I would have back at camp. I idly noted the boulder-strewn hillside in the distance. But wait! The hillside had been a smooth brownish-green that morning. Those were not boulders; the whole hill was covered with caribou.

My visions of a rest vanished as I hurried to place myself and my camera in the path of this mighty river of caribou (*la foule*, the throng) that was flowing across the tundra landscape. I hid behind a large rock, set up the movie camera, and awaited the throng. It flowed over the next ridge, down the slope, and around a small lake in the valley. Some caribou stopped to drink, some waded out and began to swim across, others swept around the edges. They spread over the marsh and then fanned out around the base of the hill from which I watched. As the thousands of hooves came up the hill, the very ground vibrated. My head was filled with the sound of the throng—the dull roar of the footfalls, a higher rattling roar as each hoof tendon clicked and popped at every step, a cacophony of sneezes, coughs, grunts, and snorts.

The throng split and surrounded me except for a narrow corridor directly downwind. A few bolted from my scent, the movement spread to a hundred, then a thousand. The roar increased as the river of caribou became a thundering torrent. The current slackened, and the stream resumed its inexorable flow. I admit that I was a bit nervous; my rock seemed a ridiculously tiny fortress. But I was seeing, hearing, smelling, and feeling the throng, a gathering of living creatures the like of which few men alive today have experienced. Only in the North and on the plains of East Africa can a spectacle such as this still be seen.

The nearly empty North

In popular literature the picture of the North is a projection of this once-in-a-lifetime experience. In adventure yarn and tourist promotion the North is presented as a hunters' paradise, teeming with moose, caribou, and grizzly, or as a place where the misfit can make a quick fortune trapping mink, marten, and white fox.

Nothing could be further from the truth. The North is in actual fact poor in animals per acre. The vast herd that surrounded me comprised about one-quarter of all the caribou in mainland Canada. Although they were antler to antler in my field of view, I could have traveled for hundreds of miles in any direction without seeing another caribou.

The tundra (a Finnish term) is a treeless, rigorous region, and animals that live in it must overcome two tough conditions. First, during three-quarters of the year, most animals can't find food. Sedges or lichens may be there but be quite inaccessible under the rock-hard, wind-beaten snow. Second, the time when animals can breed and raise their young is extremely short. Arctic animals have necessarily evolved different ways to cope with the problems.

The answer of caribou, close relatives of reindeer, is to keep moving, with the result that they do not deplete the slow-growing lichens on which they feed. In north central Canada the caribou migrate more than 1,000 miles each year, spending the winter in the sparse coniferous forest bordering the tundra and traveling northward in the spring. At the end of the spring migration fawns are born; by the age of 1 or 2 days they can run as fast as their mothers.

Because of extraordinarily effective insulation furnished by a coat of long hollow hairs underlaid by short woolly fur, caribou are virtually unaffected by low temperatures. Indeed, their one weakness lies in the

The Eskimo Curlew's Flight to Oblivion

The Eskimo curlew is a smallish wading bird (about 11 inches).

The curlew's annual migration spans 20,000 miles—a migration second only to the arctic terns'.

■ Breeding area

— Migration route

North America

South America

0 1,000
Miles

Huge flocks of Eskimo curlews once flew between the South American pampas and the North American tundra, arriving in their breeding area in May and leaving in July. Victims of incredible slaughter, the birds were thought to be extinct; recent sightings indicate a remnant population.

Crowding together on a lingering patch of snow, barren-ground caribou in Alaska seek relief from the hordes of biting summer insects. Several races of caribou roam the tundra and taiga (northern forest) of Alaska, Canada, and Greenland. The closely related but smaller reindeer range over much of northern Europe and Asia; domesticated reindeer are used for food, clothing, and transportation. Caribou and reindeer are the only kinds of deer with antlers on both sexes. The females have shorter antlers with fewer branches than those of the males.

tendency toward overheating with violent exercise; this makes them vulnerable to being chased by aircraft.

Caribou are exceedingly important to man; their meat ranks with the finest, and their skins make the best clothing for the arctic climate. Unfortunately, since the arrival of Europeans in the Far North the caribou herds have been vastly overhunted, and their numbers are probably about one-twentieth of those reported by the early explorers.

Aside from man, the chief predator of the caribou is the wolf. When wolves are not hunting, they move freely through the bands of caribou, and the caribou merely walk out of the way. But when they are hunting, the caribou sense it and flee. When a band flees as a unit, wolves seldom pursue. If, however, a caribou falters, limps, or lags behind, it is immediately pursued even though other caribou may be closer. The rest of the band stands about, watching the big show. The chase is usually short and successful since wolves rarely pursue an animal that has not shown some sign of infirmity. The remaining caribou soon regain their composure; the impact of the experience is mercifully short.

The leftovers from a wolf's kill of caribou are food for grizzly bears and wolverines. In addition to scavenging, these animals dig out voles and ground squirrels; the grizzly often grazes on grass.

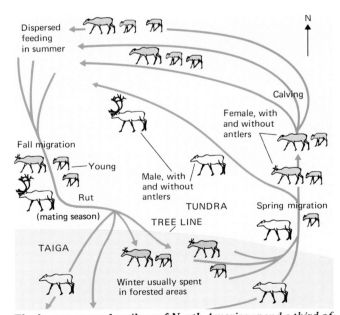

The barren-ground caribou of North America spend a third of the year in migration, moving to seasonal feeding areas and escaping from early spring insects and summer heat. After wintering in taiga forests caribou move into the tundra. Pregnant females lead this migration, giving birth in long-established calving grounds. In August the herds disperse.

121

Caribou

Short-tailed weasel

Polaris fritillaries

Willow ptarmigans

Black gyrfalcon

Collared lemmings

Arctic hares

Arctic fox

Snowy owls

Animals of the Tundra

Under the nearly continuous sunshine of the arctic summer, tundra plants and animals make up for months of scarcity. Flies, mosquitoes, and butterflies abound. About 100 species of birds nest on the tundra in summer, but only a few, such as snow buntings and rock and willow ptarmigans, remain year-round. With the arrival of shorter days and cold some tundra mammals migrate to places with more plentiful food; those that stay grow thick winter coats.

Coping with the Deep Snow and Extre

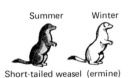

Summer   Winter

Short-tailed weasel (ermine)

Tipped by a dark tail, a white winter coat conceals the ermine as it hunts arctic hares on the snow-covered tundra.

Summer

Winter

Arctic hare

On the Canadian mainland the arctic hare changes color with the seasons; in the far north the hare is white year-round.

The wolverine is a large, powerfully built weasel with marvelous endurance and tenacity. Once, from the air, I followed a wolverine's trail on an undeviating straight line for nearly 20 miles. It ran uphill and down as if following a ruled line across a map. I have seldom seen wolverines walk. They seem to have only two gears: stop and full speed ahead.

Two kinds of foxes

Foxes prey on the smaller tundra animals: red foxes nearer forested areas and white, or arctic, foxes where there is more likely to be year-round snow cover. Both kinds eat whatever is in season: Voles, ground squirrels, birds' eggs, fish, or carrion. One important food source for arctic foxes is the remains of polar bear kills. Foxes scavenge the beaches and regularly patrol the bases of cliffs for eggs or chicks that might have fallen from the nesting ledges above. The long, thick, fluffy fur of the arctic fox furnishes such perfect insulation that the fox does not need to increase its food intake in winter.

Lemmings and hares are among the small vegetarians of the tundra. Lemmings are famous for their population explosions; in good years their great fecundity takes them just short of permanent damage to their range, and then they die off and the vegetation has a chance to recover.

One kind of lemming, the collared lemming, usually turns white in winter, one of two rodents to do

so. (Some collared lemmings on Alaskan islands that have a milder climate do not change color; their coat color continues to match the brown soil and vegetation.) In Eurasia the collared lemming is called the hooved lemming, since in winter it grows two long, double-pointed claws on each front foot—possibly an adaptation for digging through snow.

Some hares also turn white in winter, though arctic hares of the Far North are white all year. In those regions where the vegetation is too poor to support many caribou, arctic hares seem to take their place as grazers and sometimes occur in herds of as many as a hundred animals.

The amazing musk-ox

Of all mammals the musk-ox seems to be the most perfectly adapted to the tundra. Through the dense wool undercoat grow the guard hairs, which are so long in fully mature animals that they sweep the ground and form a "skirt." The musk-ox is almost totally covered with this insulation.

In summer musk-oxen congregate in the river valleys and feed on the willows and grasses. In winter they move to the windswept uplands where the vegetation, though sparse, is not covered with snow. They usually live in small herds of 10 to 20 animals.

As long as a musk-ox remains part of a social group, it is virtually immune to predation. A band standing

Musk-oxen

Pin-tailed ducks

Red-throated diver (loon)

Timber wolves

Whistling swans

Arctic terns

Grizzly bears

ld of the Long Arctic Winter

Summer

Winter

Willow ptarmigan

One of the few birds that remain on the tundra all year, the willow ptarmigan grows feathery "snowshoes" during the winter. Its feathers also change color.

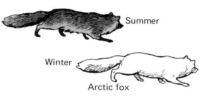

Summer

Winter

Arctic fox

The thick fur of the arctic fox turns white in the winter. This bushy-tailed hunter-scavenger stores food for the winter in rock crevices, eating its caches during lean times.

Summer

Winter

Collared lemming

A rodent that turns white in winter, the collared lemming finds warmth and plant food by tunneling in the snow. The claws on its front feet are enlarged in winter.

firm and presenting the attacker with a circle of sharp, recurved horns is highly effective against wolves and bears, though helpless against man. The musk-ox was exterminated in Alaska by about 1865; the Canadian musk-ox population, totally protected since 1917, is now recovering slowly from the earlier hunting. Most of the animals are now on the Canadian islands in the Arctic Ocean.

In climates more hospitable than the Arctic, a great diversity of plants and animals can thrive comparatively easily. Under ordinary conditions all the living things in such climates serve as a set of checks and balances

for each other, and together they provide stability. After a fire or flood or even an earthquake, such an area heals itself, given half a chance.

In the Arctic only a few species have been able to find a formula for survival. The community has a hair-spring kind of balance; a disturbed area may take more than a century to recover. It would be too easy for modern man to ruin the Arctic within a few seasons, making it unfit for both man and beast. We must very carefully consider the ecological implications of all schemes for developing the Far North; the future of the tundra depends on decisions we make now.

Why Is There a Midnight Sun?

If the earth's axis of rotation were perpendicular to its orbit around the sun, each part of the earth would have 12 hours of light and 12 hours of darkness all year. But since the axis is actually tilted, between March 21 and September 21 the North Pole is turned toward the sun, and within the Arctic Circle there is continual light; at the same time the South Pole is dark. For the other 6 months the situation is reversed, and the Southern Hemisphere has more hours of daylight than hours of darkness.

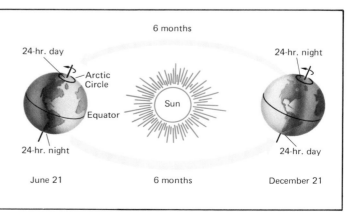

6 months

24-hr. day

Arctic Circle

Equator

Sun

24-hr. night

June 21

24-hr. night

24-hr. day

6 months

December 21

Man and the Polar World

Eskimos are the only people who have managed to live in harmony with the polar environment. European man has spared the poles no more than the land in gentler climates. Steller's sea cow and the great auk have long been extinct in the Arctic; many species, both northern and southern, are dangerously close to vanishing. Whales and bears are overhunted. Junk litters the shores near arctic and antarctic bases.

A pipeline in Siberia is blocking the migration of reindeer, and no one knows whether the new pipeline in Alaska will do the same thing to caribou. Mercury originating in the Northern Hemisphere is showing up in antarctic seals. But for most of the environment and nearly all the animals, the point of no return has not yet been reached, and wise action now could reverse the downward trend.

After shooting a walrus, Eskimo hunters pull alongside the ice to collect the carcass. Walruses and seals furnish hides for leather and fur garments, as well as meat and blubber for food. Sled dogs, necessary for transportation, eat the scraps.

An Eskimo hunter aims at fleeing caribou, which will furnish meat, clothing, tools, and tent material. In a land of few natural resources caribou are so important to the traditional life of Eskimos that the Government does not apply hunting restrictions to them.

Littering an antarctic shore, a tangled mass of plastics and rusted metal, left by a base devoted to scientific research, occupies a corner of a penguin rookery. Near the poles processes of decay and growth proceed at a slow rate; discarded materials last a long time, and no vegetation ever covers them.

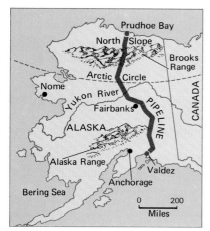

For 789 miles across mountains, rivers, and plains, the Alaskan pipeline will carry 2 million barrels of hot oil a day from Prudhoe Bay to ice-free Valdez.

Called Christmas trees, these valves cap exploratory oil wells on the tundra of Alaska's North Slope. Discovered in 1968, the Alaskan oil field is one of the largest known petroleum accumulations in the world. Its exploitation will have an immense economic and ecological effect on the area.

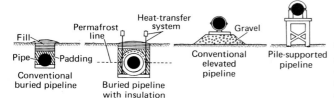

The design of the Alaskan pipeline has been influenced by the permanently frozen ground it must traverse. Heat from a conventionally buried pipeline would thaw the tundra permafrost, risking damage to the pipe and an oil spill. In areas of permafrost the Alaskan pipeline will either be elevated or buried with extra insulation; heat-transfer systems will sometimes be used to draw off excess heat.

Workers on a Japanese whaling ship process a baleen whale caught in antarctic waters. This modern floating factory is equipped with powerful winches for handling the enormous carcasses. Whales are located by sonar and killed by gunners firing cannon-propelled harpoons. These efficient methods (used by the whaling fleets of Japan and the Soviet Union, both of which operate in the Antarctic) have placed great pressure on the populations of all whale species.

Life on the Coldest Continent

Joseph M. Dukert

Remote from the everyday life of most of the world, Antarctica remains relatively wild and unspoiled.

Fluffy gray emperor penguin chicks hatched in the winter are half grown by late spring but still depend on their parents for food. The chicks cannot swim and catch their own food until water-repellent feathers have replaced their down.

Last night began in March. Not until the fourth week in September did the bright yellow edge of the sun peek over the horizon again at the South Pole. Gold spilled across a snowfield nearly 2 miles deep.

Antarctica is still an empty place, its human population scattered over more than 5 million square miles. Nature's cruelty and caprice make it dangerous in any season. But it's no longer accurate to call Antarctica a frontier. Its highest mountains have been climbed, and there is no place on its surface that man cannot reach—usually in relative comfort.

Distance and climate long kept man away from Antarctica, and this fact explains much of its value today. Its rocks, ice, and fossils, and the plant and animal life that evolved there, represent a fresh book of natural history.

The Great White Continent is nearly twice as large as Australia and has more variety than most people realize. Its snow-free "oases" are warmer than the areas around them, but hardly as lush as the name suggests: Their temperatures drop to −70°F.

Some oases contain freshwater ponds fed by melting ice; one oasis has a lake that never freezes because it is so salty, another a lake, normally covered by year-round freshwater ice, with salty bottom waters at a temperature close to 80°F. Each of these anomalies—as well as others—offers a challenge to biologists. So far, however, the search for life in these waters has located little more than microscopic plankton, usually nourished by bird droppings.

The Emperor Penguin's Year

FALL

Emperor penguins come onto ice

Penguins pair off and mate

Males huddle as they incubate eggs

All penguins feed in sea

SUMMER

WINTER

Females feed in sea

After molting chicks and adults go to sea

Chicks stay in crèche while parents hunt

Parent feeds chick

SPRING

For 2 months in winter the male emperor incubates an egg; the female returns from the sea at about hatching time. Both parents feed the chick, which joins a group of young penguins called a crèche. In summer all emperors feed in the sea.

Adélie penguins walk unconcernedly around leopard seals basking on the ice (left). But in the water these seals are the Adélie penguins' chief predators, and the birds stay away from the ice edge when they spot a patrolling seal (right).

In the dry valleys of Antarctica, where there is no snow cover protecting the surface from 100-mile-an-hour winds, most of the gray and tan soil remains lifeless. Yet even here, in the surprisingly moist permafrost less than a foot below the surface, researchers have found ancient microplants and bacteria. Some look as if they had been "freeze-dried," and of these some are capable of being restored to life.

The most important limiting factor for native plant life in Antarctica is not cold but drought. Many spots along the coast and on the Antarctic Peninsula, which is directly south of South America, experience summer-time temperatures in the high 30's, the 40's, and even the 50's. Volcanic action produces local heating. Furthermore, dark areas anywhere absorb solar heat readily, and the surface of a rock or of a peat bed may be fairly warm even with subzero air temperatures just above it. But rain falls only in the peninsula area, and even there the total precipitation from both snow and rain averages only 17 inches a year. On much of the polar plateau, the fresh snow each year is the equivalent of less than 3 inches of water.

Few plants in Antarctica

Not a single, stunted tree survives anywhere in Antarctica, though the presence of coal proves that it was not always treeless. The meager soil does support some hundreds of different kinds of colorful lichens as well as a few tiny mushrooms among the mosses. Algae sometimes splash the snow with green, yellow, or red. Near the tip of the Antarctic Peninsula there are some low-growing grasses and a single kind of flowering herb in small numbers. Botanists are convinced that some grass species now on the peninsula did not evolve

there; they were brought by winds or by sealers or whalers during the 19th century.

Lichens are relics of the ice ages. They constitute a major part of antarctic vegetation and are amazingly adaptable. Laboratory studies show that the antarctic varieties, frozen rapidly by liquid nitrogen, exhibit no ill effects after thawing. But antarctic plants develop slowly; photographs of the same lichen patch in successive seasons seem to show no growth at all.

The growing season for mosses on rock peaks near the South Pole may last only an hour or two a day for a few weeks during the year. Despite occasional temperature changes of 75°F. within a few hours—and a range twice as great as that in the course of a year—these primitive plants survive and provide shelter and food for simple animal life. Tiny insects and mites dwell there in a remarkable microcosm, spending most of their time in hibernation.

No freshwater fish has been discovered in Antarctica, and not a single land vertebrate is a native there today. The amphibians and reptiles of the distant past are known only by their fossilized bones. The largest living land animal is a wingless fly only one-eighth of an inch long.

Penguins, the trademark of the Antarctic, are sea birds with wings blunted into paddles. They drink directly from the ocean and expel salt through glands just above their eyes. Giant prehistoric penguins were almost as big as a man, but for some reason they have disappeared as completely as the great auks of the Northern Hemisphere. Besides the familiar emperor and Adélie penguins that live at many points along the coast, petrels, skuas, cormorants, and other birds nest on the continent.

The Antarctic Web of Life

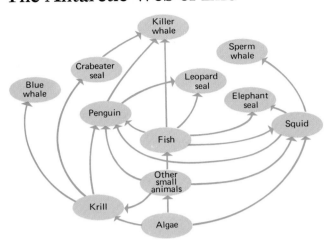

At the base of the antarctic food web are algae and other tiny plants. Only the smallest animals can live directly on them; all the rest are predators. The Antarctic Ocean supports one of the heaviest concentrations of animals in the world.

Huge, snouted elephant seals inhabit islands well north of Antarctica, but some come to the mainland every year—usually at molting time. These lumbering mammals grow to more than 20 feet in length and 4 tons in weight. Some smaller seals are full-time antarctic residents: the gentle-eyed Weddell and the voracious leopard seal, the elusive Ross's seal, which sings solitary songs from atop the ice floes, and the most numerous of all, the crabeater seal.

Human visitors to Antarctica

More than 20 tourist excursions have headed for Antarctica since the late 1950's. By the end of the 1970's, the number of commercial visitors annually will probably run to thousands instead of hundreds. Without careful briefing, those well-intentioned tourists could cause trouble.

Most people who have visited the Antarctic during this century have respected nature. The international Scientific Committee on Antarctic Research protects significant breeding and botanical sites and examples of complete ecosystems of flora and fauna. Helicopters

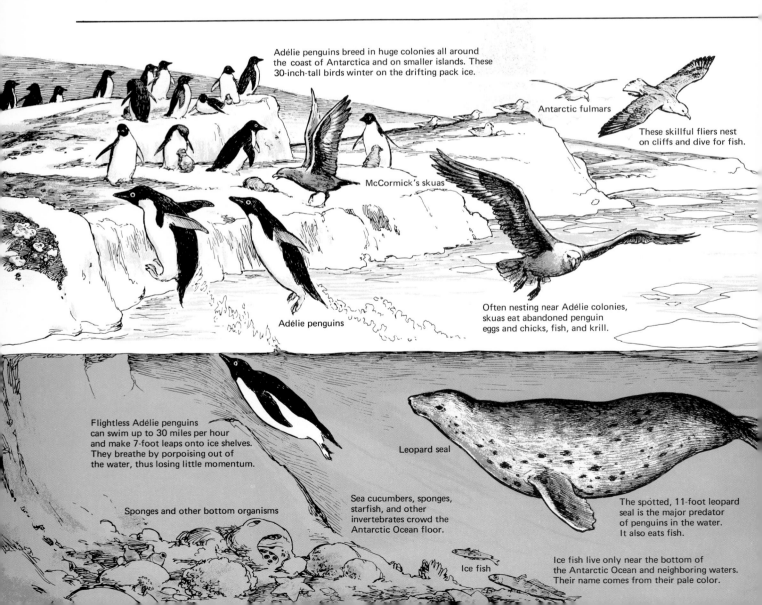

Adélie penguins breed in huge colonies all around the coast of Antarctica and on smaller islands. These 30-inch-tall birds winter on the drifting pack ice.

Antarctic fulmars

These skillful fliers nest on cliffs and dive for fish.

McCormick's skuas

Adélie penguins

Often nesting near Adélie colonies, skuas eat abandoned penguin eggs and chicks, fish, and krill.

Flightless Adélie penguins can swim up to 30 miles per hour and make 7-foot leaps onto ice shelves. They breathe by porpoising out of the water, thus losing little momentum.

Leopard seal

Sponges and other bottom organisms

Sea cucumbers, sponges, starfish, and other invertebrates crowd the Antarctic Ocean floor.

The spotted, 11-foot leopard seal is the major predator of penguins in the water. It also eats fish.

Ice fish

Ice fish live only near the bottom of the Antarctic Ocean and neighboring waters. Their name comes from their pale color.

aren't supposed to land within 650 feet of animal concentrations, and other sources of unnecessary noise are forbidden. During breeding periods of seals and birds, there is an official caution against "persistent attention from persons on foot."

Nonnative mammals have already transformed South Georgia, Marion, Kerguelen, and Macquarie Islands, as well as other islands near the continent. Apart from men, these animals include cats, rabbits, sheep, and even reindeer. The idea of alien species becoming feral in Antarctica isn't preposterous—when a Japanese expedition left its sled dogs behind at its Antarctic base, two of the dogs managed to survive the entire following winter on the continent.

A time of decision for the Antarctic

The time is fast approaching for irreversible decisions affecting antarctic conservation. Some countries are taking a new interest in the old sealing grounds. An antarctic animal with a mounting price on its head is the plentiful krill, a colorful crustacean about 2 inches long at maturity, which covers acres of ocean in dense swarms. Individual whales used to eat krill by the ton. Now there are few whales left, but Russians fish for the krill commercially to make edible products from it, and both Japan and the United States are looking in that direction. Some penguins eat krill. So do seals. Krill probably could be cropped by man, but he had better do it with some care—as to both the size and the locale of the catch.

In the 1970's the Antarctic will see a new scientific approach. Biochemists are analyzing the protein "antifreeze" that keeps fish and certain insects from turning to ice. Behaviorists are studying the way penguins protect themselves from their natural enemies—skuas, leopard seals, and killer whales. Scientists from Australia, France, the Soviet Union, the United Kingdom, and the United States are collaborating in a broad scrutiny of a vast antarctic ice-cap area to determine whether normal climate cycles and the effects of global industrialization are changing the size of the ice cap. The new day is upon us. Antarctica holds dazzling opportunities. Unless we are apathetic or unthinking, its "day" need never end.

Antarctic Animals Depend on the Sea

Antarctica—most of it under miles of ice and all of it dark for 6 months of the year—is the most unproductive continent on earth. A very few plants and insects growing in a minute area make up the total offering of food on land. But the turbulent ocean, constantly oxygenated by winds and conflicting currents, is richer in sheer tonnage of living things than any tropical jungle. In summer microscopic plants color the edges of the ice shelf and thousands of square miles of water. Tiny floating animals, about half of them the 3-inch krill, make up an estimated 10 billion tons.

Blue whale
The largest whale is solitary.

Killer whales
Feared predators, 30-foot killer whales travel in packs of as many as 40.

Weddell seals
Among the most skillful divers in the Antarctic, Weddell seals catch fish and squid at depths that exceed 1,500 feet.

Storm petrels patter on the water as they peck at the surface for krill.

Wilson's storm petrel

The most numerous of antarctic seals are the crabeater seals, which grow to lengths of 9 feet. Their main food is not crabs but krill; the seals are, in turn, preyed upon by killer whales.

Krill

Dense swarms of the shrimplike krill feed primarily on algae.

Crabeater seal

Emperor penguin

Squid are numerous in antarctic waters and apparently occur at all depths. Although they are fast swimmers and their large eyes enable them to see well, most vertebrates in the sea, including penguins, seals, and whales, prey on them.

Squid

The largest penguins, 3 to 4 feet in height and up to 90 pounds in weight, eat mostly squid but also catch fish.

The Many Miracles of the Desert

Ann and Myron Sutton

Desert plants and animals can cope with searing heat and prolonged drought, but they have few defenses against man.

In a California railroad station the American photographer Ansel Adams once met an elderly gentleman arriving from Connecticut. "When you came through that wonderful desert area," Adams asked, "what did you think of it?"

"To tell you the truth, Mr. Adams," replied the visitor, "I don't see how they ever let it get into such a terrible condition."

Thousands of people have a mental picture of deserts of North America as wild and desolate regions to be shunned for their dangers and their solitude. But others have discovered that the perils are not so terrible, that solitude can be refreshing, and that among the natural processes of desert life are a good many bordering on the miraculous.

The summer heat and the occasional storms may indeed be appalling. Close to the ground, where plants and small animals must live, air temperatures at noon may exceed 160°F., and surface temperatures approach 200°. At best, annual rainfall comes to 15 inches, and months or even years may pass with only the moisture of occasional dew. High winds mass dust into dense clouds and roll it across the desert. Sometimes cloudbursts unleash torrents of water, which gathers in gullies and rushes down gulches with savage fury. Flash floods inundate animal burrows, uproot plants. In winter great cactuses freeze and collapse. Migratory waterfowl are trapped in ice forming on ponds where they are sleeping. And blizzards bring snow, in places several feet of it.

But then comes the magic of spring. If there has been enough autumn and winter moisture, the annual wildflower display begins in January. On sheltered south-facing slopes a small cousin of the carrot breaks out its complex leaves and lifts a cluster of purple flowers to the sun. In February the creosote bush blooms yellow. From then until June one wave of color succeeds another. Whole valleys burst into fire with the orange blossoms of California poppies. Here are the scarlet torches of ocotillo, there the yellow avenues of brittlebush. Yuccas send up stalks of flowers like chandeliers with the flames of a hundred candles. The pale magenta blooms of desert catalpa are full of grace and delicacy.

The approach of summer

Day by day the rays of the sun grow hotter. April turns into May, and with the rising temperatures the flowers are fewer. By June the drought is prolonged. Week after week the sky remains cloudless. Periods of 90 consecutive days of over 100° are not exceptional.

For many desert animals, this is a time of retirement into burrows or under trees and shrubs. But the trees and shrubs, rooted in place, have nowhere to hide. They have evolved a wide variety of ways of coping with heat and aridity. Evaporation of water from leaves of plants would cool their surfaces slightly, but water is a luxury. One solution is to have small leaves; those of the prickly-pear cactus are only spines. Another solution

Strange Little Fish of the Desert

Four species of desert pupfish live in pools and streams in the Death Valley region, near the boundary between California and Nevada. Pupfish have inhabited the area since glacial times, when it was well watered. Except during occasional flooding most pupfish live only in extremely restricted areas, and the inch-long Devil's Hole pupfish has the most limited range among vertebrates. Its only home is a single spring-fed pool in the cleft of a rock, where a small amount of sunshine makes the fish's food, algae, grow. Though its ancestors have lived here for thousands of years, the pupfish now faces extinction. If pumping water for irrigation lowers the water table and pool so far that sunlight cannot reach the algae, the pupfish will starve.

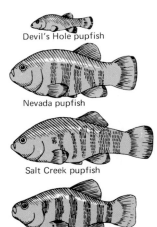

Devil's Hole pupfish

Nevada pupfish

Salt Creek pupfish

Owens River pupfish

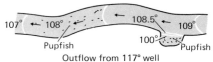

The three larger kinds of Death Valley pupfish live in a wide variety of temperatures, ranging from near the source of hot springs to streams covered with winter ice. The highest temperature that the pupfish can endure more than momentarily is 108°F.; in streams flowing from hot springs, most of the fish stay in water between 107° and 108°, since their food, blue-green algae, grows best in very warm water. A few fish may occupy a slightly cooler pocket near the main stream of hot water.

Prickliest of the cactuses, chollas glisten in the spring sunshine of the Arizona desert. Beyond the chollas and yellow brittlebush grow young, unbranched saguaros. Of the 1,700 cactus species nearly all are native to the Western Hemisphere.

A Desert Giant Grows Up

One of the world's tallest cactuses, the saguaro may reach 50 feet and take 250 years to do so. Saguaros reproduce slowly; about one seed in 12 million grows to a mature plant. These cactuses occur only in the Sonora Desert of Mexico and Arizona, where plant collecting, cattle grazing, and vandalism threaten the long-lived giants. In two U.S. national monuments the saguaros are now protected.

1 inch

Each saguaro flower, rich in nectar, blooms for about 24 hours. Bats pollinate the flowers by night, birds by day.

A saguaro seedling can get started only in the shade of another plant. Its growth is so slow that even at 25 years of age it reaches only 3 feet in height.

Nurse plant

A 50-year-old saguaro is about 10 feet tall and has produced flowers and fruits for several years.

At 70 years of age and 16 feet in height a saguaro begins to branch. Mature saguaros usually have two to seven arms.

A saguaro that has lived for a century is half grown at 25 feet tall.

A large saguaro is home for a variety of animals. Some birds burrow into the trunk; others nest in the hole after the diggers have left. Rodents and insects also shelter there.

2 years
(less than 1 in. tall)

25 years
(3 ft.)

50 years
(10 ft.)

70 years
(16 ft.)

100 years
(25 ft.)

130 years
(30 ft.)

Yucca plants and yucca moths in the arid regions of western North America have a unique relationship. Only the yucca moth pollinates yucca flowers; its caterpillars eat only yucca seeds. After mating (left), the female moth gathers pollen from yucca blossoms, which she packs into a ball suspended from her head. She flies to another plant and lays one to six eggs in the flower ovary (center) and then deposits the pollen (right). By the time the eggs hatch, the approximately 200 seeds are developed enough so that the caterpillars can get the food they need from some of them but leave plenty of others.

is to shed every leaf. The ocotillo, leafless and to all appearances lifeless during drought, puts on new leaves after moderately heavy rains, summer or winter; some years this may mean five or six crops of leaves.

The giant saguaro's pleated trunk stores water, contracting and expanding in response to the supply of moisture, withering during droughts and swelling during rains until 95 percent of it may consist of water; the folds also furnish some shade to the trunk. The leaves of some other plants, such as creosote bush, are coated with a waxy layer that keeps in moisture.

The wide-spreading roots of prickly pears soak up light rains because they are near the surface. Other cactuses send roots 30 or more feet down to underground water. The mesquite root may be 100 feet long. The creosote bush root has developed what seems to be a desperate defense: It produces a toxin that kills nearby plants and reduces competition for water.

A surprisingly high percentage of desert animals have no structural adaptations to withstand excessive heat. Most of them avoid it by spending the hottest hours in shade or in burrows.

Deserts Around the World

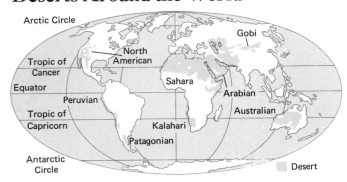

Dominated by the immense Sahara of Africa, which covers more than 3 million square miles, the deserts of the world stretch across the globe in two great belts, one near the Tropic of Cancer and one near the Tropic of Capricorn.

Desert animals don't even devote much time to searching for water. Quail and bighorn sheep find water holes on their normal routes of travel. Carnivores such as coyotes get liquid from the blood of their prey. Jackrabbits and other herbivores use the moisture of desert plants.

A web of interactions

Like all habitats the desert has a complex network of interactions among its inhabitants. When the female yucca moth lays eggs in yucca blossoms, it pollinates the flowers; the moth caterpillars hatch at the same time that the yucca seeds ripen, and the caterpillars eat some of them. Birds (which pollinate saguaros) eat saguaro fruits and drop the seeds in the shade of trees where they perch; the shade is essential to the start of saguaro seedlings.

Saguaros are in danger now because of a combination of factors. The number of wood rats, which feed on the cactuses, has increased because predators such as coyotes and snakes have been exterminated. Mesquite and paloverde, which serve as "nurse" plants by furnishing shade to young saguaros, have been taken for wood. Grazing cattle have killed many young plants. Tourists have dug up and carried away seedlings, in the process destroying many more than they have taken. Most of the damage has been done to young cactuses, and the combined result of all of the activities is that the saguaros, which do not even begin to produce seeds until they are 40 years old, cannot reproduce fast enough to maintain their numbers. Each of these factors is small and not too serious. Together, they spell trouble.

For all its seeming stability, the desert is fragile. An apparently trifling disturbance can upset the delicate balance. Overgrazing by cattle and the pumping out of groundwater for irrigation have damaged grass cover, so that erosion has been accelerated. Dune buggies also hasten erosion.

Desert flowers and rattlesnakes are gifts from the benevolent treasury of life. Since we are guests who neither created nor bestowed these gifts, we have no authority to destroy them.

How Desert Plants Cope with the Water Shortage

Confronted with extreme temperatures, strong winds, and aridity, plants of the desert have developed an array of ingenious adaptations. Immense root systems, poisons against competitors, microscopic windbreaks, and leaves that repeatedly renew themselves are some of the spectacular devices that help the desert plants survive.

The night-blooming cereus stores water in a beetlike bulb in its root system. The roots of other plants, such as the prickly-pear cactus and creosote bush, are shallow but widespread; they catch any rain that soaks into the soil in their vicinity. Still other plants, such as mesquites, send taproots deep into the soil, where the water table may lie 100 feet down.

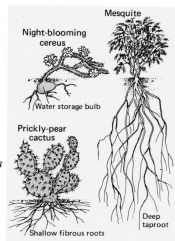

Creosote bushes, like brittlebushes and burrobushes, assure themselves of space and all the available water by poisoning the surrounding earth. Their roots give off a toxic substance that prevents other plants, even the bush's own seedlings, from growing in the immediate vicinity. As a result, the spacing of these bushes is remarkably regular.

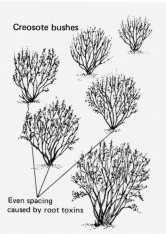

Plants lose water from their leaves. Instead of leaves, many cactuses have spines, which lose less water to the air, create shade, deter plant eaters, and cut down the wind. Other plants, such as the paloverde, smoke tree, and ocotillo, leaf out in a rainy season but promptly drop their leaves in a drought. An ocotillo may bear five or six crops of leaves in a single year.

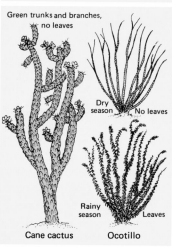

Cactuses can survive dry spells long after most other plants have perished. Many cactuses take advantage of the infrequent desert rains by storing huge amounts of water in their tissues, expanding their pleated sides. After a rain one saguaro was observed to swell from 31 to 47 inches in circumference. A barrel cactus can live on such stored water for as long as a year.

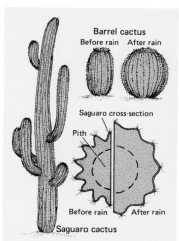

Plant leaves take in carbon dioxide and give off oxygen and water through tiny openings called stomates. The succulent leaves of the century plant have recessed stomates that greatly reduce water loss because they are shielded from the drying air currents. The leaves of creosote bushes have a waxy coating, which tends to keep them from drying.

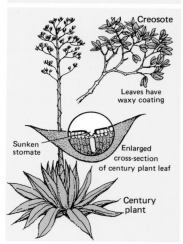

Annual plants, such as the large yellow desert primrose, wait out most of the year as seeds. Right after a heavy rain the dormant seeds germinate, and soon the plants flower and produce seeds. Most seeds sprout only after considerable soaking or abrasion, assuring that growth will begin when there is enough moisture for the plant to mature.

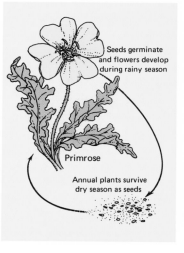

133

Yellow mesembryanthemums, or fig marigolds, bloom along Table Bay; beyond, Table Mountain rises over the buildings of Cape Town, South Africa. Few other places on earth can match the spectacular spring wildflower displays of the West Cape.

The Flowering Coast of South Africa

Leslie Brown

Renowned for its wildflowers, the Cape of Good Hope is a unique blend of North and South, a home to baboons and leopards, albatrosses and penguins.

At the southern tip of Africa is a small but remarkable region with a Mediterranean climate similar to north-western Africa's. What makes the Cape region of Africa remarkable is its extraordinarily varied plant life —an estimated 8,000 to 10,000 species of flowering plants. The terrain varies from sea level to 7,400 feet; rainfall varies from less than 10 inches a year to more than 200; landscape varies from dry, sunny slopes to mist-shrouded mountains that recall western Scotland. In these diverse habitats many small, local populations of plants have developed; the Cape Peninsula, including Table Mountain, Cape Town's spectacular backdrop, has as many kinds of flowering plants as the British Isles. Some of these flowers, such as gladiolus, agapanthus, and freesia, are in gardens all over the world.

Much of this region is covered with dense vegetation known as "fynbos," typically shrubs with small stiff or shiny leaves adapted to withstand drought. The tallest layer is usually made up of proteas—shrubs and small trees growing from 3 to 25 feet high and bearing extraordinary circular flowers as large as 12 inches across. Beneath the proteas are reedlike plants and smaller shrubs, many of them heaths.

The abundance of flowers means that nectar-feeding birds, including the beautiful, metallic-green malachite sunbird, are common. Sunbirds occur throughout most of Africa. They are not closely related to the hummingbirds of the Americas but have evolved similar adaptations: long curved bills and tongues that can be thrust deep into a flower in search of nectar and

South Africa's Endangered Wildflowers

The Cape region of South Africa harbors an unsurpassed wealth of wildflowers. Though many kinds, including the gladiolus and red-hot poker, have become garden favorites all over the world, their numbers in the wild have been drastically diminished. Overcollecting, the clearing of land for agriculture, an increased incidence of fires, and the spread of foreign plants that compete with the native ones for nutrients and water have caused this decline.

The spectacular bird-of-paradise is a member of the banana family. It is pollinated by sunbirds and sugarbirds.

Gloriosa, or flame, lilies may be orange, red, or purple. The plants climb up bushes for several feet.

The spotted-leaved yellow arum lily, one of the calla lilies, with blooms 6 or 7 inches long, is becoming increasingly rare in the wild.

Once known as the Pride of Table Mountain, the red disa is now rare. But this orchid is cultivated for florists' shops.

Related to baobabs, the impala lily shrub grows in places where the summers are hot and winters mild.

Popular in gardens, the Barberton daisy is rare in the wild and is protected.

CAPE REGION

Cape Town

Knysna

Port Elizabeth

Africa

Cape region

0   50   100
Miles

South Africa's Cape region begins west of Cape Town and stretches some 500 miles. The terrain ranges from sweeping beaches to mountain escarpments. Prevailing winds create a Mediterranean-like climate.

Brilliant spikes of the red-hot poker, a lily, cap 3-foot stalks in damp or even marshy ground. Several species grow wild in all parts of southern Africa.

Collectors who take corn lily bulbs from the dry hillsides where they grow are endangering the species.

Now rare in the wild, the waterfall gladiolus (center) is an ancestor of many hybrids cultivated throughout the world, such as the purple star (left) and the spring glory.

A Cape sugarbird perches on a protea flower, a favorite source of nectar. Sugarbirds feed mainly on nectar but also eat some insects. In spring breeding pairs build nests lined with protea fluff and rear two broods, one after the other.

insects. Sunbirds are as a rule much larger than hummingbirds; though they can hover, theirs is a clumsy maneuver compared with the rapid, whirring flight of the hummingbird, and they usually do not feed while they are hovering. Their domed nests, often suspended from the branch of a bush or small tree, are adorned with lichens, bound with cobwebs, and lined with feathers or soft plant material.

Forests are few

Natural forests are rare in the Cape; repeated fires in the fynbos and insufficient rainfall in most of the area make it a habitat that trees cannot easily colonize. Two types of indigenous forests do occur. On some of the western ranges there are stands of conifers resembling giant juniper. In the east forests of a different sort are made up of *Podocarpus* or yellowwood, a conifer with narrow, lance-shaped evergreen leaves, and several broad-leaved trees, including ironwood and the beautiful Cape chestnut, with great panicles of pale pink flowers. These eastern forests, which grow on the lower slopes of the mountains, sometimes only a few

hundred feet above sea level, are remarkably like East African forests at 6,000 to 8,000 feet. Among the typical forest birds are the handsome red-winged Knysna lourie and the large Cape parrot. The Knysna forest, on the seacoast west of Port Elizabeth, is the present southward limit of the elephant, which formerly lived on the Cape.

Mammals and birds by the sea

On the coastal plains practically nothing remains of the once abundant wildlife. The Cape lion, reputed to have been the largest and most magnificent of all races of lion, is gone for good. The strikingly marked bontebok, an antelope with white patches and lyre-shaped horns, was brought near extinction, but a few were saved on farms; they may now be seen in several reserves. The mountain zebra, frequenting terrain avoided by most zebras, is also scarce.

Of the small antelopes, a surprising number still live in the dense fynbos of the mountains. There are grysbok, common duiker, steenbuck, and vaal rhebok. The small red grysbok and the duiker live in dense cover; the steenbuck, a graceful, slender animal, in more open country. The diminutive duiker is probably the most adaptable and widely distributed mammal in Africa, inhabiting regions from the Cape to Senegal and Ethiopia, and from sea level to high altitudes, near the limits of plant growth. The vaal rhebok is found only in South Africa; it lives in pairs or small herds. This rhebok, with straight, upright horns, is strikingly reminiscent of the European roe deer—its name means "gray roebuck."

Living in colonies among the rock piles are innumerable rock hyraxes, which bear a vague resemblance to guinea pigs. But strange as it may seem, the hyrax, usually weighing between 5 and 6 pounds, is the nearest living relative of the elephant, which weighs up to 7 tons. Hyraxes are browsers, and they can evidently subsist for long periods without water. Firm pads on their feet enable them to grip the smoothest surfaces and clamber over boulders with astonishing ease.

Chacma baboons share the rock piles with the hyraxes, despite some persecution by man. Leopards, too, hang on in the mountains though relentlessly hunted, feeding on baboons, hyraxes, and small antelopes.

Many birds from Europe winter in the Cape, where they enjoy the southern summer and some even breed. Both the white stork and the rarer black stork have nested here. The colorful European bee-eater also occasionally nests in the Cape, as does the house martin. Common nonbreeding migrants include the European or barn swallow and several species of wading birds.

Among the magnificent beaches and sand dunes on the seacoast are numerous lagoons, alive with red-knobbed coots and a number of local species of ducks, while gray herons and little egrets stalk in the shallows. Five species of terns that are worldwide breeders—the Caspian, Sandwich, roseate, common, and arctic—mingle with South African terns.

The black oyster catcher is common along the west

coast. Its close relative, the European oyster catcher, visits South Africa occasionally and, while there, lives alongside its cousin. On offshore islands are large colonies of Cape gannets, strong fliers and divers very similar to the gannets of the Northern Hemisphere. Jackass penguins, named for their braying call, breed in burrows or hollows on these islands. Gulls and cormorants are common and nest colonially among the other inhabitants.

At the southern tip of the Cape Peninsula is the spectacular Cape of Good Hope. The nearly sheer sandstone cliffs of this stark promontory fall 800 feet to the sea. From here the visitor can see many of the oceanic seabirds of Antarctica. Seven species of albatrosses are recorded from waters off the Cape, and two of these, the wandering albatross and the black-browed albatross, often come close inshore. Also to be seen inshore are the giant petrel, approaching these albatrosses in wingspan, and the black-and-white petrel called the Cape pigeon. Offshore are many more species of petrels, shearwaters, and albatrosses.

In the 16th century the English admiral Sir Francis Drake called the Cape of Good Hope "the fairest cape we saw in the whole circumference of the earth." It is also remarkable as a place where one can watch such a contrast as a baboon looking for food among the rocks while out to sea soars an albatross from the Antarctic Ocean.

Among South Africa's rarest mammals, some 800 bonteboks now live in reserves. In 1930, after being killed for meat and deprived of grazing lands, these 4-foot-long antelopes numbered about 20. Local farmers are working to save the species.

South Africa's Zebras—Different Stripes, Different Fates

When Europeans settled in South Africa, they found large herds of zebras, which they slaughtered for hides and meat. Hunting and habitat destruction caused the extinction of the quagga and the South African Burchell's zebra. Two other kinds of zebra remain in South Africa. Fewer than 200 Cape mountain zebras are alive today; the Hartmann's mountain zebras, which look similar but are larger, number about 7,000.

Most of these animals live in Mountain Zebra National Park, the descendants of about 40 zebras moved there from other parts of South Africa.

The last known South African Burchell's zebra, the southern race of the common East African zebra, died in 1910 at the London Zoo. This race lacked the common zebra's leg stripes.

Quaggas roamed the southeastern plains of Africa. The last of these half-striped zebras died in 1883 in the Amsterdam Zoo.

Cape mountain zebra—endangered

South African Burchell's zebra—extinct

Quagga—extinct

A diver explores a coral canyon in the crystal-clear waters of the Outer Reef. Coral depends, in little-understood ways, on one-celled plants growing inside it. Since these tiny plants need ample light to grow, sediment-free water is vital for reefs.

Australia's Ocean Wonderland: The Great Barrier Reef

The Great Barrier Reef, some 1,250 miles long, is composed basically of 350 species of coral, living and dead. Innumerable other animals and plants live there also; new kinds are frequently found. The reef encloses about 80,000 square miles—the combined area of England and Scotland. The reef-free channel along the coast, with a few access routes to the sea, is 8 to 40 miles wide and deep enough for shipping. Rising from 1,800 feet below the surface, the massive outer wall of the reef has protected the mainland shore from the erosive force of ocean waves for millions of years, yet its ecology is surprisingly fragile and can be thrown out of balance easily. Shell collectors take great numbers of living mollusks from the reef; one of them is a predator of the crown of thorns, a coral-eating starfish. A recent population explosion of the starfish consumed about 140 square miles of living coral, and some biologists suggested that the loss of too many mollusks might have been a factor. Industry has threatened greater dangers—mining for lime and exploratory drilling for oil. No one in Australia wants to see the reef damaged, but probably only strict, well-enforced conservation laws will preserve it intact.

In a crevice on a reef wall off Heron Island two sweetlips (the black and white one is immature) swim beneath clusters of retracted cup corals. The mosslike clumps of turtle weed among the coral heads provide good grazing for some fish.

An orange-skirted sea slug crawls among bulbous blue sea squirts. Its two red, retractable tentacles lead it to food: the red structure at the left is a set of gills. This cousin of the snail has a shell only in its larval stage.

Schooling cardinal fish hover above a thicket of staghorn coral. These small carnivorous fish find prey, such as worms and crustaceans, in the coral and also find shelter from larger predatory fish among the stony, spreading branches.

How the World's Mightiest Reef Was Formed

When tiny coral animals began building the Great Barrier Reef, the water on the continental shelf was shallow. Then the land subsided or the sea rose (or both). The mountainous islands near the coast are the peaks of a range separated from the mainland by a submerged valley. The small islands of the Inner Reef are made of coral deposited on former foothills. The Outer Reef consists of coral built up from what may have been a tidal zone.

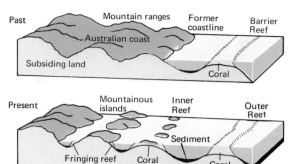

The undulating, ½-inch tentacles of the cup coral on the left are fully extended; those of the cup coral on the right are retracted. The tentacles capture bits of food from the water and bring them to the central mouth.

A sea squirt pumps in water through a siphon, traps tiny food particles on mucus sheets, and expels the waste water from another siphon. Sea squirt larvae are free-swimming, but the adults are permanently attached to the bottom.

A banded coral shrimp is conspicuous even against a confused background of corals, algae, sponges, tube worms, and sea anemones. The shrimp removes and eats external parasites from fish, which stay still for the operation.

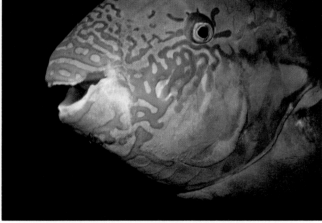

The parrot fish grazes on algae and coral with its chisel-sharp teeth, noisily crunching on the limestone skeletons. A major erosive force on the reef, the parrot fish bites out chunks of living coral and leaves easily recognizable tooth marks.

White-water rivers, fed by many springs, usually rise in high country. Constricted in their rocky beds, they break into tumultuous, foam-crested rapids whenever the descent is steep. Such rivers are clear and carry little silt with them.

Wild River, Ribbon of Life

Laurence Pringle

Though few flowing waters remain completely wild, man's pollution of rivers is not irreversible. Many rivers are becoming cleaner, and aquatic wildlife is coming back.

Rivers have quiet beginnings—the whisper of snowflakes on tree boughs, the murmur of raindrops on leaves, the drip of moisture onto forest floors, the trickle of tiny rivulets. With these sounds a roaring river is born.

"River." The word is repeatedly thrust into our consciousness. We read of worsening pollution downstream; we see pictures of dead fish. Rivers bear the brunt of our industrial society.

Remarkably, some rivers still flow clear and wild. They are not untouched; nowhere on earth is there a river unmarked by man's hand. Nevertheless, these wild rivers are the best we have, and they are very fine. Unpolluted, undammed, rich with living organisms, they are priceless laboratories for unraveling the complex skein of aquatic life.

Wild rivers are precious treasures. In the United States some have been preserved in the National Wild and Scenic Rivers System. Others are being considered for inclusion in the program, though some may not survive long enough to qualify. In northwestern Canada students spent a summer studying 20 wild rivers, such as the Yukon, with a view to saving them from the fate of too many rivers "in southern Canada and more noticeably in the United States as a result of not recognizing the value of a free-flowing river." Several organizations have banded together to save the Churchill River, which drains Southern Indian Lake into Hudson Bay and is the finest wild river left in Manitoba.

Some rivers arise from glaciers: The Columbia ice field on the spine of the Canadian Rockies sends rivers to three oceans. These rivers begin as streams formed from the meltwater at the foot of the glacier and from snow and ice melting on the glacier's surface. Some of the water in a glacial stream may have fallen as snow hundreds of years ago.

Most rivers arise from a mingling of many small streams. Trace these streams back and you will find even smaller streams, beyond which are little oozing seeps and springs fed by rain and melted snow soaking into the soil. This groundwater flows and trickles beneath the surface, coming out at low places. The amount of groundwater beneath the land is enormous, thousands of times greater than the water in rivers.

Close to the source, the origin of a river is important to the living things in it. Aquatic insects of a glacier-fed river must adapt to its daily and seasonal fluctuations in volume. Spring-fed rivers provide a quite different environment. The volume of flow is usually steady, and the temperature varies remarkably little from season to season.

Factors affecting river life

In wild rivers, as in all other habitats, living and nonliving factors affect each other in complex ways. For example, the flow of a river drops markedly as soon as the trees in the valley leaf out in the spring; they send tons of water into the atmosphere, water that otherwise might have seeped into the river. The growth of leaves also lessens the amount of sunlight reaching the water. The periods when rivers receive maximum light are spring and fall, especially in narrow streams, and it is in these seasons, rather than in full summer, that water plants receive most of the radiant energy they need for photosynthesis.

Geologists sometimes call a river "young," "middle-aged," or "mature," depending on the state of the riverbed. In the ordinary time sense most rivers are ancient—not just as old as the hills but older. They have helped carry off generations of mountains. Rivers

At a waterfall a great deal of oxygen dissolves into the stream. Each droplet of spray is surrounded by oxygen-filled air, and as the droplet falls back it carries this air with it. Active fish, such as trout, need a good supply of dissolved oxygen.

What Pollution Does to the Ecology of a River

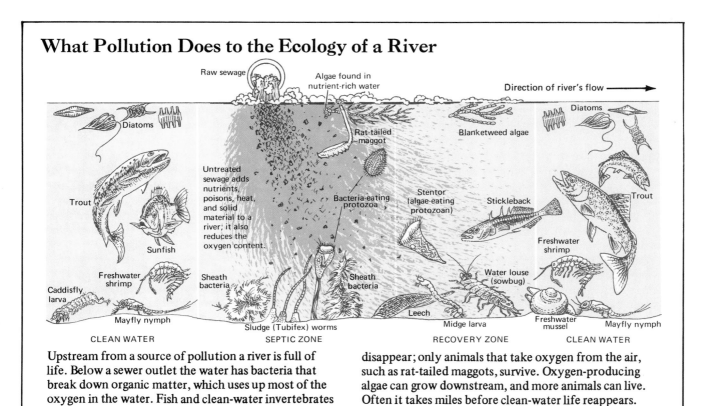

Raw sewage

Algae found in nutrient-rich water

Direction of river's flow ⟶

Diatoms

Rat-tailed maggot

Blanketweed algae

Diatoms

Trout

Untreated sewage adds nutrients, poisons, heat, and solid material to a river; it also reduces the oxygen content.

Bacteria-eating protozoa

Stentor (algae-eating protozoan)

Stickleback

Trout

Sunfish

Sheath bacteria

Sheath bacteria

Water louse (sowbug)

Freshwater shrimp

Freshwater shrimp

Sludge (Tubifex) worms

Leech

Midge larva

Freshwater mussel

Caddisfly larva

Mayfly nymph

Mayfly nymph

CLEAN WATER

SEPTIC ZONE

RECOVERY ZONE

CLEAN WATER

Upstream from a source of pollution a river is full of life. Below a sewer outlet the water has bacteria that break down organic matter, which uses up most of the oxygen in the water. Fish and clean-water invertebrates disappear; only animals that take oxygen from the air, such as rat-tailed maggots, survive. Oxygen-producing algae can grow downstream, and more animals can live. Often it takes miles before clean-water life reappears.

Salmon of the World

The seven species of salmon (one Atlantic, six Pacific) are renowned for their flesh and their unusual life history: Most salmon hatch in freshwater, spend their adult lives at sea, return to their native lakes or streams to spawn and then die. Their greatest vulnerability to man is in their final journey, when they gather in tremendous numbers for the upriver swim. King and chum salmon travel 2,000 miles up the Yukon River; others spawn in the brackish waters of tidal flats. Still others are landlocked and never migrate.

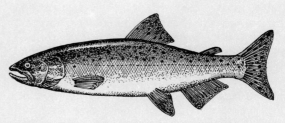

The largest salmon (up to 100 pounds), the chinook is found from the Yukon to mid-California and in Asia.

The small masu, or cherry salmon, is a game fish native to the cold rivers of the northern Japanese islands.

Pink salmon, or humpies, are Alaska's commonest species; their range extends from northern California to Japan.

A vanishing species, Atlantic salmon breed in western Europe and eastern North America (Labrador to Maine).

Chum salmon are widely distributed from Siberia to northern Japan and from the Canadian Arctic to Oregon.

The coho, a popular sport fish, occurs from the Bering Sea, south to California, and across to Japan.

Prized for their red flesh, sockeyes range from the Columbia River in the U.S. Northwest to Siberia and Japan.

such as the Rhine and the Danube drained Europe long before the Alps were uplifted.

All along the river mysteries appear. When a river's bed is made up of rocks of varying sizes, the water usually flows through a series of alternating riffles and pools. Most gravel-bed or boulder-bed rivers have riffles spaced more or less regularly every five to seven stream widths. No one knows why.

The gravel, cobbles, and boulders that make up riffles provide a diversity of habitats for aquatic life, and rivers with alternating riffles and pools support a greater variety of plants and animals than do more homogeneous streams. As fishermen know, the turbulence in riffles rips insects from their moorings, providing food for trout and other fish that lurk below the whitewater. Water and air are mixed in riffles; the water just below a riffle is usually saturated with oxygen day and night. This aeration is vital for the incubation of fish eggs. The rougher the stream bed, the higher and more stable the oxygen content of its water.

Any one or more of several factors may reduce the oxygen supply. At night aquatic plants stop producing oxygen through photosynthesis and use it instead.

In the autumn leaves from trees and shrubs fall into the water and settle to the bottom in pools and quiet backwaters. There they decay, and the bacterial action of decay consumes oxygen.

At places along the river you may see fluffs of what looks like detergent foam in little stillwater places amid the riffles. Is this pollution in paradise? No. The foam appears in the cleanest of streams; it is produced by a combination of chemicals from organic matter, mixed and stirred by the tumbling water. It contains great numbers of spores from the fungi and bacteria that are so important in the decay of once-living material.

Sit by a wild river for an hour and watch some of the workings of an ecosystem. Dragonflies patrol the shore, plucking mosquitoes and small moths from the air. A hatch of mayflies dimples the surface. Some are sucked under by trout; others are snatched up by swifts or swallows; still others flutter weakly to shore. A duck swims by and suddenly dives for a minnow.

You are witnessing strands of the community's food webs, and the interdependence of its living organisms. But some of the most important organisms and processes go unnoticed or unseen. Bacteria, fungi, and algae are growing and reproducing underwater; their presence makes possible the existence of dragonflies and trout. Perhaps you notice newly fallen birch leaves floating downstream and admire the contrast of their gold against the dark waters. For the river these and other leaves represent gold of a different sort: food energy that helps power the entire living community.

A wild river offers a wide variety of habitats for its most abundant plants and major food producers, the algae: riffles or pools, sun or shade, high or low rocks, among other choices. Scientists once assumed that algae must provide most of the primary energy of river ecosystems—the energy that flows through food webs to power the leaps of salmon, the dives of otters. However, when they were finally able to measure the primary productivity of a few rivers, a surprising picture emerged. They discovered that these rivers often consumed more—sometimes much more—than the amount of energy produced by the algae. Apparently algae provide only a part, probably a very small one, of the energy in rivers.

The importance of riverbank plants

Much of a river's living energy comes from willow leaves, beech leaves, pine needles, fern fronds, and thousands of other sources of organic matter in the river valley. Many insects and other invertebrates feed on this detritus, especially on the bacteria and fungi that contribute to its breakdown. Some insects feed on water-soaked wood. Mussels and the larvae of blackflies are filter feeders, sifting fine particles of leaves and other material from the current. The leaves that enter a river in the autumn are a ready food source all winter.

The contribution of energy from the river valley to its waters is not merely in the form of dead leaves. Flowers and fruits of trees, and even the feces of land insects, add to the river's food energy. A river is a year-round trap for organic matter from the landscape. In summer and early autumn spiders and such land insects as crickets, beetles, ants, inchworms, and grasshoppers fall, crawl, hop, or are blown into the water, where they become important food for fish.

No one knows the full scope of the dependence of a river's aquatic life on the food energy of its valley. Undoubtedly, it varies from river to river and from place to place on the same river. Lowland streams are relatively poor in aquatic life. Headwaters, however, are rich in food energy; these streams often flow through forests and are usually narrow, receiving more organic matter per stream bed unit than bigger rivers.

Facts like these tend to slip from our consciousness when we visit a river, where on some days nothing seems to be happening. No wildlife stirs on the banks, the sky is overcast, and even the trees may be uninteresting. Somewhat disappointed, we head for home; behind us, perhaps, a silent parade of dead leaves dots the dark surface, and then they sink to the bottom, one by one.

Troubles of Freshwater Fish

Besides all the difficulties faced by every animal in its natural environment—predators, climatic changes, food shortages—freshwater fish have a whole new set of problems imposed by man: Pollution, dams, stream channeling, removal of protective vegetation. What with overfishing and predatory alien species, it's a wonder native fish survive.

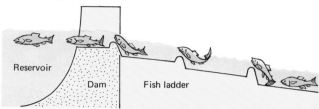

A high dam is a formidable obstacle to migrating fish. Fish ladders have been constructed beside many dams, enabling the fish to swim past the obstruction in easy stages.

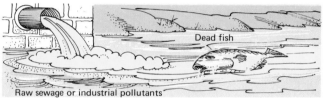

Industrial chemicals, hot water, and wastes of many kinds are poured into rivers. Some make it impossible for food plants to grow; some kill fish and other animals directly.

Cutting down trees beside a river increases erosion and decreases the amount of nutrients derived from fallen leaves. The lack of shade makes the water temperature rise.

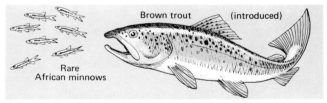

Introducing alien fish to a river or lake (often to improve sport fishing) may mean the elimination of many native fish, which are preyed upon or simply cannot compete for food.

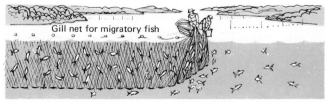

A carefully placed seine in a small body of water can catch nearly all the fish in a school. If they are taken just before spawning, the whole population could soon be wiped out.

France's Flamingo Country

Kai Curry-Lindahl

In France's coastal Camargue, rice farmers share the wetlands with one of the world's greatest concentrations of birds.

Flamingos live in Africa, in India, in South America, in the Bahamas. Who would expect these tropical and subtropical birds not only to visit but even to breed in an area on the same latitude as Yarmouth, Nova Scotia?

On the Mediterranean coast of France, the Rhône, flowing from Switzerland's Alps, has built a considerable delta. Man has occupied this delta, known as the Camargue, since before Roman times, and of its 138,000 acres, 35,000 are under cultivation, especially for rice. Many lagoons are exploited for the production of salt.

The Camargue is famous far beyond the boundaries of France for its wildlife, particularly for its birds; few places in Europe can boast so many kinds. Kentish plovers, pipits, and oyster catchers nest near the beach; farther inland are ducks, avocets, skylarks, yellow wagtails, and golden orioles.

The Camargue is the only place in Europe where flamingos nest almost every year, up to 25,000 congregating in the spring. They are the most numerous of the birds that nest here in colonies. They choose islands where no other birds except herring gulls

breed. By April each pair has usually produced its single egg, which hatches after about a month. When a flock of flamingos retreats before a visitor, it is apparent only at close range that the forest of red legs conceals grayish-brown young birds, ridiculously small in comparison with their parents. The older birds move slowly and cautiously, step by step, while the young flow like a floating carpet under them, doing their best to keep up with their elders.

Farther from the coast flocks of bee-eaters hunt insects in the air, darting as gracefully as swallows or gliding on still wings as if independent of gravity. They display a kaleidoscope of colors—green, golden yellow, reddish brown—and, depending on the angle of the sun, their undersides change from emerald to blue to almost purple. Turtledoves, hoopoes, rollers, and green woodpeckers build nests; cuckoos lay eggs in the nests of other birds. At night owls hoot pleasantly. Vultures search for carrion, and hawks, shrikes, and an occasional eagle hunt for small birds, reptiles, and mammals.

Mammals of the Camargue

There is a sizable population of hogs. They are strong swimmers and seem to enjoy water as well as mud. They eat several kinds of plant material—roots, nuts, grain, plant stems—but also eat carrion and insect larvae. In treeless areas they shelter from the sun by biting off enough grass to form a mat and then crawling under it.

But the best-known mammals in the Camargue are the half-wild white horses and black cattle that roam freely all year through the unfenced land, though they wear brands and each "rancher" keeps track of his own stock. The cattle especially seem to have reverted to their wild origins in their defense of territories, which include pastureland, drinking holes, and display areas where bulls determine order of dominance.

About 23,000 acres of what naturalists consider the most valuable parts of the Camargue are now protected in reserves. In one reserve is the headquarters of the International Wildfowl Research Bureau. The reserves are off bounds for visitors except by special permission, but all the more interesting mammals and birds can be seen from the public roads.

A farmer with whom I talked was understandably astonished to learn that people crossed all of Europe just to look at the birds around his house. He admitted that he did not take much interest in the birds except in the shooting season. Suddenly a flock of lovely rosy-white flamingos came flying over the farm, and immediately he began talking about them. He knew a great deal about flamingos and was proud that they lived in his neighborhood.

Indeed, the mass effect of hundreds or thousands of flamingos, all moving in the same direction through the water, is stunning. When the flock takes wing against a clear blue sky, it is a vision in white, rose, and black. For these birds alone, the Camargue is worth preserving.

Half-wild white horses, which feed on both grasses and aquatic plants, have roamed the Camargue since ancient times. Some have been tamed and are used to herd cattle on the local ranches. Colts have dark coats but gradually turn white.

A flock of greater flamingos wings across the Camargue. This Mediterranean region has a subtropical climate in summer and a good supply of the small mollusks and crustaceans on which flamingos feed. Each year thousands of the pink birds fly from wintering grounds in Africa to the Camargue, where they build mud nests in the shallow, brackish waters.

The Camargue of France Is Home to a Spectacular Variety of Birds

All year France's Camargue is host to great flocks of birds. Some breed there; others pause on their migration routes to rest and feed before flying on. The variety of habitats in the Camargue—saltwater, brackish water, freshwater, meadows—assures food and nesting sites for birds with many different needs. Shorebirds eat mollusks and crustaceans from estuaries and lakes; other birds eat insects, fish, or seeds.

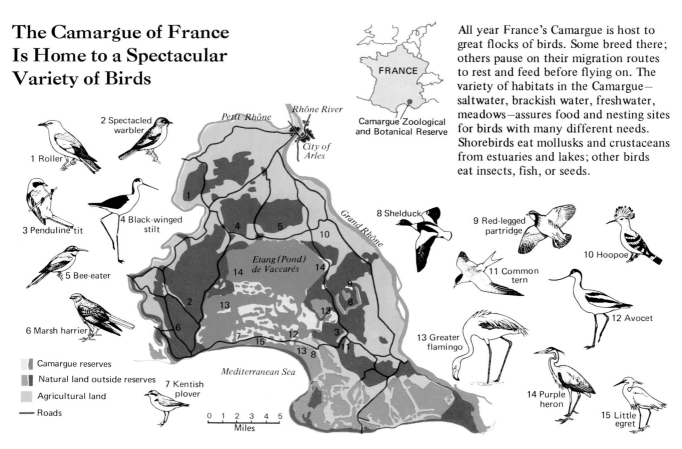

FRANCE

Camargue Zoological and Botanical Reserve

1 Roller
2 Spectacled warbler
3 Penduline tit
4 Black-winged stilt
5 Bee-eater
6 Marsh harrier
7 Kentish plover
8 Shelduck
9 Red-legged partridge
10 Hoopoe
11 Common tern
12 Avocet
13 Greater flamingo
14 Purple heron
15 Little egret

Petit Rhône
Rhône River
City of Arles
Grand Rhône
Etang (Pond) de Vaccarès
Mediterranean Sea

Camargue reserves
Natural land outside reserves
Agricultural land
Roads

0 1 2 3 4 5
Miles

Dangerous Days for Eucalypt Forests

Stanley and Kay Breeden

Like forests all over the world, Australia's towering eucalypt stands are giving way to farms and tree plantations.

Eucalypt forests rank high among Australia's natural wonders. A spring morning in such a forest is a feast for all the senses. As the first rays of the sun wink and sparkle on the dew-laden clusters of flowers, the forest explodes with sound. Flocks of lorikeets hurtle screeching through the trees, flashing green and red feathers; honeyeaters sing in more melodious voices from both treetops and undergrowth.

Seeping down to the ground, the slanting rays of the sun gleam on the pale gray trunks of the blue gums—smooth, straight pillars rising into the sky. By contrast, the neighboring yellow stringybarks have a somber and brooding appearance, their trunks clad in thick, dark-brown layered bark. Deep red stains, dripping down the yellowish, mosaiclike bark of its trunk, give the red bloodwood an appearance of anguish. But the bloodwoods have the largest clusters of flowers, with the greatest amount of nectar, and their spreading crowns are vibrantly alive with birds.

The sun is warm by the time it penetrates to the ground plants. In the tiny islands of bright light, spirals of evaporating dew curl lazily up; the air is filled with the crisp, stimulating scent of eucalyptus oil. A black-tailed wallaby pauses in a shaft of light to groom itself, rich chestnut fur shining as the animal leans back on its thick tail and scratches its chest and abdomen with long, slow strokes, eyes half shut.

Eucalypts, more than 400 species and nearly all of them evergreens, are true Australian natives; only one species is not found there. In size they range from shrubs 6 feet high in the arid zones to forest giants over 300 feet tall.

A bonanza of blossoms

Forest eucalypts do not flower every year, but when they do it is in an incredible profusion. The whole forest is heavy with the scent of honey. Branches broken by the weight of flowers litter the ground. The blossoms provide a food bonanza for countless animals from bats and possums to lorikeets and honeyeaters, and the insects drawn to the nectar nourish thornbills,

A Eucalypt's Remarkable Regenerative Ability

Eucalypt leaves have an elaborate system of defenses against insect attack, fire, and drought. Their fire-resistant bark may not even be damaged by a rapidly traveling blaze. If the bark is cut, the tree exudes a liquid that hardens into an insectproof "bandage." Most remarkable is the eucalypts' backup system of buds and tissues capable of becoming buds; leaves that have been destroyed are quickly replaced.

Every eucalypt leaf has, in the angle between the leaf stalk and twig, a structure called the naked bud. It does not develop while the leaf remains, but if the leaf is lost, the bud takes its place.

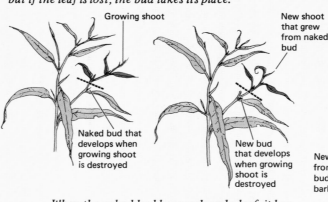

Growing shoot

Naked bud that develops when growing shoot is destroyed

New shoot that grew from naked bud

New bud that develops when growing shoot is destroyed

When the naked bud has produced a leaf, it has another naked bud waiting in case of need. Behind each leaf stalk the twig has tissues capable of producing new buds and new growth.

Under the bark of a eucalypt grows a set of dormant buds. If fire damage is severe, a new crop of leaves often grows from the bark.

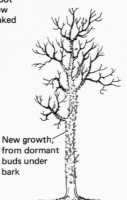

New growth from dormant buds under bark

Many eucalypts have woody, bulbous structures called lignotubers growing among the upper parts of the roots. Even if the whole trunk is destroyed, new shoots spring from the lignotuber and form trunks.

New shoot growing from lignotuber

Lignotuber

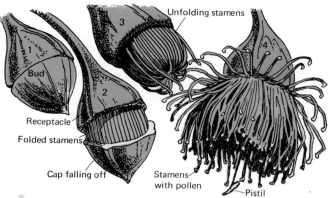

A eucalypt flower bud is covered by a sturdy cap (1); the name eucalypt means well covered. When the flower is ready to open, the cap falls off (2) and the stamens unfold (3), leaving a lovely blossom (4) that develops into a woody fruit.

whistlers, fantails, thrushes, and a host of other birds.

But the flowers do not produce this smorgasbord as a free service to the forest animals. As the animals scramble over and bury themselves in the clusters of flowers, they pick up pollen, which they deposit on the next flowers they visit and in this way cross-pollinate the eucalypt trees.

Australia imposes great hardships on its vegetation: severe insect attack, stony or sandy soils of low fertility, fire, long periods of drought. These conditions would severely stunt or utterly destroy most temperate-zone trees, but they cannot keep down the invincible eucalypts.

One of the favorite practical jokes of West Australians is to invite an unsuspecting visitor on a bush picnic to light a fire with wood from the jarrah eucalypt. No matter how hard he tries, he cannot get the fire to burn; jarrah wood is so hard and dense as to be almost completely fire resistant. In fact, fewer than 5 percent of Australia's eucalypts would be killed outright by a high-intensity bush fire. Most would survive because of the insulating qualities of the bark and the low flammability of their wood. In one experiment the flame of a blowtorch, directed at the half-inch bark of a spotted gum, melted an aluminum tag on the tree in 6 seconds. After 8 minutes the flame had not even marked the bark of the tree. It took 12 minutes to burn through the bark.

Animals that eat eucalypts

Outside Australia animals that might eat eucalypt leaves are repelled by an oil that they secrete. But in Australia many animals, including insects, have learned to live with it. Indeed, koalas, which eat more than 2 pounds of eucalypt leaves a day, are so specialized that they eat nothing else.

A visitor to a forest is invariably impressed by the clean look of a tall eucalypt. The smooth-barked trees are particularly imposing, their pale gray or even pure white trunks gleaming and immaculate. The ultimate in clean-limbed trees is the mountain ash, the tallest hardwood in the world. The loftiest known standing

The pale trunks of southwestern Australia's karris dwarf the strollers on the path below; these giant eucalypts grow to nearly 300 feet. Valued for their durable timber, the karris have been overexploited, but they are now protected by law.

Animals of the Eucalypt Forest

Australia's magnificent eucalypt forests, found mainly in the eastern part of the continent, give shelter to a unique fauna. The eucalypt trees also provide food. Honeyeaters feed on the nectar; parrots and cockatoos eat seeds; some marsupials and insects eat leaves and flowers.

EXTINCT?

ENDANGERED

Yellingbo Faunal Reserve (home of helmeted honeyeater)

The helmeted honeyeater eats the nectar of eucalypts, especially that of swamp gums. Human activity is claiming even its one small territory.

No thylacine (or Tasmanian wolf) has been seen for years, but paw marks have been found. Possibly a few of these doglike hunters may still be alive.

Fossil sites of thylacine

Last officially recorded killing of thylacine (1930)

ENDANGERED

Descendants of imported parma wallabies turned up on a New Zealand island after the species had been given up as extinct. It is still in danger.

Kawau I. (parma wallaby introduced)

North Island (New Zealand)

Present Australian range of parma wallaby

SUCCESS STORY

Koala range

ON THE INCREASE

A popular aviary bird, the turquoise parrot was heavily trapped in the 19th century, but under legal protection it is now increasing.

Range of turquoise parrot

The gentle koala eats only eucalypt leaves and was once near extinction. Under legal protection it is apparently thriving in the southeastern part of the continent.

tree of this species is 324 feet tall, but mountain ashes well over 350 feet in height once grew in the temperate south of Australia.

But in spite of their hardihood and resiliency, eucalypts are not extremely long lived. The average life-span of the more durable forest eucalypts is 300 to 400 years. The jarrah and the river red gum can survive for more than 1,000 years, but, in the end, the tree's own vigor leads to its downfall. Fast growth means brittle wood prone to decay under attack from wood-rot fungi and termites, which gain access into the older trees after a series of accidents. Eucalypts are subject to wind damage and so are usually surrounded by a litter of dead leaves and branches that feed bush fires. Though eucalypts can survive fires that would completely destroy other trees, repeated fires gradually kill patches of bark. In the early stages of the tree's life, formation of new wood proceeds much faster than the

rate of fungus-caused decay. But as the tree grows older and weaker, the amount of wood produced falls off sharply until the rate of decay overtakes growth. Eventually the tree topples in a storm.

Nothing in nature, however, has challenged the invincibility of the eucalypt as brutally as man. Annual burnings to keep land clear for agriculture have emasculated huge areas of eucalypt forests, and hundreds of acres have been flattened by timber harvests. In the 200 years of European settlement the forests have shrunk at a steadily increasing rate, and now extreme care must be exercised to preserve the remaining significant eucalypt forests.

In New South Wales and Queensland hundreds of thousands of acres of virgin eucalypt forests have been bulldozed and burned—right down to the bare soil—in order to plant neat rows of pine trees. It may be necessary to grow pines to supply Australia with soft-

Parachuting on membranes between its front and hind legs, a sugar glider can float 150 feet from tree to tree. A nocturnal feeder, this small bushy-tailed possum eats eucalypt blossoms, nectar, and insects. It is so agile that it catches moths in flight.

wood, but the choice of land and the methods used to clear it result in frightening destruction to the native forests. Australian snakes, birds, mammals, frogs, beetles, butterflies, wattles, ferns, orchids, mosses, lichens, and other living organisms have evolved to live among eucalypts; they cannot live in pine forests. Pine plantations are silent, eerie places.

The disappearing forests

Besides being felled for their own timber or wiped out to make room for other timber-producing trees, whole forests of eucalypts are being cleared from the landscape to provide grazing land, or cut down to earn export money as wood chips. These projects are often unnecessarily destructive, and they ride roughshod over values that might be considered of greater significance to Australia and Australians than a few more cattle fattened or the supply of raw material to foreign paper manufacturers.

In Tasmania, 300-foot mountain ashes are being cut down to make newsprint. The company controlling the fate of one of the most remarkable tree communities on earth has preserved patches of the tallest trees, but these are mere 40- to 60-acre plots. Once the surrounding forest has been cleared these "reserves" will soon succumb to wind damage and soil debilitation.

Eucalypts can cope with drought, with flood, with defoliation by insects, with fire. They cannot withstand the onslaught of 20th-century man and his mindless machines. It is up to the present generations of Australians to determine whether their giant eucalypt forests are to survive.

The musk lorikeet of eastern Australia lives on nectar from tree blossoms—mostly those of eucalypts but also of fruit trees. Lorikeets descend on a tree in a noisy flock and sometimes tear off flowers in their eagerness to get at the nectar.

149

A Tale of Two Edens

Roger Tory Peterson

**An ocean apart and as different
as islands can be, the
Seychelles and the Galápagos are
both remarkably vulnerable to man.**

I like to think about the whole world long, long before man started rearranging things. Few unarranged places still exist. There is the taiga, Siberia's inaccessible forest; the tangled rain forests of the Amazon basin; the vast sandscapes of the Sahara—but they are too big, too overpowering to think of as Edens.

But an island—a small, encircled place a man can walk across, or sail around, and grasp—that might be a paradise. I count myself a very fortunate man, for I have found two: a harsh, primitive Eden, the Galápagos, and a benign Eden "made over," the Seychelles.

These two island groups—the Galápagos 600 miles west of Ecuador in the Pacific, the Seychelles 1,000 miles from Africa in the Indian Ocean—are so alike, yet so different. The Galápagos are a formidable cluster of jagged cinder cones, tortured lava flows, and basalt cliffs; the Seychelles are verdant, golden-beached, palm-fringed islands. Though both lie close to the Equator, and both have evolved the flora and fauna characteristic of oceanic islands, the very stuff they're made of is different.

The Galápagos Islands are volcanic. About 2 million years ago the sea in that area began to boil as lava and rock burst from beneath its floor. With tremendous heat and force the earth sent its dark contents swirling upward, piling them in bizarre, open-topped mountains above the sea. The volcanoes are still active; in 1968 I witnessed the spectacular eruption on the youngest major island, Fernandina.

Paradise in the Indian Ocean

The Galápagos reminded Charles Darwin of the infernal regions. The Seychelles, on the other hand, could not be more inviting. These islands are made of granite, and the 600- to 800-million-year-old rocks are covered by deep humus. Plants thrive in the Seychelles. Washed with Gauguin-bright colors, set in a dazzling ocean of blue, the islands must have seemed paradise itself to the first sailors who beached there.

The porous volcanic rock of the Galápagos absorbs rainfall like a thirsty sponge. Water is scarce; there are few springs, few freshwater or brackish ponds,

Land of the Iguanas

The iguanas of the Galápagos Islands are descended from forest lizards that evidently floated there on tree trunks from Central or South America hundreds of thousands of years ago. The mainland reptiles were accustomed to plenty of vegetation and water. On the arid Galápagos they found little of either. There they evolved into two different groups. Those that remained near the sea developed into the marine iguanas, strong swimmers up to 5 feet long. Inland conditions produced the land iguanas, slightly smaller but heavier than their seagoing cousins.

The land iguana (above) eats fruit and flowers, but its main food is spiny cactus pads, from which it also gets part of its water. The world's only species of marine iguana (left, with a gull) eats seaweed at low tide and even underwater. While eating, it inadvertently swallows a great deal of saltwater, but it has specialized tear glands that secrete the excess salt.

Through the mist, *as in a prehistoric landscape, a few giant tortoises, one of them bearing a hawk, plod across Galápagos lava beds. In spite of the clouds little rain falls on these hills, but cactuses can grow and furnish food for the reptiles.*

The Galápagos: Different Islands, Different Tortoises

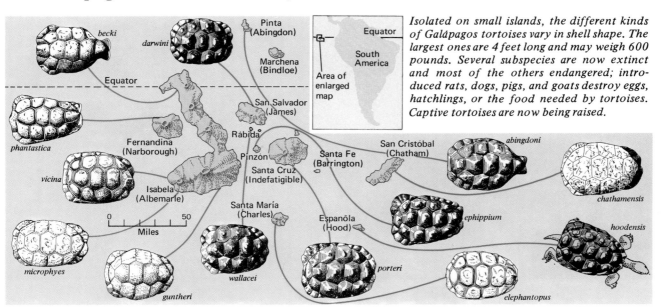

Isolated on small islands, the different kinds of Galápagos tortoises vary in shell shape. The largest ones are 4 feet long and may weigh 600 pounds. Several subspecies are now extinct and most of the others endangered; introduced rats, dogs, pigs, and goats destroy eggs, hatchlings, or the food needed by tortoises. Captive tortoises are now being raised.

and no permanent streams. In addition, the Galápagos get little rain, for the cold waters of the Humboldt Current inhibit rainfall. Geology and climate combine to make the Galápagos arid terrain.

In the Seychelles, water from drenching rains collects in innumerable hollows in the granite; streams course through the rich soil. The Seychelles have good farming land; the Galápagos do not.

Until recently few people were attracted to the Galápagos, aside from naturalists (of whom Darwin was the most famous), adventurers, and pirates. But change has come. Goats, donkeys, and other animals brought to the islands wrought havoc on the sparse vegetation. Several races of the incredible giant tortoise, a lumbering reminder of a distant past, were wiped out by hungry seafarers; once found in the hundreds of thousands on 11 of the 16 major islands, they are now numerous on only two.

Nevertheless, wildlife on the Galápagos is still relatively untouched, compared with most other islands. Large populations of lava lizards and other reptiles share the islands with blue-footed boobies and other birds. Even a moderately skilled bird watcher can find all 13 kinds of Darwin's finches, the birds that gave Darwin valuable clues to his theory of evolution. Not a single bird species has been lost in modern times; most species—though not all—are still common or abundant.

The Seychelles, on the other hand, have already lost two species of land birds—the chestnut-flanked white-eye and the Seychelles parakeet. Six others are now so close to extinction that they are classified as endangered —the Seychelles gray white-eye, the Seychelles paradise flycatcher, the Seychelles kestrel, the Seychelles brush warbler, the magpie-robin, and the Seychelles scops owl, once thought to be extinct.

Indeed, one sees very few native land birds of any sort in the Seychelles. The birds most in evidence are aliens—bright scarlet fodies (relatives of the English sparrow) introduced from Madagascar, little barred ground doves from Malaysia, and aggressive mynahs from India. Nonnative birds, along with cats and rats, are probably the major reason for the disappearance of native ones. Barn owls, for example, which were brought from Africa to eat rats on Mahé, the largest Seychelles island, preferred the abundant fairy terns; now not a single tern nests on that island. By contrast —and this is significant—no alien bird has ever been introduced into the Galápagos.

You don't see many giant tortoises in the Seychelles. They were almost completely exterminated there when people first colonized the islands; of the few that now live in the Seychelles, most were brought over from Aldabra, a coral atoll 600 miles away. Colonists completely wiped out the gentle dugong—a manateelike creature that once swam in the tidal lagoons.

What you *can* see in the Seychelles, and cannot help seeing, is people. With a total land area of about 150

Bristling with palms, *Mahé is the largest of the 91 Seychelles Islands. This Indian Ocean group is a near paradise, where fertile, well-watered soil and a tropical climate produce everything that seabirds—and men—need for pleasant living.*

The Seychelles: Native Birds, Alien Birds

At least two Seychelles bird species are extinct, and several others have fewer than 50 individuals left, all confined to one or two islands. But imported birds are thriving and have spread throughout the islands. Of these, predatory birds destroy native species, and nonpredatory ones compete with them for nesting sites and food.

square miles, the islands' human population is about 50,000. Compare this with the Galápagos, whose 3,000 square miles have only about 2,000 people.

The Seychelles are overpopulated. They are still beautiful, very beautiful, but it is not their original beauty that remains. There are no billboards, no air pollution, no auto graveyards, no rampant soil erosion. But neither are there many native trees and other plants to speak of. Instead, you see acre after acre of tea plantations, hillsides of cinnamon and vanilla, groves of cultivated coconuts. You see rows of neat pastel houses and palm-lined avenues.

Searching for paradise

Today a great many people are searching for Edens. Increasingly, they are finding the remote and little-known places—places like the Galápagos and the Seychelles Islands.

Although tourists in any Eden are a mixed blessing, the Galápagos need tourism to help support conservation programs. The 6-dollar tax paid by each visitor goes directly to the islands' wildlife protection projects, and the archipelago is now a national park of Ecuador.

The Seychelles are already remade, and more tourists there will continue the process. The islands will never regain their wildness. Perhaps the most one can hope for on most of the Seychelles is preservation of the best of civilization's changes, and a softening of the worst. Cousin Island, for example, is now a nature reserve

where the birds are thriving under strict protection.

I am emotionally attached to my two Edens. Shall I still find thin gray forests on the Galápagos' cindery slopes a few years hence? Shall I still be able to walk in peace among the frigate birds and tortoises? Shall I still find solitude and clear blue water on a Seychelles beach? If conservationists show enough concern and effort, I shall. If the value of Eden for all men is preserved, I shall. If not, the world may have to do without paradise.

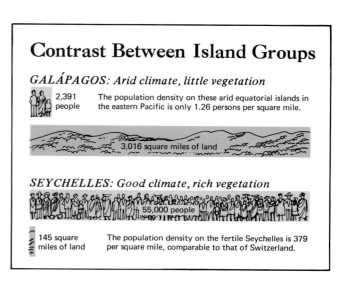

Contrast Between Island Groups

GALÁPAGOS: Arid climate, little vegetation

2,391 people The population density on these arid equatorial islands in the eastern Pacific is only 1.26 persons per square mile.

3,016 square miles of land

SEYCHELLES: Good climate, rich vegetation

55,000 people

145 square miles of land The population density on the fertile Seychelles is 379 per square mile, comparable to that of Switzerland.

Zebras and kudus share a shallow waterhole—a magnet for life—in Etosha National Park, South-West Africa. The location of water, a key element in the web of life, governs the migrations of the African grassland animals.

The Web of Life

No animal or plant lives alone. The destinies of
the prowling predator, the inconspicuous plant
eater, and the slender blade of grass are all linked.
Attempts to improve on nature often backfire
because these vital interconnections are ignored.
Ecology, the study of living things in their
environments, is yielding insights that must be
heeded as people try to meet their needs and to
preserve some of the natural world as well.

Drama of the East African Savanna

George Lindsay

Nowhere else on earth is it easier to see the vital interdependence of plant eater and plant, predator and prey.

The savannas of East Africa produce the greatest number of wild mammals in the world. Those tropical grasslands, with occasional trees and thorny thickets and a few narrow forests bordering rivers or lakes, somehow support a greater diversity of large mammals than any other natural area. They are a precious relic of the high point in the Age of Mammals and one of the most imposing ecological communities on earth.

The African savannas do not have an especially large variety of plants, though there is some diversity, and there are mammals specialized to eat each type of plant.

The different kinds of animals and plants and their interrelationships are the secret of the savannas' remarkable productivity.

All life, of course, is dependent on energy from the sun, and only green plants can capture that energy. The amount and dependability of the water supply help determine what plants grow where. In the savannas, where rain is seasonal and there is a yearly drought, grasses dominate. Their annual cycle corresponds to the rain cycle: They mature with the coming of the dry period, during which they survive in the form of seeds or through underground roots and stems.

As grasses are the most abundant plant, the grass eaters (grazers) are the most abundant animals. But there is specialization even among the creatures that eat the same kind of grass. Wildebeests and gazelles like tender new grass shoots; zebras and hartebeests take their turn as it gets further along; topi antelopes eat old dried grass not consumed by other species.

Another group of animals feeds on the thorn scrub. Like many drought-resistant plants, this vegetation has thorns and spines, but the giraffe's long, flexible tongue can wrap around and extract the leaves nestling among the thorns. The giraffe's 25-pound heart forces blood to the brain, which is 10 or more feet above it; expandable arteries engorge with blood and, together

Grazers and Browsers of the East African Savanna

Each of the savanna plant eaters shown below occupies its own niche in the interlocking ecosystem of the plains. Some are grazers, feeding on grass; some are browsers, feeding on leaves and twigs; some are both, taking whichever type of food is available. By feeding on different types of plants and on plants in different stages of growth, a large number of species can live in the same area with little competition. Most of the savanna herbivores are cud-chewing ruminants.

(The zebra, warthog, rhino, and elephant are not.) Ruminants have a four-chambered stomach (lower right) that enables them to store large quantities of food for digestion when they are not threatened by predators. As it feeds, each animal plays a role in shaping the environment.

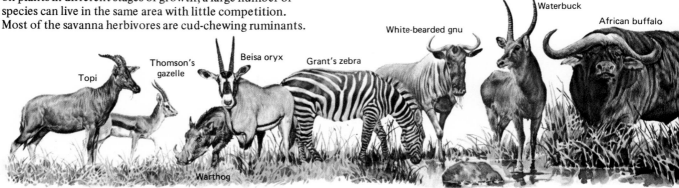

Topi — Thomson's gazelle — Beisa oryx — Warthog — Grant's zebra — White-bearded gnu — Waterbuck — African buffalo

DRY GRASSLAND — MOIST GRASSLAND

The Four Major Wildlife Zones of the Savanna

The dry grassland *is the home of species that can go without water for long periods, such as topi, gazelles, warthogs, and oryxes. Here, animals live mostly in small groups. Animals that need water daily, such as zebras, gnus, waterbucks, and buffaloes, are found in the* moist grassland, *where*

seasonal rains fill numerous waterholes. This is the region of the great herds. In the dry thorn scrub *are browsers, such as giraffes, elands, black rhinos, gerenuks, and dik-diks. Some have specialized mouths or other body parts for plucking leaves and twigs. Like the grazers of the dry grassland, most*

of these animals can endure long waterless periods and obtain some moisture from their food. The riverine forests *that fringe the savanna's lakes and streams support a dense population of moisture-loving animals, such as elephants, bushbucks, greater kudus, and duikers.*

with valves in the jugular vein, reduce pressure when the giraffe lowers its head to drink.

There are many antelope browsers, such as impalas, Grant's gazelles, and even the great elands. Most also graze occasionally.

A beautiful little antelope, the gerenuk, is specialized for browsing in thorn scrub. The gerenuk has very long legs, a long neck, and the ability to stand perfectly erect on its rear legs while it is eating.

There are several browsers of the lower thorn scrub. The black rhinoceros maintains its 2 tons of bone and flesh by nibbling leaves of clover and other leguminous plants, which it grasps with its pointed upper lip. The black rhino's even larger but better dispositioned relative, the white rhino, is a grazer. (Its name has nothing to do with its color; white is from the Afrikaans *weit* or wide and refers to the wide, square mouth.)

The insatiable elephant

The largest of land animals, the African bush elephant, consumes all kinds of vegetable matter: Grasses, reeds, papyrus, vines, and the roots, bark, branches, and leaves of trees. We have watched elephants chew branches of thorn trees that were covered with 3-inch spines and uproot cabbage palms to get at their harsh leaves and spine-edged stalks. Elephants can stand on

their rear legs while their trunks reach high to rip down branches, and they frequently push over trees to get the top leaves. A large elephant requires about 300 pounds of food a day, and it must browse or graze about two-thirds of the time. An elephant pulls up a bunch of grass with its trunk, knocks dirt from the roots by swinging it against its knees or the ground, and then stuffs the grass into its mouth.

But elephants are becoming a problem. When elephants were free to roam everywhere, the effect of a herd going through, even if they did push over some trees, was not serious. Now elephants are largely restricted to parks and reserves, which are unable to withstand the constant onslaught of the herds that no longer migrate.

The rivers and lakes of the savannas are inhabited by hippopotamuses. They are the second-largest land animal, with bulls reaching 4 tons. And although they are born, nurse, grow up, mate, and spend most of their lives in water, they feed on the adjacent grasslands. Hippos cannot survive long exposure to the tropical sun; so they must remain in the water during the heat of the day. They are powerful swimmers and can walk on the bottom of rivers and lakes, and even sleep there, automatically rising to the surface from time to time for air. But at night they take to the land and, if

Kenyan giraffe

East African eland

Gerenuk

Black rhinoceros

Dik-dik

African elephant

Bushbuck

Greater kudu

Blue duiker

DRY THORN SCRUB   RIVERINE FOREST

The savanna grasses evolved to withstand constant grazing by large animal herds. When the grass is cropped down to the ground, new shoots spring up from the roots. Different species eat the grass at different stages of development.

Eaten by gnus

Rhizome (underground stem)

The teeth and stomachs of the zebra and the gnu illustrate two different methods of living on grass. The zebra, which clips off the grass scissor-fashion between its incisors, can harvest drier, tougher grass than the gnu, which lacks upper incisors but has a hard gum pad for the lower incisors to bite against. The zebra's single-chambered stomach processes food faster than the four-chambered stomach of the gnu, but the latter extracts nourishment more efficiently.

Incisors

ZEBRA SKULL

Mouth

One chamber

ZEBRA STOMACH

Incisors

GNU SKULL

Mouth

Four chambers

GNU STOMACH

A Successful Wild Dog Hunt— Death for a Gnu, Defeat for a Lion

The most efficient predators of the African grasslands are the wild dogs. Their closely knit pack structure enables them to kill game as large as gnus and zebras and to challenge even such formidable rivals as lions. Pack size ranges from 6 to as many as 60, but the average is about 20 dogs. The pack hunts in the early morning and before dusk, locating prey by sight rather than scent. A wild dog pack approaches a herd of grazing animals slowly and cautiously; when the prey becomes alarmed and flees, the dogs give chase to an animal that is too young, sick, or weak to keep up with the herd. By culling weak or diseased animals, wild dogs are an important factor in maintaining the health of the great East African herds.

Once the prey is selected, the dogs pursue it single-mindedly, ignoring other animals in their path. The dogs can maintain a pace of 30 miles an hour for several miles and run most victims to exhaustion; they then dispatch the prey quickly with a concerted attack. Unlike most predators, wild dogs share their food freely. Dogs that arrive late at the kill are given a place or fed by regurgitation. Members of the pack also regurgitate food for pups too young to leave the home den and for mothers that have remained to nurse or guard the pups.

1 *After a brief chase wild dogs bring a young and ailing gnu to bay.*

4 *The lion swiftly kills the gnu with a bite through the neck.*

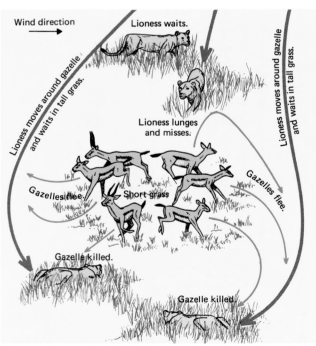

Cooperation paid off for lionesses in a hunt. Two circled around a herd of gazelles, then lay in wait in high grass until a third charged; the fourth simply waited. Boxed in, the gazelles were easy prey, and the lionesses caught two.

it is necessary, walk many miles to find savanna grass.

The far-ranging, grazing wildebeest, one of the most abundant of the grass eaters, must remain near water. Other antelopes, such as the oryxes, require less water and can feed away from waterholes, thus using food unavailable to those that must drink frequently. African buffaloes, like elephants, sometimes turn to marshes for reeds or papyrus. But their main food is grass, and they prefer lush valleys and open plains.

Most of the animals living in any area are plant eaters. It requires many plant eaters to support a meat eater, but in the East African savannas there are at least 2 dozen different kinds of carnivores, all essential to the well-being of the community.

Lions are the dominant predators of Africa, although they are restricted mostly to the grasslands. An adult male, weighing perhaps 400 to 500 pounds, probably consumes an average of 10 pounds of meat a day. But a lion can eat 40 to 50 pounds in a single meal, which lasts several hours; then it requires no more food for 4 or 5 days. Most lion food is medium-sized prey, such as wildebeests or zebras or the young of larger animals. But working in pairs or small groups, lions do drag down mature buffaloes and giraffes and, rarely, immature elephants, hippos, and rhinos. They are particularly fond of warthogs and sometimes wait by a warthog hole or even dig out its occupant. Lions also

2 *The lead dogs easily drag down the exhausted quarry.*

3 *An approaching lion has scared off the dogs; the gnu attempts to rise.*

5 *With the full pack arrived, the dogs reclaim the carcass.*

6 *The dogs devour the carcass as a vulture waits its turn.*

scavenge kills of other predators, especially hyenas.

Found everywhere except deserts, leopards are solitary hunters. An adult male weighs only about 150 pounds, but its strength, agility, and hunting ability, on a pound for pound basis, are greater than the lion's. Leopards are the natural enemy of bush pigs and of monkeys, but they also take small antelopes.

Cheetahs hunt in open grasslands, stalking and then sprinting after their prey, usually small antelopes. Cheetahs are considered the swiftest runners in the animal kingdom, but they lack great endurance.

Only recently has it been recognized that hyenas are important predators. These animals, which vaguely resemble dogs but are more closely related to cats, were long thought to be only scavengers. But at Ngorongoro Crater in Tanzania at least, hyenas kill wildebeests and zebras; they kill very young or very old lions.

Fearsome predators

The last and the most ruthless, though the smallest, of the "big five" predators are the wild hunting dogs. They have highly organized packs, numbering a few to 50 or more, which cut off an animal from a herd, pursue it until it is exhausted, bring it down, and start tearing it to pieces while it is still in shock. These animals are the most feared of the savanna's predators: Antelopes that would only watch a pride of lions will whirl and flee at the sight or smell of a hunting dog.

A balance is maintained between hunters and hunted. The predators kill only to satisfy their hunger. If food is scarce they move to another area or produce smaller litters and may desert any young that are born. Drought strikes fairly often in East Africa, but under natural conditions the animals have a breeding capacity that can permit a rapid increase after a calamity.

A savanna that for centuries has supported dozens of animal species can be ruined in only a few years by the introduction of domestic stock. One problem is that cattle and sheep eat only the grass they like, and weedy species that they will not eat take over the range. Wild animals that have adapted over millions of years to the savannas of East Africa have better digestive systems and lower water requirements; native species use the range more efficiently.

The East African savannas are a priceless asset for all mankind, an international treasure. But they must also provide food for their human inhabitants. The best solution might be to crop the wildlife for human consumption and manage it as a self-maintaining natural resource. This would be far better than destroying the savannas with farming or domestic stock.

The young African nations deserve the support and encouragement of the whole world as they bear the primary responsibility for preserving their heritage.

A mother cheetah guards her cubs. Among cheetahs mother-young bonds are strong until the cubs are mature enough to fend for themselves, but cheetahs are otherwise solitary animals. Cubs become independent at 14 to 16 months of age.

Is the Cheetah a Loser?

Norman Myers

This speedy hunter faces formidable odds in its struggle to survive. The cheetah is choosy about its habitat and has to compete for every bite of food.

One day I came upon a mother cheetah walking across the midmorning African savanna with four cubs. The mother was plainly out on a hunt. She stopped periodically to stare at small herds of Thomson's gazelles in the distance. The cubs' smoke-gray hair indicated they were about 6 weeks old. A few weeks earlier the cubs would not have been strong enough to accompany her, and she would have left them in a clump of withered grass, where their fur would have concealed them.

A cheetah with cubs must kill almost every day if she is to feed not only herself but her offspring, and this means considerable risk as long as the cubs must stay behind for the entire foray. A cheetah litter generally totals five or six cubs, and the family could well have lost two of their members already to marauding lions, hyenas, or eagles.

Eventually the cheetah mother spotted a group of gazelles about 200 yards away, grazing unconcernedly. Somehow she indicated to her cubs that this was the time for business, and they disappeared under a 6-inch-high scrub patch. The mother made her cautious way toward the prey, freezing from time to time in midstride, when she suspected she was being observed. Soon the low-slung walk accelerated to a trot and then into an all-out burst. A little cloud of dust sped across the grass-sparse plain, in pursuit of the gazelles stampeding in terror. One gazelle paused a fraction too long, and after less than 200 yards of chase, it was pinned to the ground in a silent stranglehold.

A shared meal

The cheetah lay for a while by the carcass, panting. When she recovered her breath, she started to drag her prey, but there was no convenient hiding place within reach, so, after a few minutes' effort, she gave up. Instead she trotted to the place where she had left the cubs, called them out of hiding, and returned quickly to the carcass.

But it was already too late. A vulture patrolling overhead had spotted the family. The bird alighted nearby. It was soon joined by a second, which had seen the first vulture plunge earthward. Ten vultures gathered and attracted the attention of a jackal. The jackal's expectant gait had, in turn, signaled the interesting news to a spotted hyena lying outside its den half a mile away. The hyena didn't follow yet; it merely watched the jackal.

When the cheetahs reached the carcass, there was a brief altercation as they disputed ownership of the kill with the vultures. Unless some stronger carnivore opened up the carcass, the vultures could not feed. But meanwhile they stood close guard. Having driven them 2 dozen yards back, the mother cheetah began to rip and tear at the prey's abdomen. But every few

seconds—literally, I timed her by my watch—she paused to stare around the landscape with every sign of apprehension. Perhaps she sensed that if other predators came to join the meal, the food might not be limited to the gazelle. Within a few minutes, however, she had ripped open the hide sufficiently to start feeding in earnest. The cubs licked at the tidbits.

By now the vultures had grown into a flock of 50. Every few minutes they made a concerted rush, and the mother cheetah spent more time fighting them off than feeding. The cubs had to stay close by her to avoid lethal pecks from those hefty bills. She now managed only an occasional bite at the carcass, but

A 16th-century Indian painting shows Emperor Akbar hunting game with trained cheetahs. Easily tamed, cheetahs have been kept as hunting animals for centuries. Often used in relays, they were blindfolded until it was their turn to hunt.

Vultures gather aggressively near two cheetahs and their kill, a gazelle. Although vultures can sometimes drive a lone cheetah from its kill, two cheetahs are too much for them. But cheetahs lose a high percentage of their prey to competing animals.

this was not nearly enough to serve her needs since her teeth were not strong enough to shear away chunks of meat the way lions' or leopards' teeth can.

Suddenly the mother cheetah leaped aside from the carcass. The hyena was approaching at a rush, and across the plain came others of the hyena clan. The cheetah mother did not stand and fight, hungry as she still was. The hyena is a larger and more powerful animal than the cheetah. She might soon have got a nip in the haunches that could make the flat-out chase on the next hunt a painful affair—and anything less than a 60 to 70 mph speed could mean no kill when pursuing a gazelle.

The cubs scattered. They did so in a star formation, instead of tagging after their mother. This tactic probably serves them well against a single predator, but it plays into the hands—or jaws—of pack predators. If the cubs crouch low in a close-by clump of grass, they are unlikely to escape notice from 20 hyenas milling around in the area. Even were they so fortunate as to survive this scene, they would be unlikely afterward to find the mother cheetah when the situation became safe enough for them to move.

An hour later I saw the mother cheetah striding across the plain on the lookout for prey. Only three cubs followed her, one limping so badly it could hardly keep up. The life of a cheetah family is a constant search for food, which means endless wandering. Adult lions readily team up to attack a buffalo or a giraffe. But adult cheetahs do not cooperate in hunting, so larger antelopes are beyond their capacities. And the cheetah, which is not a good climber, cannot cache its food in a tree to be secure while feeding and to ensure that the remains will be available the next day.

Other predators are doing better

The cheetah was never as numerous as the lion or the leopard in the best of times. About 2,000 lions, at least 1,000 leopards, and some 3,000 hyenas live in the Serengeti National Park and its environs, but there are only 250 cheetahs—even though there are 5,000 square miles of open habitat suitable for a speed-chase hunter and half a million gazelles available as prey. Not only do the lions and other predators dispose of quite a few cheetahs but disease seems to be more of a factor for cheetahs than for other predators. On top of all this the cheetah does not show the adaptability to a variety of wild lands that the lion does. The lion can

A leopard drags a half-eaten carcass up a tree for storage. Unlike the cheetah, the leopard is an excellent climber and has the strength to carry loads heavier than itself; kills are often cached in the fork of a tree.

survive in grasslands, savannas, woodlands, and thorn-bushes. The leopard can survive in each of these environments, and as many more again. The cheetah can manage only in semiarid areas, grasslands, and wooded savannas. Now that Africa's human population is exploding, people are spilling over from the more fertile arable areas into the next most favorable habitats—the grassland savannas.

For a variety of reasons, then, the cheetah is something of a "loser" in modern-day Africa. Its numbers have probably never been very high, but they were sufficient. Now the species is probably down to way below 20,000. This figure could well be only half as many as in 1960, when Africa's human populace began expanding its numbers and its aspirations.

Altogether Africa's parks and reserves contain only 3,000 cheetahs at most. Given the precarious position of the species, Africa's existing wildlife sanctuaries probably cannot guarantee the cheetah's survival. Were the cheetah ever to find itself in the plight of the Bengal tiger, with only some 2,000 left, it would be in far greater danger of losing the battle against extinction—and, because of the extensive tracts of land required to save it, the cost would be much higher.

Cheetahs Versus Leopards

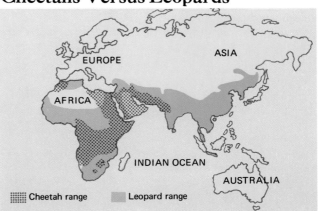

The most widespread cat, the leopard is faring better than the cheetah. The leopard population is actually increasing in some areas, while the cheetah population, especially that of the Asiatic race, has seriously declined since 1960. The leopard is more adaptable: It can exist in a greater variety of environments, and its diet is far less specialized. A cheetah needs a much larger territory to support it than a leopard does—and the cheetah's habitat, the open grasslands, is rapidly shrinking because of agricultural growth.

African Waterholes—Magnets for Wildlife

Although many large mammals of the dry African bush and grasslands are able to go without drinking for long periods, some must drink every day. And all but a few will drink whenever they have the chance. The waterhole means life to a host of animals. It also means death to some. Predators know that, sooner or later, the animals that they eat will be driven by thirst to the waterhole. So there they lie in wait. Prey animals approach a waterhole warily, sometimes taking an hour or more to cover the last few yards to the water, scanning the surroundings for suspicious movements and testing the air with sensitive nostrils. Most grazers gulp their fill in less than a minute. Among herd animals some stand guard while others drink. Only the largest and most powerful herbivores dare to approach boldly and drink at leisure.

Giraffes keep a wary alert as two of their group drink from a waterhole in Etosha National Park in South-West Africa. To reach the water giraffes must spread their forelegs wide apart; in this awkward posture, with their eyes lowered and the noise of drinking interfering with their hearing, they are especially vulnerable to predators. Like many other hoofed animals that live in arid lands, giraffes can go for weeks without drinking, obtaining all the water they need from the juicy leaves and twigs they eat. (Even during droughts such leaves may be 60 percent water.) When water is available, an adult giraffe drinks about 2 gallons a week.

Waterholes attract scavengers as well as plant eaters and predators. A dead elephant (one of its feet is the loglike object in foreground) provides a meal for hyenas, vultures, and marabou storks in the Masai Amboseli Game Reserve in Kenya.

Elephants and buffaloes *share a small waterhole, only inches deep, in Kenya's famed Tsavo National Park. There is little conflict between different species of herbivores at the waterhole. The surrounding area shows effects of heavy use.*

Every animal species has its own preferred hours *for drinking. Most plant eaters drink in the daylight, when they have the best chance of seeing predators. Elephants, safe from attack because of their size and strength, drink mostly at night. Leopards and hyenas, which hunt primarily at night and rest during the heat of the day, are usually nighttime drinkers. The dominant carnivores, lions, may drink during the day or at night. The staggered schedules may serve to lessen competition among species.*

PEAK DRINKING TIME

DAY

NIGHT

6 a.m.

6 p.m.

12 m.

12 p.m.

1 2 3 4 5 6 7 8 9 10 11

■ Leopard
□ Lion
□ Hyena
■ Elephant
■ Wildebeest, eland
■ Buffalo, zebra, giraffe
□ Warthog

*A **nighttime drink** caps a successful hunt for a pack of African hunting dogs in Botswana; the water source is a pool in a dried-out desert riverbed. Active mainly at night, these wild dogs usually drink between evening and early morning.*

*A **troop of baboons** slakes its thirst at a waterhole in Zululand's Mkuzi Game Reserve as a big male stands guard. Baboons come to the waterhole around midday, when predators are least active and most easily seen.*

Crowded Africa: Habitat for Man and Beast

Norman Myers

Africa's wildlife and people are linked in a struggle for survival as the human population rapidly expands.

A great deal has been said over the past few years about East African wildlife. Far less has been said about East Africans. Yet a prime factor in the survival of wildlife is the human population problem.

The population explosion in East Africa has resulted in a massive squeeze on animal habitats. People are already trying to grow maize in the hinterlands of Kenya's Nairobi National Park and in other savanna regions. Maize has never been grown in these places before, but it must be grown now because there are so many more people to feed. When the final division of the land takes place, the voices of African peasants are the ones that will be heard. They will be ready to go along with protection of wildlife areas only if these lands can also put food in their stomachs and cash in their pockets.

If Kikuyuland on the northern side of Nairobi Park offers a growing threat, another threat looms on the southern border. The large, migratory grazing animals in the park are dependent, for water and grazing land, upon the 400 square miles of the adjoining Masai tribal reserve. The Masai have so far ignored wildlife, but they may be less inclined to do so when zebras break down fences or rhinos wreck cattle-watering installations.

The parks and reserves account for the greater part of the $70 million a year Kenya earns from its 400,000 visitors. When the tourist stream approaches 1 million, as is expected around the end of this decade, tourism could supplant agriculture as a prime earner of foreign exchange. For this reason alone little conflict should be permitted between livestock and wildlife. While a cow or a lion costs the Government about the same amount to maintain, a lion earns 20 times as much in foreign exchange.

Compromise at Amboseli

At Amboseli in the heart of Masailand, a serious confrontation between livestock and wildlife has been avoided. The central 150-square-mile sanctuary around the lake and swamps at the foot of Kilimanjaro brings

Just a few miles from the high-rise center of Nairobi, wild zebras, hartebeests (left foreground), and wildebeests graze in Nairobi National Park, Kenya. Not only can wild animals exist close to man, in the future they may have to.

in from tourism more than half the total revenue for the entire 8,000-square-mile district. Livestock could not match this sort of income, even if the land were completely given over to the best ranching methods. Moreover, the tourist flood is still in its early stages.

As recently as 1971, Amboseli's livestock outnumbered the wild animals by three or four to one. In fact, there were more cattle to the square mile there than in any other area of East Africa, even though Amboseli was supposed to be a protected wildlife area. But when an economist and an anthropologist joined an ecologist and a local warden to balance the needs of wildlife and people, a solution was eventually worked out. The Masai are to receive water installations on the edge of the strategic wildlife sector. They will also be given compensation for grass eaten by migrating wildebeests and other wild animals. The main wildlife zone is to be upgraded to a national park.

The problems of Amboseli are similar to those in other parts of Masailand. At a time when the Masai

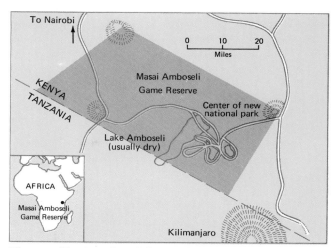

The new Masai Amboseli Park in Kenya, set apart exclusively for wildlife, occupies a swampy portion of the game reserve. A pipeline will bring water from the 150-square-mile park to points in the reserve, where cattle herding is permitted.

The Masai and Their Cattle

The Masai, proud warriors and herders in East Africa, have a way of life based on cattle. Milk mixed with the blood of cows is their main food; cow dung plasters their huts and fuels their fires. Social standing is determined by the number of cattle owned. So dependent on cattle are the Masai that they could not change to another way of life without profound cultural upheaval. Although the Masai do not hunt, their herds compete with wildlife for food and water. In the past diseases limited the size of the cattle herds, but modern medicine has removed this natural check, with effects like those shown below and at right.

Masai cattle drink from an upland stream in Kenya. Daily trampling by hundreds of cattle hooves has worn a large bare patch on the stony bank of the stream.

Masai cattle march to a water source in Ngorongoro Crater, Tanzania. Moving in a tightly packed mass, the cattle cut deep ruts in the soil with their hooves.

Masai herdsmen watch cattle near a manyatta *(encampment) in Kenya. A few years of heavy grazing will strip grass and trees from the hill, leaving it open to erosion.*

167

are being asked to share the savanna with wildlife, their population is increasing, and their livestock is increasing with it. Many of the Masai still subsist mainly on milk. A family of five needs 80 cattle, 50 of them milk cows, to see it through normal times, let alone hard times. There will not be much in the way of a final solution until the Masai can be persuaded to change their diet, but this is like telling them to change their whole social framework, to forget their Masai history and what it stands for.

One way of preserving wild animals might be to consider them a resource, like livestock. Zebra skins sell for at least $50, leaving the meat from the carcass to finance the zebra harvesting or "cropping." Zebras could make more money than cattle, as the situation now stands. And if other species besides the zebra were included in the cropping program, production undoubtedly could be greater.

The claims for cropping wild animals are being advanced more frequently as evidence of their efficiency as protein producers emerges. It seems the savanna's wild animals practice a division of labor, with different species eating different plants, while cattle tend to

Ears spread in threat, *an elephant suspiciously faces a photographer and guide in Kafue National Park in Zambia. Seconds after the picture was taken, the elephant charged, but the guide drove it off with gestures and shouts.*

Tame elands follow cattle to pasture *on a Rhodesian farm. Elands take readily to domestication and live peaceably with cattle. Although little has been done with raising elands in Africa, a large herd has thrived for decades in the Soviet Union.*

graze on fewer kinds of grass. Wild grazers also reach maturity sooner than cattle, breed more rapidly, reach slaughter size more quickly, and are more resistant to drought and disease.

Wildlife cropping could provide an additional income in many African countries. Being able to earn money from wildlife would do something for the man living on the edge of the game area who wakes up in the morning and sees his maize disappearing over the park border inside an elephant.

The poaching problem

Widespread cropping already is practiced in many parks through poaching. The Kabalega Park (formerly known as the Murchison Park) in Uganda is subject to more indiscriminate, unlicensed hunting by locals than virtually any other park in East Africa, since it is surrounded by human communities whose inhabitants do not see why their activities should harmonize with the park's needs.

The persistent poaching problem raises a question that must be asked of all the parks and reserves in East Africa. What purpose are they to serve? Ostensi-

bly they are supposed to protect nature, even if they do not always do the job well. But there are social and economic considerations as well. Kenya's gross national product amounts to only a little more than Californians spend on hunting and fishing. In the developed Western nations it is obviously in order to question what happens if commercial considerations step inside a park's borders. In East Africa one might well say that unless commercial considerations step inside a park, it is likely to stop being a park. Concerning wild country in East Africa one must accept the axiom that you use it or lose it. Otherwise, high-flown talk about national heritage is likely to be drowned out by the rumblings of empty stomachs.

At present the parks have an image as preserves for the affluent, well-fed white man. Until conservation in East Africa is considered conservation of an African environment, wild animals will lose ground. A zebra must be viewed not only as something for people from overseas to see on their vacations but also as a local resource. In the seventies East Africa must become a region where the old story of "animals versus people" is finally left behind.

The Advantages of Game Ranching

As potential ranch animals, Africa's native hoofed animals have many advantages over cattle imported to the continent. The native animals are resistant to diseases such as sleeping sickness. They can live on much less water than cattle. They thrive and grow fat on the scant forage of the savannas, while cattle stay scrawny. The different native species efficiently utilize the whole spectrum of food plants, whereas domestic stock eat only a few types. And wild animals gain weight much faster than cattle: Male elands may reach half a ton in just a year. If wildlife ranching is accepted by Africa's tradition-conscious herdsmen and farmers, it will help to preserve dwindling native species, while lessening Africa's protein shortage.

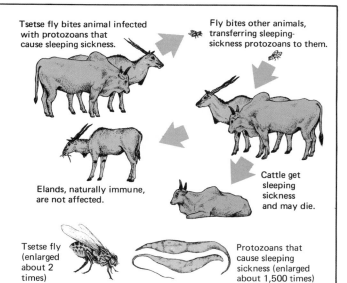

Tsetse fly bites animal infected with protozoans that cause sleeping sickness.

Fly bites other animals, transferring sleeping-sickness protozoans to them.

Elands, naturally immune, are not affected.

Cattle get sleeping sickness and may die.

Tsetse fly (enlarged about 2 times)

Protozoans that cause sleeping sickness (enlarged about 1,500 times)

Tsetse flies, abundant over much of Africa, transmit the microscopic protozoans, trypanosomes, that cause sleeping sickness in man and livestock. Infected cattle usually die, but wild animals are immune.

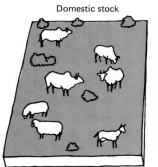

Domestic stock

Wildlife

One square mile of African savanna supports only 7 tons of domestic livestock—cattle, sheep, or goats—but it can support up to 42 tons of wild grazers and browsers. The wild animals utilize all the available food plants and do not damage the environment by overgrazing.

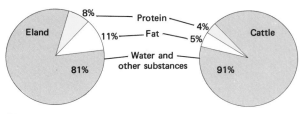

Eland — 8% Protein — 4% Cattle
11% — Fat — 5%
81% — Water and other substances — 91%

Eland milk is twice as rich in protein and fat as the milk of domestic cattle. In addition, it stays fresh longer.

A nocturnal feast on a suburban Swiss lawn lured this young wild boar from its hiding place. Though wild boars are normally shy of man, this one learned to accept the author's presence and established a regular routine of feeding visits.

Requiem for a Wild Boar

Louis J. Halle

One wild boar that ventured into the outskirts of Geneva met an untimely end, but these adaptable creatures are holding their own in Central Europe.

I hesitated to telephone my friend Paul Géroudet with a question so foolish. As one of Europe's leading field naturalists, he is constantly having to weigh the claims of observers whose enthusiasm for the identification of rare species exceeds their skill. My question was: "Do you think it at least conceivable that we might have a wild boar on our premises?"

"Our premises" are a bit of parkland sloping down to the shore of Lake Geneva. In its midst is one of those great ugly villas built about the turn of the century. As we are only about 3 miles from the crowded center of Geneva, the surrounding area became suburban long ago. At one end of our lakeshore, however, is a bed of reeds, less than 4 acres, which has been set aside by the authorities as a nature reserve. It is an oasis for waterfowl in the midst of a world of human activity.

During the week of November 12, 1972, something had been tearing up our lawn at night. I had not gone out to examine the damage until, on the 16th, a member of our household who had been brought up on the

edge of a forest in France said it looked like the work of *le sanglier*. (*Le sanglier* is the European wild boar.) I explained why this could not be; but when I went out to see for myself, I was shaken. There were even the prints of a cloven hoof. If this was not the work of a boar, it was the devil's work.

After I had put my question to Géroudet there was a moment of silence. Then he replied that yes, he supposed a wild boar on our premises was at least conceivable. He added that there had been a report of one seen near a village some miles farther up the shore, in France.

The night of the 18th was cold, cloudless, and still, the moon almost full. About 9 o'clock I stationed myself on a balcony overlooking the lawn that sloped down to the lakeshore. I had waited 10 minutes when suddenly a flock of swans, ghosts in the moonlight, all started to swim away from the shore. Half a minute later a black silhouette emerged from the reeds and moved rapidly across the lawn until it reached the trees on the other side. Here it remained. Occasionally it would move a few feet toward the house, then stop to recommence whatever it was doing. After some 40 minutes of this it suddenly walked toward the house, coming directly under the balcony.

Like a monster from a bestiary

Through the weeks that followed, although my wife and I became thoroughly familiar with the apparition, we could never quite bring ourselves to believe in it. The monster might have emerged from the pages of a medieval bestiary. I refer to the boar as a monster, for so it was in the massiveness of its head and foreparts, its thickness all over, and the four short sticks on which it was supported. However, when it walked or trotted it did so with a quick and easy grace. What was extraordinary was the lightness of its trotting gait, as if the twinkling feet carried no weight at all.

In the days that followed there were many signs of the boar, including fresh hoofprints every day. I set out potatoes, which boars are said to relish, but they remained untouched. Then I tried corn, spreading it near the corner of the house away from the lake. Shortly after dark, clearly visible in the light from the windows and from a lamp over our front door, the boar came to feed. After that, it came every evening after nightfall to spend an hour or two, with brief intervals of absence, feeding on the corn we put out.

It tended to bypass any corn that was in a heap, preferring to pick it up where the grains lay separately. Pushing its flat snout along the grass or the gravel, its forelegs slightly splayed out, it would pick up the grains as it came to them, crunching them loudly between its gleaming teeth.

The initial reaction of the gardeners in our neighborhood was that the boar must, of course, be shot. But this changed. I explained that hunting was forbidden throughout the region, that the presence of the boar was a matter of scientific interest, and that if anything happened to it the case would be one for

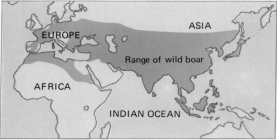

A family group of wild boars feeds in a forest in southwestern Germany (above). The striped coats of the piglets provide concealment in the brush and forest; the stripes will fade as the piglets mature. Adult male boars (above, right) sport

sharp tusks that may grow to a length of 9 inches. The tusks of the females are smaller but still effective weapons. Wild boars, the ancestors of domestic pigs, are the hardiest and the most widely distributed of all wild pig species.

the police. This word, I know, spread to the entire local population, the members of which began to appreciate the fact that our boar was, by its presence, conferring a distinction on the neighborhood.

Two days before Christmas we went off to the mountains for 3 weeks of vacation, leaving our house empty. But one of the local gardeners came every evening to put out the corn. The boar's habits were now regular. It had settled into our community. It was established. Except for the superficial damage it did by its rootings, and the paths it broke through our shrubbery, it was a most satisfactory boar, faithful in its fashion.

Before I come to the last act I should provide some background to explain the presence of such a great beast of the wilderness on the outskirts of Geneva. The wild boar, which has been known to attain a weight of 460 pounds, is one of the great mammals, a creature of the dark forests that once covered much of Europe. Unless brought to bay and in desperate circumstances, it is not a danger to human beings today. I say today because it has developed the special wariness of man that all the great beasts of the wild have acquired since he took up firearms and invented missiles to kill at a distance.

The pursuit of the wild boar by hunters on horseback, armed with long spears and assisted by packs of dogs, was widely practiced by the nobility in the Middle Ages and the Renaissance. Consequently, the species had disappeared from the British Isles by some

The Persistent Pigs

Tough, adaptable, and prolific, pigs have survived man's pressures better than many forms of wildlife. Able to eat both plant and animal food, they have spread into virtually every kind of habitat.

Pygmy hog
(wooded grassland,
northern India)

Babirusa
(tropical rain forest,
Indonesia)

African bush pig
(forest near water, Africa)

Collared peccary
(desert, scrub, and forest,
southwestern U.S.
to southern Argentina)

Warthog
(savanna, Africa)

171

Cornered at last, a large wild boar meets his end in this 16th-century Austrian altarpiece. Hunters and their dogs were often injured or killed in such hand-to-hand encounters with the ferocious and swift-moving boars.

time in the 17th century. Before the middle of the 19th century it had virtually disappeared from Switzerland, a few probably remaining only along the German border.

The wild boar is, however, hardy and adaptable, it has no predators save man, and it is capable of restoring its numbers rapidly. The litter of a mature sow may number 8 to 12 young, and she may produce as many as 3 litters in 2 years. The young are often the victims of diseases, but the possibility of population explosions is implicit in the rate of reproduction. During both the World Wars there was a notable increase of wild boars, which was attributed to the temporary cessation of hunting.

In the course of the present century they have repopulated the Jura Mountains, north and west of Lake Geneva, and the forested foothills to the south of it. Now in the 1970's, perhaps because of greatly increased plantings of corn, a population explosion is occurring in this area, as well as elsewhere. All around Lake Geneva wild boars are being reported in ever-increasing numbers, and the population pressure ap-

pears to be impelling them to venture into the outskirts of villages and towns.

Our boar, perhaps partly by swimming (for they willingly take to water), may have made its way down the lakeshore at night until it found secure conditions for establishing its lair. It was pretty much confined to the enclosed area of the reedbed and the walled property; but in the fall and early winter there were still fallen acorns and succulent roots to be dug up. Then, when the food supply was becoming exhausted, we had undertaken to make regular provision for its feeding. A tacit arrangement had been concluded.

When we returned from the mountains January 14, we looked forward eagerly to seeing our boar again. The first thing I did was to put out its corn. That evening, however, it did not come. Nor did it come the following evening, nor the evenings after. On Sunday the 21st I went into the reserve, following the trampled path through the reeds that the boar had worn by its comings and goings. At the other side of the reserve, bounded by a high mesh fence, there was a border of trees and bushes. Here the boar's highway came to an end. I looked all around, saw nothing, and was about to turn back—when suddenly I did see something. A couple of feet from where I stood the boar's snout projected from under a sort of low tent made by dead reeds that had been bent over. This was the lair our boar had made for itself, and there was the great beast itself, apparently asleep.

An apparition from the past

I knew it could not really have remained asleep through the disturbance I had been making, but it looked so much as if it were merely asleep that I was seized by what I shall call a sense of prudence. What if it should wake up to find me standing almost on top of it? I daresay I waited a full minute, not moving, before I cautiously investigated. The boar was quite dead. It had three bullet holes in its left side.

The Geneva newspapers reported the shooting of the boar and announced the offer by the Association Genevoise pour la Protection de la Nature and the Commission Cantonale de la Chasse of 1,400 Swiss francs to anyone giving information leading to the arrest of the culprit. At dawn on January 22 the carcass of the slain boar was removed. This carting away of the corpse, however, was not a satisfactory end. Something remained incomplete.

Our visitor had been a refugee from the wilderness of primeval times, now so largely obliterated by our own macadamized world. Coming to us as an apparition from an immemorial past, what it represented was not just itself, nor was its death just one death. Therefore in the evening of that day, at the hour when we had been used to looking for its visit, I played a recording of Mozart's *Requiem*—which served on this one occasion as a Requiem for a Wild Boar. When the long musical piece drew to its end, the finality of its departure had, at last, been properly solemnized and sealed.

Some Animals Get Along Well With People

Human activities have destroyed the habitats of many animal species but have provided new, bountiful sources of food and shelter for others. Some of the adaptable species, like the barn owl, rid the human environment of pests. Others, like the garbage-robbing raccoon, approach the status of pests themselves. Coyotes are regarded as enemies by some people. But most, like the cattle egret, coexist peacefully with their human hosts.

Agricultural Hangers-On

Cattle egret

Coyote

The cattle egret finds a plentiful source of food in the insects stirred up by cattle as they graze. It also eats parasites from their hides. The North American coyote supplements its normal diet of small animals and carrion with raids on domestic livestock and poultry and, occasionally, on garbage cans.

The barn owl finds small rodents around man's supplies of feed.

Suburban Foragers and Houseguests

Blue tit

Brush-tailed possum

The adaptable, omnivorous North American raccoon thrives on man's food scraps.

The suburbs, with their seminatural environment, offer food and shelter to a number of animals. European tits, for example, accept nesting boxes and eat insects around gardens. The Australian brush-tailed possum occupies a squirrellike niche in suburbs and parks.

Urban Scavengers

Herring gull

Black kite

Despite pollution and the proximity of man, a number of wild animals manage to thrive in cities, usually as scavengers. The opportunistic herring gull is a familiar denizen of garbage dumps in northern latitudes; in warmer regions the black, or pariah, kite occupies a similar niche.

India's rhesus monkeys, revered by Hindus, beg aggressively and snatch food.

The Unraveling Web of Wildness

Lee M. Talbot

Throughout history man has consistently disrupted the ecological systems on which all living things depend.

Until recently most people believed that effective wildlife conservation consisted primarily of protecting animals against wanton killing or capture. And they were right—at least in part. Since man first appeared on earth he has driven a number of species to extinction. But all the armies in the world cannot save an animal if it has no place to live, no place to hide, no food to eat.

No animal exists alone. Instead it lives at the center of a figurative spider web. The radiating strands of the web represent the animal's interrelationships with all the components of its environment—climate, water and soils, plants, animals, down to the lowest amoeba. Each of the strands, in turn, is interconnected with virtually all of the others.

If any one of these strands is significantly altered, the others will be affected, too, and the whole web may be destroyed. Change the supply of water in an area, for example, and that changes the vegetation and other conditions necessary for all of the animals. Change the types of invertebrates inhabiting that area—even the most apparently insignificant microorganisms in the soil—and the conditions essential for plant growth change, too. Change or modify plants, and you change the food supply of the plant-eating animals, which are in turn the food of the predators. Therefore, to preserve any animal you must preserve its habitat web.

Each animal has its own ecological niche, and an animal's adaptation to one niche usually rules out its occupation of any other. Polar bears and arctic foxes, adapted to extreme cold, could not survive in a desert; the desert kangaroo rat or whip-tailed lizard could not survive in the high tundra or on the ice packs. The long legs and neck of a giraffe, along with its lip and mouth structure, adapt it to browsing on savanna trees and bushes but not for survival in treeless grasslands. Burrowing rodents cannot live where rocks, soil conditions, or water preclude burrowing.

But the survival of a species requires more than

Limiting Factors and How They Affect Animal Populations

How many animals of one species can a given area support? This depends on the particular needs of the species involved, but the main factors that limit population size are food, water, and cover. Although many animals are endangered because of general habitat destruction (which includes loss of food, water, and cover), the numbers of the species shown here are kept low by one major limiting factor.

Limited by the Food Supply

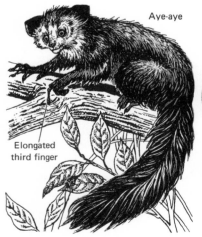

The aye-aye, a lemurlike primate of Madagascar's forests, lives chiefly on wood-boring insects that it extracts with its middle finger. These insects are found only in large old trees.

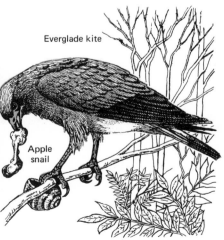

The Everglade kite of Florida lives exclusively on the apple snail. Swamp drainage, which destroys the habitat of these snails, has eliminated most of the kite's food supply.

Limited by the Water Supply

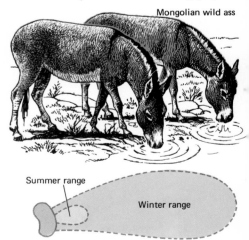

The number of Mongolian wild asses is limited by access to water, which is scarce in the arid central Asian steppes they inhabit. In summer they must remain within 6 to 12 miles of a water source.

adaptation to its environment. The perpetuation of any species also depends on the maintenance of adequate numbers. Some species, such as lynxes, need only one pair for reproduction. Others, such as penguins, must live among large numbers of their kind. Some species do not need the stimulus of large numbers to reproduce, but they range over such vast areas that they require a population high enough to ensure that male and female will actually meet and mate. Furthermore, a species with very low numbers or a single concentrated population is far more vulnerable to extermination from disease, hunting, or habitat change than a species with a larger or more widespread population.

The limiting factor

The number of a given animal that a habitat can support is known as the carrying capacity. The carrying capacity is determined by what amounts to the weakest strand in the habitat web, known as the limiting factor. The usual limiting factors are the amount and distribution of water, cover, and food.

How limiting any of these factors is depends in part on the mobility of the animal involved. A bird can make long daily flights between its feeding and resting area and its source of water, but a rabbit must meet all its living requirements within a limited range. Thus a single source of water might support a large and scattered population of birds, but only a few rabbits.

Cover, too, can be a limiting factor in several ways. Thick evergreens provide cover for some northern birds and mammals during winter storms. Some cover supplies a protection from predators.

Frequently the factors that limit the carrying capacity of a habitat are quite complex, especially so with food. For some animals the limiting factor is an insufficient quantity of food in certain seasons. Wolves may find food plentiful when migratory animals pass through, but at other times—when they must rely on resident prey—the pickings may be sparse. Similarly the carrying capacity for seed-eating birds in an area is limited by the seed supply available in winter. Backyard bird feeders increase the carrying capacity. This is why the feeders are so effective in winter and also why, once started, such feeding should be continued until a natural seed supply is available.

The quality of food is also important, especially to grazing and browsing animals, where the limiting factor is often the availability of plants with high nutritional value. With northern deer, for example, the worst period is late winter, when plants are dormant, vegetation is snow covered, and the nutritional value of the available forage is low.

But habitat is not just a particular physical place. It is the sum total of the environmental conditions

Limited by the Supply of Cover

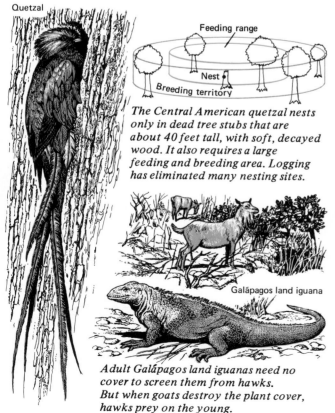

Quetzal

Feeding range

Nest

Breeding territory

The Central American quetzal nests only in dead tree stubs that are about 40 feet tall, with soft, decayed wood. It also requires a large feeding and breeding area. Logging has eliminated many nesting sites.

Galápagos land iguana

Adult Galápagos land iguanas need no cover to screen them from hawks. But when goats destroy the plant cover, hawks prey on the young.

The population of the rare Kirtland's warbler is limited by its very restricted preference in nesting sites: young stands of jack pines from 6 to 18 feet tall. Such stands are found only where forest fires have cleared the land and opened the cones of mature jack pines, releasing the seeds. Only in northern Michigan does the ground-nesting bird find the combination of cover and fast-draining soil it requires. Parasitism is an added problem; above, a male Kirtland's warbler feeds a young cowbird that has usurped its nest.

necessary for a species' health and survival. For many migratory creatures that covers a lot of territory. Many ocean fish reproduce in the shallow, nutrient-rich coastal waters, yet spend most of their life in the deeper ocean. Other fish, such as salmon, spawn in cold, swift mountain streams and then migrate to the ocean, where they grow to maturity. They ultimately return up the same river to spawn. Obviously the survival of both kinds of fish depends upon the maintenance of their total habitat web.

Successional species are usually doing well

Yet another habitat dimension is succession. Forest communities provide a good illustration, although the principles apply equally well to other communities. When a mature forest is cut or burned down, leaving essentially bare ground, there will be a succession of types of vegetation; and eventually—perhaps in tens or hundreds of years—there will be a forest again. Each stage in the recovery provides a different set of ecological niches for different animals. A mature forest, for example, is not a good habitat for deer, because it lacks the browse that was plentiful in the earlier stage.

Through lumbering, grazing, burning, and clearing, man is constantly creating more habitats for successional species and less for animals that need a stable wilderness. Maintaining habitats for these two types of animals calls for two entirely different approaches, the stable wilderness requiring complete protection from any disturbance.

Throughout history, of course, man has destroyed many animal habitats all over the world and modified most—if not all—of the rest. Species have been exterminated, forced to migrate elsewhere or to adapt to new conditions. Hardest hit have been those animals requiring large habitats, such as bison, bears, and wolves. In fact, more than half of the mammals exterminated in Africa, Asia, Europe, and North America have been large, wide-ranging predators. Most of the others were large hooved creatures, requiring extensive feeding grounds; about half the mammalian species currently threatened are from this group.

The process of habitat modification continues today, accelerated by increasing human populations and new technologies. To make matters worse, pollution has added a new and lethal dimension. Each year researchers uncover new pollutants and new facts concerning old ones. Chemical wastes, pesticides, detergents, heavy metals, oil, sewage, exhaust emissions, and heat continue to spread across the land and pour into the air and water.

More than 40 species of birds are plagued with the consequences of ingesting pesticide-contaminated foods. The birds' survival is threatened by shell thinning—their eggs become so fragile that the parent birds break them by stepping on them, while turning them during incubation, or even when laying them.

Far from being isolated tragedies, such problems are symptomatic of the health of wildlife in general. And that condition is usually a good index of any nation's natural resources. Where there is a scarcity of wildlife there also tends to be destructive exploitation of other resources. In part this situation stems from a country's policies (or lack of them) toward resource management. It also reflects the pervasive impact of land use—and abuse—on wildlife habitats.

All this does not mean wildlife is doomed. Throughout the world there is a growing appreciation of the values of wildlife in general. In 1972 more than 100 nations assembled at the United Nations Conference on the Human Environment in Stockholm. And 80 nations met in Washington, D.C., in 1973 and agreed to protect endangered species through control of international trade. Perhaps most important of all, though, people are at last beginning to realize that, in the final analysis, habitat protection *is* wildlife protection.

While still in a relatively natural state (left), Coquina Key, in Florida, furnished habitats to coastal and inshore marine life. Twenty years later, in 1972 (below), a building boom had covered the island with housing and reshaped the shoreline, destroying marine habitat.

Of Currents, Anchovies, and Seabirds

The Humboldt Current, which flows northward along the coast of Peru, is made of nutrient-rich water welling up from the cold ocean depths. Its nutrients support an incredibly dense population of plant and animal plankton. The plankton, in turn, feed great numbers of anchovies. Millions of seabirds—cormorants, pelicans, and boobies— prey on the anchovies; the excrement, or guano, that the birds deposit on their rocky nesting islands is one of the richest natural fertilizers in the world. At intervals, usually about 7 years apart, a warm countercurrent from the north pushes far southward and disrupts the Humboldt Current. This warm current is called *El Niño* (the Christ Child) because it usually appears around Christmas. Its effects are disastrous. Deprived of the Humboldt Current's nutrients, the planktonic plants die off, and with them die the animals that eat them. A chain reaction follows as the anchovies starve or migrate to cooler water. Anchovies make up 80 to 95 percent of the seabirds' diet, and so the number of seabirds drops drastically.

Seabirds such as these cormorants top the Humboldt Current food chain.

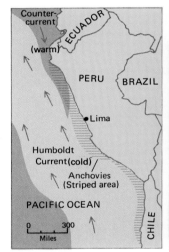

Anchovies live in the Humboldt Current off Peru.

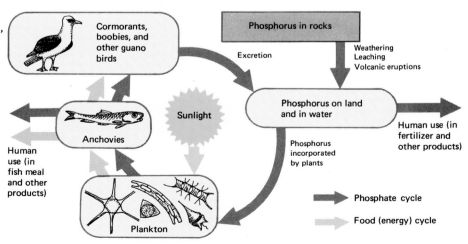

Milling cormorants throng a Peruvian island rookery. One island held an estimated peak population of 5 million seabirds, which devoured 1,000 tons of anchovies a day.

How Man Taps the Resources of the Humboldt Current

Energy from sunlight and phosphorus from mineral-laden, deep water support the dense population of plant and animal plankton on which the cycle of life in the Humboldt Current is based. In nature the cycle is self-renewing. But man intervenes at critical points, harvesting anchovies for fish meal (used in poultry feed) and oil, and mining phosphate- rich guano for fertilizer. When too many anchovies are taken, the cycle is interrupted, and the bird population declines.

The Alligator: Landscape Architect of the Everglades

David W. Ehrenfeld

The influential alligator shapes the environment, making it more attractive for a variety of wildlife.

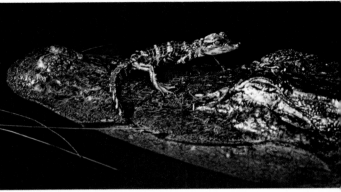

A young alligator perches atop its mother's formidable snout. Almost alone among reptiles, alligators guard their eggs until hatching and come to the aid of young ones that give the distress call, which is a loud, repetitive grunting.

The alligator is a remarkable animal—it is one of the large predators that never attack man in the wild unless badly imposed upon. Despite its agreeable disposition and its willingness to live in a variety of habitats (wild alligators inhabit a pond on the campus of the University of Florida), the alligator has been exterminated over most of its range because of habitat destruction and poaching. No population of alligators was safe from the people who raided zoos, game farms, and the Everglades National Park. Ironically, it was only as the alligator disappeared that its ecological importance began to be appreciated.

The alligator is a key species in its community. Though all animals affect the environment they live in, an alligator does so to a greater extent than most. Using its tail as a scythe, its hind feet as spades, and its mouth as a truck, an alligator rearranges the landscape.

To this reptile home is a nest, a " 'gator hole" or pond, a system of trails, and a cavelike den linked by a tunnel to the 'gator hole. As it moves between its nest and its pond and along its trails through the aquatic vegetation, the alligator helps keep the water open and clear. More important, the holes excavated or enlarged by alligators form the deepest pools in the Everglades and are the last places to become dry during a drought. In all but the worst dry spells these 'gator holes serve as oases for the dwindling life of the glades.

Enriched by the droppings of the alligator and by the remains of its meals, the water of the 'gator holes supports a rich growth of algae, ferns, and higher plants. These in turn maintain a variety of animal life. Fish, amphibians, reptiles, and invertebrates all find shelter here; birds and mammals also rely on the 'gator holes for food and water.

Nests that become islands

In addition to digging ponds, a female alligator makes a large nest mound out of sticks and mud, and hollows out the mound to make room for her 30 to 70 eggs. When built in the same place for long periods, these mounds, together with the mud dredged from the den and pool, often form islands high enough to support trees in the midst of the glades. The trees that grow on alligator islands are popular nesting sites for

Alligators bask on the edge of a limestone sinkhole in Everglades National Park. A plentiful supply of moisture is vital to the big reptiles. Sinkholes, unlike the holes the 'gators dig in swamp muck, are formed by erosion of the soft limestone rock.

How Alligators Help Wildlife

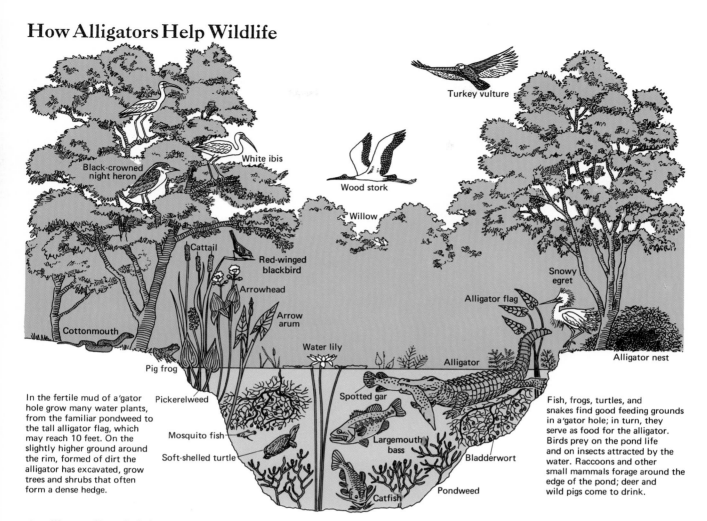

Turkey vulture

White ibis

Black-crowned
night heron

Wood stork

Willow

Cattail

Red-winged
blackbird

Arrowhead

Snowy
egret

Arrow
arum

Alligator flag

Cottonmouth

Water lily

Alligator

Pig frog

Alligator nest

In the fertile mud of a 'gator
hole grow many water plants,
from the familiar pondweed to
the tall alligator flag, which
may reach 10 feet. On the
slightly higher ground around
the rim, formed of dirt the
alligator has excavated, grow
trees and shrubs that often
form a dense hedge.

Pickerelweed

Spotted gar

Mosquito fish

Largemouth
bass

Soft-shelled turtle

Bladderwort

Catfish

Pondweed

Fish, frogs, turtles, and
snakes find good feeding grounds
in a 'gator hole; in turn, they
serve as food for the alligator.
Birds prey on the pond life
and on insects attracted by the
water. Raccoons and other
small mammals forage around the
edge of the pond; deer and
wild pigs come to drink.

An alligator digs a hole by ripping up vegetation with its powerful jaws and pushing the soft swamp muck out of the hole with its tail and feet. The alligator not only keeps the hole open but constantly enlarges it; in time a 'gator hole may *reach 25 feet across and 4 to 6 feet deep. Gator holes, which usually remain filled with water even during drought, serve as refuges for fish and other aquatic animals. But without the alligators, they quickly fill in.*

herons, egrets, and other birds; the presence of the alligator guarding her nest may frighten away raccoons and bobcats that could climb the trees and destroy the bird rookeries. In return for this "favor," however, the alligator eats baby birds that fall from the nest and fish dropped by the adult birds.

The alligator's nest mound is itself frequently used by other animals, such as turtles and snakes, as shelter for their own eggs. These "foreign" eggs also receive the benefit of an alligator guardian. For alligators are exceptional reptiles: The female guards the nest and keeps it moist for 2 months after laying the eggs. When alligator eggs are ready to hatch, the mother removes the sticks and mud that has covered them.

The alligator is a predator, and its feeding habits exert a powerful influence on the community. There is no doubt that its fondness for crunching turtles and its ability to eat and be bitten by poisonous snakes with impunity are important in Everglades ecology. But far more significant is the large number

of gars consumed by alligators. The spotted gar, which grows to a length of 2½ feet, is the most important predatory fish of the Everglades. It feeds on bass, bream, and other game fish. Where there are many alligators, the gar population is low, and smaller fish can thrive. In areas where the alligators have been exterminated, gars are numerous, the composition of the aquatic community changes, and the quality of fishing declines.

Hopefully, future research will uncover more of the ecological ties of the alligator with its community, and, hopefully, something will be done in time to prevent the extinction of the reptile—whose only close relative is nearing extinction in China—and to preserve its remaining habitat. The loss of this beneficial animal can never be compensated for by the market value of the hides it supplies. Such a loss would be a grim indictment of the health and spirit of the kind of society that values alligator shoes and handbags more than the living animals.

179

Wonders in a Woodlot

Aldo Leopold

It's an ill wind that blows nobody good, and even ailing trees play an important role in the web of life.

Soon after I bought a woodland in Wisconsin, I realized that I had bought almost as many tree diseases as I had trees. My woodlot is riddled with all the ailments wood is heir to. I began to wish that Noah, when he loaded up the Ark, had left the tree diseases behind. But it soon became clear that these same diseases made my woodlot a mighty fortress, unequaled in the whole county.

My woods are headquarters for a family of raccoons. One Sunday in November, after a new snow, I learned why. The fresh tracks of a coon hunter and his hound led to a half-uprooted maple, under which one of my coons had taken refuge. The hunter had quit coonless because a fungus disease had weakened the roots

How Dead Trees Help Wildlife

A dead tree provides food and shelter for many animal species. Tunneling insects, fungi, and bacteria weaken the standing trunk of this oak; birds, salamanders, and other animals feed on the insects. When the weakened trunk falls, the processes of decay continue, and other forms of life find shelter and nourishment there. Eventually, the fallen log becomes fertile soil, its presence detectable only by lush plant growth.

of the maple. The tree, half-tipped-over by a storm, offered an impregnable fortress for coondom.

My woods house a dozen ruffed grouse, but during periods of deep snow my grouse shift to my neighbor's woods, where there is better cover. However, I always retain as many grouse as I have oaks wind-thrown by summer storms. These summer windfalls keep their dried leaves, and during snows each such windfall harbors a grouse. The droppings show that each grouse roosts, feeds, and loafs for the duration of the snowstorm within the narrow confines of his leafy camouflage, safe from wind, owl, fox, and hunter. The cured oak leaves not only serve as cover but, for some curious reason, are relished as food by the grouse.

These oak windfalls are, of course, diseased trees. Without disease few oaks would break off, and hence few grouse would have downed tops to hide in.

Treasures in diseased trees

Diseased oaks also provide another apparently delectable grouse food: oak galls. A gall is a diseased growth of new twigs that have been stung by a gall wasp or other insect while tender and succulent. In October my grouse are often stuffed with oak galls.

Each year the wild bees load up one of my hollow oaks with combs, and each year trespassing honey hunters harvest the honey before I do. This is partly because they are more skillful than I am in "lining up" the bee trees and partly because they use nets, and hence are able to work before the bees become dormant in the fall. But for heartrots, there would be no hollow oak trees to furnish the wild bees with their oaken hives.

A flock of a dozen chickadees spends the year in my woods. In winter, when we are harvesting diseased or dead trees for our fuel wood, the ring of the ax is a dinner gong for the chickadee tribe. They hang in the offing, waiting for the tree to fall, offering pert commentary on the slowness of our labor. When the tree at last is down, the chickadees fall to. Every slab of dead bark is, to them, a treasury of eggs, larvae, and cocoons. For them every ant-tunneled heartwood bulges with milk and honey. We often stand a fresh split against a nearby tree just to see the greedy chicks mop up the ant eggs. It lightens our labor to know that they, as well as we, derive aid and comfort from the fragrant riches of newly split oak.

But for diseases and insect pests, there would most likely be no food in these trees, and hence no chickadees to add cheer to my woods in winter.

Many other kinds of wildlife depend on tree diseases. My pileated woodpeckers chisel living pines to extract fat grubs from the diseased heartwood. My barred owls find surcease from crows and jays in the hollow heart of an old basswood; but for this diseased tree their sundown serenade would probably be silenced. My wood ducks nest in hollow trees; every June brings a brood of downy ducklings to my woodland slough. All squirrels depend, for permanent dens, on a delicately balanced equilibrium between a rotting cavity and the scar tissue with which the tree attempts to close the wound. The squirrels referee the contest by gnawing out the scar tissue when it begins to shrink unduly the amplitude of their front door.

The real jewel of my disease-ridden woodlot is the prothonotary warbler. It nests in an old woodpecker hole, or other small cavity, in a dead snag overhanging water. The flash of the gold-and-blue plumage amid the dank decay of the June woods is in itself proof that dead trees are transmuted into living animals, and vice versa. When you doubt the wisdom of this arrangement, take a look at the prothonotary.

Key to the Wildlife in the Painting

(1) Downy woodpecker. (2) Pileated woodpecker. (3) Bracket fungus. (4) Winter wren. (5) Oak gall. (6) Red-backed salamander. (7) Carpenter ant. (8) Millipede. (9) Prothonotary warbler. (10) Eastern chipmunk. (11) Raccoon. (12) Garter snake. (13) Shorttail shrew. (14) White-footed mouse. (15) Long-tailed weasel. (16) Puffball. (17) Ruffed grouse.

*A **bull moose on Isle Royale** crops a mouthful of succulent water plants, mainstay of his diet in the warm months. A moose in his prime may stand 7½ feet tall at the shoulder and weigh 1,400 pounds, with an antler spread of 5 to 6 feet.*

Timber wolves trot over the hard, crusted snow on Isle Royale. The wolf population has slowly increased since the first appearance on the Michigan island around 1950. The average wolf count has been 24 but has climbed as high as 31.

Of Fire, Moose, and Wolves

Durward L. Allen

The story of an island ravaged by fire, overrun by moose, and then invaded by wolves shows that predators are essential in the natural scheme.

It was late August and another year of drought. From behind the island coastline to starboard, the gray-white pall from a burning forest billowed aloft and drifted northward.

On the bridge of a laden ore boat the master lowered his binoculars. "Looks like the whole center of the island is afire. It's worse than when we came in a week ago." The helmsman nodded. "Reckon that'll finish off the moose. I hear they mostly died off anyway. Ever been to Isle Royale, Cap'n?"

"Oh, yes. Ten years ago I took my wife there. There were plenty of moose then. Game men from the State said the moose chewed up everything they could live on and then starved. Probably you're right. This fire will fix the rest of them."

In the 1930's, the time of the "big burn," the story of Isle Royale and its moose was well known. The long, narrow wilderness island lies some 15 miles from the Canadian mainland, in the largest of North America's Great Lakes, Lake Superior. Evidently a few moose

swam to the island during the first decade of the century. Beyond any doubt, those firstcomers had found the Promised Land, for around them was vegetation nearly untouched by large browsing animals. There were no deer, and the few woodland caribou that visited Isle Royale over winter ice fed mostly on tree lichens along the moist shorelines.

With an abundance of food and no predatory enemies, the moose did what any plant-eating species would do: It reproduced at a high rate, and its population quickly increased. It took about 20 years for the herd to reach a density that may well have been more than 10 animals per square mile. Isle Royale harbored more moose than any comparable area in the world.

In the twenties it was evident that trouble was afoot. Under continued pressure by so many moose, the palatable browse was not growing back, and the supply fell steadily. Malnutrition and attendant ills spread through the moose herd. Ground cover was blighted for snowshoe hares, and new stands of poplar and birch needed by the island's beavers could not get started. Isle Royale was becoming a biological slum.

In 1930 game biologists urged immediate and heavy hunting of moose. It was the only way, they said, to avoid a disastrous die-off. But moose were protected in Michigan, and that applied to Isle Royale. Nothing was done, and the moose did die off, down to a few hundred. Those classic lakeshore tableaux, with shovel-horned bulls silhouetted in the sunset, were largely gone. Oldtimers said the moose were finished.

Most residents of the north country would have agreed that there was little future for the moose, especially after several years of drought and the burn of 1936. But the island became a national park in 1940 and was under close surveillance thereafter. As years passed, scientists began to see the fire in a new light.

In the forties normal rainfall returned. A fresh ground cover brightened the vistas of spring. Sun-loving plants took over pockets of mineral soil. Lichens and mosses began to reclaim the rocks. Stands of alder, white cedar, and other trees regenerated. Slowly the scars of fire were obscured.

The new greenery was moose browse. Favored foods proliferated on thousands of scorched acres, and the moose responded with another population increase. Then field crews in the park began finding dead moose —it appeared that the cycle of boom and bust in the moose herd might be repeating itself.

Under natural conditions most hoofed animal populations are kept from increasing beyond the limits of their food supplies by large carnivores. For the moose of North America, this meant the timber wolf, but none had reached Isle Royale. A logical solution seemed to be to bring some wolves to the island. Besides, the wolf was a threatened species that needed an undisturbed sanctuary. An island national park seemed ideal.

Plans to transplant some wolves were under way when word came that unmistakable signs of wolves were being found on Isle Royale. A breeding pack probably arrived over the ice between 1948 and 1950. After that, frequent observations left no doubt that wolves were increasing and were killing moose.

The wolves arrive

The coming of wolves to Isle Royale brought the fulfillment of a dream for many of us in wildlife research. The island had become an outdoor laboratory with "confined" populations of primitive America's wild dog and its largest antlered prey—a place to learn what uncontrolled wolves would do to moose, beavers, and smaller animals.

We knew that such a study would be lengthy and expensive—the only way to observe wolves in their hunting, for example, was on winter snow, from aircraft. Over the years we managed to get grants for a series of studies by graduate students and other researchers. This work, begun in 1958, is still in progress.

Our summer season begins when the park staff moves to the island in early May and terminates when the last boat leaves for the mainland at the end of October. In the cold months Isle Royale is left to its wild inhabitants, except for about 7 weeks when our winter camp is open. Then we reach the island by air. In nearly every hour of good weather our plane is airborne, tracking wolves, finding kills, and counting moose.

Our many years of work have all been rewarding, although sometimes it seemed that the weather was rigged to foil our every purpose. We have seen the wolves in most of their activities and have examined the bones or fresh remains of hundreds of moose. There are plenty of mysteries, but we have learned the answers to some important questions.

Picture if you can "the big pack" traveling—more than a dozen wolves strung out for half a mile on shore ice or on a frozen inland lake. They trot at about 5

An Island of Change

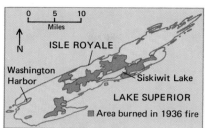

Isle Royale lies isolated in northern Lake Superior, closer to Canada than the United States. Moose probably reached the island from Canada by swimming a 15-mile strait. Wolves crossed on the ice bridges that form temporarily on very cold, calm winter days. The burned area, which covers more than a quarter of the island, has now grown back into forest.

Freezing winds and spray from Lake Superior coat the shoreline of Isle Royale with ice. In winter food is scarce for moose and wolves alike. Moose kill many young trees by stripping them of bark or breaking them down to reach twigs and leaf buds. Wolves attack adult moose by forming large packs. In summer wolves prefer the easily killed new calves, born in late May and early June. Beavers, hidden in their lodges in winter, are also eaten by wolves in summer.

Birches and maples, bright with fall color, cover a formerly burned area on Isle Royale. When small, these species furnish winter browse for moose, but the trees shown here are too tall for moose to reach. Natural forest fires would restore browse by clearing land for new young growth.

A cow moose guards the body of her calf from eight wolves on a frozen Isle Royale lake. Wolves tend to give wide berth to healthy adult moose and test their prey before attacking. Only one attack in 13 results in a kill.

miles an hour, sometimes several abreast, sometimes single file.

The wolves stop frequently to socialize, and it is clear that sexual interest is high. Sometimes a female and male may run together for several days, the bitch always slightly ahead. Each February we have seen coupling, but in the earliest years of our study there appeared to be pups only in the first year. From the fourth year on pups have numbered from one to four —the latter when the large pack's count peaked at 22. There are also lone wolves on the island, probably older animals that have become scavengers.

Wolves kill only to eat

It might be late afternoon when the traveling pack encounters or scents a moose. The stragglers catch up, and the pack pursues its intended victim. Usually the moose backs into heavy cover and, with lowered head, raised hackles, and flattened ears, defies the wolves. Frequently after a few minutes the pack moves on, and a short time later the would-be prey is calmly browsing. The wolves check out a dozen moose for every one they kill. Our finding is that they kill only to eat, and not just any moose.

A moose is long legged, and an adult moves with little difficulty in 30-inch-deep snow. If the snow is soft, the wolf must wallow. Frequently a moose leaves its attackers far behind. But some moose are less strong

Wild Dogs in Danger

The dog family includes domestic dogs, wolves, foxes, and a number of related doglike carnivores; each of the species shown here is threatened. Some dogs, such as the South American bush dog and small-eared dog, have always been rare; others have been decimated by direct conflicts with man or through loss of habitat and prey. In some instances, the decline of these carnivores has led to severe ecological disturbances as rodents and other prey undergo a population explosion.

Reflecting erroneous folklore about the savagery of wolves, a 19th-century Russian engraving shows a concerted attack on a horse-drawn sleigh by a large pack.

Status: Endangered

Nearly the size of a wolf, the Simien fox inhabits the highlands of Ethiopia. Although it lives on small rats, farmers hunt it down as a sheep killer.

The northern kit fox, native to the U.S. Great Plains, has been exterminated mainly by poison and trapping. As a result, the small rodents it preys on have multiplied.

Once a forest dweller in the southeastern United States, the red wolf has been forced into coastal marshes as forests were destroyed. It lives mainly on rodents but is poisoned by man as a suspected killer of stock.

and capable than others. The wolves quickly sense their weakness and follow closely, striking and biting at the hams. They disable a leg and bring the moose to bay. In minutes the animal may be pulled down by assailants on every side. Or hours later it may still be standing, stiffening, weakening.

Predator and prey in balance

Often the kill is made at night, and in the morning we work out the story from our circling plane. When the weather is right, we land on the nearest lake or bay, and one of us snowshoes to the kill. We collect the jaw—which reveals the age of the moose—and look for evidence of the victim's state of health. These examinations have provided the most important clue to the moose-wolf relationship. Of our first 160 winter kills, about a quarter were calves. Only seven were 2 to 5 years old, which is the age group with the most prime and capable moose. From age 6 on the moose of Isle Royale have a growing risk of being killed, as the debilities of age weaken them. The average age of adult moose eaten by wolves is 10.

Predictions that the wolves would greatly increase in number and exterminate the moose have not been borne out. The dense wolf population, now nearly one per 10 square miles, has built-in controls, involving a limited breeding by adults and heavy losses of pups.

Two dozen-odd wolves are exploiting a moose herd that averages about a thousand in midwinter; a secondary food source for the wolves is the beaver, also on the island in large numbers. For the present the predator and the two kinds of prey appear to be in a state of relative balance.

But especially in the area of the big burn, food for moose is again declining. Low brush and trees have been heavily browsed, and they are being shaded out by the natural regrowth of the forest. The time is ahead when moose will find little here, and our forecast for the future must be a decline of beavers, moose, and wolves—unless there are more fires to open up the forest and rejuvenate the system.

The Isle Royale chronicle attests that times have changed since those disaster years of the 1920's. Over the island as a whole, moose are being held within the limits of their food supply. In this process the wolves remove the elders, the ailing, the afflicted—and even, no doubt, the foolish and incompetent. For moose it is a health and welfare program of inscrutable realism.

In this relationship we have the key to why both moose and wolf are what they are, and indeed to the character of wilderness. This system and these dependencies mature through ages beyond our reckoning. The wolf manages its livestock as any husbandman must manage in order to survive. The great carnivore is inspector of the herd, liberator of the weak, and guardian of the range.

Status: Threatened

The dhole ranges over much of southern and eastern Asia. Hunting in large packs, it needs a large forest territory and an ample supply of game. Deforestation and persecution by man have greatly depleted its numbers.

The African hunting dog, threatened over much of its range, is important in maintaining ecological balance on the grasslands south of the Sahara.

The maned wolf, now limited to the thorny scrub of central Brazil, is a solitary nocturnal hunter. It has retreated as human settlement has advanced.

Status: Rare

The South American bush dog, a native of grasslands and tropical forests, is rare and seldom seen. The animal hunts by night, probably preying on large rodents. It avoids human settlements.

The small-eared dog is virtually unknown to natives of its Amazonian rain forest home. Its thick sleek fur suggests that it spends much time in the water or in heavy rains.

185

The Undesirable Aliens

David W. Ehrenfeld

Wherever man has gone, he has introduced alien plants and animals into natural communities. But he has never been able to predict the outcome.

In 1884 a visitor returning to Florida from the Cotton States Exposition in New Orleans brought back a live water plant that had been on display. It was a floating plant with large, curled, green leaves and a handsome lavender flower—a native of Central America that looked fine against the black waters of a Florida cypress swamp. Its descendants still look fine, and they please the tourists who travel to Florida. But there is no need to go out of the way to find them now; the water hyacinth, at last count, covered 90,000 acres of Florida's freshwater lakes and streams. The plants all look healthy, and with good reason; they have no natural enemies in Florida.

Water hyacinths are attractive, but they now are a major obstacle to the passage of boats on the inland waterways of the southeastern United States. Millions of dollars have been spent to control them, and millions more will be needed. They are sprayed with herbicides

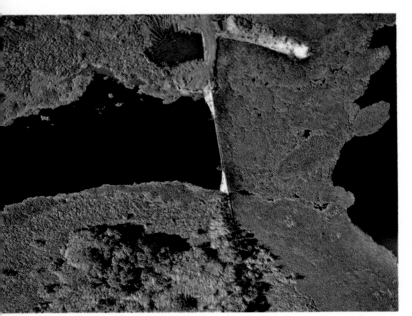

Trapped by a dam, water hyacinths form a dense, floating mat of vegetation in Florida. Introduced from Central America as an ornamental plant, the water hyacinth clogs waterways and is a major pest in the United States.

and devoured by obliging manatees, which are even transported from estuaries to inland waters for that purpose, but still the hyacinths are everywhere. Not only do they impede navigation but they shade the native water plants and retard their growth. Without this normally abundant and varied source of food, the animal community suffers. In most hyacinth-covered ponds the number of minnows, turtles, waterfowl, predatory fish, and alligators is greatly reduced.

Hyacinths are widespread and common throughout Central America. They often block streams or rivers, but only temporarily, and in most waterways are found in sheltered coves and along the banks, alternating with other water plants. After a little observation the reasons for this restrained growth become clear. Where the plants reach out into deep water, the manatees eat them by the bushel. Where the hyacinths touch the banks, one can sometimes see undulating trails of parasol ants coming out of the underbrush to meet them, and on the hyacinths themselves teams of ants snip out and carry away sections of leaves. The whole scene looks like a hyacinth assembly line run backward; the plants are chewed up at a great rate.

Water hyacinths are not new to Central America. There they are integral parts of the natural community, in which checks and balances exist to prevent one species from aggrandizing itself at the expense of the rest. That is not the case in their new home.

Transplantation is not new

Ever since man first began to travel long distances he has wittingly and unwittingly brought other creatures along with him. The dingo, Australia's wild dog, evidently came to that continent as the companion of prehistoric man during the ice ages, so transplantation is not new. As the human population increases and as rapid travel becomes commonplace, nonhuman hitchhikers abound. Insects and spiders accompany bananas; rats, mice, and even cats sneak off ships that are loading cargo at remote oceanic islands. The European traveler returning from America brings back foreign cold viruses, and the American traveler to Europe does the same.

Foreign species are also spread in other ways. Agricultural animals, such as pigs and goats, and food plants, such as coconuts, "escape" readily from domestication. People also transport and release animals and plants because they like them or because they like to hunt or fish for them. Flocks of hundreds of Australian budgerigars wheel over St. Petersburg, Florida; and schools of Pacific salmon thrive in Lakes Michigan and Superior, where they give joy to fishermen and feed on another recent arrival, the alewife.

There is no need to rely on the classic example of rabbits in Australia in an account of the damage done by imported species; few parts of the world have escaped harm. One cannot help recognizing the unpredictability of the consequences of introductions; not until we understand all the interactions of a natural community (a remote possibility) will we be able to introduce new species without risk. In marshy areas of Colombia, for example, Australian eucalypts were planted to dry the land enough for sugarcane planting. Now the water table is so low that irrigation wells have become useless.

The heaviest damage has been done to oceanic islands, whose limited and often unique floras and faunas form communities that are particularly susceptible to attack by competition-hardened invaders from the mainland. The most extreme example is the Hawaiian Islands. The American herpetologist Wayne King has described the situation there: "Approximately 60 percent of the 68 endemic land birds of Hawaii became extinct following the intrusion of rats, mongooses, rabbits, cats, goats, sheep, horses, cattle, and pigs. The list of exotic animals in Hawaii goes further, however. It also includes more than 500 species of insects, more than 50 species of birds, and numerous reptiles, amphibians, and mollusks."

Moving animals is usually bad

Generalizations in ecology are always somewhat risky, but one must be offered at this point. The introduction of exotic (nonnative) plants and animals is usually a bad thing. The damage ranges from the loss of a few native species to the total collapse of entire communities. The stock explanation for the explosive success of some introduced species is that freedom from predators and parasites gives them an unfair advantage in competition with native species. Although the truth probably exists somewhere in the vicinity of this vague notion, it is far from satisfying. There are times when introduced species do well in the face of many direct challenges. For example, five muskrats were introduced into Czechoslovakia in 1905; they multiplied and spread exceptionally rapidly, despite heavy predation by foxes, polecats, domestic cats, owls, and hunters, and despite the deliberate use of virulent bacteria. Europe now has millions of muskrats.

One of the few kinds of species introduction that is not always an unmitigated disaster is that involving sport and food fish. Many varieties of trout and salmon have been carried around the world: Brown trout have been taken from England to Tasmania to New Zealand and from Germany and Scotland to the United States. Most fishermen have welcomed the addition of this wily and handsome fish to their native waters.

On the other hand, trout introduced into Andean lakes have destroyed a number of native species of fish and have upset aquatic communities. And the largemouth bass introduced in Guatemala's Lake Atitlán has nearly led to the extinction of the lake's unique flightless bird, the giant pied-billed grebe. The bass eat the young of the grebes as soon as they leave their floating nests. These two examples of misfortunes in relatively simple lake communities should serve as a warning. The success of many sport and food fish introductions may be an illusion, fostered by our ignorance of the complex ecology of the communities that lie hidden beneath the water's surface.

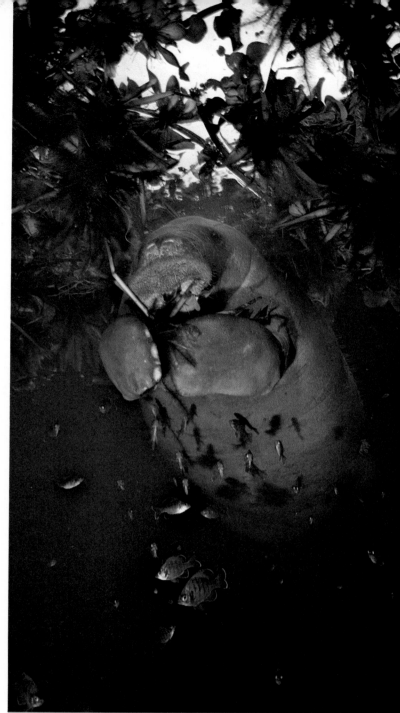

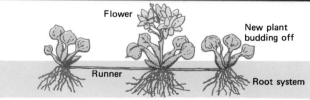

Scooping in the succulent plants with flippers and flexible lips, a manatee devours water hyacinths in a Florida waterway. A single manatee, which may grow to 12 feet and weigh 2,000 pounds, can eat 150 pounds of water hyacinths a day. The water hyacinth, admired for its lovely purple flowers, is buoyed up by its hollow leaf stalks. It reproduces rapidly by sending out runners that bud off new plants. In an 8-month growing season a single water hyacinth can produce more than 65,000 new plants, each of which reproduces in turn.

187

The Aliens: How and Why They Came

Man has transplanted many plants and animals into new environments. Some species, especially insects, have been brought in accidentally; others, especially game birds and small mammals, have been introduced deliberately, for reasons that range from sentimentality to hope of profit. Alien species that become established in their new surroundings often have disturbing effects, as the preceding and following pages indicate.

Game Animals Transplanted to a New Environment

Animals imported for hunting adapt with varying degrees of success. The golden pheasant, transplanted from China to Britain, barely gained a foothold; its cousin, the ringneck, became one of the most abundant game birds in North America.

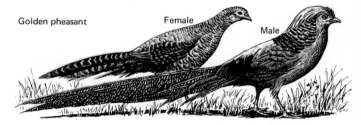

Golden pheasant Female Male

Imported to New Zealand for sport, red deer from Scotland have destroyed forests and caused massive soil erosion.

Wildlife Immigrants to New Zealand

New Zealand has played host to a variety of animals from almost every part of the world, including such unlikely guests as the North American moose and the European chamois. Most have had a destructive effect on New Zealand's environment and native animals.

ENGLAND
Hedgehog
Stoat
Ferret
Weasel
Dog
Cat
Black rat
Brown rat
Mouse
Rabbit
Hare
Cattle
Sheep
Goat
Red deer
Fallow deer
Pig
Horse
Mallard
English pheasant
Skylark
Song thrush
Blackbird
Hedge sparrow
Rook
Starling
House sparrow
Chaffinch
Redpoll
Goldfinch
Greenfinch
Yellow bunting

AUSTRALIA
Brush-tailed possum
Wallaby
Cape Barren goose
Black swan
Brown quail
Eastern rosella
White cockatoo
Laughing kookaburra
White-backed magpie
Black-backed magpie

ASIA
Tahr
Axis deer
Sambar deer
Japanese deer
Chukar partridge
Lace-neck dove
Indian mynah
Peafowl

NORTH AMERICA
Wapiti
Virginia deer
Moose
Canada goose
California quail
Bobwhite

CONTINENTAL EUROPE
Chamois
Little owl

POLYNESIA
Native dog
Maori rat

NEW ZEALAND

Alien Predators for Alien Pests

Predators imported to curb destructive alien pests are sometimes successful in their task. But the predator itself may become a problem. The giant South American toad, brought to Australia to control cane beetles, is a case in point.

The giant toad poisons cats, dogs, and waterholes.

A small snail, Gonaxis, attacks a giant African snail, which it was imported to control. The 1-pound African giant, brought to Asia by a tourist, is a serious crop pest.

The Accidental Invaders

Many animals have spread to new areas with man's unintentional aid. Rats, an outstanding example, stow away on ships. Destructive Japanese beetles and Colorado potato bugs have spread to new continents in shipments of farm or garden products. The Chinese crab (below) might well symbolize all the accidental intruders. It arrived at a German port in the ballast tanks of a ship from Asia. Now numbering in the millions, it has spread through many of Europe's river systems, destroying aquatic habitats and undermining dikes with its burrows.

Chinese crab

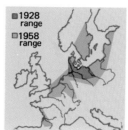
■1928 range
■1958 range

To Remember the Old Country

Man's nostalgia has brought many an animal to a new land. House sparrows and common starlings, imported to bring a touch of Europe to North America, soon wore out their welcome with their destructive habits. They raid grainfields and orchards and befoul cities with their droppings. They drive native birds such as bluebirds from nesting sites and preempt their food supplies.

CANADA
1950
1940
U.S.
1930
1910
1920
New York
MEXICO
□Starling range

House sparrow

Common starling

Profitmaking Schemes That Misfired

Many species, from furbearers to insects, have been imported in hopes of profit. In each case shown here, the profits proved illusory, but the animals escaped from captivity and became pests.

European gypsy moth caterpillars have devastated millions of acres of forest in the United States. The importer hoped to start a silk industry.

EUROPE
■ Range of raccoon dog in Europe

Imported from Siberia to Europe for its fur, the raccoon dog (left) spread over wide areas but yielded no profits. The nutria, another potential fur source, was brought from South America to Europe and the United States, where it is now a crop pest.

Able to travel over land and breathe oxygen from the air, the walking catfish, a native of Southeast Asia, was brought to Florida by tropical-fish dealers. It escaped from breeding ponds and spread to streams and lakes.

189

Alien Animals and the Wildlife They Threaten

When a species is introduced into a new environment, it often upsets a natural balance. An introduced predator may prey on animals that have no effective defenses. An introduced plant eater may deplete the food supply of the native wildlife. Although a single alien species is seldom the sole cause of decline (usually more than one factor is involved), each of the animals shown in a box has played a major part in the decline of the native animals shown to the right of the box.

The Fox and Its Victims

Swamp tortoise
(southwestern Australia)

The common European fox was introduced from Great Britain to Australia by nostalgic sportsmen. It has wreaked havoc on a number of native animals, such as the rare swamp turtle, whose eggs and young it eats. It also preys on small native carnivores, such as the rabbit bandicoot, and competes with them for prey.

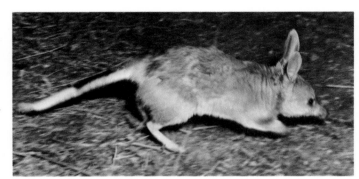

Named for its long ears, the rabbit bandicoot hunts at night for mice and insects. Once common, it is now rare.

The Rat: A Stowaway That Jumps Ship in New Lands

New Zealand bush wren

White-breasted thrasher
(West Indies)

Cahow
(Bermuda)

Saddleback
(New Zealand)

Auckland Island rail
(New Zealand)

Ships have carried rats to most of the habitable world. Aggressive, adaptable, and omnivorous, these rodents prey on the eggs and young of birds, even climbing into trees to rob nests. They also compete with wildlife for food.

The Mongoose: A Rat Killer Gone Wrong

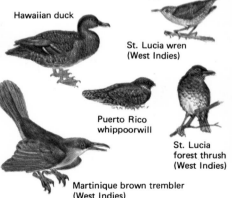

Hawaiian duck

St. Lucia wren
(West Indies)

Puerto Rico whippoorwill

St. Lucia forest thrush
(West Indies)

Martinique brown trembler
(West Indies)

Brought from India to the West Indies, Fiji, and Hawaii for rat control on plantations, the mongoose has taken a high toll of native wildlife. Some of the animals endangered by this carnivore are shown at the right.

The Fijian banded iguana has nearly been wiped out by mongooses imported to control rats.

Rabbits in a New Home: Ravenous, Prolific, and Destructive

Rabbits imported for food, fur, and sport have stripped vast areas of Australia of food and cover, threatening plant eaters, such as LeSueur's rat kangaroo. But on a Hawaiian island eradication of rabbits has meant a comeback for the Laysan finch.

Laysan finch
(Hawaiian Islands)

LeSueur's rat kangaroo
(northwestern and central Australia)

The Dog: Pet and Predator

Dog

Domestic dogs gone wild form destructive hunting packs that prey on a wide range of ground-dwelling animals, including New Caledonia's kagu (which cannot fly) and Australia's western whipbird (which nests on the ground). Island animals that have no escape patterns suffer the most severely from introduced predators.

Western whipbird (Western Australia, Victoria, South Australia)

The spectacularly crested kagu patrols the forest floor for snails and insects.

More Livestock, Less Living Space

Livestock

On all continents except Antarctica, domestic livestock has taken food and living space from wildlife, threatening species such as those shown at right. Overgrazing by livestock turns fertile habitats into deserts; goats are the worst offenders in this respect. Free-running hogs prey on small animals and compete with native species for food.

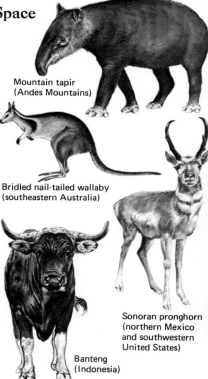
Mountain tapir (Andes Mountains)

Bridled nail-tailed wallaby (southeastern Australia)

Banteng (Indonesia)

Sonoran pronghorn (northern Mexico and southwestern United States)

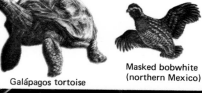
Galápagos tortoise

Masked bobwhite (northern Mexico)

Hawaii's crested honeycreeper has had much of its home destroyed by livestock.

The Deadly Domestic Cat

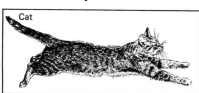
Cat

Domestic cats have been brought to many areas as pets or as rodent killers. When cats that have escaped or been released have established breeding populations in the wild, they have proved to be extremely destructive predators on native wildlife. These felines have been particularly hard on birds that nest on the ground, and they have brought some species to the verge of extinction.

New Zealand shore plover

Morro Bay kangaroo rat (California)

Hawaiian stilt

New Zealand laughing owl

A Second Chance for the Poc

Anne LaBastille

Too heavy to fly away, a rare Guatemalan water bird nearly became extinct when alien fish upset the balance of its mile-high lake.

A challenging "caow, caow, caow-uh, caow-uh, caow-uh" sounded near the shore as I steered my boat toward a pitch-black bed of reeds. To the south a cold moon silhouetted volcanic cones, shadowing the quicksilver surface of Lake Atitlán in Guatemala. Cutting the motor, I switched on a portable recorder and answered my quarry with a taped imitation of its call. Only one response.

I was taking a census of one of the world's rarest and most endangered water birds, the giant pied-billed grebe. Called "poc" by local Indians, this species of grebe lives only on mile-high Lake Atitlán and nowhere else on earth. Although it is unable to fly or walk upright on land, it is a superb diver and a veritable submarine underwater.

My investigation that moonlit spring night produced a fairly accurate estimate of its numbers. Since male pocs are fiercely territorial during breeding season, and the bright moon keeps them awake and vocal, I could rely on their responding to the taped call of a male. Thus I canvassed, by sound, the precipitous shoreline of this deep, often stormy lake for three nights. When I finished, that dawn in 1965, I estimated that some 80 birds lived on the lake.

During the preceding decades the poc population had been 200 to 300. Living on a 1,200-foot-deep lake surrounded by mountains almost 12,000 feet high, the grebes had very few predators. Food and nesting materials were plentiful. The birds were in balance with their environment.

Then in 1958 and 1960 largemouth bass and crappies were added to Lake Atitlán to improve sport fishing. They underwent a population buildup that devastated the lake's ecology. These carnivorous fish,

Indians ply the waters of Lake Atitlán, the only home of the giant pied-billed grebe. Known to the Indians as the poc, this flightless bird has so adapted to the special conditions of mile-high, isolated Lake Atitlán that scientists believe it can survive nowhere else. Essential to the poc are a plentiful supply of fish small enough for the young to swallow and extensive reedbeds for nesting. The right combination of conditions is not found in other lakes.

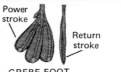

Power stroke

Return stroke

GREBE FOOT   DUCK FOOT

Virtually helpless on land, the poc has su-
perb mobility in the water. Its swimming
ability comes from its broad-lobed—not
webbed—toes, which make each foot a triple
paddle that folds to reduce drag on the re-
turn stroke (above). The poc feeds, nests,
and mates in water. A poc surfaces with a
large insect larva (left); an alert male patrols
his aquatic territory (top).

notorious predators of aquatic life, probably devoured baby grebes. Moreover, the bass ate crabs and small fish, the grebes' usual food, and the grebes could not find enough to eat. Young grebes died of starvation, and adults were hard pressed by this new competition.

The Indians of Lake Atitlán were also affected by ecological changes in the lake. For centuries their chief source of protein had been tiny native fish and crabs. Most Indians were too poor to be able to afford the proper tackle or diving gear to catch big bass, so they lost two staples of their already sparse diet.

A last-ditch stand

By 1965 the situation seemed critical: I felt certain that the giant pied-billed grebe would be extinct in 5 to 10 years. Determined to make a last-ditch stand for the bird, I began Operación Protección del Poc (Operation for the Protection of the Poc).

With grants from several organizations I approached the Guatemalan Ministry of Agriculture, obtained the support of the director of Guatemala's Museum of Natural History, and launched a conservation campaign. As the most immediate task, the ministry installed a game warden and patrol boat at Lake Atitlán and appointed me one of three honorary wardens. Dressed in khaki-green uniforms with bright yellow-and-black poc emblems, we visited the 12 villages where most of the lake's 50,000 Indians live. We met with mayors, teachers, and others to explain why and how we were trying to protect the poc. On several

occasions we lectured to schoolchildren about conservation of the poc and other natural resources.

I was especially anxious to involve the local Indians in our research and conservation efforts. If they could be convinced that the grebe was worth more alive than smoked on a skewer, our preservation program might succeed. We presented the Indians with a double inducement—money and pride. The bird could be a new tourist attraction and a motif for arts and crafts, all of which would bring economic gain to their region. And

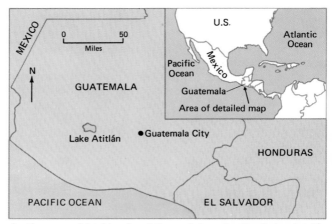

In the rugged highlands of Central America lies Lake Atitlán,
surrounded by 12,000-foot volcanic peaks. The 53-square-
mile lake, which is Guatemala's second largest, is the home of
the poc and the site of a new national park.

A newly hatched poc peers from its floating nest, woven from reed stems and other water plants. The nest is anchored to living reed stalks, preventing it from being ripped loose by the violent storms that lash Lake Atitlán.

An Indian villager cuts reeds to make woven seats and sleeping mats, one of the few local sources of cash. Humans thus compete with pocs for the reedbeds where the pocs nest. However, reed cutting is now limited to preserve nesting sites.

only in their home, Lake Atitlán, did this rare source, worthy of national pride and concern, exist.

At each village a warden warned that people who killed grebes would be prosecuted and that the shoreline vegetation could no longer be cut during part of the nesting season. Because several families relied on a cottage industry of weaving and selling seats and sleeping mats made from reeds and cattails, the remainder of each year was left open to harvesting. Every reed cutter, however, could cut only half his plot at one time and must protect any poc nests and eggs he encountered.

Poc nests are huge and heavy—the first one I found measured 3 feet deep and must have weighed 100 pounds. It was concealed by tall thickets of reeds, growing in water 4 or more feet deep. Only 3 inches of the nest protruded above the lake's surface, where it was anchored to the reeds. Underwater it was funnel-shaped, providing stability. Such mass and seaworthiness are essential because north winds and the *xocomil* (a strong south wind) often roil Lake Atitlán's water into 5-foot swells. A flimsy nest would soon disintegrate.

In the nest's damp depression the eggs lay just above the lake level. The frightened female had deserted at my approach, covering her treasures with a blanket of plants. From nearby she gave the low "poc-poc-poc" call from which the Indians derive the bird's name.

Young pocs are tiny puffballs striped in black and white from beak to tail, with bright salmon-orange areas near their bills. They are often transported on their parents' backs, huddled among the feathers between the wings. Thus they are shielded at times from predatory fish.

The chicks cheep continuously unless quieted by their parents. The persistent begging wins them water insects, crustaceans, and small fish that have been cap-

tured by both parents. Chick survival is quite low. According to my studies, less than 35 percent of the eggs hatch and develop into fledglings. The mortality of juveniles is even higher—food in Atitlán being too scarce or of a size with which the young birds physically cannot cope. Once I saw parents present their fledgling with a small bass 25 times. As much as the chick struggled, it could not swallow the fish.

In view of the ecological imbalance at Lake Atitlán, I kept hoping to find another mountain lake in Guatemala to which we might transfer grebes for safer keeping—the flightless birds, of course, cannot move to a new spot by themselves. But none of the other lakes seemed suitable; only Lake Atitlán would do.

We decided to use a tiny bay on the lake's south shore for a refuge. Here colonial Spanish priests had raised fish 2 or 3 centuries before. We rebuilt the wall that had separated the hatchery from the lake and edged it and the shoreline with fencing, leaving a 12-foot screened opening to permit exchange with the lake. The bay was treated to remove any big bass, then stocked with small native fish. One adult male grebe already lived in the bay, and we hoped that others might join him in the future.

Above the bay we built a visitors' center with an observatory, office, beach, dock, and trails. Photographs, a primitive painting of pocs, and a handwoven, poc-decorated rug are on display inside. Tourists and bird watchers can stop here to learn the story of Operación Protección del Poc and observe grebes from boats.

In June 1968 the Ministry of Agriculture officially named this small area as its first national wildlife refuge. More recently, the Guatemalan postal service issued three postage stamps and a commemorative cover featuring the grebes and Lake Atitlán.

Back from the brink

The poc's trend toward extinction has been reversed, at least temporarily: In April 1973 a new census of giant pied-billed grebes showed about 210 individuals, a dramatic increase over the population's low point! This increase, we feel, indicates that management practices are proving beneficial and that conservation efforts have been accepted by residents of Lake Atitlán.

At the same time the bass and crappie populations have peaked, dropped, and leveled off, allowing the aquatic ecosystem to readjust itself. Grebes, bass, little fish, and crabs are reaching a new and more stable balance. Meanwhile, the grebes' recent brush with martyrdom may have sounded an alert in Guatemala for the urgent need to preserve wild creatures.

But undercutting our delight was the chilling news that a large hydroelectric plant on Lake Atitlán might be ready for operation in the late 1970's. As a partial replacement for the water drawn off, long mountain tunnels would divert four rivers into the lake. At least two of these could silt up or pollute the exceptionally clear, blue waters that serve for drinking, swimming, and fishing and make the lakes a tremendous tourist attraction.

The need for electricity in this developing nation is unquestionable, but the methods by which it is produced must be studied carefully. The consequences of once again upsetting Atitlán's environment are paramount considerations. So, too, are the effects on its social and economic situation—local Indians, foreign tourists, Guatemalan vacationers, artists, photographers, anthropologists, ornithologists, and hotel owners. Surely an alternative source of power can be found that will not irrevocably damage this aquamarine gem.

We already have had a dramatic lesson on the dangers of exotic introductions and the need for solicitous stewardship of the ecological system. In the case of the bass introduction, natural biological balances and timely human ministrations gave the grebes a second chance. As I gaze over the magnificent setting that harbors a large population of Mayan Indians, plus the world's only giant pied-billed grebes, my fervent hope is that wise planning and education will save them and their environment from destruction.

Flightless Birds of New Zealand

Birds that cannot fly or fly poorly usually live in isolated places, such as high mountain lakes or oceanic islands. New Zealand, which has harbored more flightless kinds of birds than any other region on earth, is a classic example. The islands of New Zealand have no native mammals that might prey on birds; avian species that can utilize food on the ground, in the water, or within climbing distance do not need to be able to fly to survive.

Kiwi
Forest dweller. Probes ground for worms with long bill. Keen sense of smell.

Kakapo
Rare ground-dwelling parrot. Probably fewer than 100 survive. Can glide to ground but cannot fly.

Moa
Plant eater, up to 12 feet tall. Extinct about A.D. 1300. Hunted by early Maori settlers. A giant relative of the kiwi.

Weka
Eats rabbits, rats, mice, and other animals, as well as plants. Thrives near man; raids garbage cans and chicken runs. Increasing in some settled areas. Size of a large hen.

Stephen Island wren
Known only from a few specimens killed by lighthouse keeper's cat. Extinct since 1894.

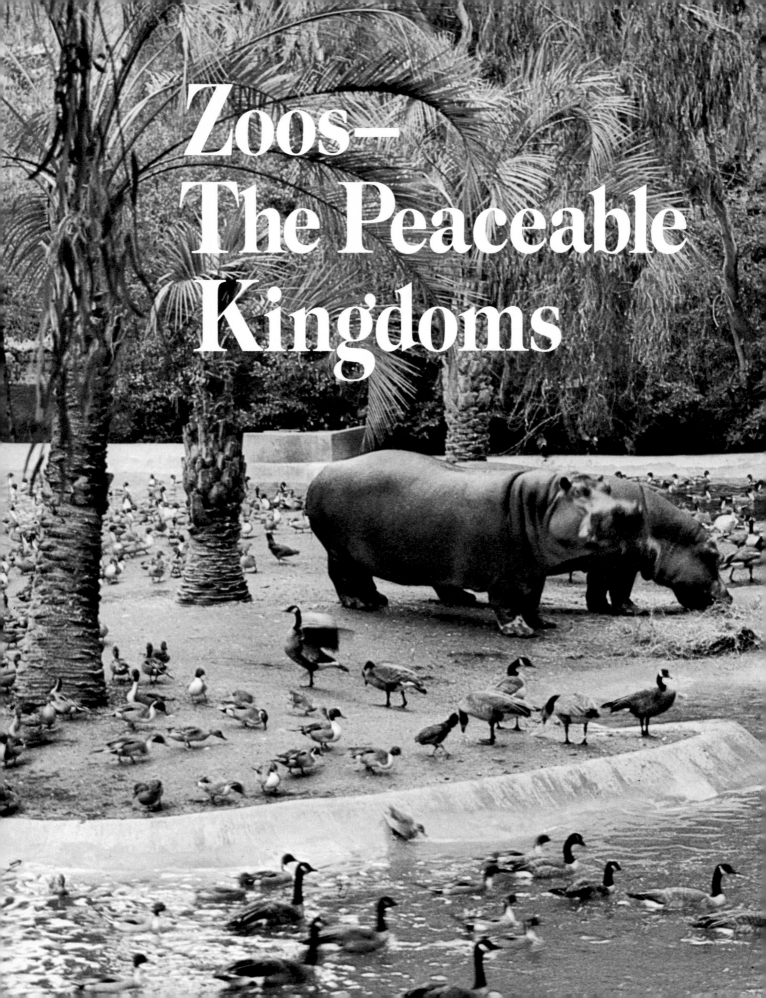

Zoos—
The Peaceable
Kingdoms

A visit to a zoo is a minisafari to foreign lands—
with a big advantage: You can get closer to a
gorilla or a tiger than you ever could in the wild.
But a modern zoo is more than a place of
entertainment—it's a living laboratory where
scientists study why animals behave as they do.
One significant discovery is that animals breed
more readily in natural-looking surroundings,
and zoos are being redesigned with this in mind.
For many species on the verge of extinction,
zoos offer refuge—and a last-minute reprieve.

*Wildlife from two continents—African hippos and
native North American waterfowl—share a spacious
enclosure at the San Diego Zoo in California. The birds
find the hippo pool an attractive wintering ground.*

Creature Comforts at the Zoo

Barbara Ford

**Life in a cage was never like this!
Bars are out. Picture windows,
pools, rocks, and greenery are in.**

Zoo directors are no longer content merely to present healthy animals in clean cages. Nowadays curators in every well-run zoo are working to make the surroundings as much like the animals' native habitats as possible. The theory is that improved space, privacy, pools, vegetation, rocks, and "natural" features that lend themselves to activity will encourage zoo animals to behave as they do in the wild.

Zoo directors and curators find that most animals do indeed become more active in tailor-made habitats. The invitation to activity also counteracts boredom:

There's more to do than just sleep, pace, or beg. Proof can be found in the World of Darkness building at the Bronx Zoo in New York. This ingenious building houses nocturnal animals in glass-fronted enclosures. The lighting turns day into night for the inhabitants. Throughout the real daytime low-level light simulates twilight, tricking the animals into staying awake for the visitors. Dim red light—invisible to the animals— is used for the species that require full darkness.

Natural settings encourage breeding

As visitors enter through the darkened hallways, their eyes take a moment to adjust. But then, under the turned-around lighting conditions, people can see bats flying, foxes trotting, and many small furry creatures scurrying through the realistic rock formations, dens, and passageways. The plastic vegetation completes the amazing effect.

William G. Conway, director of the Bronx Zoo, is committed to naturalization, and the 252-acre institution has many examples of the concept. One of the most impressive new exhibits is a naturalistic habitat for lowland gorillas and orangutans.

Displaying primates has always been a problem because these animals are strong, curious, and destructive. They tear up or throw around almost anything they can get their hands on. So far, however, the

Day Becomes Night in Zoo Exhibits Specially Designed for Nocturnal Animals

Only recently have zoos learned how to exhibit nocturnal animals successfully. In captivity these animals normally sleep by day and move about by night, just as they do in the wild, but an adroit use of lighting can reverse this cycle. Zoos in London, Amsterdam, and other cities have nocturnal exhibits. In 1969 the Bronx Zoo in New York opened the World of Darkness— probably the most impressive nocturnal animal exhibit to be found in any zoo. Here animals from every continent except Antarctica live, play, feed, and even breed in a variety of settings, ranging from a subtropical cypress swamp to a desert. One of the most unusual exhibits combines a stalactite-hung bat cave with a tropical forest. The bats' ultrasonic calls are lowered to the range of the human ear by an electronic device called a "bat translator." During the day the lights in the World of Darkness are turned very low, and the animals become active. At night bright lights are turned on, simulating daylight and triggering sleep responses.

Feet extended to seize its prey, a fishing bat skims its pool at the World of Darkness.

A vampire bat from Latin America crawls toward a glass dish of blood, its staple diet. Vampires, unlike most bats, are agile creepers and can even jump like frogs.

A hammerhead bat from tropical Africa hangs upside down in its typical resting position. These bats have a creaking, froglike call.

A tropical American long-tongued bat hovers to sip nectar from a feeder. In the wild bats pollinate flowers as they feed.

fiberglass indoor world of the Bronx Zoo's gorillas and orangutans has shown remarkably little damage. The gorillas play together in a large multilevel habitat that has artificial trees, rocks, and vines, A waterfall trickles down one corner. In an adjoining enclosure the arboreal orangutans swing back and forth in a tangle of artificial branches and vines.

Naturalistic exhibits like this go beyond entertainment for animals and visitors. They seem to have an impact on the animals' ability to breed. With the native habitats of many animals being destroyed, some rare species face extinction unless their birthrates in captivity are accelerated. The right environment may help to achieve this goal.

The Bronx Zoo was opened in 1899, in an era when the goal of zoo directors was to display exotic species in a safe, sanitary way. Little thought was given to the animals' needs. Unfortunately, this period has left a legacy. The results can still be seen in almost all city zoos: The small bathroomlike tile or concrete cages have heavy bars and perhaps the minimal comfort of a sleeping platform. Animal odors compete with those of disinfectants. The Bronx Zoo building for big cats is such a place. A leopard paces the cement floor of a bare cage; a section of tree trunk furnishes the only naturalistic touch.

"There are many exhibits that we're not proud of," Conway says. "But cats don't need as much stimulation as primates. An African lion in the wild sleeps, dozes, or rests 21 hours a day, hunts 1 hour, and feeds 2 hours."

Nevertheless, work is under way to put most of the big cats, and in fact all the animals, into naturalistic environments as soon as possible. The problem is money and what to do with the old buildings. The Bronx Zoo, a well-financed private institution run by the New York Zoological Society, has fewer monetary worries than most other U.S. zoos, particularly municipal institutions, but its buildings are still old-fashioned. "Some European zoos have one unsought advantage over their sister institutions in the United States," Conway wrote recently. "They were bombed."

New zoos for old

One U.S. zoo director envied by many other zoo officials is George Speidel, director of the new Milwaukee County Zoo. The old zoo was a small downtown installation. In the 1950's it was bulldozed for a highway. As a result, Speidel was able to build a big new zoo from scratch at the edge of the city at just the time when many of the concepts of naturalistic design were being developed.

This zoo has used almost every available naturalistic technique in its exhibits, the first of which opened

Leopard cats adapt so well to the naturalistic environment of the World of Darkness that they produce young, a fact in which the Bronx Zoo takes pride. Slightly larger than house cats, these Asian felines are skilled nighttime hunters.

The only monkeys that are active at night and rest by day, South American douroucoulis are on display in the World of Darkness. With eyes especially adapted for nighttime vision, these owl-faced primates hunt insects, spiders, bats, and birds.

Five Continents
on 185 Acres

A primary goal of the modern zoo is to display animals in open, naturalistic surroundings. Instead of cages the new 185-acre Milwaukee County Zoo in Wisconsin uses spacious outdoor enclosures and separates the animals from the public by an unobtrusive but highly effective system of moats and walls, disguised as rock formations. While grouping some of its animals traditionally by family relationships, Milwaukee also displays them in five major continental exhibits: North America, South America, Africa, Asia, and Australia. Within these continental exhibits predators must obviously be separated from prey species. Herbivores that might fight must also be kept separate. A different type of barrier is required for each animal. An Asian elephant, for example, must be contained by a moat at least 5 feet deep and 6 feet wide— too deep for the animal to clamber in and out of, too wide to step over. The jaguar, a powerful leaper, needs a moat 16 feet deep and 30 feet wide. Yet, thanks to a clever use of perspective, these moats are not apparent to spectators.

Animals from lush, tropical rain forests, bleak Andean highlands, and vast pampa grasslands live together in Milwaukee's South American exhibit. The diagram below identifies the inhabitants and shows why the jaguar does not attack the others.

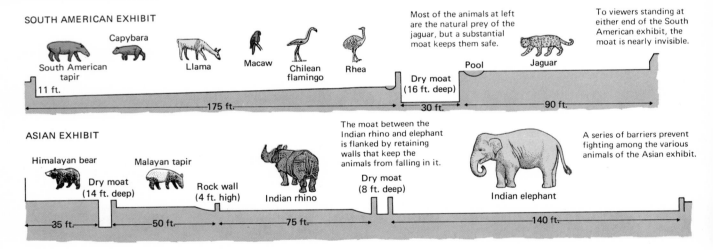

SOUTH AMERICAN EXHIBIT

South American tapir · Capybara · Llama · Macaw · Chilean flamingo · Rhea

Most of the animals at left are the natural prey of the jaguar, but a substantial moat keeps them safe.

Dry moat (16 ft. deep) · Pool · Jaguar

To viewers standing at either end of the South American exhibit, the moat is nearly invisible.

11 ft. · 175 ft. · 30 ft. · 90 ft.

ASIAN EXHIBIT

Himalayan bear · Dry moat (14 ft. deep) · Malayan tapir · Rock wall (4 ft. high) · Indian rhino

The moat between the Indian rhino and elephant is flanked by retaining walls that keep the animals from falling in it.

Dry moat (8 ft. deep) · Indian elephant

A series of barriers prevent fighting among the various animals of the Asian exhibit.

35 ft. · 50 ft. · 75 ft. · 140 ft.

in 1959. Prey and predator species from Africa, Asia, and South America are displayed in adjoining areas.

"You see that impala over there?" asked Speidel, pointing to a large grassy outdoor enclosure containing a group of African hoofed animals. "She's eyeing that cheetah, her predator, in the next enclosure. And the cheetah is looking at her. Proximity keeps both of them alert." The two species, he added, are separated by a deep, wide moat concealed from visitors.

The Milwaukee Zoo has achieved remarkable effects. Visitors can stand at certain points along the series of moated enclosures and see a dramatic African panorama. All in the same vista are lions and cheetahs, hoofed animals, big birds such as ostriches and peli-

cans, and the African giants—elephants, rhinoceroses, hippopotamuses, and giraffes. Visitors can also get a closeup view of the big cats through a picture window built into a rock wall.

Despite its advantages, naturalization creates some special problems for zoo workers. The grass in the indoor moated enclosures, for example, is regularly torn up by the large mammals, necessitating resodding each spring. Some zoos use synthetic substitutes.

Many of the warm-climate animals in the Milwaukee County Zoo have adjusted to the cold Wisconsin winters, but not the primates. Almost all of the monkeys and apes are housed in indoor cages. They are enclosed not by bars but by glass. The windows are electrified so as to give a mild shock when touched. The animals soon learn to leave the glass alone. An important advantage of glass over bars is that it allows for the installation of two separate air-circulation systems. One operates inside the cages; the other operates throughout the rest of the building. The double system protects the primates from human respiratory diseases, to which they are highly susceptible. It has the secondary advantage of keeping animals' smells in.

One example of naturalization that uses a relatively small space at the Milwaukee County Zoo is the Siberian tiger exhibit, a 54-foot by 30-foot enclosure that resembles a glass-walled patio. This area is open to the sky and viewable from the heated interior of another nearby exhibit. The animals enjoy a pool, a waterfall, rocks, and a couple of tree-trunk sections for claw sharpening. Two live trees that seem part of the enclosure are actually protected from the animals by inconspicuous fences. When snow falls, these heavily furred Siberian cats are at their best. One day last year, when the temperature plunged to 12° below zero, Orville, an adult male, was seen frolicking in the snow, plunging into the pool for a 15-minute swim, and finally emerging to lie down on a slab of ice. The setting seems to agree with Orville and his mate. They have had 14 cubs, most of which have been sent to other zoos to develop additional breeding pairs of the rare tiger.

Some of the most imaginative live-animal exhibits to be seen today are in a small nonprofit institution outside Tucson, Arizona. The Arizona–Sonora Desert Museum displays only animals native to Arizona and to the Sonora Desert, an area that includes parts of New Mexico, Arizona, and California. In one exhibit an antelope squirrel darts into a burrow built of simulated rock. In this glass-fronted world a realistic painted background provides a desert setting. "I don't like the word 'zoo,'" says director Mervin W. Larson. "It has a bad connotation—50 monkeys in a row; dirty, smelly cages. I consider this institution a combination of a zoo and a museum. But most of our staff feel closer to museums than to zoos."

A zoo museum

The real showpieces of the Arizona–Sonora Desert Museum are two-level naturalistic displays that can be viewed from outdoors or indoors. Outdoors, visitors can look down on artificial rocks, where the animals are seen as though from a small hilltop, or they can go indoors to the comfort of an air-conditioned building and view them at eye level.

One canyonlike habitat houses four species of small desert cats: Margays, ocelots, jaguarundis, and bobcats. Each species occupies a separate area that provides plenty of rocky nooks and crannies for hiding—a must for zoo animals, some zoo directors now claim. "Where are they?" I asked, peering at the ocelot exhibit from inside the building. "We think part of the fun is finding them," said a staff member, pushing a switch. A light came on in a small, windowed den. I found myself staring at two ocelots, which stared right back.

An elaborate display such as this is expensive. Larson, who designed it, says that about $250,000 has

For the Siberian tigers at the Milwaukee County Zoo, Wisconsin winters hold no terrors. Adapted to the snow and ice of Central Asia's highest mountains, these largest and most heavily furred tigers are perfectly at home in subzero temperatures.

A Unique Museum Makes the Desert Come Alive

Combining the features of museum, zoo, and botanical garden, the Arizona-Sonora Desert Museum near Tucson, Arizona, displays only species native to the southwestern United States and Mexico. The museum is well known for its naturalistic animal enclosures and ecological exhibits, which illustrate the delicately adjusted interrelationships of the desert's life forms, soils, and climate.

An Underground Zoo

The museum's 60-foot underground tunnel with glass-fronted dens lets visitors see how the desert's nocturnal animals spend the day. Realistic dens, made of plaster from latex molds of actual caves and burrows, connect with hidden open-air exercise and feeding areas.

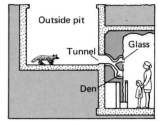

Escaping the heat of the desert sun, a kit fox rests in its den. Visitors can push buttons to light the interior of this and other exhibits in the tunnel. Like many desert animals the kit fox rests by day, seeks food at night.

Another tunnel resident is the ringtail, or cacomistle, a slender relative of the raccoon, which may grow to a length of 32 inches. A nighttime forager, the agile ringtail feeds on insects, birds, rodents, and a variety of fruits.

Otters Frolic in a Re-created Desert Stream

The Arizona-Sonora Desert Museum's otter exhibit is a meticulously reconstructed "riverbank," like those inhabited by otters before the demands of agriculture and a booming population lowered southern Arizona's water table. Visitors can view the otters underwater.

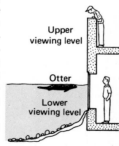

Three otters in the museum's otter exhibit expectantly await a treat of fish beside a simulated waterfall and river pool. The exhibit depicts how otters lived in the Santa Cruz River Valley in southern Arizona a century ago.

On a monorail safari visitors to the San Diego Wild Animal Park view giraffes, ostriches, and zebras in the East African area. The train affords its passengers views of animals living under near-natural conditions and creates a minimum of disturbance.

been spent on the cat enclosure, which houses only 10 individuals. A comparable display was completed a short time ago for otters, beavers, and bighorn sheep. The museum's most ambitious project, still in the planning stage, is a $1 million miniature mountain for large mammals now housed in bare little cages. "We spend more per animal than anyone else," says Larson.

A zoo park

The San Diego Zoo in California is a nonprofit institution that has recently opened its 1,800-acre Wild Animal Park in rolling country 30 miles north of the existing zoo. The park includes African and Asian species numbering about 1,000 individuals; eventually it will hold several thousand animals. The park is divided into four areas that represent North, South, and East Africa, and the Asian swamps and highlands. Each area contains appropriate species. The geographic divisions are separated by inconspicuous moats and fences, with predators kept within their own moated sites. A train carries visitors on a 5-mile trip around the park. Instead of a closeup view of animals in artificial conditions, people can see them in natural groups, with enough space to suggest their appearance in the wild. The zoo staff hopes that these naturalistic conditions will influence reproduction by providing enough privacy for the animals to breed.

It's too early to tell whether these new facilities will produce the hoped-for population increase, but early signs are favorable. In the old San Diego Zoo a rare white rhinoceros named Mandhla had lived for 10 years. In his zoo enclosure, a moated outdoor pen about 75 yards long by 15 yards wide (roomy by zoo standards), he failed to breed with his mate even once. Other captive white rhinos also showed little interest in sex. But when Mandhla was moved to the park in 1971, free to roam with 19 other white rhinos around the 92 acres of the South African area, he quickly impregnated at least four females.

Not only is Mandhla breeding, he's also healthier. According to mammal curator Clyde A. Hill: "Mandhla is much more muscular now, because he gets more exercise. White rhinos are herd animals, and they're like kids the way they play tag."

Although zoos have often operated as "scruffy little animal slums"—former zoo curator Desmond Morris' term—they have traditionally espoused aims that involve conservation, education, and research. Unfortunately, these aims have seldom been achieved. In the area of education zoos often seem torn between amusing and teaching the public. And perhaps too much zoo research once revolved around strategies for keeping individual animals alive as long as possible (longevity records have been prestigious distinctions in zoological circles), rather than being concerned about the welfare of species.

Now, with the revolution in zoos in full swing, there has been a general upgrading of priorities, which works to the benefit of both animal and man. Zoo breeding programs are becoming widespread and increasingly successful. Research into the behavior of exotic species is beginning to provide the data needed to improve endangered species' chances of survival, not only in zoos but in their natural habitats. Meanwhile, the public is getting a long-overdue look at how animals really live.

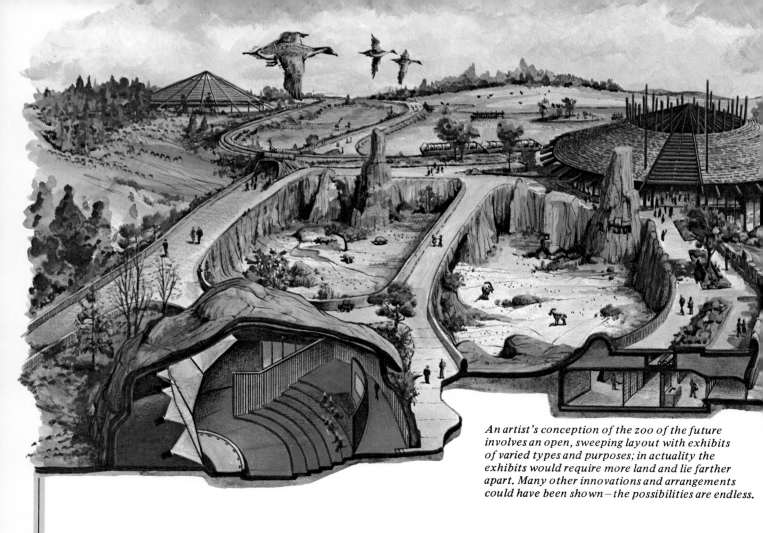

An artist's conception of the zoo of the future involves an open, sweeping layout with exhibits of varied types and purposes; in actuality the exhibits would require more land and lie farther apart. Many other innovations and arrangements could have been shown—the possibilities are endless.

Preview of the Zoo of the Future

The zoo of the future is already partly here. In imaginative ways it will combine concepts already being used successfully at many zoos, creating an environment that satisfies both animals and visitors alike. To the greatest extent possible animals will be kept in spacious enclosures, not in cages, and the design of their minienvironments will take advantage of new knowledge of animal behavior. Such factors as an animal's need for its own territory, a hiding place, a lookout rock, or soft digging soil will be provided for. Animals will be separated from the public not by bars but by unobtrusive barriers such as moats, tailored to the particular physical capabilities and behavioral makeup of each species. Every effort will be made to give the public an appreciation of the animals' intimate relationship to their environments and to enhance the visitors' feeling of involvement. The illustrations on this and the following pages were prepared by designers at California's San Diego Zoo, where a mild climate permits outdoor exhibits to be open the year round. With modifications similar exhibits can be used by zoos in regions with more rigorous climates.

Key to the Zoo of the Future

1. Entrance complex. Most visitor services are concentrated here: Parking, comfort stations, gift shop, camera shop, and vending machines. The parking lot is hidden to avoid disturbing the visual unity of the zoo; pets can be left in comfortable kennels instead of cars. An orientation plaza contains informational displays and rest areas, as well as directions to the various exhibit areas.

2. Multimedia theater. Researchers have learned that most people's enjoyment and appreciation of what they see is enhanced by understanding it. At the zoo of the future every effort is made to explain the concepts that go into each exhibit, in addition to the biology and behavior of the animals exhibited. In the multimedia theater this information is presented via films, talks, and a variety of other audiovisual techniques.

3, 4. Behavioral exhibits. Designed to highlight the unique habits of two species, these exhibits feature spectacular rock climbers—the North American mountain lion (3) and Europe's alpine ibex (4). Re-creating the animals' rugged natural habitats, the enclosures are surrounded by clifflike, unscalable walls. Galleries on the "peaks" near the ibexes give visitors views from different levels.

5. Aquatic area. Utilizing a small lake, this area is a showcase for integrated exhibits of aquatic life, showing the complex relationships between the inhabitants. The lake features native species of fish, amphibians, reptiles, and waterfowl. The island in the lake is home for a monkey colony; the water acts as a barrier between these primates and the visitors' path. A boat provides visitors with an added viewing experience.

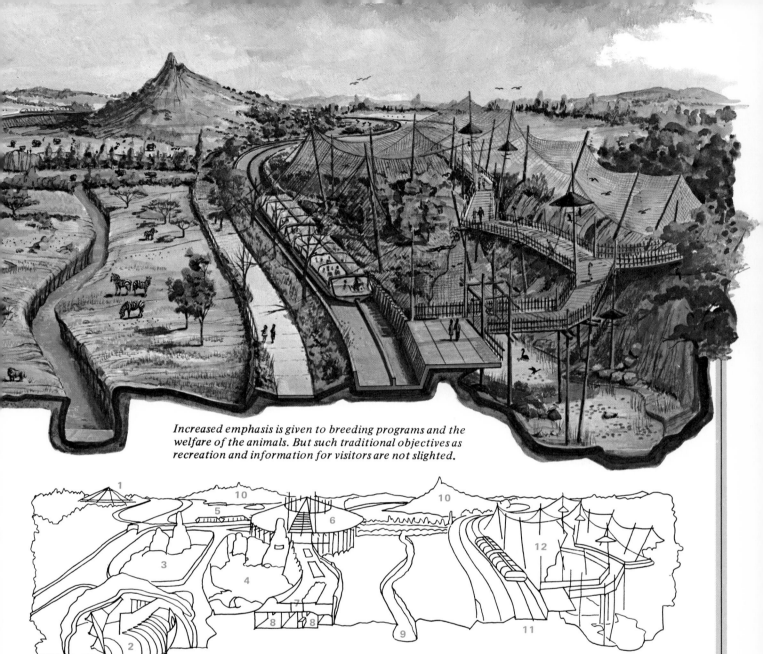

Increased emphasis is given to breeding programs and the welfare of the animals. But such traditional objectives as recreation and information for visitors are not slighted.

6. Main orientation and educational complex. Located at a major crossroads area, the building presents interpretive displays about the zoo and its animals. It could also house a small-mammal exhibit or a restaurant, overlooking one or more major exhibits. If space is limited, the multimedia theater could be incorporated into this complex.

7. Basic utilities duct. Zoos need water and electricity; some need gas. This underground duct houses the necessary pipes and powerlines and conceals them from visitors. The basic design also permits repairs and alterations to be made from the service area below without disturbing the landscaping.

8. Service areas. Located underground to isolate service and maintenance tasks from the visitors, these tunnellike areas give keepers unobtrusive access to the animal enclosures. They also contain holding cages (for animals that must be moved out of enclosures), maternity areas, and facilities for food preparation and medical treatment. Service tunnels reach every exhibit.

9. Predator-prey exhibit. Designed to dramatize the concept of flight distance—the minimum distance in which an animal feels safe from potential enemies—this enclosure holds lions and their natural prey, zebras. The two species are safely separated by a moat not apparent to visitors, and the design of the enclosure ensures that no lion can get enough of a run to leap the moat. The moat prevents the lions from coming within the zebra's flight distance.

10. Open wildlife area. A large exhibit displays animals that in nature share the same habitat. Ample space and natural features that function as boundaries (trees, bushes, hillocks) permit the animals to establish their own territories and refuges.

11. Guided-tour train. Running silently on rubber tires and propelled by a pollution-free electric motor, the train transports visitors around the entire zoo, giving them an overview of the exhibits. A zoo assistant identifies animals and gives explanations as the train moves at a slow rate for viewing. Another advantage of the train is that it permits large numbers of people to pass through the animals' environment without disturbing them, which is very important if the zoo is breeding endangered species.

12. Free-flight aviary. This walk-through exhibit permits birds to fly freely and gives visitors a chance to observe them from below and from the birds' flight levels. Plantings create a naturalistic habitat and supply shelter. At the entrances are invisible wind curtains birds will not cross.

Preview of the Zoo of the Future (continued)

The zoo of the future will contain many specialized exhibits, designed to display a particular species or to demonstrate various facets of animal behavior and ecology. The actual number and type of exhibits at any one zoo will depend, of course, on the zoo's financial resources and on the goals of its director. These pages include a few of the exhibits you can expect to find in the zoo of the future. Some, like the animal contact area and the nocturnal mammal house, already exist at several zoos.

In the animal contact area people can touch and pet common species. Orphaned animals, kept here for special care, also may be seen and sometimes touched. At left, a low fence separates visitors from animals that can be touched but not for prolonged periods. In the foreground a woman pushes a young child in a stroller past several hoofed animals roaming about freely. At right, a pond stocked with pinioned water birds attracts wild birds in a pageant that changes with the seasons.

Hovering in a manmade wind current, a bat flies about in the nocturnal animal house. Visitors can study the bat's flight, and the bat gets ample exercise despite the relatively small size of its cage. Glass separates the bat's realistically sculptured "cave" from viewers. A large fan behind a protective screen drives air from right to left.

Nocturnal animals are housed in a windowless building with an exterior resembling a rock outcropping. Normally asleep by day, the animals are tricked into daytime activity by the use of low-intensity or red lights, which they cannot see. At night bright lights are turned on, triggering their sleep reflexes.

The entrance complex houses an attractive building with kennels for visitors' pets, vending machines, toilets, and a cafeteria; film is also sold here. Outside are parking lots and an orientation plaza with displays about the zoo. The building overlooks an exhibit of wildebeests, contained by a wide moat and a low wall.

A year-round, all-weather habitat for gorillas permits the great apes to seek the conditions most comfortable for them, whatever the weather may be. The covered area is kept at a temperature and humidity similar to those of the gorillas' native rain forests. The sturdy jungle gym in the outside enclosure provides the gorillas with stimulation, exercise, and shade. Moats with vertical walls, which gorillas cannot scale, separate apes and visitors.

Bears and moose share an enclosure modeled after their native habitat—the lake-studded northern forests. Each side represents a type of habitat the animal would frequent in nature: for the bears, a craggy glen; for the moose, a pond's shore. The barrier between the species, with overhangs to prevent the animals from surmounting it, is also a path for visitors.

The giraffe enclosure makes use of a unique barrier: a wide, shallow moat with a steeply sloping inner edge. An inborn fear of climbing down a steep incline prevents the giraffes from wading across the moat. The moat's width prevents the animals from stretching their heads into the visitors' area. This type of barrier works only with giraffes.

The beaver pond has four observation areas. Galleries overlook the pond at water level and above; a submerged tunnel permits visitors to watch beavers swimming underwater. Another tunnel (not shown) affords an unusual view of the lodge interior.

Bernhard Grzimek of the Frankfurt Zoo

Jack Denton Scott

He speaks for the animals. The man who saved the herds of Serengeti has devoted his life to them.

Bernhard Grzimek (pronounced *zhim-ek*) rebuilt the Frankfurt Zoo after World War II, starting with a few bombed-out buildings and only one animal, a male hippopotamus that had survived the bombing by submerging in his pool. When Grzimek was appointed director of the zoo, he was told by the mayor that the establishment must be entirely self-supporting.

A city zoo always needs space. Knowing this, Grzimek had signs printed, by which he claimed three bombed-out city blocks. It wasn't legal, but no one protested. Grzimek and a crew of volunteers spent weeks clearing debris and began rebuilding. Then he toured the countryside in a charcoal-burning car, collecting animals from destroyed zoos and circuses.

During the war Grzimek had placed his research animals with the Leipzig Zoo. Just as the Russians were about to occupy the city, he raced into Leipzig and retrieved his animals, plus eight others.

Grzimek's efforts to rebuild the Frankfurt Zoo brought great popular response. Children roamed the city's streets collecting money for the zoo; workmen donated weeks of their time rebuilding cages and houses; boys took turns leaving the zoo on bicycles,

King penguins swim in their climate-controlled tank at the Frankfurt Zoo's Exotarium, a zoo within a zoo. The Exotarium houses other marine animals, from sea anemones to elephant seals, as well as a large collection of reptiles and insects.

carrying rhesus monkeys on their backs and pedaling to the Autobahn where they asked American soldiers for fruit for their animal friends. With slim funds Grzimek bought a pair of camels and a female hippopotamus from the Nuremberg Zoo. Shrewdly exchanging his rapidly breeding deer, goats, camels, and monkeys for species the zoo lacked, he gradually enlarged the zoo's collection.

While building the Frankfurt Zoo, Grzimek made many research trips to Africa to study animals in their natural environment. To his distress he found that the animals were distributed over small parts of East Africa—in particular, the grassland savannas (where wildebeests, zebras, and gazelles exist in millions) that form 10 percent or less of the East African landscapes. "The result," Grzimek said, "is that whereas 95 percent of the children in England have seen lions and elephants, 95 percent of the Africans have not. Already man has wiped out scores of wild species. I fear by this century's end children will learn about elephants, rhinoceroses, leopards, and hippopotamuses only through films and books."

Grzimek made a film showing African animals in danger, which was widely shown and commercially successful. He offered the profits to the British administrators of the Serengeti National Park in Tanzania (then Tanganyika) to acquire more land for this last home of the large wild herds. They suggested that he use the money to take a census of Serengeti herds.

A flying zebra

Grzimek and his son Michael bought a single-engine airplane. *The Flying Zebra* was painted black and white so it could easily be seen in case of emergency. As there was no map of Serengeti, the Grzimeks made one, marking off small sections that they crisscrossed daily, counting animals. Whenever they landed, they took soil and plant samples, sending them to Frankfurt for analysis. They wanted to discover how the zoo animals' diet compared with food eaten by the same species in the wild.

Then tragedy halted the expedition; in 1959, 25-year-old Michael Grzimek was killed when his plane collided with a vulture. Bernhard Grzimek buried his son on the rim of the nearby Ngorongoro Crater, where, he says, "God keeps his own zoo." Inscribed on Michael's gravestone is: "He gave all he had, including his life, for the wild animals of Africa."

That dedication drove Grzimek on to finish the film *Serengeti Shall Not Die!* and write a book with the same title. The film was viewed by millions, and the book was translated into Swahili and other dialects to show Africans the problems facing their wildlife. In all, it was translated into 23 languages and sold about a million copies over the years. Together, the film and book brought worldwide action: Foundations and individuals donated money to save the Serengeti.

Although untiringly active in conservation, Grzimek is still dedicated to his zoo work. His accomplishments are on view at the Frankfurt Zoo. Grzimek pioneered

Hoofed Animals That Live Together Often Fight Together

Zoos sometimes keep different species of hoofed animals in the same enclosure. One large living area usually gives each animal more space and opportunity for exercise than several smaller ones; it also provides a more interesting spectacle for visitors. But mixing species in captivity may lead to fighting, especially between males. The risk is greatest when combatants are unequal in size or when one has much longer horns than the other. Some hoofed animals, such as bantengs (wild Asiatic cattle), are such dangerous fighters that they cannot be kept with other species.

Peaceful Coexistence

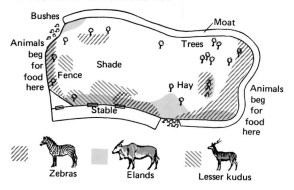

Zebras   Elands   Lesser kudus

At the Frankfurt Zoo three hoofed species sharing an enclosure avoid conflict by occupying different areas. Zebras, the dominant animals, have the largest territory; kudus, the smallest.

To Fight or Not To Fight

Fights are most likely to take place between different species when their threat postures and rituals are similar, as with the threatening blackbuck and sika to the right (top). Below them, the nilgai threatens by stretching its neck forward, but the sika, not recognizing the threat, does not respond. The sequence of threat-and-response is interrupted; no fight will occur. The circumstances are similar for the threatening blackbuck and the nilgai (bottom).

Fights Between Unequal Adversaries

Male hoofed animals are "programmed" for ritualized fighting with their own species. In confinement the fighting urge may be directed at other species. The contenders are often unequally matched.

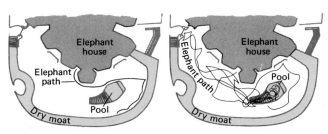

An aggressive male zebra bites a Watusi bull on the neck. The bull responds by lowering its head.

Each recognizing the other's threat, a Cameroon dwarf goat and a Watusi bull spar playfully.

Kneeling with lowered heads, an oryx and a gnu prepare to charge. The long horns of the oryx give it an advantage over the gnu.

A giraffe wards off a bull eland with a powerful forward kick. Giraffes can also deliver smashing blows with their heads.

---

in the use of glass to replace iron bars. His Ape House is an impressive example: Half-ton glass windows front each cage, set obliquely so reflections aren't cast from either side. And he is probably the first to make his a "speaking zoo," with an FM station running tape recordings that explain the exhibits.

Grzimek has long prohibited visitors from feeding animals and threatened to fine those who do. "Feeding animals," he says, "is similar to feeding hospital patients. They need special diets. Indiscriminate feeding is unhealthy, cruel, and sometimes fatal."

With his special magic Grzimek took several bombed-out buildings and converted them into what may be the world's outstanding zoo. Recently, as he watched a gorilla (his favorite animal) bathing at the Frankfurt Zoo, Grzimek said, emotion in his soft voice, "This is my whole life."

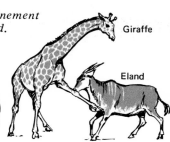

Feeding the elephants was popular with visitors to the London Zoo. But this deprived the elephants of needed exercise and caused them digestive upsets. Zoo officials plotted the actual movements of an elephant (above, left) and found that it spent most of its time begging for food along a limited stretch of its boundary moat, ignoring the pool and other features of its large enclosure. When feeding was banned, the elephant bathed in the pool, played with logs, tires, and sand, and explored the enclosure thoroughly (above, right).

209

Heini Hediger of the Zurich Zoo

Claus Gaedemann

**What makes a good zoo?
It may be a waterhole, a tree trunk
to rub against, or soil to dig in, says
a world-famous Swiss zoo designer.**

No animal lives a really 'free' life, in the sense of far-ranging movement," says Professor Heini Hediger. Animals do not roam the countryside at will. Each is bound to its own fixed territory; within it an individual moves at fixed times, along fixed paths, and to fixed places.

As we toured the Zurich Zoo, where Professor Hediger was director, we stopped at the enclosure of a family of vicuñas. "You'd think that these llamalike creatures, accustomed to roaming the South American Andes, would require a huge enclosure," said Hediger. "But look!" And sure enough, their tracks showed that the vicuñas weren't using even half of the area at their disposal. Yet evidence of their well-being stood on still-uncertain legs before us: a newborn vicuña.

"The well-being of zoo animals," Hediger explains, "is not a question of mere space, but of what they find in it. It's up to man to furnish them with surroundings that approximate their natural habitats—a well-defined 'home' where they feel secure and fixed sites for feeding and watering. Beasts and birds of prey must have a place where they can tear apart their food. Elephants and buffaloes need a waterhole for bathing, lions a solarium. Other animals require a spot where they can see without being seen, or a hiding place. It is also important that the denizens of our zoos be able to stake out their territories as they do in the wild, over roughly similar terrain. If all this is provided for, animals in captivity can get along with only a fraction of the space they require in the open."

Small amenities help too. Zebras at the Zurich Zoo, for example, are supplied with imitation concrete termite hills to rub against. Brown bears have their own gnarled tree trunks to which they affix their glandular secretions that tell other bears to stay away. In a Dutch zoo an armadillo kept running in circles because the concrete floor frustrated its digging instinct. The solution, according to Hediger, was an 8-inch layer of soil, which at once calmed the animal. A lion at the Frankfurt Zoo, enfeebled with age, became more relaxed after he was furnished with a big boulder behind which to hide from the more robust of his companions.

Given the choice, animals conditioned to the security of zoo life may prefer captivity to liberty. A keeper at the Bern Zoo once inadvertently left a gate open, and the deer promptly went out to explore the world. Even though a woods was only about 30 yards away, they returned to their enclosure after browsing.

Hediger's pioneering work on zoos has gained worldwide recognition, and invitations come from all over: "We want a zoo. Please come and build one for us!" One "client" was São Paulo, Brazil. Its 3 million inhabitants were clamoring for an island of living nature in the asphalt desert. The city fathers made available approximately 93 acres of jungle that contained a small lake, hills, and gorges.

"The Brazilians were so keen on getting their zoo

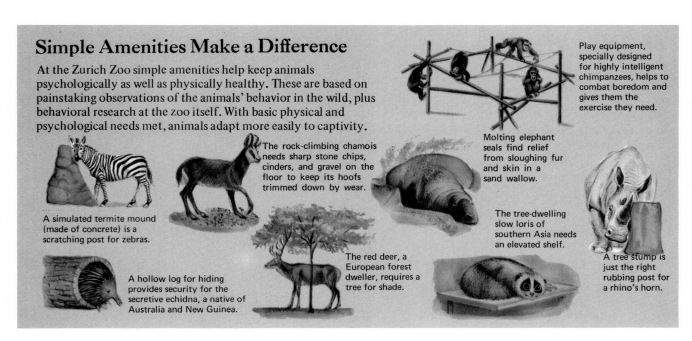

Simple Amenities Make a Difference

At the Zurich Zoo simple amenities help keep animals psychologically as well as physically healthy. These are based on painstaking observations of the animals' behavior in the wild, plus behavioral research at the zoo itself. With basic physical and psychological needs met, animals adapt more easily to captivity.

A simulated termite mound (made of concrete) is a scratching post for zebras.

The rock-climbing chamois needs sharp stone chips, cinders, and gravel on the floor to keep its hoofs trimmed down by wear.

Play equipment, specially designed for highly intelligent chimpanzees, helps to combat boredom and gives them the exercise they need.

Molting elephant seals find relief from sloughing fur and skin in a sand wallow.

The tree-dwelling slow loris of southern Asia needs an elevated shelf.

A hollow log for hiding provides security for the secretive echidna, a native of Australia and New Guinea.

The red deer, a European forest dweller, requires a tree for shade.

A tree stump is just the right rubbing post for a rhino's horn.

Monkey islands designed by Heini Hediger at Brazil's São Paulo Zoo are isolated by a lagoon that also serves as a swan lake. Dead trees on the islands are for climbing, and little houses on posts provide shelter. Catwalks lead from island to island.

that a veritable miracle took place," Hediger recalls. "No sooner had I drawn up a sketch of enclosures, buildings, and roads than a bulldozer clanged into the area to clear away the undergrowth. In August 1957 I was still stalking through virgin jungle, and the following March there was a zoo, complete with a thousand animals gathered from all over the world."

Hediger got up at sunrise every day to plan and organize. His first order was: "No wire fence or bars anywhere." Even the birds were not caged. Instead, Heini Hediger used glass-domed aviaries in which visitors and birds mingle.

A zoo close to the source

Professor Hediger started his next zoo in Simla, high up in the Himalayas. Says Hediger: "It is an especially gratifying project because this rugged mountain world, with its magnificent cedar forests and tree-size rhododendrons, abounds in rare specimens not usually found in zoos, such as the giant panda, the yak, and the musk deer." Many of them will find a new home in Simla— without bars, of course.

The international list of zoos that bear the stamp of Hediger's collaboration is long. Washington's National Zoo is on it, as are Innsbruck, Verona, Nairobi, and Toronto, to name but a few. His latest innovation is the world's first "alpinarium," located at an elevation of 9,000 feet in the Swiss Alps. Here, in an open-air preserve, visitors may observe the ibex, marmot, snow rabbit, and chamois at close range.

When I asked Professor Hediger what made him devote his entire life to the study and care of animals, he answered: "I believe that we basically want to communicate with our four-footed and feathered friends. It has been my life's ambition to help break down the barriers between us."

Living evidence of its parents' well-being, a baby vicuña rests in its enclosure at the Zurich Zoo. Animals do not breed unless their psychological needs are satisfied; a successful breeding program is one sign of a well-designed zoo.

Why Zoos in Africa?

Robert R. Golding

Like most city people all over the world, urban Africans have little contact with wildlife.

Many non-Africans believe that the whole African continent is teeming with wildlife and that every African sees animals every day. This is not true. As a country develops and more land is taken for agriculture and industry, habitats for wild animals dwindle. Direct contact with wild nature diminishes just as it does, of course, in the more developed countries.

At the University of Ibadan Zoo in Nigeria most visitors had never seen an elephant or a chimpanzee before coming to the zoo. The idea of rapport with animals was new to them, and an element of suspicion and fear was present. When our gorillas and chimpanzees were young and were brought out of their cages for exercise, as often as not visitors ran in panic.

On the other hand, when keepers known to the animals entered the cage and played with them, talking to them, chasing them, being chased by them, the spectators became more relaxed and enjoyed the whole performance. Afterwards the animals could be brought outside the cage without frightening the audience.

This kind of introduction is useful with many species of animals, especially with snakes. The greatest obstacle to be overcome is the deep-rooted belief that all wild animals, especially reptiles and amphibians, are dangerous to man. Once convinced that there is no danger, schoolchildren will compete enthusiastically in their attempts to touch or even hold a tame python. If the children had seen the same snake in the bush, they probably would have run away as fast as they could or would have tried to kill the animal.

There are special problems in establishing zoos in developing countries. Many Nigerians, for example, are aware that some foreigners think of them as living in the bush "with" the animals. They rightly resent this. So fear of the bush is compounded by a wish to be dissociated from a backward image.

Running a zoo in Africa has special challenges too. Few African countries have money to spare; so costs for zoo cages and enclosures must be kept as low as possible. But inexpensive structures need not necessarily be poorly designed nor hard to maintain. And there is nothing that says a zoo has to be large; a small, well-run zoo can be a perfect gem.

Gambling Gorillas Delight Visitors to the Ibadan Zoo

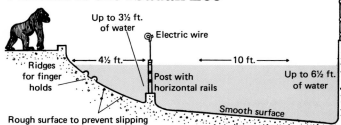

A 2,870-square-foot enclosure gives young gorillas at the Ibadan Zoo in Nigeria ample room for activity; an identical enclosure serves a group of chimpanzees. A roof extension shelters portions of the enclosures from sun and rain. Each yard is bounded on two sides by a moat with a sloping floor, ridged and roughened for the animals' safety and divided by a metal barrier. The shallow inner side has a maximum depth of 3½ feet; the side nearest the visitors slopes down to 6½ feet, too deep for an ape to maneuver in. Electric cattle-fence wires above the underwater barrier discourage the animals from crossing the moat. The chimpanzees do not like the water and avoid it, but the gorillas thoroughly enjoy it and take frequent dips on hot days. They leap in, splash, and even have learned to swim for short distances—but never put their faces in the water. Although wary of humans at close range, the gorillas do not seem disturbed by the crowds of visitors standing on the far side of the moat.

Like most children these young Nigerians are fascinated by snakes. A keeper at the University of Ibadan Zoo shows them that a python can be beautiful and interesting, and some of them will soon overcome their prejudices enough to want to touch it.

A gorilla at the Ibadan Zoo demonstrates its feelings about its favorite keeper—as a matter of fact, the only keeper the gorillas tolerate within their enclosure. Gorillas are fond of the company of those human beings whom they trust.

One of the gorillas leaps into the water to make certain that another keeper, cleaning the outer moat, does not cross the fence into gorilla territory. Like people, gorillas sometimes dislike others for no apparent reason.

One practical problem during the early days at the University of Ibadan Zoo was that of finding keepers with experience or with a feeling of compassion for animals. Now, however, there is an experienced staff of Nigerian keepers who take a great interest in their work. In some instances these keepers have made economic sacrifices in order to work at the zoo. In the past it was not easy to attract people of good general education to take up zoo work on the professional level, because men with the right qualifications preferred more traditional white-collar jobs. But attitudes in this part of Nigeria have changed markedly in the past few years, and applicants for zoo posts are better qualified as the years pass. If the increasing numbers of zoos are to maintain contact with the public and with other zoos throughout the world, their employees must be people of experience and practical ability who can also write reports and articles, keep records, correspond with other zoos, and address school groups and television audiences.

What of the advantages of a zoo in Africa? Many suitable species of animals are near to hand. Local birds, reptiles, and small mammals can generally be obtained cheaply and without difficulty. Large quantities of fresh fruits, seeds, tubers, leaves, and grass are readily available. A camel costs nothing to feed: It is merely taken out and tethered in the bush.

A new zoo may, through lack of planning, acquire a haphazard collection of animals. Despite such pitfalls and economic problems, small zoos have an important part to play in the preservation of wildlife in Africa. By presenting living animals to the public in safe surroundings, such zoos can encourage people to watch animals without a stick in the hand or a gun.

Bored when they have nothing to do, gorillas are fascinated by any new object, and they find the tools brought by a keeper for cleaning up rubble a source of delight. Gorillas' hands look clumsy, but they are capable of surprisingly delicate manipulations.

Rearing Primates in a Zoo

Mating and giving birth are only the first steps in the successful breeding of zoo animals: The ultimate goal is to have the zoo-born young themselves mate and give birth. For this purpose it is usually desirable to have the mother of a zoo infant raise her own offspring, although zoo keepers are prepared to take over if she cannot (or will not) care for her infant. When keepers give warmth and individual attention to a young primate, they increase its chances of becoming an adult capable in its own turn of raising young.

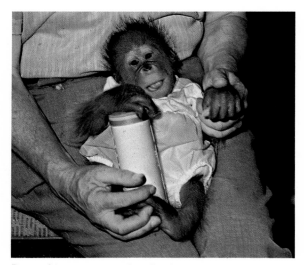

Dressed in rompers and with a firm grip on its bottle, an orangutan seems content to live in the human world.

A gibbon infant, clinging to its mother's abdominal fur by reflex action, frees her arms for locomotion.

In the Basel Zoo this gorilla mother and infant (the second born to her) trust the keeper completely.

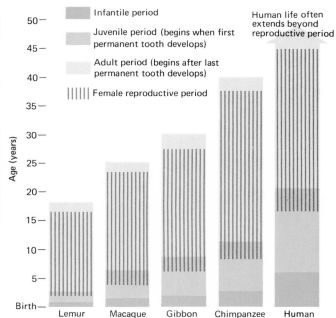

All primates follow a parallel pattern of development, but for higher primates the various stages are more prolonged.

Panda-monium Reigns

Rare, elusive, and difficult to capture, giant pandas are seldom seen in zoos. Aside from a pair presented to the Emperor of Japan in A.D. 685, the first live panda to leave its native China was a 2-month-old cub that went to Chicago's Brookfield Zoo in 1936. A few additional pandas went to various U.S. and European zoos before World War II. After the war the Moscow Zoo acquired two males, Ping-Ping and An-An, and the London Zoo got one female, Chi-Chi. International politics prevented the export of any more pandas until 1972, when Hsing-Hsing and Ling-Ling were presented to the National Zoo in Washington, D.C., and another pair went to Tokyo's Ueno Zoo. The first captive pandas did not live long. Their specialized diets made it difficult to keep them in good health. However, much more is known about pandas today, and one panda at the Peking Zoo lived to be at least 20. But even healthy pandas are hard to keep. Their strength, agility, and cunning make them first-rate escape artists. And they have a playful habit of tearing up everything within reach—including unfamiliar keepers. Highly publicized attempts to mate Moscow's An-An and London's Chi-Chi failed. But the Peking pandas have produced at least 10 healthy cubs; and perhaps when Hsing-Hsing and Ling-Ling mature, they too will increase the world's panda population.

Ling-Ling cautiously sniffs an apple before eating it. In their native mountains pandas feed mainly on bamboo but occasionally raid farmers' cornfields and beehives. They also eat birds and small mammals.

Star attractions of the National Zoo, Ling-Ling (Cute Little Girl) and Hsing-Hsing (Bright Star) relax in typical playful panda fashion. Although apparently friendly, they must be kept in separate enclosures, for pandas are solitary animals and resent intruders in their territory. Only at mating time does a panda of the opposite sex become a welcome visitor.

A hoop is to climb through, roll in, or toss about. Pandas a

Cooling off on a hot day is a necessity for a panda, adapted to the year-round cold of mountains up to 12,000 feet high. With a 2-inch coat of fur, pandas suffer greatly from heat, and during Washington's hot, muggy summers Hsing-Hsing and Ling-Ling must often remain in their air-conditioned dens. Though some pandas living in zoos avoid water, the pair in Washington seems to enjoy it.

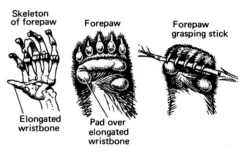

Skeleton of forepaw   Forepaw   Forepaw grasping stick

Elongated wristbone   Pad over elongated wristbone

An elongated wristbone forms a thumblike projection that gives the panda an almost human grip. Though the "thumb" does not move, a panda's fingers can clamp down against it in a pincer action that is powerful yet delicate enough to handle a straw.

...scinated by toys, though with their great strength they soon destroy them. This specially designed plastic hoop lasted several months.

From a treetop-level balcony in the South American rain forest exhibit, visitors to the World of Birds at the Bronx Zoo in New York watch a startlingly realistic thunderstorm. Undisturbed by the storm and the crowds, the birds behave as if in the wild.

Wonder World of Birds

Jean George

The tropics come alive in the Bronx Zoo's newest birdhouse. Flowers bloom, warm rain falls, birds are everywhere.

Set on a quiet, wooded knoll in New York City's Bronx Zoo is an extraordinary Garden of Eden—the Lila Acheson Wallace World of Birds. Eleven years in creation, the $3.5 million cluster of circular towers, walkways, curving galleries, and flying-buttress ramps has drawn visitors by the thousands. They explore habitats that are alive and whirring with birds—the world's most sophisticated display of its kind.

The World of Birds is crowned by skylights tilted to catch the sun. Floodlights mounted above the glass add the precise minutes of extra "daylight" necessary to re-create any season anywhere in the world. Inside, toucans, thrushes, hummingbirds, sunbirds—500 individuals of 200 species, each in the proper, controlled climate—fly over visitors' heads, sing in man-made tropical thunderstorms, alight on living trees, vines, and flowers.

Corridors lead past simulated riverbanks and desert floors, where ground birds dwell. Outdoor ramps wind up to the structure's second story, where bridges put you right in the jungle treetops.

Here zoo history is being made. A pair of motmots —long-tailed, green-and-turquoise birds from South America—is nesting before the public. A male satin bowerbird from Australia has built a trysting place of sticks that he decorates daily with bits of blue paper (no other color will do). Recently the female stepped into the bower, looked approvingly at the arranged paper, and mated with him. She will now build a separate nest in which to lay her eggs.

The birthrate attests to the success of the World of Birds from the birds' point of view; birds bred there within months after taking up occupancy in the new building. It's also a hit with ornithologists. Says Roger Tory Peterson, dean of American bird watchers: "I'm seeing things I've never seen before. I'm getting photographs I've never been able to get in the wild, where jungle canopies are too dense and birds too cautious."

Designed without barriers

The World of Birds had its genesis in 1961, when William G. Conway, general director of the Bronx Zoo, began work on a new exhibit of water birds which would test the old theory that given a good natural environment, birds would stay within it, without restraints of glass or wire. Today in the aviary for aquatic birds, terns and sandpipers fly over simulated beaches, with no barrier at all between the birds and the corridors where people walk.

Conway had ideas about zoo visitors, too. "Today," he says, "people want to see more than just birds.

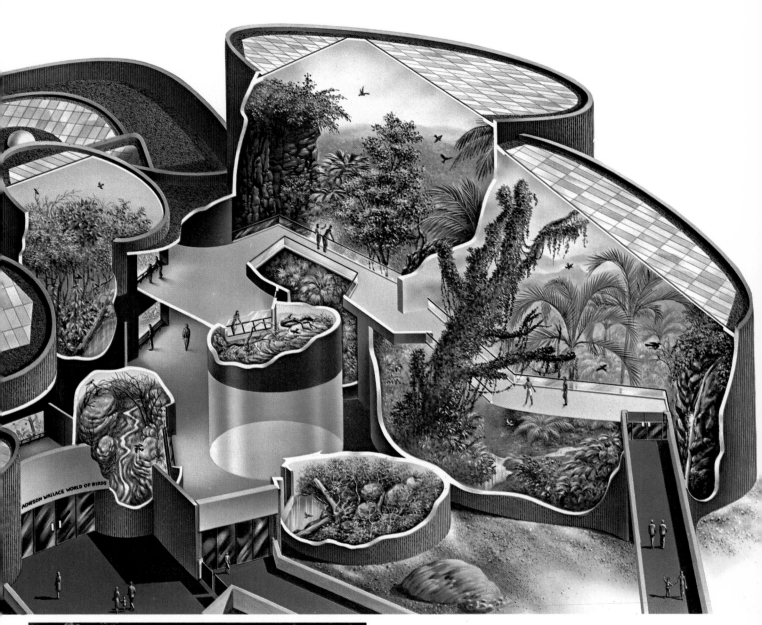

The World of Birds Brings People and Birds Together

The World of Birds building, with its sun-catching skylight roofs, is a striking example of functional design. The photograph (left) highlights the portion of the building that is enlarged and cut away in the painting (above). This section of the building contains a variety of free-flight exhibits, ranging from a rocky hillside to a wooded swamp, from the dry Australian scrub to the tropical rain forests of Africa and South America. While most exhibits feature habitat groupings, others explore such aspects of bird behavior as nesting and mating. Several major exhibits can be viewed both from ground and treetop levels. An ingenious layout leads visitors past every exhibit without once turning back; ramps eliminate the need to climb stairs.

A Bowerbird at the Bronx Zoo

Surely the bowerbirds of Australia and New Guinea are among the most remarkable birds in the world. The male builds an elaborate courtship arena (the size and shape of which varies according to species) and decorates it. He then attracts a female to the bower, but after mating, she leaves him and builds a conventional nest for her eggs in a tree. In the Bronx Zoo's World of Birds, where these pictures were taken, a male satin bowerbird has felt so completely at home that he has built his bower in full view of visitors.

To build his "avenue" bower the male satin bowerbird erects parallel walls of twigs about 9 inches long, 12 inches high, and 4 to 5 inches apart. The tops of the walls sometimes meet to form a tunnel. In the wild, males often rob one another of building materials.

Some bowerbirds paint their bowers. The satin bowerbird uses chewed-up plant material, preferably charcoal.

The satin bowerbird has what seems to be a passion for bright blue baubles, and he adds as many of them as he can find to his bower.

A male satin bowerbird displays a straw as part of his courtship ritual. Next to blue, the bird prefers yellowish or yellow-green colors. This preference influences his choice of display objects.

The female satin bowerbird crouches in the bower and watches the male display. The display includes moving the ornaments, dancing, posturing, flashing his wings, and making churring or scolding noises.

Wall of sticks about 1 foot high and 2 inches thick

Male

Female

Bower decorations

They want to see what they do, and how and where they do it." Thus he began thinking about a dream aviary with free-flying birds in various habitats—indoor jungles, swamps, rain forests, mountaintops, deserts, and underground and hollow-tree environments.

With approval from his board of trustees, Conway showed the early sketches to Lila Acheson Wallace, cofounder of *The Reader's Digest*. She is a woman who has given millions in support of the arts and conservation and has kept many birds in her own home. Looking over the plans carefully, she said, "I would like to do that."

Ground was broken in 1969. "For 4 years we never had the World of Birds off our minds," says curator Joseph Bell. "Going to and from work, on vacation, over weekends, all of us on the zoo staff kept our eyes open for specific ferns and mosses, new electrical fixtures, different ways of piping water. Once, when somebody found a dead tree we wanted, nine of us went to bring it in."

To make a natural 50-foot waterfall for the tropical rain forest, the exhibit curator sent a crew to the steep cliffs of the New Jersey Palisades, across the Hudson River from New York City, to take measurements and

220

make molds. Cast in fiberglass, the molds were mounted on steel girders. Painted backgrounds on the rocks created the illusion of damp, wide forest vistas. There are no sharp corners anywhere, because flat walls give the viewer the feeling of a cage.

Finally, the first birds were moved in. Stretching their necks, cocking their heads, most of them explored their new homelands like kids in a haunted house—with mixed reactions. The glorious orange Bolivian cock-of-the-rocks at first huddled in the cracks of a rain forest cliff and refused to fly in the periodic sprinkler-system rainstorms. Keepers and staff watched anxiously as the storms, with their real downpours and taped thunder, came and went. Still the birds withdrew. Then, one morning while the men were testing the system, the birds soared out into the rain and darted through the tinkle and splash like exploding Roman candles. The rain forest was a success!

A home away from home

Other birds made themselves right at home. The green wood hoopoes, turned free in the African Forest Edge exhibit, swooped down on the plants and quickly stripped them of their leaves. A male burrowing owl not only adapted to his desert on sight but aggressively defended his territory against the keeper who came in to feed him. Four hummingbirds, which curators feared might fight each other to death as they have been known to do, set up territories around the four feeders, settling their differences with invisible fences. Two Uganda double-toothed barbets disappeared into the African jungle and were not seen for several weeks. The touracos, in contrast, received from a private aviary, have proved too friendly. They alight on the rail of the jungle bridge to greet visitors.

Ten years ago most of the creatures on display in zoos were captured in the wild. Today, zoos have an "animal pool" to trade surplus birds and beasts among themselves and use it to replace a large part of the animal loss. In fact, the breeding of wildlife in zoos is saving certain species from extinction. "Zoos may become the last survival grounds for some," says Conway. A brooding room, hospital, and incubator have been installed in the World of Birds.

"We have another, equally important job to do," Conway adds thoughtfully. "Today three-fourths of our population is urban. If people are to learn about man and his environment, it is vital to concentrate that education right here in the cities, where the crowds are."

As I stood recently before the motmots, the truth of this point was strongly brought home. A woman beside me suddenly exclaimed to her young daughter, "Look! The birds are building a nest!" Obviously they had never seen such a thing before, and for 15 minutes they stood transfixed, whispering excitedly. As they finally turned away, the mother said, "We must come back every day to see what happens!"

And that, to me, reveals the real success of the World of Birds.

A gray-necked rock fowl from West Africa's rain forests tiptoes delicately along a log at the Bronx Zoo's World of Birds. Never common, the rock fowl is now endangered by man's pressures. Secretive in nature, it is friendly in captivity.

One of the most colorful inhabitants of the World of Birds, the quetzal is native to Central America's mountain forests. Considered sacred by ancient Aztecs and Mayas, the quetzal is threatened by loss of habitat to farming and lumbering.

Spectacular relative of the domestic chicken, a blue peacock perches on a railing in the walk-in aviary at Jurong Bird Park. This bird, the common peafowl of antiquity, is native to southern India and Sri Lanka. Males reach a length of 8½ feet.

Singapore's United Nations of Birds

Betty Godfrey

Imagination and international cooperation turned an entire Asian valley into an immense birdcage.

On a cool Sunday in January 1971, 30 diplomats gathered at the foot of a hill in Singapore's industrial satellite town Jurong to witness the official welcome of 7,000 new settlers. The diplomats had special reason to be there: Each had personally sponsored the arrival of many of the newcomers. The occasion was the opening of the $5.2 million, 50-acre Jurong Bird Park; the settlers were birds.

The park is the brainchild of Defense Minister Goh Keng Swee. He took time off from a World Bank meeting in Rio de Janeiro to visit the zoological garden. Impressed by the large free-flight aviary, he conceived the idea of a bird park for Singapore. Jurong was an ideal location for such a park. The bold design included caging a whole valley for a free-flight aviary—putting a wire mesh over 5 acres of the park within a box canyon. Nineteen cables, each 450 feet long and weighing 2.5 tons, were lifted with a motor winch to the valley perimeter, where each cable was anchored to a thrust block planted 20 feet in the ground, pulled taut, and fixed to a thrust block at the other end. Then a wire mesh was thrown over the cables, 73 feet above the ground.

A 100-foot, man-made waterfall, the highest in the

Aviaries Past and Present

Aviaries date back at least to the time of the Roman Empire. The design and purpose of aviaries have, like those of other zoos, changed over the centuries. In Roman times the birds were almost secondary to monumental buildings built to impress visitors. The Victorian period brought a new concept: the display of the greatest possible number of different species. The birds were often exhibited in small cages or display cases, like scientific specimens, with little thought given to the birds' comfort or psychological needs. Buildings were still grandly monumental and formal. In the 1960's, with new findings in animal psychology—many based on in-depth studies of birds—aviaries reflected a new concept of zoo design. The traditional small cages gave way to large, free-form enclosures in which birds have ample flying room and visitors can observe them flying, feeding, courting, and even nesting under near-natural conditions.

The captive birds were overshadowed by the monumental style of private aviary, designed by a wealthy Roman in the first century

world, was also constructed. Two pumps pour 6,000 gallons of water over the falls every minute. The water then runs into a stream that winds picturesquely through the free-flight aviary and out into a chain of lakes, where it is recycled to the falls.

While the park was being built, Jurong Park Committee Chairman Woon Wah Siang urged ambassadors and other foreign dignitaries in Singapore to contribute birds. "I attended every National Day cocktail party just to ask for birds," he said.

The diplomats cooperated, and soon birds began arriving from all over the world. From Taiwan came finches, pheasants, herons, sparrows, and teals. Britain sent mallards, owls, waxbills, finches, and pheasants. From the United States came blue jays, mockingbirds, robins, owls, hawks, quail, geese, and ducks. The German Federal Republic sent lapwings, and Italy gave buntings, siskins, thrushes, and hooded crows. Australia contributed white-backed magpies, pink cockatoos, and Cape Barren geese. From the sultan of Johore State, West Malaysia, came peacocks and Japanese pheasants. By opening day, 12 countries, 7 zoos, and 40 private donors had given birds to the park.

Color and motion

The aviary presents a scene of extraordinary beauty. Like daubs on a Monet canvas, mynahs, weavers, doves, pigeons, starlings, thrushes, and egrets are scattered along the valley slopes. White ibises stand on the eastern side of the valley; pheasants cluster on the western bank. Herons and Chinese egrets perch silently on the Rainbow Bridge that spans the stream from the waterfall.

The park's manager, veterinary surgeon Velupillai Mukundhan, and I wound over roads and paths, for a look at some of the 78 display aviaries. (Visitors may tour the park on foot or take a 15-minute tram ride along the main roads.) Stopping at one fenced paddock, we saw 12 sarus cranes begin a courtship dance.

The graceful, long-legged birds paired off for a minuet. Then, dancing round the females, the male cranes spread their wings wide and swayed and bowed, their vivid red heads forming a dipping ribbon of color. Nearby, poised imperturbably on one leg, was one of the world's largest storks, the lovely white and scarlet jabiru from the forests of South and Central America.

A white stork stood in a separate enclosure. "He is a new arrival," explained Mukundhan. "Storks do not welcome newcomers and may beat him to death. He is segregated for his own safety until they get used to his presence. Then he moves in with them."

From a colony of small aviaries across the way came shrill choruses and a high-pitched melody. Eight rust-colored Chinese nightingales were in full song. Prima donnas of the park, they are major attractions, with their range of notes—and bouts of bad temper.

One of the park's keepers, Lim Thiam Hock, joined us. "These birds have individual personalities," he said. "Like people, they can be cheeky, selfish, friendly, aloof, or affectionate." Then, pointing to a whistling black and white magpie robin, he asked: "You wouldn't think him anything but mild, would you? There were once eight males and eight females in the cage. This little fellow killed the other males. Now he is king of his cage. We gave him one consort."

At the end of my visit I took a look at the 17 transit aviaries and the sick bay. An ostrich with a cold peered sourly from a corner in the sickroom. A cassowary glared from a cage where bullying birds go for a period of isolation. "He has shown no repentance," Mukundhan said. "He is to be sold." A tribute to the park's standard of care is that there are usually fewer than four patients a week in the sickroom. And the mortality rate so far has been less than 1 percent.

So far, four peahens, a peacock, four Egyptian geese, six mallards, and dozens of smaller birds have hatched at the park. There is no better sign of success than breeding, say the keepers.

A striking innovation in the 1850's was the London Zoo's first hummingbird house. The birds were displayed in glass cases.

The newest concepts in aviaries—openness and freedom— are exemplified by the London Zoo's Snowdon Aviary.

A French Paradise for Birds

Betty Werther

Two wars destroyed Jean Delacour's collections. Undismayed, he rebuilt his peaceable kingdom.

As a child, I was always intrigued by the story of the Garden of Eden," says naturalist Jean Delacour, "where man, animals, and plants lived in peace and harmony."

Delacour has spent a lifetime constructing his own idea of Eden and has succeeded so well that French author Colette called his Parc Zoologique de Clères just that—a terrestrial paradise.

Delacour's park is set in 600 acres of green Normandy countryside. A medieval castle looks out over ancient trees, a stream, lawns, meadows, and wooded hills. Waterfowl of 120 species live in the high reeds of a small lake, tend their young, and chase each other in and out of a forest of spindly flamingo legs. Peacocks decorate the lawns, displaying their regal plumage among giant beeches, while parrots fly freely in the branches above.

A herd of blackbuck antelopes grazes, wallabies jump along the shaded paths, while, on a small island in the lake, a pair of white-cheeked gibbons performs a breathtaking trapeze act in the poplar trees.

Clères was created as a private collection in 1920 and today contains nearly 3,000 birds from 590 species, many rare and some extinct in the wild. The waterfowl and pheasant collections are among the best in the world.

Jean Delacour is a sturdily built man with gentle blue eyes. His nearly 6-foot frame is now slightly bent under the weight of more than 80 years. Through two World Wars he has spent his life building and rebuilding his collection.

Son of wealthy landed gentry in northern France, Jean Delacour discovered his passion for birds at age 3, when he raised a fluffy chick into an affectionate white-bearded hen. Serious collecting began at 10, when his father gave him as a birthday present some abandoned aviaries on the family's 6,000-acre estate. At 15 he had one of the largest collections of birds then in existence.

In the first decade of this century Delacour was one of the first persons to observe that birds were decreasing alarmingly. He helped set up the French Ligue pour la Protection des Oiseaux (League for the Protection of Birds). In 1922 he helped organize the International Committee (now Council) for Bird Preservation, serving as its president from 1938 to 1958.

"Despite all our efforts in limiting the feather trade, enacting and obtaining better enforcement of protective legislation, I would say there are only a tenth as many birds around today as there were 20 years ago," he says. "People have become too numerous. For our food supply we destroy theirs. For our housing and highways we do away with their habitats. When the world is cemented over, where can they go?"

Jean Delacour was 24 years old when World War I was declared. He had already earned a doctorate in botany and had built his collection to 1,500 birds of 380 species.

Crowned cranes patrol the gardens of Clères in search of insects, their natural prey. These 38-inch-tall natives of Africa are typical of the free-living, exotic species that Jean Delacour has gathered in his 600-acre "terrestrial paradise."

The Zoo Has a Long Tradition in France

France has long been a leader in the development of zoos, beginning in the 1600's with the private animal collections of noblemen, which were often extensive and maintained in lavish style. The world's first public zoo was established in 1794 at the Jardin des Plantes, Paris, with animals taken from the Royal Menagerie at Versailles.

Built in the 1600's as a showplace for Louis XIV, the Royal Menagerie at Versailles included some modern zoo features, such as the grouping of closely related animals.

By the mid 1800's the menagerie at the Jardin des Plantes boasted a number of imposing structures—this elephant house, a museum of comparative anatomy, and a library.

During the war Marshal Ferdinand Foch set up his high command in the Delacour château. But the château with all its treasures was completely destroyed during the second Battle of the Somme. It was "a misfortune without parallel in the history of aviculture," according to one ornithology journal.

After the war Delacour set out to rebuild his collections. Near the small market town of Clères, 15 miles north of Rouen, he found a lovely Gothic château and established there the present park.

Disaster strikes again

During World War II, Clères suffered violent bombings in May and June 1940, and the collections were wiped out. There was nothing to do but begin again.

Today, in the 5 acres of gardens at Clères, this indomitable man has rebuilt his Eden. Cranes, ibises, and egrets move gracefully among richly planted flower beds or between sculptured yew hedges. Sometimes they are joined by big flocks of the rarer species of geese (emperor, red-breasted, Ross's, snow, and others) on the lawns that extend to the lower part of the park. There, on the 4-acre lake, one of the world's greatest waterfowl collections lives freely along with four species of flamingos. In addition to the geese, one can observe almost all the swans, as well as shelducks, tree ducks, and many other species. Northern sea ducks—eiders, goldeneyes, scoters, buffleheads, and harlequins—do exceptionally well in the lake's cold, clear waters.

The assortment of animals is strange: In nature many would never see one another. But under the spell of Clères they live together in peace and safety.

Peering from its mother's pouch, a young wallaby enjoys a spring day at Clères. Wallabies imported from Australia by wealthy animal fanciers did so well that they once actually ran wild in parts of Europe until killed by hunters.

Insects Are Animals Too

Jiro Wakamiya

An extraordinary zoo presents the miniature world of fireflies, butterflies, and other tiny creatures.

The two Butterfly Glasshouses at the Insectarium of the Tama Zoo in Tokyo are the first exhibits of their kind in the world. Unlike conventional exhibits where visitors admire the insects only from the outside, the Glasshouses let you come right in. Around you the butterflies sip nectar from flowers and lay their eggs just as in their natural habitats.

Year-round the luxuriant foliage and bright blossoms shelter such common butterflies as small whites and pale clouded yellows, as well as rarer swallowtails, great mormons, and chestnut tigers. Even on a cold winter day the aromas of bougainvillaeas, sweet peas, begonias, cyclamens, and poinsettias waft through the air. Tangerine, orange, and pepper trees spread their branches under the enclosing glass roofs.

At least 10 butterfly species are on display summer and winter. The butterfly eggs are hatched and the caterpillars reared so that there will always be at least 100 butterflies in flight. The system used to accomplish this "staging" is relatively simple: Low temperatures delay the development of a species until it is needed.

Like zoos that display mammals and birds, the Butterfly Glasshouses present numerous opportunities for scientific research. Observations have revealed that certain species of butterflies are more belligerent than others, something quite unexpected from an insect as dainty as a butterfly. Among the species living at the Tama Zoo, the *Byasa alcinous* butterfly has the nastiest disposition: It chases away any butterfly that dares to cross its path.

In the Glasshouses, as in the wild, male butterflies usually emerge earlier than females. The result is that at certain times males outnumber females, sometimes by as many as eight to one. The males wait for the females to emerge from the resting pupal state, and the moment a female is full-fledged a prospective mate is by her side.

On a tour of the Glasshouses, curator Minoru Yajima pointed at the tail of a female *Luehdorfia japonica*. A close look revealed an object that looked like a small bag. "It's a chastity belt," Yajima said. He picked up several newly emerged female butterflies and put them on the branch. Hardly had they settled themselves than males came swarming toward them and started to mate. (The courtship of some butterflies does not involve fighting among males; the only thing that matters is speed in getting to the females.) After mating, the males secreted a fluid that sealed the sex organs of the females, forming the "chastity belts."

A caterpillar's business is eating

Visitors to the Butterfly Glasshouses often marvel at the voracious appetite of the caterpillars there. A young spangle butterfly, for example, eats an average of 60 tangerine leaves during its existence. This means that a 20-inch-tall, 2-year-old seedling is needed in order to raise just one caterpillar.

The Tama Zoo's Insectarium has much more than butterflies. There are breeding farms for locusts and grasshoppers, where their life cycles can be observed, and a firefly farm. Many other live insects—from the singing crickets so popular as pets in Japan to the tiger beetles and walkingsticks—are on display in the Insectarium Center, a two-story exhibition building with a museum and lecture hall. Downstairs in the Center are nocturnal animals, such as slow loris and great galagos, marsupials and fruit bats, armadillos and owls —all fed with insects raised in the Insectarium.

Morio Kita, the author of the best-seller *The Entomological Diary of Dr. Mambo*, has pointed out an important service provided by the Glasshouses and the Insectarium: "At a time when butterflies are getting scarcer, people who come to this fantastic exhibit will acquire firsthand knowledge of these lovely insects without having to catch them." The fascinating ways of insects were once appreciated by relatively few specialists. Now many people can watch and enjoy the beauty of the insect's fleeting, flitting world.

Fascinated schoolboys watch bright yellow sulfur butterflies in one of the Butterfly Glasshouses of Tokyo's Tama Zoo. Here butterflies fly about freely, alighting on flowers to feed on nectar; signs help visitors identify the various species.

The Brilliant Butterflies of the Tama Zoo

Many formerly common butterflies are becoming increasingly rare as herbicides, insecticides, and habitat destruction through highway and building construction take their toll. The problem is particularly acute in a densely populated land such as Japan. However, the Glasshouses at the Tama Zoo—and other insectariums—offer hope on two fronts. Their highly successful breeding programs help to ensure survival for some threatened species. And, by bringing butterflies within easy view of the public, they revitalize the appreciation of city dwellers for their natural treasures.

Pierrot adult

Pierrot larva

In an unusual partnership ants feed and groom larvae of the gray-pointed pierrot, getting sweet fluid in return. A display of this relationship is planned for Tama.

A feeding ox-eye pansy butterfly spreads its wings, displaying prominent eyelike spots that may frighten off predators. A widespread species ranging from Asia to Africa, it is closely related to the mourning cloaks.

This strikingly patterned insect is known in Asia as the "paper butterfly" because of its tough, papery wings, which span nearly 8 inches.

A mountain dweller from Japan, the rare chestnut tiger (right) is on view the year round at the Tama Zoo.

The common grass yellow butterfly, one of the sulfur butterflies, is found in the Tropics around the world. It is a close relative of the great orange tip.

An Old World swallowtail sips nectar from a red flower—its favorite kind. Its larvae feed on parsley.

The great orange tip, measuring 4 inches with wings outspread, is one of the giants of its family.

Striking orange and black wing markings gave the common tiger butterfly its popular name.

An Aquarium Is an Underwater Zoo

Though many people would not think of it as one, an aquarium actually is a zoo—but a zoo specializing in animals that live in water, not on land. Although fish have been raised in captivity for more than 2,000 years, the first public aquariums did not appear until the 1850's. Originally the goal was to display live specimens; little thought was given to providing naturalistic habitats. Today, however, the emphasis is on showing how aquatic animals live together in the wild, rather than on merely exhibiting as many specimens as possible. Like zoos, aquariums have made great technological strides. Once limited to creatures that could be kept in relatively small tanks, many aquariums now display animals as large as elephant seals and killer whales. In learning how to keep their charges alive, aquariums have made valuable contributions to our knowledge of marine and freshwater biology.

Ready for mating, a male pink salmon attacks a smaller rival. At the Vancouver Public Aquarium in British Columbia visitors can follow salmon through every phase of their life cycle.

Feeding time is always an important event, especially when combined with a performance. At Germany's Stuttgart Zoo, a trainer rewards a sea lion with a tidbit of fish, while an elephant seal begs.

Tropical fish swim in a re-created coral reef habitat at the New York Aquarium. Such realistic displays of several different species sharing the same living space as they might in nature have long been a feature of aquariums, predating zoos' adoption of the approach by years. For practical reasons the mixed-habitat concept works best with small fish.

A beluga whale returns a young visitor's wondering gaze at the Vancouver Public Aquarium. Native to the Arctic, belugas, also known as white whales, reach a length of 12 to 16 feet and can weigh 1,500 pounds.

Skana the killer whale leaps clear of her pool at a trainer's command. One of the star attractions at the Vancouver Public Aquarium, she is 20 feet long and weighs 5,500 pounds. She shares a pool with a smaller male and several dolphins.

A giant cylindrical tank with 50 species of sea animals is an innovative feature at Boston's New England Aquarium. The spiral ramp around the 3-story tank makes possible a cross-sectional view of marine life, with each species occupying its own preferred depth.

The London Zoo's "fountain system," devised in the 1850's, was the first system to circulate water in an aquarium, preventing stagnation. More sophisticated techniques have replaced it.

A pioneer in many fields, the London Zoo opened the first public exhibit of marine life in 1853. Emphasis was on displaying a variety of species, rather than on showing how fish live.

The world's largest herd of Père David's deer — more than 200 animals — lives at Woburn Abbey in England. In 1898 the Duke of Bedford saved these rare Chinese deer from almost certain extinction by assembling the last 18 individuals at Woburn.

The Rescue of Père David's Deer

Philip Street

This animal, with the antlers of a deer, the hooves of a cow, the neck of a camel, and the tail of a donkey, wouldn't be around today if it weren't for zoos.

Père David's deer is unique because it owes its survival to the activities of one man, the 11th Duke of Bedford.

For a long while the existence of this species was known to only a handful of people in China. The deer probably became extinct in the wild in the second century B.C. In the 1860's its sole living representatives were a herd living in the Imperial Hunting Park, a few miles south of Peking. This was an immense walled park containing many deer herds, which were hunted by members of the Imperial Court. The park was so strictly guarded that few Chinese and no foreigners had ever been privileged to enter it.

In 1861 a young French priest, Jean Pierre Armand David, was sent by the Vincentian (Lazarist) order in Paris to open a school in Peking. Young Père David already had a reputation as a naturalist, and it was expected that in addition to his missionary duties he would study Chinese natural history and send collections of material to the National Museum of Natural History in Paris.

Père David discovered the strange species of deer that now bears his name in 1865. For a long time he

had been curious about what kind of animals lived in the Imperial Hunting Park. He often walked along the boundary wall, hoping to catch a glimpse inside. One day Père David found a large heap of sand against the wall where workmen were making repairs. When no one was near, he climbed the heap and looked over the wall. Describing what he saw, he wrote to Professor Milne-Edwards of the Paris museum: "From the top of the wall I could see, rather far off, a herd of more than 100 of these animals, which looked to me like elks. They had no antlers at this time; what distinguished the animal was the length of its tail, which seemed as long as that of a donkey."

Père David later wrote Milne-Edwards: "I have made fruitless attempts to get the skin of this species. It seems quite impossible. And the French Legation feels incapable of unofficial approaches to the Chinese Government to procure this curious animal. Fortunately I know some Tartar soldiers who are going to do guard duty in this park, and I am sure, by means of a bribe, that I shall get hold of a few skins, which I shall hasten to send you. The Chinese give to this animal the name of *mi-lou* or *sseupou-siang*, which means 'the animal with the four unusual features,' because they consider that this deer takes after the stag by its antlers, the cow by its hooves, the camel by its neck, and the mule or even the donkey by its tail."

A midnight tryst

Eventually a rendezvous was arranged with the soldiers outside the wall, and in the middle of the night the skin and bones of a male and a female were dropped over to the waiting naturalist. He immediately packed them up and sent them to Paris.

When the Chinese learned that news of their deer herd was out, they raised no objection to requests for living specimens, and quite a few reached various European zoos. In 1874 Père David left China, and no more specimens of this species were sent out of the country. Those in European zoos maintained their numbers by occasional breeding.

Then in the early 1900's zoo specimens became the sole hope of survival for the species; the Peking herd had been killed off through a series of calamities. As a result of serious floods in 1894, the walls of the Imperial Hunting Park had been breached in several places, and most of the deer escaped into the surrounding countryside. The animals were killed and eaten by the starving peasants. The small remnant herd within the walls survived for 6 years. During the disorders of the Boxer Rebellion in 1900 and the 1911 Revolution all but two deer were killed; both of these were dead by 1921.

It was at the time of the Boxer Rebellion that the 11th Duke of Bedford, in England, made the decision that saved the species from extinction: He would collect the few Père David's deer in Europe into one herd in a place where they would have ample space to live normally and breed. He purchased all the Père David's deer in zoo stocks and released them into his own magnificent 4,000-acre deer park at Woburn Abbey near London. The total world population of Père David's deer stood at fewer than 20.

The spaciousness of the park obviously suited them, and their numbers increased steadily. By the outbreak of World War I in 1914 the herd was up to 88. This small success was jeopardized by wartime food shortages. Despite losses, however, there were enough animals to keep the species going. On the eve of World War II in 1939 the herd numbered about 250.

By this time the 11th Duke had been succeeded by his son, who was also a great naturalist and a man intent on preserving the deer. His worry was not so much that the herd might be starved, as that it might be bombed or that an epidemic might kill off the deer. It was known that Père David's deer were susceptible to Johne's disease, an incurable infection.

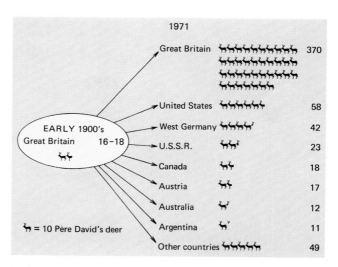

Perhaps the alltime zoo success story is that of Père David's deer. This native of China is now found in zoos and parks on every inhabited continent. On the brink of extinction only 70 years ago, Père David's deer now number more than 600.

It seemed too great a risk to keep all the living representatives of a species in one place. The 12th Duke decided to build up satellite herds elsewhere. With the help of the Zoological Society of London, a herd was built up at Whipsnade, a zoo near Woburn.

The Duke of Bedford's plans were judged a success when a calf was born to the new Whipsnade herd on April 5, 1947. Since then calves have been produced at Whipsnade every year, and small stocks have been sent from Whipsnade to many other zoos.

Perhaps the most satisfying of all these exports occurred in 1957, when four young Père David's deer, in the charge of a keeper from the London Zoo, traveled to the Peking Zoo to form the nucleus of a herd in China. After an exile of nearly 60 years, this species once again found a home in its native country.

The World's Rarest Horses

Small herds of the last truly wild horses left in the world are occasionally sighted in their native Mongolia, where their major problem is competition with the livestock of nomads for food and water. Some 200 of these small rugged horses now live in zoos—certainly far more than still exist in the wild. Fortunately the species is breeding well in captivity.

The zoo population of Przewalski's horses doubled from 1964 to 1974, rising from about 100 to 200. But only one or two dozen animals survive in the wild.

One Last Chance: Captive Breeding

Leland Stowe

Where can an animal breed when its natural habitat is gone? The zoos of the world are providing an answer.

Just as head keeper Cecil Jackson carried breakfast in to the 7-year-old gorilla Mahari one January morning at Ohio's Cincinnati Zoo, the gorilla let out such a hair-raising scream that Jackson almost dropped the tray. "Mahari lay heaving and twisting around," Jackson recalls. "No doubt about what was happening! Another scream, a few moans, and suddenly I saw Mahari pulling at an emerging mass. After a few more seconds she was cleaning her baby. Much later I learned that I was the first U.S. zoo employee to see a gorilla being born."

Mahari's offspring was the first of six captive gorilla births in a 3-year period in Cincinnati—triumphs in the desperate battle currently being waged by a number of zoos around the world to rescue scores of endangered species. Some lions, tigers, and rhinos may be saved in national parks and preserves as a result of efforts by a host of national and international, governmental and nongovernmental conservation organizations. But until more land is set aside for wildlife, the only chance for dozens of other species may reside in a "survival crusade"—captive breeding in zoos.

Captive breeding is a precarious undertaking, complicated by the physical, social, and psychological requirements of each species. Successful matings have often been followed by stillbirths and deaths from maternal neglect, outright killing, or recurrent diseases. Consider how recently these crucial zoo firsts were recorded for surviving births: lowland gorilla (in Columbus, Ohio), 1956; and cheetah (in Philadelphia, Pennsylvania), 1956.

After countless failures zoos have learned some requisites for success. One of these is preferential mating. Male-female compatibility—as unpredictable with some animals as with humans—is a must for the great apes and most felines. At Chicago's Brookfield Zoo a 475-pound gorilla named Babe repeatedly repulsed one female so viciously that he was written off as a "killer." Then a newly acquired female became his next-cage neighbor. Babe registered deep interest at first sight and, once they were united, became an ardent and surprisingly gentle mate.

Orangutans insist on choosing their mates. At Washington's National Zoo, a huge male, Butch, scornfully disdained one familiar female after another. "Finally we shipped Butch out to Colorado's Cheyenne Mountain Zoo, and he immediately fell for a new female face," reports curator William Xanten. "He's been siring offspring ever since. Meanwhile, we obtained Archie from Toronto for our jilted Jennie, and they've produced six infants in 8 years."

Although zoos obtained hundreds of orangutans in this century, great numbers died from tuberculosis. Since then, high-iron diets have markedly improved progeny production. With only about 5,000 orangutans surviving in their native Borneo and Sumatra, zoo breeders were cheered by 30 births in 1971. "We haven't yet got many births from captive-born parents, but I'm confident that we will," says Brookfield curator Benjamin Beck. "I believe the breeding problems with orangutans and gorillas may be nearly licked."

First Moments of Life at the San Diego Zoo for a Newborn Addax—A Rare Dese

Obscured by the shadow of its mother's body, the calf, still in its placenta, emerges as the birth process nears completion.

The mother stimulates the newborn by licking it with her tongue, and at the same time she learns its particular odor.

Pheasants Rescued from Extinction by Captive Breeding

Set up specifically to save pheasants that are threatened with extinction in their native habitats, the Pheasant Trust carries on intensive breeding programs in a reserve on the east coast of England. The birds come from such diverse localities as the rain forests of Southeast Asia, the wooded mountains of Taiwan, and the nearly inaccessible high valleys of the Himalayas; yet all have adapted favorably to the cool, damp English climate. The six species shown here are breeding so well that pairs are being sent out to restock refuges in their homelands.

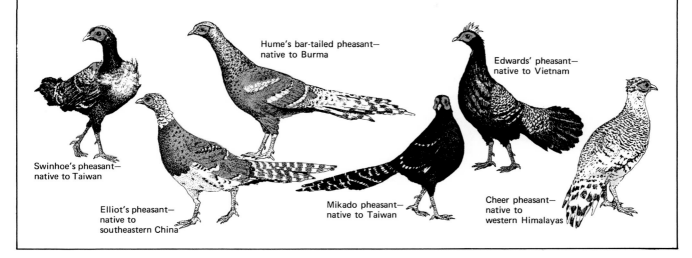

Swinhoe's pheasant—native to Taiwan

Elliot's pheasant—native to southeastern China

Hume's bar-tailed pheasant—native to Burma

Mikado pheasant—native to Taiwan

Edwards' pheasant—native to Vietnam

Cheer pheasant—native to western Himalayas

Rigid separation of sexes appears to be another propagation must for many species. Cheetahs, for instance, seldom mate unless they have been kept out of sound and sniffing range of one another. Keepers only bring a male to a female when she suddenly becomes very submissive and utters low, stuttering sounds. At Britain's famous Whipsnade Park, this technique paid off: five fuzzy-gray litters in 6 years. Even so, cheetah breeding still demands extreme care because of the many factors involved.

Pygmy hippos are now scarce in West Africa's streams, and captive breeding is vital to the species' survival. Sexual segregation of pygmy hippos is usual in zoos; the 600-pound males are ferocious fighters, and although the smaller females are aggressive, they can be injured in the melee. Another serious obstacle to successful breeding is the fact that hippos normally mate in water, with copulation lasting 5 minutes or more; the female's head is often submerged, and mating is interrupted by her struggles to escape drowning.

ntelope from Africa

With the mother's gentle nudging the infant is on its feet within minutes—for a prey animal, the sooner the safer.

The calf nuzzles its mother's body until it finds what it needs: the source of its meals for the next few weeks.

Rare African white rhinos graze placidly at the Whipsnade Zoo near London. This zoo-born calf proves the success of the zoo's breeding program. Actually light gray in color, the big, two-horned animals can weigh 4,000 to 6,000 pounds when full-grown.

Head keeper Herbert T. Stroman, of the National Zoo in Washington, D.C., reports that when the water depth in a pygmy hippo's tank was lowered to 18 inches, all went well. "In general," he says, "pygmy hippos are easy to breed now."

Another key to successful zoo propagation is suitable terrain and climate. Since these conditions are most readily supplied for hoofed animals, such species are often easier to breed than other mammals. Disparities between natural and zoo conditions have generated great difficulties with two favorites—snow leopards and polar bears.

A polar bear mother needs solitude

For years most polar bear females crushed or ate their newborn. At Ohio's Toledo Zoo only two of 10 babies survived. Everywhere the reason was the same: Mothers need utter seclusion until cubs are big enough to scramble around. In the wild dens dug in arctic snowdrifts provide this isolation.

After losing several litters, Brookfield's director Peter Crowcroft chanced to read a Dutch breeder's survival prescription: Provide a pregnant female with the equivalent of a polar bear den. The zoo constructed one. "It worked beautifully with both our females," says Crowcroft. "During the first winter we wondered for

days—not a squeal to be heard. Then one mother emerged with a cub, and the other mother with two!"

Rare in zoos and in the wild, the snow leopard is adapted to life at altitudes up to 11,000 feet in Central Asia. Infant snow leopards seem to have almost no resistance to human infections. "The mother's milk contains antibodies that provide immunity against bacteria during an infant's first days," says Brookfield curator Christen Wemmer. "Our snow leopard mothers refused to nurse all their infants, and, because the newborn have little chance of survival in city air, we keep ours in incubators for 2 weeks."

Under the supervision of curator Brad House, more than half of the snow leopards at the Bronx Zoo were born and raised there. "We're greatly encouraged because a captive-bred male sired a litter of cubs," he reports. The species' prospects are indeed brighter: In 1971, 31 cubs were born in zoos around the world.

Captive breeding has now entered a crucial phase. Fast-dwindling wildlife resources and recent protective curbs on international trade in threatened species have made zoo-managed propagation essential. Hence, major zoos have initiated widespread animal exchanges that either provide for mutual sharing of resultant progeny or barter, whereby the supplying zoo later collects in other desired species. For example, every other snow leopard offspring sired in California's San Diego Zoo by the male loaned by Cincinnati will be given to Cincinnati. While playing host to 4 guest species, Brookfield had 9 of its own species, totaling 21 animals, out on loan.

But for any species' survival, sustained birth by second and third generations is essential. Now just under way for most endangered mammals, this takes decades to assure success. A comprehensive survey found that only eight endangered species (seven hoofed animals plus the Siberian tiger) are as yet believed to be secure.

Leading zoo officials strongly endorse the conclu- sion of that survey: "If survival is to be of species, rather than of individuals, many zoo practices must be radically changed." Among the reforms advocated are the following: 1) Zoos should specialize in fewer species and give up the traditional objective of trying to exhibit "something of almost everything." 2) Zoos should adopt *long-term* breeding programs for selected species, generally in much-enlarged groups. 3) Zoos should be prepared to engage in cooperative breeding programs. 4) Zoos should establish in-zoo survival centers, plus rural breeding farms wherever possible. 5) Research should be greatly expanded to identify and overcome obstacles to breeding.

Penguins Parade at Scotland's Edinburgh Zoo

In 1919 a pair of king penguins at the Edinburgh Zoo in Scotland made history by producing a chick—the first time these birds had ever bred outside their native subantarctic range. Since then the Edinburgh penguin colony has grown to some 100 birds. Four species live and breed there. The 3-foot-tall king penguin, second largest of the penguins, comes from islands in the distant South Atlantic. The 2-foot macaroni penguin, with its bushy "eyebrows," comes from the same area. The 2½-foot gentoo and chinstrap penguins inhabit small, rocky islands off the Antarctic coast. So successful is Edinburgh's breeding program that its penguins are exported to zoos all over the Northern Hemisphere. Already in step with the Northern seasons, they seem to thrive better than birds from the Antarctic, which must adjust to a complete reversal of summer and winter. A factor in Edinburgh's success is its cool summers, for penguins do poorly in hot weather. Adapted to withstand severe cold, they succumb easily to heat exhaustion. In some zoos their quarters must be air-conditioned. But climate is not the only problem in keeping penguins. Naturally programmed to strike at living prey, which is impractical for zoos to provide, some must be fed their rations of fish by hand.

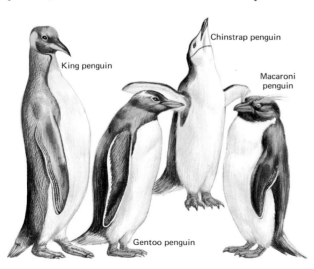

King penguin

Chinstrap penguin

Macaroni penguin

Gentoo penguin

The Edinburgh Zoo's "penguin parade" is a daily event in summer. Just before feeding time the birds leave their enclosure and waddle through delighted crowds of visitors.

A Manor Becomes a Menagerie

Timothy Green

**Can one individual start
his own zoo? Gerald Durrell
proved it can be done.**

Threatened by man's inroads on its native habitat in Madagascar, the ring-tailed lemur thrives in captivity; several zoos have successful breeding programs. This wary-looking individual is exploring its surroundings at Gerald Durrell's zoo.

The trouble with me," said Gerald Durrell, "is that I was born with this thing about animals. Being quite uneducable, the only job I could ever do was animal collecting." From earliest childhood he has been a walking menagerie, with field mice, toads, or grass snakes overflowing his pockets. Even then Durrell had a single ambition: to have his own zoo.

Today Durrell presides over a unique zoo—the Jersey Wildlife Preservation Trust—on one of the British Channel Islands.

"I got desperate at what I saw going on all over the world," Durrell says. "The forests were being chopped down, and new deserts were being created in their place. Everyone loves to put up money to save a giraffe, but not for some obscure, cross-eyed little animal with a snub nose. But ugly ones have just as much right to be saved as a giraffe. Take the solenodon from Cuba and Haiti—it looks rather like a large rat, with beady eyes, heavy claws, and a naked, scaly tail. Not an animal many people want to cuddle, but I believe it deserves to be preserved."

A tolerant sister

But where to start a zoo? "I had come back from a collecting trip to West Africa with everything from chimps to cobras, and for a while I parked them in my sister's back garden in Bournemouth."

His natural enthusiasm soon fell afoul of red tape. No one was ready to grant him permission to found a private zoo. Durrell called on Major Hugh Fraser, who lived in a 15th-century manor house, Les Augres Manor, on Jersey. "What a marvelous place for a zoo," Durrell remarked to him. "I thought Fraser might go white and faint," he recalls, "but he simply said: 'Would you like to rent it? It's too big for me.'"

So in 1959 Durrell became not only a zoo owner but Lord of the Manor of Les Augres. The manor and its 40 acres of park have proved perfectly adaptable to a zoo. The old stables, dating from 1795, have been converted into the mammal house. Two Bornean orangutans, Oscar and Bali, occupy the ground floor with their daughter Surabaja, who was born at the zoo in April 1971. Above, red-handed and saddle-back tamarins and mouse lemurs are in residence. A stream lazing through the meadows below the house has been dammed into a series of ponds, which are now bustling with waterfowl.

The zoo has had spectacular breeding success with the white-eared pheasant. These rare birds were found only in China and Tibet, where they may now be extinct in the wild. The white-eareds have bred so well that the Jersey Wildlife Trust now has the largest collection outside China (and possibly in the world). By the end of 1971, 35 white-eareds had been successfully reared, and 11 of them lent to zoos in France, Belgium, England, and the United States against the possibility that an epidemic might hit Jersey. Durrell hopes eventually to send some of the white-eareds to China and Tibet. "It would be ideal to ship 20 or 30 of them to their original habitat," he says.

Adequate financing is a problem for all zoos, public and private. In the early days the Jersey zoo had what Durrell calls "a stamp collection"—a wide selection of popular animals to attract the public. Without its support the zoo could not prosper. "But once we had the gate money coming in and made the zoo viable," Durrell explains, "we turned it into a scientific trust. The purpose is to build breeding colonies of mammals, birds, and reptiles, whose numbers are so reduced in their normal habitat that they can no longer cope with the natural hazards of their environment."

The Jersey Wildlife Trust now relies heavily on subscriptions and on a popular and growing form of animal support—adoption. One new enclosure in the park houses Pedro, a spectacled bear from the Andes Mountains of South America. For a while a plaintive sign outside his compound requested financial aid in finding Pedro a mate. The money was raised, and a female spectacled bear has joined him. Virtually every mammal, bird, and reptile has been "adopted," either by an individual or by a school. The "parent" pays the annual food bill and, in return, gets regular reports about the animal. At last count there were 5,650 Trust subscribers in 38 countries and hundreds of "parents."

Bred in an Island Zoo

The five animals shown below come from different parts of the world and are quite different in their needs, especially in their particular requirements for mating. Each species is being bred successfully at the Jersey Wildlife Trust.

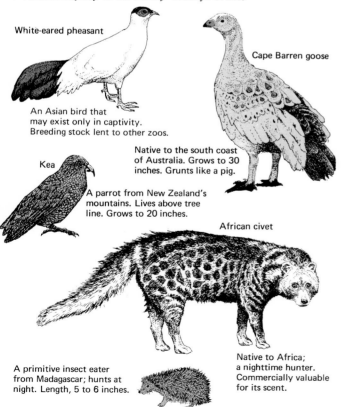

White-eared pheasant

An Asian bird that may exist only in captivity. Breeding stock lent to other zoos.

Cape Barren goose

Native to the south coast of Australia. Grows to 30 inches. Grunts like a pig.

Kea

A parrot from New Zealand's mountains. Lives above tree line. Grows to 20 inches.

African civet

A primitive insect eater from Madagascar; hunts at night. Length, 5 to 6 inches.

Native to Africa; a nighttime hunter. Commercially valuable for its scent.

Pygmy hedgehog tenrec

Return of the Nene

Once on the verge of extinction the nene, a native Hawaiian goose, was saved by the captive breeding program of Britain's Wildfowl Trust at Slimbridge. Nenes numbered about 25,000 before whaling crews reached Hawaii, but by 1800 the nenes had begun to decline. By 1947 only 50 remained in existence, most of them in small, privately owned flocks. Slimbridge obtained two nenes in 1950; but both birds turned out to be females. A gander was promptly brought from the Hawaiian Islands, and he fathered nine healthy goslings the next year; by the time he died he had more than 230 descendants. So successful was the Slimbridge breeding program that more than 50 nenes were sent to Hawaii to aid in rebuilding the wild nene population there.

A Slimbridge warden removes a nene egg from the nest, leaving a wooden substitute. For protection against predators, most eggs are hatched artificially.

Nene goslings feed as a vigilant parent looks on. When fully grown, they will be 23 to 28 inches long and will have a weight of 4 to 5 pounds.

A group of male chimpanzees interrupts its grooming activities to vocalize. Chimps communicate emotions, ranging from affection and satisfaction to hostility and fear, by a remarkably varied repertoire of grunts, hoots, barks, moans, and screams.

How To
Watch Monkeys

Patricia Gowaty, Barbara Ribakove, and Sy Ribakove

What's that monkey doing? And why? Here are some tips that will help you interpret the oddities of monkey behavior on your next visit to the zoo.

Watching monkeys at the zoo can be a rewarding study in animal behavior if you know what to look for. Because human beings identify so closely with other primates, we tend to interpret their behavior as we would our own. Some primate behavior actually is similar to human conduct; a friendly-looking gesture —a pat or a caress—generally *is* friendly.

Most social animals, be they chickens or baboons, have a clear social hierarchy, a "pecking order." Rank has its privileges; superiors and inferiors can be identified by the way they behave toward each other. The monkey that gets first choice of food, space, mates— the one that causes others to back off, cringe, or scuttle for safety—is dominant. Usually, this is a mature male.

All monkeys groom their fur; they carefully separate the hair, search for dirt, insects, and dandruff, and

delicately remove such particles. Monkeys also perform this service for one another. Mutual grooming seems to promote harmony in the group. This hygienic behavior, which keeps the monkey's fur clean, comfortable, and free of disease carriers, is apparently highly pleasurable, and monkeys devote hours to it. Generally, the dominant members of the group get the longest turn at being groomed. Monkey mothers with newborn young are always especially interesting to other members of a group, and they are groomed a great deal. But every member of the group, regardless of rank, gets some grooming, and this clearly serves to promote amicable relations.

Where primate behavior is most often misunderstood by human beings is in the way they express their feelings. When Ham, the first space chimpanzee (an ape, not a monkey), returned to earth and her capsule was opened, observers saw her grinning widely. "She loved the ride!" they exclaimed. They couldn't have been more mistaken. When a chimpanzee or hamadryas baboon draws its lips back so that the teeth show, retracts its ears, and seems to look away, it is not smiling but grimacing in stark terror. And what looks like a yawn—mouth opened wide, teeth partially covered by the lips—is not an indication of sleepiness or boredom but of hostility. Not only are these expressions the opposite of human behavior, but each species of ape and monkey has its own characteristic forms of facial expression.

Another widely misunderstood form of behavior in primates is the act of presenting. A juvenile male monkey will ward off the anger of a dominant male by backing up to him, exactly as a female might present

How Monkeys and Apes Signal Their Moods

Next time you're watching monkeys or apes at the zoo, just consider that we're primates too. Sometimes these animals remind us so much of ourselves that it is tempting to think of them as people. We interpret the facial expressions of these animals as though they were human and *mis*interpret what they are telling each other. To help you understand what you see, here are some of the things scientists have learned about how monkeys and apes reveal their emotions and signal their intentions to one another.

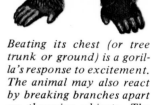

Expressions of Hostility and Threat

A chimpanzee's frowning face, with wide-open eyes and tightly closed lips, conveys a threat of attack.

The South American ouakari threatens by staring and by opening its mouth.

A hamadryas baboon displays its eyelids and formidable canine teeth in a "yawn" that means threat.

Beating its chest (or tree trunk or ground) is a gorilla's response to excitement. The animal may also react by breaking branches apart or throwing objects. The display is used to intimidate an intruder.

Expressions of Appeasement and Fear

A young chimpanzee's pouting face and whimpering cries beg for an adult's attention; cries may become shrieks.

A mandrill signals submission by baring its teeth on each side of the nostrils.

The rhesus monkey shows terror, not pleasure, with its "grin" of bared teeth and staring or evasive eyes.

The chimp's open mouth, bared teeth, and raised eyebrows express fear.

herself to solicit mating. This is a form of appeasement behavior. The dominant male may mount the juvenile, but likelier than not the presenting gesture will suffice to quiet the older animal's ire. Presenting may look like a sex act; in reality it is a form of self-defense.

In most instances, when you see a monkey group that looks active, where rearing of young is under way, you are safe in assuming that it is an established group and that the individuals are contented. When the group seems quarrelsome, it may be because there are young adults present. When a young male in a troop of monkeys grows large enough to become competitive with his elders, he may begin to fight.

Monkeys seek to establish their position in the troop as they reach maturity, squabbling with their equals, occasionally testing themselves against older, stronger animals. (That is why humans who have kept pet monkeys happily during the animal's early years are often dismayed to find a formerly docile pet becoming pugnacious and aggressive as it matures.) At first the outcome is generally defeat, which may be signaled by presenting. But the young animal may persist, and in cases where the troop is already large or space is too confined for such quarreling, the young animal may be removed from the troop to prevent injuries. The social order may also be thrown into turmoil when a new individual is introduced into an established troop. A restless period of squabbling can always be expected in a newly assembled troop of monkeys as each member establishes its place in the social structure.

If you want to communicate with the monkeys when you go to the zoo, wear colorful clothes—monkeys are attracted by bright colors. Don't tap on the glass, jump up and down, wave your arms, or shout. Even behind glass, monkeys can see and hear you, but zoo monkeys have observed these human behavior patterns thousands of times and are generally bored by the behavior.

Watch the monkeys to see what they do that you can imitate. You might try an aggressive stance, bending forward at the waist, opening your mouth, staring directly into a monkey's eyes, even hooting. If you are successful, the monkey may make a submissive gesture or threaten back in response.

Or you might try a friendly, submissive gesture yourself, though it's hard for humans, however uninhibited, to do a really good "present." Our bodies aren't constructed for it. If a monkey tries to attract your attention, a friendly gesture on your part (smacking your lips and tongue together, as if you were noisily tasting something delicious) may reward you with a further gesture.

Don't look for a strong response. Unknowing people will turn away in frustration from a monkey that was actually paying close attention to them. A slight gesture or a swift movement of the eyes may be all the monkey shows. It's important to keep in mind that any real contact between a monkey and a human will be brief; even though we humans might wish for a 3-minute "encounter" with a monkey, 3 seconds are usually enough for the monkey.

Grooming and Appeasement—Vital Social Rituals

Monkeys and apes are social animals that instinctively seek the company of their own species. As each animal grows up, it establishes its own social rank and position in the troop. An important social bond between troop members involves grooming: Dominant animals receive the most grooming, but every member of the troop receives some attention.

Comfort Through Grooming

While a chacma baboon mother holds her infant, another female grooms it—a coveted privilege.

A moustached monkey grooms her youngster. Grooming is a soothing ritual for each participant.

A gelada baboon male grooms a female. Dominant animals receive the most grooming attention.

One female patas monkey grooms another, searching for and removing insects and other foreign matter.

How a Hierarchy Preserves the Peace

A chacma baboon presents its rump to a dominant animal as a gesture of submission and appeasement or before taking food.

A dominant male chimpanzee (right, above) reassures a cowering subordinate male with a gentle touch. Gradually the subordinate relaxes enough to face his superior (right).

Growing Up in a Primate Society

The prolonged infancy of monkeys and apes (1½ years for macaques to 3½ for orangutans and gorillas) is usually an idyllic period. Occasionally a juvenile or adult in a fit of exuberance or rage may treat an infant like an inanimate object, and at such times the toughness of the little one is a decided advantage. But usually even ill-tempered old males are extremely tolerant of the gaucheries and high spirits of the very young. By the time the youngster is weaned, however, its education as a member of a group with its own strict code of conduct proceeds rapidly and, now and then, painfully as respect for the others in the group is enforced.

Chimpanzee Playtime

When a chimpanzee mother tickles her offspring, their "play faces" show that both are enjoying the contact.

Young male chimpanzees wearing "play faces" wrestle. Juvenile male primates often engage in rough play.

An Infant Is the Center of Attention

An infant chimpanzee is a source of fascination to other troop members; but while it is very young, its mother carefully repulses all their efforts to touch it.

More than most primates, langur monkeys are tolerant of the attentions of other adult females; they will help protect the infant.

Under its mother's watchful supervision other troop members are allowed to touch this slightly older rhesus monkey infant. Thus it begins to learn social contact.

Transporting Offspring Is One of a Baboon Mother's Responsibilities

For its first few weeks a chacma baboon infant does most of its traveling upside down, clinging with hands and feet to its mother's fur.

By the time the infant is 5 weeks old, it is able, by following its mother's tail, to climb onto her back. Here it lies, holding securely to her fur.

At 3 to 4 months of age the youngster usually rides sitting up, but it still lies down for safety when the mother is running or climbing.

Success Stories

All over the world, wildlife success stories are making news. Some species once on the brink of extinction have been rescued; others thought to be extinct have been rediscovered; land threatened by development has been made secure for wildlife. The heroes of these success stories are sometimes governments or private organizations, sometimes just concerned individuals. There are still a host of conservation battles left to fight, but the heartening fact is that such efforts so often do pay off.

The Thames: A River Reborn

Jeffery Harrison, Peter Grant, and John Swift

A farsighted antipollution program changed London's smelly and lifeless river into a haven for wintering birds.

By the late 1950's the once teeming wildlife of the River Thames had been virtually wiped out. Increasingly since the days of the Industrial Revolution the river had been used as a convenient place in which to dump the waste of London's industry and population. The riverside marshes that sheltered so many animals had gradually been filled.

The water was so polluted that it lacked oxygen, was black in color, and emitted the evil-smelling and destructive gas hydrogen sulfide. Most fish and underwater life had disappeared, and only hardy, air-breathing eels survived. A few mallards, mute swans, and gulls remained, feeding on spillages around the grain wharves and pickings from what had become more like an open sewer than a river.

As far as wildlife was concerned, the whole of the Inner Thames (the 25 miles from London to Tilbury) was virtually dead. The picture was grim, and naturalists could well be excused for believing that the Thames had lost its wildlife forever.

In this respect London's river was typical of other industrial waterways of the world. But on the Thames timely action was taken to improve the situation. In the late 1950's the Port of London Authority and the Greater London Council began cleaning up the river.

Small, overloaded sewage works along the Thames were replaced by larger, more efficient units. Industrial concerns were required to channel wastes through these new sewage plants instead of pouring them directly into the river.

Wildlife returns to the Thames

By 1963 the Inner Thames was showing signs of improvement. Dissolved oxygen was present in the water throughout the entire year, and small numbers of fish were returning. By early 1974 a total of 73 species had been taken from the previously fishless zones. And the increase in birdlife has been little short of miraculous.

Records of the London Natural History Society show that, at least during this century, no duck flocks with more than 50 birds had been seen on the Inner Thames. Yet numbers along this section now regularly approach the 10,000 mark, and probably often exceed it. Given a severe winter, when wildfowl are driven from European areas, the normally unfrozen waters of the Thames could be crucial to the very existence

Graceful necks erect, mute swans sail past a gravel barge in the heart of London's dock district. As late as the early 1960's only a few mute swans survived on the heavily polluted Inner Thames. By 1973 more than 600 swans were counted there.

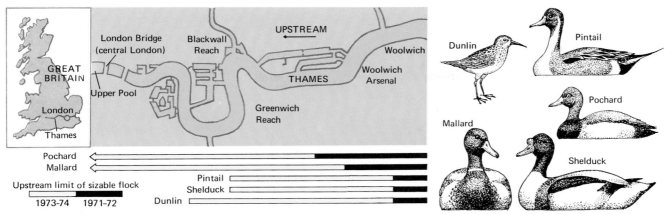

As the Thames cleanup progressed, the water became less polluted and richer in food. Birds penetrated farther upstream toward London, the source of the greatest pollution; the arrows indicate the change in five species' distribution over a 2-year period.

of many thousands of migrating ducks and other birds.

Perhaps the most exciting trend is that each winter ducks are turning up progressively nearer central London, and in increasing numbers—presumably taking advantage of the steady improvement in the water's condition.

Fortunately several factors combine to make the Thames a ready-made reserve for its newfound bird population. Shooting is illegal on the Inner Thames, and wide expanses of the soft, low-tide mud keep human disruption to a minimum. River traffic is much reduced now that most of the central London docks have been closed down, with the result that the huge rafts of resting ducks are largely undisturbed. But if the future presence of these birds is to be ensured, certain important areas of riverside open ground and the low-tide shallows on which the birds feed must be preserved.

For the time being, however, the riverfront throughout London has been totally transformed by an unrivaled wildlife spectacle. The Thames is once again a river fit for people to live beside and to work on, a river fit for fish to swim in and for waterfowl to inhabit. It is a triumph without parallel—the successful restoration of a river once all but dead. It should give hope to conservationists the world over.

Flying birds darken the sky at London's West Thurrock power station. Since the cleanup large flocks of dunlins, snipes, and other waders have roosted near this Thames-side plant at high tide. As many as 10,000 birds have been counted at one time.

A Bright Future for the Musk-Ox

Jack Denton Scott

With a little help from man, this contemporary of the ice-age mammoth is making a comeback in the Arctic.

The arctic morning mist smoked around them, reminding me of the Cro-Magnon paintings on cave walls. They lifted yoke-shaped horns and wheeled to face us. But I couldn't detect whether they were alarmed, or even whether they were staring at us, for their eyes were hidden in a long, tangled mass of hair.

The setting was perfect for this encounter with the musk-ox. Norway's Svalbard is a mountainous, fjord-slashed archipelago that includes Spitsbergen. It lies in the Arctic Ocean about halfway between mainland Norway and the North Pole, close to the spectacularly beautiful polar ice pack, which was now gleaming with sun sparks of color.

It was late July. Nearing Svalbard, the captain of our vessel had asked if I wanted to see the North's most remarkable animals. Not knowing what to expect, I went ashore to meet the first herd of musk-oxen I had ever seen. As we walked closer, a big bull grumbled and did a graceful little two-step forward, threatening us. Our first mate began using his camera, and this action seemed to agitate the musk-oxen.

Nosing the three calves into the center of a quickly formed semicircle, the adults closed the circle. Their horned heads were down and moving from side to side.

The recurving horns form a bony helmet across the head about 10 inches wide at their bases. Both males and females have them, those of the males being heavier and longer. Horns have been measured at 30 inches, but 25 is more common.

Musk-oxen are smaller than domestic cattle, their bodies blocky, legs and necks short, shoulders slightly humped, tails stubby. The hair covering their bodies is brownish-black, paling on the middle of the back and on the lower legs. Males may weigh 700 to 800 pounds, females about one-third less.

The musk-ox's scientific name, *Ovibos moschatus*, means "musky sheepcow." Though musky, the animal

is not a sheep, a cow, or even an ox. Its nearest surviving relative is probably the takin, a goat antelope from the highlands of central Asia. There are two subspecies: the barren-ground musk-ox of the North American mainland and the northern musk-ox of Greenland and the arctic islands.

A northern desert

Musk-oxen are adapted for survival in the high Arctic, the world that edges the polar seas. Here vegetation is sparse, wind is high, and temperatures are low. Strangely, though, there is little snow. The high Arctic is, in effect, a far northern desert, with a yearly precipitation of about 10 inches; snowfall is never more than 30 inches.

Musk-oxen cannot survive for long where there is deep snow. With their sharp, horny hooves, they can penetrate some ice and snow for food, but they prefer feeding on exposed, wind-bared slopes where they can easily find whatever scrubby vegetation there is. They eat mainly dwarf shrubs, sedges, and grasses. Crowberries, willows, and beach rye grass are favorites, but they do not care much for lichens. Lichens are the main food of caribou, and so the two species do well on the same range.

Social animals, musk-oxen gather in herds of 4 to

End of the trail for a horned veteran: A male arctic wolf inspects the carcass of a musk-ox cow that died of natural causes during the harsh winter. The blood on the wolf's face and throat came from another carcass on which he fed.

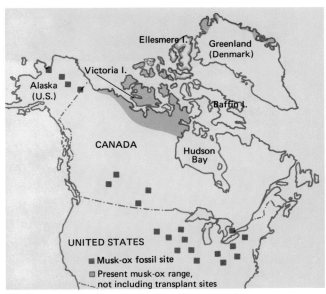

Farflung fossil sites prove that during an ice age musk-oxen crossed a land bridge from Asia to North America and ranged south of the great ice sheet. Scientists theorize that during the ice ages hunters killed off mainland herds in both Eurasia and North America; the only remaining musk-oxen lived in an isolated, ice-free zone in northern Canada and Greenland. When the glaciers melted, their descendants spread slightly south.

A herd of wild musk-oxen forms a defensive circle with calves at the center. Few predators can break through the ring of horns and hooves.

247

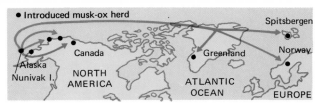

Wildlife officials release young musk-oxen from Nunivak Island (descendants of a small herd imported from Greenland in 1930) on Alaska's arctic coast near the Prudhoe Bay oilfields. The transplant, made in 1970, is part of a program to reintroduce musk-oxen to their former range. The herd that these animals joined is now breeding and slowly increasing its size (estimated in 1974 to be some 30 to 50 animals), an indication of successful adjustment. The map at right indicates sites of other relocation projects.

15 or occasionally more. Herds are headed by a bull and include cows, calves, and other immature animals. In warm weather bulls without harems are loners, but in winter they join harems or make up bachelor groups.

The late summer breeding time produces mighty combats as bulls contest for harems. A single calf, 20 inches long and weighing about 20 pounds, is born in April or early May, when temperatures may still be −30°F. The curly-haired calf huddles under its mother until it is dry. A few hours later it can keep up with the herd. Although it feeds on its mother's milk, rich in sugar, protein, and fat, for several months, at about 2 weeks of age it also begins to nibble on grass. Growth is rapid in the first year; the calf puts on as much as 200 pounds. But it is not full grown until it is 5 or 6 years old.

Musk-oxen are not prolific; females usually breed only every other year and never bear more than a single calf. And under the Arctic's stern system of population control, many calves are lost. Large herds without any calves are often seen.

Musk-oxen look clumsy; but as I saw in Svalbard, they are agile and fast. They can make right-angle turns at a gallop over rough country. Their hooves are constructed to spread on slippery surfaces, with edges sharp enough to grip the ground.

Ancestors of the musk-ox roamed the arctic prairies, steppes, and tundra of north central Asia during the ice ages. They were contemporaries of the mammoth, woolly rhinoceros, and two kinds of giant musk-oxen —all now extinct.

The musk-ox came to North America during a glacial period when so much water was frozen that the sea level was low enough to permit animals to travel across a land bridge joining Siberia and Alaska. When the glaciers extended into what is now the United States, the musk-ox ranged as far south as Iowa. But when the glaciers melted and retreated, the musk-ox managed to survive only in the far north of North America, including Greenland. In Europe and Asia it became extinct.

When white men—traders and whalers—came to the Arctic, they shot thousands of musk-oxen for food and for the prized undercoats. The Hudson's Bay Company bought nearly 20,000 hides. By the middle of the 19th century only remnants of the species were left.

New homes for musk-oxen

The 15 musk-oxen we saw in Svalbard were among about 50 descendants of 17 Greenland animals released there in 1929. In 1932 musk-oxen were also transplanted to a mountain plateau in Norway; from there five animals emigrated to Sweden in 1971.

In 1930 the United States Congress appropriated $40,000 for the purchase of Greenland musk-oxen. Thirty-four animals were turned over to the University of Alaska for study, and of these 31 were released on Alaska's Nunivak Island in the Bering Sea, reserved for them as a national wildlife refuge. By the time the herd had reached 750, they were outgrowing the island and were beginning to be transplanted to other areas. Protected by law in Alaska, Canada, Greenland, and Norway (although some hunting is allowed), musk-oxen seem to be facing a bright future.

Musk-Oxen Are Being Domesticated on an Alaskan Ranch

Just 7 miles from Fairbanks, Alaska, the University of Alaska maintains an experimental musk-ox ranch. Here the animals, dehorned for safety, are raised, bred, and stripped annually of the fine, woolly undercoats that protect them from the coldest arctic winds. This wool, called qiviut by the Eskimos, is soft, light, and finer than cashmere. One pound makes 25 miles of yarn—and a grown musk-ox yields 6 pounds a year. Unlike sheep, musk-oxen cannot be shorn: The valuable qiviut must be plucked or combed out by hand when the animals shed in early summer. Though aggressive in the wild, the musk-oxen on the ranch have proved to be tame, friendly, intelligent, and playful. The university herd will produce breeding stock for private domestic herds, providing Eskimos and Indians with a valuable product for sale as well as meat to replace the dwindling supply of game. It will also mean a new lease on life for the musk-ox, which was almost extinct 70 years ago.

A calf (above) takes its first meal at the University of Alaska's ranch. Musk-oxen breed readily in captivity; the calf survival rate is high.

An Eskimo handler (left) pulls matted qiviut from a musk-ox at the university ranch. The wool must be cleaned and carded before it can be spun.

Year-old musk-oxen at the university ranch form a defensive circle as their handler, aided by a pair of well-trained sheep dogs, prepares to head them into their barn. The animals try to stand their ground, but the dogs will keep them moving.

The Noisy Scrubbird Calls Again

Vincent Serventy

Lost since 1889, the noisy scrubbird was rediscovered by an alert naturalist who heard a strange, loud call.

Christmas Eve 1961. The phone rang. I picked it up casually. It was a reporter. Would I comment on the reported discovery of the noisy scrubbird?

"If it's true, it's the most exciting find of the century," I exclaimed, and demanded more information. My excitement mounted as he filled in the details. A bird thought to be extinct had suddenly reappeared.

The story began in the last century, when the British ornithologist John Gould decided to learn and write about the birds of Australia. He started to publish material in 1837 but soon realized that little information was available. Since one man alone could not gather the necessary data, Gould sent John Gilbert to Australia. There Gilbert discovered the first noisy scrubbird known to science.

Details of Gilbert's find were lost for more than a hundred years. Then a long-overlooked notebook was

A 19th-century lithograph by John Gould shows a mature male noisy scrubbird (lower) and a young male. The scrubbird is a poor flier and relies on its concealing coloring for protection. Despite its name, it has a melodious voice.

discovered in 1950 at the Queensland Museum in Brisbane. In its pages Gilbert had described what he knew of the noisy scrubbird:

"This is without exception the loudest of all the songbirds inhabiting Western Australia. It inhabits the densest and rankest vegetation, on the sides of hills, and the thick grass around swamps or small running streams. . . . It runs along the ground with the utmost rapidity; and as it invariably utters its loud notes while on the ground perfectly sheltered from view by the overhanging vegetation, it is nearly impossible to get a shot at it. When I first heard its extraordinary loud notes, many of which are sweet and melodious, I was perfectly convinced it was a new bird, and watched and waited about for it for hours together without so much as seeing it. . . . This species appears to be confined to the limit of about 40 miles from the coast, for I have in no instance heard it in the interior or at a greater distance than this."

A specimen of the noisy scrubbird was collected in 1889. After that, many well-known naturalists unsuccessfully searched for the bird. So it was thought to be extinct. Then came the dramatic month of December 1961. Here is the story in the words of the noisy scrubbird's rediscoverer, Harley Webster:

"On December 17, 1961, in an area where I had

A triumphant Australian ornithologist, D. L. Serventy, examines the first noisy scrubbird ever caught alive. After being weighed, measured, photographed, and banded, the bird was released, and it bounded—not flew—back into the scrub.

been spending a good deal of time observing and photographing birds, my attention was caught by a series of bird calls which were quite new to me. They were fairly long and were also loud and frequent. I had to move over 200 yards and into very dense high scrub surrounding a small swamp before I was close to the bird. In spite of the noise I made in my approach, it continued to call, and I halted to listen about 20 feet from it. The loudness and richness of the calls were remarkable, and I began to hope that it was indeed that will-o'-the-wisp that had lured ornithologists in the past 70-odd years into the thick scrubs of the Southwest, the noisy scrubbird. . . ."

So it proved. After that more and more of the birds were discovered in the dense vegetation of some nearby gullies and ravines.

The authorities moved swiftly to put a total ban on the taking of any scrubbirds or any other animals within a radius of 4 miles of Mount Gardner, on Two People Bay, the center of the newly found colonies.

Encounter with a scrubbird

It was to this area that I went with Harley Webster to see my first scrubbird. It was a beautiful day, and we drove out in the afternoon. Webster slammed the car door. Immediately from the greenery came the challenging call of the noisy scrubbird. We walked down a footpath. The bird's call came closer. My ears rang with the clamor of the hidden singer as he poured

out his melody. First from one side, then from the other, and finally right at my feet came a burst of song. I looked but could see nothing. Suddenly there was a disturbance at the foot of a nearby tree, and a brown shape flitted in the shrubbery.

Webster, with all the knowledge he had gained of this bird's habits, took me to a new spot.

"Sit there and it will cross the path," he said. I waited. Closer and closer came the call. I lifted my binoculars. A circle of green came sharply into focus. Out of the shrubbery a long-tailed bird came striding. It smoothly crossed the open space and was gone. I saw the scrubbird several times and even managed to film it as it dashed across.

What has been done to prevent the noisy scrubbird from disappearing for a second time, perhaps forever? The Western Australian Government has set aside the 13,600-acre Two Peoples Bay Wildlife Sanctuary to protect the two to three hundred noisy scrubbirds known to exist. But then came word that a small town might be built on the margins of this limited area.

Naturalists brought pressure to bear. Protests, including a plea from the Duke of Edinburgh, poured in from around the world. By 1969 the housing development project had been abandoned. A warden for the reserve was appointed, and public access to the scrubbird area has been strictly limited. In addition, it may be possible to trap several pairs of scrubbirds and transplant them to new areas.

More Rediscoveries From Australia and New Zealand

A number of New Zealand and Australian animals, including the noisy scrubbird, were believed extinct until "rediscovered," usually in small numbers in isolated places. The status of each of the species shown here is precarious, and even the number of survivors is in some cases unknown.

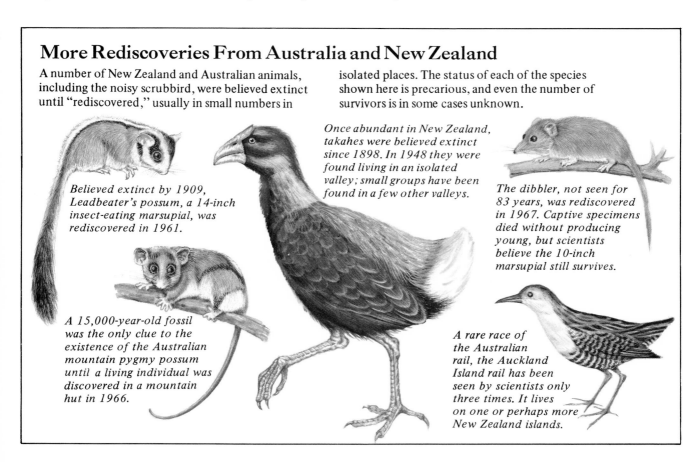

Believed extinct by 1909, Leadbeater's possum, a 14-inch insect-eating marsupial, was rediscovered in 1961.

A 15,000-year-old fossil was the only clue to the existence of the Australian mountain pygmy possum until a living individual was discovered in a mountain hut in 1966.

Once abundant in New Zealand, takahes were believed extinct since 1898. In 1948 they were found living in an isolated valley; small groups have been found in a few other valleys.

The dibbler, not seen for 83 years, was rediscovered in 1967. Captive specimens died without producing young, but scientists believe the 10-inch marsupial still survives.

A rare race of the Australian rail, the Auckland Island rail has been seen by scientists only three times. It lives on one or perhaps more New Zealand islands.

Rescue in Bermuda

David R. Zimmerman

For 300 years scientists thought that the cahow was extinct. When this seagoing bird was rediscovered, it was saved by a man who wouldn't give up.

A fledgling cahow exercises its wings outside the opening of its burrow in preparation for flight. Young cahows perform this routine each night for about a week before they are able to fly. Their parents are gone, and instinct guides their actions.

Many fond farewells have been written to the several hundred animals that human activity has put on the road to extinction. Far less has been said about whether some might be pulled back from the brink, and if so, how—and by whom.

There is one man who is succeeding, through his own passionate commitment, at the task of saving one highly endangered bird. The man is David Wingate, Bermuda's chief conservation officer and resident ornithologist. The bird is the cahow (pronounced ka-HOW), a tube-nosed seabird or petrel, named for its weird mating cry. The place is the Atlantic island of Bermuda—more specifically, four or five windswept rocky islets off its coast.

The cahow is an ocean wanderer. When it leaves the long burrow in which it hatched, it goes to sea—and stays there. It feeds on small fish and squid, drinks salt water, takes its rest afloat, and returns to its natal islet only to breed. Once tens or even hundreds of thousands of cahows bred on the main island of Bermuda. Following its discovery in 1515, man and his animal retinue—especially hogs and rats introduced by early Spanish sailors and later British colonists—took so great a toll so quickly that for 300 years the cahow was presumed to be extinct.

In 1906 a naturalist, Louis L. Mowbray, killed a strange petrel on an island in Castle Harbour, Bermuda. Thinking the cahow extinct, he identified it as a windblown stray of a New Zealand species. Ten years later, when another naturalist, R. W. Shufeldt, described the abundant fossils of the cahow in Bermuda caves, Mowbray recognized that his 1906 specimen was identical and redescribed it as a cahow.

The cahow's downfall had been rapid, but its rediscovery was haltingly slow. In 1935 zoologist William Beebe heard a cry one night on Nonsuch Island, one of the islets in Castle Harbour. He thought it might be a cahow and tracked the bird down. It was not, but now Beebe's interest was whetted. He alerted the keeper of St. David's Lighthouse, which looks out over the islets and the shore where cahow remains had been found. Later that year the keeper sent him a dead petrel that had struck his light. Beebe sent it to The American Museum of Natural History, where the world expert on petrels, ornithologist Robert Cushman Murphy, identified it as a cahow.

During World War II a young American soldier, Fred Hall, found several dead birds that he believed to be cahows. Hall also found rats eating the birds' remains and put out rat poison. In 1948, having sent

The Breeding Cycle of an Ocean Wanderer

A cahow's reproductive cycle begins when the bird reaches breeding age 4 to 5 years after hatching. The cycle follows a yearly rhythm. In late October the cahows return to their rocky nesting islets off Bermuda, clean out their old cliffside burrows, and build nests of twigs and leaves. Mating takes place in late November and is followed by a brief period at sea. One large egg is laid in January; incubation takes about 8 weeks. For nearly 3 months the parents feed the chick, finally abandoning it to live on its huge fat reserves. When the chick has grown adult plumage, it exercises outside the burrow for several days, mastering the art of flight. By mid-June it is ready to begin its adult life at sea, returning to land only to breed.

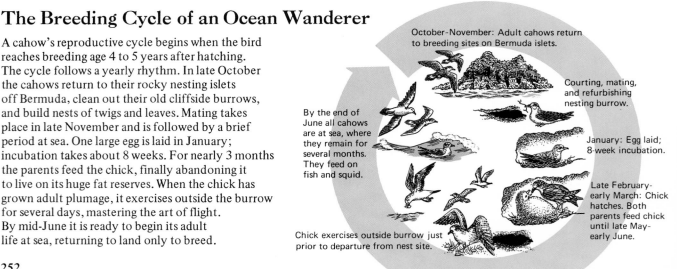

October-November: Adult cahows return to breeding sites on Bermuda islets.

Courting, mating, and refurbishing nesting burrow.

By the end of June all cahows are at sea, where they remain for several months. They feed on fish and squid.

January: Egg laid; 8-week incubation.

Late February-early March: Chick hatches. Both parents feed chick until late May-early June.

Chick exercises outside burrow just prior to departure from nest site.

Cahows searching for food skim a turbulent sea in this detail from a painting by Guy Coheleach. The 15-inch birds (wingspread, 20 inches) spend their first 4 to 5 years entirely at sea before returning to Bermuda to seek a mate.

the birds' remains to the Smithsonian Institution for identification, Hall exchanged letters with ornithologist Richard Pough, a conservation activist.

In the autumn of 1950 petrel expert Murphy, urged on by Pough, decided to make one last stab at finding a live cahow. Murphy journeyed to Bermuda, where local arrangements were made by the curator of the Bermuda Aquarium, Louis S. Mowbray, son of the man who had rediscovered the cahow. The younger Mowbray invited David Wingate to join in the search. Wingate was then 15, a local schoolboy who had grown up with the cahow's colorful history vividly imprinted on his mind.

"For days," Wingate later recalled, "gales prevented any visit to the offshore islands. The weather finally moderated on January 28, 1951, and with a heavy sea still running, one last-ditch attempt was made. After several difficult landings we finally found an islet that offered some evidence of occupancy: a patch of greenish-white excreta and a half-obliterated footprint at the entrance of an extremely deep and curved tunnel in the cliff. After much digging a bird was finally revealed sitting on an egg."

As it was hauled forth with a wire noose, Murphy exclaimed: "By gad, a cahow!"

The Murphy expedition found seven nesting cahow

In its cramped burrow on a Bermudian islet, a cahow chick sits on a crude twig nest (above). Below, an artificial cement burrow placed on high ground, where tropic birds do not normally nest, separates cahows from their enemies.

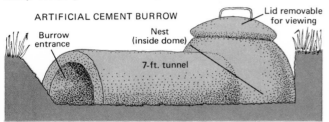

ARTIFICIAL CEMENT BURROW

Lid removable for viewing

Burrow entrance

Nest (inside dome)

7-ft. tunnel

pairs on two islets. Chicks hatched in only four burrows. When Mowbray checked the burrows a month or so later, all four chicks were dead. Rat bones were found nearby, so Murphy helped organize subsequent expeditions to trap and poison the rats.

Yet even chicks that hatched after the rats were poisoned died. A dismaying new menace was found. Ironically this menace was itself a bird: the beautiful white-tailed tropic bird. Boldly marked in black and white, the bird has two plumes that extend out far behind its body and hence is known to Bermudians as the longtail. Like the cahow, it is an ocean wanderer, which returns only to breed in cliffside burrows. This was—and is—the source of the longtail's deadly conflict with the cahow.

On the tiny, rocky islets where the cahow was making its last stand, there were few places to dig. The cahows were forced to use rocky crevices and cliffside holes, many of which the longtails also found suitable. In preparing their own nests, the longtails destroyed the cahows' egg or killed the chick.

Differences in the two species' use of the burrows provided the first possibility for helping the cahows. The cahows arrive in Bermuda in late autumn, mate, and then return to sea. Usually the female lays her one enormous egg in January. She incubates the egg for more than 50 days, during most of which time the longtails are nowhere about. They return in late March and April—just in time to kill the cahow chicks. The cahows leave the burrows unattended by day, while they fish at sea. They return at sundown or later with food for their young. By dawn they have gone. As the sun rises, the longtails, which spend their nights at sea, return and leave again by late afternoon. Thus the adults of the two species rarely meet.

Murphy and Pough worked up a plan to keep the longtails out by putting chicken-wire screens across the burrow openings early in the morning and removing them late in the afternoon. That was a tough task, for it meant staying on the tiny, storm-torn islets overnight. Wingate by now was in college in the United States, and there was no one else in Bermuda who could accept the assignment. But in New York a 26-year-old conservationist named Richard Thorsell ran into Pough at the Museum of Natural History. After hearing about the problem, Thorsell agreed to go to Bermuda. He arrived early in March of 1954.

With Mowbray's help Thorsell attempted to screen two burrows, each occupied by a cahow chick. But bad weather forced him off the islet; and when he returned, a longtail had killed one of the chicks. Thorsell dispatched his boatman back to tell Mowbray.

The all-important size difference

That day Pough was in Bermuda, and Mowbray brought him out to the islet. Pough suggested that they exploit another possible difference between cahows and longtails: their respective sizes. The cahows, it appeared, were slightly smaller. If so, it might be possible to build permanent or semipermanent doorways—or baffles—just wide enough to admit the cahows but too narrow for the longtails.

After days of experimentation, Thorsell produced a baffle 5 inches wide, just wide enough for the birds' folded wings to pass through, and 2¼ inches high. It worked. A cahow could pass through it, but a longtail could not. Thorsell and Pough had created what apparently was the first device with which humans have been able to intervene in the field to enhance reproductive success in an endangered bird.

The next year, in February of 1955, Thorsell went back to Bermuda but soon left, never to return. His earlier report, containing the baffle specifications, became lost from sight in Mowbray's files.

Mowbray continued to work with the baffles, experimenting with the shape and size of the hole. But when Wingate returned from college in 1957, he found that cahow reproduction had not improved. Baffles had not been erected on three islets; and where they had been, they were not working. The longtails were getting through.

Wingate spent 6 weeks researching baffle dimensions again, and the measurements he came up with virtually duplicated Thorsell's. He also discovered that baffles only work against new and nest-searching pairs of tropic birds. (Tropic birds, like cahows, return year after year to the same nest site, and once it is established, they are determined to return to it. A baffle cannot stop them from forcing an entry.) To solve the problem once and for all, those few pairs of tropic birds already in cahow burrows had to be eliminated.

By 1961 Wingate succeeded in installing baffles in all cahow burrows on the known breeding islets. Since then, he has not lost a single cahow to longtails. The breeding population by 1961 was 18 adult pairs, which

In the early 1900's the Laysan teal population totaled 7 because rabbits had devoured the vegetation on which the teals lived. With the rabbits destroyed, these ducks slowly recovered and now number several hundred.

Laysan's Birds—Almost Off the Danger List

An isolated, low-lying coral island in the Hawaiian archipelago, Laysan once supported an immense bird population. Several species were unique to Laysan, including the Laysan teal and finch. Both these birds were brought close to extinction in the early 1900's when rabbits, imported by a resident guano miner to vary his diet, multiplied and devoured the vegetation on which the birds depended for food and shelter. The teals, almost flightless, could seek no distant source of food; the finches were not strong enough to fly to another island. In 1909 Laysan and other islands in the leeward group became the Hawaiian Islands National Wildlife Refuge. By the 1920's U.S. biologists had eliminated the rabbits, and the vegetation began to grow again. The finches are no longer scarce; the teals, vulnerable to storms that sweep them out to sea, are increasing but are still in a precarious position.

The Laysan finch—a honeycreeper with a heavy bill adapted for seed eating—was another near victim of the rabbits. The Laysan population now numbers 10,000, with more on nearby islets.

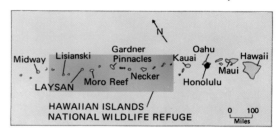

produced 12 young. The breeding success, at one young per successful attempt, thus was 66 percent.

But then the fledging rate began to fall again. By the mid-sixties only about one pair in three, or 33 percent, successfully reproduced. This was too few to replace natural loss. Again the cahows appeared doomed.

The cause of this new decline soon was identified by Wingate and environmental biologist Charles Wurster, Jr. Wurster analyzed dead cahow eggs and chicks. He found DDT and its breakdown product, DDE. The evidence suggested that the cahows' oceanic food chain —floating plants, eaten by tiny animals, eaten by small fish, eaten by squid that are eaten by cahows—had been poisoned by chemicals dispersed into the ocean from continents hundreds or thousands of miles away.

As DDT use rapidly declined in North America in the late 1960's, the reproductive success of the cahows climbed back toward its earlier 66 percent fledging rate. In 1971, for the first time, Wingate's work was richly rewarded: He counted 13 fledglings, about double the previous year's total. In 1972 there were 27 breeding pairs that produced 17 fledglings.

Although the spectacular gains of the 1971 and 1972 seasons were reversed in the following two breeding seasons due to abnormally high adult mortality and a lack of newly established pairs, the annual production of young has nevertheless remained at 12 chicks. Unless some new problem develops, we can soon expect these chicks to return and bolster the population by breeding, thus continuing or even improving on the average gain of one pair per year since 1961. It's agonizingly slow progress, but it's progress.

For the cahow there seems to be a future. Its breeding grounds are small enough so that one highly dedicated man can monitor and manage them. And Wingate does not seem to have grown tired of his efforts to save the cahows.

What do the cahows give him back? In spring Wingate has the pleasure of peeking in on the vigorous chicks by day, while their parents are out fishing. In winter there is the eerie wail of their mating cry when he braves the rolling seas to visit the islets; occasionally he may glimpse the adult birds in silhouette flying against the full moon or the setting sun.

255

Return of the Elephant Seal

Jim Tallon

Mexico and the United States protect the largest of the seals, once killed for its hide and oil. Offshore islands are now home to flourishing herds.

On San Benito and Guadalupe Islands, off the coast of Baja California in Mexico about 250 miles south of San Diego, lives an animal that looks like a moldy, 5,000-pound sausage. Its social hierarchy resembles the pecking order of the domestic chicken; it will snooze nonchalantly while man, once its greatest enemy, stands no more than 10 feet away. A few decades ago this odd mammal teetered on the brink of extinction. But since 1970 I have seen hundreds of animals lying like close-packed driftwood on beaches at Guadalupe and hundreds more congregating in sandy coves just beyond the surf on San Benito. These were cheering sights—visual proof of the return of the northern elephant seal.

The largest seal, the elephant seal weighs more than twice as much as the walrus. Mature bulls may weigh more than 5,000 pounds and reach lengths of 17 feet; cows average around 1,700 pounds and are 7 to 9 feet long. Seal pups are born black, but as adulthood overtakes them their colors may soften to a yellowish-brown or slate gray. Semiannually they shed both hair and an outer layer of skin, which peels off in large patches. At this time the newly exposed skin is as sensitive as sunburned skin is to humans. When old hair and skin have been fully replaced by new, the elephant seal's coat appears dark brown.

On land the big mammal's nature demands company, and plenty of it. Elephant seals often mass into a literal sea of blubber, seemingly drawn together like iron filings to a magnet. Unfortunately this "piling on" may have drastic effects on pups in an elephant seal colony. Those caught in the line of march of a bull may be crushed; bulls crawl over the pups as if they did not exist.

A deep diver

At sea the elephant seal prefers to be alone. The ungainly creature that, on land, drags itself around so awkwardly with its foreflippers becomes capable of surprisingly graceful movements in the water. Hindflippers, so useless on the beach, become powerful propellers, thrusting the great bulk along with surprising speed. The elephant seal's diet includes small amounts of seaweed, plus squid, skates, dogfish, puffer sharks, ratfish, shellfish, and other marine life native to the ocean floor. It is worth noting that the ratfish, never found in water less than 300 feet deep, forms part of this diet. Thus the elephant seal forages to depths where daylight is filtered to dimness.

The seal's front flippers serve a purpose beyond navigation. The seal, snoozing in the sun, may be pestered by flying insects, and its short hair offers little defense against attack. With its foreflippers the seal shovels sand across its back as a protective screen. Elephant seals also have been known to fling sand or stones quite accurately at humans who step too close.

The elephant seal is polygamous, and bulls may have as many as 30 cows in their harems. Generally, however, only one bull in seven maintains a harem. The "elephant" forename of the species derives from the trunklike proboscis of the male, said to be a secondary sex characteristic. Bulls hold their places in their pecking order by both fighting and bluffing, although the actions are directed wholly toward pos-

Northern Elephant Seal Colonies Proliferate Off California and Mexico

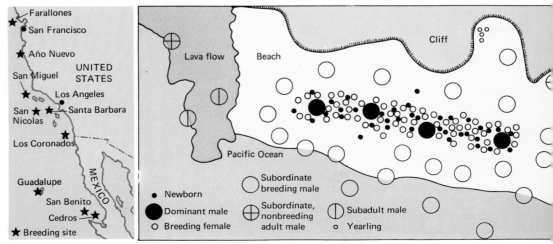

From a single small herd on the Mexican island of Guadalupe, northern elephant seals have recovered enough to recolonize a 1,000-mile stretch of islands. (See map at right.) The map at far right shows the division of territory in a typical breeding colony. Most of the beach is occupied by a few dominant bulls, plus their harems and young. Other seals are crowded out to less favored sites.

Farallones
San Francisco
Año Nuevo
San Miguel
UNITED STATES
Los Angeles
San Nicolas
Santa Barbara
Los Coronados
Guadalupe
San Benito
Cedros
★ Breeding site

MEXICO

Lava flow
Beach
Cliff
Pacific Ocean

• Newborn
● Dominant male
○ Breeding female
⊕ Subordinate, nonbreeding adult male
◐ Subordinate breeding male
◖ Subadult male
∘ Yearling

Undeterred by bleeding neck wounds from earlier encounters, two bull elephant seals face off in a duel for dominance.

A savage lunge for the throat throws one of the combatants off balance. Despite the carnage, such battles are seldom fatal.

The beaten bull prepares to escape. Temporarily defeated in this encounter, he may immediately challenge another bull.

Instinctively seeking bodily contact, elephant seals huddle together on a beach at Mexico's San Benito Island. These seals are mostly females and pups; a single large male (upper right) rests his pendulous proboscis on the back of a much smaller female.

session of harems rather than food or territory. In fact, the bulls fast during the breeding season.

When a contender approaches a bull's harem, the defending animal rises on his foreflippers and rears his head, allowing the long proboscis to hang into his open mouth. From two large air chambers in the snout the bull emits short blasts. The inside of the mouth acts as a resonance chamber, creating a loud, low-pitched sound so strange as to rival the fabled cry of the loon. Should the contender roar back, the pair may engage in a battle lasting from several seconds to more than 15 minutes. On San Benito Island I saw two full-grown bulls fight bloodily for half an hour. More often, however, the antagonists back off.

If the master of a harem loses a battle, he relinquishes his harem to the winner but may be back to fight for repossession after a short rest. Eventually an especially strong bull works his way up the pecking order to become an "alpha bull." The animal then becomes the elephant seal equivalent of king of the hill and as such will mate with more females than any other bull in the colony.

The fall to near extinction

Aside from man the elephant seal's only enemies are large sharks, parasites, and particularly killer whales. Although the birth rate of the species is quite low, the seal was always in balance with its natural predators. The operations of modern man, however, were disastrous.

Between 1855 and 1870 hide and oil hunters exterminated the fur seal and sea otter along Baja California and its offshore islands. The hunters then turned their lances on the elephant seal, and tens of thousands of the huge animals were slaughtered. From one good-sized adult elephant seal could be made 200 gallons of an oil considered especially fine for lubricating machinery. Extinction of the seals seemed imminent and, indeed, was presumed to be a fact by some biologists. In 1892, however, a small herd was discovered on Guadalupe Island, and in 1911 the Mexican Government gave full protection to the remaining seals.

Today Guadalupe's original tiny colony of elephant seals has expanded into a healthy population estimated at more than 15,000 animals—a magnificent comeback. Some of the descendants of that Guadalupe herd have since migrated north to the islands of the California coast—they may be seen today on Santa Barbara Island in Channel Islands National Monument off the southern coast of the State—and may range as far north as southern Alaska. Mexico still prohibits killing of the elephant seal, and the United States has extended this protection to its own west coast. Barring the unforeseen, the survival of the elephant seal seems assured.

Six Seals Struggling for Survival

While the elephant seal's survival seems assured—given continued protection—the situation is still precarious for the six seals pictured on this page. Ruthlessly slaughtered by man for their flesh, blubber, hides, and valuable furs, these formerly numerous seals have been reduced to small remnant populations. All but the Japanese sea lion are protected by law, although the quality of enforcement varies from country to country. The Mediterranean monk seal is still killed by fishermen who regard it as a fish thief. The Juan Fernandez fur seal is slaughtered for its meat, which is used to bait lobster traps. Tourists visiting the breeding beaches may inhibit mating or panic nursing seals. Pollution is becoming a serious problem in some areas.

Seals are divided into two families: the "true," or earless, seals, which lack external ears, and eared seals, which include the fur seals and sea lions. The true seals, more completely adapted to aquatic life, are thought to be descended from an otterlike ancestor; the eared seals probably had a bearlike ancestor.

True Seals

True seals get most of their swimming power from their rear limbs. In adapting to this propeller role, their rear legs became buried within their bodies. They cannot be turned under for walking.

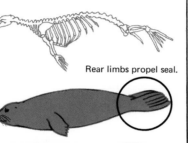

Rear limbs propel seal.

Hawaiian monk seal

Almost exterminated by blubber hunters, the Hawaiian monk seal now numbers perhaps 1,000. Though protected, it will not breed where humans visit; sharks also take a toll. Monk seals are the only warm-water seals.

Saimaa seal

Left landlocked by the receding Baltic Sea some 8,000 years ago, the Saimaa seal inhabits a few freshwater lakes in Finland. Once reduced to 40, it now numbers about 250. Its principal menaces are fishermen and pollution.

Mediterranean monk seal

Once abundant from the Black Sea to the northwest coast of Africa, the Mediterranean monk seal now exists only in a few colonies; as few as 500 may remain. The outlook is gloomy since it lacks protection in much of its range.

Eared Seals

The massive bone structure of the eared seals' chests reveals that most of their swimming is done with their front limbs. The rear limbs can be turned under the body to act as clumsy legs.

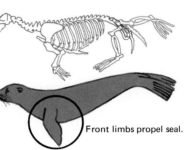

Front limbs propel seal.

Formerly numbering an estimated 2 to 3 million, the Juan Fernandez fur seal has about 500 poorly protected survivors on two islands off Chile.

Juan Fernandez fur seal

Probably never numerous, the Japanese sea lion may now be extinct. Korean soldiers may have wiped out the last colony.

Japanese sea lion

Galápagos fur seal

Fur seals are not tropical animals, but a cold oceanic current enables the Galápagos fur seal to live near the Equator. Recovering slowly under protection, this seal now numbers about 1,000, in many small colonies.

Floating on its back, a sea otter uses a stone on its stomach as an anvil to smash open a clam—one of the few known examples of tool using outside of man. To maintain its body temperature, an adult sea otter must consume about 20 pounds of food a day.

The Sea Otter Story —A Qualified Success

The sea otter, which can reach a length of 4 feet and weight of 80 pounds, is a large cousin of the river otter. Most sea otters inhabit the kelp beds of North America's Pacific coast (from Baja California to Alaska); a smaller number live on the other side of the Pacific, in Russian waters. Lacking an insulating fat layer, the sea otter is protected from the water's chill by thick brown fur. But this fur proved to be the otter's undoing. Fur hunters slaughtered the animals with such ruthless efficiency that by 1900 they were almost extinct. Protected since 1911, otters have increased slowly. The northern herds have reached their optimum size, and some surplus otters have had to be moved to new locations. But the California herds of sea otters, threatened by oil spills and illegally killed by fishermen who regard them as competitors, are not yet out of danger.

Anchored by a strand of giant kelp, a sea otter gnaws open a sea urchin, one of its major sources of food. The otter eats the urchin's soft inner parts and discards its spines and shell. Where otters are killed off, sea urchin populations boom.

With a heavy rock for a hammer, a sea otter (left) skillfully pounds a stubbornly clinging abalone loose from its foothold on an undersea boulder. This photograph, by Ron Church, is the first ever taken of a sea otter dislodging an abalone underwater. The sea otters' taste for abalone has brought them into conflict with commercial divers (above), who harvest abalones for the gourmet market.

The main food items of sea otters are sea urchins, abalones, and mussels, all denizens of the giant kelp beds of the Pacific. The mussel feeds on tiny organisms that it filters out of the water. The abalone, prized by human epicures, grazes on rockweeds and other algae that flourish in association with the kelp. The sea urchin feeds on the kelp itself, destroying the habitat of the abalone. By preying on sea urchins, otters keep the kelp ecosystem in balance, ultimately ensuring survival for the abalones.

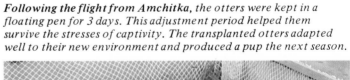

Abalone

Rockweed, kelp, and other algae

Microorganisms

Sea urchin

Sea otter

Mussel

Sea otters from an oversized herd on Alaska's Amchitka Island were moved to Washington State (part of their former range) in 1970. Chilled water tanks cooled the otters during the flight.

Following the flight from Amchitka, the otters were kept in a floating pen for 3 days. This adjustment period helped them survive the stresses of captivity. The transplanted otters adapted well to their new environment and produced a pup the next season.

Cranes Over Kyushu

George W. Archibald

A cultural treasure of Japan returns each fall to a warm welcome and plenty of food on the plains of Areseki.

Beaks stretching skyward, a pair of white-naped cranes performs the "duet ceremony," a ritual that lasts from 5 to 15 seconds. The combination of calls and postures warns away intruders and strengthens the bond between the two cranes.

The Areseki plains on the island of Kyushu are Japan's last major wintering area for the rare white-naped crane. A traditional subject for oriental art, the white-naped crane, like many of the world's 15 crane species, has been in danger of extinction.

As its name suggests, this crane has a graceful white strip down the back of the neck, ending in a crescent-shaped flare at the shoulders. Except for the bare red skin of the cheeks the bird is predominantly gray. It stands over 4 feet high, has a wingspread of about 7 feet, and weighs from 12 to 15 pounds.

The cranes are roosting on a spacious, isolated rice paddy. Here on one small plot of earth stand the remnants of a species that once wintered in tens of thousands over all the major islands of Japan.

At 7 A.M. a local farmer and crane warden loads his jeep with sacks of corn, wheat, and fish. Several enthusiastic schoolchildren help him scatter the cranes' breakfast over the dry, gravel-coated dike in front of his home, about half a mile from the roosting area. Soon the majestic cranes meander or fly across the plain for their morning handout.

From an observation tower beside the house a group of crane lovers watches the winter visitors. By mid-morning the cranes have had their fill, and the flock disperses. Each family unit, consisting of the parents with or without one or two chicks, separates from the flock and flies to a second feeding area, where it remains until late afternoon.

Red-cheeked threats

The family stays close together—frequently the chick is between the parents. If other cranes approach the pair's territorial boundary, the resident cranes assume a rigid, upright posture. Their bare, red cheek areas expand backward to beyond the ears, transforming the whole head into an aggressive signal. With rigid, swaying steps the female approaches her mate. Side by side, upright, with beaks slightly lowered, they continue this "cakewalk" toward the intruders. Then they stop the approach.

Suddenly the female catapults her head and neck back toward her tail and simultaneously emits a chilling scream. An eighth of a second later the male emits a long, low-frequency call, elevates his inner wings high above his back, and lowers the slate-colored flight feathers toward the ground in a "turkey strut."

As their remarkable unison call continues, the female's head and neck again return to the upright position. She emits two high-frequency cackling notes for each low-frequency trumpet call of the male. With each call the male elevates, then quickly lowers, his wings. The effect of this wing motion is striking. The inner wing feathers are almost white, and when thus displayed, they produce a flash of light that is visible for a great distance.

Occasionally the male and female of a mated pair, or a group of immature birds, engage in the famed crane dance, common to other crane species all over the world. With long, exaggerated strides the birds

Japan's Imperial Crane

Even rarer than the white-naped crane is the Japanese crane, which has a bright red patch on its head. (Its Japanese name, *tanchō*, means "crimson crest.") Formerly breeding over much of Japan (and also on the Asiatic mainland), the *tanchō* in Japan was virtually wiped out by hunters. Only one colony, on the island of Hokkaido, survived; in 1924 it numbered about 20. Declared a "nature monument" in 1925, the colony is legally protected and now numbers about 200.

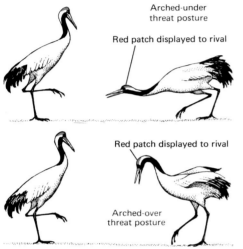

Arched-under threat posture

Red patch displayed to rival

Red patch displayed to rival

Arched-over threat posture

To threaten a rival, a Japanese crane arches its neck over or under. Such aggressive behavior is common, but fights rarely occur.

An 18th-century artist painted these Japanese cranes on a silk scroll. A favorite motif of oriental art, cranes symbolize long life.

Largely ignored by their fellow cranes, a pair of tanchō *perform the leaping courtship dance for which they are famed.*

The last major wintering area of white-naped cranes in Japan is located near the small village of Areseki. Ricefields, drained for the winter, double as winter feeding stations for the cranes as well as for mallard ducks, pintails, and other waterfowl.

circle about each other, bowing, throwing sticks or pieces of turf into the air, leaping several feet straight up, then bouncing down to continue the circling. The dance usually ends with the pair running side by side for 50 to 100 yards, partly flying with wings flapping in a rigid manner and tails slightly elevated. Presumably the dancing solidifies the pair bond and synchronizes the cranes' sexual states in preparation for breeding.

Late in the afternoon the cranes congregate back at the feeding station for a final handout. As dusk approaches, they gradually make their way toward the roost. Before dark the entire Areseki crane population

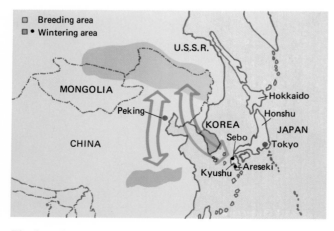

The breeding grounds of the white-naped crane are marshes along the Amur and Ussuri Rivers in the Soviet-Chinese border zone. Sizable flocks winter in South Korea and along the Yangtze River in China. Arrows show migration routes.

is huddled together in a tight flock. Some rest, others sleep, and several are alert, watching. One short, low alarm call and the flock is instantly in the air.

Day of departure

Migration day arrives on a bright, windy February morning. By 9:30 the cranes have fed, but pairs are not leaving for their usual feeding territories. They stand in small, scattered groups between their roost and the feeding station, unusually passive, facing the breeze. Something is urging them to leave Japan. With wing flaps and long, running strides, several cranes mount the breeze. They circle southward toward the mountains, then back over the feeding station, emitting quick, loud flight calls. The birds then begin a spiral that winds continuously up, up into the blue, windy sky until they are practically lost to human vision.

More cranes take off. Soon a spiral of glistening white, red, and gray extends from the Areseki plains to altitudes unknown. When the birds reach the northerly wind currents they need, they head out over the Sea of Japan, north toward Korea and the first rest on their long migration to breeding grounds near the Soviet-Chinese border.

Several hundred people gather to observe the departure of the cranes. A feeling both sad and happy prevails. The cranes will return in November. Perhaps there will be more of them. Certainly, as long as the breeding habitats are protected, and the birds are not destroyed during migration, the white-naped cranes will continue to return to the loving care extended to them by the people of Areseki.

Japanese Wildlife Is Imperiled

Japan, with a deep-rooted tradition of nature appreciation, has long been a leader in wildlife protection. Yet Japan's animals, like island-dwelling species elsewhere, are more than usually vulnerable. The area available to them is shrinking steadily, and most have no way of moving to a new habitat. Although large areas of land have been set aside as national parks and refuges, the amount of wildlife they can support is limited, and the future of some species is uncertain. The animals shown on this page are a case in point. One, the crested shelduck, slid into extinction more than half a century ago. Though now protected, the others are still rare or endangered. For example, the giant salamander, found only in a few mountain rivers between 1,000 and 3,000 feet, lost much of its habitat when riverbanks were deforested or paved with concrete. But protection alone is not enough for Japan's endangered animals; it remains to be seen whether active measures, such as habitat restoration and captive breeding, will succeed.

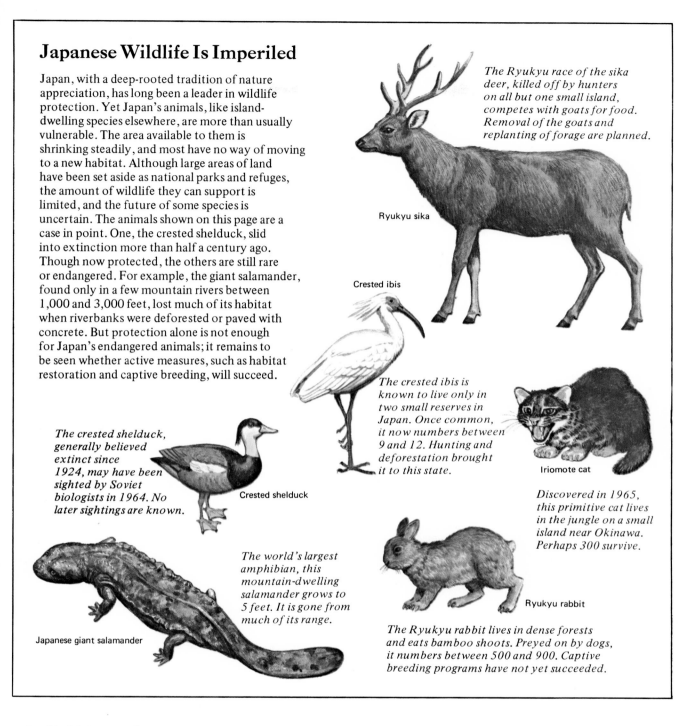

The Ryukyu race of the sika deer, killed off by hunters on all but one small island, competes with goats for food. Removal of the goats and replanting of forage are planned.

Ryukyu sika

Crested ibis

The crested shelduck, generally believed extinct since 1924, may have been sighted by Soviet biologists in 1964. No later sightings are known.

Crested shelduck

The crested ibis is known to live only in two small reserves in Japan. Once common, it now numbers between 9 and 12. Hunting and deforestation brought it to this state.

Iriomote cat

Discovered in 1965, this primitive cat lives in the jungle on a small island near Okinawa. Perhaps 300 survive.

The world's largest amphibian, this mountain-dwelling salamander grows to 5 feet. It is gone from much of its range.

Japanese giant salamander

Ryukyu rabbit

The Ryukyu rabbit lives in dense forests and eats bamboo shoots. Preyed on by dogs, it numbers between 500 and 900. Captive breeding programs have not yet succeeded.

In feudal Japan white-naped cranes were protected by the ruling classes and fed by the peasants. Between 1869 and 1871 Emperor Mutsuhito abolished the feudal system and with it the protection of cranes and their habitat. By 1920 they were reduced to perhaps fewer than 200 individuals, with Areseki as their last stronghold. In 1921 the Areseki fields came under Government protection. The cranes benefited and rapidly increased from a known population of 158 in 1936 to 469 in 1939. They again suffered during the bleak days of World War II and the American occu-pation. Somehow a small core survived. Government-supported feeding began in 1952, and subsequently crane numbers, although still perilously low, have in-creased to about 300.

Several years ago a few pairs of white-naped cranes began to winter near Sebo, a rural Kyushu area several hundred miles north of Areseki. Recently they were reported as brief visitors to other areas in Kyushu. If their numbers continue to increase, this spectacular bird may again be a winter reality in many areas of southern Japan.

Miracle of the Saiga

Bernhard Grzimek

A Soviet ban on hunting turned near extinction into abundance—and a unique antelope thrives on the arid steppes.

It was not an easy matter to see the saiga antelope. I had to journey to Kazakhstan, near the Soviet border with China—a long but rewarding trip. In Kazakhstan a dying species has been transformed in a little more than 50 years into the most prolific hoofed animal in the whole Soviet Union. The story of the saiga is a model example of nature conservation.

Saigas are clumsy-looking antelopes of the Eurasian steppes; about the size of sheep, they have thin little legs and misshapen, swollen noses, which function as dust extractors. The males also have horns.

Because people believed that the saiga's horns had medicinal or aphrodisiacal value, the animals were slaughtered in the 19th century. They were shot from ambush; horsemen drove whole herds toward lines of armed hunters; tribesmen hunted them with grey-hounds and trained eagles. Only their horns were taken; their flesh was left to rot.

The advance of the plow and the harvesting machine also had its effect. By the end of World War I the saiga faced extinction. Only a few were to be found at the eastern limit of Europe, several dozen in Kazakhstan, and some at scattered points in Asia—a bare 1,000 in all.

At the last possible moment, in 1919, an early decree of the revolutionary regime banned hunting of the saiga; in 1923 the Republic of Kazakhstan followed suit. A group of Russian and Kazakh zoologists, headed by Professor A. T. Bannikov of Moscow, began investigating the migratory and breeding habits of this vanishing animal.

Running from the wind

Bannikov's research revealed that saiga antelopes are constantly on the move. They are extremely sensitive to the slightest change in the weather that may presage drought or snow. When they graze, their progress is very slow—2 to 4 miles an hour. If the winter is very cold and the snowfall heavy, the saigas run with the wind at their backs. They follow precisely the direction of the wind, even if it carries them over railroad tracks or through villages—they pay no heed to danger. Since they all start running in the same direction once snow begins to fall, the herds coalesce and move forward at a speed of between 6 to 12 miles an hour, often for 6 days without stop.

Over a period of several years Bannikov and his assistants pieced together details of the saiga's breeding behavior. Mating begins in late November. By this time the bucks are carrying 2-inch layers of fat, chiefly on their hindquarters; during the mating season they will eat nothing but snow. Bucks in rut also have noses that are considerably more swollen than usual.

A buck may have 2 or 3, 20 or even 50 mates, which he is constantly striving to keep in a tight pack. Saiga bucks at first mate with the older females in their harem, then with the young does of that year's brood. Finally the mating herds join up to form one great herd. The males now cease their rivalry.

Male saigas face the winter in a weakened condition. In March they often die in masses; in a hard winter nearly all the adult males may die. The scarce winter fodder is thereby kept for the pregnant and young animals, ensuring the continuance of the species. Young bucks are not sexually mature by their first November, as their sisters are, and therefore eat during the breeding season. Because of this they survive the winter in far greater numbers than the mature males and are ready to mate the following autumn.

The remarkable recovery

The fertility of the saiga is amazingly high. More than 95 percent of the older does and 85 percent of the yearling does conceive each year; three out of four give birth to twins. The high fertility and the animal's ability to run away from bad weather have allowed the

A saiga fawn nestles with its mother in the scanty grass of the steppe, their coloration making them almost invisible. Saiga fawns can run a few hours after birth and begin to eat grass when 4 days old. At 10 days they can run as fast as adults.

saiga to make a remarkable recovery. At first the ban against hunting did no more than ensure that the last few hundred saigas remained alive. Then, in the 1920's, their numbers began to increase. By 1970 more than 2 million saigas roamed the steppes. As the herds grew to the maximum size that the arid land would support, a state corporation was set up to hunt the saiga. Every year a census is taken at calving time and again in the autumn. Game licenses are issued, and the animals are hunted in the fall, just before the start of the mating season.

The saigas are cropped for their meat, which tastes rather like mutton, and for their hides. A fully grown saiga yields up to 37 pounds of meat. The Soviet Union thus gathers an annual harvest of 6,000 tons of meat and 24,000 square yards of leather, all from desert areas that, if the saigas had been exterminated, would today yield nothing for man.

The example of the saiga shows what madness it is to allow any form of natural life to die out completely. An animal species that evolved in the struggle for existence over millions of years often has capabilities of which we are quite unaware. The saiga produces meat and leather from the arid salt wastes of the steppes, something domestic animals cannot do. Yet if it hadn't been for the firm action of a few determined and intelligent men, these remarkable animals would have vanished from the earth forever.

What a Saiga Eats

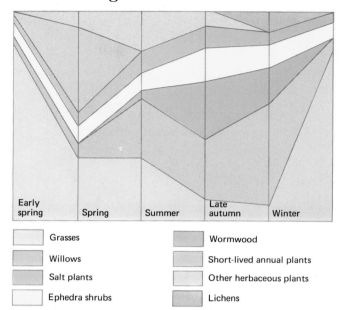

| Early spring | Spring | Summer | Late autumn | Winter |

Grasses · Willows · Salt plants · Ephedra shrubs · Wormwood · Short-lived annual plants · Other herbaceous plants · Lichens

Grasses, weeds, and lichens are the mainstay of the saiga's diet, which changes according to the seasons. In the chart above the varying width of the band for each food plant shows the varying proportion of that food in the saiga's diet. Recently the saigas have found an additional source of food during the spring and summer—newly developed wheat fields.

Three phases of the saiga's life cycle are shown in these unusual photographs taken in the Soviet Union. Left, a small group of saigas graze. Center, a buck and his harem migrate to fresh pasture. Right, a herd scrapes for fodder on a snow-covered flat.

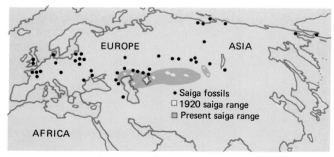

Saigas once ranged over much of Eurasia, as the sites of fossil finds indicate. By 1920 hunting had reduced the saiga population to a few small herds. Under legal protection the number of saigas and their range have increased greatly.

EUROPE · ASIA · AFRICA · • Saiga fossils · □ 1920 saiga range · ▪ Present saiga range

A male saiga antelope in midleap graces a Soviet postage stamp. Both males and females (which do not have horns) make periodic observation leaps as they run along with heads lowered. Saigas have only one fast gait: the trot.

The Orangutans Are Going Wild

Carl Mydans

In their native Borneo captive orangutans are being retrained so they can live free in the forests.

A mustache, a beard, and bulging cheeks identify an adult male orangutan, which may weigh as much as 250 pounds. In captivity these apes often become obese from lack of exercise. Orangutan is Malay for "man of the woods."

Joan had never before paid any attention to me. She seemed always to be looking for something, fussing around among the vines and leaves, shifting her baby absentmindedly from hip to hip. Whenever I tried to approach her, she kept her distance.

Then one morning there she was, dressed in glowing auburn red, coming directly up to me. She climbed onto a log and sat, somberly taking me in.

"Good morning," I said. And she hoisted her baby and spread him on his back across her head like a hat. Then she took the baby by both feet and hung him upside down.

Joan and her baby Johnnie are orangutans, one of the least-known species of man's closest relative, the apes. Joan and Johnnie live in the forest of Sepilok in northeastern Borneo. They are not quite wild, but it is hoped that they soon will be—for that is the goal of the extraordinary experiment being carried out here. Animal scientists of the Forestry Department of the Malaysian State of Sabah, directed by assistant game warden G. Stanley de Silva, are retrieving captive animals and teaching them to be wild again, so that they can be put back in the rain forest habitat to procreate.

A rain forest laboratory

The "laboratory" for this experiment is the rain forest itself, a vast wilderness of saraca trees, which rise to tremendous heights and spread a canopy far overhead, and of ironwoods, bamboos, palms, and thick-sprouting undergrowth, all exuding the rich smell of wet plant life. In a tiny clearing a small board bungalow on stilts shelters the rangers who protect the orangutans brought there and who keep a record of their success in adapting to jungle life.

The program was started in 1964, after a law was passed making it a serious offense to kill orangutans or hold them in captivity. So far 51 animals have been absorbed into the project. Sixteen have died, but all except eight of the remaining 35 have gone into the forest to feed, roam, and survive on their own. These eight—Joan among them—keep returning to the bungalow, to wait for the fruit they know will be given them.

To an untrained observer a released semiwild orang is indistinguishable in the forest from a wild one. The animal scientist, however, discerns many differences. One day, for example, when I was in the forest with De Silva, Joan came down to the forest floor and joined us. Showing off for his benefit, she used a dead branch as a club, as though to pound a pole into the ground, much as a man might pound in a fence post. "If an anthropologist saw this, he might be excited at first," De Silva said. "A wild animal using tools! But what you are seeing is not an ape that has discovered the use of tools but one that is simply remembering something she has seen humans do."

Of all the orangs brought to Sepilok, Joan has provided the richest material for behavioral study. She's been there longest (since 1964), and has often left (twice she came back pregnant), but never for good.

Orangs once ranged over much of eastern Asia; at their peak they may have numbered 500,000. Today a few thousand survive in the dwindling rain forests of Sumatra and Borneo.

Joan protectively cuddles her infant Johnnie at the Sepilok training center. Female orangutans are devoted parents, caring for their young until the offspring are about 3 years old.

That morning when Joan looked me over so carefully, I had the feeling that we were establishing a rapport for the days ahead. In my jungle treks I was accompanied by Sundang Sarim, a young ranger who could find Joan even during her times of concealment, spotting her far up in the forest canopy and calling out in his melodious Malay, "Joan, *makan!* Joan, *makan!* Joan, eat!" And he would hold up some fruit.

We would follow her for hours, and sometimes I worked so close to her with my cameras that when she unpredictably changed course, swinging from vine to vine, we had to dodge each other to avoid collision. Once, when I was absorbed in taking photographs, she reached out and gently tapped me on the head.

Each day she seemed to get busier and busier, moving branches, performing all kinds of nonsensical acts. And I saw with astonishment that she was wearing that transparent expression of make-believe preoccupation that self-conscious people put on for the camera. She seemed very human to me.

Thus I was unprepared for Joan's attack, especially unprepared that her rage should be directed at her friend Sundang. He was offering bananas to her, and her mouth was full and white with fruit, when suddenly she threw him to the ground with a flying tackle and bit his leg viciously.

Sundang had to go to the hospital for treatment of the bite. Next morning, limping on his bound leg, he showed no heart for a jungle trek. Lest the experience

influence his career, I urged him to go back into the forest with me. After a while he took some bananas, and we went off again.

When we found Joan, high in the forest canopy, she at first refused to answer Sundang's call of "Joan, *makan!*" But then she came down fast, until she hung on a trellis of vines just above us. There was a soft, inquiring look on Joan's leathery face. Johnnie held one of her enormous callused hands in his tiny black ones, and with her other hand she reached out toward Sundang. Was it a gesture of friendship? Nervously, Sundang stepped up and gave her the bananas. She took them, slipped the ripe fruit out of the skins one by one, and ate them, poking little pieces into Johnnie's mouth. Then she climbed to a branch overhead and began to fold small branches in under her.

"She's going to sleep now," Sundang said as we moved off. I looked back and saw her crouching on her leafy bed with little Johnnie clutching the fur of her chest. She was gazing after us as though we puzzled her.

From all this it somehow seems reasonable to hope that when Joan's little Johnnie—and the offspring of other rehabilitated orangutans—grow up alone beneath the sheltering saraca canopy, they will do no more than shyly hide themselves at the approach of humans, watching us from a safe perch. And if this happens, the chances of any other human having the experiences I had among the orangutans at Sepilok will have ended.

Orphan, a young golden eagle, perches on the wrist of his trainer, coauthor Maryrose Spivey. First conditioned to fly to his trainer for food, Orphan then had to learn to track and catch a moving lure. The leash prevents his escape.

A School for Birds of Prey

Maryrose Spivey with Nathan Zabarsky

Volunteers at the San Francisco Zoo are teaching captive birds of prey how to live in the wild.

Still on his tether, Orphan pounces on a live white rabbit. The novice hunter made several false strikes before succeeding, for eagles acquire their hunting skill slowly. Had he been released without training, he might have starved.

I was on one side of a long grassy field behind the San Francisco Zoo, excited and scared. Across the field was Jupiter, a golden eagle. I stood with my arm extended at a right angle to my body and gave as loud a whistle as I could manage. Jupiter cocked his head and shifted his taloned feet. I whistled again, and he was off, flying at me in a gliding arc. He came in smoothly, talons extended, and the sudden contact rocked me backward.

From that moment on I was committed to the zoo's bird of prey (raptor) project, which began in February 1971. For some time it had been obvious that the zoo's raptors were not doing well. Some had broken feathers and bad foot conditions (often a problem in captive birds of prey). Few had the vital appearance that marks a prospering confined animal. So the birds in the worst condition were removed from their cages and tethered by means of leather bracelets and leashes in a grassy fenced area. Jupiter, partially blind in one eye, was the first to come out, followed by a bald eagle called Charlie and two red-tailed hawks. Calling

themselves Raptors Lib, volunteers began training the birds, using the ancient methods of falconry. Today the San Francisco Zoo is one of the few places in the world with a release program for birds of prey. So far 16 birds have been returned.

During the summer of 1971 we were given two young golden eagles in the hope that we could act as substitute parents, teach them to fly and hunt, and then reintroduce them to the wild. They were both males, only a few months old. We called them Orphan and Geronimo. Orphan was picked up from a nest, after his parents had been shot, and brought to us by the Fish and Wildlife Service. Geronimo had been stolen from his nest, apparently by someone who wanted him as a pet. In any event Geronimo had subsequently got loose and was found wandering around San Francisco. Although in the United States it is illegal to shoot or capture golden eagles, as well as other endangered birds of prey, the fates of Orphan and Geronimo are not uncommon.

First both young birds had to become accustomed

to their human foster parents. Both were young enough that they quickly became unafraid and learned to fly to our gloved fists for their food.

Geronimo was as friendly with humans as a golden eagle ever gets. He liked to have his head scratched and was very slow to show aggressive behavior. Orphan was another matter. The most beautiful eagle any of us had ever seen, he was fearless and very aggressive.

After 2 months' work Orphan and Geronimo were firmly conditioned to fly to us for food. The next task was to help the two eagles learn to hunt. This task fell to mountain climber and teacher of yoga Larry Caughlan, photographer Nat Zabarsky, and me.

First we constructed a fake rabbit out of rabbit fur and compacted soft filler. We used this lure to start teaching the two young eagles how to use their feet to grasp and kill their prey.

By April 1972 both young eagles were flying well to the lure. I would hold Orphan at one end of the field, while 15 yards away Larry would begin running as fast as he could, dragging the lure well behind him. Orphan learned to intercept the "game" no matter how fast Larry ran.

Training with live prey

Now we began to "provide" the eagles to live game (rabbits). This was decidedly an unpleasant task for all of us, but it was vital that Orphan and Geronimo have this experience before they were released.

A wild golden eagle dives on its prey, landing and gripping hard with its powerful talons. Death for the prey is almost instantaneous. Because of their youthful inexperience, however, Orphan and Geronimo were clumsy and slow at first. Orphan never lacked aggression, but he needed know-how. Geronimo was actually afraid of live rabbits. We didn't know whether to laugh or cry as one morning we watched a rabbit chase him in circles.

As their schooling progressed, we began taking both birds for varied hunting and flying exercises to ranches where the sympathetic owners let us use their property. By late spring we felt we had taught the eagles as much as we could. We began to think about a place for their release—a spot as far away as possible from human habitation and yet a place where there was someone to monitor them.

Finally in late June we found Joe and Lois Smith, an exceptional couple who had spent their last two summers manning a fire tower on a private ranch high in the mountains. Game was plentiful on this isolated ranch, the owner was willing to let us release the birds there, and the Smiths were enthusiastic.

For the release of the two golden eagles we decided to use a method falconers call "hacking out." We built special perches at which the birds would be tethered and fed for 2 weeks while they became accustomed to the site. After their release the Smiths would continue to put out food in case either eagle needed help.

The 2 weeks passed, and early one July morning we once again made the 75-mile trip to the fire tower. It was an extremely hot and dusty day, but we told ourselves it was perfect for soaring above the mountains. Larry lifted Geronimo to his arm and carried him to a bluff overlooking the mountain. We slit Geronimo's leather bracelets, and with an exultant cry of "Be free, Geronimo!" Larry cast him into the air. The eagle immediately flew off, and we watched until he was only a dot.

Then it was my turn. I urged Orphan into the air, and he took quickly and eagerly to flight. Both eagles were now aloft and free. We spent the rest of that day and the next watching through binoculars, once in a while catching sight of the birds.

Since we released the two eagles at the fire tower, the Smiths have faithfully kept watch over them. They have seen Geronimo periodically return for food, but Orphan has never come back. He flies over the tower now and then in the company of two other immature eagles and is obviously doing splendidly.

The Ancient Sport of Falconry

A medieval French illustration shows details of falconry—the art of hunting with trained birds of prey. The birds kill the prey but do not retrieve it.
Falconry has been practiced for at least 4,000 years; today its traditional techniques are used in programs for training captive birds to hunt for themselves.

Scotland's Ospreys Come Home

John Ennis

Birdwatchers maintain a 24-hour vigil at Speyside so that the ospreys can nest in peace. These cherished birds are now spreading to other parts of the Highlands.

Each spring, for more than a decade, a female osprey has left her winter quarters in Central Africa and flown north to keep a date in Scotland.

On her 5-foot wingspread the great fish hawk glides over the Mediterranean, crosses Europe, and flies a confident course up the length of Britain. In the second week of April she arrives in the Spey Valley, below Scotland's Cairngorm Mountains. Wheeling high over the aerie at Loch Garten is her mate, who has been on the lookout for her since his own arrival a few days earlier.

Human eyes are watching, too, and within minutes the word will go out: "The Speyside ospreys are back!" From that moment until the birds leave in the autumn, their nest will have a guard of birdwatchers 24 hours a day in what has become one of the most remarkable bird-conservation programs in Europe.

On meeting, the two ospreys cry a high, joyous "chee-chee-chee" of greeting, then celebrate by chasing each other through the chill sky. Occasionally the male swoops to pick up a stick for the great 4-foot, 100-pound nest they will build in a 40-foot Scotch pine, which still holds the remains of last year's nest. The Speyside ospreys have chosen their tree with care. Near lochs containing pike and trout, its isolated position in a forest clearing gives the birds an uninterrupted view round the nest where human egg stealers or other predators might lurk.

Winged pioneers

Such caution is vital. For centuries ospreys lived untroubled on Speyside. Then, during the 19th century, these magnificent birds were driven from their ancient Scottish aeries by landowners reluctant to share their fishing rights and by a popular mania for collecting eggs and stuffed birds. Ospreys abandoned Britain as a breeding ground and, except for passing migrants, were not seen there for more than 50 years. The Speyside pair are the pioneers.

The osprey is a proudly handsome bird, standing some 2 feet high and weighing between 3 and 4 pounds. Brown-bodied with white underparts, it has a snowy-white head broken by black streaks circling its fierce yellow eyes and running back on either side

Wings outspread and feet extended, an osprey comes in for a landing in its nesting tree at Speyside. By 1973, 11 pairs were nesting at Speyside and nearby sites, an encouraging gain over the lone original pair. Nine nest locations are top secret.

of its head. Its legs are equipped with powerful talons to grip slippery fish.

Ospreys appear to mate for life. Arriving first from his tropical winter, the male gathers sticks for a nest; he dives hard onto dead pine branches, snapping off up to 3-foot lengths that he adds to the unwieldy mass atop the tree. When his mate joins him, she collects moss and turf, shaping them into a soft lining. To shore up their home, the ospreys use anything handy. Ornithologist Clinton Abbott noted more than 40 different items in ospreys' nests, including oilcloth, fish netting, barrel staves, seashells, and a wheel from a child's cart. When the nest is complete, sparrows move in as basement boarders, poking their little nests between the lower sticks and catching the morsels of fish that fall from the big birds' table.

Breeding begins in April or early May. The female

A female osprey returns to her nest, where the male has taken his turn caring for the half-grown chicks. Alert and well feathered, the chicks will be ready to try their wings in a few weeks. Ospreys may use the same nest for many years, adding to it annually until it assumes huge proportions. In the United States pesticides, destruction of habitat, and nest robbing by raccoons and other predators have been major factors in the osprey's decline. In Scotland the chief dangers are depredation by human egg collectors and shooting by ill-informed gamekeepers.

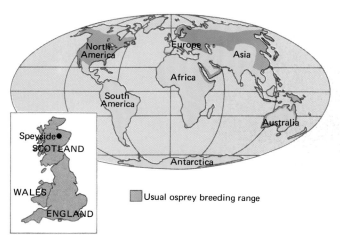

Ospreys breed on every continent except Antarctica and South America; these far-ranging birds may also be seen in wintering grounds far from their nesting sites. The inset map shows the location of Speyside.

lays three 2½-inch brown-spotted eggs, and while she incubates, the male leaves twice a day on fishing trips. Slowly flapping, he flies at 30 feet above the water, his keen eyes seeking the dark shape of a fish basking near the surface. Seeing one, he folds his wings and dives with talons held ahead of his curved beak, sighting his victim like a fighter pilot. He hits the water with a splash, right on target. Coming up with his prey, he hovers an instant to adjust his hold and shake the water from his plumage, then makes for his "feeding tree." There he eats his share before his mate's annoyed calls persuade him to bring over what he has not eaten.

Incubation takes some 35 days. At last the chicks appear, striped in brown and fawn down. For a month the mother stays with them while the father continues to fish. At first she feeds them with strips torn from

An osprey devours a freshly caught fish on its feeding tree, which is usually some distance from its nest and serves as a lookout. Ospreys always hold their prey in their right feet, an unusual example of "right-handedness" in birds.

273

Bringing the Eagle Owl Back to Sweden

Concerned by the disappearance of the eagle owl from large parts of its former range, a group of Swedish ornithologists at Göteborg began a captive breeding program in 1969. After some trial and error the captive owls' egg production rate surpassed that of wild owls. More important, a greater percentage of the eggs laid by captive birds were fertile, and the survival rate of hatchlings was higher. Protection from predators and from bad weather played a part, and a scientifically planned diet may have been equally important. Two years after the breeding program began, the scientists were able to release four young eagle owls; since then, increasing numbers have been returned to the wild. Trained to hunt before their liberation, the captive-bred birds have thrived and are reportedly raising their own broods.

Still with its soft downy feathers, a young eagle owl huddles close to its mother in a breeding cage at Göteborg. When full-sized 3 months after hatching, the owlet will stand up to 27 inches tall, with a 62-inch wingspread.

the fish provided by the male osprey; then, after 4 weeks, the chicks start to feed themselves.

By early August, some 8 weeks after hatching, the oldest chick is ready for flight. Fully grown, it vigorously flaps its wings. It has been practicing for a week or two, but this time the flapping takes it on a short vertical flight, up a few feet and back down on the nest. It soon learns. Within a week of its first flight, a Speyside chick has acquired enough skill to fly boldly up to its father and snatch a fish from his talons.

Once they can fly, the young birds are given a week of fishing lessons. Instead of bringing food regularly to the nest, the parents tantalize the youngsters by repeatedly dropping a fish, diving, and catching it just before it hits the water. Screaming with hungry rage, the young ospreys first learn to catch a dropped fish in the air, then to scoop one off the water.

Soon they try fishing for themselves. A Speyside observer, John Buxton, describes a young osprey making its first lone dive. "He was diving straight down, when at about 10 feet above the surface he tried to stop. The result was a 'belly flop'—and a bedraggled osprey came up spluttering."

When the young ospreys have proved their self-reliance, the family unit gradually dissolves. The male and female abandon the nest until next year, leaving soon for their long flight south. The young ones, too, set out on a migration to Africa.

"Operation Osprey" began in 1958 when repeated sightings of the Speyside pair indicated that the osprey had at last come back to Scotland. George Waterston, then Scottish representative of the Royal Society for the Protection of Birds (R.S.P.B.), realized that without protection the birds would stand no chance against human nest robbers, willing to risk a fine for osprey eggs worth twice the fine on the black market.

The day the first R.S.P.B. team arrived at Speyside, the vital need for a round-the-clock guard was demonstrated. Suddenly the ospreys shot up from the nest, circling and screaming alarm. Quickly skirting the marsh in their jeep, the R.S.P.B. men caught a well-known egg collector from southern England. He explained unconvincingly that he was "only having a look." The guards warned him off. But his appearance told them that news of the ospreys had traveled at disturbing speed.

For a month a handful of men crouched in a makeshift sackcloth blind, safeguarding the birds. Any day now the first chick, using its tiny, temporary egg tooth, would hack its way into the world.

A master fisherman, the osprey soars above the water (1) until it spots a fish near the surface. Diving sharply with partly folded wings (2), it extends its feet (3) just before striking the water (4). Waterproof plumage, not found on other birds of prey, permits the osprey to completely submerge without risk. Seizing the fish in its talons, the osprey beats its way free of the water with a sweeping horizontal wing motion, then flies off to eat its prey (5).

Almost perfectly camouflaged, three young wild eagle owls sit on the rocky ledge where they hatched. Eagle owls do not build nests but lay their eggs in rock clefts or hollow trees, using the same site year after year.

Then, on a dark night, the enemy struck. At 2:30 A.M. on June 3, Philip Brown, then the R.S.P.B. national secretary, spotted through his night glasses the silhouette of a man climbing the tree. Brown pulled the alarm string attached to the wrist of his fellow watchman, who was sleeping in a tent nearby. They sprinted toward the tree, but when they reached it the man was gone. Two broken eggs lay on the ground, each containing a pathetic embryo.

The 1958 disaster faced R.S.P.B. officials with the need for a bold decision. Newspaper headlines told of the robbery: With the secret revealed, the ospreys became the concern of an interested nation, as bird-watchers and tourists flocked to Speyside. Pressed by Waterston, the R.S.P.B. decided to enlist the direct support of its members and other interested bird-watchers, and "Operation Osprey" was born.

It was an immediate success. Every year the osprey watch attracts 100 or so volunteers—students, city clerks, housewives, retired admirals—who take turns in the day and night watch from a wooden blind some 200 yards from the nesting pine. Farther back is a visitors' center with a telescope for viewing the osprey nest close up. In 1973 more than 100,000 people, many from overseas, visited the Loch Garten Reserve. They leave contributions in a box, and one man impulsively handed over his expensive binoculars for the use of the wardens. The Countess of Seafield's estate, owner of the ospreys' territory, leaves 677 acres unworked so as not to disturb the birds. As an extra precaution the base of the nesting tree is now swathed in barbed wire.

Recently I visited Speyside just before the ospreys hatched three chicks. Manned by Jimmy Richardson, a retired Scottish oilman who was on his fourth annual stint as a volunteer warden, the blind contained a rough bed, an oil heater, and a bottled-gas ring for making coffee. A truncheon hung on one wall; on another, a heavy full-length coat. A microphone at the tree, switched on after dark to pick up any noise, made a thunderous sound whenever the sitting bird moved.

Richardson let me look at the huge nest through fixed binoculars. Only the female osprey's head could be seen, the feathers of her crest lifting in the strong breeze. The male sat watchful on his favorite spot, the branch of a dead tree nearby. As I watched, a buzzard came past; the male spread his wings and chased it away. Returning, he brought a bit of bark to add to the nest, as his mate stretched and peered about her. Then the male took over, sitting on the eggs while she flew to her retreat, another dead tree 250 yards away. There she sat and preened for an hour.

Watching their every move

Every move by the birds was entered by the warden in a log, which reads like a battle report:

"01.23: Male circles, tries to land on nest—is put off by female. Flies N. and engages hooded crow. Battle continues to E. of nest for a minute; finally, both fly out of sight.

"10.50: Female starts calling from nest.

"10.55: Male flies in from N.E. over forest, bringing fish."

The R.S.P.B.'s remarkable effort at Speyside is paying off. In 2 decades the nesting pair has produced a total of 29 young. In 1973, 11 new pairs of ospreys —themselves probably offspring of "Operation Osprey"—produced 21 chicks in other Highland aeries kept secret by the R.S.P.B. George Waterston said of "Operation Osprey," "In 1800, before persecution began, a dozen pairs at most, with their young, formed the entire Scottish osprey population. The return of that number would mean complete success. We believe we have made the breakthrough."

This 2½-week-old whooping crane was hatched from an egg laid in Canada and transported by plane to Patuxent. Eventually eggs laid by captive whoopers at Patuxent may be flown back to Canada for hatching by wild cranes.

Patuxent's Offspring

Dennis Farney

Some of North America's rarest animals are being reared at a Federal research center near Washington, D.C.

They are the survivors. One-fourth of all the whooping cranes left on earth are here, halfway between Baltimore and Washington, D.C. As the orange-gold sunlight of a late afternoon slants across their grassy enclosure, they stroll with the stately deliberation of dignified old gentlemen, their red-and-black caps bobbing.

The day is ending at Patuxent Wildlife Research Center, home of perhaps the most dramatic wildlife program in the United States. What a handful of experts is attempting here is nothing less than a last-ditch program to rescue a number of species from extinction.

Most of Patuxent's projects are still years away from the payoff stage. Moreover, Patuxent has experienced several frustrating failures. But the program recently got a badly needed psychological boost with its first apparently successful reintroduction into the wild, spelling good news for the nearly extinct Aleutian Canada goose.

In 1963 wildlife biologists and coastguardsmen had retrieved 16 goslings from the one rocky islet in the Aleutians where the Aleutian Canada goose still bred. At Patuxent these birds multiplied into a flock of 112. In the spring of 1974 the center flew 41 geese back to the Aleutians, toughened them up in holding pens, and then released them. At last report all were still alive, five pairs had nested, and some goslings had been sighted.

Breeding bobwhites

Since 1970 the Patuxent program has been tantalizingly close to success with another kind of bird. That was the year when wildlife officials first released the masked bobwhite, an endangered quail with a black mask around its eyes.

The research center's captive flock had begun in 1966 with only eight birds. Slowly the staff built up a large flock. While the quails were being reared, the Federal Government was restoring the habitat (which had been destroyed by drought and overgrazing) at three sites in their former Arizona range. Then the quails were flown to Arizona and released—some 3,000 birds between 1970 and 1974.

Each time the quails were released, they vanished. The best estimate is that not more than a handful of descendants survive today. Just what went wrong is still open to question, but Patuxent isn't giving up just yet, and last year saw the release of 300 more birds.

So far, Patuxent has concentrated on birds, but late in 1971 the center began working with six weasellike animals—black-footed ferrets, one of the world's rarest mammals. But soon after the six ferrets were brought from South Dakota, four died of distemper. The apparent cause was the distemper virus in the vaccine used to inoculate them. The two survivors have since been supplemented by three additional ferrets, and the center has switched to a different kind of vaccine. So far, the ferrets have not mated.

The black-footed ferret, the masked bobwhite quail, and the Aleutian Canada goose—each breeding program presents its own unique challenges. But for sheer drama none of these projects matches the center's work with the whooping crane.

The whooper's struggle for survival—the slow, tenacious comeback of the wild migratory flock, from 15 birds in 1941 to 48 today—has become a metaphor for man's larger struggle for environmental quality. So United States and Canadian wildlife experts knew they were dealing with a symbol as well as an endangered species when, in the spring of 1967, they traveled into the remote lake-and-muskeg country of northern Canada to retrieve some whooping-crane eggs.

Wild whooper pairs normally rear only one chick a year, although the female usually lays two eggs. It seems that either the mother abandons the nest after the first chick hatches or that the stronger of the two chicks pecks the weaker one to death. So the United States-Canadian team left one egg in each nest it found, put the second into a warm carrier, and rushed it back to Patuxent's big incubator. A total of five egg-gathering trips brought 50 eggs to Patuxent.

The program may be only a year or two away from hatching the offspring of whooping cranes mated in captivity. Eventually whooper juveniles, or juveniles and adults together, may be released. But perhaps the most intriguing plan is to "release" not whoopers but their eggs. Under this approach fertile whooper eggs laid at Patuxent would be slipped into the nests of wild sandhill cranes, which are more common. In theory, the sandhill cranes would hatch the whoopers and shepherd them through their first flight south. Scientists would have to be certain, however, that the sandhill and the whooping cranes would not interbreed.

Looking ahead, Dr. Ray Erickson, assistant director for endangered wildlife research, anticipates working with a growing number of species. As he puts it: "People are coming to realize that these animals don't have to be lost."

A male Andean condor, one of the world's largest soaring birds, is a stand-in for the closely related, extremely rare California condor in Patuxent's breeding experiments. Knowledge gained here may help the California condor.

Captive Breeding for the Peregrine Falcon

Programs like Patuxent's are helping a number of endangered species. A notable example is the Cornell University project for the peregrine falcon, which has vanished from much of its former range due to the effects of DDT. At Cornell (in Ithaca, New York) breeding pairs of falcons, including peregrines, are provided with the physical and behavioral stimuli needed for mating (nesting shelves that simulate cliffside ledges, for instance). When the first eggs are laid, they are taken from the nest. As a result, the birds produce one or two additional clutches. All the eggs removed are hatched in an incubator, and chicks are raised by hand for the first few weeks. This procedure eliminates competition between chicks that in nature would cause the death of half the hatchlings. The chicks are later returned to their parents or to other adult birds for rearing. Cornell scientists hope eventually to produce 200 young peregrines a year for release into the wild; the first releases were made in Colorado in 1974.

Crops bulging with a specially prepared meal, these 3-week-old peregrine falcon chicks were hatched in captivity at Cornell.

Proof of successful preparation: Courting peregrine falcons at Cornell University display near a scratching rock. The male is at left.

Breeding range of peregrine falcon

The peregrine falcon once had an unusually extensive breeding range (see map), but DDT has caused its decline in many areas.

The Bison of Bialowieza

Edward R. Ricciuti

The European bison, saved by captive breeding, once again roams free in an ancient Polish forest.

Massive head raised warily, a European bison bull sniffs the air in a Bialowieza glade. Bulls join cows and calves during the August-to-December rutting season, then spend the rest of the year alone or in the company of other males.

A chill drizzle accompanied dawn in the Bialowieza Forest of Poland. It was only early October, but the oaks and maples had already lost their golden leaves. I stood on a rutted woods road, watching a great, shaggy bull wisent, or European bison, a creature whose kind roamed most of Europe when forests covered the land.

The bison breeding season was ending, and shortly the bull would join an all-male herd. Today, however, he was still with a herd of a half-dozen cows and calves. Sensing human presence, the bull raised his head and moved slowly toward the cows and young. They in turn began to fade into the trees with surprising stealth for such large beasts. Within a few minutes the herd had vanished into the forest with only an occasional snap of a twig to mark their passing.

Half a century ago about 50 European bison survived. Today more than 1,000 exist, and some 350 live free in Bialowieza Forest. Bison also inhabit several other forests in Poland and the Soviet Union, but Bialowieza is rather special. Like the bison, it is a reminder of Europe's past, for in all the central part of the Continent only the woodland of Bialowieza remains as it was almost 2,000 years ago.

Woodland wilderness

By car the Bialowieza Forest is a 5-hour drive from Warsaw, which lies to the southwest. The highway enters the forest like a breach in the ramparts of the wilderness, passing by hundred-foot trees that seem to belong to another age. The forest is shared by the Soviets and the Poles, with the Polish section including somewhat less than half of its total 280,000 acres.

Spring, when wildflowers carpet the forest floor, and early autumn, when the trees yellow in Poland's famed "golden autumn," are perhaps the best times of year to visit Bialowieza Forest.

A band of Bialowieza bison faces an intruder. Taller and rangier than their North American relatives, these European bison do not form large herds. They wander in small groups through the forest, feeding on seedlings, bark, and leaves.

The Great European Broadleaf Forest Is Gone

From the end of the ice ages until about 2,000 years ago, broadleaf forests covered most of central Europe. (See map below.) Usually dominated by such trees as oaks and hornbeams, the temperate forests provided food and shelter for a large and varied population of animals. But as agricultural activities expanded and more trees were cut for use in industry and building, the forests shrank. New forests of quick-growing conifers were planted and harvested. A few natural tracts were set aside as hunting grounds for noblemen, but most of these disappeared, too. Bialowieza, on the border of Poland and the U.S.S.R., is the last central European forest remaining in a relatively undisturbed state.

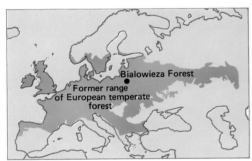

A 19th-century German artist painted this fanciful scene of nymphs and a stag in a mature broadleaf forest much like Bialowieza.

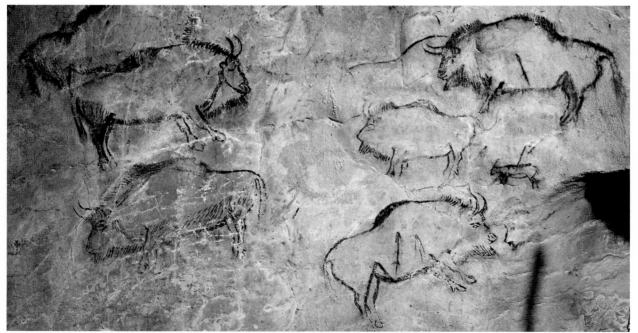

Cave paintings prove bison once ranged over Europe. Ice-age hunters created these likenesses 14,000 years ago at Niaux in southwestern France. Anthropologists believe the paintings played a part in hunting rituals.

One day in October I arrived in the Bialowieza at dusk with Zbigniew Wolinski, the assistant director of the Warsaw Zoo. Foresters and scientists attached to the forest's research center keep tabs on the bison of Bialowieza; so I felt it would not be difficult to track down a small herd.

We arose before dawn and set out by car, bumping over unpaved woods roads until we came to a great meadow. Apparently the bison had already been there and left. We found their prints in the soft, wet ground and saw where they had bent the tall meadow grass. Disappointed, we went back to the car, while a fine, cold drizzle began to turn us and our spirits soggy. As we headed down the road, we saw a man on a bicycle pedaling furiously after us. The forester, it turned out, had found our bison.

The herd was browsing among the trees, under the eye of the bull. Accustomed to humans but nevertheless wary, the bison drifted off as we edged closer. Near me Wolinski smiled with satisfaction, for the bison indeed is Poland's pride.

The pride is justifiable, for although Poles, Germans, and Russians contend for the honor of saving the bison, the history of the European bison is in part the history of Poland.

Throughout medieval central Europe, the combined pressures of hunting and habitat destruction led to the end for bison herds. By the 19th century wild bison existed only in the Caucasus and in Bialowieza Forest.

Protected by nobility as a hunting preserve, the Bialowieza Forest was maintained when land around it was cleared. In 1589 the forest became the private preserve of the Polish kings, who in 1798 were succeeded by the Russian czars.

Wildlife of Poland's Bialowieza Forest

The glory of 280,000-acre Bialowieza Forest, on the border of Poland and the Soviet Union, is its groves of huge ancient trees, many of them several centuries old and up to 10 feet in diameter. Today there are 12 distinct kinds of forest communities in Bialowieza, each with a different combination of trees. Bialowieza also has sunny open glades, streams, lakes, marshes, and scrub growth. The wide variety of habitats supports a diversity of animal inhabitants. In addition to the famed European bison (also called wisent), there are moose (rare in central Europe), roe deer, red deer, beavers, and wild boars. Wolves, lynxes, foxes, and an occasional brown bear prey on the abundant small mammals. The alert visitor may see black and white storks, spotted eagles, hoopoes, and capercaillies, the turkey-sized, forest-dwelling grouse famed for their mating duels. While most of Europe's remaining forests are managed for maximum timber yield, the forest in Bialowieza National Park has been deliberately left untouched. Mature trees are not harvested; they are allowed to age, die, and decay undisturbed. A natural plant succession is thus preserved, along with the animals that thrive in each kind of plant community. Old as it is, Bialowieza is not identical with the ancient forest that blanketed central Europe at the end of the ice ages. Climatic changes since that time have eliminated or reduced the numbers of some plant species, allowing others to become established in the area. But through all its natural changes Bialowieza has remained a forest unaltered by the human hand.

Widespread in northern European and Siberian forests, birch mice feed by night on berries, seeds, and insects. Agile climbers on bushes and shrubs, these rodents travel on the ground by leaping.

Extinct in 1851, the tarpan (a small, wild ancestor of the horse) was gradually "re-created" by breeding horses with tarpan blood. A small herd now lives in Bialowieza.

During the 19th century the number of bison in the forest varied, because of disease and the fighting in the forest between Polish rebels and the Russians.

By the outbreak of World War I, 727 bison lived in Bialowieza. As the front swept through the forest, fighters slaughtered the bison. The last wild bison in Bialowieza was killed in 1921. Within a few more years all of the bison in the Caucasus suffered the same fate, and only 56, all captive, remained.

Building up bison numbers

In 1923 the tide turned for the European bison. Careful records of purebred European bison (those not mixed with American animals) were compiled, and zoo people the world over turned their efforts to increasing the numbers of captive bison.

By World War II, 100 bison existed in zoos. Scat- tered in many nations, the bison did not suffer as severely from the second world conflict as they had from the first, and herds grew rapidly in the postwar years. By 1952 bison had been freed in Bialowieza, and other releases elsewhere followed.

Although the bison roam Bialowieza freely, they do not exist independently of man. In winter they receive supplementary food. Individuals are removed or introduced into the wild herd on occasion to provide fresh blood and to stock the forest's breeding center. Here bison are kept in large paddocks and carefully tended.

Zoos continue to breed bison in captivity, and the global herd is still growing—so much so that in 1973 the International Union for the Conservation of Nature announced that the European bison is now "relatively secure because effective conservation measures have been taken."

A young female roe deer peers through ferns growing in an opening in the forest. Numbering about 1,000, roe deer are the most abundant of Bialowieza's large mammals. Red deer also find plentiful browse in the lush undergrowth.

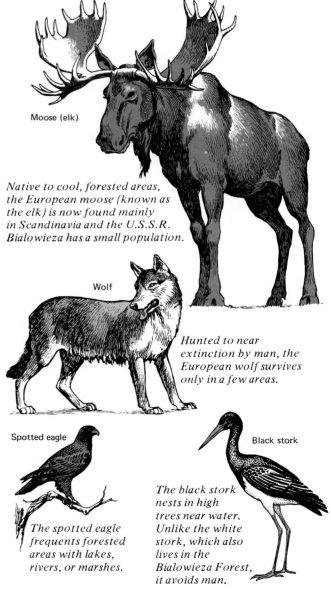

Moose (elk)

Native to cool, forested areas, the European moose (known as the elk) is now found mainly in Scandinavia and the U.S.S.R. Bialowieza has a small population.

Wolf

Hunted to near extinction by man, the European wolf survives only in a few areas.

Spotted eagle

The spotted eagle frequents forested areas with lakes, rivers, or marshes.

Black stork

The black stork nests in high trees near water. Unlike the white stork, which also lives in the Bialowieza Forest, it avoids man.

White Birds
and Redwoods

Harold Gilliam

An oil spill, a proposed marina, and land developers threatened a heron refuge, but people acting together saved birds, trees, and lagoon.

In the dark early-morning hours of Monday, January 18, 1971, two tankers collided in the fogbound Golden Gate, the entrance to San Francisco Bay. Over the next few hours several hundred thousand gallons of fuel oil spilled across the waters of the channel and into the bay on a flood tide. Then the tide reversed, and a northerly current moved the black mass 10 miles along the precipitous coast of Marin County toward the entrance to Bolinas Lagoon.

There, for the next 36 hours, the major battle against the great San Francisco oil spill was waged. The lagoon, with miles of tidal flats, is a superb wildlife habitat that centers at Audubon Canyon Ranch, designated as a natural landmark by the National Park Service. The oil was a potential death warrant.

On Tuesday morning Audubon naturalist Clerin Zumwalt arrived at sunrise and found the ocean off Bolinas Lagoon coated with oil. He quickly telephoned for help from Standard Oil Company of California—owner of both the tankers—and then went to the lagoon entrance, where he found scores of people already at work.

After the San Francisco oil spill a volunteer swabs solvent on a cormorant to remove the gummy petroleum residues that clog its feathers. In this way nature lovers saved several hundred seabirds that would otherwise have perished.

"Everybody seemed to sense the danger," Zumwalt recalls. "Nobody was in charge, but someone had found ropes and gunnysacks, and somebody else had brought a tennis net, and by the time I got there two makeshift booms already were rigged across the channel. They had to swim out in that icy water to do it."

Zumwalt doubted the booms would hold back much oil, so he searched the countryside for straw. He finally located a load and had it dumped into the water between the booms to soak up the oil.

Keeping the oil out

Meanwhile, a battered cattle truck painted in psychedelic colors deposited a band of long-haired residents of a nearby commune. The newcomers hauled six telephone poles off the truck and lashed them to a cable, which was hauled across the channel by a small boat. At the same time, from the opposite shore 100 yards away, hard-hatted workers from Standard Oil were setting up their own boom—a polyethylene skimmer, like the kind used at refineries.

When the tide came that afternoon, the crowd of workers and spectators watched and hoped. The polyethylene boom soon broke, but the others held, and the straw soaked up immense quantities of oil.

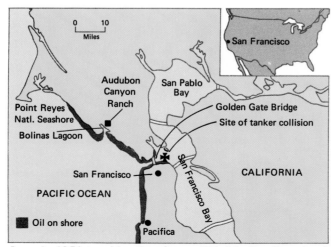

In early 1971 two big oil tankers collided in San Francisco's Golden Gate Strait (cross marks site), spilling nearly a million gallons of fuel oil into the water. Tides and currents spread the sticky, black mass along 55 miles of coastline.

Cleaning Up Oil Spilled at Sea

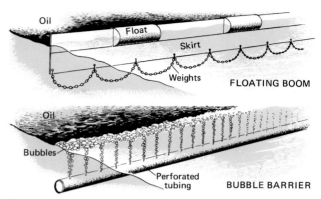

Floating booms supporting plastic skirts are among the best means of confining spilled oil at sea until it can be disposed of. However, waves and turbulence can carry oil over and under the boom. Bubble barriers work in calm water but cannot be used in rough weather. Various chemical agents that concentrate the oil and sink it are also being tried.

In a last-ditch effort to combat the San Francisco oil spill, volunteers spread bales of straw on the contaminated beach (above, top), then collected the oil-soaked debris (above, bottom) and carried it to disposal sites inland.

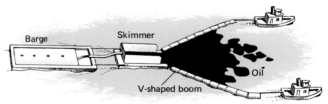

In one of many techniques used to clean up spilled oil, tugboats tow a V-shaped boom that funnels oil to a skimmer. The skimmer picks up the oil, separates it from most of the water, and pumps it into a storage barge.

Overnight and through the next day hundreds of students from local schools, the hard-hats from the refinery, and the longhairs from the commune worked together to save the wildlife of Bolinas Lagoon. By Wednesday the main mass of black death had moved out to sea. The lagoon with its unique habitat was saved—after the most sudden and dramatic of a long series of threats to its existence.

I first saw Audubon Canyon Ranch on a spring morning some 10 years ago. I had driven north from San Francisco. The lagoon, drained by a low tide, was a maze of channels winding among glistening sand flats. Diaphanous mists billowed from the retreating water. Out of one drifting fogbank appeared a bird so large that at first I thought it was an illusion. It was standing motionless on reedlike legs, its long neck slightly arched.

Then, graceful and dignified, the bird spread long wings and with powerful strokes took flight. It was an egret adorned with plumes of the breeding season. I kept the egret in sight as it soared against the backdrop of Bolinas Ridge. Beyond the great white bird were grassy hillsides where cattle pastured 1,000 feet above the Pacific, steep canyons where streams cascaded through redwood groves, and high ridges tufted

by Douglas firs. After a short flight the egret turned into a canyon and disappeared.

I continued along the lagoon and turned off at the same canyon. I parked and took a trail along the steep hill. After a few minutes' hike I was beyond the fog, and sunlight sifted through the branches of the laurels and live oaks. A half mile up the canyon I came upon an opening in the live oaks. The view through that forest window was unforgettable.

Congregated in the upper branches of a grove of redwoods were at least 100 egrets and great blue herons. Some stood over nests containing two or three young birds. Others were settled on soon-to-hatch eggs. Every redwood tree was, in effect, a high-rise apartment house, with separate living quarters on several levels. For more than 2 hours I watched the comings and goings at the heronry, and it was with reluctance that I finally walked back down the trail and away from the birds.

That the redwoods still stand in the canyon near Bolinas Lagoon is nearly a miracle. By 1960 a dozen breeding colonies of egrets and great blue herons had disappeared from the area, particularly along the San Francisco Bay shoreline. One by one the heronries had been displaced by shopping centers and marinas.

Stately great egrets roost in the redwood forests of Audubon Canyon Ranch in California. The egrets, 3-foot-tall birds that nest on all continents except Australia and Antarctica, breed in this sanctuary and winter in nearby areas of the State.

Birdwatchers at Audubon Canyon Ranch observe a distant egret roost (a closeup of the birds appears at left). Audubon Canyon and the adjacent marshlands are one of the major bird sanctuaries on the California coast.

Egret Plumes: A Near–Fatal Fad

Two ladies pose in egret-plumed hats, which were the height of turn-of-the-century fashion.
To satisfy the demand, egrets were shot by the hundreds of thousands. It took a concerted campaign by pioneer conservationists to ban the use of egret plumes in the United States, thus eliminating a major market and ending most of the slaughter.

But at Canyon Ranch, then a dairy farm, the birds remained, undisturbed by the cows that grazed the grassy hillsides. Nevertheless, the dairy business was on the wane there, and the ranch was just 15 miles from the growing city of San Francisco.

In 1961 Dr. Martin Griffin, president of the Marin Audubon Society, learned that a new owner was planning to log the redwoods and subdivide the ranch. Dr. Griffin knew that the canyon was the last major refuge for the great wading birds in central California. He knew he had to make some effort to save it.

Dr. Griffin alerted Marin Audubon Society board member William S. Picher, and the two plotted an audacious strategy. They approached the owner in San Francisco and asked if he would sell the 507-acre ranch. He was agreeable, but his price was a staggering $337,000. Griffin and Picher may have been inwardly dismayed, but they persuaded the board of directors of the Marin Audubon Society to launch a campaign to raise the money. The society at that point consisted of precisely 125 people. The largest sum of money it had ever raised was $200 to help send a state park ranger to a National Audubon Society summer camp. To even consider raising a third of $1 million was hardly rational. So the society made an irrational decision: It could not allow Canyon Ranch to be destroyed without making some attempt to save it.

The most urgent need was to stall for time until

A winter sun sets over the tidal flats of Bolinas Lagoon, feeding area for thousands of birds. The purchase of Audubon Canyon Ranch (bordering part of the lagoon) by conservationists stimulated many other conservation efforts.

long-range plans could be made. The owner agreed to wait 90 days if he was paid $1,000 as an option. Griffin and Picher spent most of the next 48 hours on the phone and persuaded 10 people, mainly Marin Audubon members, to contribute $100 each. Having bought 3 months' time, they set about raising another $3,000 for a further 6-month option.

They described the plight of Canyon Ranch to anyone who would listen. With the help of a growing corps of volunteers and the 1,000-member Golden Gate Audubon Society, which joined Marin Audubon as a cosponsor, they parlayed donations into a series of options that staved off the bulldozers for 15 months.

Griffin and Picher and their associates took increasing numbers of people on tours of Canyon Ranch. Few visitors were able to gaze through the forest window at the avian city in the redwoods without offering their help to save it. Many pledges were made on the spot.

Help from across the country

Pictures and news stories typed by volunteers went out to every newspaper in California. Pledges began to arrive from across the country. Two Audubon members made a film on the ranch, with impressive footage of the egrets and herons on the wing and in their nests. A Cincinnati businessman who saw the film contributed $3,000. Another viewer promised to donate $5,000

a year. A New York family made a memorial gift of $50,000, making possible a down payment and a contract to purchase the ranch.

Payments were scheduled to run through 1972. But the campaign had snowballed, and the full price of $337,000 was paid off—in what surely must be a record in conservation fund raising—by 1965. When money kept flowing in, Audubon members bought several hundred acres of tideland plus 234 acres adjoining South Canyon.

Audubon Canyon Ranch is now an environmental education center. The ranch is being managed to preserve natural values. Parking and improvements are restricted to the immediate area of the ranch house. A few trails have been built. And the old milking barn has been converted into a museum of the geology, ecology, and history of the Bolinas area. Hundreds of children from local schools are bused to the ranch for nature education every year.

The redwoods of Audubon Canyon, once a needle's breadth from the sawmill, should stand for centuries to shelter their contingent of egrets and great blue herons. But whether there will be egrets and herons left to return to Audubon Canyon in years to come depends on many imponderables. Not the least of these is the will of the thousands of people who come to the ranch on Bolinas Lagoon out of curiosity and leave with a sense of wonder.

The Seychelles fodi, or toq toq, named for its call, is holding its own on Cousin Island; it numbers about 600. This sparrow-sized bird, a member of the weaver bird family, feeds primarily on insects and fruit; it also eats terns' eggs.

One of the rarest birds in the world, the Seychelles warbler numbered only 30 in 1960. Now more than 70 of the insect-eating birds inhabit the dense brush of Cousin Island, and a few have been sighted on nearby Cousine.

Beacon of Hope in the Indian Ocean

Tony Beamish

The sign reads: "This island belongs to the birds." And so it does—for Cousin Island is now an international reserve, set up to save its rare species.

I have yet to find an atlas with a good map of the Seychelles Islands in it. They are either on the edge of a page or printed so small in the vast expanse of the Indian Ocean as to be unrecognizable as land. In 1967, on my first visit to the Seychelles, I had to wait until I reached Port Victoria, capital of the archipelago, to pinpoint the position of Cousin Island, the new nature reserve of the International Council for Bird Preservation (I.C.B.P.).

Cousin Island is very small, just a 60-acre coconut plantation surmounted by a rocky hill. At first sight it looks insignificant, certainly not worth the tremendous efforts by the I.C.B.P., the World Wildlife Fund, and thousands of nature lovers to acquire it.

A special island

Why did the I.C.B.P. choose Cousin and not one of the other 95 islands of the Seychelles? Not only did Cousin have the biggest concentration of seabirds in the islands, but it was also the last refuge of several threatened species of land birds and of a distinct form of the giant tortoise.

Cousin has been fortunate in its owners, especially the last two, France Jumeau and his widow Martha. As naturalists they took positive steps to protect the teeming wildlife of their island.

Mrs. Jumeau was on the white sand beach of Cousin Island to greet me. "Listen to my little bird singing!" she cried excitedly. Above the crashing of the sea on the reef I heard the melodious warbling of a bird. It was the Seychelles brush warbler, a bird that lives only on this 60-acre island.

At first glance Cousin appears to have been taken over by the fairy terns. They flutter to within a few feet of your face, standing in the air and shrieking loudly. You have to be careful where you walk to avoid treading on an egg or a chick. They lay eggs just anywhere—in the fork of a small branch, in the shallow step on a palm tree, on the rocks underfoot where the parents have to be wary of marauding lizards.

The warden of the reserve estimates that there are 15,000 pairs of fairy terns on the island and the same number of lesser and greater noddy terns as well. Other terns are present but are far less numerous.

Numerous on Cousin Island, dainty fairy terns have declined greatly on other Seychelles islands. Fairy terns lay only a single egg. People collect and eat them; marauding lizards and introduced predators, such as rats, cats, and barn owls, also take a toll.

The most striking of the seabirds are the frigate birds and the white-tailed tropic birds.

The hordes of seabirds are so arresting that you do not at first notice the land species—and when you do, it is hard to realize that you are looking at some of the world's scarcest living creatures. I saw my first land birds, apart from the warbler near the beach, around the houses where the laborers live. One of the wives was feeding the chickens, and two of the native species were joining the banquet: the toq toq and the Seychelles rufous turtledove. Other land birds that nest here are the Seychelles sunbird, the Madagascar fodi, the Seychelles moorhen, and the barred ground dove, probably an immigrant from Asia.

The ghostly wailing of the wedge-tailed shearwaters in their burrows on top of the hill is much louder now than it has been in the past. For years the chicks were cropped for the tables of the island inhabitants; now they are left unmolested. There is still a danger from poachers, but the birds should continue to increase.

At dusk, as I was walking home along the beach, I saw two hawksbill turtles coming up to lay their eggs. Formerly these reptiles were killed here for their valuable tortoiseshell, usually as they lay off the reef waiting to come ashore to make their nesting holes in the sand. Now at last they have a safe refuge—though, again the small resident staff has to be on a constant lookout for poachers.

The Cousin Nature Reserve is the first entire Indian Ocean island to be given international protection. It can become a breeding base from which other islands may be repopulated by species that once frequented them. It will provide valuable opportunities for scientific study of tropical plants and animals.

The new nature reserve is important on a wider front, too, for it has drawn local attention to the need for conservation. And it has done so in a way that is likely to impress doubters. Since the island is still earning revenue from the sale of coconuts, which helps to pay for upkeep, it has demonstrated that conservation and cultivation are not necessarily incompatible.

New hotels are going up on other islands in the Seychelles, roads are being built and improved, and there are numerous housing developments. So as the old dangers have receded, new ones have arisen. The tourist invasion has, however, a hopeful side to it. Wild animals in their natural habitat are a powerful tourist magnet. The example of Cousin may inspire other island owners to take steps to protect their wildlife. On one island the owner is cutting old palm trees to make room for a colony of sooty terns.

Cousin is a beacon of hope. If all goes well, its influence on the whole archipelago may at last put the island squarely back on the map—at least figuratively.

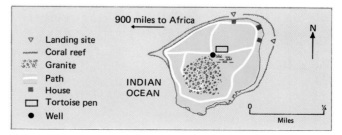

Ringed by a coral reef and traversed by paths for visitors, Cousin Island is the first entire island in the Indian Ocean to be given international protection. Tens of thousands of birds and a colony of giant tortoises live on the 60-acre preserve.

A Guide to Enjoying and Preserving Our Wildlife Heritage

From a suburban backyard to the great open spaces, wild creatures share the earth with us and add a special excitement to our lives. On the following pages you will find suggestions on where to find them, how to watch them, and how to help them survive.

CONTENTS

Herring gulls at Malibu Beach, California.

Invite Wildlife to Your Backyard

Jack Ward Thomas, Robert O. Bush, and Richard M. DeGraaf

Step by step, by planting the right trees and shrubs, you can create your own wildlife sanctuary. Here's a three-stage plan, with planting lists for your region. It's an exciting family project – and good conservation too.

Go out to your backyard and look around. Watch the fish weaving among the water lilies, the dragonflies moving in glittering arcs above the little pool. Don't move—the robins are busy feeding their youngsters in that nest above your head; squirrels are edging down the beech trunks behind you and darting into the shrubbery. The trumpet vine on your stone wall is almost irresistible to the hummingbird that just appeared, and song sparrows are adding their notes to the birdsong sifting down from the oaks and maples. If you're really patient, that timid rabbit might bring her brood onto the grass.

This isn't your yard, you say? It could be. If you have even a quarter acre of crabgrass right now, you can turn it into your own wildlife haven. Even a few square yards can become a wildlife refuge in miniature.

Where do you start? This backyard habitat plan is divided into three stages. No matter what your backyard looks like now, it will fit into one of them, give or take a few years' growth. But before you do anything, put your plan on paper, no matter how crudely. This is important because the planning you do at the outset will determine the whole course of your backyard program for attracting wildlife.

Stage 1. If you start with only a bare back lawn, then plant the trees, shrubs, and herbs suggested in the backyard plantings chart (page 293). Your yard will now be in Stage 1. At this point you will already have a usable wildlife habitat. In the early years you will need to augment food and water resources with artificial feeders and birdbaths. Bird nesting will be limited, but you can help with nesting boxes. Robins will feed on the lawn, and ground-feeding sparrows and finches will forage among shrubs and flowers.

If your yard already has trees and shrubs, but the kind, numbers, and placement don't fit the ideal backyard habitat plan illustrated here, work out

your own version. Use what you have to best advantage. Remove undesirable plants and relocate others.

Leave enough open space so you can observe the wildlife without disturbing it. Consider the eventual heights of your plantings so the taller ones will be in the rear. Vary the heights of masses of plants for a visually pleasing growth.

Stage 2. It takes about 5 to 10 years for a yard to progress from the initial plantings of Stage 1 to the fairly mature shrub conditions of Stage 2. The trees will be about 25 feet tall. If your yard is in this stage now but is too densely wooded with young trees and shrubs, plan to thin out the vegetation.

In Stage 2 there will be enough flowers and fruits to attract a variety of birds and insects, which will in turn attract reptiles and amphibians. You may want to replace the birdbath with a small pool. Robins will raise broods in the trees. Catbirds, cardinals, and song sparrows will nest in the denser shrubbery. Dusk will bring rabbits to browse in the security of your yard. Mornings will find chipmunks emerging from holes in your stone wall to search for food under the trees.

Stage 3. Starting from scratch, you can expect your backyard to look like Stage 3 about 30 to 40 years after the initial planting. This means a yard with a variety of mature trees producing fruits and nuts, plus mature shrubs and sufficient open areas. If, however, your yard already has a reasonable number of mature trees, you can plant shrubbery and low vegetation to achieve Stage 3 in 5 to 10 years.

This stage attracts the maximum number of wildlife species. Orioles and tanagers will nest in the higher branches; foliage-gleaning warblers will feed in the treetops. Rabbits may even raise their young in well-hidden nests. Squirrels will live in tree hollows or nest boxes. Chipmunks, field mice, garter snakes, toads, and butterflies and other insects may make your backyard home.

Four wildlife needs

All wildlife, indeed all life, requires four basic elements to survive: Food; water; cover, as protection from natural enemies and the elements; and areas where it can reproduce and bear its young in safety. Combinations of these four elements differ for each species, but you can plan a habitat that offers enough combinations to attract the greatest number and variety of wildlife your area will support.

Food for wildlife is easy to furnish. You can supplement natural growth with a variety of products, especially those for seed-eating birds. In fact, many people who don't have enough

In Stage 1, just after the initial plantings, the shrubs will be low and the trees scattered. Although the backyard is already a wildlife habitat, artificial aids such as feeders, nesting boxes, and birdbaths will attract more species.

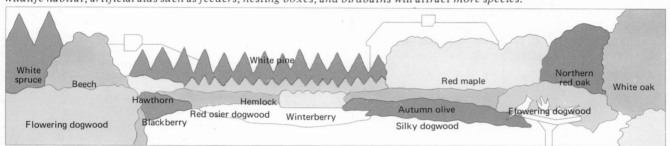

White spruce

Beech

White pine

Red maple

Northern red oak

White oak

Flowering dogwood

Hawthorn

Blackberry

Hemlock

Red osier dogwood

Winterberry

Autumn olive

Silky dogwood

Flowering dogwood

In Stage 2 below, 5 to 10 years after planting, the shrubs are almost full grown and the trees about 25 feet tall. A small manmade pond replaces the birdbath. Although some birds will still use nesting boxes and feeders, others will nest in the shrubs and feed on the fruits. The key above shows the locations of the plantings in the Stage 2 backyard, which is in the northeastern United States. For species that do well in other areas, see the chart on page 295.

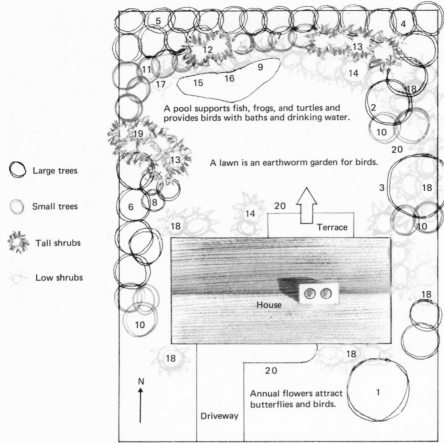

Large trees

Small trees

Tall shrubs

Low shrubs

A pool supports fish, frogs, and turtles and provides birds with baths and drinking water.

A lawn is an earthworm garden for birds.

Terrace

House

N

Driveway

Annual flowers attract butterflies and birds.

A view from above shows the vegetation in a home wildlife refuge; the chart on page 293 indicates the particular species planted. The stages in the development of the refuge, shown on pages 291 and 293, are viewed from the terrace.

land to provide water and cover can enjoy numerous kinds of animals through feeding alone.

The ideal wildlife management plan, however, supplies as much food as possible through the vegetation that you plant. Variety is necessary to meet the full year-round needs of many species.

Be sure to select your plants carefully to provide the maximum overlap of flowering and fruiting times. Food should be available as needed. For birds this means a year-round supply. If you have bird feeders, continue to fill them through the spring until new vegetation takes over.

You can fulfill wildlife's critical water needs—drinking and bathing—with a simple birdbath or ground-watering device. Most desirable, however, is a small pool with an area large enough to support plants that grow in water and around the edge. Your pool will become the site of a broad range of fascinating wildlife activity.

In addition to its wildlife value, the water area will provide a focal point in the landscape design. Locate it so as to provide maximum visibility from the terrace or windows of the house. You can encourage winter activity by keeping a section of the pool ice free, using a livestock trough warmer.

Cover is any place that protects animals from their predators and the weather. Different species have different cover requirements. These include rock piles or stone walls for chipmunks and lizards; brush piles or dense shrubs for cottontails and towhees; evergreens for chickadees and squirrels; water for frogs and turtles.

Cover also serves as home base—the farther an animal must venture from cover, the more vulnerable it is to predators. So try to provide cover close to food and water. Many cover plants can also be food plants.

All wildlife needs a specific kind of cover where it can reproduce and, in most cases, raise its young. Each reproductive area must offer protection from the elements and relative safety—either inaccessible to predators or well hidden.

The diversity of cover you need for a complete habitat requires mature trees, which provide den sites for squirrels and nesting places for birds. Until your habitat is complete, you can compensate for a lack of big trees with nest boxes for squirrels and some birds—for instance, house wrens, bluebirds, tree swallows, and woodpeckers.

When do you start? Today. Of course, the best time to plant trees and shrubs is spring or early fall. But you can make your all-important plan, clear out unproductive growth, and prepare your soil almost any time. Maybe you can build a bird feeder the first rainy or cold weekend.

What's the cost?

The answer to this question is also a question: How much do you want to spend? You can make your own plans, do your own work, and, if you don't mind waiting a little while for noticeable results, you can start with quite small plants.

On the other hand, you can hire a landscape architect to design your backyard and a landscape firm to do the installation. This is expensive, but you will see the fastest results in the shortest time.

You will have additional expenses for periodic maintenance. But the costs of fertilizer, water, and labor are no more for a wildlife backyard than for a lawn.

How big a backyard?

The backyard brought to life on these pages is about 100 feet by 120 feet (about ¼ acre). If your yard is smaller, it may be impossible to provide food, water, and cover for many species. But it *is* still possible to provide one or more of these needs and attract *some* wildlife.

While this backyard plan is designed for the Northeast, you can apply these same principles wherever you live. In Miami, fill your yard with night-blooming jasmine and lemon trees and listen to the mockingbirds. In Tucson, plant flowering cactuses and enjoy white-winged doves. In Vancouver, grow lupines and attract western bluebirds. Refer to the "Regional Equivalents" list for suitable plant materials for any yard, regardless of its location.

Your county agricultural agent or state university landscape specialist can give you advice on a wide variety of problems. Your local nurseryman can also assist you. If you live in a soil conservation district, you can get help on water and soil problems from the district office. Some State and Provincial

Stage 3, reached about 30 years after planting, attracts the maximum number of animal species. Trees are mature and producing fruits; the treetops, the higher branches, the lower branches, and the shrubs all host different species.

A well-chosen combination of plants provides food and cover for a variety of wildlife throughout the year, each plant filling a different need with the changing seasons. The plants have been positioned to create a "forest-edge" environment, which attracts the greatest variety of species. The plants shown here are some of those that grow well in the northeastern United States and southeastern Canada; a list of plants for different regions is found on page 295.

	SPECIES	FLOWERS	FRUITS	LIGHT	SOIL MOISTURE	WILDLIFE SERVED
TREES	1. Beech		Sept.-Oct.	Lt. shade or sun	Moist	Nuts, seeds, acorns: fall and winter food for squirrels, large songbirds. Spring, summer foliage: cover, reproductive areas for songbirds, tree-dwelling mammals, insects. Leafless branches: winter roosting for birds. Flowers not important to birds or mammals.
	2. Northern red oak		Sept.-Oct.	Lt. shade or sun	Moist	
	3. White oak		Sept.-Nov.	Lt. shade or sun	Moist or dry	
	4. Red maple			Shade or sun	Moist or well drained	
	5. White pine		Aug.-Sept.	Sun	Dry	Cones: fall, winter food for squirrels, songbirds. Boughs: year-round cover, reproductive areas for songbirds, tree-dwelling mammals, insects. Flowers not important to birds or mammals.
	6. White spruce		Aug.-Sept.	Sun	Dry	
	7. Hemlock			Shade or sun	Moist	
	8. Red cedar		Sept.-May	Sun	Moist or dry	
SMALL TREES	9. Winterberry	May	Oct.	Lt. shade	Wet or moist	Flowers: food for butterflies, other insects. Fruits: fall, winter food for songbirds. Spring, summer foliage: cover, reproductive areas for songbirds. Leafless branches: winter cover, roosting for songbirds.
	10. Flowering dogwood	Mar.-June	Aug.-Nov.	Sun	Well drained or dry	
SHRUBS	11. Hawthorn	June	Oct.-Mar.	Sun	Dry	
	12. Crab apple	Mar.-May	Sept.-Nov.	Sun	Moist or dry	
	13. Autumn olive	May-July	Sept.-Feb.	Sun or lt. shade	Moist or dry	
	14. Silky dogwood	May-July	Aug.-Sept.	Sun or lt. shade	Wet or dry	
	15. Red osier dogwood	May-Aug.	July-Oct.	Sun	Moist or wet	
	16. Elderberry	June-July	Aug.-Sept.	Sun	Moist or wet	Spring, early summer flowers: food for butterflies, other insects. Berries: food for songbirds, mammals, reptiles, amphibians, insects. Dead branches: winter cover for ground-dwelling mammals and birds.
	17. Blackberry	May-July	July-Sept.	Sun	Moist	
	18. Rhododendron	May-July	Aug.-Dec.	Shade	Moist	Spring flowers: food for butterflies, other insects, hummingbirds. Foliage: dense cover, reproductive areas for songbirds, mammals. Rhododendron foliage: winter cover for songbirds, mammals.
	19. Honeysuckle	June-July	July-Sept.	Sun or shade	Well drained or dry	
FLOWERS 20.	Sunflower	Aug.-Oct.	Sept.-Nov.	Sun	Moist or dry	Flowers: food for butterflies, other insects. Seeds: late summer, fall, winter food for many seed-eating birds, especially sparrows.
	Aster	Aug.-Oct.	Sept.-Nov.	Sun	Moist	
	Daisy	June-Aug.	July-Sept.	Sun	Dry	
	Marigold	Aug.-Oct.	Sept.-Nov.	Sun	Moist or dry	
	Black-eyed Susan	June-Sept.	July-Sept.	Sun	Dry	

game departments have staff biologists who may be able to help you. Your local zoo, natural-history museum, or nature center can tell you the specific needs of wildlife in your area. And some commercial nursery catalogs are gold mines of information.

You don't have a backyard?

If you have no yard, you can still provide food and water, using containers set in a window box or a glass-top window feeder. These can bring a bit of nature even into the lives of apartment dwellers—provided some birdlife is already present and your apartment is not too high above ground. With a little luck, birds will make your window a part of their daily routine.

As the trend toward urbanization continues, green space for people and plantings for wildlife will become increasingly important. Your small backyard island will be a happy haven for some wildlife. But you'll be more successful if you can persuade your neighbors to cooperate in a backyard habitat program. By working with your neighbors, you can create "wildlife neighborhoods" that will aid wildlife and make life more fun for you and your family.

Informally, you can share plant materials and ideas. Formally, you can plan together. For example, if your yard is in Stage 1, with only grass and shrubs, and next door a neighbor's yard has 25-foot trees, the combined habitat would be close to Stage 2 in completeness. If you are lucky enough to have a neighbor with a stream or pond, or with a fairly wild woodlot or field, your total habitat will attract wildlife much more successfully than your yard could alone. And if your neighbors like wildlife too, they are not as likely to complain if rabbits wander into their vegetable garden or lettuce patch.

Let's face it, some wildlife tenants are unwelcome. Rabbits may nibble the bark off shrubs. Squirrels may rob bird feeders or get into attics. Snakes repel some people, and bees and wasps may sting. You can accept the situation, or you can control it.

If you decide on control, you can either alter the habitat to eliminate the life requirements of the unwanted animals or remove the offending individuals. You can discourage squirrels by using bird feeders that are squirrel-proof, sealing the attic, and covering tree holes with tin. Or you may want to livetrap and transplant them. Move the bird feeder out of the reach of dogs and cats; move it closer to a hedge or other cover to which birds can retreat for safety; install tin cat guards on the poles that support feeders and birdhouses. Or chain the dog, bell the cat, build a fence.

What's the payoff?

As your habitat develops and grows, it will become an increasingly exciting and important part of your family's life. Your backyard can become a stage where wild animals are the stars and people the audience. Inviting wildlife to your backyard is probably the best way for children to learn a basic tenet of the complex science of ecology. Life operates in one large system, and everything in that system is interconnected.

The case presented here is simple: The human habitat can be wildlife habitat too. If we are to maintain any contact between city and suburban dwellers and nature, we must share our living space. Our society has been alerted to the deterioration of our environment, and we have heard the call to great crusades. Yet there is a question in many minds: What can one person do?

You can improve your own environment with a plan like this and, in doing so, exhibit a faith in the possibility of a solution to environmental problems. And you can do it where it means most to you—in your own backyard.

Build a Minipond for Wildlife

One of the easiest, quickest, and least expensive ways to attract wildlife is to provide water. Birds will visit the simplest birdbath, especially if there is cover nearby; a drip bath (a pan beneath a water-filled pail with a nail hole in the bottom) is also effective. A lily pond (below) or a more sophisticated, concrete-lined waterfall pool (right) will bring a delightful variety of animals to your backyard.

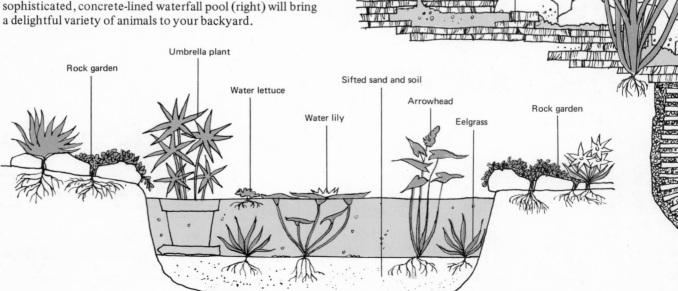

Border planting for wind protection
Plastic pipe
Rough mortared stones
Rock garden
Umbrella plant
Water lettuce
Sifted sand and soil
Water lily
Arrowhead
Eelgrass
Rock garden

What To Plant in Your Area

Few plants flourish in every region. The list below suggests food and cover plants that are known to thrive in the various climatic regions of the United States and southern Canada. These, of course, are only a few of the many possible species. You may well prefer to use others that are more readily available in your area.

TALL TREES		SMALL TREES	TALL SHRUBS	LOW SHRUBS	HERBACEOUS GROWTH
Northeast White pine Hemlock Colorado spruce Sugar maple White oak Red oak Beech Birch **Southeast** Longleaf pine Loblolly pine Shortleaf pine Ash Beech Walnut Live oak Southern red oak Tupelo Pecan Hackberry	**Northwest** Douglas fir Ponderosa pine Western white pine Lodgepole pine Colorado spruce Oregon white oak California black oak Big-leaf maple **Southwest** Arizona cypress Pinyon pine Live oak Black cherry	**Northeast** Flowering dogwood Crab apple Hawthorn Cherry Serviceberry Red cedar **Southeast** Holly Dogwood Serviceberry Cherry Persimmon Red cedar Palmetto Hawthorn Crab apple **Northwest** Serviceberry Dogwood Hawthorn **Southwest** Serviceberry Dogwood Mesquite Crab apple	**Northeast** Sumac Dogwood Elderberry Winterberry Autumn olive Wisteria **Southeast** Sumac Dogwood Elderberry **Northwest** Sumac Bitterbrush Russian olive Elderberry Buckthorn Madrona **Southwest** Mulberry Lotebush Sumac Manzanita Madrona	**Northeast** Blackberry Blueberry Bayberry Spicebush Huckleberry **Southeast** Blackberry Blueberry Bayberry Spicebush Huckleberry **Northwest** Blackberry Blueberry Snowberry Oregon grape **Southwest** Utah juniper Blackberry Spicebush Prickly pear Agarita	**Northeast** Panic grass Timothy Sunflower **Southeast** Lespedeza Panic grass Sunflower **Northwest** Turkey mullein Timothy Sunflower Filaree Lupine Fiddle-neck Tarweed **Southwest** Turkey mullein Sunflower Filaree Lupine Fiddle-neck

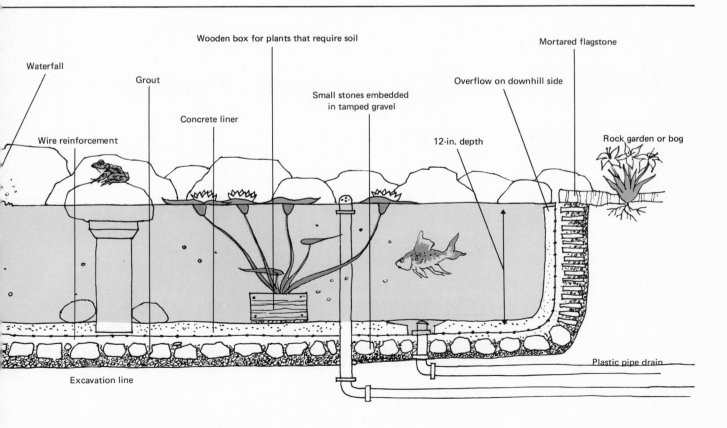

Bed and Board for Backyard Birds

Thomas P. McElroy, Jr.

Whether or not you make your own feeders and houses, you'll be fascinated by the birds that come to visit or nest.

Success in attracting birds to any yard or garden is a matter of providing them with what they need—a continuous supply of food and water, protective cover, and secure nesting sites.

Of all the ways of attracting birds, none is more successful—or gives more pleasure to backyard owners—than winter feeding. If in early fall you put out several well-placed feeders, they will soon find steady customers.

This extra food does not make wintering birds indifferent to their natural food supply; birds will leave well-stocked feeders to feast upon weed seeds, insect eggs, and grubs. But once you start a winter feeding program, you should continue it until there is again enough natural food to support birdlife.

What birds eat

The birds attracted by an artificial food supply can be divided into two groups—insect eaters, such as woodpeckers and warblers, and seed eaters, such as finches and sparrows. Some birds—blue jays, chickadees, and nuthatches, for instance—eat both types.

Suet. Beef suet is a favorite of all insect-eating birds. Chickadees, nuthatches,

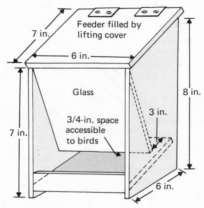

A hopper feeder filled with seeds attracts many species of birds. Its hinged cover makes it easy to fill, and its glass front shows at a glance when the seed supply needs replenishing.

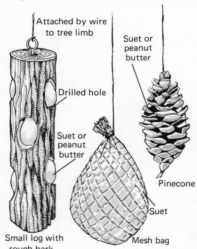

Easy-to-make feeders that hold suet or peanut butter bring insect eaters, such as woodpeckers, chickadees, and nuthatches, to your backyard. Seeds may be mixed with suet or peanut butter.

tufted titmice, brown creepers, and blue jays are extremely fond of it. Suet is practically the only food that will attract woodpeckers. Juncos, white-throated sparrows, and tree sparrows will feed on it during cold spells. Finely chopped suet will often attract wintering warblers.

Suet mixtures. The addition of any or all of the following ingredients to melted suet will make a very acceptable winter delicacy: Millet, sunflower seeds, raisins, cornmeal, oatmeal, rice, cracked corn, chopped peanuts, and cooked noodles or spaghetti. Suet mixtures can be used to make molded cakes or can be poured into coconut shells or other containers.

Peanut butter. A favorite of chickadees, peanut butter is eaten readily by tree sparrows, juncos, and many other species. The peanut oil helps provide the extra warmth and energy needed in cold weather. To attract brown creepers and nuthatches, peanut butter should be spread on rough-barked trees.

Sunflower seeds. Chickadees, titmice, nuthatches, cardinals, purple and house finches, goldfinches, evening grosbeaks, cardinals, and crossbills will eat great quantities of these large seeds.

Hemp seeds. Most seed-eating birds prefer hemp seeds to other seeds. Hemp oil makes the seeds extremely nourishing as a winter food, but they are expensive.

Millet. A favorite of sparrows and goldfinches, millet is an inexpensive bulk filler for any seed mixture.

Buckwheat. The best customers of buckwheat are bobwhites, pheasants, mourning doves, and blue jays.

Cracked corn. The smaller sizes of cracked corn are acceptable to seed eaters, especially tree sparrows and juncos. Cracked corn also makes a good filler when mixed with millet and hemp.

Seed mixtures. There are numerous mixtures of wild-bird food on the market. Many mixtures are expensive. If you expect to use large amounts, you can combine your own ingredients and save money. A recommended formula follows: Sunflower seeds, 25 percent; hemp seeds, 25 percent; millet (small yellow), 20 percent; millet (large yellow or white), 20 percent; buckwheat, 5 percent; fine cracked corn, 5 percent.

Nutmeats. Accepted readily by blue jays, chickadees, cardinals, nuthatches, and titmice, nutmeats are expensive.

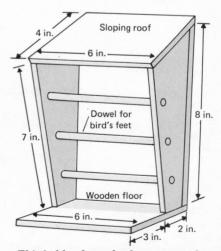

This ladder-front feeder, mounted on a tree or pole, holds suet cakes and also makes a handy perch. Use an aluminum can as a mold for the suet, or buy commercially prepared suet cakes.

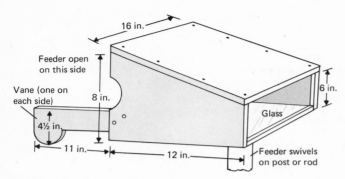

The weather-vane feeder, pivoted to swing with the wind, keeps its open side away from driving wind or snow. The seeds inside stay dry, and the birds are protected.

The glass-top window feeder allows closeup observation of birds while protecting the food from rain and snow. Adding a holder for suet or peanut butter attracts even more birds.

They should not be included in any mixture to be kept for a long time, as they often become rancid. Finely ground dog biscuits are good substitutes for nutmeats.

Raisins. Catbirds, mockingbirds, hermit thrushes, and robins eat raisins readily. Catbirds prefer them cut in small pieces.

Dried berries. The fruits of the dogwood, viburnum, mountain ash, bittersweet, and bayberry are favorites.

Oranges. Orioles, rose-breasted grosbeaks, catbirds, blue jays, and flickers find oranges to their liking. Secure orange halves to posts or trees or put oranges in your feeders.

Bananas. Scarlet and summer tanagers like bananas. Partially peel them and place them out in the open.

Bread. Pieces of bread on the lawn will attract grackles, starlings, sparrows, red-winged blackbirds, and robins.

Other foods. Rabbit food (in pellets), cooked noodles and potatoes, fatty meat, and apple peelings are accepted by many birds.

Grit. When the ground is covered with snow, birds will welcome an accessible supply of grit. Clean sand or fine gravel can be added to a seed mixture or placed in separate containers. Finely crushed clam or oyster shells are also a good dietary addition.

Homes for birds

When you improve your yard or garden to attract birds, don't overlook the possibility of providing nest facilities: More than 50 species of American birds will accept nesting boxes.

Before you build or buy a birdhouse, ask yourself these questions: Is the house designed for a specific kind of bird? Does the house provide drainage and ventilation? Can it be cleaned easily? Although well-built and properly designed birdhouses are now on the market, you can save money by build-

Plant a Garden for Hummingbirds

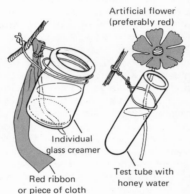

(A) Quince. (B) Wall with trumpet vine, honeysuckle, clematis. (C) Beauty bush. (D) Wall with honeysuckle, clematis. (E) Albizzia (tree). (F) Butterfly bush. (G) Weigela. (H) Hedge with honeysuckle, Siberian pea shrub. (★) Artificial hummingbird feeders.

(1) Columbine. (2) Hollyhock. (3) Coralbells. (4) Salvia. (5) Dianthus. (6) Delphinium. (7) Petunia. (8) Nicotiana. (9) Gladiolus. (10) Bee balm. (11) Foxglove. (12) Scabiosa. (13) Snapdragon. (14) Phlox. (15) Cleome.

Ever since the discovery that hummingbirds would accept an artificial nectar in the form of sugar water, thousands of people have been using this substitute food to attract the birds to their gardens. Studies and observations made during the past few years, however, indicate that a continuous diet of sugar water may do more harm than good.

Honey water, which contains a high percentage of carbohydrates, proteins, and minerals, is an acceptable substitute. To make it, mix one part honey with three parts boiled water. A small amount of red food coloring added to this syrup will make it more enticing and is especially helpful in establishing new feeders. The honey syrup can be used in any homemade or commercially manufactured hummingbird feeder.

One of the most practical feeders is an inverted container with a small feeding hole at the bottom. This type of feeder will be used less by insects than open-top styles. Attractive and practical feeders can be made from vials, test tubes, pillboxes, chemists' bottles, individual cream bottles like those used in restaurants, and similar small glass containers. The bottle-type feeder can be made more attractive to hummingbirds by rimming the top with an artificial flower of aluminum or plastic and painted bright red. Attach the feeders to individual stakes and place them in your flower beds.

The surest way to attract hummingbirds is to plant a section of your garden especially for them. The garden, through the correct selection of plants, should be in continuous bloom from spring until fall.

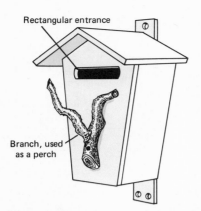

Rectangular entrance

Branch, used as a perch

Wrens will nest in a small wooden box with a letter-slot opening and a stick perch. The top is hinged to permit easy cleaning after the young birds have flown away in the late summer.

ing your own; most practical bird-houses are very simple in design and construction.

Wrens. The easiest of all birds to attract to artificial nest sites, wrens will build in almost any type of box. It is better, however, to provide boxes specially designed for them.

A house with a rectangular entrance facilitates nest building and the feeding of young. Boxes for house wrens should have an entrance 7/8 inch high by 2 or 2½ inches wide, small enough to prevent competition from house sparrows. If you have both house wrens and Bewick's wrens, the height of the entrance should be 1 inch. Carolina wrens need a 1½-inch opening.

Wrens will use nesting boxes placed on posts, the sides of buildings, or tree

branches, but stationary boxes located in open areas are preferable.

Bluebirds. In many areas the bluebird population has decreased alarmingly because the birds cannot find suitable natural nesting cavities. Putting up boxes for bluebirds in the country is a worthy conservation endeavor; bluebirds will seldom nest in urban or suburban places.

Houses intended for bluebirds are often invaded by house sparrows. To discourage the sparrows, place the boxes rather low (5 feet) on a post out in the open and as far away as possible from buildings. Bluebirds nest early and usually rear two broods a year. Boxes should be ready by mid-March.

Tree swallows. Tree swallows like a box out in the open, preferably along the borders of a pasture, meadow, swamp, or pond where flying insects are abundant. The box should be on a post 6 to 15 feet in height, away from shade trees. Unlike most songbirds, tree swallows tolerate neighbors of their own species if boxes are at least 50 feet apart.

Woodpeckers. The downy, hairy, and redheaded are the woodpecker species most likely to use nesting boxes. They prefer the log type of house that closely duplicates a natural nest site. Boxes are most acceptable when they are placed on dead tree stubs in groves, semiopen woodlands, or old orchards. An inch or more of sawdust, fine wood chips, or dry rotted wood should be placed in the bottom of a woodpecker house so the birds can shape a nest.

Nuthatches, titmice, and chickadees. These woodland birds like woodland borders but can be enticed to nest in

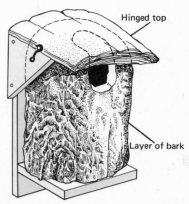

Hinged top

Layer of bark

A hollow-log house with a hinged roof is a design that can be adapted to suit the needs of a wide variety of birds. The chart on page 299 gives the house dimensions required by each species.

garden areas that are not too open or sunny. Boxes may be placed on posts, trees, or tree stubs. Use log-type boxes.

Robins and phoebes. Robins will accept a shelf or bracket type of box with one or more open sides. Boxes placed under the overhanging eaves of a shed, garage, or porch roof, or on an arbor in the garden, will be most acceptable. Phoebes will use the same type of shelf or bracket. The shelves will have a natural appearance if stained a dull color or made of weathered lumber.

Purple martins. Many people who are interested in birds want a colony of martins, but often their efforts go unrewarded. There isn't any magic formula that will guarantee success in enticing martins, but if you offer them a properly constructed house in a well-chosen

Bringing Back the Bluebird

The eastern bluebird—a gaily colored, sweetly warbling insect eater—is in trouble because of a shortage of nesting sites. One of three North American bluebird species, it nests east of the Rocky Mountains in dead trees (which are now often removed) and in wooden fenceposts (which are being replaced by metal ones). In addition, many of the cavities that could be used by nesting bluebirds have been usurped by the house sparrow and the starling, two nonnative species introduced from Europe.

If you have a backyard or an open area in a small town, a suburb, or a rural area, you can help the bluebird by putting out nesting boxes in late winter. Bluebird boxes don't have to be elaborate; the one shown here can give bluebirds protection against starlings and house sparrows, predators such as raccoons, and bad weather. The houses should be placed out in the open and mounted on posts at a height of 3 to 5 feet.

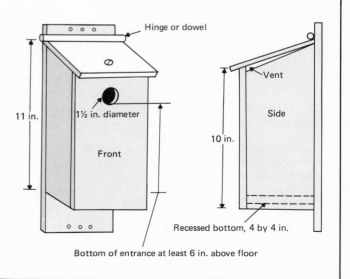

Hinge or dowel

11 in.

1½ in. diameter

Front

Bottom of entrance at least 6 in. above floor

Vent

Side

10 in.

Recessed bottom, 4 by 4 in.

location, you will have met two essential requirements.

The house illustrated here, recommended by the U.S. Department of Agriculture, is a practical and successful design. The house should be erected out in the open, well away from trees and buildings, on top of a pole 15 to 20 feet in height. A nearby body of water offers additional enticement.

Once a colony is established, the birds will return to the same location year after year. For this reason the supporting structure should be a permanent one, preferably a 15- to 20-foot wooden pole or a 3-inch steel pipe. (See illustration below.) The pole may be mounted with two bolts between a pair of channel irons set in concrete.

Screech owls and saw-whet owls. Screech owls will accept nest boxes more readily than other owls. Screech owls frequent old orchards and open groves of trees. Houses that are covered with bark or made of hollow logs are excellent; fasten the box rather high in a tree, preferably to the main trunk. The same type of box and location may prove attractive to saw-whet owls.

Locating and mounting boxes

Birdhouses often fail to attract the tenants for which they were intended. This difficulty can frequently be attributed to a bad choice of location. The average garden, lawn, or backyard should contain a limited number of nesting boxes. Most birds of the same species do not like to nest near one another. In a small area you will attract more tenants by putting up one house for each of a few species rather than by attempting to attract a family to every post and tree.

Trees or shrubs near feeders afford birds an easy escape from hawks and cats. Evergreen trees and hedges provide excellent cover.

Points to remember

• Design every birdhouse for a specific kind of bird.
• Never build a box with more than one compartment (except for martins).
• Build your houses of wood, not of tin or other metals.
• Include provisions for drainage and ventilation in each house.
• Use brass or galvanized hardware.
• Use dull colors for painting or staining—brown, green, or gray.
• Place boxes where cats cannot obtain access, or use metal cat guards.
• Place boxes out in the open. Avoid dense foliage and deep shade.
• Clean boxes thoroughly after each brood of birds leaves the nest.

Different Birds, Different Nesting Boxes

Successful birdhouses follow the recommended dimensions exactly. Too large an entrance may let in predators and competitors; one too small will keep out the desired species. The height above the ground is also an important factor.

SPECIES	FLOOR OF CAVITY	DEPTH OF CAVITY	ENTRANCE ABOVE FLOOR	DIAMETER OF ENTRANCE	HEIGHT ABOVE GROUND
	Inches	Inches	Inches	Inches	Feet
Bluebird	5x5	8	6	1½	5–10
Robin	6x8	8	(a)	(a)	6–15
Chickadee	4x4	8–10	6–8	1⅛	6–15
Titmouse	4x4	8–10	6–8	1¼	6–15
Nuthatch	4x4	8–10	6–8	1¼	12–20
House wren	4x4	6–8	1–6	1–1¼	6–10
Bewick's wren	4x4	6–8	1–6	1–1¼	6–10
Carolina wren	4x4	6–8	1–6	1½	6–10
Violet-green swallow	5x5	6	1–5	1½	10–15
Tree swallow	5x5	6	1–5	1½	10–15
Barn swallow	6x6	6	(a)	(a)	8–12
Purple martin	6x6	6	1	2½	15–20
Song sparrow	6x6	6	(a)	(a)	1–3
House finch	6x6	6	4	2	8–12
Starling	6x6	16–18	14–16	2	10–25
Phoebe	6x6	6	(b)	(b)	8–12
Crested flycatcher	6x6	8–10	6–8	2	8–20
Flicker	7x7	16–18	14–16	2½	6–20
Golden-fronted woodpecker	6x6	12–15	9–12	2	12–20
Redheaded woodpecker	6x6	12–15	9–12	2	12–20
Downy woodpecker	4x4	8–10	6–8	1¼	6–20
Hairy woodpecker	6x6	12–15	9–12	1½	12–20
Screech owl	8x8	12–15	9–12	3	10–30
Saw-whet owl	6x6	10–12	8–10	2½	12–20
Barn owl	10x18	15–18	4	6	12–18
Kestrel	8x8	12–15	9–12	3	10–30
Wood duck	10x18	10–24	12–16	4	10–20

(a) One or more sides open   (b) All sides open

A Home for Purple Martins

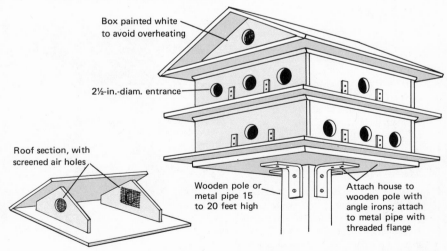

Box painted white to avoid overheating

2½-in.-diam. entrance

Roof section, with screened air holes

Wooden pole or metal pipe 15 to 20 feet high

Attach house to wooden pole with angle irons; attach to metal pipe with threaded flange

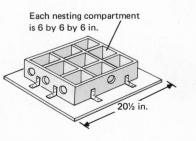

Each nesting compartment is 6 by 6 by 6 in.

20½ in.

Purple martins are welcome guests not only because of their insect consumption but also because of their rich color and graceful flight. Highly social birds, they nest in colonies. This "apartment house," made of durable wood painted white to reflect heat, is attractive to martins. This design provides nesting compartments for 16 families of purple martins; even larger houses have been used successfully.

A New Way To Watch Birds

Jean George

A hobby may become an absorbing lifetime interest when you know how to interpret the secrets of bird behavior.

In the wild and windy months of spring, thousands of birds—flickers, bluebirds, tanagers, sparrows, and finches—are moving north. And on the way they're providing a new kind of pleasure in an unprecedented number of homes across the land. Purveyors of birdseed mixtures used in backyard feeding stations report record-breaking business, and sales of bird books are surging rapidly upward. In addition, memberships in the National Audubon Society and the National Wildlife Federation have increased at an unparalleled rate during the past 5 years.

A new kind of pleasure? Decidedly. A few years ago amateur birdwatchers contented themselves with adding up the number of species they could record in their "life lists." Today they are more interested in bird behavior—bird reading, it's called.

People study birds not only in the country and suburbs but in cities. (The parks of New York City alone are hosts to more than 400 species every year.) I myself first caught the bird-reading bug one winter day in college when I saw a bird alight in the newly fallen snow. It was a junco, and it began to stir up a tiny blizzard by flicking its wings and swirling the snow into its breast feathers and over its back. The next day I learned that the bird was not bathing in snow, as I had thought, but was aligning its feathers. "The snow straightens the feathers out," my ornithology professor said, "forming an airtight insulating layer beneath the feathers that holds in the body heat." I was won to the game.

One fascinating—and encouraging—aspect of bird reading is that many of the breakthroughs in behavioral understanding have been made not by professional ornithologists but by amateurs. Consider the experiences of an English businessman, H. Eliot Howard, who for years took detailed notes on bird activity around his home in Birmingham.

An inspired amateur

Howard observed that the male of a mated pair would sing from the same branch or treetop each morning, and that when he approached, the bird did not fly away; it moved around and around in the general area of its "singing post." He mapped these posts and, in a flash of insight, saw that each pair had a piece of property and that the males were singing not for joy or love but to let it be known that "No Trespassing" signs were up. When Howard published his *Territory in Bird Life* in 1920, ornithologists the world over hailed the book with embarrassed enthusiasm. This nonprofessional had seen

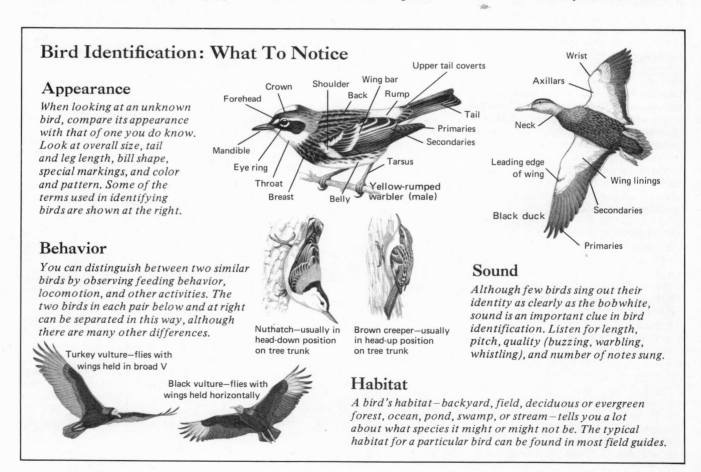

Bird Identification: What To Notice

Appearance

When looking at an unknown bird, compare its appearance with that of one you do know. Look at overall size, tail and leg length, bill shape, special markings, and color and pattern. Some of the terms used in identifying birds are shown at the right.

Forehead • Crown • Shoulder • Wing bar • Back • Rump • Upper tail coverts • Tail • Primaries • Secondaries • Mandible • Eye ring • Throat • Breast • Belly • Tarsus • Yellow-rumped warbler (male)

Wrist • Axillars • Neck • Leading edge of wing • Wing linings • Secondaries • Primaries • Black duck

Behavior

You can distinguish between two similar birds by observing feeding behavior, locomotion, and other activities. The two birds in each pair below and at right can be separated in this way, although there are many other differences.

Nuthatch—usually in head-down position on tree trunk

Brown creeper—usually in head-up position on tree trunk

Turkey vulture—flies with wings held in broad V

Black vulture—flies with wings held horizontally

Sound

Although few birds sing out their identity as clearly as the bobwhite, sound is an important clue in bird identification. Listen for length, pitch, quality (buzzing, warbling, whistling), and number of notes sung.

Habitat

A bird's habitat—backyard, field, deciduous or evergreen forest, ocean, pond, swamp, or stream—tells you a lot about what species it might or might not be. The typical habitat for a particular bird can be found in most field guides.

what had been staring them in the face for years.

Seven years later, another amateur, Margaret Morse Nice, a housewife in Columbus, Ohio, put up a feeder to learn about the birds around her. She became enthralled with the song sparrow and its beautiful, bubbling voice. Over the next 10 years she banded hundreds of these birds, traced them from egg to death, charted territorial fluctuations, and compiled voluminous notes on song variations and postures. The result of her work, *Studies in the Life History of the Song Sparrow,* is today a model for Ph.D. candidates in ornithology as well as a bible for bird readers.

What to watch for

In reading bird behavior, you observe what an individual is doing, then go on your hunches. For example, while studying the Wilson's storm petrel, British bird reader Brian Roberts noticed that when one of these birds took off, the white band on its rump flashed, and instantly its flock took off with it. The white band, Roberts concluded, was a visual signal to get up and move. This observation has since been applied to many other birds that travel together in flocks.

Another readily observable law is that of species dominance: A cardinal will run off a redpoll, a mockingbird will replace a cardinal. Dominance is also exercised among individuals of the same species. A neighbor of mine studied this by placing a mirror on a feeder. Seeing himself, a male bird generally reacts in one of two ways. If he stands tall, flattens his feathers, raises his crest and tail, and finally flips his wings and tail, he is being intimidated. On the other hand, if he puffs up his feathers to look larger, then crouches and vibrates his wings, he is dominating the bird in the mirror. The excessively dominant will attack.

Occasionally, some strange bird activity and a shrewd deductive hunch will add to the general store of behavioral knowledge. Several winters ago, while up in the Far North, bird artist George Miksch Sutton was puzzled to see a snowy owl puff up its feathers, open its beak, and tilt its whole body to one side in a most bizarre manner. It was midday, and the sun was shining full upon the owl. Suddenly, it occurred to Sutton that even nocturnal animals require direct warm sunlight. The owl was taking sun on its body by turning up its feathers and opening its bill. It is now known that this is done by all birds, and bird readers regularly see birds sunning themselves in the bushes surrounding feeding areas.

Another facet of bird reading is the interpretation of physical characteristics. Wings can tell much about a bird. Short, compact wings carry a bird through thick underbrush. Long, tapered ones are found on birds of the open sky. A bird's legs tell where and how it feeds. Birds that spend most of their time catching insects on the wing have tiny feet and legs. On the other hand, towhees, doves, and sparrows—ground feeders that seek seeds and creeping insects—have appropriately long, strong legs.

Birds' bills tell us what they eat. Witness the powerful nutcrackers of the grosbeak and finch, the sharp chisel of the woodpecker that drills for tree-dwelling insects. Most astonishing of all is the crossbill's beak, a deformed-looking thing intertwined at the tip. I once lured a flock of these engaging birds to my yard with branches of cone-laden pines and dried stalks of weeds. Climbing about like little parrots, the crossbills opened cones and seed coverings by pressing the top bill down, the bottom bill up, and prying like a staple remover while the tongue snatched the seed.

Why bird reading is vital

In addition to providing enjoyment for millions of people, bird reading has a serious purpose. For today the birds of North America have been put to work, serving as, what one noted ornithologist calls, "monitors of the environment." It is known, for example, that DDT makes the eggshells of many species so thin that they break under the weight of incubating parents. And it is known that nestlings receiving food contaminated with lead or other harmful chemicals quickly die off. Eight years ago, to keep track of chemical contamination across the country, Cornell University's Laboratory of Ornithology started a computerized Nest-Record Card Program. To date, there are 120,000 cards on file from bird readers who keep tabs on the robin nesting on the porch or the catbird in the bush. A lab technician told me recently: "The avian birthrate is a sure indicator of environmental conditions. A deteriorating ecosystem can be spotted quickly and checked before it gets to the catastrophe stage. This has happened a few times already."

I for one never weary of bird reading. Late one recent afternoon I listened to the chirps and calls that mark the end of day. Birds were darting to cover; a few sparred for toeholds in a bush; then the "All's well" signal was sounded by a finch that was settling into a juniper tree nearby. I moved closer and saw it squat on a twig—a tendon tightened its toes around the twig so it would not fall off while asleep. The wind blew, the sky darkened. Then, as my own vision faded, the finch closed its eyes and tucked its head into its shoulder feathers. At that precise moment the whole flock fell silent, and I, too, was at one with the world.

Tips for Birding

First steps. Borrow a field guide and binoculars; ask a knowledgeable friend to take you to a favorite birding spot.

Choosing a field guide. Some bird books cover a country or a continent, some a region. Get advice from birders or visit a good bookstore. Most guides group closely related species together; others classify birds by habitat.

What binoculars? Select a pair that is comfortable for you to handle. For most birding 7 x 35 center-focus binoculars are the best choice.

When to go. The best times are early morning (until 10 in the summer) and late afternoon (after 4).

What time of year? Each season has its bird bonuses. Spring migration usually brings a parade of temporary visitors. Summer is the time to look for nesting birds; there are even field guides to recognizing birds' nests. Fall and winter bring flocks of waterfowl. A hard winter will force seed-eating birds and snowy owls to fly far south. After a violent storm windblown strays may be far from their normal range.

How to behave. Wear dark or neutral-colored clothing. Walk slowly and don't talk. Avoid sudden, jerky movements. Find birds with your naked eye; then, without moving your eye from the spot, slowly raise your binoculars. You can coax elusive species into the open with imitations of birdcalls and whistles or squeaking sounds; try kissing the back of your hand.

Join a group. You can learn a lot on your own by visiting bird collections in your local museum and by studying a field guide. But by joining a group, you benefit from its collective experience.

Involve your children. Most youngsters learn to spot and recognize birds faster than adults. There's no better time of life to take up this richly rewarding hobby.

A final word. When birding, carry a small notebook and a checklist of the birds of your area. (Many bird clubs publish such lists.) Use the list as a permanent record and the notebook for descriptions or rough sketches. When you return home, study the illustrations and descriptions of every new bird and fix them firmly in your mind. If you learn even one or two species in this way every time you go out, you will build up your bird knowledge at a surprising rate.

How To Photograph Wildlife

Heather Angel

You don't need an expensive camera, but you do need to know how to approach or attract animals. An expert wildlife photographer tells how.

Bird photography does not require elaborate and expensive equipment. A long-focus lens or a focal-length extender is essential for photographing most birds, but neither of these need be an expensive item. And groups of birds can be photographed with a basic camera.

One worthwhile project is to strive to collect a series of pictures covering the complete life history of a species—even one as common as a robin or house sparrow. Such a series would illustrate the difference between the sexes, courtship displays, nest building, eggs, hatching, development of fledglings, feeding by parents, preening, drinking, bathing, flight, territorial behavior, and differences in seasonal plumages.

Birds in the garden

The best place to begin photographing birds is in the garden. But garden birds, even those fed daily, are naturally timid. Unless the camera is on a tripod and triggered from a distance with a pneumatic cable release, a long-focus lens will be necessary.

A window near a flat-topped bird feeder makes an effective blind. Try to position the feeder so that the background will not conflict or merge with the birds. Birds can also be photographed on a perch near the feeder. The photograph will look authentic if the background and perch look natural and if the feeder is not in the picture.

Birds at the nest

Locating a nest suitable for photographing is often a time-consuming preliminary. You can systematically search such likely places as hedges or observe with binoculars the route taken by an adult bird with food. Once you find a nest, see whether there are eggs or fledglings inside. If the interior of the nest is not visible from the ground, tie a mirror on a pole to view the inside.

Most birds at the nest are best photographed from a blind. For photographing birds such as ducks and geese, gulls, sandpipers, and other shorebirds whose young leave the nest soon after hatching, the blind should be put in place a few days before the eggs hatch; at that time the adults are least likely to desert the nest. For species whose young remain in the nest for some time, the blind can be set up a few days after hatching.

There are two essential requirements for a blind: It must be rigid, and it must be opaque. Readymade blinds are available. But a blind can be made from burlap or canvas, supported by a rigid framework of four vertical poles, connected at the top with four crosspieces and steadied with guy ropes if necessary. The opening should be away from the nest and always tied down.

One point worth stressing is the importance of approaching the blind with another person, who can then leave. Most birds will be fooled into believing the blind has been deserted.

Wait until the parents have fed the young several times before taking any pictures. This will make the birds less nervous and also indicate their direction of approach and whether they alight on a perch before entering the nest.

A noisy shutter will disturb most birds and may even frighten them away. This problem can be partly overcome by muffling the camera with a padded cover or blimp.

A car, with the engine turned off, can make a useful blind for photographing birds perched on fences or trees beside the road. Longer exposure times will be possible if the camera is clamped by a ball-and-socket head to the base of the car window.

Birds in flight

Flocks of birds are easier to photograph in flight than individual birds:

Photographing Zoo Animals

Choose a day when the zoo will not be crowded. Most zoos are really busy only during the summer and on weekends. Get there as early as possible—many animals are more active in the morning than later in the day. Animals behave in special ways at different times of the year, so walk around to check what is happening. Keep your eyes open for distinctive behavior, such as courtship in birds or play in mammals.

Take advantage of weather conditions. On warm sunny days many mammals sunbathe; vultures pose with their wings half opened. In warm rain birds sing and preen their feathers. Hazy days are best for photographing animals enclosed by high bars or wires, since the shadows from the barrier will not show then. Snow makes an excellent background for polar bears or penguins.

Positioning your camera

Once you have chosen your animals, decide the best distance and angle for photographing them. Try to find a position from which you can take a picture without clutter but with interesting colors, textures, or shapes. Take into account the design of the cage; see if it will help frame your picture.

By getting lower (bending your knees and crouching), you can often make the animal look more imposing or find a better background for your picture. A high viewpoint is less often desirable. An animal seen from above looks squat, with very short legs. If the design of the cage means that you cannot avoid a high viewpoint, photograph the animal when it is standing away from the barrier.

Working around the barriers

Where there are still old-fashioned bars keeping people away from the cages, photographing is difficult—if you photograph the animals, you also photograph the bars. Unless you actually *want* a picture with bars (in order to create a special effect), you should choose exhibits without bars.

If you can get your camera close up to the barrier, you can take good pictures by making sure that no bar or wire is in front of the lens. A strand of wire in front of the lens will not show if the camera is really close to it, preferably

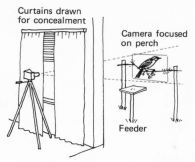

A simple backyard photographic setup can yield naturalistic photographs like this mockingbird (left). A feeder out in the open attracts birds; a branch tied to posts serves as a perch. Photographer and camera are concealed indoors.

The working distances are greater, and focusing is not as critical.

If possible, observe the birds' flight patterns before starting to photograph. Birds tend to rise into the wind, so a good waiting position for you is upwind.

The sky makes a fine background for solitary birds in flight. Be careful not to underexpose birds viewed against a clear blue sky. Dark birds will always be silhouetted against the sky. Light-colored birds will be silhouetted only if the sun is high in the sky.

Long-focus lenses are usually essential for photographing birds in flight. A 135-mm, 200-mm, and possibly even a 300-mm lens can be handheld on a 35-mm camera, but a longer lens must be steadied either with a shoulder pod or a tripod. Sharp pictures of birds in flight will be possible only with careful focusing and a fast shutter speed.

Speeds of 1/500 or 1/1,000 of a second are needed for photographing a bird crossing the line of sight; but if it is flying head-on toward the camera, 1/125 of a second is sufficient to freeze it. Even when taken at 1/1,000 of a second, birds with rapid wing beats will have blurred wings. This blur can be effective for suggesting movement. Fast films are essential for taking flight pictures by available light, when using fast shutter speeds combined with small apertures.

Finding mammals to photograph

The first consideration is finding the subjects. Mammals tend to be creatures of habit. In dry tropical regions the animals will congregate at a waterhole. Deer will usually move to a favorite area to feed at dawn or dusk.

Most mammals have an acute sense

of smell, and so the photographer must always stalk them from downwind. A long-focus lens is essential for photographing wild animals by stalking, and a shoulder pod will help to steady the camera. Gradually move forward from tree to tree when the animal is feeding or has its head turned away. If there is no cover, it is better to keep walking or crawling slowly than to freeze suddenly.

Attracting small mammals

Small mammals active during the day are best stalked by crawling on your hands and knees or even by inching forward on the belly. Squirrels can be attracted by laying out nuts and raisins on stumps and logs; rabbits can be lured by baiting with food pellets bought in a pet shop.

A bait mixture that attracts nocturnal mammals can be made in this way: Melt fat or suet; add grain; allow mixture to set. In the evening place it in an open area near long grass or other cover; in the morning look for small teeth marks. The next evening cover a flashlight with red cellophane and sit downwind to wait. The most likely visitors are wood mice; but voles, moles, raccoons, and opossums may also be attracted.

Provided that the camera and flash are set up in advance, you should be able to photograph these small mammals feeding in the open, but when the flash is fired, they will disappear. More than one picture can be taken on a single evening by using a red filter over a flash or a continuous red-light source.

---

with the diaphragm wide open and a correspondingly fast shutter speed.

Pick the moment at which you take your picture with great care. Try to choose the instant when the subject is in just the right place, doing just the right

thing. Most animals look best when their eyes are open. If your subject is walking, pick a moment when all four legs are visible; if one leg is hidden behind another, the animal in the photograph will not look right.

Above all, try to photograph that little bit of action that makes all the difference. If the animal is sunbathing, catch it yawning and stretching. Details like this are well worth waiting for.
—*Michael Boorer*

21 days

84 days

165 days

An extra dimension can be added to animal photography by following a young animal through the various stages of its development. This can most easily be done with zoo animals, such as the Malayan tapir (above) photographed at the San Diego Zoo.

Where To See Wildlife

Each continent has it's wildlife exclusives—animals found nowhere else. Here are more than 200 places to see wild animals, including parks, reserves, and zoos. Some are close to home, some across continents or oceans. Visit any of them and your life will be enriched, your imagination stirred by one of the great experiences of the wild world.

AFRICA

Survivors from the age of giant mammals live on in many parks and reserves.

Nakuru National Park. In Africa's first bird reserve, pink clouds of flamingos—the world's largest concentration—line the lake's shore.

Awash

Masai Amboseli

Kabalega Falls

Aberdare

Nairobi

Tsavo

Rwenzori

Virunga National Park. Snow-topped volcanoes tower above the forest home of gorillas and okapis.

Ngorongoro Conservation Area. Grasslands at the bottom of a huge crater are alive with animals.

Serengeti National Park. Its plains support immense herds of antelopes and their predators.

Kafue

▲ National park

● Wildlife reserve

1-19 See page 311

Etosha

Kalahari Gemsbok National Park. Herds of rare oryxes thrive amid the dunes of this desert habitat.

Wankie

Kruger National Park. Africa's oldest reserve, Kruger offers an unequaled variety of typical birds and mammals.

Bontebok

Hluhluwe and Umfolozi

Ethiopia

AWASH NATIONAL PARK

Southeast of Addis Ababa lies Awash National Park, the best developed and most accessible park in Ethiopia. The excellent Addis-Awash road divides a landscape of open grassland, dense thorny brush, and blistered lava fields, dominated by the towering slopes of Fantalle Crater; the elevation ranges from 3,000 to 6,000 feet.

Miles before reaching the park entrance, you will see ostriches, Soemmering's gazelles, and beisa oryxes with their distinctive black-and-white facial markings. An unpaved road, called a track, leads from the entrance to the park headquarters, lodge, and camping grounds on the banks of the Awash River. Around the tent area blue vervet monkeys gather in the morning and evening, chattering and begging.

Most animals at Awash feed early in the morning or at dusk. Some of the best places for animal viewing are within walking distance of the lodge and campgrounds, along the rim of Awash Canyon. Here greater kudus, defassa waterbucks, bushbucks, small duikers, and dik-diks pick their way through the brush to drink at the river's edge, and solitary anubis baboons survey the scene from the cliffs. Farther along the gorge at a forested spot striking black-and-white colobus monkeys frolic.

The park has many miles of good roads as well as tracks that require four-wheel-drive vehicles. One track follows the Kudu Valley, frequented by oryxes and other antelopes. During the day cheetahs hunt there, and bat-eared foxes gambol at the entrances of their dens. Along the valley's upper rim the Aware-Melca-Awash track leads to the hot springs at Filwoha, where hippos and crocodiles gather in the evening and leopards, lions, and serval cats are sometimes seen. Spectacular birds, such as turquoise Abyssinian rollers and carmine bee-eaters, perch in the palms.

Fantalle Crater dominates the landscape north of the Addis-Awash road. It can be reached by the Fantalle track; eventually you must leave your vehicle, but the view from the rim is worth the rugged climb. The high crater walls surround a wooded valley whose surface is broken by spouts of volcanic steam.

Outside the crater, as far as the eye can see, the land is rocky and arid. In the Fantalle foothills you are likely to see greater and lesser kudus, oryxes, dainty klipspringer antelopes, and heavy-winged ground hornbills. Farther along, the Aware-Melca track turns toward Filwoha, along a plain where kudus and Grevy's zebras feed. A short track leads northward to the Cassem River, with beautiful spots for picnics, fishing, and swimming.

How To Get There: *By car from Addis Ababa (90 miles). Airstrip for light aircraft. By train to Awash station.* **When To Go:** *Open year round.* **Where To Stay:** *Lodge, trailer camp, tent site.*

Kenya

ABERDARE NATIONAL PARK

Although it does not offer the spectacle of vast herds of game, Aberdare National Park in Kenya's Central Highlands is one of the best places for observing such rare species as the bongo, a forest-loving antelope, and the giant forest hog, as well as large groups of elephants and buffaloes.

The park, about 100 miles north of Nairobi, contains 228 square miles. With a range of elevation from 6,600 to 13,000 feet, Aberdare includes zones of rain forest, bamboo forest, giant hypericum (St.-John's-wort) scrub, and rolling alpine moorland with thickets of giant heather. Many streams cascade down the deeply ravined slopes.

A "panhandle" extending down the eastern slope of the range leads to the famous Treetops hotel, built high in the branches of a grove of trees and overlooking a flood-lit waterhole. From the hotel balconies black rhinoceroses, elephants, buffaloes, warthogs, and other animals can be observed at night visiting the waterhole and salt licks.

At other places in the park, the best time for observing the large mammals is just after dawn. The elusive bongo frequents the upper edge of the bamboo forest and the scrub; on the moorlands are elands, duikers, and rhinos.

Birds are abundant in the park. Most conspicuous are the colorful sunbirds. There are also francolins, crowned and ground hornbills, crowned cranes, green ibises, barbets, widow birds, hawk eagles, and eagle owls.

How To Get There: *By car from Nairobi, via Nyeri, or alternate, scenic route, via Rift Valley. By train to Nyeri or Naivasha.* **When To Go:** *Open all year. Best times, January and February.* **Where To Stay:** *Treetops hotel in park;* four campsites (bring your own food). *Near park, Outspan and White Rhino Hotels.*

MASAI AMBOSELI GAME RESERVE

The glistening, snowcapped volcanic cone of Kilimanjaro rising to the south of this 1,259-square-mile area on the border of Tanzania makes an incomparable backdrop for the Masai Amboseli Game Reserve. Open plains, dense thornbush, and woodlands of yellow-barked acacias (called fever trees) vary the terrain. The whole region is owned by Kenya's Masai tribe.

The Masai have traditionally pastured their large herds on the scanty grass of the plains, contributing to the destruction of the fragile, semiarid habitat and endangering Amboseli's great variety of wildlife. Lake Amboseli is dry for most of the year, but it is bordered by swamplands fed by underground streams, whose source is the melting snows of Kilimanjaro. The Kenyan Government has set aside 150 square miles of the swamp and lake region as Amboseli National Park and will encourage the Masai to graze their cattle elsewhere.

A network of roads and trails opens up a wildlife paradise in this swamp and lake region. A drive of 50 or 60 miles from Ol Tukai Lodge, the reserve headquarters, is almost certain to provide encounters with the black rhinos for which Amboseli is famous. Elephants (among which are some notable tuskers), Masai giraffes, African buffaloes, zebras, elands, Coke's hartebeests (kongoni), white-bearded gnus (wildebeests), and several species of smaller antelopes and gazelles are also common. Troops of yellow baboons are always present, and bat-eared foxes sun outside their dens. Lions, cheetahs, and leopards are all likely to be seen.

Among the birds of the swamps are Madagascar squacco herons, long-toed lapwings, African jacanas, saddle-bill storks, hammerheads (storklike wading birds), several species of ibises, many kinds of ducks and geese, herons, and African spoonbills.

In the dry bush country around Namanga, graceful long-necked gerenuks balance on their hind legs while browsing. Here, too, live fringe-eared oryxes. Birds include francolins (partridges), guinea fowls, and bustards.

Birds of prey are represented by 47 species—tawny, bateleur, and Wahlberg eagles, African fish eagles, and long-crested hawk eagles; goshawks, falcons, kites, and harriers. The superb glossy starling with its long tail, green head, amethyst throat, and golden-yellow underparts is among the gaudiest of the many smaller birds. Taveta golden weavers are a species not likely to be seen anywhere else in Africa.

How To Get There: *Two routes (both about 150 miles) from Nairobi—the Mombasa road to beyond Emali, then the main Loitokitok road to branch off to Ol Tukai Lodge; or the Kajiado-Namanga-Arusha road, with a branch to Ol Tukai.* **When To Go:** *Open all year. Best time, July through March.* **Where To Stay:** *Ol Tukai Lodge, a tented campsite (bring your own food); Amboseli New Lodge (hotel and restaurant with tented camp); Namanga Hotel.*

NAIROBI NATIONAL PARK

One of the unusual features of this popular park is its location on the outskirts of Kenya's capital, Nairobi. Also unique is its Animal Orphanage, where young animals that have lost their parents are raised to maturity.

Nairobi National Park is situated on the edge of a highland plateau. Although only 44 square miles in area, it provides a well-diversified range of wildlife habitats. On the Nairobi side of the park is a highland forest zone, dominated by flowering Cape chestnut and Kenya olive trees. Beyond the forest lies a broad savanna with scattered groves of acacias, cut by deep, rocky valleys and gorges, and finally a wooded river valley. One hundred miles of road take visitors' cars to almost every part of the park (walking is forbidden).

Most of the mammals are typical grassland species: Impalas, kongoni (hartebeests), elands, gnus (wildebeests), Thomson's and Grant's gazelles, and zebras. Giraffes may be seen browsing on the scrub vegetation. A few black rhinos keep mostly to the forest zone. The great cats—lion, leopard, and cheetah—are all represented, with lions the most numerous. Spotted hyenas are also common. Hippos and crocodiles inhabit the river. There are no elephants.

Ostriches, bustards, hornbills, secretary birds, helmeted guinea fowls, francolins, and quails can be seen in the open country. Crowned cranes, yellow-billed storks, and waterfowl frequent the streams and pools; numbers of almost tame marabou storks can be observed around the park's manmade ponds. Smaller birds include mousebirds, touracos, sunbirds, and weavers.

There are numerous hawks, vultures, and eagles of four species.
How To Get There: *By car from Nairobi.* **When To Go:** *Open all year.* **Where To Stay:** *Hotels in Nairobi.*

NAKURU NATIONAL PARK

At certain seasons almost 2 million of East Africa's 3 million lesser and greater flamingos (half the world population) gather at Lake Nakuru (an alkaline lake in Kenya's Rift Valley).

Nakuru National Park, originally established in 1961 to encompass just the lake and its immediate environs, has been tripled in size (to about 40,000 acres) by a 1973 World Wildlife Fund land purchase. The shallow, sedge-bordered lake is about 8 miles long by 3 miles wide. Small stands of acacias, dense bushes, rocky outcrops, and pools add variety to the terrain.

Most of the birds at Nakuru are lesser flamingos; about 1 in 50 belongs to the larger 6-foot species. The biggest concentrations of these algae feeders frequent the west side of the lake, where the water is only inches deep. The water level depends on rainfall; as local conditions and food supplies vary, so do the number of flamingos. Water pollution is a real problem at Lake Nakuru and is being studied at the research station.

Altogether Nakuru has 370 resident species of birds and about 30 species of wintering migrants. Since the introduction of tilapias for mosquito control, the lake also supports fish-eating pelicans, cormorants, darters, spoonbills, yellow-billed storks, grebes, and terns. Predatory marabou storks prey on the flamingo population. The waterfowl include Cape widgeons and stiff-tailed maccoa ducks. Several species of plovers are resident, and during spring migration flocks of little stints, greenshanks, curlews, and marsh, wood, and green sandpipers can be seen.

Birds of the acacia woodlands include several species of kingfishers and bee-eaters, lilac-breasted and rufous-crowned rollers, African hoopoes, drongos, tropical boubous, paradise flycatchers, and honey guides.

The northeast corner of the lake, where springs have created a series of reed-choked pools, harbors a small herd of hippos. Reedbucks, bushbucks, bush duikers, and klipspringers can frequently be sighted around the edges.

How To Get There: *By car or train from Nairobi to Nakuru Township, 2 miles from Lake Nakuru (less than 100 miles). Tour day trips from Nairobi.*

TSAVO NATIONAL PARK

Located halfway between the Kenyan coast and Nairobi, Kenya's main wildlife sanctuary and one of the largest of Africa's national parks comprises 8,000 square miles. Tsavo National Park is world-famous for its huge herds of elephants. The park is divided by the Nairobi-Mombasa railway and highway into two sectors: Tsavo Park West and twice-as-large Tsavo Park East.

Of the four rivers that drain the area only two are permanent—the Athi and the Tsavo. These two unite to form the Galana River above picturesque Lugard Falls. In the dry season elephants dig waterholes in the sandy beds of the Voi and Tiva Rivers; these holes serve many other animals, from bulky black rhinos to dainty duikers. Roads running alongside these rivers provide convenient lookout points for observing wildlife.

Tsavo lies on a vast plain that varies in altitude from 1,000 to 2,000 feet. Rainfall ranges from 16 inches a year in the arid east to more than 80 inches in the forested Chyulu section. Most of the park is grassy savanna, spotted with acacias, baobabs (a favorite food of elephants), and succulents, such as aloes and euphorbias.

Near Kilaguni Lodge in West Tsavo is Mzima Springs, where millions of gallons of crystal-clear water gush out from below a ridge of lava. Many hippos and scavenging fish live in the springs and can be observed from a submerged glass observation chamber.

Although elephants appear in fantastic concentrations, especially at the Mudanda Rock catchment area, they are by no means Tsavo's only attraction. Black rhinos, spiral-horned lesser kudus, long-necked gerenuks, fringe-eared oryxes, and impalas are almost always in evidence. You are also likely to encounter leopards and lions, Masai giraffes, warthogs, kongoni, buffaloes, klipspringers, and steenboks.

Among the park's varied bird population of some 250 species, the white-headed buffalo weaver with its red rump is conspicuous; 17 other weaver species are listed. The numerous starlings include the brilliant golden-breasted and the rare Fischer's starling. There are eight species of hornbills and many birds of prey. Colorful sunbirds and finches of many species are prevalent. The thick-trunked baobabs provide nesting sites for parrots, barbets, and rollers. Peter's finfoot, a rare aquatic bird, frequents the waters downstream from Mzima Springs.

How To Get There: *By car or train from Nairobi or Mombasa (150 miles). Landing strips inside the park.* **When To Go:** *Open all year. June to September, warm; January to March, dry and dusty.* **Where To Stay:** *In West Tsavo, hotel-style Kilaguni Lodge, 22 miles from Mtito Andei; Kitani and Murka Lodges (bring your own food). In East Tsavo, Aruba Safari Lodge, 22 miles from Voi. Camping sites.*

Rhodesia

WANKIE NATIONAL PARK

This great reserve (more than 5,000 square miles) contains large concentrations of wildlife. Elephant and buffalo populations in Wankie National Park each number well into the thousands; a single herd of buffaloes can easily include more than 400 animals. Wildebeests and zebras roam freely in extensive herds, and impalas, giraffes, and kudus are numerous in limited areas.

Wankie has a varied terrain. The sands of the Kalahari Desert reach their eastern extremity here. Savannas and grassy plains are dotted with acacias, palms, and other trees; there are scattered forests of Rhodesian teak. Here warthogs, steenboks, and duikers graze among the buffaloes and drink at the shallow watering places called pans.

The northwestern corner of the park is hilly; here mopani trees, typical of the African bush, grow on outcroppings of basalt rock amid acacias, baobabs, and wild date palms. Waterbucks, sassaby, roan, and sable antelopes, reedbucks, klipspringers, and impalas are numerous only in this section. Lions are here probably because prey is plentiful.

Leopards, cheetahs, hyenas, and two types of jackals hunt throughout the park. White rhinos have been reintroduced, and black rhinos also occur. Crocodiles lie submerged or doze at the edge of the pans, and ostriches wander on the plains. There are multitudes of other birds, including various vultures and eagles common to Africa.

Nyamandhlovu Pan, located only a short distance from the park's main camp, is a good place for animal viewing. During the dry season you can visit the observation platform on moonlit nights, when great numbers of animals visit the waterhole.

Because Wankie is a wildlife sanctuary as well as a tourist attraction, only

When To Go: *Open all year. Best times, June to September, January to March.* **Where To Stay:** *Hotel in Nakuru Township. Camping permitted.*

one-third of the area is open to visitors. **How To Get There:** *By air from Salisbury, Victoria Falls, and Bulawayo. By rail on Bulawayo-Victoria Falls route. By car on Victoria Falls-Bulawayo Road.* **When To Go:** *Open all year. Best time, August through November.* **Where To Stay:** *Lodges and chalets at Main, Robins, and Nantwich open from June to November; Main Camp and Sinamatella open year-round. Camping sites at each location.*

South Africa

BONTEBOK NATIONAL PARK

This small reserve is a good example of what wise conservation can achieve. By 1931 the beautifully marked antelope known as the bontebok (meaning "variegated buck" in Afrikaans) had been reduced to a score of individuals. Local conservationists organized what was called the National Bontebok Park, an 1,800-acre enclave near Bredasdorp.

The starting stock was 22 individuals, all that were left of what European travelers in 1777 had described as an "abundant" population. By 1953 the reinvigorated population had grown to about 120, but in the meantime it had become apparent that the site was unwisely chosen (parasites abounded, and seasonal floods threatened the habitat). In 1960 the bonteboks were transferred to their present home, a sandy depression in the Langeberg foothills, 150 rocky miles east of Cape Town. The countrywide population, including those animals in a few nearby sanctuaries, is now nearly 1,000.

Another rare animal, the red hartebeest, thought to be extinct in the late 1960's, has been reintroduced to Bontebok National Park. The park also shelters other species of African plains animals; these include the springbok, eland, gray rhebok, gray duiker, steenbok, Cape grysbok, reedbuck, bushbuck, and Cape buffalo. Some 170 species of birds, including guinea fowls and ostriches, have been reported. Against the backdrop of the Langeberg Mountains the park is a scenic spot. **How To Get There:** *By car, 2 miles southeast of Swellendam. By rail to Swellendam.* **When To Go:** *Open all year. All seasons equally good.* **Where To Stay:** *Hotels at Swellendam. Campsite not far from park.*

HLUHLUWE AND UMFOLOZI GAME RESERVES

Home of one of the world's largest remaining populations of rhinoceroses, these two neighboring reserves together occupy more than 200 square miles of the rugged, hilly highlands of eastern Zululand. A 15-mile-wide corridor of farmland separates the two. Grass and thornbushes cover most of the reserves' rolling landscape and support the abundant wildlife. The Hluhluwe and Umfolozi Rivers flow through the reserves named for them, and there are also numerous tributaries and waterholes. The river valleys are densely forested.

The features of the reserves are their white and black rhinoceroses. Hluhluwe has an estimated 90 white rhinos and a much larger number of black rhinos; Umfolozi has more than 1,000 white rhinos and probably as many black rhinos. The two species do not compete for food: The white rhino eats grass, while the black rhino browses on leaves and twigs. The Umfolozi-Hluhluwe area is the only region where their natural ranges overlap.

In addition to the rhinos, the reserves contain large herds of zebras, gnus (wildebeests), and buffaloes. Giraffes, elands, nyalas, impalas, and duikers are among the other notable grazers and browsers. Waterbucks, reedbucks, and bushbucks favor the concealment of river-valley forests. Warthogs and bush pigs are common, and troops of baboons roam the bushland. Leopards are present but seldom seen. Crocodiles live in the rivers. Due to the low number of predators, the herbivores have become too abundant for the good of the environment. A number of surplus white rhinos have been shipped to other African parks and reserves.

Both Hluhluwe and Umfolozi are rich in birdlife, with about 240 species reported. You are sure to see those ubiquitous scavengers, the marabou storks and vultures, but there are also ground hornbills, crested guinea fowls, francolins (partridges), night herons, and bee-eaters. There is an unusual variety of eagles, including the fish eagle, martial eagle, bateleur, and others.

Almost alone among African parks, Umfolozi offers guided nature hikes. The hikes, lasting from 2 to 5 days, must be booked in advance through reserve headquarters in Mtubatuba. You may also tour the reserve in your own car, accompanied by a native guide. Hluhluwe has no hiking trails, but again accompanied by native guides, you may leave your car to approach resting or sleeping rhinos. **How To Get There:** *By car from Durban via Mtubatuba (about 180 miles). By train to Mtubatuba (about 32 miles*

from both reserves) and Hluhluwe village. Nearest airport, Durban. Tours from Durban and Johannesburg. **When To Go:** *Reserves open all year. Best time, May through August.* **Where To Stay:** *Rest camps with cottages and rondavels (cook's services included, but except on conducted tours you must bring your own food).*

KALAHARI GEMSBOK NATIONAL PARK

A rolling, open expanse of colorful red and pink sand dunes covered with sparse grass and dotted with scattered acacia trees and thornbushes—this is Kalahari Gemsbok National Park. It is located in the northwestern finger of South Africa that juts up between South-West Africa and Botswana. Thanks to the deep, porous sand, which absorbs and holds the scanty rainfall, the 3,700-square-mile park supports enough vegetation to sustain sizable herds of hoofed animals and the predators that live off them. The park is crossed by two dry rivers, the Nossob and the Auob, which flow only once or twice a century after exceptionally heavy rains. The rivers' wide, empty, level beds constitute the main roads.

The chief attraction is the gemsbok, a large oryx with magnificent straight horns up to 4 feet in length; an estimated 10,000 head of gemsboks live in the park. The most numerous large animal is the gazellelike springbok, which can be seen grazing in huge herds of 1,000 to 1,500. These two are true desert animals, able to obtain most of their moisture requirements from the plants they eat. There are also big herds of wildebeests (gnus) and elands. Red hartebeests are abundant but hard to see until they move, since their coloring blends with the dunes. If you are lucky, you may see an occasional kudu, far from its normal range.

Preying on the herds of grazers are lions (now declining in number), leopards, cheetahs, and wild dogs. The most abundant predator is the hyena. Bat-eared foxes, scavenging the kills of larger predators, are a common sight. Honey badgers and termite-eating aardwolves are other interesting predators.

Kalahari Gemsbok supports an abundant population of birds, mainly groundbirds, scavengers, and predators. You are likely to see ostriches, kori bustards, and francolins. You'll see secretary birds stalking about in search of snakes and small lizards. Other predators include the chanting goshawk and the big spotted eagle owl. There are several species of vultures, including the endangered lammergeier, largest of the native scavengers. Larks and weaverbirds are also numerous, and one of the park's most striking sights is the huge communal nests built by weaverbirds.

Human encroachments on the environment are few. Small bands of Bushmen still hunt in the park, using their age-old, highly economical techniques. **How To Get There:** *By car from Upington (200 miles), Pretoria (650 miles), or Cape Town (690 miles). By air to Upington; air-taxi connections from Upington to park.* **When To Go:** *Open all year. Best time, March through October.* **Where To Stay:** *Cottages and campgrounds at three sites in park. Visitors should bring food, cooking gear.*

KRUGER NATIONAL PARK

In the northeastern uplands of South Africa lies Kruger National Park, believed to contain more species of animals and birds than any other park in the world. Kruger's nearly 8,000 square miles extend in a narrow, irregular oblong along the Mozambique border, from the Crocodile River in the south to the Limpopo River in the north, a distance of about 200 miles. Its varied terrain ranges from wide plains to rugged hills, kopjes (small rocky knolls), and low mountains. The plant communities include open grasslands, savannas, thorn scrub, and deciduous forests.

Despite limited rainfall, coming mostly as thunderstorms in summer (October through March), Kruger supports an estimated million mammals, including such rare and threatened species as the leopard, cheetah, crocodile, and white rhinoceros (formerly native to the area and reintroduced). Huge numbers of impalas roam the grasslands and scrub, as do their rare cousins the sassaby, roan, and sable antelopes. In all, the park is home for 17 species of antelopes, among them the imposing eland, greater kudu, reedbuck, and blue wildebeest (gnu). The thornbush provides browse for giraffes; hippopotamuses, crocodiles, and clawless otters inhabit the few rivers that flow year-round. The great herds of herbivores support a large population of lions and other predators, most notably hyenas, jackals, and wild dogs.

Elephants are best seen in the northern section of the park, especially around Olifants and Shingwidzi camps. In the southern grasslands are rhinos, buffaloes, and lions; the road from Lower Sabie to Skukuza is famous as the "Road of the Lions." Crocodiles and hippos are concentrated near Crocodile Bridge, Letaba, and the Hippo Pool near Pretoriuskop.

Some 400 species of birds have been recorded in Kruger Park. Ostriches, secretary birds, and kori bustards stalk through the grassland and scrub; there are also crowned and crested guinea fowls, francolins, crowned plovers, hornbills, and a great variety of smaller birds, such as lilac-breasted rollers, finches, and weavers. Along the streams can be seen storklike hammerheads, colorful saddle-billed storks, herons, ducks, geese, and other waterfowl.

Drought is an increasingly severe problem at Kruger. However, numerous dams and wells have been constructed. During the dry season these manmade waterholes are gathering places for great concentrations of wildlife. **How To Get There:** *By car from Pretoria (235 miles) or Johannesburg (250 miles). By bus or limousine tour.* **When To Go:** *Best season, winter (April 1 to October 14); northern portion closed from October 15 to March 31.* **Where To Stay:** *Cottages, huts, and campsites in 14 rest camps (early reservations advised).*

South-West Africa

ETOSHA NATIONAL PARK

The semiarid northwestern corner of South-West Africa is the site of this 8,000-square-mile park. Its heart is the Etosha Pan, a muddy depression about 80 miles long. At one time the Kunene River ran through the region, emptying into what was then Etosha Lake. When the river changed its course, a vast salt pan remained. Water fills the pan only during the rainy season, but several waterholes in the area remain available to wildlife throughout the year.

There is no vegetation in the Etosha Pan, but surrounding it are open grasslands with scattered deciduous mopani bushes. A little farther to the east the soil supports trees and shrubs, such as wolf's thorn, wild fig, wild date and other palms, and various acacias. In this setting live the characteristic savanna animals of southern Africa. Burchell's zebras, gemsboks, wildebeests, and springboks are the commonest species. Greater kudus are frequently seen in the bushy areas, and giraffes are in evidence everywhere. Near the waterholes red hartebeests can be found. Somewhat rarer are roan antelopes, elands, steenboks, and warthogs.

Prides of lions and the more elusive leopards are among the predators of the large mammals. Cheetahs live mainly on springboks. Highly vocal black-backed jackals are often heard at night and sometimes met during the day. Bat-eared foxes can be seen occasionally. Hyenas are very shy, but once in a while a pack can be sighted. Honey badgers, mongooses, South African lynxes, genets, and wildcats are common. Early risers at Namutoni, one of the park rest camps, may be rewarded with a glimpse of the tiniest of all antelopes, the Damara dik-dik, or the exceedingly rare black-faced impala. Black rhinos appear at waterholes in the park's western section. Elephants wander in herds that may number 80 individuals.

During the rainy season, when the Etosha Pan is full of water, greater and lesser flamingos breed by the hundreds of thousands; Egyptian geese, spoonbills, marabou storks, and several species of ducks also abound. Ostriches, kori and giant bustards, secretary birds, eagles, vultures, guinea fowls, francolins, blue cranes, and many kinds of finches are common.

Etosha National Park has three rest camps. Namutoni, an old renovated fort, includes a lookout tower complete with telescope. Halali has bungalows, dormitories, and tents. Okaukuejo is the park administrative center; within sight of the cabins there is a spring attractive to animals. At night floodlights play on the scene. **How To Get There:** *By car from southern border of South-West Africa, best way. Bus tours available. Regular flights to Windhoek, where cars can be rented. Light aircraft fly directly to rest camps.* **When To Go:** *Open from March 16 to October 31. Rainy season (shortly after the park opens), best time to see birds.* **Where To Stay:** *Three rest camps (early reservations advised).*

Tanzania

NGORONGORO CONSERVATION AREA

Set in the highlands of northern Tanzania, 3,200-square-mile Ngorongoro Conservation Area includes sweeping, grass-covered plains where Masai herdsmen graze their long-horned cattle, rugged highlands, and a chain of extinct and still active volcanoes.

The heart of the area is Ngorongoro Crater, a gigantic volcanic caldera, which provides a magnificent setting for a microcosm of East African wildlife. Surrounded by mountains with several peaks more than 10,000 feet high, the crater averages 10 to 12 miles across and covers 102 square miles. Its rim rises steeply 2,000 feet above the floor.

Streams and springs feed extensive swamps and a salt lake; for the rest the crater landscapes range from dry, open grassland, through scrub, to dense forests of broad-leaved trees and bamboo.

The wildlife of the conservation area is much like that of the neighboring Serengeti Plains, with great herds of zebras, gnus (wildebeests), elands, impalas, Grant's gazelles, and other antelopes. Ngorongoro Crater itself contains many of these grazing animals, plus others not found on the plains. One of the crater's chief attractions is its large population of black rhinoceroses, estimated at more than 100. A small colony of hippopotamuses inhabits a swampy area in the east of the crater. Waterbucks and reedbucks frequent the marshy Lerai Forest.

The abundant predator population includes lions (the Ngorongoro race is known for its luxuriant black mane), leopards, cheetahs, and hyenas. Packs of hunting dogs visit the area.

The crater has a rich birdlife. Hawks and eagles, among them Verreaux's eagle and the bateleur eagle, nest in rocky outcrops on the crater wall. Six species of vultures scavenge the large predators' kills, and a huge lammergeier visits the crater occasionally. Solitary kori bustards and small groups of ostriches patrol the open grasslands. Another grassland bird is the crowned crane, a sociable bird that is almost always seen in large flocks. Numerous plovers nest in the grass.

Water birds include large flocks of ducks and geese. A number of European species winter in the crater. The European stork also winters there, and lucky visitors may see the rare hammerhead and saddle-billed stork, both permanent residents. Marabou storks scavenge the wetlands. African spoonbills and sacred ibises are plentiful in the marshy areas, and great flocks of greater and lesser flamingos are always present at the lakes, though they do not breed there.

Ngorongoro must be visited by four-wheel-drive vehicles (ordinary cars cannot negotiate the steep tracks down the crater walls). At Olduvai Gorge, 32 miles from the main lodge and part of the conservation area, a guide conducts visitors around the sites where Dr. L.S.B. Leakey discovered relics of man's remote ancestors. **How To Get There:** *By car from Arusha (112 miles) or Nairobi (290 miles) or from Seronera in Serengeti National Park (87 miles). By plane to Arusha and Seronera; air taxis to crater rim. By train to Arusha.* **When To Go:** *Open all year. Best time, December.* **Where To**

Stay: *Three lodges and one guesthouse on crater rim; one campsite on rim and three on crater floor.*

SERENGETI NATIONAL PARK

Foremost among the world's great national parks for its spectacular pageants of hoofed animals, Tanzania's Serengeti National Park never fails to impress visitors. From March to May (when most of the rains fall), the seemingly limitless green expanses of the Serengeti Plains support tremendous herds—estimated at more than 2 million animals—of about 20 species: zebras, 600,000; wildebeests, more than 1 million; Thomson's and Grant's gazelles, 500,000; impala, roan, and topi antelopes; hartebeests, kudus, and elands.

During this season of lush grasses the herd animals give birth to their young. These newborn, together with old, sick, or crippled animals, furnish abundant food for the Serengeti's numerous lion prides (one of the largest lion populations in Africa), its solitary leopards and cheetahs, and its packs of spotted and striped hyenas, golden and black-backed jackals, and hunting dogs. Giraffes, buffaloes, and black rhinos complete the roll of plains mammals.

In addition to the vast plains with their characteristically African granite outcroppings, or kopjes, Serengeti's more than 5,700 square miles embrace woodlands of flat-topped acacias, swamps and pools surrounded by dense vegetation, forest-bordered rivers, and rolling hills, particularly in the western extension known as the corridor. With this extension park territory reaches to within 5 miles of Lake Victoria.

As the dry season begins in June, fires blacken the grasslands, and the herds start to migrate—long, orderly processions heading west and north toward the hills and wooded valleys. These wooded areas also shelter fringe-eared oryxes, waterbucks, small duikers, dik-diks, and suni antelopes, preyed on by the lesser spotted predators—genets, servals, caracals, and African wildcats. Clawless otters and hippos occur in the rivers; rock hyraxes and mongooses inhabit the kopjes.

In wooded areas near water are found many of the Serengeti's 400 species of resident and transient birds: Shrikes, sunbirds, weavers, and bishop birds; forest kingfishers, rollers, and waxbills; spur fowls, cuckoos, and touracos—to name only a few. Flocks of francolins and guinea fowls cackle their way through the scrub. Over woodland, scrub, and plains soar the rare martial

and Verreaux's eagles, bateleur eagles with their tumbling flight, and a dozen other large raptors. Saddle-billed and marabou storks join the six species of vultures at scavenger duty. Inconspicuous hen ostriches brood their enormous eggs in nests hollowed out of the dusty ground. Ploverlike coursers, bustards, and sandgrouse haunt dry areas. And on the alkaline flats of Lake Magadi flamingos feed in a pink crescent.

For the visitor Serengeti National Park offers a centrally located complex at Seronera. Here are food and shelter, guide service, and a small museum. **How To Get There:** *By car from Arusha, Tanzania, via Lake Manyara and Ngorongoro Crater (206 miles). Four-wheel-drive cars may be rented at Arusha. By plane from Nairobi, Kenya.* **When To Go:** *Open all year. Best time for viewing herd migrations, late May.* **Where To Stay:** *Seronera Wildlife Lodge in park; Fort Ikoma Lodge and tented camp outside park. Campsites.*

Uganda

KABALEGA FALLS NATIONAL PARK

Formerly Murchison Falls National Park, this is Uganda's largest reserve—1,500 square miles of rolling grasslands and savannas, with swamps and scattered woodlands. The Victoria Nile flows through the park from east to west. Near the park's western edge the river bursts from a narrow gorge—only 20 feet wide at one point—to cascade down the 140-foot escarpment of the world-famous Kabalega Falls into a huge pool where hippos and crocodiles congregate by the hundreds.

Under protection elephants have increased to 15,000 or more. With their destructive habits and voracious appetites, this number of elephants imposes a severe stress on the environment, and periodic culling is necessary.

The river is crowded with 12,000 hippos and Africa's largest concentration of crocodiles. You are certain to see warthogs, bush pigs, and some of the park's 14,000 buffaloes. With luck you may see the rare black and the reintroduced white rhinoceroses as they feed on the plains or drink at the river. The grasslands and savannas support many species of antelopes, including the oribi and Uganda kob. Giraffes are fairly abundant, and baboons can be seen in forested areas.

Predators range in size from lions to shrews. The great cats are well represented, with leopards dominating the woods and scrub, and lions, the open country. There are also hyenas, wild-cats, and servals.

In Kabalega 423 species of birds have been recorded, including 14 species of herons, 11 eagles, 8 falcons, and 4 horn-bills. Of special interest are the whale-headed (shoebill) and saddle-billed storks. Bee-eaters, sunbirds, and touracos abound.

The highlight of a visit to Kabalega Falls National Park is the 7-mile launch trip up the Nile from Paraa Safari Lodge to the foot of the falls. The boat passes crocodiles sunning on sandbanks and hippos resting in the shallows. Elephants and buffaloes feed along the banks, and black-and-white colobus monkeys leap through the forests that line the river. A foot trail leads to the top of the falls. Two nearby salt licks attract many animals.

Most areas of the park can be reached by road, and ranger guides can be hired for auto trips. A drive around the Buligi circuit at the western edge of the park is particularly rewarding.
How To Get There: *By car from Kampala, via Masindi (190 miles). By air from Entebbe.* **When To Go:** *Open all year. Best time, December through April.* **Where To Stay:** *Paraa Safari Lodge below falls, Chobe Safari Lodge on Nile.*

RWENZORI
NATIONAL PARK
Flanked by the towering (16,500 feet) snowcapped Rwenzori Range ("Mountains of the Moon"), the 860 square miles of this reserve, formerly called Queen Elizabeth National Park, lie athwart the Equator at an altitude of 3,000 to 4,500 feet. This Ugandan park offers a remarkable range of habitats—large lakes, grassy plains, tropical forests, rivers, swamps, and volcanic craters with emerald lakes in their depths.

Forming part of the park's western boundary is Lake Edward, joined by the 20-mile Kazinga Channel to Lake George, which fills most of the north-eastern quarter of the reserve. The northern grasslands, dominated by a rare species of euphorbia (a strange, cactuslike tree), are separated from the rolling plains of the southern Kigezi section of the Maramagambo Forest.

A characteristic feature of Rwenzori National Park is the flourishing hippopotamus population, currently about 13,000, three times the desirable number. This means that the wardens must regularly crop the herds to keep them from destroying their habitat. Even so, the remaining hippos crowd the water and shores of the lakes and channel.

The Maramagambo Forest is crossed by a main road, from which you can observe black-and-white colobus monkeys, an occasional rare red colobus, blue monkeys, red-tailed monkeys, and perhaps a chimpanzee or two. The rolling Kigezi parkland, home of tree-climbing lions, has great herds of topi antelopes, waterbucks, and lyre-horned Uganda kobs. Giant forest hogs are frequently sighted. Rare whale-headed (shoebill) storks patrol the shores of Lake George. There are elephants, buffaloes, and leopards.

Recorded species of birds are close to 500. Malachite and pied kingfishers are abundant and relatively approachable for observation and photography. The juncture of the Kazinga Channel and Lake George is the sole known habitat of the Uganda cormorant, only recently recognized as a species. Noisy fish eagles haunt the area. Bird counts during a single launch trip through the channel often reach 60 to 70 species. Pelican Point at the mouth of the Nyamagesant River is a gathering place for many water birds.
How To Get There: *By road from Kampala, Uganda, via Masaka and Mbarara (271 miles), or from Kabalega Falls National Park, via Hoima and Fort Portal (300 miles). Scheduled flights to Kasese, 40 miles from Mweya. By train from Kampala to Kasese.* **When To Go:** *Open all year. Best time, October-November and March-April.* **Where To Stay:** *Mweya Safari Lodge in center of park; Hotel Margherita in Rwenzori foothills. Campsites available.*

Zaire

VIRUNGA
NATIONAL PARK
Glacier-capped peaks rising above baking equatorial savannas, giant lakes, winding rivers lined with wild date palms, extinct and active volcanoes—all are part of Zaire's Virunga National Park (formerly Albert National Park).

The 3,124-square-mile park adjoins Rwenzori National Park in Uganda and Volcanoes National Park in Rwanda. The land rises from an altitude of 3,000 feet in the Rift Valley to 15,500 feet in the snowcapped Rwenzori Mountains at the north end of the park. The vegetation ranges from open savanna to rain forest and dense jungle; on the higher alpine slopes are tree-sized heath plants, giant senecios (15-foot-tall cousins of the groundsel), and giant lobelias (also up to 15 feet).

Hippopotamuses, estimated at more than 22,000, may well be the most abundant of Virunga's large mammals. The greatest concentration of hippos is found in Lake Edward. Antelopes and buffaloes are abundant.

The dense forests of the Virunga Range, a chain of extinct volcanoes in the southeast of the park, shelter the threatened mountain gorillas. It was here that George Schaller conducted his pioneering studies of gorilla behavior. The gorillas are still numerous enough (one source estimates 300) to give you an excellent chance of seeing one or more family groups during a stay of 3 to 4 days. Other forest animals include elusive okapis and bongos (found in the lowland area north of Lake Edward) and giant forest hogs.

In the grasslands the most common animals are kob and topi antelopes; defassa waterbucks and sitatungas (swamp bushbucks) haunt the marshy areas along the lakes and rivers.

Chimpanzees and tree hyraxes live in the sparse forests of the active volcano zone in the southwest of the park, a geologically interesting region with lava flows and hot springs. Large troops of olive baboons and vervet monkeys forage noisily on the savannas.

Lions are the dominant carnivores of Virunga. Both spotted hyenas and leopards are common, though rarely seen by visitors.

With its diversity of habitat Virunga Park has a great variety of birds, including eagles, vultures, kites, pigeons, and francolins. But waterfowl and wading birds seem to dominate the birdlife, thanks to the abundance of water. Notable species include pelicans and cormorants, ducks, gallinules, storks, and herons. From September to April thousands of migratory birds from Europe winter in Virunga's rich feeding grounds.
How To Get There: *By road from Kisangani; also from neighboring Tanzania, Uganda, and Rwanda. Nearest airport, Goma, on Lake Kivu.* **When To Go:** *Open all year. Best time, September-December and March-May (rainy seasons).* **Where To Stay:** *Rwindi Hotel in park.*

Zambia

KAFUE
NATIONAL PARK
Slightly more than half the size of Switzerland, Kafue National Park spreads over 8,650 square miles of amply watered highland plain in the southwest of Zambia, about 3 hours by car from Lusaka, the capital. The Kafue River winds through the north-

east of the park and borders it on the east before emptying into the mighty Zambezi. Numerous tributaries of the Kafue cross the park, and there are extensive floodplains and swamps in the extreme north and south. Thanks to the abundant moisture, the vegetation, which ranges from grasslands to brush and forest, affords year-round forage.

Most numerous are the antelopes, ranging from giant elands and kudus to little duikers. If you are lucky, you may see a herd of sable antelopes grazing on the plains or galloping off in alarm. Little oribis are often observed, waterbucks graze along the riverbanks, and the rare red lechwe, a semiaquatic antelope nearly exterminated by poachers, still survives in the swamps at the north and south ends of the park. The sitatunga, another water-loving antelope, is found in the extreme north.

Large herds of buffaloes, sometimes numbering a thousand or more, frequent the river flats, and hippos and crocodiles live in the rivers. You are almost certain to see elephants and the very common warthogs. With luck a black rhinoceros may be sighted. Zebras and gnus round out the list of large herbivores. Lions and leopards range over the entire park, although the leopards are rarely seen by day. Cheetahs hunt on the grasslands of the north.

Kafue has more than 600 species of birds, most notably waterfowl and waders. The greatest bird concentrations are found in the floodplains and swamps. Of special interest are the four species of eagles, including the fish eagle, Zambia's national bird, and the bateleur eagle, noted for its acrobatic flight. Four species of vultures, among them the rare lappet-faced vulture, soar over the plains. Along the watercourses visitors can see the picturesque openbill and saddle-billed storks and wattled and crested cranes.

A network of dirt roads links points of major interest. There are guided nature walks, and motorboats with a pilot can be rented.

How To Get There: *By car from Lusaka (3 hours). Nearest airport, Mumbwa.* **When To Go:** *From end of rainy season (usually mid-June to early November).* **Where To Stay:** *Hotels and cabins at seven park sites. Trailer facilities. Camping at Chunga.*

More Places To See Wildlife in Africa

1. MOUNT KENYA NATIONAL PARK, Kenya. Forested slopes; alpine moorland with giant lobelias, groundsels, heathers. Wildlife highlights: Elephants, buffaloes; bushbucks, duikers, bongos; giant forest hogs; colobus monkeys. Many birds of prey, including lammergeiers.

2. MASAI MARA GAME RESERVE, Kenya. Upland savanna; adjoins Serengeti. Wildlife highlights: Lions, leopards, cheetahs, wild dogs; topi and roan antelopes, elands, bushbucks, reedbucks, gazelles; zebras, giraffes, buffaloes, black rhinos.

3. ARUSHA NATIONAL PARK, Tanzania. Rain forests, crater lakes, grassland. Wildlife highlights: Elephants, black rhinos, buffaloes, hippos, giant forest hogs; bushbucks, waterbucks, reedbucks; colobus monkeys; leopards. Flamingos, pelicans.

4. LAKE MANYARA NATIONAL PARK, Tanzania. Salt lake bordered by Rift Valley escarpment. Wildlife highlights: Elephants, black rhinos, hippos, buffaloes, giraffes; zebras, impalas, suni antelopes; tree-climbing lions, leopards; vervet monkeys. Flamingos, pelicans, goliath herons, sacred ibises, spoonbills, crowned cranes, jacanas; marabou, saddlebill, and openbill storks.

5. RUAHA NATIONAL PARK, Tanzania. Woodland and savanna between rivers. Wildlife highlights: Kudus, impalas, elands, sable and roan antelopes, dik-diks (pygmy antelopes), waterbucks; black rhinos, hippos; lions, leopards, hyenas, jackals, bat-eared foxes. Ostriches.

6. KASUNGA NATIONAL PARK, Malawi. Woodland and savanna. Wildlife highlights: Elephants, black rhinos, buffaloes; zebras, impalas, kudus, elands, hartebeests, sable and roan antelopes, reedbucks, waterbucks, oribis (pygmy antelopes); lions, leopards, cheetahs, serval cats. Carmine bee-eaters.

7. NYIKA NATIONAL PARK, Malawi. Hilly, high savanna. Wildlife highlights: Zebras, roan and sable antelopes, reedbucks, bushbucks, duikers, klipspringers; lions, leopards, hyenas, jackals; blue monkeys. Sacred ibises, wattled cranes, marabou storks; secretary birds, fish eagles; bustards, ground hornbills.

8. SUMBU GAME RESERVE, Zambia. On shore of Lake Tanganyika; bush, grassland, forest. Wildlife highlights: Elephants, hippos, buffaloes; zebras, elands, sable and roan antelopes, waterbucks, duikers, klipspringers; warthogs. Crocodiles. Fish eagles.

9. LUANGA VALLEY NATIONAL PARK, Zambia. Parklike savanna with meandering river. Wildlife highlights: Elephants, buffaloes, giraffes, black rhinos, hippos; zebras, elands, kudus, impalas, gnus, waterbucks; lions, leopards, wild dogs. Crocodiles. Six species of eagles; carmine and little bee-eaters.

10. VICTORIA FALLS NATIONAL PARK, Rhodesia. Spectacular falls and gorges of Zambezi River; savanna and rain forest. Wildlife highlights: Elephants, buffaloes, hippos, giraffes; kudus, impalas, elands, roan and sable antelopes, bushbucks; baboons, vervet monkeys; lions, leopards, cheetahs. Crocodiles. Egyptian geese, fish and bateleur eagles; crowned guinea fowl, fishing owls, trumpeter hornbills.

11. CHOBE GAME RESERVE, Botswana. Tree-lined rivers, wetland, dry scrub. Wildlife highlights: Kudus, elands, sable antelopes, sitatungas, and lechwes (swamp antelopes). Crocodiles. Spurwinged and Egyptian geese, crowned and blacksmith plovers; red-faced mousebirds, hornbills; boubou, fiscal, and long-tailed shrikes; glossy starlings, bronze mannikins, fire finches, blue waxbills.

12. GORONGOSA NATIONAL PARK, Mozambique. Grassland, scrubland, palm jungle. Wildlife highlights: Lions, leopards, caracals, cheetahs; elephants, buffaloes, hippos, hartebeests, bushbucks, reedbucks, elands; vervet and blue monkeys, bush babies. Crocodiles. Openbill storks, crowned cranes, African spoonbills, pelicans; Mozambique rollers.

13. AMBRE MOUNTAIN NATIONAL PARK, Malagasy. Extinct volcano with crater lakes, moss-covered rain forest with tree ferns. Wildlife highlights: Gentle lemurs, Sanford's lemurs, crowned lemurs.

14. GOLDEN GATE HIGHLANDS NATIONAL PARK, South Africa. Geologically interesting, with colorful rock formations; alpine flora. Wildlife highlights: Elands, hartebeests, gnus, springboks, klipspringers, blesboks. Rare black eagles and lammergeiers.

15. NDUMU GAME RESERVE, South Africa. Low wooded plain, marshes. Wildlife highlights: Hippos, nyalas, impalas, bushbucks, reedbucks, suni antelopes, duikers. Crocodiles (breeding station). Dwarf and Egyptian geese; kingfishers, bee-eaters, hornbills, cuckoos and coucals, barbets; crested francolins, crested and crowned guinea fowl; shrikes, honey guides, sunbirds, finches.

16. QUIÇAMA NATIONAL PARK, Angola. Highland savanna. Wildlife highlights: Elephants, lions, leopards, cheetahs; elands, reedbucks, bushbucks, roans; wild dogs, spotted hyenas; West African manatees; vervet monkeys. Crocodiles.

17. "W" NATIONAL PARK, Dahomey-Niger-Upper Volta. Forest savanna, semidesert. Wildlife highlights: Elephants, buffaloes, hippos; kob, roan, and topi antelopes, hartebeests, oribis (pygmy antelopes), sitatungas (swamp antelopes); lions, cheetahs, leopards, caracals; red monkeys. Crocodiles. Guinea fowl, secretary birds, ground hornbills, fish and martial eagles, bustards.

18. WAZA NATIONAL PARK, Cameroons. Forest, savanna; in Lake Chad basin. Wildlife highlights: Kob, topi, and roan antelopes, reedbucks, waterbucks; elephants, giraffes, lions, leopards, cheetahs. Pelicans, jabiru and marabou storks, sacred ibises, crowned cranes, secretary birds, ostriches.

19. NIOKOLO-KOBA NATIONAL PARK, Senegal. Grassland, woodland. Wildlife highlights: Hippos, bush pigs; reedbucks, hartebeests, oribis, duikers; lions, leopards, jackals, hyenas, wild dogs. Crocodiles, monitor lizards. Guinea fowl, francolins, bustards.

ASIA

More sanctuaries may yet save the endangered animals of this overpopulated continent.

▲ National park

● Wildlife reserve

◆ Sanctuary

1-18 See page 315

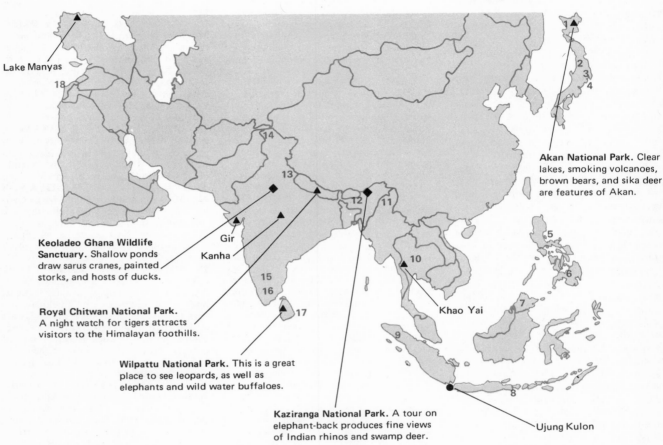

Lake Manyas

18

Akan National Park. Clear lakes, smoking volcanoes, brown bears, and sika deer are features of Akan.

14

13

Gir

Kanha

Keoladeo Ghana Wildlife Sanctuary. Shallow ponds draw sarus cranes, painted storks, and hosts of ducks.

15

16

12 11

Royal Chitwan National Park. A night watch for tigers attracts visitors to the Himalayan foothills.

17

10

Khao Yai

5

6

7

Wilpattu National Park. This is a great place to see leopards, as well as elephants and wild water buffaloes.

9

8

Kaziranga National Park. A tour on elephant-back produces fine views of Indian rhinos and swamp deer.

Ujung Kulon

India

GIR
NATIONAL PARK

The last stronghold of the Asiatic lion —India's national animal—is a 500-square-mile tract of arid, overgrazed scrub forest of stunted acacia and teak trees on the Kathiawar Peninsula, about 550 miles northwest of Bombay. Some 7,000 tribesmen known as maldharis, with 20,000 domestic buffaloes, live in the park, and their herds compete for food with the wild hoofed mammals— the lions' normal prey.

The feature of the Gir National Park is the "lion show," held in late afternoon during the tourist season. Lured by the bleating of a goat, led by an armed guard, a group of lions stalks

leisurely past the viewing area. This policy ensures visitors a good view of the park's star attractions.

Other carnivores in the Gir Forest include leopards, hyenas, sloth bears, and jungle cats; however, these are rarely seen. Hoofed animals include nilgais, spotted chital and sambar deer, chinkara gazelles, four-horned antelopes and serows (goatlike antelopes). Wild boars root in the forest floor. Bands of langur monkeys range through the treetops, often feeding together with chital deer and peafowl in a three-way mutual warning system.

Peafowl are the most numerous as well as the most conspicuous of the park's birds. Others are green pigeons, quails, partridges, sandgrouse, golden orioles, and paradise flycatchers.

How To Get There: *By road from Ahmadabad in Gujarat State to park headquarters at Sasan (about 250 miles). By train from Bombay to Sasan. By air from Bombay to Keshod, about 50 miles from Sasan. Guided tours from Junagadh and Keshod.* **When To Go:** *Open November through June. Best time, January and February.* **Where To Stay:** *Resthouse at Sasan.*

KANHA
NATIONAL PARK

Situated in the central highlands of India, Kanha National Park is one of the best places in India for viewing wildlife. It is among the nine areas in India where a special tiger conservation project, called Operation Tiger, has been launched. Spotted deer, barasinghas, sambars, blackbucks, wild boars, and gaur (wild oxen) feed in the extensive grassland, called maidan, at the center of the park's 178 square miles. Here at Kanha the endangered barasingha, the central Indian subspecies of the swamp deer, finds its last refuge.

Enclosing the maidan are semievergreen and deciduous forests and dense bamboo thickets. Birds include peafowls, red jungle fowls, gray partridges, pigeons and doves, kingfishers, and Malabar pied hornbills.

Supported by an ample base of wild herbivores, tigers thrive in Kanha. Viewing a tiger in this park is a near certainty. Leopards, sloth bears, and dholes, or Indian wild dogs, are other predators; the scavengers are hyenas and jackals. Observation towers are located along the roads, and trained elephants are available for animal viewing. **How To Get There:** *By road from Jabalpur (104 miles) or Mandla (44 miles), both in Madhya Pradesh State. Nearest airport, Nagpur (170 miles), where taxis can be hired.* **When To Go:** *Best time, April to June. Open except during monsoon season (July to October).* **Where To Stay:** *Resthouses at Kanha and Kisli.*

KAZIRANGA WILDLIFE SANCTUARY
The main attraction of this remote but rewarding sanctuary is the great Indian, or one-horned, rhinoceros. This largest of rhino species, like other rhinos in Asia and Africa, was once hunted nearly to the brink of extinction for its "horn." The current population is estimated at 700, of which about 400 roam the open grasslands and reedbeds of the Kaziranga reserve—166 square miles of amply watered, often swampy plains south of the Brahmaputra River.

Kaziranga also has good stocks of wild Asiatic buffaloes, wild elephants, tigers, leopards, civet cats, barasinghas, barking and hog deer, sloth bears, Himalayan black bears, and otters.

Birds are abundant in the reserve. Among the large, easily seen species are spotted-billed pelicans, openbill storks, Pallas' fishing eagles, water cocks, Indian darters (related to the anhinga), cormorants, egrets, and herons. Barheaded geese and thousands of ducks winter in the pools.

A few trails suitable for travel by jeep are open from December to March. The best method for observing wildlife, however, is by trained elephant. **How To Get There:** *By air from Calcutta to Gauhati or Jorhat airports, then by*

road (135 miles from Gauhati, 60 miles from Jorhat). By car from airports. **When To Go:** *Open all year. Best time, November to April.* **Where To Stay:** *Tourist lodge and bungalow on main road from Gauhati.*

KEOLADEO GHANA WILDLIFE SANCTUARY
A former duck-hunting preserve of Indian royalty, Keoladeo Ghana Wildlife Sanctuary (or Bharatpur Bird Sanctuary, as it is also known) lies on the northern Indian plain about 30 miles west of Agra. The 11-square-mile sanctuary lies in a sparsely wooded, shallow basin, which monsoon rains turn into a vast expanse of lake and marsh that attracts huge flocks of water-loving birds.

From July through October, when the water is high, visitors can count on an overwhelming spectacle. The variety of species and the sheer number of birds make Keoladeo Ghana the best location in India for seeing ducks, geese, and wading birds. Outstanding are the tall, stately sarus cranes, with deep-red heads setting off their light gray plumage. Sarus cranes perform their nuptial dances and build their nests on marshy islands. Openbill and painted storks nest in the acacia trees.

The vast concentrations of waterfowl support a number of predatory birds, including steppe eagles, Pallas' fishing eagles, and marsh harriers. In the scattered trees and brush perch blue kingfishers, green bee-eaters, rose-ringed parakeets, and a host of other colorful small birds. Peacocks strut around the sanctuary. Altogether 250 species of birds have been recorded.

Visitors can reach most of the sanctuary on foot, using the roads and embankments that crisscross it, or explore it in small boats poled by guides. **How To Get There:** *By road from Delhi (100 miles) and Agra (30 miles). By train from Delhi and Agra to Bharatpur, 2 miles from sanctuary. Taxis available in Bharatpur.* **When To Go:** *Open all year. Best time, August and September.* **Where To Stay:** *Furnished guesthouse with cook in sanctuary. (Visitors must bring food.)*

Indonesia

UJUNG KULON NATURE RESERVE
Far off the beaten track, the Ujung Kulon Nature Reserve lies at the western tip of Java. Here the last survivors of the nearly extinct Javan rhinoceros are making a slow comeback under strict

protection, supported by the World Wildlife Fund.

Ujung Kulon is mostly lowland with many streams and swamps. The greater part of the area is covered by dense tropical vegetation, dominated by palms, bamboos, giant ferns, or large forest trees.

The Javan rhino was once common in Southeast Asia, but in this century it has been nearly exterminated. From the low point of an estimated 25 individuals in Ujung Kulon in 1967, the rhinos had increased to 44 in 1973.

Another notable denizen of the reserve is the banteng, a threatened species of wild ox. About 200 bantengs live in Ujung Kulon, and groups of up to 40 may be seen grazing in open patches of meadow. Other hoofed animals include muntjacs (barking deer), chevrotains (lesser mouse deer), and wild pigs.

The forest trees are lively with giant squirrels, Javan macaques, two species of leaf monkeys, and Javan gibbons, whose tiny population inhabits a small area at the reserve's eastern border. Flying lemurs glide from tree to tree, and large numbers of fruit bats soar in the evening sky.

Reptiles thrive everywhere. Most fascinating are monitor lizards that reach 6 feet in length and flying lizards called dragons. Pythons sometimes grow to enormous size. Along the shore sea turtles and saltwater crocodiles occasionally can be seen.

More than 100 species of birds have been recorded. Outstanding visitors to the grazing areas are green peafowls and red jungle fowls. Among the forest dwellers are hornbills, barbets, and shama thrushes.

Visitors can best reach Ujung Kulon by boat. The boat trip has the advantage of permitting visits to the crater of Krakatoa and the island bird sanctuary of Pulau Dua en route. Because of the difficulties of organizing such a trip, visitors may find it preferable to join an organized ship tour. **How To Get There:** *By boat from Labuan (reached by car or bus from Djakarta).* **When To Go:** *Open all year. Best time, April through October.* **Where To Stay:** *Accommodations on tour vessels. Guesthouses in Labuan, bungalows on Peutjang and Handuleum Islands.*

Japan

AKAN NATIONAL PARK
This mountainous, forested park in eastern Hokkaido, Japan's northern-

most major island, has some of the most dramatic scenery in the entire island chain. Between stretches of virgin conifer forests, volcanic peaks—two of them still spouting steam—rise as high as 4,500 feet.

The lakes of Akan are famous for their beauty. Kutcharo, the largest crater lake in the world, is noted for its reflections of the surrounding forests and mountains. Mashu is known for its transparent, indigo-colored waters, so clear that one can look down to the incredible depth of 130 feet. Akan, also a crater lake, with four picturesque tree-covered islands, is renowned for an unusual deep-green water plant, found in only a few spots in the world, which forms small velvety balls and is called marimo. These balls float just below the surface of the water, and boats take visitors to see them.

Fine spots for viewing Akan's magnificent scenery are Bihoro and Sempoku Passes and the Sodokai Plateau. These areas are spectacular from late September to early November, when the maple and birch trees turn crimson and yellow. In spring rhododendrons and azaleas set the park aflame. The deep forests shelter Eurasian brown bears, raccoon dogs, sika deer (small Asiatic relatives of the European red deer), badgers, ermines, sables, and varying hares.

Between the city of Kushiro and Akan a refuge for the endangered Japanese, or red-crested, crane has been established. Called Tanchō-zuru National Park after the Japanese name for the bird, it is a marshy area where migrating cranes from Siberia winter and where tame cranes are raised.

How To Get There: *By plane from Tokyo to Sapporo, capital of Hokkaido. From Sapporo to Kushiro, 40 minutes by plane or 6 hours by train. From Sapporo to Obihiro, 4½ hours by train. Bus and train to park.* **When To Go:** *Open all year. Best times, May through October; late September to early November, for fall foliage.* **Where To Stay:** *Three spas in the park; lodges and youth hostels. Hotels in Kushiro and Obihiro.*

Nepal

ROYAL CHITWAN NATIONAL PARK
One of four national parks planned by Nepal to conserve examples of the country's unique range of habitats—from low plains, or Terai, to the icy heights of Mount Everest—Royal Chitwan (or Chitawan as it is often spelled)

has recently been given full national park status. The new park is Nepal's last stronghold of the great Indian rhinoceros. It is also one of the best places in Asia to see the vanishing tiger.

Royal Chitwan embraces 212 square miles of the Rapti River Valley in the Terai and the Himalayan foothills southwest of Katmandu. From the park's undulating grassy plains, the visitor can turn to a magnificent view of snowcapped Himalayan peaks.

Most of the mammals of the Terai and foothills are present in Chitwan. Tigers and leopards are the chief cat species. Both Himalayan black bears and sloth bears are fairly common. The endangered gaur, or wild ox, is the park's most important bovine. Herbivores are plentiful—sambars, spotted deer, hog deer, and barking deer. Serows (a species of rock goat) are sometimes spotted. Rare Asian elephants occasionally enter the park from the adjoining reserve forest.

Schools of sightless Gangetic dolphins, a small, exclusively freshwater species, inhabit the Narayani River. There are two species of freshwater crocodiles.

Water birds include darters, cormorants, bronze-winged jacanas, common gallinules, ruddy shelducks, teals, pintails, and shovelers. Other birds of the riverbanks and marshes are ospreys, cattle egrets, black ibises (a larger relative of the more familiar glossy ibis), adjutant and white-necked storks, and fishing eagles.

Chitwan's pride is Tiger Tops jungle lodge on the Rapti in the western part of the park. Elephants for rhino viewing, boats for mahseer (carp) fishing, and of course opportunities for tiger watching are Tiger Tops' specialties.

How To Get There: *By air from Katmandu to Meghauli airstrip (40 minutes); then by elephant to Tiger Tops (8 miles). By jeep taxi from Katmandu to Saurah campsite.* **When To Go:** *Best time for viewing rhinos, February and March when grass is low.* **Where To Stay:** *Tiger Tops lodge; Saurah campsite (bring camping gear and food).*

Sri Lanka

WILPATTU NATIONAL PARK
Of Sri Lanka's two major national parks, Wilpattu and Ruhunu, the former is noteworthy for its great concentration of leopards. Wilpattu National Park covers 507 square miles of dry jungle in northwestern Ceylon.

Wilpattu includes a 5-mile-wide

coastal strip, as well as shorelines along Portugal and Dutch Bays. These waters are important as the last refuge in the area of the nearly extinct dugong.

The leopards of Wilpattu, the only large predators, are bolder and less solitary than elsewhere in Asia and sometimes hunt in pairs or in even larger groups. Sightings are frequent during early morning and late afternoon. Sambars, spotted deer, muntjacs (barking deer), and mouse deer are the leopards' usual prey.

The marshes, freshwater lakes, and shore areas of Wilpattu attract many water-loving birds, such as five species of herons, egrets, spoonbills, white ibises, cormorants, spot-billed pelicans, and numerous terns—whiskered, bridled, gull-billed, and crested, among others. Painted, white-necked, and openbill storks stalk for insects and small aquatic animals. In winter flocks of migrating shorebirds from Europe and Asia throng the edges of lakes and shores. Other birds include hornbills and Ceylon jungle fowls.

How To Get There: *By car from Colombo (81 miles).* **When To Go:** *Open all year. Best time, May through July.* **Where To Stay:** *Several furnished bungalows, each with cook and housekeeper. (Food and linen not provided, but linen may be rented.)*

Thailand

KHAO YAI NATIONAL PARK
In the lush tropical rain forests of Thailand's oldest and largest national park, visitors can see many of Southeast Asia's colorful tropical birds and large mammals. Located 130 miles northeast of Bangkok, Khao Yai (the name means "Big Mountain") takes in more than 800 square miles of upland, dominated by forested peaks nearly 5,000 feet in height. There are many scenic waterfalls. Ferns and epiphytes (air plants) clothe the trees; at certain seasons orchids are plentiful.

The heavy forest cover of palms, bamboos, evergreens, and deciduous trees provides shelter for a splendid variety of wildlife. Small herds of Asian elephants, numbering as many as 20 individuals, frequent the area north of Khao Kieo Mountain. During the day sambar deer and barking deer can be seen from a lookout tower above an artificial salt lick. At night mouse deer, and occasionally elephants, gaurs (wild oxen), and wild boars, seek the salt and can be seen by flashlight from the tower. Two species of gibbons are common, and pig-tailed macaques and slow lorises are also present. Carnivores include sun bears, tigers, and leopards.

More than 200 species of birds are listed at Khao Yai. Hornbills are present in great numbers. After the breeding season (January to May) great and wreathed hornbills can be seen roosting for the night in big flocks, as many as 200 in a single tree. Colorful smaller birds include emerald doves, fairy bluebirds, and racquet-tailed drongos.

Khao Yai has about 25 miles of paved road and many miles of hiking trails. There are guided hikes and organized tours at night—the best time for viewing the large mammals. **How To Get There:** *By car from Bangkok (130 miles).* **When To Go:** *Open all year. Best time, November through February.* **Where To Stay:** *Cabins, motels, and campgrounds.*

Turkey

LAKE MANYAS NATIONAL PARK

Although it encompasses only 125 acres near the south shore of the Sea of Marmara, Lake Manyas National Park is a veritable "bird paradise" (its original name in Turkish). The shallow lake, fringed with willows and reedbeds, and the nearby woods and low-lying, often-flooded areas provide a welcome haven for birds migrating from Europe to North Africa and back. Much of the region had been privately protected for years, but in 1959 the Turkish Government established Lake Manyas as a bird sanctuary and has since set up a research station and a bird museum.

The parade of migrants includes white storks, glossy ibises, squacco herons, and white-winged black terns. Huge flocks of Dalmatian and white pelicans pass through the park on the way to and from their breeding grounds in the Danube Delta.

In addition to sheltering migrants, Lake Manyas is a breeding place for many species of birds. The most plentiful breeders are great and pygmy cormorants. Gray and purple herons, black-crowned night herons, little egrets, and European spoonbills abound. Elusive little bitterns nest in the reeds.

Many species of waterfowl—ferruginous ducks, ruddy shelducks, teals, and mallards—share the lake. Savi's and great reed warblers nest in the reeds; penduline tits suspend woven nests from reeds or bushes.

How To Get There: *By car from Istanbul across the Bosporus (100 miles). By ferry from Istanbul to Bandirma; then by taxi. By air from Istanbul to Bandirma.* **When To Go:** *Open all year. Best time, summer to early October.* **Where To Stay:** *Hotels at Bandirma and at Erdex, 25 miles from Lake Manyas.*

More Places To See Wildlife in Asia

1. DAISETSUZAN NATIONAL PARK, Japan (Hokkaido). Rugged volcanic mountains with lakes, gorges, waterfalls. Wildlife highlights: Asiatic black bears, sika deer, Japanese macaques; badgers, sables, pikas. Pine grosbeaks, three-toed and black woodpeckers.

2. NIKKO NATIONAL PARK, Japan (Honshu). Volcanic craters, hot springs, waterfalls. Wildlife highlights: Japanese serows, Japanese macaques, Asiatic black bears, sika deer. Rare azure-winged magpies.

3. TAMA ZOO, Japan (Honshu). Picturesque site near Tokyo. White-naped and Japanese cranes; huge aviaries. Unusual insectarium with butterfly farms.

4. FUJI-HAKONE-IZU NATIONAL PARK, Japan (Honshu). Mountains, seacoast. Wildlife highlights: Sika deer, Japanese macaques, raccoon dogs, giant flying squirrels. Japanese auks, goshawks, kingfishers.

5. QUEZON NATIONAL PARK, Philippines (Luzon). Virgin rain forest on mountain peaks. Wildlife highlights: Crab-eating macaques, Philippine deer, Javan wild pigs. Monitor lizards. Pompadour pigeons, fairy bluebirds, megapodes (mound builders), Philippine cockatoos, Philippine falconets.

6. MOUNT APO NATIONAL PARK, Philippines (Mindanao). Mountains, waterfalls, lakes; rain forests. Wildlife highlights: Philippine deer, wild pigs; Philippine tarsiers, flying lemurs, slow lorises, crab-eating macaques; Malay and palm civets. Rare monkey-eating eagles, Apo lorikeets, Apo sunbirds.

7. KINABALU NATIONAL PARK, Malaysia (Borneo). Lofty forested mountains, tropical lowlands. Wildlife highlights: Orangutans, gibbons, leaf monkeys, macaques, slow lorises, tarsiers, flying lemurs; rare Sumatran rhinos; giant ground squirrels, pygmy squirrels, scaly anteaters. Broadbills, spider hunters, babblers, minivets, rhinoceros hornbills.

8. BALURAN GAME RESERVE, Indonesia (Java). Seashore, savanna, mountains. Wildlife highlights: Bantengs, water buffaloes; Javan sambar, barking, and mouse deer; Javan wild pigs; tigers, black leopards; leaf monkeys, crab-eating macaques. Green and red jungle fowls, green peafowls, hornbills.

9. LOSER GAME RESERVE, Indonesia (Sumatra). Forested mountains, tall-grass lowlands. Wildlife highlights: Rare Sumatran rhinos; Asiatic elephants, orangutans; Sumatran serows; Malayan sambar, barking, and mouse deer; white-handed gibbons, pig-tailed and crab-eating macaques; tigers, clouded leopards, Malayan sun bears, Argus pheasants.

10. TUNG SLANG LUANG NATIONAL PARK, Thailand. Forested upland plateau, deep gorges. Wildlife highlights: Asiatic elephants, gaur; sambar and mouse deer; gibbons; tigers, leopards. Silver, fireback, and gray peacock pheasants, red jungle fowls, wreathed hornbills, trogons, barbets, lorikeets.

11. PIDAUNG GAME SANCTUARY, Burma. Grassy plains, jungle. Wildlife highlights: Asiatic elephants, bantengs, water buffaloes; sambar, hog, barking, and mouse deer; tigers, leopards, Malayan sun bears; gibbons, leaf monkeys, pig-tailed macaques. Kalij pheasants, red jungle fowls, green peafowls, painted quails, pied and great hornbills, black-necked storks.

12. MANAS WILD LIFE SANCTUARY, India. River gorge and plains in Himalayan foothills of Assam. Wildlife highlights: Great Indian rhinos, Indian elephants, water buffaloes; hog and barking deer; Asiatic black bears, tigers. Pelicans, egrets, ibises, hornbills.

13. CORBETT NATIONAL PARK, India. Forested Himalayan foothills, river valley. Wildlife highlights: Tigers, leopards; sloth and black bears; Indian elephants; sambar, chital (spotted), barking, and hog deer; Himalayan gorals (rock goats). Gavial and mugger crocodiles. Red jungle fowls, peafowls, kingfishers, bulbuls, mynas, drongos.

14. DACHIGAM WILD LIFE SANCTUARY, India. Kashmir valley with alpine meadows; deodars (cedars), firs, and spruces. Wildlife highlights: Kashmir stags, snow leopards, musk deer, Asiatic black bears. Paradise flycatchers, Himalayan bulbuls, rock thrushes.

15. MUDUMALAI WILD LIFE SANCTUARY, India. Rolling woodland at foot of Nilgiri hills. Wildlife highlights: Tigers, leopards, sloth bears; Indian elephants; gaur; sambar, chital, barking, and mouse deer, four-horned antelopes; langurs, bonnet macaques. Red spur fowls, gray jungle fowls, peafowls, hornbills, paradise flycatchers, Malabar trogons, racket-tailed drongos, crested hawk eagles.

16. PERIYAR WILD LIFE SANCTUARY, India. Manmade lake set among wooded hills. Wildlife highlights: Elephants, gaur; sambar and barking deer; wild pigs; Nilgiri langurs, giant squirrels. Egrets, herons, Indian darters.

17. RUHUNU NATIONAL PARK, Sri Lanka (Ceylon). Lagoons, plains, scrub forest. Wildlife highlights: Ceylonese elephants, leopards, sloth bears; spotted and sambar deer; wild pigs; langurs. Saltwater and mugger crocodiles, monitor lizards. Gray pelicans, Indian darters, Ceylonese hawk eagles; painted, open-billed, and white-necked storks.

18. HULEH SWAMP NATURE RESERVE, Israel. Papyrus marshes. Wildlife highlights: Otters, jungle cats. Herons, egrets, black-necked stilts, spur-winged plovers; pied and Smyrna kingfishers.

AUSTRALIA and NEW ZEALAND

A bountiful supply of parks in widely varying habitats protects unique marsupials and birds.

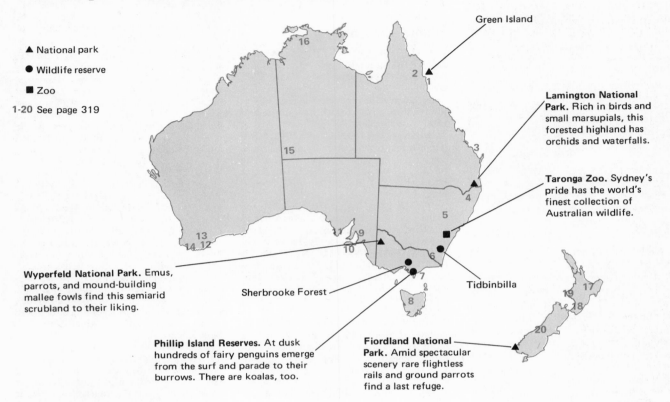

▲ National park

● Wildlife reserve

■ Zoo

1-20 See page 319

Green Island

Lamington National Park. Rich in birds and small marsupials, this forested highland has orchids and waterfalls.

Taronga Zoo. Sydney's pride has the world's finest collection of Australian wildlife.

Wyperfeld National Park. Emus, parrots, and mound-building mallee fowls find this semiarid scrubland to their liking.

Sherbrooke Forest

Tidbinbilla

Phillip Island Reserves. At dusk hundreds of fairy penguins emerge from the surf and parade to their burrows. There are koalas, too.

Fiordland National Park. Amid spectacular scenery rare flightless rails and ground parrots find a last refuge.

Australia

GREEN ISLAND, Queensland

This small coral cay, 18 miles offshore from Cairns, gives its visitors convenient access to the wonders of the Great Barrier Reef, the huge coral expanse that stretches along 1,250 miles of Australia's northeastern coast. Glass-bottomed boats travel over the coral gardens of the surrounding Coral Sea, which are slowly recovering from the damage done by the crown-of-thorns starfish. A privately owned underwater observatory offers a spectacular view of reef life.

Green Island is covered by a dense vegetation of coconut palms, white cedars, wild plums, pandanuses, and casuarinas. Torres Strait and red-crowned pigeons frequent this tiny patch of forest, and a splendid variety of seabirds—silver gulls, noddies, and little, Caspian, crested, and sooty terns—visit the dazzling white beaches. Reef herons, whimbrels, and curlews stalk the shallow waters.

Green Island National Park covers about 17 acres, and 7,500 acres of surrounding waters have recently been set aside as the Marine National Park. Visitors may swim or snorkel, but spearfishing and removal of reef shells and coral are forbidden. Because of damage to the fragile coral habitat and also the possible danger of stepping on a poisonous stonefish, walking on the reef itself is not advisable.

Nature photographers can have a deep-sea field day at the underwater observatory. Through its 22 thick plate-glass windows thousands of free-living, unbelievably brilliant fish and other coral-loving sea animals are visible as they come and go amid staghorn, golden leaf, brain, and many other species of living corals. Huge schools of silvery small fish scatter before the larger predators, such as Spanish mackerels and trevallies. Cleaner fish remove parasites from their clients; gaily striped parrot fish nibble at the coral with their sharp beaks. Amid the waving fronds of sea anemones small clown fish nestle, immune to the poisonous tentacles. Gi-

ant clams, up to 4 feet wide, open their mantled, serrated jaws and strain the seawater for food.

How To Get There: *Daily launch service from Cairns.* **When To Go:** *Open all year. Best time, April to November.* **Where To Stay:** *In Cairns; island guesthouse (April to November).*

LAMINGTON NATIONAL PARK, Queensland

A rugged volcanic plateau, deeply cut by winding river gorges that sparkle with literally hundreds of waterfalls, is the setting for Lamington National Park. Its 70 square miles stretch along the boundary of New South Wales.

Plentiful rainfall supports a richly varied plant life. There are areas of lush rain forest, dominated by towering, buttressed trees, and open eucalyptus forests, sometimes with an understory of grass trees—short black trunks crowned with a tuft of grasslike leaves. In small, high areas gnarled antarctic beeches, some believed to be more than 1,000 years old, grow at the northern limit of their range. In moist spots rosettes of staghorn, elkhorn, and bird's-nest ferns decorate trees and rocks; tree trunks are laced with pothos vines and climbing ferns. More than 20 species of orchids—some spectacular like the golden king orchid, others small and fragrant like the orange-blossom orchid–bloom on trees, rocks, and cliff ledges.

Aside from its magnificent forested setting, Lamington chiefly attracts visitors by its colorful birds: King parrots, crimson rosellas, rainbow lorikeets, golden whistlers, black-and-gold regent bowerbirds, and deep-blue satin bowerbirds. Pied currawongs, noisy crow-sized birds, and brush turkeys, which incubate their eggs in enormous mounds of rotting vegetation, are plentiful and conspicuous. Nine species of pigeons, six of honey eaters, five of thornbills, and four of scrub wrens keep bird watchers busy with identification. Among less-often-seen birds are Albert lyrebirds, paradise riflebirds (a species of bird of paradise), eastern whipbirds (named for the whiplike crack of their call), and rufous scrubbirds.

Although most of the park's mammals are nocturnal and therefore difficult to observe, red-necked wallabies can be seen feeding in late afternoon or early morning in clearings near the park entrances; bandicoots frequent guesthouse lawns; and brush-tailed and ringtailed possums and sugar gliders come to feeding stations.

Lamington has about 90 miles of trails that climb in and out of ravines and lead to waterfalls or lookouts over valleys, mountains, and distant plains. The park with its cool climate is a walker's paradise.

How To Get There: *By car or tourist bus from Brisbane, Queensland (75 miles).* **When To Go:** *Open all year. Best time, May through November.* **Where To Stay:** *One guesthouse in park, one at park boundary.*

PHILLIP ISLAND RESERVES, Victoria

Washed by the chilly waters of Bass Strait, Phillip Island lies just off the Australian coast, some 80 miles south of Melbourne. Once a farming community, the island now contains several small but noteworthy nature reserves. They total a mere 1,300 acres but offer visitors unusually good opportunities for seeing such typical Australian animals as the fairy penguin and the koala.

In the sand hills along the shores are large breeding colonies of muttonbirds, or short-tailed shearwaters, whose migration route takes them as far north as the Aleutian Islands. But the outstanding wildlife attraction of Phillip Island is the fairy penguin, the only species of penguin native to Australia. Standing a mere 15 inches, this is the smallest of all the penguins. Phillip Island has Australia's largest penguin colony.

The penguins spend the day at sea, feeding, and return en masse at dusk. The "Penguin Parade" at Summerland Beach, when hundreds of penguins emerge from the surf and waddle back to their burrows, is an unforgettable sight. Their courting display (August to mid-October) is another fascinating spectacle: The birds face each other with vibrating flippers and beaks, and occasionally slap each other on the back to the accompaniment of throaty wails.

Two small reserves are devoted to koalas. These teddy-bearlike marsupials are often hard to spot in the wild, but the manna-gum trees they inhabit on Phillip Island are relatively small, and the koalas can be easily observed and photographed.

How To Get There: *By road from Melbourne (about 70 miles). Bus tours from Melbourne.* **When To Go:** *Reserves open all year. Best time for viewing penguins, October through May.* **Where To Stay:** *Hotels and motels in Melbourne and the resort town of Cowes. Several campgrounds, one with trailer facilities.*

SHERBROOKE FOREST PARK, Victoria

Even if these 2,000 acres of mountain forest, in the Dandenong Ranges, only 30 miles east of Melbourne, had no wildlife to offer, Sherbrooke Forest would be worth a visit just to see its almost tropical beauty. Luxuriant tree ferns canopy its walks; its towering mountain ashes (a variety of eucalyptus) are among the world's tallest hardwoods. But Sherbrooke also has superb lyrebirds—about 120 of them—and they are indeed superb as an attraction.

The male lyrebird is a dancer with a magnificent feathered display and a singer with an incredible repertoire, which blends faultless imitations of the songs of other birds with his own clear, ringing calls. When he is not showing off, the male is an inconspicuous brown and gray bird, somewhat resembling a pheasant with a long, trailing tail of filmy feathers. During most of the year visitors can usually see a male and three or four females, duller and shorter of tail, scratching in the damp forest debris with powerful backward kicks.

To observe the male lyrebird's display is another matter. For one thing, lyrebirds breed in the Australian winter, when the forest can be dank and chilly. For another, the male requires a certain amount of privacy if he is to perform. The display areas are slightly raised mounds of bare earth some 4 feet in diameter. Within his territory of 6 to 10 acres, a male may have a series of these mounds, located near the territories of his various females.

The truly fantastic exhibition begins as the male mounts his mound, utters a few soft clicks and churrs, then gives a selection of loud calls and songs. If the bird is undisturbed by too insistent watchers, he will soon go into his dance. The two long, silver-marked outer tail feathers forming the "lyre" and the filmy inner train are both raised and spread forward so that they cover the bird's head and body with a shimmering, diaphanous veil. Dancing back and forth, the bird quivers its tail feathers.

How To Get There: *By car from Melbourne. By electric train to Belgrave (30 miles); hourly bus connections to park. Scheduled bus tours from Melbourne.* **When To Go:** *Open all year. Best months for lyrebird display, May and June.* **Where To Stay:** *Hotels and motels in Melbourne or nearby towns.*

TARONGA ZOO, New South Wales

Although Taronga Zoo, the pride of Sydney, exhibits animals from all parts of the world, its outstanding feature is the world's most comprehensive collection of the animals that are unique to Australia and its nearby islands.

The Australian Section is close to the main entrance, so that visitors who want to see the Australian animals need not walk through the whole of the zoo's 75 acres. Here are 16 different types of kangaroos, ranging from giant red kangaroos that can rear to a height of 7 feet, to potoroos that are less than 1 foot high. Most of the kangaroos are displayed in irregular moated paddocks against a background of native vegetation. Numbats, beautiful and rare little animals that live on an exclusive diet of termites, are exhibited outdoors.

Most of Australia's mammals are shy and inactive by day and are seldom seen. It is difficult, for example, to get close to a koala in the wild, but, at Taronga Zoo, visitors can walk up a spiral ramp and observe koalas in their treetop habitat, only a few feet away.

Australia is the home of the egg-laying mammals known as monotremes. Two platypuses are on view for 1 hour twice a day in a 20-foot-long aquarium in a large building devoted to their support. The other egg-laying mammal, the echidna, or spiny anteater, may be seen in several kangaroo enclosures.

Taronga's collection of Australian birds (more than 300 kinds) is so large that it is distributed over the whole zoo. In the Australian Section native black swans, ducks, geese, coots, and other waterfowl can be seen in a series of cascading ponds. Here, too, is the rain forest aviary, where visitors walk on a causeway through rain forest vegetation and come within arm's length of bellbirds, whipbirds, bowerbirds, lyrebirds, pigeons (including enormous crowned pigeons), parrots and parakeets, honey eaters, and fantails.

The reptile department, in the Australian Section, displays a wide range of Australian lizards, from the giant monitors to tiny dragons and skinks, pythons, and a collection of venomous snakes, which includes deadly taipans and tiger snakes.

Near the lower entrance of the zoo (where visitors can depart for the cross-harbor ferry) is a large aquarium devoted mainly to Australian fish and other aquatic animals. Here may be seen colorful fish from the Great Barrier Reef, as well as the crown-of-thorns starfish that is destroying parts of the reef. The Australian lungfish has an exhibit to itself, and air-breathing mudskippers climb among mangroves.

In addition to its wealth of animals and its gardens—with the accent on Australian native plants—Taronga Zoo offers as a special bonus a splendid panorama of Sydney Harbor and the downtown city area.

Visitor Services: *Cafeteria, picnic areas. Contact area where children can feed and touch tame animals.*

TIDBINBILLA NATURE RESERVE, Australian Capital Territory

Cradled within the Tidbinbilla and Gibraltar Ranges, this reserve is a treasury of plant and animal life and striking geological formations.

Large enclosures on the valley floor hold indigenous gray kangaroos, introduced red kangaroos, and reintroduced flightless emus. The koalas' enclosure, on the lower western slopes, is placed where one of their food trees, the ribbon gum, is plentiful. As the visitor ascends the ranges, many different eucalypts—brown barrel, manna gum, narrow-leafed peppermint, alpine ash, and snow gum—grow at varying levels of altitude.

Many arboreal marsupials, such as brush- and ring-tailed possums and greater gliders, can be found on the forested slopes. Terrestrial marsupials include gray kangaroos, red-necked and swamp wallabies, and wombats. In lightly wooded and grassland areas the spiny anteater, an egg-laying mammal, is sometimes seen as it wanders in search of food.

Tidbinbilla has a bird list of more than 100 species. There are kookaburras, cuckoos, wonga and forest bronzewing pigeons, honey eaters, fantails, wood swallows, and cockatoos and other parrots. Predators are wedge-tailed eagles, peregrine falcons, and nocturnal boobook owls. Male satin bowerbirds, frequent visitors to the bird-feeding area in winter, build bowers to attract females in spring and summer. The protected slopes are the habitat of the superb lyrebird, the master mimic whose loud, ringing calls can often be heard in the winter months.

Waterfowl enclosures will produce indigenous black ducks, wood ducks, and reintroduced gray and chestnut teals. To increase the variety of Australian waterfowl on exhibit, black swans, Cape Barren geese, musk ducks, and pink-eared ducks have been introduced. Ponds and wet areas induce many waders to visit the reserve. White-faced herons and royal spoonbills are among the larger visitors.

A number of trails traverse the western slopes. The Turkey Hill Geology Trail features groups of granite boulders known as tors, exposed by weathering and erosion. The Red Hill Nature Trail leads through a ribbon gum forest and a wet gully with tree ferns and shield ferns up to a lookout with a fine view. White cockatoos, wombats, and swamp wallabies may be seen.

How To Get There: *By car or tourist bus from Canberra (25 miles).* **When To Go:** *Open all year.* **Where To Stay:** *Hotels and motels in Canberra.*

WYPERFELD NATIONAL PARK, Victoria

Essentially, this 220-square-mile reserve in Victoria's semiarid northwestern corner has been set aside to protect one bird, the mallee fowl, to save an area of typical mallee flora and fauna, and to preserve part of the rich flood plain of the Wimmera River. "Mallee" is an aboriginal word for several varieties of dwarf, drought-resistant eucalypts.

The mallee flora and its associated wildlife are vulnerable to fire. Wyperfeld has been swept by two great fires since it was established in 1921. The heaviest loser in such conflagrations is the mallee fowl, one of the remarkable family of birds known as mound builders. About the size of a small turkey and beautifully patterned in soft gray, brown, and black, the mallee fowl lays its eggs deep in mounds of rotting vegetation heaped by the breeding pair. The eggs are hatched by the combined heat of the sun and the heat of fermentation inside this natural incubator. The heat is carefully controlled by the male, who opens the mound each morning, checks the temperature with his sensitive tongue and beak, then either closes the mound or leaves it open for all or part of the day to maintain a uniform temperature. After hatching, the precocial chicks struggle out unaided and are able to feed themselves.

More than 200 other bird species have been recorded at Wyperfeld, with 91 listed as breeding. There are few hours of the day when wedge-tailed or whistling eagles are not to be seen wheeling in the sky. On the flood plain, flocks of parrots—Regent, red-backed, ringneck, and galah—and smaller numbers of cockatoos—both pink and white —fly in to feed and drink. The ventriloquial notes of crested bellbirds ring through the mallee. Black-faced cuckoo shrikes are common.

The "big" bird feature of Wyperfeld is the emu, largest of living birds after the ostrich. Emus are present in force—females lead parades of striped young and pose for photographs along the ring road. Emus and black-faced kangaroos can often be seen feeding together in the dried lake beds.

How To Get There: *By car from Melbourne, via the Henty Highway through Hopetoun or the Western Highway through Dimboola and Rainbow (271 miles).* **When To Go:** *Open all year. Best time, winter and spring.* **Where To Stay:** *No accommodations in park, but camping permitted. Hotel in Hopetoun, motel in Dimboola.*

New Zealand

FIORDLAND NATIONAL PARK, South Island

With 4,725 square miles, ranging from rugged coast to mountain heights above 9,000 feet, Fiordland National Park is one of the world's largest national parks and one of the most unspoiled. This southwestern corner of New Zealand's South Island, visited by Captain James Cook in 1777, offers a wide variety of habitats, including a dozen mountain ranges, beech forests and rain forests, dozens of lakes, 14 fiords, many rivers and waterfalls.

The 33-mile Milford Track permits

hiking from Lake Te Anau (largest in the park, 133 square miles) to magnificent Milford Sound at the park's northwestern corner. Milford is also accessible by air or by road, both dramatic approaches. At Milford Sound launches take awed visitors for one of the world's most spectacular boat rides.

Besides two of the three species of the kiwi, national symbol of New Zealand, Fiordland's birdlife includes two flightless, nearly extinct birds—the takahe, a large rail; and the kakapo, a large greenish-yellow ground parrot. Both of these birds exist only in Fiordland.

From 1849 until 1898 just four living takahes were recorded; for the next half century not a single one was sighted, and the species was written off as extinct. But in 1948 a few takahes were discovered in an isolated glaciated valley 2,200 feet above Lake Te Anau; the population was estimated at no more than seven pairs. From this precarious rebirth conservationists have nursed the species back to about 200 pairs.

The kakapo was also rediscovered in recent years. This nocturnal ground parrot is confined to New Zealand's high beech forests and grasslands, where it is still endangered by habitat destruction and predators.

A third endangered New Zealand bird, the South Island wattled crow, or kokako, may survive in scattered Fiordland localities near the timberline.

Besides these rare birds Fiordland is a refuge for crested penguins, blue ducks, paradise ducks, pukekos (dark-blue rails with red faces and legs), yellow-crowned parakeets, fantails, yellow-breasted tits, bush robins, tuis, and bellbirds.

All land mammals in New Zealand are introduced species. Native fur seals and sea lions are present in the fiords.

How To Get There: *By car or bus to Te Anau from Queenstown (113 miles), Dunedin (181 miles), or Invercargill (98 miles). By air to Milford Sound or Te Anau.* **When To Go:** *Open all year. Best time, December through April (local summer). Trails closed in winter.* **Where To Stay:** *Hotels at Milford Sound, Te Anau, and Manapouri. Hostels at Milford Sound, Te Anau, Cascade Creek, and Manapouri.*

More Places To See Wildlife in Australia and New Zealand

1. BELLENDEN-KER NATIONAL PARK, Australia (Queensland). Rugged mountain range, coastal lowland. Wildlife highlights: Tree kangaroos, ringtail and striped possums, brown and spotted cuscuses. Golden and tooth-billed bowerbirds, Prince Albert riflebirds; white-tailed kingfishers, brush turkeys and scrub fowl (mound builders), cassowaries.

2. LAKE BARRINE NATIONAL PARK, Australia (Queensland). Volcanic crater lake; tropical rain forest with tall kauri trees. Wildlife highlights: Platypuses, brushtail, ringtail, and striped possums, sugar gliders. Prince Albert riflebirds, tooth-billed bowerbirds, whipbirds, brush turkeys, cassowaries.

3. HERON ISLAND NATIONAL PARK, Australia (Queensland). Wooded coral island on Great Barrier Reef. Wildlife highlights: Wedge-tailed muttonbirds, white-capped noddies, sea eagles. Nesting sea turtles.

4. GIBRALTAR RANGE NATIONAL PARK, Australia (New South Wales). Rocky upland, deep gorges; subtropical rain forest, spectacular wildflowers. Wildlife highlights: Platypuses, echidnas (spiny anteaters), wombats, koalas, gray kangaroos, wallabies, marsupial tiger cats. Rufous scrubbirds (rare), paradise riflebirds, superb and Albert lyrebirds; satin bowerbirds, buff-breasted pittas, spine-tailed log runners, whipbirds.

5. WARRUMBUNGLE NATIONAL PARK, Australia (New South Wales). Eroded volcanic range with unusual rock formations. Wildlife highlights: Koalas, echidnas; gray kangaroos, wallaroos (mountain kangaroos), rock wallabies. Wedge-tailed eagles; 18 species of parrots, including rainbow and scaly-breasted lorikeets; 16 species of honey eaters.

6. KOSCIUSKO NATIONAL PARK, Australia (New South Wales). In Australian Alps; tundra with many wildflowers. Wildlife highlights: Platypuses, echidnas, red-necked wallabies, wombats, gray kangaroos. Wedge-tailed eagles, emus, ganggang cockatoos, crimson rosellas, flame robins, superb lyrebirds.

7. WILSON'S PROMONTORY NATIONAL PARK, Australia (Victoria). Mountainous seacoast. Wildlife highlights: Echidnas; pygmy, ring-tailed, and brush-tailed possums, koalas, wombats, wallabies. Crested terns, silver gulls; pied and sooty oyster catchers, spur-winged plovers; musk ducks, whistling and sea eagles; white cockatoos, blue-winged parrots, crimson and eastern rosellas; kookaburras; magpie larks; superb blue wrens.

8. MOUNT FIELD NATIONAL PARK, Australia (Tasmania). Rugged, forested mountains; waterfalls, high bogs. Wildlife highlights: Platypuses, Tasmanian devils, Tasmanian echidnas; bandicoots, wombats, wallabies. Tasmanian native hens (gallinulelike birds), yellow wattlebirds, green rosellas.

9. CLELAND CONSERVATION PARK, Australia (South Australia). Rugged upland with scrub forest. Large enclosed reserves for native fauna: Red and gray kangaroos, wallabies, euros, wombats, koalas, echidnas; emus, parrots, Cape Barren geese. Unusual peat bog area.

10. FLINDERS CHASE NATIONAL PARK, Australia (South Australia). On Kangaroo Island; cliffs, dunes, beaches. Wildlife highlights: Echidnas, platypuses; ring-tailed, brush-tailed, and pygmy possums, seals. Black cockatoos, black swans, Australian pelicans, brush turkeys.

11. LINCOLN NATIONAL PARK, Australia (South Australia). Sandhills, mallee scrub, spectacular coastal cliffs. Wildlife highlights: Scrub kangaroos. Sea eagles, ospreys; mallee fowl, emus; Port Lincoln and rock parrots.

12. TWO PEOPLES BAY WILDLIFE SANCTUARY, Australia (Western Australia). Hilly, semiarid coastland, covered with dense scrub. Wildlife highlights: Rare dibblers (tiny marsupials long thought extinct), honey possums. Noisy scrubbirds.

13. STIRLING RANGES NATIONAL PARK, Australia (Western Australia). Rugged peaks with cloud forest remnants, dry eucalypt forest, mallee heath; rare wildflowers. Wildlife highlights: Gray kangaroos, wallabies, wombats. Emus, purple-crowned lorikeets, many species of honey eaters.

14. WALPOLE-NORNALUP NATIONAL PARK, Australia (Western Australia). Heavily timbered coastal hills with magnificent karri trees, flowering shrubs and creepers. Wildlife highlights: Gray kangaroos, short-nosed bandicoots, ring-tailed possums. Purple-crowned lorikeets, red-capped parrots, black cockatoos; red-winged and splendid blue wrens.

15. AYERS ROCK–MOUNT OLGA NATIONAL PARK, Australia (Northern Territory). Fantastic sandstone domes rising from desert plain. Wildlife highlights: Dingoes (wild dogs), bandicoots. Emus, Australian bustards, other desert birds.

16. WOOLWONGA WILDLIFE SANCTUARY, Australia (Northern Territory). Tropical wetland with swamps and lagoons. Wildlife highlights: Magpie geese, green pygmy geese, Burdekin ducks; jabirus (storks), white ibises, jacanas. Agile wallabies.

17. UREWERA NATIONAL PARK, New Zealand (North Island). Densely forested mountains, waterfalls, lakes. Wildlife highlights: Kiwis, wekas (rails); paradise and blue ducks; kakas (parrots), shining cuckoos, New Zealand pigeons, moreporks (owls), tuis (throat-tufted honey eaters).

18. MOUNT BRUCE BIRD RESERVE, New Zealand (North Island). Breeding sanctuary for takahes and wekas (rails), kiwis; saddlebacks (New Zealand wattlebirds), flightless kakapo parrots.

19. EGMONT NATIONAL PARK, New Zealand (North Island). Forested mountains. Wildlife highlights: Brown kiwis, kakas (parrots), shining cuckoos, North Island tomtits, North Island wattled crows, or kokakos.

20. WESTLAND NATIONAL PARK, New Zealand (South Island). Adjoins spectacular Mount Cook. Wildlife highlights: Keas and kakas (parrots), pukekos (rails), paradise and blue ducks, yellow-crowned parakeets, tuis, New Zealand pigeons.

EUROPE

In a continent with little space for wildlife, reserves and zoos ensure survival.

Rondane National Park. This unspoiled northern wilderness has lakes, peaks, and tundra with wild reindeer.

Slimbridge. Almost all the world's ducks, geese, and other waterfowl are on display in this Severn Valley preserve.

Frankfurt Zoo. A polarscape with penguins, jungles with crocodiles and pythons, and a gorilla family are some of the wonders here.

Camargue Reserve. Europe's only flamingos feed in the brackish lagoons and sometimes even breed.

Coto Doñana National Park. One of Europe's most important sanctuaries shelters the endangered Spanish imperial eagle and Spanish lynx.

Gran Paradiso National Park. This alpine refuge for ibexes and chamois has 1,500 species of flowers and a great view of Mount Blanc.

Neusiedlersee Reserve. Colonies of great egrets and spoonbills, rare in Europe, nest in the reedbeds of this shallow steppe lake.

Stora Sjöfallet
Fair Isle
Lindisfarne and Farne Islands
Cairngorms
London and Whipsnade
Norfolk
Minsmere
Skanes Djurpark
Texel and Terschelling
Carl Hagenbeck
Berlin
Bialowieza
Antwerp
Bavarian
Jersey
Basel
La Vanoise
Zurich
Swiss
Marchauen-Marchegg
Danube Delta
Valle de Ordesa

▲ National park
● Wildlife reserve
■ Zoo

1-16 See page 329

Austria

MARCHAUEN - MARCHEGG NATURE RESERVE

A few years ago the area occupied by this wildlife reserve, one of the most luxuriant of Europe's remaining riverine forests, was about to be destroyed for commercial land development. The 2,000 villagers of nearby Marchegg raised a large sum of money, the World Wildlife Fund guaranteed a matching amount, and this invaluable habitat of wet meadows and woodland was saved.

The 2,760 acres of the Marchauen reserve lie along the west bank of the March, a Danube tributary, about 40 miles east of Vienna. They are part of a plain that extends to the foothills of the Carpathian Mountains. The birdlife is varied. Ponds attract migrating waterfowl: Mallards, gadwalls, garganeys, pochards, goosanders (common mergansers), and greylag geese. The reserve has the last surviving colony of cormorants in Austria and two large colonies of herons. For many years the biggest tree-nesting colony of white storks in Austria (18 pairs) has flourished there.

Seven species of woodpeckers, including the uncommon Syrian woodpecker, and four species of owls nest there. Among the predators are black kites, white-tailed eagles, hobby falcons, goshawks, sparrow hawks, and honey buzzards. Marshy and wooded habitats abound in warblers.

Marchauen's mammals include red deer, roe deer, and wild boars. Martens are sometimes visible, and a lynx occasionally ambles into the nature reserve. **How To Get There:** *By car or bus from Vienna to Marchegg (40 miles).* **When To Go:** *Open all year. Best time, spring.* **Where To Stay:** *Hotels in Vienna, Marchegg, and nearby villages.*

NEUSIEDLERSEE AND SEEWINKEL RESERVES

Center of a region of great ecological value, known among bird observers for its unusual species, the Neusiedlersee is a remarkable steppe lake, the only example in Western Europe. It is 22 miles long, from 5 to 10 miles wide, and yet at no point more than 6 feet deep.

The combined areas of the Neusiedlersee Reserve and the adjoining Seewinkel Reserve (including Lange Lacke) total more than 85,000 acres. The Seewinkel is a zone of shallow marshes, pools, and small salt lakes. Both reserves are administered by the World Wildlife Fund. The town of Neusiedl-am-See has a museum and a bird observatory.

The area of the Neusiedlersee and the Seewinkel forms a vast breeding ground that attracts more than 300 species of birds. Hidden among the reeds are small clearings sought out by such elusive species as Baillon's crake (a small raillike marsh bird). The frog chorus is punctuated by the songs of warblers and bluethroats. Penduline tits build hanging nests of reed fluff, and bearded tits secure nests to reed stalks.

These reedy fastnesses are Europe's most westerly home of the great egret. European spoonbills also nest. (Both egrets and spoonbills are rare in the rest of Europe.) The edges of the small ponds attract migrating waders—broadbilled sandpipers en route to northern breeding grounds and red-necked (northern) phalaropes.

Lange Lacke harbors numerous species of ducks and geese. (A visiting naturalist once recorded some 5,000 waterfowl of 13 different species in a single day.) In late fall up to 30,000 migrating white-fronted and bean geese may pause on the two larger lakes.

White storks nest on chimneys in every nearby village, notably in the town of Rust. Black storks are occasionally seen soaring over the plains.
How To Get There: *By car or bus from Vienna to Neusiedl-am-See (30 miles).* **When To Go:** *Open all year. Best months, April and May.* **Where To Stay:** *Hotels and pensions in Neusiedl-am-See. Campground at Podersdorf. Camping at St. Andra. Youth hostel at Neusiedl.*

Belgium

ANTWERP ZOOLOGICAL GARDEN

Opened in 1843 and rebuilt after World War II, Belgium's national zoo, in the heart of Antwerp, maintains a traditional garden atmosphere. Yet, for all its antique charm, this is one of the most scientifically oriented, research-minded zoos in the world, and its facilities are among the most modern and innovative anywhere. In 1945, for example, the Antwerp Zoo invented a new way to exhibit birds, which was later widely copied throughout the world: In a number of indoor exhibits nothing but a difference in lighting separates visitors from birds—no glass,

wires, or bars. While the birds bask in "sunlight" amid living plants, visitors view them from a darkened gallery. The realistic twilight world of the Nocturama makes visible the activities of pottos and bush babies (small lorises and lemurs), jumping mice, opossums, and fennecs (big-eared desert foxes).

Within this unique combination of Old World tradition and modernity the zoo displays some 8,000 animals, representing about 500 different species. Many are notable for their rarity. Antwerp was the first zoo to import okapis, forest-dwelling cousins of the giraffe. It is one of the few zoos to display mountain gorillas and was the first to breed this endangered species. Other rarities include white, black, and Indian rhinos; three kinds of African buffaloes, including the seldom-seen red buffalo; African manatees; South American maned wolves; and pygmy chimpanzees.

In addition, the Royal Zoological Society has established a breeding station for endangered animals such as Père David's deer and European bison at Planckendael, south of Antwerp.
Visitor Services: *Regular performances by dolphins. Lectures, films. Restaurants and terrace café.*

France

CAMARGUE ZOOLOGICAL AND BOTANICAL RESERVE

One of Europe's most important bird sanctuaries, the Camargue Reserve is famous for its great variety of species —more than 320 have been recorded— and for its large colony of greater flamingos, the only one in Europe.

The reserve occupies 26,000 acres in the heart of the Camargue, the vast, low-lying marshy plain formed where the Rhone River meets the Mediterranean. Surrounded by grazing lands, rice farms, vineyards, and saltworks, the reserve is run by a conservation society.

Much of the reserve consists of saltwater and brackish lagoons, studded with low islands. The lagoons are the feeding grounds of flamingos, which may number as many as 25,000 in a favorable year. Black-headed gulls and at least four species of terns—gull-billed, whiskered, little, and common—breed here, and the Kentish plover nests along the foreshore.

Inland, on higher and drier ground, there are bee-eaters, rollers, great spotted cuckoos, and a number of different warblers. In winter as many as 100,000 migratory ducks—pochards, mallards, teals, European wigeons, gadwalls, and tufted ducks—feed in the lagoons.

From mid-July on, shorebirds from northern Europe congregate on the mud flats; among them are lapwings, black-tailed godwits, pratincoles (swallowlike shorebirds), and sandpipers.

The Camargue Reserve is operated as a living laboratory, and admission is by permit only. This is no drawback to the Camargue's visitors, however, since excellent views of the rich birdlife may be had from its boundaries.

Outside the reserve the Camargue contains much the same assortment of birds, plus hoopoes, black kites, falcons, and three species of woodpeckers. Here, too, flourish some of Europe's last beavers. Wild boars are increasing, but the most numerous large mammals are the semiwild black cattle and white horses, traditional symbols of the Camargue.
How To Get There: *By train to Arles, Aigues-Mortes, or Le Grau-du-Roi. By plane to Marseilles. By car to the Camargue. One-day guided train tours from Avignon.* **When To Go:** *Best seasons, spring, early fall, and winter.* **Where To Stay:** *Hotels at Arles, Saintes-Maries-de-la-Mer, other nearby resorts.*

LA VANOISE NATIONAL PARK

The first national park established in France, LaVanoise is as notable for its magnificent alpine scenery as for its wildlife. Located in the Savoy Alps, east of Grenoble, La Vanoise extends from about 3,280 feet above sea level to 12,670 feet at its highest point.

The park's steep slopes are marked by several zones of vegetation. As you ascend the mountains, grassland gradually gives way to coniferous forest, heath, and alpine meadowland, where gentians, buttercups, and edelweisses bloom. Still higher are talus slopes (fallen rock fragments) and bare rock face, where hardy plants such as moss campions have found a niche. Finally there are glaciers and permanent snow.

By far the most common mammal is the marmot, which inhabits the high meadows and talus slopes. Never venturing far from their dens, they can be observed if approached cautiously.

The star attraction of La Vanoise is the ibex, recently on the verge of extinction but now increasing under protection. At last count there were about 300 ibexes in the park, mainly in the rock and talus zones. More numerous (about 3,000) but less approachable are the chamois.

About 115 species of birds inhabit La Vanoise for at least part of the year. In summer birds include water pipits and stonechats; alpine accentors, snow finches, black grouse, and alpine choughs are permanent residents. Ptarmigans live high among the rocks, and golden eagles soar above the peaks.

La Vanoise is closed to automobiles, but visitors may explore it along 180 miles of well-marked hiking trails. Tours led by naturalists are available.

How To Get There: *By car from Grenoble, via Lanslebourg; from Geneva, via Annecy and Albertville. By train to Modane, Bourg-Saint-Maurice, Moutiers.* **When To Go:** *Best time, May to October.* **Where To Stay:** *Hotels at Val-d'Isère and other nearby villages. Furnished rooms in farmhouses. Overnight cabins in park. Camping outside park.*

Germany, West

BAVARIAN FOREST NATIONAL PARK

The Bavarian Forest National Park, the first in the Federal Republic, combines the concepts of recreation, bioecological research, and wildlife conservation. The park spreads over 50 square miles of forest land, in the Bayerischer Wald highlands of southeastern Germany.

When the national park was created in 1969, some of the wildlife species native to this area along the border with Czechoslovakia had been exterminated. There are plans to reintroduce the species that made up the original fauna, particularly the northern lynx, beaver, Ural owl, and raven. Measures have already been taken to restore the original forest of spruce, beech, and fir. The most significant mammals now are roe and red deer, martens, badgers, and some of Germany's last otters.

The heavy forest provides excellent cover and food for three rare species of grouses—the capercaillie, black grouse, and hazel hen. Other forest birds are three-toed woodpeckers and ring ouzels. Predatory birds include Tengmalm's owls and goshawks.

The Bavarian Forest National Park is laid out in three zones, each for a different use. Along the southern rim is a recreational zone, containing an information center and large enclosures where you can view and photograph animals in natural surroundings. The largest of the three zones is the one for hikers, with trails laid out for nature study. The innermost zone is the nature reserve proper. This area is intended for the preservation of rare plants and animals and for scientific studies. Guided tours are conducted throughout the park.

How To Get There: *By car from Munich, Nürnberg, and other major cities.*

By train to Grafenau. **When To Go:** *Open all year.* **Where To Stay:** *Inns, guesthouses, and campgrounds near park and in nearby towns.*

BERLIN ZOOLOGICAL GARDENS

This fine zoo has chosen comprehensiveness for its theme. As if bringing a wildlife encyclopedia to life, it has gathered more than 13,000 specimens belonging to about 2,400 species.

Berlin's comprehensive approach involves exhibiting all members of the animal kingdom—mammals, birds, reptiles, amphibians, fish, and invertebrates (relatively few zoos include the last two classifications). Biological characteristics determine the way animals are grouped for display. More than 40 kinds of meat eaters are shown in the new carnivore house, for example.

The "something of everything" approach prevails even in specific exhibits. Numerous zoos have both African bush and Indian elephants, but few have the African forest elephant. In the zebra house you will be able to compare the stripe patterns of four different species.

Superlatives are the rule at the Berlin Zoo. The world's largest birdhouse, for instance, displays nearly 300 parrots of 75 species. The aquarium holds the world's largest collection of fish, reptiles, amphibians, and invertebrates: 1,450 species, totaling 9,000 specimens. More than 250 tanks display a wide variety of freshwater and saltwater fish, including such curiosities as lungfish.

Another common denominator at Berlin is rarity. The deer park includes two species that are seldom encountered in zoos—Burmese brow-antlered deer and South American pudus (the world's smallest deer). Among the wild cattle are red buffaloes, mountain and lowland anoas, and Indian gaur.

Visitor Services: *Performances by Asian elephants. Children's zoo. Group tours. Pavilion restaurant.*

CARL HAGENBECK ZOO

The history of the modern zoo began at this flower-decked animal park in suburban Stellingen, near Hamburg. Carl Hagenbeck, a 19th-century animal dealer, developed innovative methods of training animals for his own circus. He learned much about the heights and distances that predatory animals can leap and used that knowledge to design a revolutionary zoo. His animal park, which opened in 1907, featured open-air enclosures in which tigers and lions were safely separated from spectators

by concealed ditches. Moreover, the enclosures were designed to simulate native habitats. Hagenbeck's principles were adopted by zoos all over the world.

Today, when you enter the main gate, you need walk only a short distance to see Hagenbeck's original moated panorama. Chapman's zebras, warthogs, and ostriches roam across an African plain, and, immediately behind them, a pride of lions prowls along a rocky expanse. The lions, in turn, have as background a cluster of craggy cliffs occupied by aoudads (Barbary sheep).

Directly opposite, a miniature mountain is the playground for a flock of rarely exhibited goats from the Juan Fernández Islands off Chile, a species made famous by *Robinson Crusoe.*

Elephants from Africa and Asia (including the Ceylonese subspecies) enjoy a roomy enclosure. Next to the elephants is the zoo's pride—a pair of great Indian rhinoceroses. The Hagenbeck Zoo is one of the very few zoos where this endangered species has reproduced.

For animal life on a smaller scale there is the Troparium (primarily fish, reptiles, and amphibians) and the combined small-mammal house (sloths, lemurs, gerbils) and aviary (tropical and subtropical birds).

Visitor Services: *Daily performances by dolphins and sea lions. Pony and elephant rides. Playground. Restaurant.*

FRANKFURT ZOO

Many people come to the Frankfurt Zoo just to visit the Exotarium, a one-building zoo-within-a-zoo. Entering the Exotarium's Climatic Landscape Hall, you are confronted by a large polarscape so realistic it appears to have been imported intact from the Antarctic, along with the emperor, king, and gentoo penguins. Across the hall is a South American river inhabited by endangered river turtles and arapaimas, the world's largest freshwater fish.

In the Aquarium Hall common seals from the North Sea are viewable above and below the water. Nearby, a Chinese giant salamander, the world's largest amphibian, lives in a mountain stream. The tropical-sea exhibit plays host to a multicolored array of tiny reef fish and sea anemones; in another display are blood-thirsty Brazilian piranhas.

On the Exotarium's second floor the Reptile Hall has a jungle atmosphere. Concealed amid the tropical foliage are giant pythons from Asia and Australia, anacondas from South America, cobras and mambas from Africa, and frilled lizards from Australia.

The Insectarium offers insights into

insect societies—among other exhibits, a working beehive, a swarm of migratory locusts, and a colony of parasol ants that harvest leaves and carry them home over their heads.

Outside the Exotarium most of the rest of the approximately 5,000 animals in the Frankfurt Zoo can be viewed without the separation of bars. The Frankfurt Zoo was the first to exhibit gorillas in this way; only a wall of glass panels separates you from a large gorilla family that has produced a number of young.

Visitor Services: *Bilingual (German and English) communication facilities. Performances by elephants, sea lions, apes. Film shows on weekends.*

Great Britain

CAIRNGORMS NATIONAL NATURE RESERVE, Scotland

In the heart of the Cairngorm Mountains in the Scottish Highlands is Britain's largest wildlife reserve. Most of its 100 square miles are on privately owned land, administered under agreement with the Nature Conservancy Council. The reserve is located on a gently rolling plateau, from which rises a number of ancient granite peaks, worn and rounded by glacial action. The highest point is Ben Macdui (4,296 feet). Owing to the high latitude, snow patches often remain throughout the year. A chair lift gives easy access.

Much of the Cairngorms area was formerly used for sheep grazing or as deer-hunting preserves; as a result, the predominant vegetation is heath and grass. Portions of the original forests of Scotch pine remain, however, and a forest regeneration program is being carried on. Above timberline many alpine plants add interest to a mountain hike.

The most numerous mammal is the red deer. Small brown roe deer find browse and concealment in the forests. In the northeast portion of the reserve is a herd of reindeer, introduced from northern Sweden.

Birds are abundant, particularly in the forests along the Spey River. A few pairs of golden eagles nest in the crags overlooking the river; kestrels, merlins, and peregrine falcons also breed in the reserve, and ospreys nest at nearby Loch Garten. In the pine forests you should watch for capercaillies (turkey-sized grouse), Scottish crossbills, and crested tits—all specialties of the Cairngorms. Moorland birds include red and black grouses, pipits, skylarks, greenshanks, and wheatears.

The Cairngorms Reserve is roadless, but there are about 75 miles of old drovers' paths and other foot trails, including two self-guided nature trails.

How To Get There: *By car or train to Aviemore (north of reserve) or Braemar (southeast of reserve); by foot from there (a walk of several miles).* **When To Go:** *Open all year. Spring and summer, best time for wildflowers; spring for mating displays of birds. Portions of reserve closed between July 1 and February 15 for deer culling.* **Where To Stay:** *Hostels and campsites outside reserve. Lodge in north of park. Hotels at Aviemore and Braemar.*

FAIR ISLE BIRD OBSERVATORY, Scotland

Fair Isle is a tiny (1½ by 3 mile), rocky island lying midway between the Orkneys and Shetlands in the North Sea. Although the island is slightly off the principal migratory routes between Scandinavia and the Arctic regions and the wintering areas of southern Europe and Africa, its isolation makes it an ideal site for the study of migration.

As a bonus to its visitors Fair Isle's magnificent bird cliffs support a breeding population of black guillemots, razorbills, kittiwakes, and fulmars. Storm petrels and puffins nest in burrows; great and Arctic skuas colonize the moorland; flotillas of eider ducks sail the many coves.

A bird observatory since 1948, Fair Isle is owned by the National Trust for Scotland. Its basic mission is to conduct migration studies and train young ornithologists in the techniques of trapping, banding, laboratory examination, and fieldwork.

Since 1948 more than 100,000 birds of some 225 species have been banded. Recoveries of Fair Isle banded birds have been reported from North America, Greenland, Spain, Italy, Greece, Turkey, and West Africa. Many vagrant and migrant species recorded are land birds—wood pigeons, collared doves, European cuckoos, fieldfares, song thrushes, redwings, blackbirds, Greenland wheatears, warblers, and finches.

May is the best month to observe Fair Isle's spring migrants and breeding birds; autumn migrants start to arrive in August, reaching a peak in October.

How To Get There: *By boat (2½ to 3 hours) from Sumburgh, Shetland, twice weekly (Tuesday, Friday) May through September. By air from Sumburgh; May through September, weekly plane (Saturday) connects with flights from Glasgow, Edinburgh, or Aberdeen.* **When To Go:** *Open all year. Best season, May through September.* **Where**

To Stay: *Hostel-type accommodations with meals at observatory. Apply to Fair Isle Bird Observatory Trust, 21 Regent Terrace, Edinburgh, Scotland.*

JERSEY ZOOLOGICAL PARK, Channel Islands

What distinguishes the Jersey Zoological Park—the personal project of naturalist and author Gerald Durrell—from other zoos is that its sole purpose is conservation through breeding. The park is administered by the Jersey Wildlife Preservation Trust, and its 200 species of mammals, birds, and reptiles are all in the rare or endangered categories. For zoo enthusiasts it offers the opportunity to see many unusual animals, such as South American spectacled bears, African crested rats, and Jamaican and Cuban hutias (rodents).

Trust headquarters are in the ancient manor house of Les Augres. Lawns, shrubberies, and flower beds, ponds and meadows surround the zoo buildings. Groves of trees and open fields separate the aviaries, pheasant runs, and other exhibits. The displays are not literal recreations of habitats. Emphasis is on providing for the animals' every need, so that they will breed.

One of the Jersey Trust's more notable successes is with the white-eared pheasant, a bird that is nearly extinct in its native China and Tibet. The Jersey flock has hatched so many chicks that the zoo has been able to send breeding stock to other zoos.

Many mammals have been equally productive. Jersey has built up large colonies of ursine black-and-white colobus monkeys from West Africa, Asian tree shrews, and African civets. West African striped squirrels and serval cats are producing a second generation, and two species of tenrecs are even into a fourth generation. Tenrecs, small insect eaters from Madagascar, can be seen under artificial moonlight in the Nocturnal House.

How To Get There: *By air to Jersey Airport. By car or train from London or other points to Weymouth, then by ship to Jersey (6 hours).* **When To Go:** *Open all year.* **Where To Stay:** *Hotels and pensions on Jersey.*

LINDISFARNE AND FARNE ISLANDS RESERVES

More than 1,200 years ago Christian missionaries used Lindisfarne (Holy Island) and the nearby Farne Islands, off the coast of Northumberland, as bases for their work among the pagan Saxons. Today these islands, some of them bearing ruins from their historic past, are famous as nature reserves.

The Lindisfarne reserve comprises the sand dunes and salt marshes on and around Holy Island, together with the intertidal sand and mud flats between the island and mainland—a total of more than 7,700 acres. The Farne Islands are a group of 28 small rocky islets within sight of Lindisfarne.

The most numerous species at Lindisfarne is the European wigeon, with up to 25,000 wintering there annually. Perhaps the most interesting is the brent (brant) goose, for this is the only regular wintering ground in Britain for the light-bellied race that nests on the Arctic islands of Spitsbergen. Whooper swans regularly reach 450, the largest flock wintering in England; among them, if you are lucky, you may see a Bewick's swan, a tundra visitor.

A great variety of ducks visit the reserve, including scoters, teals, scaups, common goldeneyes, red-breasted mergansers, and long-tailed ducks, while mallards, eiders, and shelducks are year-round residents. Knots, dunlins, and bar-tailed godwits patrol the beaches and tidal shallows, and you may also see gray (black-bellied) plovers, redshanks, ringed plovers, and ruddy turnstones. Sea ducks, divers (loons), and grebes are numerous off the coast in winter.

The craggy rocks of the Farnes have large colonies of seabirds. Arctic, common, roseate, and sandwich terns can all be seen. Kittiwakes nest on tiny ledges on the cliff faces. The larger ledges are often shared by shags (small cormorants). Great cormorants nest on two low islands.

Guillemots (common murres) are concentrated on columnar formations, and a few razorbills may be seen. Puffins dig nesting burrows where the rock has a covering of soil. Several hundred eider ducks nest on the Farnes, often near paths and buildings.

Adding to the variety of animal life is a colony of some 7,000 gray seals, a dangerously large population for their limited breeding grounds.

Only two of the larger Farne Islands are open to visitors. On these the wildlife can be seen from well-marked footpaths.

How To Get There: *By car from Berwick-upon-Tweed or Alnwick to Holy Island. By boat to the Farne Islands from Seahouses, south of Bamburgh.* **When To Go:** *Late April to mid-July for nesting season on Farne Islands. September and October for migration at Lindisfarne.* **Where To Stay:** *Accommodations in Berwick and Seahouses.*

LONDON ZOO AND WHIPSNADE PARK ZOO, England

Opened in 1828, the London Zoo in Regent's Park is one of the world's oldest zoos. Over the years it has been the home of many animal celebrities, like Jumbo, the famous African elephant, and, more recently, Chi-Chi, the much-lamented giant panda. The present-day animal collection is one of the largest and most comprehensive on earth.

Although it is a historic place, London Zoo has been transformed into a very modern exhibition. Perhaps the most exciting architecture is the large free-flight aviary. Designed by Lord Snowdon, it consists of four giant triangles suspended high in the air, with wire mesh stretched over them.

Another building, the Charles Clore Pavilion, holds the world's largest collection of small mammals. Among them are red (or lesser) pandas, ocelots, brush-tailed porcupines, mongooses, sloths, tree kangaroos, martens, ruffed lemurs, vizcachas, tree shrews, and fire-footed squirrels. The underground level of the pavilion houses the Moonlight World, where nighttime lighting stimulates the activities of nocturnal mammals, such as owl monkeys, bush babies, lorises, and elephant shrews.

In 1931 the Zoological Society of London opened a 500-acre country zoo called Whipsnade Park, about 30 miles north of London. At this pioneering "open-space" zoo (since copied by many others) animals roam in apparent freedom over acres of fields and woods. Whipsnade has one of the finest breeding records of any zoo. Its collection includes a fine herd of rare Père David's deer. Other endangered species, such as Przewalski wild horses, European bison, and musk-oxen, have also bred.

Visitor Services: *At London Zoo a water-bus service on Regent's Canal (mid-April to mid-October). At both zoos, children's zoos, camel and pony rides for children. At Whipsnade only, daily dolphin-training sessions.*

MINSMERE BIRD RESERVE, England

One of Britain's outstanding bird reserves, Minsmere is famous for the numbers of species attracted to its varied habitats. A visit to this 1,500-acre reserve on the Suffolk coast will give you a wide view over reedy marshes and pools, woodland, heathland, and hedgerows. A unique area is "The Scrape," a 50-acre system of shallow lagoons and islands; 1,500 pairs of birds now nest there.

More than 250 species, the great majority of them waterfowl and shorebirds, visit Minsmere each year. Half of them are passing migrants or winter visitors; half are nesting species. Hundreds of pairs of sandwich and common terns are residents, and the scarce little terns are also breeding. Of special interest are the European avocets (one of two breeding colonies reestablished in England after an absence of 125 years). Bitterns, gray herons, and bearded tits nest in the reeds, and a few pairs of marsh harriers patrol the reedbeds.

Many species of warblers, six different tits including the long-tailed tit, three-toed woodpeckers, thrushes and nightingales, nuthatches, and treecreepers nest in the woods and hedgerows. Heathland birds include nightjars, yellowhammers, tree pipits, redpolls, and rare red-backed shrikes.

Winter brings many species to Minsmere, including small groups of Bewick's swans, hen harriers, snow buntings, and great gray shrikes. Spring and fall bring spotted redshanks, curlew sandpipers, and black terns. Summer migrants include sandpipers, phalaropes, and many other waders and shorebirds, even European spoonbills.

The reserve, on privately owned land, is administered by the Royal Society for the Protection of Birds. Access to most portions of the reserve is forbidden, but a well-laid-out system of footpaths permits views of all areas. If you are a photographer, you will appreciate the excellent observation blinds.

How To Get There: *By car, from Ipswich, Suffolk. By train from London to Darsham, where taxis can be hired.* **When To Go:** *Open all year, but access by permit only. Apply to Royal Society for the Protection of Birds, Sandy, Bedfordshire, England.* **Where To Stay:** *Hotels in Ipswich, Aldeburgh, and other nearby towns.*

NORFOLK WILDLIFE PARK AND PHEASANT TRUST, England

A small country park at Great Witchingham, Norwich, near Britain's east coast, is the site of two highly specialized zoological institutions—the Norfolk Wildlife Park and the Pheasant Trust.

The Pheasant Trust's collection of rarities, the largest ever assembled, includes such exotically plumaged types as greater Bornean crested firebacks, Siamese firebacks, brown-eared and white-eared, bartailed, common koklases, Malay and Bornean great arguses, Sonnerat's jungle fowl, and Palawan peacock pheasants. In some instances enough breeding stock has been produced to repopulate wild areas.

The emphasis on fertility is no less pronounced among the European animals in the Wildlife Park. Virtually all of them have reproduced, some for the first time under captive conditions. Like the Pheasant Trust, the park maintains a policy of restocking depleted wild populations. It has distributed numerous eagle owls (largest of European owls) in areas of Germany and Sweden where the species had become extinct.

Shy, seldom-seen creatures like European lynxes and wildcats can be viewed at close range. Alpine ibexes scamper around a scaled-down mountain. European susliks (similar to ground squirrels) scurry in and out of burrows. You can see badgers through windows in their underground home and beavers in a realistic replica of their lodge. In the nocturnal house "moonlight" illuminates the nighttime behavior of genets, porcupines, mongooses, hedgehogs, weasels, rats, mice, and voles. In the most dramatic demonstrations of animal behavior, trained owls and eagles are allowed to fly freely.

How To Get There: *By car from London via Newmarket to Norwich, Norfolk, then 12 miles to Great Witchingham. Bus service.*

THE WILDFOWL TRUST (SLIMBRIDGE), England

Part bird sanctuary, part specialized zoo, the Wildfowl Trust at its Slimbridge headquarters in Gloucestershire maintains the world's largest collection of waterfowl: 140 species of swans, geese, ducks, South American screamers (distant relatives of geese), and flamingos—totaling 2,500 birds. The site, in water meadows along the Severn Estuary, is a natural haven for birds.

Slimbridge seems to be a sanctuary for people, too, as they walk among the birds in a setting of sweeping green pastures and ponds. The captive birds that wander across the lawns—emperor and bar-headed geese from Asia, Magellan and ashy-headed geese from South America, among others—appear to be "loose," but, actually, most are pinioned to keep them from straying.

At the entrance building a picture window provides a panoramic view of the biggest exhibit, one populated largely by flocks of geese representing most of the world's species.

For the most part the exhibits are based on continental groupings. The African pen has flamingos (greater and lesser) and fulvous tree ducks. The South American enclosure features a colony of Chilean flamingos. Mandarin ducks from China paddle around an Asian pond. The global view of wildfowl is rounded out by birds from North America, Europe (every native species), Australia (featuring black swans), and New Zealand.

Winter is the best time to see the wild birds. More than 6,000 white-fronted geese winter at Slimbridge, and as many as 600 Bewick's swans migrate from their Siberian breeding grounds.

The results of Slimbridge's breeding programs literally surround you. About 1,800 ducklings, goslings, and cygnets hatch each year. Less than 50 Hawaiian geese, or nene, existed in the world in 1947. Starting with three, Slimbridge boosted the population to the point where 200 geese could be released in their native habitat.

How To Get There: *By car from London (115 miles), Bristol (24 miles).* **When To Go:** *Open daily; from 12 noon on Sundays.*

Italy

GRAN PARADISO NATIONAL PARK

Here in one of the most beautiful parts of the Italian Alps, near the Val d'Aosta, lies a refuge for wildlife that dates back to the last century. Originally intended as a final retreat for the disappearing ibex, the park today boasts a population of some 3,000 of these mountain goats.

Besides the ibex many other species of alpine animals are found in this 245-square-mile park, named for Italy's highest peak and containing some of the country's most extensive glaciers. At its southwest corner Gran Paradiso National Park is contiguous with France's La Vanoise National Park.

The Paradisia Botanical Garden, near the Cogne entrance, provides information about 1,500 species of alpine plants. Alpine meadows are gay with flowers, among which are bellflowers, anemones, and several species of gentians.

The most satisfactory way to view the park's wildlife is an early-morning walk along some of the 250 miles of trails. From these trails you will be able to see ibexes at fairly close range. With caution they can be approached within a few yards, thus ensuring excellent photographs. Large numbers of chamois share the rocky slopes with the ibexes. Nervous animals that dart away at the slightest provocation, chamois can be observed only at a distance.

If you are patient, you will also be rewarded with the sight of alpine hares, ermines, squirrels, and snow voles. Although some pine martens, polecats, badgers, and otters also live in the park, they are more difficult to spot.

The chances of your seeing a golden eagle are good, for these great predators feed extensively on the plump marmots that scramble all over the rocks. Other high-altitude birds are crag martins, alpine swifts, crowlike alpine choughs, snow finches, black grouse, and ptarmigans. Near a rapidly flowing stream you may spot a dipper perched on a rock or plunging beneath the surface to feed on the bottom. Another unusual species that prefers a damp, rocky habitat is the wall creeper, a small, grayish bird with startlingly brilliant crimson wings edged with black and spotted with white.

How To Get There: *By train to Aosta or Turin. By car from Aosta to Cogne, Valsavaranche, Rhême-Notre-Dame, or Pont. By car or bus from Turin to Ceresole Reale.* **When To Go:** *Open all year. Best season, June to September.* **Where To Stay:** *Shelters and campsites in park. Hotels in Cogne, Rhême-Notre-Dame, Valsavaranche. Campsites at Cogne and Valsavaranche.*

Netherlands

TEXEL AND TERSCHELLING RESERVES

Between the northern coast of the Netherlands and the low-lying Frisian Islands lies the Waddenzee, a huge expanse of tidal flats and shallows, where hundreds of thousands of birds forage for food. Covering about 1,100 square miles, the Waddenzee empties and fills twice a day with the tides.

Between these protected shallows and the stormy North Sea the Frisian Islands of Texel (pronounced Tessel) and Terschelling slope down from high barrier dunes to tidal flats on the inshore side. The natural vegetation of the dunes is mostly beach grasses, sea buckthorns, and crowberries. Pines and other trees have been planted on many of the dunes. Much of the tideland has been diked, drained, and reclaimed for farmland (called polders), but on the untouched portions a number of small bird reserves have been established. Not all are open to the public, but some of the most interesting, on the islands of Texel and Terschelling, are easily accessible.

Breeding species on Texel and Terschelling are eiders, shelducks, black-headed gulls, herring gulls, terns, European oyster catchers and avocets, black-tailed godwits, redshanks, lapwings, and curlews. Of outstanding interest are the three breeding colonies of spoonbills, the most northern ones in Europe. Another unusual nesting species is the ruff, a large sandpiper noted for its spectacular breeding plumage and courtship rituals.

In spring and fall the bird population of the Waddenzee swells to more than a million as the great flocks of migrants stop off to rest and feed. Plovers, bar-tailed godwits, oyster catchers, whimbrels, greenshanks, and redshanks are among the most numerous species. Many migrant birds spend the winter in the rich feeding grounds of the Waddenzee: An estimated half million dunlins (sandpipers), up to 150,000 eiders, 250,000 oyster catchers, thousands of brent (brant) and barnacle geese.

The paths and roads among the dunes are always open to visitors, but during breeding time (April 15 to July 15) the nesting colonies are either inaccessible or only accessible under the guidance of a keeper. On Texel many birds can be seen fairly well from the surrounding roads or dikes. An observation tower gives an excellent view of the spoonbill nesting colony.
How To Get There: *By car from Amsterdam to Den Helder for Texel, to Harlingen for Terschelling. By daily car ferry to islands.* **When To Go:** *Best seasons, end of March to early June, mid-September to early November.* **Where To Stay:** *Hotels, guesthouses, campsites on both islands.*

Norway

RONDANE NATIONAL PARK
Established as a reserve in 1962, Rondane became Norway's first national park in 1970. Magnificently situated in a high mountain range in central Norway, approximately 150 miles north of both Bergen and Oslo, the park boasts 10 peaks that rise above 6,000 feet. A beautiful lake, Rondvatnet, lies between the two highest peaks.

Rondane National Park, along with the surrounding territory, is largely unspoiled country. No roads exist within park boundaries, only trails for walkers. Terminal moraines of sand and gravel, steep-walled cirques, or basins, and deep kettle holes all give evidence of a relatively recent glacial period. Trees are restricted to sparse conifers and dwarf birches. Reindeer moss gives much of the terrain a yellowish-white tinge. Of the few flowers glacier crowfoots are the most plentiful.

Lapp reindeer herds are not found within Rondane, but wild reindeer are present; one of their regular calving

places is at Dorälen, in the northern end of the park. In addition, there are hares, red foxes, wolverines, stoats, weasels, and squirrels. Near the streams and lakes minks and otters occur. Musk-oxen can occasionally be seen in the park; there is a free-roaming herd at Dovrefjell, 25 miles north.

About 125 species of birds have been recorded in Rondane. Ptarmigans, snow buntings, meadow pipits, and wheatears are typical species. Whenever small rodents are abundant, you are likely to see a few rough-legged buzzards (hawks) and kestrels hovering in search of prey.
How To Get There: *By car from Oslo via Lillehammer to western entrances. By train from Oslo, with connections to nearby Otta and Sel stations.* **When To Go:** *Open all year. Best season, June to mid-September.* **Where To Stay:** *Two cabins in the park; meals served. Lodges and hotels nearby.*

Poland

BIALOWIEZA NATIONAL PARK
The Bialowieza Forest, site of the Bialowieza National Park, has for centuries been the principal home of the once greatly endangered European bison, or wisent. Although the park was established in 1947, Bialowieza has been a protected area since 1921 and, with the neighboring Soviet area, preserves the last remnants of the primeval forest of the central European plains.

This is the setting to which the European bison has returned. Compared with the American bison, the European species is a bit smaller with a less dense coat but with longer horns. Centuries ago this magnificent animal roamed freely throughout the vast forests of Europe. But the disappearance of many large forests, disease, and threats from various predators, including man, so reduced the bison population that during World War I most of the last free specimens had been wiped out.

Through the combined efforts of several organizations, in 1929 Bialowieza imported from Sweden and Silesia a few captive bison. Careful breeding has since been responsible for the bison's increase.

Elks, deer, lynxes, wolves, and beavers are among Bialowieza's other mammals. And an attempt to breed horses resembling the extinct tarpan (a close relative of the primitive Przewalski horse) is under way.

Bird fanciers may see several species of owls and eagles, white and black

storks, white-backed and three-toed woodpeckers, red and black kites, capercaillies, and black grouse. Among the more unusual smaller birds are collared and red-breasted flycatchers, hoopoes, rollers, ortolan buntings, red crossbills, and thrush nightingales.

Bialowieza National Park contains a museum and a research station. Visitors must proceed through the park on foot and must have a guide.
How To Get There: *By car from Warsaw (about 210 miles). By train to Bialystok (about 170 miles from Warsaw).* **When To Go:** *Open year round. Best time, May to September.* **Where To Stay:** *Park lodge; hotels and other accommodations in Bialystok.*

Romania

DANUBE DELTA RESERVE
Composed of silt, sand, and gravel brought down by the Danube River on its long journey across central Europe to the Black Sea, the Danube Delta is a 1,700-square-mile maze of shifting channels, reedy swamps, treacherous sandbars, low islands, and floodplains rising barely above water level. Flooded spring and fall, often to a depth of 13 feet, it has remained largely wild.

Reeds are the dominant vegetation, sometimes growing to twice the height of man, though on some of the higher islands there are open woods of oak and ash, and poplar and willow trees cover large tracts.

Large herds of wild boars live in the reedbeds and woodlands; wolves, almost extinct in the rest of Europe, are also numerous. Other mammals include wildcats, foxes, otters, minks, ermines, muskrats, and nutrias (the last two introduced or escaped from fur farms).

Crossed by five major European flyways, the rich feeding grounds of the Danube Delta attract many thousands of migratory birds and also support a large population of year-round residents. Outstanding among its nearly 200 recorded species are the white and Dalmatian pelicans, each with breeding colonies of several thousand pairs.

In this watery wilderness, split by the three main arms of the Danube, are three major wildlife sanctuaries, included in the overall Danube Delta Reserve, plus a number of smaller reserves. The largest of the three reserves, Rosca-Buhaiova-Hrecisca (38,050 acres), lies inland in the northern part of the delta near the Russian border. Its reedbeds shelter Europe's largest colony of pelicans, as well as nesting pygmy cormorants, glossy ibises, night herons, several species of egrets, and many species of warblers.

In the southeast of the delta is the Perisor-Zatoane Reserve (35,200 acres), where proximity to the Black Sea creates a mosaic of freshwater, brackish, and saltwater habitats. Mute swans, egrets, night herons, squacco herons, gray and purple herons, black-winged stilts, avocets, greylag geese, and rare white-headed ducks nest in the marshes, and in the autumn thousands of cranes fly in from the north. Huge flocks of red-breasted, bean, and barnacle geese, many kinds of ducks, divers (loons), and grebes spend the winter in the reserve. But the greatest spectacle takes place with the arrival and departure of the migratory birds.

Just west of Perisor-Zatoane is the Periteasca-Leahova Reserve, a 9,640-acre tract of dry sandbanks and shallow lagoons, where waterfowl, waders, and several uncommon species of seabirds—Mediterranean and slender-billed gulls, gull-billed and Caspian terns—nest.

The best way to see the Danube Delta Reserve is by boat. The Romanian Government tourist agency conducts 2- and 3-day boat trips, starting from Tulcea, at the head of the delta. The agency also arranges longer trips in the boats of local fishermen, who act as guides; their small boats can reach remote areas that the large tour vessels cannot penetrate.

How To Get There: *By tourist bus or car from Bucharest to Tulcea.* **When To Go:** *Open all year. Best time for migratory birds, early spring and fall.* **Where To Stay:** *Hotels in towns around delta and in Black Sea resorts; overnight accommodations on tour vessels and with families of local guides.*

Spain

COTO DOÑANA NATIONAL PARK

Amid the sand dunes and marshes of the Guadalquivir River Delta in southwest Spain lies the Coto Doñana, one of the most important wildlife areas in Western Europe. About half of Europe's bird species can be seen in the Coto Doñana, and it is one of the last refuges of the endangered Spanish imperial eagle and the Spanish lynx.

Created around a former hunting preserve of the dukes of Medina Sidonia (later a biological reserve), Coto Doñana National Park encompasses about 130 square miles of varied habitats—coastal dunes; freshwater, brackish, and salt lagoons; creeks; scrubby

thickets and woodland, in addition to the extensive *marismas*, or marshes.

Wild boars are abundant, especially in the wooded areas and scrubland. Here, too, toward dusk, you may catch a glimpse of strikingly spotted lynxes on the hunt. An estimated 60 to 80 lynxes survive in the Coto Doñana. Red deer and fallow deer are so prolific that their numbers must be controlled.

But it is the birds for which the Coto Doñana is famous. The most noteworthy bird is the Spanish imperial eagle. Six or seven pairs nest in the cork oaks and stone pines on higher ground. Another rarity, the azure-winged magpie, is a year-round resident.

A sampling of birds that breed or feed on or near the lagoons includes avocets, black-winged stilts, slender-billed gulls, black and gull-billed terns, crested coots, black-necked grebes, marsh harriers, and white-headed and ferruginous ducks. Drier-area nesting birds are short-toed larks, pratincoles, sand grouse, and stone curlews (large, elusive birds belonging to the thick-knee family). Unusual land birds include bee-eaters, great gray shrikes, and great spotted cuckoos.

Then there is Doñana's multitude of herons and egrets—squacco, purple and night herons, little and cattle egrets—spoonbills, and white storks. The storks, spoonbills, herons, and egrets prefer the ancient cork oaks for nesting. Each species nests at a different level, and a fully occupied tree is a striking sight.

Giants among Doñana's birds are the huge griffon vultures and the less common black vultures. Both these scavengers are wary, but, if you are patient, you will be rewarded with a chance for close-up photographs.

Entrance to Coto Doñana National Park is by permit only, obtainable from the Estación Biológica de Doñana in Seville. The wildlife is best observed on foot, but off-road transportation by horse or motor vehicle can be arranged. **How To Get There:** *By air to Seville. By car from Seville via La Palma and El Rocío. By train to La Palma.* **When To Go:** *Open all year. Best weather, January through July.* **Where To Stay:** *Limited accommodations in Palacio; visitors must bring own food. Hotels, pensions, campgrounds nearby.*

VALLE DE ORDESA NATIONAL PARK

Just south of the high peaks of the Pyrenees on the border with France lies the Spanish valley of Ordesa, set off from the surrounding territory by its spectacular crags and escarpments.

In this setting the Valle de Ordesa National Park covers about 5,000 acres at an average altitude of 8,000 feet, with some peaks towering to 11,000 feet. You can explore Ordesa either on foot or horseback, following its many paths and trails that lead to waterfalls and cascades, mountain meadows and caves. Torrential rivers slicing through the valley teem with trout. The rocky terrain is an excellent habitat for Spanish ibexes and chamois; the thick evergreen forest gives protection to wild boars, wildcats, pine martens, European brown bears, and northern lynxes.

Chief glory of the Ordesa wildlife, however, is the magnificent population of birds of prey. The cliffs and crags of the Ordesa may well be the world's most favorable habitat for the rare lammergeier, often called the bearded vulture. This great bird, with its 9-foot wingspread, is remarkable for its habit of crushing large bones by dropping them onto rocks from a great height.

Besides the raptors many species of smaller birds enliven the valley. Hoopoes murmur their mellow yet penetrating *hoop-hoop*. Nightingales pour out their fabled song. European goldfinches and linnets stitch the woods with flashing color. Wild rock doves, ancestors of our familiar street pigeons, nest on the cliffs, and wood pigeons patrol the valley floor. On the heights there are alpine swifts, alpine choughs, ptarmigans, rock thrushes, and stonechats.

How To Get There: *By rail and bus from Barcelona or Madrid. By road from Lérida, via Barbastro, Torla (116 miles); from Madrid, via Saragossa, Huesca, Torla, and Ordesa (Huesca to Ordesa, 175 miles).* **When To Go:** *Best season, June to September.* **Where To Stay:** *Hotels and inns in nearby villages; Refugio Nacional and campgrounds in park.*

Sweden

SKANES DJURPARK

A visit to this country zoo is like a trip around the wild areas of southern Sweden. The 250-acre site is typical of this rather remote part of Sweden in its natural state: pine and spruce forests intermingled with rolling meadows.

The Djurpark (Animal Park) concentrates solely on Scandinavian animals. Enclosures are occupied by 60 species of mammals, birds, and reptiles. Pine martens scamper along tree limbs, wild boars nose along forest floors, badgers waddle across meadows.

Brown bears roam barless, moated enclosures. Atlantic gray seals splash around a big pool. Otters and beavers dive and frolic in woodland ponds. Streams are populated by white and black storks, gray herons, cranes, and 21 kinds of ducks and geese. To see the wolves, you follow a fenced-in path through the center of their territory.

During visiting hours breeding herds of large hoofed mammals are confined to relatively smaller areas. This arrangement gives you better views of moose, reindeer, roe deer, fallow deer, and European bison.

The only exception to the no-building policy is the Djurpark's farm, built in typical local style with stone foundations, red-painted gables, and thatched roofs. The pastures contain domestic animals customarily kept by Swedish farmers: Mountain cattle, Gotland ponies and sheep, Jämtland goats, and Skåne geese. A minifarm offers the chance for children (and adults!) to make contact with young animals. **How To Get There:** *By ferry from Copenhagen to Malmö. By train or plane from Stockholm to Malmö. By car from Malmö to Höör (32 miles).* **When To Go:** *Open all year.* **Where To Stay:** *Inn at nearby Frostavallens, hotels at Malmö.*

STORA SJÖFALLET NATIONAL PARK

Moose, brown bears, and golden eagles are a few of the attractions of Stora Sjöfallet National Park, more than 60 miles above the Arctic Circle in Swedish Lapland. Stora Sjöfallet (the name means "great waterfall") covers 534 square miles of rugged mountain and lake country. Although damaged by hydroelectric developments, this is still an exceptional forest area. Two other large national parks—Padjelanta, a rich botanical area, and Sarek, in almost inaccessible mountain country—adjoin Stora Sjöfallet; together they form a continuous protected area of more than 2,100 square miles, by far the largest in Europe. Sjaunja Bird Sanctuary also adjoins the three-park complex.

Primeval coniferous forests, chiefly pines, clothe Stora Sjöfallet's lower slopes up to about 1,650 feet. Above this, birch woods, often open and park-like, climb to about 2,300 feet. A broad belt of dwarf birch and willow scrub fringes the upper edge of the birch woods. Above this lie alpine heaths and tundra. At all levels there are extensive areas of marsh and bog.

Brown bears are often seen in summer, grazing on alpine lettuce and giant angelicas. Wolves, now rare, hunt for small rodents, their main prey, in the birch forest and at higher elevations. Wolverines are occasionally seen in the willow belt. Lynxes are abundant in the pine forest, though you probably won't see one because of their nocturnal habits; another pine-forest dweller is the marten. A few otters inhabit the lakes.

Moose, now abundant under protection, feed in the wetlands and willow thickets in summer, retreating to the pine forests in the winter. Semiwild reindeer, herded by their Lapp owners, graze in the park. Lemmings proliferate in the highlands.

Most spectacular of the park's birds is unquestionably the rare golden eagle, and, if you are lucky, you may also see gyrfalcons, merlins, and rough-legged buzzards (hawks). Several species of owls, including snowy and Tengmalm's owls, inhabit the forests, along with many species of woodpeckers, tits, and thrushes. The birch woods produce willow warblers and bluethroats and redwings (both small thrushes). The scrub zone shelters woodcocks and willow grouse; wheatears and golden plovers nest on the moors. Ducks and other waterfowl throng the waterways, and whooping swans summer in the park.

A road traverses Stora Sjöfallet from southeast to northwest, and there are many miles of well-marked foot trails. You can also see a good deal of the park and its wildlife by boat. **How To Get There:** *By rail from Narvik, Norway, to Porjus; or from Stockholm, via Boden to Porjus. By mail bus or car from Porjus to Saltoluokta, at entrance to park, or Vietas, in the park.* **When To Go:** *Open late June to early September.* **Where To Stay:** *Hotel in Saltoluokta; cabins and huts along trails; campground and cafeteria at Vietas. Campers must bring own food.*

Switzerland

BASEL ZOOLOGICAL GARDEN

One of the most visually appealing of all zoos, Basel conveys a first impression of groves of tall pines and shade trees, ponds filled with waterfowl, and lawns where cranes wander freely. Yet landscaping is hardly the chief attraction; nor are the ultramodern exhibition techniques or rare animals (though Basel has an abundance of both). What most distinguishes this zoo is babies.

The Basel Zoo has won the respect of zoo professionals for its exceptional success with species regarded as difficult to breed. One example is the great Indian one-horned rhinoceros. When the first two Indian rhinos arrived in 1951 and 1952, this species had never bred in captivity. By 1973 the Basel rhinos had produced 12 offspring.

A high percentage of the world's zoos keep sea lions, but for some reason the animals rarely produce pups. In Basel they do—regularly. Echidnas (spiny anteaters), the strange, egg-laying mammals from Australia, often have long lifespans in captivity but do not reproduce. The Basel echidnas have laid eggs, hatched them, and even raised one young to a weight of 12½ ounces.

The zoo recorded the first gorilla birth in Europe in 1959, and since then the gorilla colony has produced babies regularly. Basel now has the largest gorilla group living together in a zoo.

Zoos exhibited pygmy hippos for years with no reproductive success. Since Basel made the breakthrough, pygmy hippos have seemed almost as prolific as rabbits. Somali wild asses, acquired from one of the last surviving herds, have started to increase. Proboscis monkeys from Borneo have only begun to breed in zoos, and Basel is one of them. **Visitor Services:** *Performances by elephants and sea lions. Children's zoo. Rides for children.*

SWISS NATIONAL PARK

The only official national park in Switzerland is set in the rugged Engadine Alps at the eastern end of the country, on the Italian border. The Swiss National Park was established in 1914 in a small area of 5,000 acres that had previously been disturbed by lumbering and iron mining.

Since its founding the park has been enlarged to include impressive peaks of dolomite rock, remote untouched valleys (some with small hanging glaciers), and, above all, miles of magnificent pine forest.

Although timber regrowth in the logged areas has been slow, the lower slopes of the mountains are now forested up to about 7,200 feet. Pine predominates at the lower levels; larch is plentiful at the upper levels. Rhododendrons grow abundantly in the woods. Above timberline alpine meadows are bright with gentians, alpine primroses, anemones, alpine asters, and edelweisses.

If you want to see wildlife, the most rewarding areas of the Swiss National Park are above timberline. Ibexes, reintroduced to the park, are plentiful on the high, rocky slopes, such as Piz Albris and Piz dal Diavel; chamois can be seen almost anywhere. Numerous marmots have their dens in the high zone.

Unusual birds of the alpine heights include ring ouzels, alpine swifts, snow finches, ptarmigans, black grouse, and alpine choughs. Ravens and nutcrackers are common. Huge grouselike capercaillies and several woodpeckers, among them the rare three-toed species, haunt the forest zone. Hawks and owls are often sighted, and golden eagles nest in the upper levels. As a special treat a park guide can show you a cliff face where you may be lucky enough to see a pair of wall creepers, small grayish birds with brilliant wing markings.

A main highway traverses the Swiss National Park. There are about 50 miles of foot trails, which visitors are forbidden to leave. The park guides conduct tours in the summer, and other walking tours are suggested in park-guide booklets.
How To Get There: *By car, bus, or train to Zernez, northeast of St. Moritz. By air to Sameden, 15 miles from Zernez.*
When To Go: *Open all year. Best season, mid-June to mid-November.*
Where To Stay: *Hotel at Il Fuorn, inside park. Hotels and pensions at nearby villages. Camping and trailer sites at Schuls and Zernez.*

ZURICH ZOO
Vistas of snowcapped mountains surround this zoo, perched on a thickly wooded hilltop. Among the groves of tall pines and other trees, nearly 2,000 animals representing about 420 species are exhibited in spacious, open-air replicas of their native habitats. Reproductive success is high. One of many examples is the herd of vicuñas. These endangered cousins of the camel from the Andes have thrived in this Swiss mountain zoo—almost all on exhibit were born there.

Every effort is made to create exhibits that stimulate not only breeding but all facets of natural behavior. In the South African exhibit for Chapman's zebras, for example, a large manmade termite hill provides the animals with the same sort of scratching post they use in the wild.

White and black rhinos and hippos occupy Africa House. The walls and floors of the barless displays, both outside and in, are contoured to suggest the curving geometry of the animals' environment—no unnatural right angles. Another naturalistic touch is the birdlife. Cattle egrets and oxpeckers dart about the big mammals, land on them, and peck at their tough hides to remove parasites—an example of symbiosis (living together).

Otters live in a realistic woodland setting, with a glass-fronted pool that allows you to watch them underwater. Canadian beavers are so at home that they have reproduced regularly.

In the aquarium underwater behavior demonstrates several symbiotic relationships. Remoras, or shark suckers, glean leftover food from sea turtles, poisonous sea anemones protect clown fish from predators, and tiny cleaner fish groom large tropical groupers. The zoo's main building, where the aquarium is located, also contains an open aviary with colorful birds.
Visitor Services: *Guided tours and lectures. Miniature railway.*

More Places To See Wildlife in Europe

1. SKAFTAFELL NATIONAL PARK, Iceland. At the foot of Europe's largest glacier; meadows and bogs, black lava beaches. Wildlife highlights: Arctic foxes (rare), seals. Greater and arctic skuas, fulmars, arctic terns, European oyster catchers, gyrfalcons.
2. BORGEFJELL NATIONAL PARK, Norway. Remote highland with rivers, lakes, marshes. Wildlife highlights: Moose, reindeer, wolverines, red foxes, hares. Bean geese, long-tailed ducks (old squaws); golden eagles, rough-legged buzzards (hawks), ospreys, snowy owls; red-throated phalaropes, golden plovers; ptarmigans, snow buntings.
3. OULANKA NATIONAL PARK, Finland. Gorge of Oulanka River; subarctic spruce and birch forests. Wildlife highlights: Moose, reindeer, European brown bears. Golden eagles, eagle owls, whooper swans, black woodpeckers, reed buntings, rare red-flanked bluetails.
4. TIPPERNE RESERVE, Denmark. Meadows and salt marshes. Pintail ducks, shelducks, mute swans, black-tailed godwits, European avocets, gull-billed and sandwich terns, black-headed gulls; marsh harriers.
5. KRKONOSE NATIONAL PARK, Czechoslovakia. Forested mountains, alpine meadows. Wildlife highlights: Red and roe deer, mouflons (introduced), wild boars. Black storks, black grouse, dotterels, eagle owls, goshawks, nutcrackers, black woodpeckers, dippers, ringed ouzels.
6. TATRA NATIONAL PARKS, Poland/Czechoslovakia. Rugged, conifer-clad mountains. Wildlife highlights: Chamois, wild boars, wolves, brown bears, lynxes, wildcats, marmots. Capercaillies, black grouse, black storks; golden and spotted eagles, peregrines, kites; wall creepers, scarlet grosbeaks.
7. SREBARNA NATIONAL WILDLIFE SANCTUARY, Bulgaria. Large lake with extensive reed swamps. Wildlife highlights: European susliks (ground squirrels), steppe polecats. Dalmatian pelicans, mute swans, little bitterns, squacco herons; whiskered terns, ferruginous ducks; penduline tits, rollers, golden orioles, hoopoes.
8. PLITVICKA JEZERA NATIONAL PARK, Yugoslavia. Limestone crags, canyons, waterfalls. Wildlife highlights: Brown bears, wolves, badgers, otters, wildcats. Woodpeckers (eight species), Ural and eagle owls, golden eagles, kites, capercaillies, black grouse, hazel hens, Hungarian partridges.
9. ABRUZZO NATIONAL PARK, Italy. Precipitous, forested mountains. Wildlife highlights: Brown bears, wolves, badgers, chamois, roebucks. Golden eagles, lesser kestrels; crag martins, alpine accentors, alpine choughs, blue rock thrushes, black redstarts.
10. PYRÉNÉES-OCCIDENTALES NATIONAL PARK, France. Striking mountain scenery. Wildlife highlights: Brown bears, lynxes, chamois, ibexes. Lammergeiers, griffon and Egyptian vultures; golden, Bonelli's, and booted eagles, peregrines, kites; wall creepers, alpine accentors, rock thrushes, black redstarts.
11. JARDIN DES PLANTES, France (Paris). Historic zoo buildings. Przewalski horses, saiga antelopes, European bison, markhors, addaxes, clouded leopards; Cape Barren geese, New Zealand kagus, rare pheasants.
12. HAUTES FAGNES NATIONAL RESERVE, Belgium. Highland and forest. Wildlife highlights: Red and roe deer, wild boars, wildcats (rare). Honey buzzards, curlews, red grouse, European kingfishers, red-backed shrikes, meadow pipits, migrating cranes.
13. LÜNEBURGER HEIDE NATURE RESERVE, West Germany. Rolling heather-covered moors, bogs, coniferous woods. Wildlife highlights: Red, roe, and fallow deer; wild boars, badgers, pine and stone martens, polecats; traditional moorland sheep. Honey buzzards (hawks), goshawks, harriers, falcons, owls; stock doves, tree and tawny pipits, stonechats; black woodpeckers, wrynecks.
14. OUSE WASHES RESERVES, Great Britain (England). Meadows and marshes with remnants of original fen vegetation; canals and dikes. Wildlife highlights: Bewick's swans, pintails, pochards, teals, tufted ducks, European wigeons; lapwings, golden plovers, snipes, redshanks; reed and sedge warblers.
15. SKOMER ISLAND RESERVE, Great Britain (Wales). Rocky island with seabird cliffs. Wildlife highlights: Gray seals. Puffins, Manx shearwaters, guillemots (common murres), razorbills, kittiwakes, fulmars. Migrating thrushes, larks, other land birds.
16. WEXFORD SLOBS REFUGE, Great Britain (Ireland). Extensive tideland. Wildlife highlights: Bewick's and whooper swans; white-fronted, pink-footed, and greylag geese; European wigeons, pintails, and golden-eye ducks; black-tailed godwits, ruffs, whimbrels, curlew sandpipers.

NORTH AMERICA

An unequaled network of national parks and wildlife refuges is the pride of Canada and the United States.

Mount McKinley National Park.
Unspoiled tundra, glacial streams, and North America's highest peak are the background for grizzly bears and moose.

Glacier National Park. Breathtaking peaks, the home of mountain goats and bighorn sheep, are crowned with glaciers.

Algonquin Provincial Park. Timber wolves roam this glaciated landscape and participate in an annual howl with human visitors.

Olympic National Park. A unique temperate-zone rain forest is draped with mosses and ferns. Seals and whales play offshore.

Yellowstone National Park. In this mountain wonderland of lakes, geysers, and canyons roam herds of bison and elks.

San Diego Zoo. Rare animals and plants from around the world are displayed in a spectacular setting of ravines and canyons.

▲ National park

● Wildlife refuge

■ Zoo

1-40 See pages 340-41

Arizona-Sonora Desert Museum. Fascinating desert creatures, from horned lizards to jaguarundis, are at home in re-created habitats.

New York Zoological Park. The incredible World of Birds has jungles and rain forests with breeding tropical species.

Wind Cave National Park. This primeval grassland area on the edge of the Badlands has bison, pronghorns, and prairie-dog towns.

Map labels: Kenai, Wood Buffalo, Banff, Mount Rainier, National Bison, Point Pelee, Metro Toronto, Grand Teton, Chicago, Philadelphia, Sequoia and Kings Canyon, Bear River, Los Angeles, Washington, Great Smoky Mountains, Rocky Mountain, Haleakala, Big Bend, Aransas, Everglades

---

Canada

ALGONQUIN PROVINCIAL PARK, Ontario

Only 175 miles from Toronto, Algonquin Provincial Park, Ontario's largest reserve, extends across 2,910 square miles of the Canadian Shield, the exposed bedrock that covers much of the northern portion of the Province. The remote central portion may be reached only by canoe or on foot, but a highway traverses the southern portion.

Algonquin crests in a high domelike shape (1,850 feet above sea level), off of which flow many rivers. Prehistoric glacial activity was responsible for creating these rivers, as well as numerous picturesque lakes.

One of Algonquin's outstanding attractions is the presence of many white-tailed deer. Other large mammals include timber wolves, red foxes, black

bears, and moose. Beavers are common throughout the park. Martens, fishers, otters, and minks are more elusive.

The most impressive of Algonquin's birds is the common loon. The wail of a loon piercing the silence of a summer evening is an unforgettable experience. Another song that rings through the woods is the sweet call of white-throated sparrows. Other typical birds are ruffed grouse, ospreys, mergansers, ravens, gray jays, and three-toed and pileated woodpeckers.

Thirty canoe trips have been mapped for Algonquin's lakes and rivers. A visitor center and museum are open daily throughout the summer; there are daily hikes and nature trails.

How To Get There: *By car from Toronto via Huntsville; from Ottawa via Pembroke. By train to north side of park. By air to a number of small airfields.* **When To Go:** *Open from late*

April to mid-October. Best time, July and August. **Where To Stay:** *Four lodges, eight campgrounds.*

BANFF NATIONAL PARK, Alberta

Noted for its spectacular mountain scenery—with several 11,000-foot peaks, mighty glaciers, and turquoise-blue lakes fed by glacial meltwaters—Banff National Park also has a fine assortment of wildlife, including such endangered species as mountain goats, bighorn sheep, and golden eagles. Canada's oldest national park, Banff originally consisted of 10 square miles around a hot spring; today it spreads over 2,564 square miles of the Canadian Rockies.

Banff National Park is heavily forested with lodgepole pines, firs, and spruces. Above timberline (about

7,000 feet) are alpine meadows where hardy wildflowers—paintbrushes, gaillardias, crocus anemones, and small orchids—bloom during July and August.

Bighorns and mountain goats inhabit the park's highest zones (you will need binoculars to see them really well). Majestic elks browse the high forest slopes in summer, sometimes moving up into the lush alpine meadows.

Autumn is a time of activity in the park. Elks and other deer move down to the sheltered valleys. September is mating season, and at that time you can hear the bulls bugling out their challenges to rivals.

Large predators include cougars and timber wolves. Grizzly bears are found in the remote highlands—give these formidable, rarely seen carnivores a wide berth. Black bears are common.

The park has many species of birds, but they are thinly distributed. Most likely to be noticed are gray jays, Clark's nutcrackers, and black-billed magpies. If you travel above treeline, you may see ptarmigans, water pipits, and golden eagles. Forest birds include varied, hermit, and Swainson's thrushes, mountain bluebirds, pine and evening grosbeaks, and three-toed woodpeckers. Waterfowl frequent the lakes and marshes.

The Trans-Canada Highway crosses the park from east to west. However, the park is best seen from its 700-mile network of foot and horse trails. Naturalists lead hikes throughout the summer. Bus tours and launch trips are scheduled regularly.

How To Get There: *By car, from Calgary or Vancouver. By bus or train to Banff and Lake Louise. By air to Calgary; landing strip for small planes near Banff.* **When To Go:** *Open all year; some stretches of road may be closed by snow in winter. Summer and fall, best time for observing wildlife.* **Where To Stay:** *11 campgrounds, open May 15 to September 15. Hotels and motels in and around Banff and Lake Louise.*

METRO TORONTO ZOO, Ontario

One of the world's newest (1974) and largest (710 acres) zoos occupies a sizable segment of the Rouge River Valley, 25 miles northeast of downtown Toronto. A visit to the Metro Toronto Zoo is like a miniexcursion around the world because the animals—about 5,000 mammals, birds, reptiles, amphibians, invertebrates, and freshwater fish—have been arranged geographically.

Large moated, open-air exhibits predominate. A major feature of the Eur-

asian segment is a "mountain range" where Siberian ibexes, Asian argali sheep, and European chamois scamper along rugged cliffsides; Tibetan yaks graze in the foothills. Not far away a series of hills, with camouflaged barriers between them, alternate predator and prey species: Siberian tigers and small Asian deer called muntjacs, Chinese clouded leopards and Dybowski's sika deer from Korea.

The outdoors flows inside without a break. Outside the African pavilion a broad savanna is home to white rhinos and herds of zebras and waterbucks. Each geographic region is visually separated from the others by landscaping and careful placement.

In some instances there are no actual barriers between people and animals. At the foot of the Eurasian mountain range, a walk-through woodland allows visitors to stroll along ponds and streams in close proximity to rare Père David's deer, muntjacs, Chinese water deer, ducks, geese, swans, and cranes.

At the Canadian Domain you pass by a prairie dog village at the entrance. After viewing small mammals from the Ontario region, you can ride through some 300 acres of the Rouge River Valley and enjoy the sight of free-roaming herds of wood bison, mule deer, and woodland caribou.

Visitor Services: *Two restaurants, three snack bars. Electric trains.*

POINT PELEE NATIONAL PARK, Ontario

Very much a people's park, Point Pelee National Park encompasses 3,500 acres of sandy beaches, forests, and ponds and marshes. The park's unusual shape is an inverted isosceles triangle, dipping into Lake Erie.

Minks and muskrats live in Point Pelee's many marshes, while the forest land is inhabited by whitetailed deer, coyotes, raccoons, foxes, weasels, gray squirrels, skunks, and rabbits. But it is the park's role as a way station for migrating Canadian birds that has made it famous as an observation center.

Every spring and fall Point Pelee, where two major flyways overlap, is visited by enormous flocks of birds en route to, or from, northern breeding areas. The spring migration occurs between March 15 and June 1; the warbler migration is at its peak in May. The fall migration begins in August and extends through October. Thousands of hawks and tremendous flocks of blue jays and blackbirds pass over during these months. Canada geese, whistling swans, and many species of wild ducks

are some of the northern migrants that also pass through the area. Numerous southern birds, rare elsewhere in Canada, are frequently sighted.

For the butterfly enthusiast the fascinating migration of monarch butterflies through Point Pelee is a must. To see it, visit the park in late September or early October when great numbers of monarchs gather on the trees at the tip of the point.

To help you fully appreciate your visit, an information center offers guides, slide shows, and lectures. Here you can learn about the park's free transit system and arrange to join beach walks, conducted hikes, or a "muskrat ramble" along the boardwalk trail.

How To Get There: *By car or bus from Windsor, London, Niagara Falls, or Toronto to Leamington.* **When To Go:** *Open year round, but some visitor services are seasonal. Peak bird migrations, autumn and spring.* **Where To Stay:** *No individual campsites. Many types of accommodations in nearby Leamington.*

WOOD BUFFALO NATIONAL PARK, Alberta

Established in 1922 to protect the last remaining herd of wood bison in North America, Wood Buffalo National Park is on the boundary between Alberta and the Northwest Territories. It encompasses a vast wilderness area of 17,300 square miles, making it by far the continent's largest national park.

Lying between Lake Athabasca and Great Slave Lake, the park is made up of gently rolling plains; immense forests of spruces, tamaracks, and jack pines are interspersed with grasslands.

The bison of Wood Buffalo National Park are hybrid animals of migratory habits. Wood bison, larger and darker than plains bison, were the first park residents. But by 1928, more than 6,000 plains bison had been shipped to Wood Buffalo, where they interbred with wood bison. A recent count placed their numbers in excess of 12,000. In 1957, however, a pure strain of wood bison was discovered, and these bison have since been kept isolated. Two breeding herds have been established, one near Great Slave Lake and the other at Elk Island National Park.

In addition to bison other large mammals include moose, mule and white-tailed deer, woodland caribou, black bears, and timber wolves. The numerous streams and marshes provide suitable habitats for many small mammals: Beavers, muskrats, varying hares, ermines, and

More than 200 species of birds have been recorded in Wood Buffalo National Park. Hawks, eagles, owls, and ravens are among the common predators. Three species of grouse—spruce, sharp-tailed, and ruffed—are present. Great flocks of Ross', white-fronted, snow, and Canada geese stop over during migration, as do many ducks.

More notably, Wood Buffalo National Park is famous as the only known nesting ground of whooping cranes. These birds had not been recorded in the area from 1922 to 1955, when two Canadian Wildlife Service officers spotted a crane nesting in one of the park's marshes.

Whooping cranes are so rare that in 1973 the total wild population was 48. The cranes' normal clutch is two eggs, but seldom is more than one young reared. A number of Canadian and U.S. wildlife agencies cooperate to protect this greatly endangered species in its transit to winter quarters at Aransas Wildlife Refuge in Texas.
How To Get There: *By car from Edmonton, Alberta, via the Mackenzie Highway to Hay River, Highway 5 to Fort Smith and Peace Point. By air from Edmonton and Yellowknife to Fort Smith.* **When To Go:** *Open year round. Best seasons, spring and fall.* **Where To Stay:** *Campgrounds within the park. Limited accommodations at Fort Smith and Fort Chipewyan.*

United States

ARANSAS NATIONAL WILDLIFE REFUGE, Texas
The tidal flats, saltwater marshes, grasslands, woods, and freshwater ponds of the Aransas Wildlife Refuge, covering 85 square miles along the Gulf of Mexico, hold a variety of bird and animal life throughout the year. Aransas is the main wintering ground of endangered whooping cranes. American alligators haunt the refuge waters. Woods and grasslands give protection to such unusual mammals as red wolves.

The whoopers arrive in October to late November from their northern Canadian breeding ground in Wood Buffalo National Park. They feed in the ⎯⎯ and brackish marshes of ⎯⎯ the winter, then leave ⎯⎯ ⎯ril.

⎯⎯ ⎯rotective of
⎯⎯ which spend
⎯⎯ ⎯ransas refuge
⎯⎯ Although the
⎯⎯ ⎯oached closely,
⎯⎯ from boats in the
⎯⎯ an observation

tower. They share their feeding range with the slightly smaller sandhill cranes.

The species of ducks at Aransas include pintails, American wigeons, gadwalls, mottled ducks, northern shovelers, and blue-winged and green-winged teals. Canada, lesser snow, and a few white-fronted geese winter in the refuge. Shorebirds include western sandpipers, long-billed dowitchers, long-billed curlews, killdeers, black-necked stilts, American avocets, plovers, gallinules, and rails. Among the larger wading birds are great, snowy, and cattle egrets, plus seven kinds of herons.

White-tailed hawks and great horned owls nest in the refuge. Swallow-tailed flycatchers perch on wires or fences. In spring the trees of Aransas are thronged with thrushes, tanagers, buntings, vireos, and warblers on their way to northern nesting grounds.

White-tailed deer feed in the grasslands. The woods, mostly bay trees, live oaks, and blackjack oaks, give cover to raccoons, opossums, pocket gophers, and striped skunks. Coyotes are often seen, and gray foxes are increasing in number.
How To Get There: *By car from Houston or Rockport.* **When To Go:** *Open year round. Best time, November to March.* **Where To Stay:** *Motels, trailer parks, and campsites in Rockport and Port Lavaca.*

ARIZONA-SONORA DESERT MUSEUM, Arizona
This highly praised institution, in the rugged mountains 14 miles west of Tucson, limits its perspective to the ecology of its own region, the Sonora Desert that extends over the States of Arizona in the United States and Baja California and Sonora in Mexico. Within this scope the Arizona-Sonora Desert Museum presents a total ecological picture —wildlife, plants, earth, and water.

When you visit the Desert Museum, you'll be assisted in understanding what you see by interpretative devices—audiovisual displays, graphics, and models. In the orientation room, for example, a life-size model of an American horned lizard disappears, then rematerializes as a thorny devil (an Australian desert lizard). This is an illustration of parallel evolution: Different species on opposite sides of the world evolved into look-alikes because they adapted to similar arid habitats.

Because of the ways man has altered the environment, some animals have virtually disappeared from the Sonora Desert—otters, for example. From an elevated walkway you can watch these

water-loving mammals in their aquatic playground. Opposite the otters a stream tumbles over rocks and splashes into the beavers' pond, then trickles into a desert watering hole frequented by bighorn sheep. By moving underground you can watch the otters and beavers underwater through large plate-glass windows, or you can light up their dens when the animals move inside.

Many desert animals are active only at night. To see how they live during the day, you enter "the Tunnel." By pressing buttons you can illuminate the underground burrows of prairie dogs, kit foxes, ringtail cats, pack rats, skunks, porcupines, badgers, and rattlesnakes; there is also a bat cave.

Outdoor features include fenced areas for mountain lions, jaguars, deer, and peccaries, or jabalinas, and there is a walled area where prairie dogs dig their tunnels. The bird enclosures display desert hawks, burrowing and other owls, jays, quail, and waterfowl.

The museum's aquarium features desert-dwelling fish as well as saltwater types from the Gulf of California. Especially notable are the endangered desert pupfish and Mexican chubs. In the adjacent amphibian room frogs, toads, and salamanders inhabit accurate representations of a temporary rainpool, a permanent pool, a canyon stream, and a Mexican river.
Visitor Services: *Lectures, classes, and demonstrations. Desert garden showing desert plants in home landscaping.*

BEAR RIVER MIGRATORY BIRD REFUGE, Utah
This national refuge is situated on the vast delta of the Bear River where it empties into Great Salt Lake. The more than 110 square miles of the Bear River Migratory Bird Refuge serve as a resting and feeding area for hordes of waterfowl that nest in Alaska and Canada. Nesters include gadwalls, cinnamon teals, redheads, mallards, pintails, northern shovelers, and ruddy ducks. Egrets, herons, and many kinds of shorebirds breed in the marshes and on the mud flats, islands, and dikes. A figure of 5,000 breeding pairs of American avocets is a conservative estimate.

Duck populations in early fall occasionally exceed half a million. Late fall brings large numbers of whistling swans; up to 30,000 swans can be seen by mid-November each year. During the winter bald and golden eagles move in, along with rough-legged hawks.

The refuge also hosts a number of rare species, such as the white-faced ibis, long-billed curlew, snowy plover.

peregrine falcon, and prairie falcon.

A 12-mile loop road around one of the five major impoundments allows you to view the great bird concentrations from the dikes. Birds certain to be seen while driving include white pelicans, western grebes, yellow-headed blackbirds, avocets, black-necked stilts, snowy egrets, California and Franklin gulls, Forster's and black terns, Canada geese, willets, dowitchers, godwits, sandpipers, killdeers, and Wilson's phalaropes. Turnouts and observation towers are provided along this route.
How To Get There: *By car from Brigham City.* **When To Go:** *Open March through December. Portion of refuge open to hunting during fall.* **Where To Stay:** *Motels at Brigham City and neighboring cities. Camping area near refuge headquarters.*

BIG BEND
NATIONAL PARK, Texas
This desert park on the Mexican border, in the elbow of the Rio Grande, encompasses 1,100 square miles of ruggedly beautiful wilderness, with the Chisos Mountains at its heart. Wide expanses of arid flatlands, sheer canyons, forested slopes, and mountain meadows make for a great variety of wildlife habitat.

In the spring the desert vegetation produces an amazing array of colors: Scarlet blossoms on ocotillos, brilliant pink on strawberry cactuses, yellow on prickly pears, and gold on the sotol's 15-foot flower stack. Yuccas, agaves, spiny allthorns, lechuguillas, candelillas, creosote bushes, and mesquites dot the rocky landscape. More than 1,000 kinds of plants are native to Big Bend, and some, like the longspur columbines, can be found nowhere else.

In among the desert plants the hardy desert animals may be glimpsed. White-tailed antelope squirrels skitter up cactuses, chittering wildly. Desert mice nose around for seeds. Also present are pronghorns, mule deer, kit foxes, and peccaries (jabalinas). Cactus and canyon wrens flit and call; roadrunners race in front of you; brown towhees and pyrrhuloxias sing from their perches.

At higher elevations the vegetation and wildlife change dramatically. Oaks, piñon pines, Texas madronas, and junipers cover the slopes; Douglas firs and ponderosa pines appear on the heights.

At dusk white-tailed deer come out to feed; on rocky ledges coyotes watch for prey. Later, mountain lions (cougars) and gray foxes are on the prowl.

Big Bend National Park, with more than 385 recorded species, offers bird watchers the chance to add many unusual species to their life lists. Quite common are white-throated swifts, Mexican jays, Scott's orioles, and poorwills (Western relatives of the whippoorwill). With luck you may spot a rare Colima warbler at its only nesting area in the United States. The park's rocky hillsides harbor an unusual lizard, the checkered whiptail.

Big Bend has self-guiding nature trails, trails for hiking and horseback trips, and primitive roads for four-wheel-drive vehicles. Naturalists explain park geology, plants, and animals.
How To Get There: *By car from San Antonio via Marathon (410 miles); from El Paso via Alpine (323 miles).* **When To Go:** *Open all year. Best time for desert blooms, February to June.* **Where To Stay:** *Chisos Mountain Lodge at basin. Camping at basin and Rio Grande Village; trailer parks at Rio Grande Village and Panther Junction.*

CHICAGO
ZOOLOGICAL PARK, Illinois
Most people know the Chicago Zoological Park as the Brookfield Zoo because of its location. But the zoo's influence isn't limited to its immediate surroundings; it actually extends to Australia, where it has established a 14,000-acre refuge for the hairy-nosed wombat.

Wombats (resembling overgrown guinea pigs) are a feature of Australia House. Brookfield specializes in immersing people in animal environments, and this building provides a "Down Under" walk-through. The first stop is an orientation hall. Displays explain how the continent's geographic isolation produced its unique fauna and how its pouched marsupials differ from the placental mammals that dominate the rest of the world. You then enter a twilight scene with a warren housing three hairy-nosed wombats (outside Australia only six zoos display them). The path leads through a dry desert and a eucalyptus forest with kangaroos, wallabies, opossums, cuscuses, and phalangers.

In the Tropic World of Primates three large rain forests represent South America, Southeast Asia, and Africa. Troops of monkeys and apes range through the trees. Only open spaces and waterways separate animals from people. Even orangutans and gibbons roam freely (at a safe distance). The only exception to this is the African forest, where gorillas are behind bars (disguised as bamboo).

The Cat Ecology House places you inside naturalistic depictions of an Old World desert, two northern mountain slopes, and two tropical forests. Five dioramas with curving walls create the illusion of limitless space. Illumination simulates dawn and dusk, the time when the small carnivores displayed here are most active—fishing cats actually hunt their prey in a stream.

Brookfield has also bridged the gap between people and animals by pioneering some unusual graphics, such as those at the Baboon Island. To uninformed visitors the activities of the lively Guinea baboon colony might be entertaining but meaningless. But large pictorial displays explain the facial expressions and postures with which the baboons communicate.
Visitor Services: *Train tours on the Brookfield, Salt Creek, and Western Railroad (powered by antique steam locomotives). Children's zoo. Performing porpoises. Self-guided tours.*

EVERGLADES
NATIONAL PARK, Florida
A unique experience for most visitors, the only subtropical national park in the United States was established in 1947 to protect the complex plant and animal communities of Florida's southern tip. Within Everglades National Park's more than 2,100 square miles (larger than the State of Delaware) are the slow-flowing "River of Grass" with its elevated hardwood "islands," or hammocks; stands of Caribbean pine and dwarf cypress; one of the world's largest mangrove swamps; and the bird-haunted shallows and keys of Whitewater and Florida Bays.

Continually under threat from manmade or natural water shortages, fires, hurricanes, chemical pollution, and proposed airport and highway encroachments, Everglades National Park nevertheless provides a home for a number of North America's endangered (and seldom seen) animals: Florida cougars, North American manatees, sea turtles, saltwater crocodiles, Everglade kites, and white-crowned pigeons. Freshwater alligators, raccoons, opossums, otters, and white-tailed deer are more frequently encountered.

But the glory of the Everglades has always been the remarkably varied and abundant birdlife; some 300 species have been recorded in the park. Nesting species include wood storks (North America's only example of this family), white ibises, roseate spoonbills, gre white herons (a rare color phase great blue herons), reddish egrets, nificent frigate birds, and bald

Everglades National Park is

tered by way of the Headquarters Visitor Center, 12 miles south of Homestead, where an orientation program explains the natural wonders you will encounter. At the Royal Palm Visitor Center nearby, the raised boardwalk of the Anhinga Trail gives you an intimate view of Everglades wildlife—purple and common gallinules pattering over lily pads, anhingas spreading their wings to dry, alligators sunning on the banks of the slough. A circuit of the Gumbo Limbo Trail introduces you to the atmosphere of a tropical hammock.

From the main park road to Flamingo short spurs diverge to other trails, ponds, a boardwalk and observation tower at Pa-hay-okee (Grassy Waters) Overlook, and Mahogany Hammock. At Flamingo, on Florida Bay, at the end of the road, ranger-naturalists give talks and lead nature walks. There are marked canoe trails and scheduled boat trips into Florida and Whitewater Bays. Finally, a tram tour takes in the Shark Valley Loop.

How To Get There: *By car from Miami, via Homestead (about 40 miles to main entrance); from western Florida resorts by Tamiami Trail.* **When To Go:** *Best time to see wildlife, dry winter months; May through November, very warm and wet.* **Where To Stay:** *Campgrounds at Long Pine Key and Flamingo. Motels, houseboats, marina at Flamingo. Motels at Everglades and Homestead.*

GLACIER
NATIONAL PARK, Montana

Nearly 1,600 square miles of steeply rising peaks and open, parklike valleys scooped out by glacial ice make up Glacier National Park. Its coniferous forests, rocky crags, and alpine meadows shelter bighorn sheep, mountain goats, grizzly bears, and 235 species of birds, including bald and golden eagles and ospreys. Heavy snowfalls replenish the park's more than 40 glaciers and innumerable lakes and streams. Canada's Waterton Lakes National Park adjoins Glacier on the north.

The Continental Divide roughly bisects Glacier. The well-watered western portion has dense forests dominated ~ spruces, firs, lodgepole pines, and ~st of the divide the climate ~sively drier.

~ndant from June ~ most convenient ~an Pass. The ~ heads of bear ~nber of the lily ~ glacier lilies light ~ows. At lower elevations ~ colorful flowers as

magenta fireweeds, scarlet Indian paintbrushes, and purple pasqueflowers.

In early morning and evening elks and white-tailed and mule deer graze the meadows. Hoary marmots and pikas make their dens at the foot of rockslides. On the rocky upper slopes you may see bighorn sheep and mountain goats; the goats sometimes come within camera range. Moose feed in the lowland ponds and lakes; beavers and otters frequent the streams. Grizzly bears are most often encountered in the high country, while black bears range through the lower altitudes. Wolverines, timber wolves, and coyotes are also present, as are northern bog lemmings, porcupines, golden-mantled ground squirrels, pine martens, and fishers.

Among the birds are Clark's nutcrackers, gray jays, mountain bluebirds, and varied thrushes. Common loons, western grebes, and three species of mergansers inhabit the lakes; dippers feed in the streams. Ruffed, blue, and spruce grouse, pileated and northern three-toed woodpeckers, pine siskins, and red crossbills prefer wooded areas; white-tailed ptarmigans, gray-crowned rosy finches, and water pipits live above the tree line.

A 50-mile scenic drive, the Going-to-the-Sun Road, traverses Glacier National Park, and there are a number of spur roads and about 700 miles of foot and horse trails, most of them in wilderness areas. Ranger-naturalists lead walks from several centers in the park.

How To Get There: *By car or bus from Great Falls or Missoula. By air to Great Falls or Kalispell. By train to East or West Glacier (Belton) stations. Park buses connect with planes, trains, and buses.* **When To Go:** *Open year round. Going-to-the-Sun Road closed from mid-October to early June. Park accommodations open from early June to early September.* **Where To Stay:** *Hotels, motels, cabins, and campgrounds in park; back-country camping by permit only. Hotels in nearby towns.*

GRAND TETON
NATIONAL PARK, Wyoming

Long famous as a scenic area, Grand Teton National Park also offers visitors an ever-changing panorama of wildlife.

The eastern half of the 485-square-mile park is a high, open plain broken by occasional low ridges. The western portion is dominated by the Rockies' mighty Teton Range, whose pyramidal peaks rise abruptly above the plain, soaring to 13,770 feet at Grand Teton.

Cottonwoods, willows, and blue spruces fringe the banks of the Snake

River and its tributaries. Sagebrush and grasses cover the valley floor. Lodgepole pines, Douglas firs, and aspens hide the base of the Tetons. Subalpine firs, Engelmann spruces, and whitebark pines dominate the forests on the slopes. Above timberline are alpine meadows bright with forget-me-nots, columbines, and glacier lilies. In the lowlands—particularly along the Indian Paintbrush Trail—pentstemons, larkspurs, blue lupines, painted cups, wild geraniums, and other wildflowers provide a colorful display from May to mid-August.

Moose are easily seen in all seasons. In spring they feed in lowland ponds and browse the willow groves. In summer they move up to the alpine meadows, where they can be observed from scenic highway overlooks. In fall and winter many moose band together in open country.

Elks, the most numerous of the large mammals, summer in the alpine meadows and in the valleys. Since they retreat to the forest during the midday heat, they are best observed in early morning and late afternoon. The fall mating season brings elks down to the lowlands. In early winter large bands of elks migrate to their winter range in the National Elk Refuge, adjoining the park.

Small bands of bighorn sheep inhabit the high country, and a herd of bison thrive in the northeast section of the park. Mule deer summer on the lower forest slopes, and pronghorns graze on the sagebrush flats. Beavers flourish in the streams and ponds of the bottomlands. Black bears are common but are not frequently sighted. Grizzlies, fewer in number, prefer remote mountain country. Smaller predators include coyotes, lynxes, bobcats, otters, martens, and foxes. A few cougars survive in the wilder areas.

More than 200 species of birds have been recorded in Grand Teton National Park. Trumpeter swans are year-round residents, nesting in the more remote ponds, and Barrow's goldeneye ducks and Canada geese are present at all seasons. Other birds of special interest include bald eagles and ospreys. Great blue herons feed in the wetlands, and white pelicans stop over on their spring and fall migrations. In the forests there are many songbirds, such as mountain bluebirds and western tanagers. High in the mountains you may see the black rosy finch, nesting among rocks and snow. Magpies, ravens, gray jays, and Clark's nutcrackers are common.

Two paved roads cross Grand Teton National Park to the east of the mountains, but most of the park is best seen from the 200 miles of foot and horse trails. There are guided nature hikes and pack trips. Float trips on the Snake River are a favorite way of seeing scenery and wildlife. Nature programs are presented nightly during the summer. **How To Get There:** *By car from Yellowstone National Park, Idaho Falls, Idaho, or Cheyenne, Wyoming, via Rock Springs. By bus from Rock Springs to Jackson, south of park. By air to Jackson.* **When To Go:** *Open all year. Best time for observing wildlife, June through September.* **Where To Stay:** *Five campgrounds, trailers permitted at all but Jenny Lake (closed from late September to early June). Lodges and dude ranches at Jenny Lake and Jackson Hole open year round.*

GREAT SMOKY MOUNTAINS NATIONAL PARK,
Tennessee-North Carolina

Established to preserve remnants of the eastern hardwood forest, Great Smoky Mountains National Park preserves an area of botanic interest. The Smokies, part of the Appalachian system, were named by early settlers for the bluish haze that shrouds the mountains on warm days. The park, which straddles the Tennessee-North Carolina border, contains 16 peaks over 6,000 feet high.

At lower elevations the park is heavily forested with a rich variety of hardwood trees—oaks, maples, basswoods, beeches, yellow poplars, cucumber trees, yellow buckeyes, sweet and yellow birches, mountain silver bells, and many others, often of record size. Eastern hemlocks grow up to about 5,000 feet, mingled with the hardwoods. Above this level lies an unusual belt of typical Canadian forest.

Mountain laurels, azaleas, and rhododendrons grow to treelike proportions throughout the park. Their blooming season, extending from May through July, is one of the park's highlights.

The park's only large mammals are the white-tailed deer, abundant around Cade's Cove in the western end, and black bears, commonly seen along the transmountain road.

Because of the varying forest habitats, the park is rich in bird species. Wild turkeys forage for acorns in the oak woods; you are most likely to see turkeys at Cade's Cove. Ruffed grouse are common at all elevations; in April and October you may hear the males drumming out their noisy challenges. Other year-round residents of the park's lower levels include cardinals, Carolina wrens, tufted titmice, Carolina chickadees, and several species of woodpeckers. Nesting birds in the highland spruce-fir zone include juncos, vesper sparrows, veeries, and red crossbills (which rarely nest south of Canadian forests).

Paved roads are limited, but there are about 600 miles of foot and horse trails. The Appalachian Trail traverses the park from end to end. Unfortunately, the park's capacity has been severely strained by the sheer number of visitors, bringing with them problems of trail erosion and littering. Park authorities have imposed a limit on the number of overnight hikers on the Appalachian Trail.

How To Get There: *By car over Blue Ridge Parkway. Bus tours from Knoxville, Tennessee, and Asheville, North Carolina.* **When To Go:** *Open all year. Best seasons for migratory birds, late spring and fall. Best time for wildflowers, May through late July; October for spectacular foliage display.* **Where To Stay:** *Campgrounds and campsites in park. Lodge on Mount LeConte; hotel at Elkmont. Hotels and motels in nearby towns.*

HALEAKALA NATIONAL PARK, Hawaii (Maui)

A refuge for several rare or threatened species of native Hawaiian birds, 34-square-mile Haleakala National Park includes the spectacular crater of Mount Haleakala, a dormant volcano, and an 8-mile-long gorge that leads down to a black-lava ocean beach.

Most of the crater is arid and supports only a sparse plant growth; but the northeast corner receives up to 300 inches of rain a year, and here a lush rain forest flourishes, with such unusual native plants as the ape-ape, which has circular leaves up to 5 feet in diameter. In the arid portion grow spectacular silverswords, which are found in the wild only on the islands of Maui and Hawaii.

Birds are found mostly on the western slope of Haleakala and in the crater rain forest. Some of the native honeycreepers are strikingly colorful: Iiwis, scarlet with black wings and tail; scarlet, black, and white apapanes; and the green-and-yellow amakihis. The nene, a rare, land-dwelling goose formerly extinct on Maui and on the verge of extinction elsewhere, has been successfully bred at Slimbridge in England and reintroduced. More common native birds include Hawaiian short-eared owls and white-tailed tropic birds. Golden plovers, which migrate across thousands of miles of the Pacific to nesting grounds in Alaska, are abundant from September through May.

A road winds through the western portion of Haleakala National Park; inside the crater are 30 miles of foot and horse trails. If you are in top condition, you can climb down and back in a day, but the average visitor is advised to plan on taking 2 to 3 days. Horses for guided trips of 1 to several days can be rented. **How To Get There:** *By air from Honolulu or Hilo to Kahului airport; then by car to park.* **When To Go:** *Open all year. Best season, summer.* **Where To Stay:** *Three overnight cabins, three campgrounds, backpack camping by permit. Hotels and motels in Maui.*

KENAI NATIONAL MOOSE RANGE, Alaska

Home of one of North America's most impressive moose populations, Kenai National Moose Range occupies 2,700 square miles of the Kenai Peninsula. About two-thirds of the area is undulating lowland, with spruces, aspens, willows, and birches on the higher ground, in addition to vast stretches of water and muskegs (peat bogs). The remainder is mountainous, rising to 6,612 feet. There are more than 2,800 lakes.

Above timberline—only 2,000 feet at this latitude—are stretches of tundra and alpine meadows, where cushion pinks, columbines, forget-me-nots, azaleas, lupines, and fireweeds blossom during the brief arctic summer.

Caribou were once by far the most numerous mammals in the range, but a series of fires destroyed most of their feeding grounds, and few if any have survived. The deciduous trees that sprang up after the fires furnished ideal browse for the moose population, which expanded to fill the newly opened ecological niche. Today about 7,500 moose inhabit the lowlands of the range.

In the mountains live Dall sheep and mountain goats. You may have difficulty seeing these shy, white-coated animals, especially since their favorite precipitous slopes are often shrouded in clouds. The numerous marmots in the alpine meadows are hard to miss. Other mountain dwellers include giant Alaskan brown bears (rare) and wolverines (seldom seen). Black bears are numerous in almost every part of the range. Beavers are common in the wetlands.

With its variety of land forms and habitats, the range is rich in birdlife—146 species have been recorded. Among the nesting birds are rare trumpeter swans and bald eagles. Great horned owls and goshawks are common. The most abundant waterfowl are mallards, common and Barrow's goldeneyes, and green-winged teals. Common and arctic loons fish in the lakes, and glaucous-winged gulls forage for anything eatable. Black-billed magpies, gray jays, ravens, spruce grouse, ptarmigans (rock, willow, and white-tailed), and redpolls are year-round residents of the high forests. White- and golden-crowned sparrows, boreal chickadees, varied thrushes, and Bohemian waxwings are among the summer visitors.

Much of the Kenai Moose Range is best seen by water, and two extensive canoe systems have been laid out. The Sterling Highway traverses the range, and there are two scenic drives.

How To Get There: *By car, via Sterling Highway from Anchorage (about 12 miles). By light plane to designated lakes and airstrips.* **When To Go:** *Open all year. Best time for observing wildlife, June through September.* **Where To Stay:** *14 campgrounds, most accepting trailers. Motels in Kenai and Soldotna.*

LOS ANGELES ZOO,
California

The modern Los Angeles Zoo approaches wildlife exhibition through the concept of zoogeography. That is, it displays its 2,500 animals in continental groups, a more realistic approximation of nature than the conventional plan that places all cats or all bears together. To add regional realism, each "continent" (North and South America, Africa, Eurasia, and Australia) is planted with appropriate botanical specimens.

The Los Angeles Zoo also stresses conservation in its exhibits. It claims to have more endangered species (about 60) on display than any other American zoo, and it has bred a high percentage of them. One major success is with the golden lion-maned marmoset. This tiny monkey, nearly extinct in its native Brazil, has been difficult to breed in captivity. But in Los Angeles several litters have been born. The marmosets are now housed in a climate-controlled shelter in "South America." Nearby, maned wolves (often described as "red foxes on stilts") have also been reasonably prolific, despite a record of rarely reproducing in zoos. Spectacled bears and bush dogs are among the other vanishing South American species that can be seen. An unusual exhibit is the World of Tapirs. Los Angeles is the only zoo with four species.

In the Eurasian section the Arabian oryxes have reproduced so well that the zoo has had to construct larger quarters for them. Now almost extinct in the wild, they can be seen elsewhere only in private Arabian collections and in

two other zoos (Phoenix and San Diego). Other Eurasian rarities are Indian rhinos, onagers (Persian wild asses), Przewalski wild horses, and tarpans (replicas of an extinct wild horse produced by careful breeding).

The only exceptions to the geographic display scheme are the sections devoted to various forms of animal specialization: Birds and amphibians, reptiles and fish. The reptile collection is one of the world's largest and most varied. For example, Los Angeles exhibits 31 of the 32 species of rattlesnakes.

Visitor Services: *Tours for groups. Minibuses to exhibit areas. Elephant training sessions. Live animal demonstrations in Children's Zoo.*

MOUNT MCKINLEY
NATIONAL PARK, Alaska

Only 250 miles south of the Arctic Circle, Mount McKinley National Park is world famous for its rugged scenery as well as its abundant wildlife. Including a portion of the snowcapped Alaska Range, the park is the site of 20,320-foot Mount McKinley, the highest peak in North America. This immense subarctic wilderness (larger than the States of Delaware and Rhode Island combined) contains several other peaks over 12,000 feet high, snowfields, glaciers, and vast stretches of taiga (swampy coniferous forest) and tundra.

Moose, Mount McKinley's largest mammals, feed in the lowland marshes and forests; grizzly bears dig for roots and ground squirrels and forage for berries on the open tundra. The rare Dall sheep feed at the higher elevations on the precarious rock slopes. In late June and July migrating herds of barren-ground caribou pass through the park. Wolves, lynxes, and wolverines are present but rarely seen. Smaller mammals include beavers, porcupines, martens, and coyotes.

About 130 species of birds, many of them long-distance migrants, frequent the park in summer. Permanent residents include golden eagles, gyrfalcons, ravens, black-billed magpies, Canada jays, boreal chickadees, and willow and rock ptarmigans. The park waters produce common and arctic loons, red-necked grebes, common goldeneyes, and harlequin ducks. Among the summer visitors are yellowlegs, sandpipers, whimbrels, wandering tattlers, varied thrushes, northern shrikes, water pipits, tree sparrows, and Lapland longspurs. American golden plovers reach the Mount McKinley area from wintering grounds in Hawaii, wheatears come

from the Asian mainland, and surfbirds arrive from South America.

An 88-mile gravel road, open from about June 1 to September 10, traverses the eastern half of Mount McKinley National Park. About 20 miles of foot trails, some of them self-guided nature trails, radiate from the McKinley Park Hotel, at the main entrance of the park. Guided bus tours leave the hotel daily. Transportation into the interior is by free buses.

Cross-country hikers should check their intended routes with a park ranger, for the tundra and the glacial streams can be treacherous. Be sure to bring warm clothing, rain gear, and insect repellent.

How To Get There: *By car from Anchorage (240 miles) or Fairbanks (120 miles); in summer from Paxson (160 miles) by the Denali Highway. By train from Anchorage or Fairbanks. By air taxi or private plane to hotel airstrip.* **When To Go:** *Open late May to mid-September. Best time, late May and June.* **Where To Stay:** *McKinley Park Hotel. Seven campsites along park road —trailers permitted (no hookups). Limited accommodations at Camp Denali, just outside park.*

MOUNT RAINIER
NATIONAL PARK, Washington

Best known for its mighty glaciers and the spectacular wildflowers of its mountain meadows, Mount Rainier National Park also has more than 50 species of mammals, including cougars and mountain goats, as well as 130 species of birds. The park, which lies in the rugged Cascade Range in west-central Washington, is dominated by the massive bulk of 14,410-foot Mount Rainier.

Moisture-laden winds from the Pacific dump an average of 50 feet of snow a year on Mount Rainier's upper slopes and summit, feeding more than 25 glaciers. Most of the glaciers are active, so that if you make the strenuous climb to the glacier fields, you can observe glacial processes at work. At Paradise Glacier are the noted ice caves.

Most of the 378-square-mile park lies between 2,000 and 4,000 feet. Dense forests—dominated by Douglas firs, western hemlock, and western red cedars—extend up to timberline, giving way to broad alpine meadows at the higher levels. Among the wildflowers are mountain buttercups, pasqueflowers, avalanche lilies, and glacier lilies, which often bloom through several inches of melting snow.

Small bands of hardy mountain goats —an estimated 400 live in the park—can often be seen grazing the high rock slopes near the glaciers. Marmots and pikas are abundant in the rockslides and alpine meadows. Beavers thrive along the streams, and mule deer find abundant browse in the forests. Elks are seldom seen except by back-country hikers. Chipmunks and golden-mantled ground squirrels are common at overlooks and campsites.

Birds are plentiful, especially near water. Several species of woodpeckers, thrushes, and warblers, golden- and ruby-crowned kinglets, and mountain chickadees are the dominant species in the forest zone. In the alpine meadows you are almost certain to see Clark's nutcrackers, mountain bluebirds, ravens, and gray jays. Above timberline the most noticeable species are white-tailed ptarmigans, water pipits, and gray-crowned rosy finches. Hikers often hear the booming call of the blue grouse. Several species of hawks and an occasional golden eagle cruise the sky.

Mount Rainier National Park has almost 120 miles of roads and 300 miles of trails, ranging from short, self-guided nature walks to the 90-mile Wonderland Trail encircling Mount Rainier. Intersecting a number of paved roads, the Wonderland Trail can easily be reached by car for short hikes. Nature walks are led by ranger-naturalists.

How To Get There: *By car from Tacoma (about 60 miles). By daily bus from Tacoma or Seattle (late June to early September).* **When To Go:** *Open all year; most facilities closed winter and spring. Best time, July through mid-September.* **Where To Stay:** *National Park Inn, Paradise Inn; six campgrounds, four primitive sites (one campground open all year). Back-country camping by permit.*

NATIONAL BISON RANGE, Montana

Lying in a broad valley flanked by mountains, the National Bison Range embraces 25 square miles of rolling grassy plains, steep hills, and narrow canyons. Parklike forests of firs and ponderosa pines grow on the high slopes and ridges, and on the creek bottoms there are thick growths of alders, aspens, and cottonwoods. Many colorful prairie wildflowers—Indian paintbrushes, clarkias, pentstemons, lupines, and larkspurs—bloom in May and June.

Established in 1908 to protect the almost-extinct American bison, the range began with 34 animals bought from a private herd, plus seven donated from other sources. Later, other species were added, including elks, mule and white-tailed deer, bighorn sheep, and pronghorns. Each of these species is able to take advantage of a different ecological niche: Bison graze on the grasslands, while elks browse in the upland forests in summer and the creek-bottom thickets in winter. Mule deer forage in the highlands, while whitetails feed on the lush creek bottoms. Pronghorns seek out arid scrub; bighorns, high elevations.

A few beavers live along the streams. Yellow-bellied marmots and ground squirrels provide food for badgers and weasels. A few bobcats and coyotes and an occasional black bear wander through the range.

Due to the lack of large predators, the bison and other herds must be kept within limits to avoid overgrazing and destruction of habitat. The annual bison roundup in October is a major event.

The upland game birds you are most likely to see are introduced species: Ring-necked pheasants and chukar and gray partridges. Common birds include rock wrens, western meadowlarks, Brewer's blackbirds, short-eared owls, hawks (marsh, red-tailed, and rough-legged) in the grasslands, red-breasted and pygmy nuthatches, mountain and black-capped chickadees, and Lewis' woodpeckers and Clark's nutcrackers in the highland forests. Golden eagles may often be seen soaring above the ridges.

Because of the danger from rattlesnakes and the unpredictable nature of bison, hiking is limited to designated trails. A 19-mile self-guided auto tour (road open June 1 to September 30) offers a good chance of seeing most of the large herbivores.

How To Get There: *By car from Missoula to refuge headquarters at Moiese (about 50 miles). By air to Missoula.* **When To Go:** *Open all year; portions closed by snow in winter. Best time, June through September.* **Where To Stay:** *Motels nearby.*

NATIONAL ZOOLOGICAL PARK, District of Columbia (Washington)

At this branch of the Smithsonian Institution there is no question about the star attraction: two giant pandas. This is the only zoo in the Western Hemisphere that has pandas, and long lines wait to see Hsing-Hsing (male) and Ling-Ling (female).

Only animals as appealing as pandas could outshine some of the other rare creatures in the National Zoo's collection of more than 3,000 animals—white tigers, for instance. Not many white tigers (a color phase of the Bengal tiger) exist either in the wild or in captivity, but in Washington they have reproduced cubs regularly. Now in Chicago's Brookfield Zoo while a new lion-tiger complex is being built, they are expected to return by 1976.

The pandas are not the only diplomatic windfall to the National Zoo. A rare forest elephant (smaller than the African species) was presented by the Republic of the Congo; Komodo monitor lizards, by Indonesia; dorcas gazelles, by Tunisia; a pair of kiwis, by New Zealand; and pygmy hippos, by Liberia.

The National Zoo has an outstanding record in the reproduction of rare and endangered animals. A pair of bald eagles hatched and reared an eaglet, which is highly unusual in captivity. The zoo also recorded births of a kagu, an endangered chicken-sized bird from New Caledonia, and a bongo, an African forest antelope, which was the first bred in captivity. Golden lion marmosets bred so well that a special building was erected just for them.

The National Zoo's most striking structure is the outdoor aviary, a series of parabolic arches strung with wires. Free-flying cormorants, mynas, magpies, ducks, and other birds accompany you as you follow a path that winds down a hillside past waterfalls and natural vegetation.

Visitor Services: *Tractor train. Guided tours.*

NEW YORK ZOOLOGICAL PARK (BRONX ZOO) AND AQUARIUM, New York

The Bronx Zoo's chief aim is to present a wide variety of natural habitats, showing the many specialized ways animals have adapted to different environments. The elaborate and beautiful World of Birds, for example, offers 24 habitat replicas, ranging from luxuriant tropical jungle to dry desert. North American burrowing owls use underground tunnels; South American torrent ducks occupy riverbanks; and African weaver finches build colonies of drooping, baglike nests. Some displays are viewable at both ground and treetop level, and others (like the South American and African rain forests) are open-fronted with no barriers.

The World of Darkness displays nocturnal animals by reversing day-night cycles. Primitive primates like African galagos, or bush babies, scamper through jungle treetops. Kit foxes patrol a southwestern desert panorama. Bats flit in and out of a cave.

Survival of a more urgent sort is the concern of the Endangered Species

Range. Here more than an acre of moated, natural landscape is provided for each of three animals whose existence now depends on captive breeding: Père David's deer, European bison, and Przewalski wild horses. The rarest animals in the Bronx collection are shaggy goat-antelopes from Burma, called takins.

Some of the newer exhibits contain wildlife grouped by geographic region. You enter tropical Asia through an orientation building that has ecological displays in addition to live exhibits of orangutans, Komodo monitor lizards, and other Asian animals. From an exterior platform you can observe gibbons frolicking on their island, then board a monorail that transports you past Siberian tigers, and elephants.

On the other side of the city the New York Aquarium sits by the ocean in Brooklyn's Coney Island section. The prime attraction is the exhibit of beluga or white whales.

Reef tanks hold brilliant tropical fish, large sharks, and sea turtles. Four 600-gallon tanks contain the freshwater fish of North America. Smaller tanks offer lethal stonefish, primitive lungfish, clown fish in a symbiotic relationship with poisonous sea anemones, and an electric eel that lights up a neon sign. **Visitor Services at the Bronx Zoo:** *Skyfari cable-car ride. Free guided tours on weekends. Children's zoo.* **At the Aquarium:** *Performances by dolphins and beluga whale. Children's Cove with "touch-it" tank.*

OLYMPIC
NATIONAL PARK, Washington
Renowned for its extraordinary rain forest and its Roosevelt elks—the largest herd of this subspecies in the United States—Olympic National Park embraces most of the rugged Olympic Range. In addition, the park includes a 50-mile strip of seacoast.

In the sheltered valleys of the western portion grow the Olympic rain forests, extending up to the 2,000-foot level. Sitka spruces, Douglas firs, and western hemlocks dominate the rainforest community, often towering 200 to 300 feet above the forest floor. Sprawling vine maples and pink-flowered rhododendrons form a shrubby layer. Luxuriant mosses and ferns drape the trees and carpet the ground. A broad zone of silver firs and western white pines lies above the rain forest. Above timberline stretch alpine meadows where avalanche lilies, larkspurs, painted cups, wild phloxes, and lupines bloom from July to September.

In summer the majestic Roosevelt elks (estimated at 4,000 to 5,000 head) graze the upland meadows in early morning and evening, and black bears forage for berries and other plant foods. Other large mammals include black-tailed deer, cougars (relatively plentiful but rarely seen), and introduced mountain goats. Beavers and otters are abundant in the streams, while mountain beavers, large burrowing rodents that sometimes cut down trees, are found throughout the park. The whistling calls of Olympic marmots are a common sound in high country. Bobcats, preying on the smaller mammals, are numerous.

In the Pacific coast area of the park seals and sea lions sun on the offshore rocks. Gray whales pass close to shore on migrations to and from their Mexican breeding grounds.

More than 300 species of birds are recorded in Olympic National Park. About half the species are seabirds, shorebirds, and ducks and other waterfowl. Bald eagles and glaucous-winged gulls search the beaches for fish. Auklets, tufted puffins, and common murres nest on offshore rocks. Mountain birds include Lewis' and pileated woodpeckers, ravens, mountain bluebirds, gray and Steller's jays, and rosy finches.

About a dozen roads penetrate varying distances into the park from the encircling U.S. 101; all stop short of the central wilderness area, which is reached on foot trails. In July and August ranger-naturalists lead nature walks. **How To Get There:** *By car from Olympia, Aberdeen, or Hoquiam, Washington. Car ferries from Victoria, British Columbia, and Seattle. By bus to Port Angeles, near park boundary. By air from Seattle or Tacoma to Port Angeles.* **When To Go:** *Open all year (some areas and most facilities closed in winter). Best time, mid-June through October.* **Where To Stay:** *Cabins and lodges; 17 campgrounds.*

PHILADELPHIA
ZOOLOGICAL GARDEN,
Pennsylvania
A formal charm marks the Philadelphia Zoo with its green lawns, flower beds, and rose gardens. The zoo's ponds and streams are home to one of the largest waterfowl collections in the world.

At the Hummingbird Exhibit you follow an elevated walkway through the American "tropics" for unbarred close-up looks at tiny, exotically colored hummers. Flitting amid the 2,500 tropical plants are some 20 other species of tropical birds, such as jaçanas, bellbirds, and honeycreepers—plus assorted

species of lizards, frogs, turtles, and fish.

In the Reptile House a southern cypress swamp harbors rattlesnakes, cottonmouths, turtles, and small alligators. An arid, desert-isle seascape authentically reproduces the Galápagos Islands for giant tortoises. Opposite them crocodiles lurk along a tropical riverbank. Several times daily, crocodiles and visitors are treated to a jungle storm.

The Small Mammal House features a South African veld. Meerkats (a type of mongoose) scurry around a sleepy aardvark; rabbitlike hyraxes huddle on rocky outcrops. In the Rare Mammal House young gorillas frolic in a man-made equatorial forest of trees and vines. Nearly every year a baby orangutan is on view in this building.

Outdoors a pack of timber wolves engages in its normal, highly structured social behavior on a rocky site. Five acres of African plains give you an unhindered look at antelopes, giraffes, zebras, and ostriches.
Visitor Services: *Children's zoo and pony rides. Elevated monorail loop. Recorded lectures at 50 locations.*

ROCKY MOUNTAIN
NATIONAL PARK, Colorado
Less than 70 miles by road from Denver, Rocky Mountain National Park sits astride the towering Front Range of the Rockies. Its 410 square miles include rugged peaks, deep gorges, and a large expanse of alpine tundra.

Forests—mainly Engelmann spruces, Douglas firs, and ponderosa pines—clothe the slopes up to about 1,500 feet, giving way to tundra. Herds of mule deer browse chiefly on shrubs; elks graze the meadows. Pine martens stalk squirrels by night. Beavers build dams along the many streams. Coyotes, bobcats, and foxes are plentiful but too wary to be seen often. With luck you may spot a black bear or cougar. Look for the rare bighorn sheep in the Never Summer Mountains and at Sheep Lake.

About 240 species of birds are recorded in the park; among them golden eagles, Clark's nutcrackers, Steller's and gray jays, black-billed magpies, western tanagers, purple finches, black-capped and mountain chickadees, and western meadowlarks are plentiful. There are also red crossbills, pine and black-headed siskins, grosbeaks, Townsend's solitaires, blue grouse, and ravens.

To many visitors the alpine tundra is the most interesting part of the park. Here, such colorful flowers as yellow paintbrushes, deep-red king's crowns, golden marsh marigolds, deep-blue gentians, and alpine forget-me-nots brighten the uplands during the brief 6-week blooming season. In early summer snow buttercups may push yellow petals through melting snowbanks.

Yellow-billed marmots and pikas make their dens in rock piles; pocket gophers dig into grassy areas. Water pipits, rosy finches, white-crowned sparrows, and horned larks nest during the brief tundra summer, while white-tailed ptarmigans are year-round residents.

The Trail Ridge Road gives you a fine view of the tundra. Or you can walk a paved nature trail. Below timberline there are more than 300 miles of foot and horse trails. Daily walks are conducted by ranger-naturalists during the summer months. But many areas of Rocky Mountain National Park can be reached by road, including the Alpine Visitor Center.

How To Get There: *By train, bus, or plane to Denver. By car or bus from Denver.* **When To Go:** *Open all year. Best time for tundra flowers and wildlife, June through September; fall, winter, and spring for observing elks and deer. Trail Ridge Road closed from mid-October to late May.* **Where To Stay:** *Hotels, motels, dude ranches at Estes Park and Grand Lake. Public campsites in park.*

SAN DIEGO ZOO AND WILD ANIMAL FARM, California

Perhaps the world's most spectacular zoological exhibition, the San Diego Zoo added to its laurels by opening a second zoo in 1972. The original zoo in Balboa Park follows traditional patterns but with an unusually open, outdoor quality.

A pathway winds through a canyon past grottoes for bears, lions, and tigers. Moated displays of hoofed animals stretch across broad mesas. Rocky ravines furnish authentic settings for wild goats and sheep. A bridge leads into Cascade Canyon, the "African" home of semiaquatic antelopes (sitatungas and oribis), crowned cranes, spur-winged geese, and comb ducks. An elevated boardwalk leads through this habitat and twists down a canyon greened with groves of palm and eucalyptus. Just beyond are the hippo pools. Close by, a large walk-through aviary rises over a steep incline.

The San Diego Zoo has enhanced the naturalness of its displays by making them part of one of the foremost botanical gardens in the United States. More than 56,500 trees plus comparable numbers of flowering plants, vines, and shrubs from around the world fill the spaces between exhibits.

Even before the second zoo was built, San Diego boasted the world's largest collection of mammals, birds, and reptiles—about 5,000 specimens of nearly 1,400 species and subspecies. It is the only non-Australian zoo to display koalas, the cuddly teddy-bearish marsupials. Other Down Under curiosities include tree kangaroos, wombats, Tasmanian devils, and a variety of kangaroos, wallabies, and wallaroos. Kiwis (small, almost wingless birds from New Zealand) probe a "moonlit" forest floor for earthworms.

Animals that are nearly as rare in the wild as they are in zoos can be viewed in San Diego. A random sampling includes pygmy chimpanzees, okapis (the giraffe's only close relatives), and aardwolves (termite-eating cousins of the hyena) from Africa; gorals (goat-antelopes) from the Himalayas; and fossas and red-ruffed lemurs from Madagascar. Even in the case of more familiar zoo exhibits, there is extraordinary diversity. Not many zoos, for example, display two species of giraffes (baringo and reticulated) or two kinds of piglike peccaries (collared and white-lipped).

The San Diego Zoo's Wild Animal Park is set in the San Pasqual Valley, 30 miles north of the parent zoo. This 1,800-acre zoo resembles a cross between a zoological park and a wildlife reserve. About 600 acres have thus far been developed for exhibits—primarily five habitat panoramas. Each habitat re-creates an existing ecosystem in which several species of mammals and large birds are mixed as they would be in nature.

You can ride a minitrain through representations of Asian swamps and plains, northern African mountains, and two African savannas. The animals are sometimes fairly distant (binoculars are recommended), but the journey will still give you many of the thrills of an actual trip through African and Asian wildlife refuges. The 90-acre South African savanna, for instance, contains zebras, ostriches, nine species of antelopes, and more than 20 white rhinos.

The Wild Animal Park also functions as a survival center where breeding and research projects aid endangered species. The white rhinos are a noteworthy case. During the park's first year six white rhino babies were born. More recently, several litters of cheetahs have been born—this endangered species has seldom reproduced in captivity.

Visitor Services at Balboa Park: *Guided bus tours. Skyfari cable-car ride. Children's zoo. Sea lion performances. Buses to the Wild Animal Park.* **At San Pasqual:** *One-hour excursions on*

WGASA Bush Line trains. The Kraal (children's zoo). Elephant wash.

SEQUOIA AND KINGS CANYON NATIONAL PARKS, California

In 1890 Sequoia National Park was established to prevent impressive groves of ancient sequoia trees from becoming lumber. Kings Canyon National Park was founded a half-century later to preserve the superb mountain scenery.

Administered as a single unit, the parks cover 1,324 square miles, rising from dusty, chaparral-covered foothills to the crests of the High Sierra. The high point of the park is 14,495-foot Mount Whitney, the tallest peak in the United States outside Alaska.

As you ascend the Sierra's gentle western slope, the chaparral scrub eventually gives way to oak forests. The famed sequoias—including the tree named General Sherman, the world's largest known tree in terms of sheer bulk—grow mainly between 4,500 and 8,000 feet. Often topping 250 feet in height, and in exceptional cases measuring more than 100 feet around the base, some of the sequoias are estimated to be at least 3,000 years old. Between the sequoia groves are 200-foot sugar and ponderosa pines. Pines and firs dominate the higher levels, with gnarled, stunted junipers at timberline and alpine meadows on the higher peaks.

Bighorn sheep are rarely seen, but mule deer are abundant, and black bears range widely. Golden-mantled ground squirrels are common. Marmots and pikas sun on rockslides. Cougars and fishers are rare, but the small mammals furnish prey for large numbers of coyotes, bobcats, gray foxes, and badgers. The pine forest is the haunt of swift, agile martens. Raccoons are abundant.

The outstanding birds of Sequoia-Kings Canyon National Parks include golden eagles; blue grouse, whose booming call fills the woods in spring; mountain quails; dippers in the streams; Clark's nutcrackers at higher elevations; and gray-crowned rosy finches nesting near the snowline. Evening grosbeaks, purple finches, Steller's jays, pygmy and red-breasted nuthatches, several species of woodpeckers, western bluebirds, and western tanagers inhabit the forest. Large and small hawks find good hunting. In all, the twin parks have nearly 170 species of birds.

Roads lead to the sequoia groves and other points of interest, but Sequoia-Kings Canyon is primarily a hiker's park, with about 800 miles of trails. Guided nature walks are conducted, and there are also self-guided nature trails.

How To Get There: *By car from Fresno (75 miles). By bus and plane to Fresno, Tulare, and Visalia, where there are bus connections to park. By train to Tulare.* **When To Go:** *Open all year (portions closed by snow in winter).* **Where To Stay:** *Lodges and cabins in parks; 14 campgrounds; backpack camping by permit.*

WIND CAVE
NATIONAL PARK, South Dakota

Nestled in the southern reaches of the Black Hills, Wind Cave National Park is named for the spectacular limestone cavern that was its original attraction. The cave, discovered in 1881, functions as a natural barometer. When the pressure of the outside atmosphere drops, air rushes from the cave with a loud, whistling noise; when atmospheric pressure rises, air rushes into the cave.

Wind Cave National Park spreads over 44 square miles of hilly country. It is mostly grassland with areas of park-like forest, dominated by ponderosa pines at higher elevations. Elms and cottonwoods grow along the streams.

The two chief wildlife attractions are the herd of American bison (about 400 head) and the prairie dog towns. These prairie dogs are relics of an animal community that once spread all over the Great Plains. Two of the biggest prairie dog towns lie along the main park road. The prairie dogs and other abundant small rodents become prey for golden eagles, badgers, coyotes, and other predators, including endangered black-footed ferrets. The largest predators, except for an occasional roving cougar, are coyotes and bobcats. Elks are often seen along the roads in the early morning; pronghorns, in the late evening.

Sharp-tailed grouse, bobwhites, and western meadowlarks thrive in the grasslands, and black-billed magpies are also abundant. Red-tailed, Swainson's, and ferruginous hawks hunt for small rodents by day; great horned owls hunt by night. A few golden and bald eagles live in the park.

Two paved roads and two dirt roads (not passable when wet) reach most areas of interest. A self-guided nature trail leads to a scenic lookout. Wind Cave itself can be visited only with a ranger-guide. If you visit it, dress warmly.

How To Get There: *By car from Custer (21 miles) or Hot Springs (11 miles). By bus from Hot Springs, Custer, Edgemont, and Rapid City. By air to Rapid City.* **When To Go:** *Open all year; best time, April through October. Wind Cave closed in winter.* **Where To Stay:**

Campground in park (closed in winter). Motels, hotels in Hot Springs, Custer.

YELLOWSTONE
NATIONAL PARK, Wyoming

The oldest and largest national park in the United States, Yellowstone is world-famous for its spectacular geysers, steaming fumaroles, boiling hot springs, and colorful mud pots. The park also provides a refuge for some of the most important concentrations of large mammals outside of Alaska.

Yellowstone National Park spreads over 3,400 square miles of high, rolling volcanic plateaus bounded by rugged mountains—an area almost three times the size of Rhode Island. With an average elevation of 7,500 feet, Yellowstone contains a dozen peaks over 10,000 feet. Forest covers about 90 percent of the park area. Lodgepole pines are the dominant trees, but firs, spruces, and junipers add variety. Aspens grow at lower levels, and willows and cottonwoods border the streams. There are meadows and stretches of sagebrush.

The most numerous of Yellowstone mammals are the elks, which number around 20,000. The most noticeable mammals are the ubiquitous black bears. About 250 grizzly bears occur mostly in the remote backcountry.

Bison often graze the meadows along Nez Perce Creek, though most of the park's herd of some 600 head remain in the rugged backcountry. Moose browse along the streams or wade into ponds for succulent water plants. Mule deer browse in the forests, and pronghorns feed on the open plains. Wary bighorn sheep are confined to the rocky upper slopes. Streams and lakes contain beavers, otters, and muskrats. Small mammals include pikas, ground squirrels, and yellow-bellied marmots.

Perhaps the most notable birds are golden eagles and trumpeter swans. Ospreys nest along the 1,200-foot-deep Grand Canyon of the Yellowstone River. White pelicans nest on Yellowstone Lake. There are also California gulls, sandhill cranes, and sharp-tailed grouse. Among the small birds are western and mountain bluebirds, gray jays, dippers, black-headed grosbeaks, and brown-capped rosy finches.

The park contains about 340 miles of roads, including the 145-mile Grand Loop, which touches many of the park's scenic features. More than 1,000 miles of horse and foot trails have been laid out, some leading into the wild back-country.

As many as 40,000 people a day may visit Yellowstone during the peak

months of July and August. But you can escape the crowds by going in winter. The northern portion of the park is open year-round. Transportation by snow coach or snowmobile is available, and great concentrations of elks and bison can be seen from the road, especially in Lamar Valley.

How To Get There: *By car to park entrances. By bus to Cody, Gardiner, and West Yellowstone. By train to Livingston, Montana. By air to Jackson and Cody, also Billings and Bozeman, Montana; summer service to West Yellowstone. Park buses connect with trains and airlines.* **When To Go:** *Park open May 1 to October 31; northern portion open all year. May, June, September, and October, best time for observing wildlife.* **Where To Stay:** *Hotels at Old Faithful (open all year), Mammoth Hot Springs, and Lake Village; lodge at Canyon Village. Cabins and 17 campsites; trailer court. Camping in wilderness areas by permit.*

More Places To See
Wildlife in North America

1. PACIFIC RIM NATIONAL PARK, British Columbia. Sandy and rocky shores of Vancouver Island. Wildlife highlights: Sea lions, migrating gray whales. Black oyster catchers, black turnstones, bald eagles.

2. KOOTENAY NATIONAL PARK, British Columbia. Mountains, canyons, glacial valleys. Wildlife highlights: Elks, mule deer, bighorn sheep; cougars, lynxes, grizzly and black bears; wolverines, beavers, snowshoe hares.

3. ELK ISLAND NATIONAL PARK, Alberta. Wooded hills, lakes. Wildlife highlights: Plains and woodland bison, moose, elks, white-tailed deer; beavers, coyotes.

4. PRINCE ALBERT NATIONAL PARK, Saskatchewan. Forests and prairies. Wildlife highlights: Moose, elks, white-tailed and mule deer, woodland caribou; gray wolves, badgers, beavers. Bald eagles, ospreys, white pelicans, ravens, pileated woodpeckers.

5. RIDING MOUNTAIN NATIONAL PARK, Manitoba. Wooded plateau, grasslands, lakes. Wildlife highlights: Moose, white-tailed deer; black bears, gray wolves, coyotes, lynxes; beavers. Migratory whistling swans.

6. GATINEAU PARK, Quebec. Wooded, glaciated hills, lakes. Wildlife highlights: White-tailed deer, black bears, gray wolves; beavers, minks, otters, porcupines. Loons, ospreys, barred owls, ravens; boreal chickadees.

7. FORILLON NATIONAL PARK, Quebec. Sculptured coast with rocky headlands. Wildlife highlights: Harbor seals on beaches, pilot and other whales offshore; moose, black bears, lynxes. Double-crested cormorants, kittiwakes, black guillemots.

8. BONAVENTURE ISLAND WILDLIFE SANCTUARY, Quebec. Sea cliffs, spruce forests. Wildlife highlights: Tremendous gannet colony; Atlantic puffins, common murres, kittiwakes.

9. FUNDY NATIONAL PARK, New Brunswick. Rugged seashore, forested hills. Wildlife highlights: Moose, white-tailed deer; black bears, porcupines, beavers. Gray jays, boreal chickadees; 18 species of warblers, evening grosbeaks, white-throated sparrows.

10. CAPE BRETON HIGHLANDS NATIONAL PARK, Nova Scotia. Mountainous coast with cliffs, treeless plateau. Wildlife highlights: Moose, woodland caribou, black bears, lynxes, beavers. Gannets, arctic terns, black guillemots; bald eagles, goshawks; ringnecks, goldeneye ducks, mergansers; spruce and ruffed grouse, pine grosbeaks, crossbills.

11. MALHEUR NATIONAL WILDLIFE REFUGE, Oregon. Marshes, meadows, shallow lakes, sagebrush and juniper uplands. Wildlife highlights: Pronghorns, mule deer. Sandhill cranes, white pelicans; whistling swans; sage grouse.

12. HART MOUNTAIN NATIONAL ANTELOPE REFUGE, Oregon. Desert range, partly wooded mountains. Wildlife highlights: Pronghorns, bighorns. Sage grouse, mountain bluebirds.

13. CAMAS NATIONAL WILDLIFE REFUGE, Idaho. Meadows and marshes in mountain valley. Wildlife highlights: Pronghorns, elks, moose, beavers. Longbilled curlews, whistling swans, sage grouse.

14. TULE LAKE NATIONAL WILDLIFE REFUGE, California. Marshes, lakes, grainfields; on Pacific Flyway. Wildlife highlights: Tremendous concentrations of waterfowl — white-fronted, Canada, Ross, and snow geese; whistling swans, ducks; western grebes.

15. IMPERIAL NATIONAL WILDLIFE REFUGE, California-Arizona. Marshes on Colorado River. Wildlife highlights: Desert bighorns, Yuma clapper rails, scaled and Gambel's quails, white-winged doves.

16. SAGUARO NATIONAL MONUMENT, Arizona. Desert with giant saguaros, many other species of cactuses. Wildlife highlights: Mule deer, peccaries, kangaroo rats. Desert tortoises. Roadrunners, Gambel's quails, Gila woodpeckers, elf owls, curve-billed thrashers.

17. RED ROCKS MIGRATORY WATERFOWL REFUGE, Montana. Shallow lakes, marshes. Wildlife highlights: Shiras moose, pronghorns. Trumpeter swans (main breeding area); scaups, redhead and ruddy ducks; blue, sage, and ruffed grouse; great horned owls.

18. UPPER SOURIS NATIONAL WILDLIFE REFUGE, North Dakota. Marshes, impoundments. Wildlife highlights: Western grebes, white pelicans, sandhill cranes, sharp-tailed grouse.

19. FORT NIOBRARA NATIONAL WILDLIFE REFUGE, Nebraska. Rolling shortgrass prairie. Wildlife highlights: Exhibition herds of bison, elks, longhorn cattle; beavers, coyotes, bobcats. Sharp-tailed grouse.

20. SQUAW CREEK NATIONAL WILDLIFE REFUGE, Missouri. Wetlands on Central Flyway. Wildlife highlights: Migrating snow, white-fronted, and Canada geese; white pelicans; wintering bald eagles.

21. WICHITA MOUNTAINS NATIONAL WILDLIFE REFUGE, Oklahoma. Outstanding prairie habitat. Wildlife highlights: Bison, elks, pronghorns, longhorn cattle; coyotes. Wild turkeys.

22. LAGUNA ATASCOSA NATIONAL WILDLIFE REFUGE, Texas. Desert, marshes, coastal scrub. Wildlife highlights: Peccaries, coyotes, ocelots. Mottled ducks, fulvous and black-bellied tree ducks, reddish egrets, American avocets; white-tailed kites, caracaras; roadrunners, cactus wrens.

23. LACASSINE NATIONAL WILDLIFE REFUGE, Louisiana. Wetlands on Mississippi Flyway. Wildlife highlights: Otters, armadillos. Alligators. Wintering white-fronted and snow geese; mottled ducks, fulvous tree ducks, roseate spoonbills, white ibises.

24. AGASSIZ NATIONAL WILDLIFE REFUGE, Minnesota. Marshes, timberlands; on the Central Flyway. Wildlife highlights: Massive concentrations of migrating waterfowl; nesting black terns, Franklin's gulls, blue-winged teals, gadwalls, northern shovelers, redheads, ringnecks, bald eagles, giant Canada geese (rare subspecies).

25. ISLE ROYALE NATIONAL PARK, Michigan. Forest-covered islands. Wildlife highlights: Timber wolves, moose, beavers. Wood ducks, sharp-tailed grouse, pileated woodpeckers.

26. HORICON NATIONAL WILDLIFE REFUGE, Wisconsin. Restored marshes. Wildlife highlights: Up to 100,000 migrating Canada geese, whistling swans, blue-winged teals.

27. MILWAUKEE COUNTY ZOO, Wisconsin. Many rare species: African kongoni, bongos; Indian rhinos, Malayan tapirs, Himalayan black bears, Siberian tigers. A 65,000-gallon tank holding 35 species of native fish.

28. HAWK MOUNTAIN SANCTUARY, Pennsylvania. Wooded mountain, on major fall migration route. Wildlife highlights: Migrating bald and golden eagles; sharp-shinned, red-tailed, red-shouldered, and broad-winged hawks; peregrines, merlins, kestrels, goshawks, gyrfalcons; ospreys, marsh hawks.

29. BAXTER STATE PARK, Maine. Forested mountainous area including Mount Katahdin. Wildlife highlights: Moose, white-tailed deer, caribou, black bears, beavers. Three-toed woodpeckers, ruffed and spruce grouse, redpolls, evening and pine grosbeaks.

30. MONTEZUMA NATIONAL WILDLIFE REFUGE, New York. Managed wetland with dikes. Wildlife highlights: Mallards, gadwalls, northern shovelers, redheads; wood, black, and ruddy ducks; shorebirds.

31. BRIGANTINE NATIONAL WILDLIFE REFUGE, New Jersey. Tidal marsh with impoundments. Wildlife highlights: Migratory and nesting ducks and geese. Herons, egrets, glossy ibises; Forster's and gull-billed terns, black skimmers, oyster catchers, willets, whimbrels.

32. BOMBAY HOOK NATIONAL WILDLIFE REFUGE, Delaware. Salt and fresh-water marshes. Wildlife highlights: White-tailed deer, opossums, raccoons, red foxes. Migratory and nesting ducks and geese, clapper and Virginia rails, common gallinules, willets, black terns, black skimmers, short- and long-billed marsh wrens.

33. BLACKWATER NATIONAL WILDLIFE REFUGE, Maryland. Forested wetlands. Wildlife highlights: Delmarva fox squirrels (endangered); Canada geese, ducks, clapper and Virginia rails, bald eagles, marsh hawks, bluebirds, indigo buntings.

34. CHINCOTEAGUE NATIONAL WILDLIFE REFUGE, Virginia. Low, sandy barrier island. Wildlife highlights: Feral ponies, otters, introduced sika deer. Migratory waterfowl, waders, shorebirds.

35. NOXUBEE NATIONAL WILDLIFE REFUGE, Mississippi. Flooded timberland, levees. Wildlife highlights: White-tailed deer, beavers, otters, bobcats, raccoons. Migratory waterfowl; wild turkeys, bobwhites, bald eagles, rare red-cockaded woodpeckers.

36. CAPE ROMAIN NATIONAL WILDLIFE REFUGE, South Carolina. Salt marshes, beaches, wooded Bulls Island. Wildlife highlights: Otters, white-tailed deer. Alligators, loggerhead turtles. Brown pelicans, wood storks, royal terns, American oyster catchers, other shorebirds; bald eagles, wild turkeys, pileated and red-cockaded woodpeckers.

37. OKEFENOKEE NATIONAL WILDLIFE REFUGE, Georgia. Primeval cypress swamp. Wildlife highlights: Black bears, white-tailed deer, otters. Alligators. Sandhill cranes, white ibises, anhingas, limpkins; swallow-tailed kites, bald eagles, wild turkeys.

38. J. N. "DING" DARLING NATIONAL WILDLIFE REFUGE, Florida. On Sanibel Island in Gulf of Mexico; beaches famous for seashells; fresh and salt marshes. Wildlife highlights: Otters. Alligators, loggerhead turtles. Roseate spoonbills, white ibises, wood storks; mottled ducks, brown pelicans, anhingas, magnificent frigate birds; swallow-tailed kites, bald eagles; burrowing owls.

39. CORKSCREW SWAMP SANCTUARY, Florida. Virgin cypress swamp with many orchids, other air plants; wet prairies, pinewoods. Wildlife highlights: Alligators. Wood storks, limpkins, egrets, purple gallinules; pileated woodpeckers, bald eagles.

40. SCAMMON LAGOON WHALE SANCTUARY, Baja California, Mexico. Protected bay area; mating and calving grounds for gray whales.

CENTRAL and SOUTH AMERICA

Growing interest in nature is producing new parks in rain forests and Andean tundra.

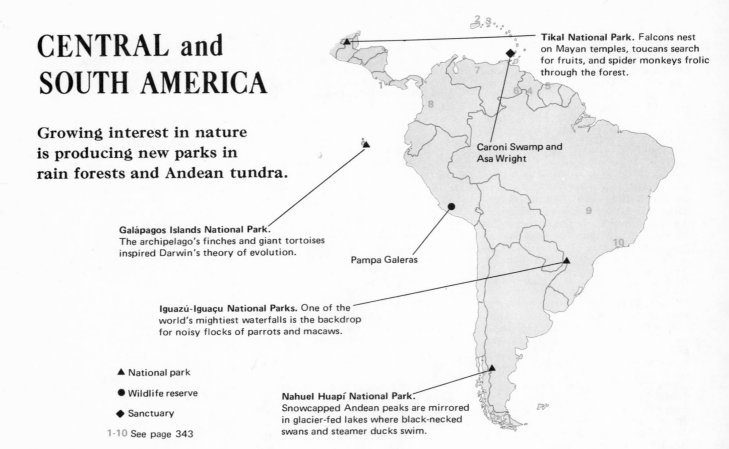

Tikal National Park. Falcons nest on Mayan temples, toucans search for fruits, and spider monkeys frolic through the forest.

Caroni Swamp and Asa Wright

Galápagos Islands National Park. The archipelago's finches and giant tortoises inspired Darwin's theory of evolution.

Pampa Galeras

Iguazú-Iguaçu National Parks. One of the world's mightiest waterfalls is the backdrop for noisy flocks of parrots and macaws.

▲ National park

● Wildlife reserve

◆ Sanctuary

1-10 See page 343

Nahuel Huapí National Park. Snowcapped Andean peaks are mirrored in glacier-fed lakes where black-necked swans and steamer ducks swim.

CARONI SWAMP WILDLIFE SANCTUARY AND ASA WRIGHT NATURE CENTER, Trinidad

The outstanding attraction of the Caroni Swamp Wildlife Sanctuary, on the island of Trinidad, is its population of scarlet ibises, estimated at about 10,000. In the late afternoon the mass flight of these brilliant birds to their treetop roosts on small, mangrove-covered islands is an unforgettable spectacle.

The brackish, shallow waters and mud flats of Caroni Swamp Wildlife Sanctuary, 800 acres in all, provide an ideal habitat for wading birds. In addition to scarlet ibises, there are cattle egrets, roseate spoonbills, limpkins, and white, little blue, and Louisiana herons.

Not far from Caroni Swamp is the Asa Wright Nature Center. Beautifully situated in the Northern Range, the center is surrounded by rain forests, rich in birdlife.

You will not need to leave the immediate vicinity of the center to see a multitude of small colorful birds: Blue-gray, palm, silver-beaked, white-lined, and bay-headed tanagers; blue-hooded and violaceous euphonias; purple, red-legged, and green honeycreepers. The flowers attract many hummingbirds.

The center is renowned for its colony of oilbirds, which nest in a gorge reached by a forest trail. Oilbirds are white-spotted, medium-sized brown birds that roost in caves, emerging at night to feed on palm fruit.

How To Get There: *By car or taxi from Port of Spain to Caroni Swamp or Asa Wright Nature Center.* **When To Go:** *All year round.* **Where To Stay:** *Hotels in Port of Spain. Guesthouse at Asa Wright Nature Center (reservations necessary).*

GALÁPAGOS NATIONAL PARK, Ecuador

"Still a primitive Eden" is the description naturalist Roger Tory Peterson gave of the Galápagos Islands, which lie 600 miles west of Ecuador.

A visit to the Galápagos is a never-to-be-forgotten experience. You cruise among the islands by ship, live on board, and go ashore at selected points in the company of a naturalist.

There are 16 major islands and many more smaller ones, spread over 2,000 square miles of ocean. Landscapes vary from the damp forests of Santa Cruz (Indefatigable) to the cinder cones and craters of Santiago (James). Inland there are land iguanas, giant tortoises, Galápagos hawks, and 13 species of Darwin's finches. Huge colonies of magnificent frigate birds, waved alba-trosses, and masked, red-footed, and blue-footed boobies nest in the seemingly most uninviting terrain.

The richest wildlife is found at the shoreline, where marine iguanas, flightless cormorants, swallow-tailed gulls, and brilliant red crabs populate the rocks. The cold Humboldt Current makes it possible for seals and penguins to live on the Equator. The Galápagos penguins, smallest of these flightless birds, are found only here.

How To Get There: *By cruise ship from Guayaquil, Ecuador. By plane from Quito or Guayaquil to the Galápagos island of Baltra; cruise ship from there.* **When To Go:** *November to July.* **Where To Stay:** *Aboard ship.*

IGUAZÚ NATIONAL PARK, Argentina IGUAÇU NATIONAL PARK, Brazil

Iguazú or Iguaçu—however the name is spelled—the mighty falls of the river the Guarani Indians called "Great Waters" are one of the world's spectacular sights. The thundering torrent breaks into a multitude of falls and cascades, foaming over rocky ledges and plunging between wooded islets in a wide arc.

Luxuriant tree ferns, bamboos, and palms border the falls; bromeliads, orchids, and vines festoon the forest trees. Metallic-blue morpho butterflies drift overhead. And through the rainbow-tinted mists flash flocks of macaws, parrots, and parakeets. Trogons, toucans, and small tropical birds haunt the forest edges. Plumbeous kites, black hawk eagles, and crested caracaras soar over the trees; even the rare harpy eagle occurs in the park.

In the Brazilian park a paved path leads to the brink of the falls. From this path you can see the whole thrilling panorama, including the deep lower gorge called the Devil's Throat. From the Argentine side you can approach the base of the falls very closely.

How To Get There: *By plane from São Paulo, Brazil; by plane or car from Asunción, Paraguay; by plane or bus (15 hours) from Curitiba, Brazil.* **When To Go:** *Open all year. Best time for viewing falls, August to November.* **Where To Stay:** *Hotel on Brazilian side; several hotels on Argentine side.*

NAHUEL HUAPÍ NATIONAL PARK, Argentina

Rising from the bleak Patagonian pampas to the snowcapped Andes along the Chilean border, Nahuel Huapí National Park is Argentina's largest.

Most of the park's 3,015 square miles are covered with a dense forest of antarctic beeches, myrtles, and larches. Above timberline are perpetual snowfields and glaciers. The highest peak, Mount Tronador ("Thunderer"), towers to nearly 12,000 feet.

One of Nahuel Huapí's most unusual mammals is the pudu. The smallest of deer, it stands only a bit over a foot tall. Another native deer is the guemal, a small, almost tailless species that lives at high altitudes. Vicuñas and guanacos are other high-altitude mammals.

Many exclusively South American species of waterfowl—among them black-necked swans, ashy-headed geese, and steamer ducks (they propel themselves over the water like paddle-wheel steamers)—can be seen on the lakes. Blue-eyed cormorants nest on the cliffs, Chilean flamingos wade in the shallows.

The forests shelter austral parakeets, austral pygmy owls, and Magellanic woodpeckers. There are many species of South American ovenbirds, such as cinclodes, rayaditos, and tree runners, and a wide variety of tyrant flycatchers. The Andean condor, with its 10-foot wingspan, often soars above the peaks.

At lower elevations Nahuel Huapí has marked trails for hiking and horseback riding. Much of the park can also be explored by boat.

How To Get There: *By bus, train, and plane from Buenos Aires and other major cities to resort village of San Carlos de Bariloche.* **When To Go:** *Open all year. Best time, November through April (summer).* **Where To Stay:** *Hotels and hostels in the park. Campgrounds.*

PAMPA GALERAS NATIONAL RESERVE, Peru

Once numbered in the hundreds of thousands throughout the Andes, the graceful vicuña was ruthlessly slaughtered for its silky wool; by the 1950's only a few thousand were left. To save this valuable animal, the Pampa Galeras National Reserve was established.

Located on the bleak, windswept *altiplano* (high plateau) of Peru, some 450 miles southeast of Lima, the reserve covers 230 square miles of rolling, treeless grassland, with broad valleys separated by flat-topped ridges.

A one-species reserve, Pampa Galeras harbors some 9,300 vicuñas that live in small family bands consisting of a male and several females with their young. Each family occupies its own territory, sleeping near a ridge top and moving down to the valley to feed.

How To Get There: *By car, via Pan American Highway from Lima to Nazca; from Nazca to Pampa Galeras.* **When To Go:** *May to November (dry season).* **Where To Stay:** *Hotel in Nazca.*

TIKAL NATIONAL PARK, Guatemala

Although wildlife preservation is slow in gaining acceptance in Central America, a heartening exception is Guatemala's Tikal National Park. Created around a restored Mayan temple city whose tall pyramidal edifices emerge from the surrounding jungle, the park covers 222 square miles of dense tropical forest.

The mammals include brocket deer, peccaries, agoutis (small, piglike rodents), jaguars, pumas, ocelots, coatimundis, and kinkajous. In late afternoon bands of spider monkeys leave the forest for the temple area.

Screaming flocks of toucans and parrots make a brilliant display as they search for edible fruits. Trogons, woodpeckers, tanagers, motmots, and honey creepers are abundant. Painted buntings and hummingbirds flash through the forest fringe. Ocellated turkeys, crested guans, and curassows are plentiful. Bat falcons and orange-breasted falcons nest on the high temples.

How To Get There: *By air from Guatemala City. By car on partially paved roads from Guatemala City.* **When To Go:** *Open all year. Best season, dry months (December through April).* **Where To Stay:** *Lodges near park.*

More Places To See Wildlife in Central and South America

1. SANTA ROSA NATIONAL PARK, Costa Rica. Seashore, mangrove swamps, dry forests. Wildlife highlights: Tapirs, peccaries, jaguars, pumas, ocelots, monkeys. Ridley, green, and leatherback turtles. Macaws, curassows.

2. LUQUILLO NATIONAL FOREST, Puerto Rico. Rain forest surrounding peak of El Yunque. Wildlife highlights: Puerto Rican parrots (endangered), Puerto Rican tody flycatchers.

3. BUCK ISLAND REEF NATIONAL MONUMENT, Virgin Islands. Thriving coral reef community. Underwater trail for snorkelers and scuba divers. Wildlife highlights: Blue-head wrasses, sergeant majors, squirrelfish.

4. KAIETEUR FALLS NATIONAL PARK, Guyana. Tropical forest, savannas. Wildlife highlights: Jaguars, ocelots, sloths; howler, capuchin, and spider monkeys; capybaras, tapirs, giant and dwarf anteaters, giant otters. Toucans, parrots, macaws, trumpeters, curassows, tinamous.

5. WIA-WIA NATIONAL RESERVE, Surinam. Coastal wetland. Wildlife highlights: Ridley, leatherback, green, hawksbill, and loggerhead turtles. Scarlet ibises, flamingos.

6. CANAIMA NATIONAL PARK, Venezuela. Tropical rain forest, spectacular Angel Falls. Wildlife highlights: Jaguars, tiger cats; tapirs, peccaries, brocket deer, giant armadillos, capybaras. Caimans (crocodiles). Cocks of the rock, hoatzins, harpy eagles.

7. HENRI PITTIER NATIONAL PARK, Venezuela. Seacoast and forested mountains. Wildlife highlights: Peccaries, agoutis, pacas, brocket deer; sloths, howler and capuchin monkeys; jaguars, pumas, jaguarundis. Guans, tinamous; toucans, cotingas, tanagers, manakins, parakeets.

8. PURACÉ NATIONAL PARK, Colombia. Snowcapped volcano; grasslands and forests. Wildlife highlights: Spectacled bears, mountain tapirs, pudu deer. Black-tailed trainbearers and viridian metaltails (hummingbirds); spinetails (ovenbirds), white-capped dippers, flower-piercers.

9. BRASILIA NATIONAL PARK, Brazil. Wooded upland savanna. Wildlife highlights: Giant armadillos, giant anteaters, pampas deer; maned wolves, bush dogs, black howler monkeys. Great teju lizards. Tinamous, burrowing owls.

10. ITATIAIA NATIONAL PARK, Brazil. Mountainous tropical rain and cloud forests. Wildlife highlights: Maned wolves, jaguars, ocelots, crab-eating foxes; tapirs, giant anteaters, woolly spider monkeys, sloths. Harpy eagles, guans, toucans.

343

Guide to Conservation Organizations

Whatever your interest in nature—observing wildlife, protecting natural habitats, safeguarding endangered species—there are many conservation-minded organizations you will want to know about and probably a number you will wish to join. This guide features international and national organizations. In addition, many excellent State, Provincial, and local societies in Canada and the United States are listed in the *Conservation Directory* (published by the National Wildlife Federation) and in the *Canadian Conservation Directory* (published by the Canadian Nature Federation).

INTERNATIONAL

American Committee for International Wildlife Protection, Inc., c/o The Wildlife Society, 3900 Wisconsin Ave. NW., Washington, D.C. 20016.

Arctic Institute of North America, The, 3458 Redpath St., Montreal 109, Quebec, Canada; 1619 New Hampshire Ave. NW., Washington, D.C. 20009. Publications: *Arctic Journal*; *The Arctic Bibliography*.

Caribbean Conservation Association, P.O. Box 4187, St. Thomas, Virgin Islands 00801.

European and Mediterranean Plant Protection Organization, 1 Rue Le Nôtre, Paris, France.

Fauna Preservation Society, c/o Zoological Society of London, Regent's Park, London NW. 1, England. International wildlife tours. Publication: *Oryx*.

Friends of the Earth, 620 C St. SE., Washington, D.C. 20003. Affiliates in several other countries. Publication: *Not Man Apart*.

International Atlantic Salmon Foundation, The, P.O. Box 429, St. Andrews, New Brunswick, Canada.

International Council for Bird Preservation, c/o British Museum (Natural History), Cromwell Rd., London SW.7, England.

International Institute for Environmental Affairs, 345 East 46th St., New York, New York 10017.

International Union for Conservation of Nature and Natural Resources, 1110 Morges, Switzerland. Wildlife and environmental projects throughout the world, emphasizing endangered species. Publications: *Red Data Books* (five volumes); *IUCN Yearbook*; *United Nations List of National Parks and Equivalent Reserves*.

International Wild Waterfowl Association, P.O. Box 1075, Jamestown, North Dakota 58401.

Project Jonah, 12 Dacotah Ave., Toronto 128, Ontario, Canada; P.O. Box 476, Bolinas, California 94924. Whale conservation.

World Wildlife Fund, 1110 Morges, Switzerland. Dedicated to saving threatened and endangered species and habitats through grants to other organizations. National appeals in 22 countries (U.S. appeal: 910 17th St. NW., Washington, D.C. 20006). Publications: *World Wildlife Yearbook*; *Progress Report*.

AFRICA

African Wildlife Leadership Foundation, Inc., 1717 Massachusetts Ave. NW., Washington, D.C. 20036. Publication: *African Wildlife News*.

East African Wild Life Society, The, P.O. Box 20110, Nairobi, Kenya. Nature tours. Publication: *Africana*.

Ethiopian Natural History Society, The, P.O. Box 1160, Addis Ababa, Ethiopia. Publication: *Walia*.

Wildlife Protection and Conservation Society of South Africa, The, P.O. Box 487, Pinetown, Natal, South Africa. Publication: *African Wildlife*.

ASIA

Association for the Conservation of Wildlife, Thailand, The, 4 Old Custom House Lane, Bangkok, Thailand.

Bombay Natural History Society, Hornbill House, Shahid Bhagat Singh Road, Bombay, India. Publication: *Journal*.

Holy Land Conservation Fund, Inc., 150 East 58th St., New York, New York 10022.

Nature Friends of Israel, P.O. Box 4142, Haifa, Israel. Nature trips.

Nature Reserves Authority, 16 Hanatziv St., Tel Aviv, Israel. Wildlife reserves.

Society for the Protection of Nature in Israel, 4 Hashfela St., Tel Aviv, Israel. Field study centers, nature tours.

Wildlife and Nature Protection Society of Ceylon, Chaitiya Road, Fort, Colombo, Sri Lanka. Reserves. Publication: *Loris*.

Wildlife Preservation Society of India, 7 Astley Hall, Dehra Dun, Uttar Pradesh, India. Publication: *Cheetal*.

AUSTRALIA and NEW ZEALAND

Australian Conservation Foundation, P.O. Box 91, Eastwood, New South Wales, Australia.

Federal Department of the Environment, Canberra, Capital Territory, Australia.

Royal Forest and Bird Protection Society of New Zealand, Inc., P.O. Box 631, Wellington, New Zealand. Reserves. Publication: *Forest and Bird*.

Victorian National Parks Association, 23 Camdon St., Pascoe Vale, Victoria, Australia. Publication: *Nature Conservation in Victoria*.

EUROPE

Association of Nature Conservation (County) Trusts, The, The Manor House, Alford, Lincolnshire, England. Many reserves, field courses.

Austrian Society for the Protection of Nature, 8010 Graz, Hamerlingasse 8/1, Vienna, Austria.

British Trust for Ornithology, Beech Grove, Tring, Hertfordshire, England. Publication: *Bird Study*.

Council for Nature, c/o Zoological Society of London, Regent's Park, London NW. 1, England. Publications: *A Handbook for Naturalists*; *Nature Trails in Britain*.

Finnish Association for Nature Protection, The, Fredrikinkatu 77 A 11, Helsinki, Finland. Publication: *Suomen Luonto*.

Jersey Wildlife Preservation Trust, Les Augres Manor, Trinity, Jersey, Channel Islands, Great Britain.

League for the Protection of Nature, Faculdade da Ciéncias, Rua da Escola Politécnica, Lisbon, Portugal. Publication: *Protecção da Natureza*.

National Society for Protection of Nature and Acclimatization in France, 57 Rue Cuvier, Paris, France. Publication: *La Terre et la Vie*.

Nature Conservancy Council, 19 Belgrave Sq., London SW. 1, England. Regional offices in England, Wales, Scotland. Many reserves.

Royal Society for the Protection of Birds, The, The Lodge, Sandy, Bedfordshire, England. Regional offices in Scotland, Wales, Ireland. Many reserves. Publications: *Birds*; *Bird Life* (children's periodical).

Scottish Wildlife Trust, The, 8 Dublin St., Edinburgh, Scotland. Many reserves. Publication: *Scottish Wildlife*.

Society for the Promotion of Nature Conservation, c/o British Museum (Natural History), Cromwell Rd., London SW. 7, England. Reserves and nature trails.

Society for the Promotion of Nature Reserves, The Manor House, Alford, Lincolnshire, England. Publication: *Handbook*.

Swedish Society for the Conservation of Nature, The, Kungsholms Strand 125,

Stockholm, Sweden. Reserves. Publication: *Sveriges Natur*.

Swiss League for the Protection of Nature, Wartenbergstrasse 22, Basel, Switzerland. Reserves. Publications: *Schweizer Naturschutz*; *Du und die Natur* (children's periodical).

Wildfowl Trust, The, Slimbridge, Gloucestershire, England. Wildfowl refuges. Publications: *Key to the Wildfowl of the World*; *Wildfowl*.

Wildfowlers Association of Great Britain and Ireland, 104 Watergate St., Chester, Cheshire, England. Wildfowl reserves.

Zoological Society of London, The, Regent's Park, London NW. 1, England. Publications: *International Zoo Yearbook*; *Journal of Zoology*.

NORTH AMERICA

American Cetacean Society, P.O. Box 22305, San Diego, California 92122. Whale-watching trips. Publication: *The Whalewatcher*.

American Forestry Association, The, 1319 18th St. NW., Washington, D.C. 20036. Publication: *American Forests*.

American Littoral Society, Sandy Hook, Highlands, New Jersey 07732. Publication: *Underwater Naturalist*.

American Museum of Natural History, The, Central Park West at 79th St., New York, New York 10024. International field tours. Publication: *Natural History*.

American Ornithologists' Union, Inc., Smithsonian Institution, Washington, D.C. 20560.

American Rivers Conservation Council, 324 C St. SE., Washington, D.C. 20005.

Appalachian Mountain Club, 5 Joy St., Boston, Massachusetts 02108. Hikes, canoe trips, outings. Publication: *Appalachia*.

Appalachian Trail Conference. P.O. Box 236, Harpers Ferry, West Virginia 25425.

Atlantic Salmon Association, 409-1405 Peel St., Montreal, Quebec, Canada.

Bureau of Land Management, Department of the Interior, Washington, D.C. 20240. Publication: *Our Public Lands*.

Bureau of Sport Fisheries and Wildlife, Department of the Interior, Washington, D.C. 20240. Wildlife refuges.

Canadian Forestry Association, 185 Somerset St. West, Ottawa, Ontario, Canada.

Canadian Nature Federation, 46 Elgin St., Ottawa, Ontario, Canada. Publications: *Nature Canada*; *Canadian Conservation Directory*.

Canadian Wildlife Federation, 1419 Carling Ave., Ottawa, Ontario, Canada. Publication: *Wildlife News*.

Canadian Wildlife Service, Place Vincent Massey, Hull, Quebec, Canada.

Defenders of Wildlife, 2000 N St. NW., Washington, D.C. 20036. Publication: *Defenders of Wildlife News*.

Desert Bighorn Council, 1500 North Decatur Blvd., Las Vegas, Nevada 89109.

Desert Fishes Council, 407 West Line St., Bishop, California 93514.

Desert Protective Council, Inc., The, P.O. Box 33, Banning, California 92220.

Ducks Unlimited, Inc., P.O. Box 66300, Chicago, Illinois. Publication: *Ducks Unlimited Magazine*.

Ducks Unlimited (Canada), 1495 Pembina Highway, Winnipeg, Manitoba, Canada. Publication: *Duckological*.

Environmental Defense Fund, Inc., 162 Old Town Rd., East Setauket, New York 11733.

Florida Audubon Society, P.O. Drawer 7, Maitland, Florida 32751. Nature tours. Publication: *The Florida Naturalist*.

Forest Service, Department of Agriculture, Washington, D.C. 20250.

Foresta Institute for Ocean and Mountain Studies, 6205 Franktown Rd., Carson City, Nevada 89701.

Friends of the Sea Otter, Big Sur, California 93920. Publication: *The Otter Raft*.

Hawk Mountain Sanctuary Association, R.D. 2, Kempton, Pennsylvania 19529.

Izaak Walton League of America, The, 1800 North Kent St., Arlington, Virginia 22209.

Laboratory of Ornithology, Cornell University, Ithaca, New York 14850. Publication: *The Living Bird*.

Massachusetts Audubon Society, Inc., South Great Rd., Lincoln, Massachusetts 01773. Nature tours.

National and Provincial Parks Association of Canada, 43 Victoria St., Toronto, Ontario, Canada. Publication: *Park News*.

National Audubon Society, 950 Third Ave., New York, New York 10022. Ecological workshop tours, nature centers. Publications: *Audubon*; *American Birds*.

National Coalition Against Poisoning of Wildlife, P.O. Box 14156, San Francisco, California 94114.

National Park Service, Interior Building, Washington, D.C. 20240.

National Parks and Conservation Association, 1701 18th St. NW., Washington, D.C. 20009. East African nature tours. Publication: *National Parks and Conservation Magazine*.

National Wildlife Federation, 1412 16th St. NW., Washington, D.C. 20036. Wildlife tours. Publications: *International Wildlife*; *National Wildlife*; *Ranger Rick's Nature Magazine* (children's periodical); *Conservation Directory*.

Natural Resources Defense Council, Inc., 15 West 44th St., New York, New York 10036.

Nature Conservancy, The, 1800 North Kent St., Arlington, Virginia 22209. Many reserves.

Nature Conservancy of Canada, 2200 Yonge St., Toronto, Ontario, Canada.

New York Zoological Society, Bronx Park, New York, New York 10460. Publication: *Animal Kingdom*.

Rachel Carson Trust for the Living Environment, Inc., 8940 Jones Mill Rd., Washington, D.C. 20015.

Save-the-Redwoods League, 114 Sansome St., San Francisco, California 94104.

Save the Tall Grass Prairie, Inc., P.O. Box 453, Emporia, Kansas 66801.

Sierra Club, 1050 Mills Tower, San Francisco, California 94104. Chapters coast to coast. Wilderness trips, foreign tours. Publication: *Sierra Club Bulletin*.

Smithsonian Institution, 1000 Jefferson Dr. SW., Washington, D.C. 20560. Tours. Publication: *Smithsonian*.

Society for the Preservation of Birds of Prey, P.O. Box 891, Pacific Palisades, California 90272. Field trips in California and the eastern U.S. Publication: *The California Condor*.

Student Conservation Association, Inc., Olympic View Dr., R.D. 1, Box 573A, Vashon, Washington 98070.

Wetlands for Wildlife, Inc., P.O. Box 147, Mayville, Wisconsin 53050.

Whooping Crane Conservation Association, Inc., 3000 Meadowlark Dr., Sierra Vista, Arizona 85635. Publication: *Grus Americana*.

Wilderness Society, The, 1901 Pennsylvania Ave. NW., Washington, D.C. 20006. Wilderness trips. Publication: *The Living Wilderness*.

Wildlife Society, The, 3900 Wisconsin Ave. NW., Washington, D.C. 20016. Publications: *The Journal of Wildlife Management*; *A Manual of Wildlife Conservation*; *Wildlife Monographs*.

SOUTH AMERICA

Brazilian Institute of Forestry, Ministry of Agriculture, Rio de Janeiro, Brazil.

Charles Darwin Foundation for the Galápagos Islands, Santa Cruz, Galápagos Islands, Ecuador. Publication: *Noticias de Galápagos*.

National Park Service, Ministry of Agriculture, Santa Fe 690, Buenos Aires, Argentina. Publication: *Anales de Parques Nacionales*.

Trinidad Field Naturalists' Club, The, 64 Roberts St., Port of Spain, Trinidad. Publication: *Journal*.

Bibliography

The editors wish to acknowledge their indebtedness to the following books and periodicals consulted for reference. Publications of interest to the general reader are marked with an asterisk (*).

CONSERVATION

*ALLEN, THOMAS B., *Vanishing Wildlife of North America*. Washington, D.C., National Geographic Society, 1974.

*CARAS, ROGER A., *Last Chance on Earth*. New York, Chilton Company, 1966.

*CROWE, PHILIP KINGSLAND, *World Wildlife: The Last Stand*. New York, Charles Scribner's Sons, 1970.

CURRY-LINDAHL, KAI, *Let Them Live*. New York, William Morrow & Company, Inc., 1972.

*DASMANN, RAYMOND F., *No Further Retreat*. New York, The Macmillan Company, 1971.

DORST, JEAN, *Before Nature Dies*. New York, Houghton Mifflin Company, 1970.

EHRENFELD, DAVID W., *Conserving Life on Earth*. New York, Oxford University Press, Inc., 1972.

*FISHER, JAMES, and others, *Wildlife in Danger*. New York, The Viking Press, Inc., 1969.

GREENWAY, JAMES C., JR., *Extinct and Vanishing Birds of the World*, rev. ed. New York, Dover Publications, Inc., 1967.

*GRZIMEK, BERNHARD, *Wild Animal White Man*. New York, Hill and Wang, Inc., 1966.

GUGGISBERG, C. A. W., *Man and Wildlife*. New York, Arco Publishing Company, Inc., 1970.

*LAYCOCK, GEORGE, *America's Endangered Wildlife*. New York, W. W. Norton & Company, Inc., 1968.

*MILNE, LORUS, and MILNE, MARGERY, *The Cougar Doesn't Live Here Any More*. Englewood Cliffs, N.J., Prentice-Hall, Inc., 1971.

*PRINCE PHILIP, H. R. H., Duke of Edinburgh, and FISHER, JAMES, *Wildlife Crisis*. New York, Cowles Book Company, Inc., 1970.

Red Data Book (Vol. 1: Mammalia; Vol. 2: Aves; Vol. 3: Amphibia and Reptilia; Vol. 4: Pisces; Vol. 5: Angiospermae). Morges, Switzerland, International Union for Conservation of Nature and Natural Resources (revised periodically).

*ROBINS, ERIC, *The Ebony Ark*. New York, Taplinger Publishing Company, 1970.

*SERVENTY, VINCENT, *A Continent in Danger*. New York, Reynal & Co., 1966.

*SILVERBERG, ROBERT, *The Auk, the Dodo, and the Oryx*. New York, Thomas Y. Crowell Company, 1967.

Threatened Wildlife of the United States. Washington, D.C., Bureau of Sport Fisheries and Wildlife, 1973 (revised periodically).

*ULLRICH, WOLFGANG, and others, *Endangered Species*. New York, Hart Publishing Company, Inc., 1972.

Vanishing Species. New York, Time-Life Books, 1974.

ECOLOGY

ALLEE, W. C., and others, *Principles of Animal Ecology*. Philadelphia, W. B. Saunders Company, 1949.

BROWN, LESLIE, *Africa—A Natural History*. New York, Random House, 1965.

CARLQUIST, SHERWIN, *Island Life*. New York, The Natural History Press, 1965.

CURRY-LINDAHL, KAI, *Europe—A Natural History*. New York, Random House, Inc., 1964.

DORST, JEAN, *South America and Central America*. New York, Random House, Inc., 1967.

KEAST, ALLEN, *Australia and the Pacific Islands*. New York, Random House, 1966.

MATTHIESSEN, PETER, *The Tree Where Man Was Born*, and PORTER, ELIOT, *The African Experience*. New York, E. P. Dutton & Co., 1972.

*MILNE, LORUS, and MILNE, MARGERY, *The Nature of Life*. New York, Crown Publishers, Inc., 1972.

*MYERS, NORMAN, *The Long African Day*. New York, The Macmillan Company, 1972.

PFEFFER, PIERRE, *Asia—A Natural History*. New York, Random House, 1968.

Secrets of the Seas. Pleasantville, N.Y., The Reader's Digest Association, Inc., 1972.

INTRODUCED SPECIES

ELTON, CHARLES S., *The Ecology of Invasions by Animals and Plants*. London, Chapman and Hall, Ltd., 1958.

*LAYCOCK, GEORGE, *The Alien Animals*. New York, The Natural History Press, 1966.

NATIONAL PARKS

CURRY-LINDAHL, KAI, and HARROY, JEAN-PAUL, *National Parks of the World*. New York, Golden Press, 1972, 2 vols.

*LAYCOCK, GEORGE, *The Sign of the Flying Goose*. Garden City, N.Y., Anchor Press (Doubleday), 1973.

MORCOMBE, MICHAEL, *Australia's National Parks*. Melbourne, Australia, Lansdowne Press Pty. Ltd., 1969.

*MURPHY, ROBERT, *Wild Sanctuaries*. New York, E. P. Dutton & Co., Inc., 1968.

ROSS-MACDONALD, MALCOLM (ed.), *The World Wildlife Guide*. New York, The Viking Press, 1972.

United Nations List of National Parks and Equivalent Reserves. Brussels, Hayez, 1971 (supplements published periodically).

VERTEBRATES

AUSTIN, OLIVER L., *Birds of the World*. New York, Golden Press, 1961.

Book of British Birds. London, Drive Publications Limited for the Reader's Digest Association, Inc., and the Automobile Association, 1969.

*CARR, ARCHIE, *So Excellent a Fishe*. New York, The Natural History Press, 1967.

EWER, R. F., *The Carnivores*. Ithaca, N.Y., Cornell University Press, 1973.

Fascinating World of Animals. Pleasantville, N.Y., The Reader's Digest Association, Inc., 1971.

MACKINTOSH, N. A., *The Stocks of Whales*. London, Fishing News (Books) Ltd., 1965.

MOCHI, UGO, and CARTER, T. DONALD, *Hoofed Mammals of the World*. New York, Charles Scribner's Sons, 1971.

*SCHALLER, GEORGE B., *Golden Shadows, Flying Hooves*. N.Y., Alfred A. Knopf, 1973.

*VAN LAWICK-GOODALL, HUGO, and VAN LAWICK-GOODALL, JANE, *Innocent Killers*. Boston, Houghton Mifflin Company, 1971.

*VAN LAWICK-GOODALL, JANE, *In the Shadow of Man*. Boston, Houghton Mifflin Company, 1971.

WALKER, ERNEST P., *Mammals of the World*. Baltimore, Md., The Johns Hopkins Press, 1968, 2 vols.

ZOOS

*CRANDALL, LEE S., *A Zoo Man's Notebook*. Chicago, Ill., The University of Chicago Press, 1966.

*GERSH, HARRY, *The Animals Next Door*. New York, Fleet Academic Editions, Inc., 1971.

*HAHN, EMILY, *Animal Gardens*. New York, Doubleday & Company, Inc., 1967.

HANCOCKS, DAVID, *Animals and Architecture*. New York, Praeger Publishers, 1971.

HEDIGER, H., *The Psychology and Behaviour of Animals in Zoos and Circuses*. New York, Dover Publications, Inc., 1968 (original publication, 1955).

HEDIGER, H., *Wild Animals in Captivity*. New York, Dover Publications, Inc., 1964 (original publication, 1950).

KIRCHSHOFER, RODL (ed.), *The World of Zoos*. New York, The Viking Press, 1968.

Zoos and Aquariums in the Americas. Wheeling, W.Va., American Association of Zoological Parks and Aquariums (revised periodically).

PERIODICALS

Africana. Marketing & Publishing Ltd., Nation House, Tom Mboya Street, P.O. Box 49010, Nairobi, Kenya.

Animal Kingdom. New York Zoological Society, The Zoological Park, Bronx, N.Y. 10460.

Audubon. National Audubon Society, 950 Third Avenue, New York, N.Y. 10022.

Biological Conservation. Applied Science Publishers Ltd., Ripple Road, Barking, Essex, England.

Frontiers. Academy of Natural Sciences, 19th and the Parkway, Philadelphia, Pa. 19103.

International Wildlife. National Wildlife Federation, 1412 16th Street NW., Washington, D.C. 20036.

The Living Wilderness. The Wilderness Society, 1901 Pennsylvania Avenue NW., Washington, D.C. 20006.

National Parks and Conservation Magazine. National Parks & Conservation Association, 1701 18th Street NW., Washington, D.C. 20009.

National Wildlife. National Wildlife Federation, 1412 16th Street NW., Washington, D.C. 20036.

Natural History. The American Museum of Natural History, Central Park West at 79th Street, New York, N.Y. 10024.

Nature Canada. Canadian Nature Federation, 46 Elgin Street, Ottawa, Canada K1P 5K6.

Oryx. Fauna Preservation Society, c/o Zoological Society of London, Regents Park, London NW1 4RY, England.

Smithsonian. Smithsonian Associates, 900 Jefferson Avenue, Washington, D.C. 20560.

Wildlife (formerly *Animals*). 21-22 Great Castle Street, London W1N 8LT, England.

Index

Page numbers in bold type refer to illustrations/captions.

Page numbers in bold type refer to illustrations/captions.

Picture Credits

Cover: R. F. Head/National Audubon Society.
Pages 2-3 René Pierre Bille. 5 (top) G. D. Plage/Bruce Coleman Inc.; (bottom) M. Philip Kahl, Jr. 6 (top) William R. Curtsinger/ Rapho Guillumette; (bottom) Peter Johnson. 7 (top) San Diego Zoo; (bottom) Harry Engels. 8-9 G. D. Plage/Bruce Coleman Inc. 10 New York Zoological Society. 11 (top) Lee Ames; (bottom) Enid Kotschnig. 12 (top) Ingeborg Lippman; (bottom) Nick Calabrese. 13 Enid Kotschnig. 14 (top & bottom left) Les D. Line; (bottom center) Enid Kotschnig; (bottom right) Nick Calabrese. 15 Nick Calabrese. 16 Alan Goodall. 17 (top) Lee Ames, after Schaller; (bottom) Nick Calabrese. 18-19 (top) Larry B. Jennings/National Audubon Society; (bottom) Lee Ames. 20 George Kelvin. 21 & 22 (left & center) Lee Ames; (right) Edward S. Ross. 23 (top) W. J. C. Murray/Bruce Coleman Inc.; (bottom) Lee Ames. 24 Edward S. Ross. 25 Victor Kalin. 26 Edward Malsberg. 27 (top) Helen Cruickshank; (bottom) Enid Kotschnig. 28 & 29 (top & bottom left) Edward Malsberg; (bottom right) Glenn Titus. 30 & 31 (bottom) Lee Ames, after Carr; (top) D. Hughes/Bruce Coleman Inc. 32 Howard Friedman. 33 (left) Enid Kotschnig; (right) Ramon Bravo/ Frank Shiel. 34 Roger Tory Peterson. 35 (top) Lee Ames; (bottom) Stan & Kay Breeden. 36 & 37 (top left & right) Michael K. Morocombe; (bottom left) Lee Ames. 38 & 39 (top) Frederick Kent Truslow; (bottom) Lee Ames. 40 Bernard Pertchik. 41 John E. Swedberg. 42 (left) Soren Noring; (right) Enid Kotschnig. 43 René Pierre Bille. 44-45 Edward Malsberg. 46 & 47 (top) Charles Nicklin, Jr.; (bottom) Howard Friedman. 48 Charles Nicklin, Jr. 49 (top) Howard Friedman; (center & bottom) Enid Kotschnig. 50-51 M. Philip Kahl, Jr. 52 Enid Kotschnig. 53 G. B. Schaller/Bruce Coleman Inc. 54 Erwin A. Bauer. 55 Enid Kotschnig. 56 (left) Edward Malsberg; (right) The British Museum. 57 G. B. Schaller/Bruce Coleman Inc. 58 & 59 (left & top right) Willis Peterson; (bottom right) Lorelle Raboni, after Norris. 60 & 61 (bottom left) Marvin E. Newman; (top) Conrad Moulton; (bottom right) The Metropolitan Museum of Art, Gift of Dr. Sidney A. Charlat, 1949, in memory of his parents, Newman & Adele Charlat. 62 (center) Lorelle Raboni; (bottom) Michel Brosselin/Jacana. 63 Lorelle Raboni. 64 (top) Edvin Nilsson; (center) Lee Ames. 65 Conrad Moulton. 66 A. Gutierrez E./ Östman Agency. 67 Edward Malsberg. 68 & 69 (top) J. A. Fernandez/Bruce Coleman Inc. 69 (bottom) Edward Malsberg, after Valverde. 70 & 71 (right) Harry A. Thomson; (left) Conrad Moulton. 72 (top) E. R. Degginger; (center) Edward Malsberg. 73 Harry A. Thomson. 74 Tony Florio/National Audubon Society. 75 (top) Enid Kotschnig; (bottom) U. S. Fish & Wildlife Service. 76 (top) Edward Malsberg; (bottom) Ed Bry. 77 E. R. Degginger. 78 (top left) Fred W. Lahrman; (top center & right) Lorelle Raboni. 78-79 (bottom) Wood Buffalo National Park. 79 (top left) John Borneman/National Audubon Society; (right) Patricia Caulfield. 80 (left) Lorelle Raboni; (right) David Muench. 81 Erwin A. Bauer. 82 (top) David Muench; (bottom) Conrad Moulton. 83 (top) Cecil W. Stoughton/National Park Service; (bottom) Lorelle Raboni. 84 & 85 Harriet Pertchik. 86 Jerry Lang. 87 (top & bottom) Francisco Erize; (center) Conrad Moulton. 88 Jerry Lang. 89 (top) William L. Franklin; (center) Edward Malsberg; (bottom) Conrad Moulton. 90 Simon Trevor/Peter H. Schub. 91 (top) Lorelle Raboni, after Myers; (center) Leonard Lee Rue, III; (bottom) Lee Ames. 92 Lorelle Raboni. 93 Photo Trends. 94 Marion Kaplan. 95 (top & center left) South African Tourist Corp.; (center right & bottom right) Marion Kaplan; (bottom left) Andy Miller. 96-97 (top) N. Myers/Bavaria-Verlag; (bottom) Edward Malsberg, after Myers. 98 H. Schmied/Bavaria-Verlag. 99 (top) Simon Trevor/Bruce Coleman Inc.; (bottom) Patricia Ryan, after Myers. 100 & 101 (right) Michael K. Morocombe; (left) Edward Malsberg. 102 Michael K. Morocombe. 103 Edward Malsberg. 104-105 William R. Curtsinger/Rapho Guillumette. 106 Enid Kotschnig. 107 (top) Patricia Caulfield; (bottom) Enid Kotschnig. 108 Lorelle Raboni.

109 (top) Enid Kotschnig; (center left) Amon Carter Museum of Western Art; (center right & bottom) Sy Seidman/Photo Trends. 110-111 (bottom) Lee Ames; (top) A. L. Goldman/ Rapho Guillumette. 112 (top) Kyuzo Tsugami; (bottom) H. Reinhard/Bruce Coleman Inc. 113 (left) H. Reinhard/Bruce Coleman Inc.; (right) J. Markham/Bruce Coleman Inc. 114 Loren McIntyre. 115 (left) Enid Kotschnig; (right) Edward Malsberg. 116 & 117 (top) Loren McIntyre; (bottom) Enid Kotschnig. 118 (top & left) Loren McIntyre; (right) Enid Kotschnig. 119 (top & bottom) Loren McIntyre; (center) Jerry Lang. 120 Lorelle Raboni, after Richards. 121 (top) Charlie Ott/ Bruce Coleman Inc.; (bottom) E. Kotschnig. 122-123 (top) Lee Ames; (bottom) George Kelvin. 124 (left) Bill Strode/Black Star; (top right) Joseph S. Rychetnik; (bottom) George Holton/ Photo Researchers. 125 (top left) Enid Kotschnig; (top right) Alyeska Pipeline Service Co.; (center) Jerry Lang; (bottom) Photri. 126 (left) Guy Mannering/Bruce Coleman Inc.; (right) Edward Malsberg. 127 William R. Curtsinger/Rapho Guillumette. 128 (top) Edward Malsberg; (bottom) & 129 Lee Ames. 130 Lorelle Raboni, from "The Desert Pupfish," by James Brown, Copyright © 1971 by Scientific American, Inc. (all rights reserved). 131 (top) Josef Muench; (bottom) Victor Kalin. 132 (top) Robert W. Mitchell; (bottom) Enid Kotschnig. 133 Victor Kalin. 134 Gerald Cubitt. 135 (illustrations) Victor Kalin; (map) Enid Kotschnig. 136 Gerald Cubitt. 137 (top) Anthony Bannister; (bottom) Lorelle Raboni. 138 (top & bottom left) Ron Taylor; (center & bottom right) Valerie Taylor. 139 (top) Jerry Lang; (center right) Ron Taylor; (center left & bottom) Valerie Taylor. 140 Donna Harris. 141 (top) Ray Atkeson; (bottom) Jerry Lang. 142 Kyuzo Tsugami. 143 Edward Malsberg. 144 & 145 (top) H. W. Silvester/Rapho Guillumette; (bottom) Enid Kotschnig, after Weber. 146 Victor Kalin, after Breeden. 147 (left) Jerry Lang; (right) Michael K. Morocombe. 148 Edward Malsberg. 149 Stan & Kay Breeden. 150 Les D. Line. 151 (top) Tui A. De Roy; (bottom) Enid Kotschnig, after Carlquist. 152 R. Zanatta/Bruce Coleman Inc. 153 (top) Enid Kotschnig (bottom) Edward Malsberg. 154-155 Peter Johnson. 156-157 Eva Cellini. 158 (top) Norman Myers/Bruce Coleman Inc.; (bottom) Lorelle Raboni, after Schaller. 159 & 160 Norman Myers/Bruce Coleman Inc. 161 The Victoria & Albert Museum. 162 & 163 (top) Norman Myers/Bruce Coleman Inc.; (bottom) Jerry Lang. 164 (top) Norman Myers/Bruce Coleman Inc.; (bottom) Bob Campbell/Bruce Coleman Inc. 165 (top) Helen Cruickshank; (center) Patricia Ryan, after Weir & Davison; (bottom left) Clem Haagner/Bruce Coleman Inc.; (bottom right) Peter Johnson. 166 John S. Flannery. 167 (top) Lorelle Raboni; (center & bottom) Norman Myers/Bruce Coleman Inc. 168 (top) George H. Harrison; (bottom) Jen & Des Bartlett/Bruce Coleman Inc. 169 Jerry Lang. 170 Mary M. Thacher. 171 (top) H. Reinhard/ Bruce Coleman Inc.; (center right) Lorelle Raboni; (bottom) Juan Barberis. 172 Chorherrenstift Klosterneuburg. 173 (illustrations) Juan Barberis; (top right) Eric Hosking/National Audubon Society; (center left) Leonard Lee Rue, III/National Audubon Society; (bottom right) T. S. Satyan/Black Star. 174 & 175 (left) Juan Barberis; (right) Ron Austing/Bruce Coleman Inc. 176 Airflite. 177 (top & center right) Francisco Erize; (center left & bottom) Jerry Lang. 178 (top) Thase Daniel; (bottom) Patricia Caulfield. 179 Jerry Lang. 180-181 (left) Harriet Pertchik; (right) Patricia Ryan. 182 (left) Durward L. Allen; (right) Rolf O. Peterson. 183 (top & center) Durward L. Allen; (bottom) Lorelle Raboni. 184 (top) Durward L. Allen; (bottom left) New York Public Library, Prints Division; (right) & 185 Jerry Lang. 186 R. E. Pelham/Bruce Coleman Inc. 187 (top) Ron Church/Tom Stack & Assoc.; (bottom) Patricia Ryan. 188 (top left) Jurg Klages; (top center & bottom left) Jerry Lang; (top right) Bruce Coleman Inc.; (center) Edward S. Barnard; (bottom center) Juan Barberis; (bottom right) R. Tucker Abbott. 189 (top) Charles L. Trainor; (crab illustration & map) Juan

Barberis; (center right) Edward S. Barnard/Bruce Coleman Inc.; (pheasant illustration) Juan Barberis; (bottom left) M. F. Soper/ Bruce Coleman Inc.; (bottom right) Jerry Lang. **190** (illustrations) Eva Cellini; (top right) Australian Information Service; (center right) Bruce Coleman Inc. **191** (illustrations) Eva Cellini; (top center) Nina Leen; (center right) Richard E. Warner. **192 & 193** (top) David G. Allen; (center) Jerry Lang; (bottom) Lorelle Raboni. **194** David G. Allen. **195** Juan Barberis. **196-197** San Diego Zoo. **198** (center) Nina Leen; (bottom) Jerry Lang. **199** E. R. Degginger. **200** (top) Milwaukee County Zoological Park; (center) Lorelle Raboni. **201** Mary Fran Cahill/Milwaukee County Zoological Park. **202** (illustrations) Lorelle Raboni; (center & bottom right) Richard Jepperson; (bottom left) Thase Daniel. **203** San Diego Zoo. **204-205 & 206-207** Charles Faust & Joseph Ferarra. **208** Ernst Müller/Zoologischer Garten. **209** (top & center) Lee Ames, after Walther, Backhaus, & Frädrich; (bottom) Lorelle Raboni, after Crompton. **210** Edward Malsberg. **211** (top) Marvin E. Newman; (bottom) Jurg Klages. **212 & 213** (bottom) Robert Golding; (top) Jerry Lang. **214** Robert Golding. **215** (top left) Calgary Zoological Society/Walt Browarny/ "Dinny's Digest"; (top right) Jurg Klages; (bottom left) Paul Steinemann; (bottom right) Edward Malsberg, after Schultz. **216 & 217** (top left & bottom) Donna K. Grosvenor; (top right) Conrad Moulton. **218** Robert Phillips/Reader's Digest. **219** (top) Alex Ebel; (bottom) Louis Checkman. **220** (top, center, & bottom left) William Conway/N.Y. Zoological Society; (bottom right) Lee Ames. **221** (top) Robert Phillips/Reader's Digest; (bottom) E. R. Degginger. **222** (top) Carl Mydans; (bottom) N.Y. Public Library. **223** (left) N.Y. Public Library; (right) Ian Yeomans/ Woodfin Camp & Assoc. **224** Yolka/Atlas Photo. **225** (top left) New York Public Library; (top right) S. R. D. Bablin/Museum d'Histoire Naturelle; (bottom) Pitch. **226** Paul Chesley. **227** (top right) Lee Ames; (top left & center right) M. Yajima; (top center & all three bottom left) H. Uchida; (bottom right) E. Hamano. **228** (top left) Hartmut Noeller/Peter Arnold; (top right) Murray A. Newman/Vancouver Public Aquarium; (bottom) New York Zoological Society. **229** (top) Pierre Dow/Vancouver Public Aquarium; (bottom left) New England Aquarium; (center right & bottom right) New York Public Library. **230** Susan Griggs. **231** (top & bottom left) Jerry Lang; (bottom right) Francisco Erize. **232 & 233** (bottom) Kenneth W. Fink; (top) Jerry Lang. **234** Donald C. Thomas. **235** (left) Edward Malsberg; (right) Russ Kinne/Photo Researchers. **236** G. Harrison/Bruce Coleman Inc. **237** (left) Jerry Lang; (top right) Joanna M. Lub-

bock; (bottom right) George Harrison. **238** Teleki-Baldwin. **239, 240, & 241** Kyuzo Tsugami. **242-243** Harry Engels. **244 & 245** (bottom) Pamela & Jeffery Harrison/ Susan Griggs; (top) Kyuzo Tsugami. **246 & 247** (top) Philip S. Taylor; (bottom right) Jerry Lang. **248** (top) Larry B. Jennings/National Audubon Society; (center) Jerry Lang. **249** Joseph S. Rychetnik/Black Star. **250** (top) New York Public Library; (bottom) Graham Pizzey. **251** Edward Malsberg. **252** (top) Bermuda News Bureau; (bottom) Lee Ames. **253** Guy Coheleach. **254** (top) Bermuda News Bureau; (center) Jerry Ferguson. **255** (top) Erwin A. Bauer; (center) Lorelle Raboni. **256** Lorelle Raboni, after Bartholomew. **257** Warren Garst/Tom Stack Assoc. **258** Donald Rutherford. **259** Kyuzo Tsugami. **260** Jeff Foott/Bruce Coleman Inc. **261** (top) Ron Church; (center) Jerry Lang; (bottom) Karl W. Kenyon. **262** International Crane Foundation. **263** (top left) Lee Ames, after Keith; (top right) Courtesy of Mrs. Cornelius Crane; (bottom) Orion Press/Tom Stack Assoc. **264** (top) International Crane Foundation; (bottom) Jerry Lang. **265** Kyuzo Tsugami. **266 & 267** (center & bottom right) Texas Tech University; (top) Lorelle Raboni, after Bannikov; (bottom left) Jerry Lang, after Bannikov. **268** F. Lane/Bruce Coleman Inc. **269** (left) Carl Mydans; (right) Lorelle Raboni. **270** Nathan Zabarsky. **271** New York Public Library, Picture Collection. **272** Ian Yeomans/ Susan Griggs. **273** (top) Kenneth W. Fink/National Audubon Society; (center) Lorelle Raboni; (bottom) Arthur Christiansen. **274** (top) Peter Lindberg/N; (bottom) & **275** (bottom) Edward Malsberg; (top) Viking Olsson/N. **276 & 277** (top) Patuxent Wildlife Research Center; (center right & bottom left) The Peregrine Fund; (bottom right) Jerry Lang. **278** Foto de Biasi/Madeline Grimoldi. **279** (top left) Lorelle Raboni; (top right) Courtesy of Schackgalerie, Munich; (bottom) Yan/Rapho Guillumette. **280 & 281** (left) Foto de Biasi / Madeline Grimoldi; (right) Lee Ames. **282** (top) The Sea Library; (bottom) Lorelle Raboni. **283** (top left) Clerin W. Zumwalt; (center left) David Cavagnaro; (top right) Lee Ames. **284** (top) Clerin W. Zumwalt; (bottom) National Audubon Society. **285** David Cavagnaro. **286** Peter Johnson. **287** (top) Erwin A. Bauer; (bottom) Lorelle Raboni. **288** David Muench. **290-295** Edward Malsberg, after National Wildlife Federation. **296-299** Lee Ames, after McElroy. **300** Guy Tudor. **303** (top left) Karl H. Maslowski/National Audubon Society; (top right) Jerry Ferguson; (bottom) San Diego Zoo. **304, 312, 316, 320, 330, & 342** Lorelle Raboni.

Picture Editor: Robert J. Woodward

Acknowledgments

CHIMNEY PETS OF EUROPE, adapted with the permission of Hill and Wang, a division of Farrar, Straus & Giroux, Inc., from *Wild Animal, White Man*, by Bernhard Grzimek; translated from the German by Michael Glenny. Published in Great Britain by André Deutsch and Thames and Hudson. © 1966 by Bernhard Grzimek. Published originally by Kindler Verlag. MONARCH OF THE NORTH, by Fred Bruemmer, condensed from *Natural History*. © The American Museum of Natural History, 1968. BUTTERFLIES IN JEOPARDY, adapted from "How To Kill a Butterfly," by Jo Brewer, from *Audubon,* the magazine of the National Audubon Society. © 1972. THE SOCIABLE, CURIOUS PRAIRIE DOG, by Mary Cable, condensed from *Smithsonian*. © 1972 Smithsonian Institution. PERIL POINT FOR SEA TURTLES, adapted from *So Excellent a Fishe*. © 1967 by Archie Carr. Used by permission of Doubleday & Co., Inc. Distributed in Great Britain by Cassell & Co.,

Ltd. THE INCREDIBLE KANGAROOS, by Roger Tory Peterson, condensed from *International Wildlife*. © 1972 National Wildlife Federation. THE BALD EAGLE: SYMBOL AND VICTIM, by George Ott, condensed from *National Wildlife*. © 1970 National Wildlife Federation. GREAT GOATS OF THE GRAN PARADISO, by Verna Mays, condensed from *International Wildlife*. © 1973 National Wildlife Federation. IN SEARCH OF THE RIGHT WHALE, by Roger S. Payne, condensed from *Report From Patagonia: The Right Whales*. © 1972 New York Zoological Society. THE CHALLENGE OF SOUTH ASIA, by George B. Schaller, condensed from *Report: A Naturalist in South Asia*. © 1971 New York Zoological Society. ELEPHANTBACK IN NEPAL, by Erwin A. Bauer, condensed from *Treasury of Big Game Animals*. © 1972 Erwin A. Bauer. Reprinted by permission of Popular Science Publishing Co., Inc. LAST STAND OF ASIA'S LIONS, by Eliot Elisofon, condensed from

Smithsonian. © 1973 Smithsonian Institution. BRINGING BIBLICAL ANIMALS HOME, by Martin Zucker, condensed from *Animal Kingdom.* © 1972 New York Zoological Society. SPANISH HAVEN FOR WILDLIFE, condensed from *Gaçeta Ilustrada.* © 1972. WILD NATURE IN OTTAWA'S BACKYARD, condensed from "Gatineau Park: Wild Nature Near a City," by Sheila C. Thomson, reprinted from *Nature Canada,* Volume 2, Number 1 (January/March 1973), by permission of the Canadian Nature Federation and Sheila C. Thomson. SANCTUARIES FROM SEA TO SEA, condensed from *Wild Sanctuaries.* © 1968 by Robert Murphy and reprinted by permission of E.P. Dutton & Co., Inc., and Harold Ober Associates, Inc. EL DORADO ON THE MANÚ, by Tony Morrison, condensed from *Animals.* © 1970 *Animals* magazine and Tony Morrison. TSAVO: TOO MANY ELEPHANTS? by John Reader, condensed from *Smithsonian.* © 1972 Smithsonian Institution. LIVING LABORATORY OF THE SERENGETI, by Niko Tinbergen, condensed from *Animals.* © 1966 *Animals* magazine and Niko Tinbergen. AUSTRALIA'S RAIN FOREST WONDERS, by Allen Keast, from *Australia and the Pacific Islands.* © 1966 by Random House, Inc. Reprinted by permission of Random House, Inc., and Chanticleer Press, Inc. THE VANISHING PRAIRIE, by John Madson, condensed from *Audubon,* the magazine of the National Audubon Society. © 1972. HIDDEN WORLD OF THE HEDGEROW, by Ted Walker, condensed from *Audubon,* the magazine of the National Audubon Society. © 1972. FABULOUS FOREST OF THE AMAZON, taken from *The Nature of Life,* by Lorus and Margery Milne. Used by permission of Crown Publishers, Inc. THE FRAGILE NORTHLAND, by William O. Pruitt, Jr., condensed from *Animals.* © 1964 *Animals* magazine and William O. Pruitt, Jr. LIFE ON THE COLDEST CONTINENT, by Joseph M. Dukert, condensed from *Smithsonian.* © 1971 Smithsonian Institution. THE FLOWERING COASTS OF SOUTH AFRICA, by Leslie Brown, condensed from *Africa.* © 1965 by Random House, Inc. Reprinted by permission of Random House, Inc., and Chanticleer Press, Inc. WILD RIVER, RIBBON OF LIFE, adapted and abridged from *Wild River,* by Laurence Pringle. Copyright under International Copyright Union. All rights reserved. Reprinted by permission of J.B. Lippincott Company. FRANCE'S FLAMINGO COUNTRY, by Kai Curry-Lindahl, condensed from *Europe: A Natural History.* © 1964 by Random House, Inc. Reprinted by permission of Random House, Inc., and Chanticleer Press, Inc. A TALE OF TWO EDENS, by Roger Tory Peterson, condensed from *International Wildlife.* © 1973 National Wildlife Federation. DRAMA OF THE EAST AFRICAN SAVANNA, by George Lindsay, condensed from *Pacific Discovery.* © 1970 California Academy of Sciences. IS THE CHEETAH A LOSER? by Norman Myers. © 1975 by Norman Myers and reprinted by permission of Curtis Brown, Ltd. CROWDED AFRICA: HABITAT FOR MAN AND BEAST, by Norman Myers, condensed from *Animal Kingdom.* © 1974 New York Zoological Society and reprinted by permission of Curtis Brown, Ltd. REQUIEM FOR A WILD BOAR, by Louis J. Halle, condensed from *Audubon,* the magazine of the National Audubon Society. © 1974. THE UNRAVELING WEB OF WILDNESS, by Lee M. Talbot, condensed from *National Wildlife.* © 1974 National Wildlife Federation. THE ALLIGATOR: LANDSCAPE ARCHITECT OF THE EVERGLADES, by David W. Ehrenfeld, from *Conserving Life on Earth.* © 1970 by Holt, Rinehart and Winston, Inc.; © 1972 by Oxford University Press, Inc. Reprinted by permission. WONDERS IN A WOODLOT, by Aldo Leopold, from *A Sand County Almanac with other essays on conservation from Round River.* Copyright 1949, 1953, © 1966 by Oxford University Press, Inc. Reprinted by permission. THE UNDESIRABLE ALIENS, by David W. Ehrenfeld, from *Conserving Life on Earth.* © 1970 by Holt, Rinehart and Winston, Inc.; © 1972 by Oxford University Press, Inc. Reprinted by permission. A SECOND CHANCE FOR THE POC, by Anne LaBastille, condensed from *Audubon,* the magazine of the National Audubon Society. © 1972. CREATURE COMFORTS AT THE ZOO, by Barbara Ford, condensed from *Satur-* *day Review.* © 1972 and reprinted by permission of Saturday Review Publishing Assets Industries, Inc. BERNHARD GRZIMEK OF THE FRANKFURT ZOO, by Jack Denton Scott, condensed from the January/February 1973 issue of *International Wildlife.* © 1973 National Wildlife Federation. WHY ZOOS IN AFRICA? by Robert R. Golding, condensed from *Animals.* © 1966 *Animals* magazine and Robert R. Golding. A FRENCH PARADISE FOR BIRDS, by Betty Werther, condensed from *Smithsonian.* © 1971 Smithsonian Institution. THE RESCUE OF PÈRE DAVID'S DEER, by Philip Street, condensed from *Animals.* © 1965 *Animals* magazine and Philip Street. A MANOR BECOMES A MENAGERIE, by Timothy Green, condensed from *Smithsonian.* © 1972 Smithsonian Institution. HOW TO WATCH MONKEYS, by Patricia Gowaty, assisted by Sy and Barbara Ribakove, condensed from *Animal Kingdom.* © 1973 New York Zoological Society. THE THAMES: A RIVER REBORN, by Peter Grant, Jeffery Harrison, and John Swift, condensed from *Animals.* © 1973 *Animals* magazine, Peter Grant, and Jeffery Harrison. A BRIGHT FUTURE FOR THE MUSK-OX, by Jack Denton Scott, condensed from *International Wildlife.* © 1972 National Wildlife Federation. THE NOISY SCRUBBIRD CALLS AGAIN, by Vincent Serventy, condensed from *A Continent in Danger: A Survival Special on Australian Wildlife.* © Vincent Serventy, 1966. Published by André Deutsch Ltd. and Reynal & Co. RESCUE IN BERMUDA, by David R. Zimmerman, condensed from *The New York Times Magazine.* © 1973 by The New York Times Company. Reprinted by permission of the New York Times Company and Julian Bach Literary Agency, Inc. RETURN OF THE ELEPHANT SEAL, by Jim Tallon, reprinted and condensed by permission from *National Parks & Conservation Magazine,* March 1973. © 1973 National Parks & Conservation Association. CRANES OVER KYUSHU, by George W. Archibald, condensed from *Animal Kingdom.* © 1973 New York Zoological Society. MIRACLE OF THE SAIGA, adapted with permission of Hill and Wang, a division of Farrar, Straus & Giroux, Inc., from *Wild Animal, White Man,* by Bernhard Grzimek; translated from the German by Michael Glenny. Published in Great Britain by André Deutsch and Thames and Hudson. © 1966 Bernhard Grzimek. Published originally by Kindler Verlag. A SCHOOL FOR BIRDS OF PREY, by Maryrose Spivey with Nathan Zabarsky, condensed from *Smithsonian.* © 1973 Smithsonian Institution. PATUXENT'S OFFSPRING, by Dennis Farney, condensed from *Defenders of Wildlife.* © 1974 Dennis Farney. THE BISON OF BIALOWIEZA, by Edward R. Ricciuti, condensed from *Animal Kingdom.* © 1973 New York Zoological Society. Reprinted by permission of Curtis Brown, Ltd. WHITE BIRDS AND REDWOODS, condensed from *The San Francisco Experience.* © 1972 by Harold Gilliam. Used by permission of Doubleday & Company, Inc. Appeared originally in *Audubon* magazine. BEACON OF HOPE IN THE INDIAN OCEAN, by Tony Beamish, condensed from *Animals.* © 1969 *Animals* magazine and Tony Beamish. INVITE WILDLIFE TO YOUR BACKYARD, by Jack Ward Thomas, Robert O. Brush, and Richard M. DeGraaf, condensed from *National Wildlife.* © 1973 National Wildlife Federation. BUILD A BACKYARD MINI-POND, by George H. Harrison, condensed from *National Wildlife.* © 1974 National Wildlife Federation. ATTRACT BIRDS WITH FEEDERS AND BIRDHOUSES, by Thomas P. McElroy, Jr., excerpts from *The New Handbook of Attracting Birds,* second edition, revised and enlarged by Thomas P. McElroy, Jr. Copyright 1950, © 1960 by Alfred A. Knopf, Inc. Reprinted by permission of the publisher. HOW TO PHOTOGRAPH WILDLIFE, by Heather Angel. Taken from *Nature Photography,* published by the Fountain Press, Station Road, Kings Langley, England. PHOTOGRAPHING ZOO ANIMALS, by Michael Boorer. © 1971 Michael Boorer.

The editors would like to give special thanks to Jack Anderson, Archie Carr, Peter Crowcroft, Brad House, Wayne King, Alexander Klots, Arline Schneider, George Speidel; the staff of the Cornell University Laboratory of Ornithology; and Nicholas Eze, Patrick Ogbodu of the Ibadan Zoo.